The Sanitarian

by Agrippa Nelson Bell

Copyright © 2019 by HardPress

Address:
HardPress
8345 NW 66TH ST #2561
MIAMI FL 33166-2626
USA
Email: info@hardpress.net

The Sanitarian

Medico-Legal Society, New York

Population and Registration at most recent Estimates and Dates.	Deaths under 5 years	Total number of deaths [from all] causes.	Per 1000.	By Violence.	Small-pox.	Diphtheria.	Scarlatina.	Measles.	Croup.	Whooping Cough.	Typhoid Fever.	Typhus Fever.	Puerperal Diseases.
New York, 1,060,800; 4 weeks, ending Jan. 30..	997	2536	31.07	95	140	210	60	......	......	......	26	......	...
Philadelphia, 775,000; " " "	561	1247	20.40	21	......	41	102	2	57	......	26	1	1
Brooklyn, 450,000; " " "	434	1005	29.63	14	15	81	59	2	49	7	4	1	
St Louis, 450,000; " " "	219	501	14.47	16	109	7	15	......	2	......	12	......	
Chicago, 400,000; " " 23...	211	495	16.08	16	......	7	11	4	8	......	11	......	1
Boston, 375,000; " " "	......	665	23.05	......	......	......	......	......	......	......	......	......	...
Baltimore, 350,000; " " 30...	250	636	23.62	13	......	11	59	......	27	6	16	1	1
Cincinnati, 260,000; 2 weeks, " 25...	101	279	27.90	......	2	7	9	......	3	10	7	......	...
New Orleans, 207,000; year, 1874............	......	6798	32.84	*159	587	102	......	......	......	......	......	......	...
" 210,000; month ending Jan. 31...	168	572	32.68	15	32	1	1	......	7	1	2	......	
Washington, 150,000; 4 weeks, ending Jan 30..	156	315	29.90	12	......	3	1	5	6	16	4	......	
Pittsburg, 140,000, month ending " "	132	285	24.43	......	2	2	33	2	......	6	18	......	
Richmond 65,000; 4 weeks ending " "	38	109	21.80	3	......	3	......	......	1	......	3	......	...
New Haven, 60,000; month ending Jan. 31....	40	100	20.00	3	1	...	......	......	4	......	3	......	
Charleston, 50,000; " " " "	50	98	25.48	2	......	5	......	......	......	......	1	......	
Toledo, 50,000; month ending " 31...	22	55	13.20	......	......	......	......	......	1	1	......	......	
Paterson, 40,000; year 1874	31	32	26.65	4	......	17	1	......	1	......	......	......	...
Wheeling, 27,000; month ending Jan. 31.........	18	46	28.44	2	......	4	6	......	......	......	1	......	
" " year 1874	195	306	14.66	9	......	7	21	1	5	12	18	......	
Dayton, 34,000; month ending Jan. 31	12	46	+16.23	2	......	......	......	......	1	......	1	......	...
Salem (1870), 24,117; month ending Jan. 31.....	......	47	......	1	......	......	2	......	......	......	......	......	
" year 1874	161	496	20.56	7	......	1	5	......	6	6	21	......	
Poughkeepsie, 24,000; year 1874.............	145	400	16.66	8	......	11	15	3	7	......	9	1	
Elmira, 21,000; month ending Jan 31..........	7	25	14.09	1	......	......	4	......	......	......	......	......	...
Norfolk, 21,000; year, 1874......................	243	554	26.03	16	8	11	3	......	3	20	11	......	

Other Causes.

New Orleans ...Congestive Fever, 2[illegible]4.
" Jan. ...Other Fevers, 10.

1837
ARTES
VERITAS
SCIENTIA
LIBRARY OF THE
UNIVERSITY OF MICHIGAN
SI QUAERIS PENINSULAM AMOENAM
CIRCUMSPICE

2597

THE

SANITARIAN.

A MONTHLY JOURNAL.

A. N. BELL, M.D., Editor.

VOLUME II.

NEW YORK:

324 BROADWAY.

Entered accordiug to Act of Congress, A. D. 1875, by
A. N. BELL,
in the Office of the Librarian of Congress, at Washington.

THE SANITARIAN.

A MONTHLY JOURNAL.

VOL. II.] APRIL, 1874. [NO. 1.

DRAINAGE FOR HEALTH.

By JOSEPH WILSON, M. D., Medical Director U. S. Navy.

There is something astonishing in the effect of drainage on growing plants.

We take an ordinary red earthern flower-pot, with a hole in it; we fill this pot with earth, and cultivate plants successfully. But if we undertake to cultivate a plant in a bowl, or any ordinary jar, we fail; and even if we take the flower-pot and cork up the hole, so as to destroy this arrangement for getting rid of a little superfluous moisture, our plants do not flourish. Whether we water them or whether we neglect them, makes but little difference,—they do not flourish—they will not flourish.

The clay soil of a meadow, like the bowl in this case, does not allow the rains to penetrate and filter through it; partly the water flows off over the surface, and partly it evaporates; but the plants do not flourish. The farmer, when he prepares his field for wheat, tries to remedy this evil by ploughing his land into ridges and hollows, thus making surface drains. The earth, to the depth stirred by the plough, is permeable to water, which thus finds its way to the surface drains without flowing so much over the surface. The wheat grows best on the centre of the ridges—the highest part; and scarcely any grows in the hollows. This peculiarity of the growing crop is seen all over the field.

WHEAT ON CLAY SOIL.

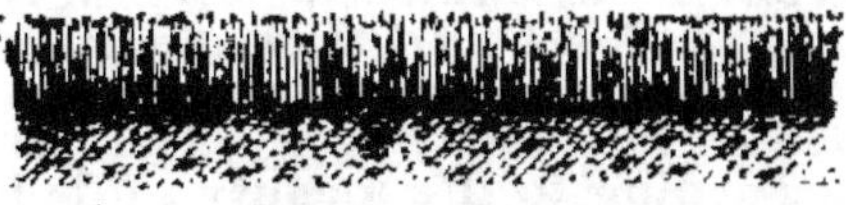

ON THE SAME LAND DRAINED.

This difference in the appearance of the crops is seen, not only on marshy land, but on any ordinary soil resting on clay. Some plants can hardly be made to grow at all on such land; but nearly all plants flourish on it when drained. Such drainage as we have just described—the ridges and surface drains of the wheat field—does pretty well for wheat and grass crops, having all the roots near the surface; but apple trees and grape vines, having deep roots, will not flourish without deeper and more effective drainage. This is mostly done by channels of earthern pipes, three or four feet beneath the surface. The English rule, reached by a good deal of expensive experience, is to place the drains four feet deep and forty feet apart. If the clay be very adhesive, four feet is a little too deep, and the drains should be placed a little closer together.

The influence of this subsoil drainage is very difficult to comprehend. It is seen not only in flat and marshy places, where there would seem to be a superfluity of water, but even in hilly and dry countries. Any piece of land with its immedi te sub-stratum of impermeable clay is unproductive, no matter how well manured or how well watered, until it is provided with underground drainage. The moisture, much or little, stagnating in the soil, poisons vegetation; and, indeed, it has been suggested that the plants secrete poisons into the soil—a sort of poisonous excrement—which, unless it be dissolved and removed by percolating water, poisons the plants. This is the only explanation which has been offered.

There certainly is a very deadly poison in just such places, very destructive of human life. This poison we know only by the havoc it makes—by the disease and death which it causes. It is called *malaria*, marsh miasm, marsh fever poison, etc. The diseases which it principally causes are the various types of periodic fever, intermittent, remittent, congestive, and pernicious, ague-cake, malarial anæmia, diarrhœa, dropsy, marasmus, etc. Leaving out the deaths of infancy and old age, probably more than one-third of all the deaths in the world are caused by malarial poisoning. During the first two years of our Civil War 20,675 deaths of our soldiers were reported from malarial fevers, and 71,192 deaths from all causes; so that more than two-sevenths of all the deaths were from malarial fevers. This is perhaps a fair average through a somewhat protracted war in a healthy country. Of course, special service in the less healthy districts caused much greater mortality. In 1809 a British army of 39,214 men embarked for Holland, and was nearly destroyed in four months, about nineteen-twentieths of the deaths and disabilities being from malarial disease. (*Bondin*, An. d'Hygiene, vol. xxxv.)

We may avoid this kind of disease and death by keeping away from malarious land. We may sometimes do still better by draining the land, and thus making it healthy—increasing the crops two or three fold, according to the situation, and greatly lessening the labor of cultivation. The arrangements for drainage must vary according to the locality and character of the soil.

Natural Subsoil Drainage.—In a hilly country with a light soil—soil with a due proportion of sand or gravel—not much need be done. When the forest is first cleared off and the soil turned up, the place is likely to be unhealthy the first autumn; but after the land is fairly cleared, and ploughed into ridges and surface drains, in the direction of its slopes, as in ordinary wheat culture, it immediately bears good crops and is quite healthy; there is no more appearance of malarial poisoning. Such land in the older parts of the country is instantly recognized by the elegant houses and big barns. The farmers occupying such land may be known by their florid complexions and fine forms; they are above the average size of men, bright and cheerful. They mostly have large families, a very large proportion of whom live much beyond the average duration of human life. The land undergoes sub-division from generation to generation, till the farms become too small for further dividing, and then these healthy and fertile farms send a constant stream of emigrants to the large cities and new countries. Nearly all the prosperous merchants, physicians, lawyers and clergymen, philosophers and sages, have to refer to such healthy places as the homesteads of their fathers and grandfathers.

In the malarious district and on the farm of much malarious land, all this is reversed. The crops are so poor that there is no need of a big barn; the inhabitants are so poor that they are unable to build a good house or even to repair an old one. The house has probably been built by some unfortunate or imprudent man raised on a better place: he has scarcely raised any family, has probably died of the fever, and one of his unfortunate children may have inherited the place—to be still poorer and more wretched. The land needs no sub-dividing; an occasional stranger becomes an unfortunate owner, because there is not enough native population to occupy the land. There is no surplus population to supply the learned professions—none to become prosperous merchants. The children of these malarious districts are a sad sight—sallow, dwarfish, hatched-faced, pot-bellied little creatures—but very few of whom ever become men and women—very wretched men and women. Even the cattle, the very horses and cows, are dwarfish, worthless beasts.

All this contrast comes of naturally gentle slopes, a moderate quantity of sand or gravel in the subsoil, and a sufficient elevation above the water-courses for good drainage, or the land being without one or more of these advantages. The first of these pictures is seen in Byberry, Philadelphia, where nearly all the land is divided into very small farms, with elegant buildings, mostly owned and occupied by people bearing the names which crossed the ocean with William Penn; and in the east end of Bucks County, from Bristol to Trenton, where the same division of land has occurred, and the same Quaker names prevail; and in healthy districts all over the country except where overrun by manufacturing villages. The second picture is seen in some parts of New Jersey, and in Pennsylvania it is seen immediately south of Philadelphia, where Tinnicum seems to have but one house for the whole township. This second picture is also seen in large districts of Delaware and Maryland, Virginia and Carolina—principally east of the main lines of north and south railroad. All this level country, except the bluff banks of rivers and the Pine Barrens, is thus wretched. By careful study and systematic labor, we can do much to relieve the misery here hinted at—these ague-cakes and sallow skins—this sickness, poverty, and premature death.

Valleys and Meadows.—Immediately contiguous to the land of natural subsoil drainage, there is nearly always found a less healthy variety—small tracts less productive of men and crops. The rains that water the healthy hills, wash down some of the soil, and this, settling in the course of time, forms nearly level valleys or meadows along the brooks and rivers. The material thus deposited in level layers may be principally clay—scarcely permeable to moisture. The water coming from the hills, in underground channels, meets this clay in the side of the meadow, and can go no further without rising to the surface; hence beautiful clear springs of the best drinking water. Such meadows produce no good crops, not even good grass; they produce a great variety of sedges called meadow-grass, which half-starved cattle sometimes eat. They poison the atmosphere, causing malarial fevers, and destroying the health of all who live within the range of their influence. The remedy for this is simple enough, though it involves some labor and expense. It is merely drainage,—something equivalent to the hole in the bottom of the flower-pot.

The drainage of meadows is most economically effected by a system of underground drains—made with drain pipes of red-brick clay, the cheapest possible material, and lasting for ages. The first thing to be done is to survey the land, determine the highest and lowest parts, and observe the conformation of contiguous lands and hills. Between two elegant fertile slopes, we may have a strip of *worthless marsh*, with a sluggish stream flowing through its middle. We draw a small map of this, and starting where the stream flows off—the lowest part—we trace dotted lines of equal elevation. And as the ground is very level, we must trace the lines for the drains very nearly at right angles to these lines of equal elevation, in order to give the drains enough fall to make them work well. Commonly we can give all the drains sufficient fall, by arranging most of them parallel with each other, in two or three directions. Thus in our strip of worthless marsh, the first work is to trace a drain along each side, near enough to the foot of the hills to catch all the springs; next trace drains about twenty feet from the boundary lines, so as to drain our own land with the least possible interference with our neighbor; trace a drain on each side of the stream, nearly parallel to it and thirty or forty feet distant, for the stream itself is probably the best drain for its banks, and, besides, is liable to wash out pipes placed too near it. The rest of the land may have its drains drawn nearly parallel with each other, and as nearly perpendicular to the lines of level as possible, without too much complication of plans. In practice it seems sufficient to place the drains four feet deep, about forty feet apart; if but three feet deep they must be much nearer together.

Heavy Land.—Soil principally composed of adhesive clay is nearly impermeable to water and is called heavy land. It sometimes occurs on the tops of pretty high hills, so that the highest land of a hill-side farm is sometimes the most marshy, and has the greatest need of artificial drainage. The object in this case is accomplished in the same way as in the flat meadow; but we need not look for springs, and there is so much slope that there is very little trouble in giving the drains enough fall, without being so particular about the direction of the slopes.

Sometimes this heavy land has a deep stratum of permeable gravel. Much land about Philadelphia is of this character; so that after working the surface into bricks, there remains well-drained gravelly lands for building lots. Land of this character may be very well and cheaply drained by means of a series of sinks cut through the clay. These are made with an earth auger, such as is used in planting telegraph poles, the hole being somewhat enlarged at the top with a spade. The opening thus made is filled with gravel or coarse sand, or chips; and the whole arrangement is levelled and worked over with the plough. Thus all marks of our labor quickly disappear, except the good health and the good crops of the farmer.

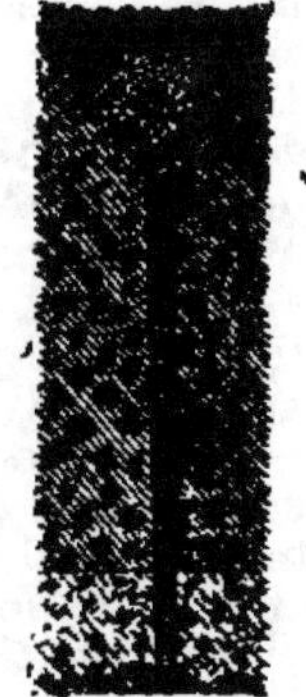
SINK FOR DRAINAGE.

Sandy Loam.—A large part of the malarious region of the United States is sandy loam, so flat and so nearly on a level with the ocean that it is very imperfectly drained. There is some of it in New Jersey, Pennsylvania, Delaware, and Maryland; and in Virginia it includes nearly all the country east of Fredericksburg and Richmond. Many of the farm-houses of this district are built of bricks imported from England by the early settlers. It still continues in farms of 1,000 acre tracts, or even larger. The poor owner does not know how to do any better, and he really has not the means to improve his land. The healthy spots of this region are the bluff banks of rivers, the pine forests, and some sea-coast islands. This border of level sandy land extends along our coast from Maryland to Mississippi, varying from twenty miles to a hundred and fifty miles in width. For half of its breath, there is hardly any of it thirty feet above the level of the ocean. With an average slope of not more than one foot to the mile, of course this land is not well drained, and it would seem nearly useless to attempt to drain it; but things may be improved. The worst parts may be cultivated in rice, where no one should think of fixing a dwelling—the workmen living in healthy villages at no great distance. And if no such convenient healthy place can be found on land, the workmen, while tending and harvesting the rice crop, may live in boats anchored in the middle of the streams, only landing to work in the daytime; for it has been abundantly proved that there is no danger from malarial poison in the daytime, and little if any danger in a boat half a mile from the malarious shore at any time. There are healthy spots, the bluff banks of rivers and the pine groves, even in this desperate strip of country; and these spots may be improved.

The western half of this sandy plain is considerably more elevated, some of it even reaching two hundred feet above the level of the ocean. This is the region of Pine Barrens; it is too level and too much under water for cultivation without some system of artificial drainage. It is partially occupied by an unhappy, malaria-poisoned people. The lumber men, while in this forest, are healthy; but as soon as they clear a patch for cultivation, they have the fever, and the weeds, bushes and forest again take possession. An attempt has been made to drain some of it by open ditches along the roads; and in some places these ditches are made to serve the purpose of boundary lines and fences. But there are not enough of them to drain the land; they breed an awful quantity of mosquitoes; and they rapidly fill with weeds and dirt, so as to need constant cleaning out.

There are several ways of improving this land. In the first place, it is necessary to recognize the fact that, but for the growth of pine timber, it is deadly malarious; and hence it must be insisted on that the people who work it are to live in villages, in healthy spots protected by a growth of pine trees. They can walk to the fields in the morning and return in the evening. We thus secure healthy workmen in the first place.

Next, in place of the open ditches, which only half do the work, and really cost a good deal of labor and money, let us have good drain pipes, carefully set, from three feet to ten feet below the surface; and let us have at least ten times as many such drains as there are now of open ditches. These will carry off the water steadily and certainly, will breed no mosquitoes, will need no repairs. The drains need not be so close together here as in clay soil, for the water filters very rapidly through the sand into these drains.

With such arrangements as these, nearly all this land may be made healthy and productive. The mere swamps along the banks of sluggish streams, though not habitable for human beings, may be made valuable as rice fields.

Pine Forests.—There is something astonishing in the salubrity of the pine forests of this region, which, by the way, are not "barren" at all. There are immense tracts of this flat land occupied almost exclusively by pine timber. The trees grow pretty close together, so as to destroy the side branches as they grow up; and thus the earth is covered some inches deep, with dead branches and pine leaves. The ground is generally quite dry, the water disappearing very rapidly after a rain. These forests supply tar, timber, and turpentine for the markets of the world; but, much more interesting to us, they are quite healthy—quite clear of malarial fevers. Various attempts have been made to account for this good health. It has been suggested that turpentine is wholesome and neutralizes in some way the malarial poison. There may be something in this notion, but there is plenty of fever about the turpentine stores, except in the forest. The thick carpeting of pine leaves has been supposed to prevent the malarial poison from rising; and it doubtless has a beneficial influence in this way.

It seems to me that the pine trees act principally by draining the land; and this they do by the peculiar manner in which the roots of pine trees decay. As the trees of the forest get too thick to thrive, the weaker die and decay, root and branch, but much more rapidly and completely the roots; and thus the whole situation of the pine stump becomes a very extensive and effective sink, resembling somewhat the artificial-drainage sinks already described. The roots near the surface form an extensive series of radiating drain channels, and the deep roots form deeper channels by which the water rapidly sinks to its lowest level. These stump holes are very nice dens for coons and foxes. My attention was first called to this subject by observing some deep holes in the pine grove of the Norfolk Hospital. These holes were four or five feet in diameter to an apparent bottom of loose twigs and leaves. I asked many questions about these holes, and could only elicit the conjecture that they might have been made by the diggers for Captain Kidd's money. As there was no visible pile of dirt, this was not a satisfactory explanation. One of these holes was near a surface drain that was being opened, and I directed the drain to be opened to the money hole with a view of filling it up. But after the next heavy rain I saw quite a large stream, eighteen inches wide and two inches deep, running into the hole and disappearing—a small Niagara. Kidd's treasure must have knocked a hole in the bottom of the Hospital Woods, and a stream of water was running down through it. I accidentally obtained an explanation by trying my cane on an old stump overgrown with smilax (green briars). The strongest part of the stump was its bark; the rest was black dust, the cane passing easily its whole length in any direction. All the men about the place seem to know that the pine stump, in this manner, decays very quickly and completely, even to the ends of the smallest roots. Thus the whole matter is plain enough. These pine-stump sinks may be made much more permanent, so as to be useful after the clearing of the forest, by filling them with clean course sand or gravel from a brook, or even oak chips; they do not then fill up with surface dirt, and they continue to transmit water much longer.

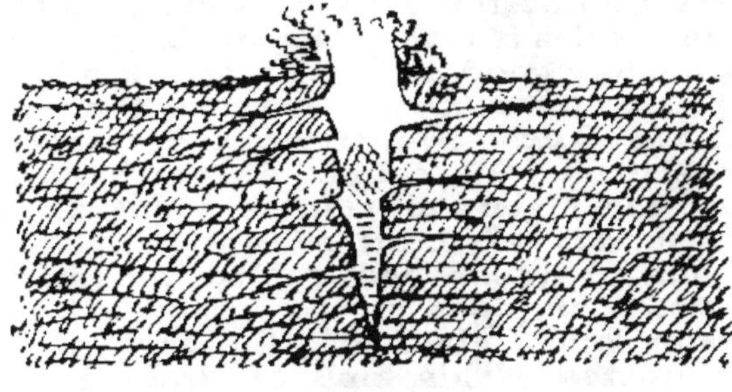

NATURAL DRAINAGE SINK OF THE PINE FOREST.

This action of pine trees in draining the land begins when the trees are quite small. The first year from the seeds the young trees are a foot high; the second year they are four feet; and the the third year they are eight feet, and more than half of those that started are dead and decaying. Every year, while the forest lasts, there are some trees thus going to decay; and they have amazingly deep tap-roots. It thus appears easy to make a healthy place for a village almost anywhere—as we have but to scatter a few pine cones on any suitable piece of land, and wait three or four years. The Naval Hospital at Norfolk, Va., is separated from very malarious fields, naturally pine forest, by a pine grove about three hundred yards wide; and this is found to be amply sufficient. The *Eucalypti* of Australia are just now exciting much interest as fever-preventing trees; but there certainly is no need of anything better than our own Southern pines. However, let us have the Eucalyptus; one of the species is a very elegant large tree, and there is no danger of too many good things of this kind; and besides, this tree may be suitable for some places where the pine does not flourish.

Flat Rock.—Sometimes we find marshy land on a surface of nearly level rock. We cannot do much here with the ordinary tools, but the same general plan is adopted. The rock is likely to be limestone, not very hard, so that, with the aid of picks and crowbars, the trenches are opened, not so deep as in heavy land, or so far apart. Instead of pipes in the bottom of the trenches, we arrange some fragments of the rock; the earth is levelled, and thus the work is completed. This kind of drainage is much practised about Sandusky City, Ohio; and thus rather poor wheat land worth twenty dollars an acre becomes worth four hundred dollars for the cultivation of grapes, and the country is becoming healthy.

The water enters such drains as we have described, by filtering through the soil, and finding entrance to the pipes by the loose joints. Where drain-water is discharged into a brook, it may be made to pass through a mass of gravel, thus imitating a natural spring. In draining *meadows*, subject to the overflow of the tide, the drainage is collected into a pool, near a sluice-gate, discharging into the river at low-tide. These *Bank Meadows* everywhere south of New England are dangerously malarious, destroying the health or life of nearly every person who undertakes to live near them.

It might be inferred from the preceding discussion, that the malarial poison which kills so many thousands of men, is the same that prevents our plants from thriving; but this would be a mistake. The marshy meadows of New England produce nothing but meadow-hay, good only to pack crockery; but malarial fevers are hardly known in New England. The land occupied by the Panama Railroad has an abundance of marshy places, but not at all in proportion to the deadly character of the climate. The lives of more than eighty thousand workmen were destroyed by malaria while building this railroad; one man died for each yard of the track, 1760 died for each mile, and in round numbers 81,000 lives were destroyed in building these forty-six miles of railroad. I fear that five times as many will be destroyed in the contemplated enterprise of building a canal in the same region. There appear to be at least three distinct species of marsh poison, removable by drainage: (*a*) First, there is the poison that interferes with vegetation, so that many meadows produce scarcely anything, except sedges in place of grass. (*b*) Second, there is some poison which determines that typhoid fever mostly occurs on heavy land and flat land, though this disease appears to be contagious like measles, and whooping-cough. (*c*) Third, the most important is malarial poison—the poison of the periodic fevers—killing its hecatombs, say one thousand victims every day, and keeping a large portion of the earth's surface in the condition of a howling wilderness.

The proper drainage of buildings is a matter of great importance. Cellars may be wet, stables not very dry, water may drip from the eaves, cutting holes into the earth and making puddles. The water from such puddles filters directly into the cellar, so that old houses in the country are very frequently dangerous to life on account of the water settling into the cellars. A damp cellar may sometimes be made dry by making a sink in it, as already described for the fields. Cellars are sometimes made in such wretched places that they need drain-pipes to carry off the water. In arranging any of this kind of work about a stable, it is necessary to be careful that the drainings of the stable do not filter into any water required for domestic use. Water should on no account be allowed to drip from the eaves; it is a great nuisance, undermining foundations and rapidly destroying buildings.

The inlets of drains require attention. When they empty into an offensive sink or sewer the gaseous emanations follow up the pipes for very great distances. This nuisance is prevented by various arrangements called traps; the most simple and generally available is a simple curve in the pipe, so that at a particular spot it remains full of water. Inlets have traps not only to stop offensive gases, but to prevent the drains from becoming choked by rags, gravel, kitchen-slush, etc. These inlets are of various forms, according to the object to be accomplished.

It seems very important to ventilate the interior of these drains about buildings. Air confined anywhere, even in a clean room, becomes offensive, probably unhealthy, with a disagreeable smell of closeness, and confined with filth in a drain or sewer, it must be infinitely worse. Drains built tight, with traps, etc., so that there is no ventilation of their interior, generate very poisonous gases, which are ready on the occurrence of any small leak to escape and poison everybody who happens to go near them. The best arrangement for ventilators in houses is to have a separate flue built in the chimney-stack expressly to receive the ventilator pipes. Thus the air from the drain is discharged high in the atmosphere in a position to be mixed with smoke; and the noxious properties are destroyed, the smoke, whether of wood or coal, containing about the best chemical disinfectants known.

The great importance of this neglected subject must be my apology for writing plainly about it. In all parts of New England hundreds of people are dying every year of typhoid fever; a large tract of the city of Boston is now building on made land, nearly as flat as the prairies about Chicago; and in a few years it will doubtless have to be re-graded and rebuilt to get rid of this pestilence. From Maine to Pennsylvania there are flat undrained fields, and wet cellars, nearly as bad. All over the country further south, but principally in the Mississippi valley and the flat country bordering the ocean, the half-drained land is infected with intermittent fever and the other malarial pestilences to such an extent as to destroy many thousands of people every year; so that, in spite of constant immigration, extensive tracts of country are about as sparsely peopled as they were when Pocahontas saved the life of John Smith. Some parts of this desert is the most fertile land in our country, and the most easily cultivated, but for the failure of health among those who unfortunately undertake to occupy it. I have known men as long ago as 1843, to purchase tracts of this land, as they supposed, remarkably cheap. They commenced by raising fine crops of early vegetables for the Northern markets. The crops of the first year paid for the land five times over; but before the next spring some of the family were probably dead, and the rest so broken down in health that no other such crop was ever raised. These migrations from healthy districts to these pestilential regions are constant; and on visiting the same district in 1868, I found the same desert – the same paradise of mosquitoes. It would be well if this migration could be stopped until it can be undertaken with a fair appreciation of the difficulties. When it is done with such precautions as I have indicated, I feel sure that these fertile regions will become the happy homes of millions of happy and prosperous people; and beautiful groves of long leaf pine will surround, beautify, and protect their thousands of delightful villages.

Concerning College Life.—In addressing you at the commencement of your higher academic course, I am fully aware how slight is the chance of your following any advice I may presume to offer. * * * * * * To quote Lord Derby: "Take two men, if they could be found, exactly alike in mental and bodily aptitudes, and let the one go on carelessly and idly, indulging his appetites, and generally leading a life of what is called pleasure, and let the other train himself by early hours, by temperate habits, and by giving to muscles and brain each their fair share of employment, and at the end of two or three years they will be as wide apart in their capacity for exertion as if they had been born with wholly different constitutions."

So far as to matters which are within your own control. You can't help the dampness or defective drainage of the basement lodging allotted to you in one or two colleges I could name, nor the want of ventilation in overcrowded class-rooms (I know of one institution of learning where lectures on hygiene are given in an atmosphere so close that few students can stand it for half an hour without feeling nausea and headache). If, instead of the ordinary curriculum of arts, you are following some more specialized course—*e. g.*, "polytechnic"—you are not responsible for the exhausting, if not exhaustive, plan of instruction which seeks to compress within three years the proper work of five, and which entails such excessive labor that men sometimes faint during examination. But for the very reason that you are exposed to many inevitable insalutary influences, it concerns you all the more to shun the outside risks which you can avoid, and to maintain with prudent care sufficient bodily health to insure mental soundness for the next three or four years. Remember that after that (unless you're fortunate enough to inherit an independent income and fall into a life of ruinous leisure) you have your profession to study or your way to make in business, either of which will test the vigor and endurance now within your power to cultivate or to impair.

Dr. Ollapod.—*The World.*

THE HUDSON RIVER STATE HOSPITAL.

In the legislative session of 1866, the pressing need of hospital accommodation for the insane of Eastern New York, was made so evident as to result in the creation of a Commission, who were empowered to select a hospital site on or near the Hudson River. The report of the Commissioners was presented in January, 1867, showing that after an extensive and careful examination, during which they had received from both sides of the river, several highly eligible offers, they had finally fixed on a site near the city of Poughkeepsie. The beautiful ground thus selected, consists of more than 200 acres, and was a gift to the State from the people of Duchess County. The organizing Act was passed in March. A Board of Managers was forthwith appointed, and entered, without delay, upon their duties. Dr. Joseph M. Cleaveland, who had been one of the State Commission, was chosen as Superintendent, and Mr. James S. Weeks, of Poughkeepsie, was appointed Treasurer. Eighty-four acres of adjoining ground, which were regarded as essential to the future of the institution, and which have since been turned to excellent account, were immediately secured by purchase. Messrs. Vaux, Withers & Co. were requested to prepare plans for a hospital in conformity with a carefully planned interior, already devised by the Superintendent. The plans, elevations, specifications and estimates produced by the architect, were adopted by the Board, and received the approval of the State officers, as by law required. The design thus prepared under the direction of the Building Committee of the Board, is decribed by the architect as follows :

"The hospital is planned to accommodate about three hundred patients of each sex. The wards for men, constituting the entire wing to the south, and the wards for women, the entire wing to the north of the central building, which is devoted to the various departments of general management. The chapel is placed between the wings, and in the rear of the central building, so that patients of one sex are prevented from looking into the wards and yards of patients of the other sex. The kitchen and general service department is located in the rear of the chapel.

"The department for each sex consists of four wards on the principal floor, four wards on the second floor, one ward on the third floor, and an infirmary on the third floor, separated entirely from the rest of the wards.

"Each ward is furnished with a hall and staircase on the front line of the building, and roads of approach are to be arranged so as to give a separate access to the entrance-hall thus attached to each ward. A hall, with staircase communicating with an airing court, is arranged also in each ward on the rear line of the building.

"The wards for excited patients are farthest removed from the central building, and have bedrooms on one side only of the corridors.

The wards for quiet patients have their bedrooms on both sides. In the parts of the building which are thus arranged, open spaces are left for light and for circulation of air. These spaces are intended to furnish opportunity for open-air exercise in mild weather.

"It will be observed that in the wards containing bedrooms on both sides, the living-rooms, lavatories, etc., are arranged on one side only of a separate corridor that runs at right angles with a bed-room section. Every ward, in addition to its dormitories, has a living-room of large dimensions, with windows on three sides; a dining-room, with pantry attached, communicating by lifts with the basement corridor, and thus connecting with the service department; a lavatory, whose wash-pipe and water-tight floor and sides admit the thorough cleansing of a patient in any posture; a bath-room, having the bath in the centre, with screened dressing-space attached; a room containing water-closets and urinals, and a sink for the use of the attendant; a linen and clothes-room, and a soiled linen shaft, large enough to be used also for hoist-way purposes.

"Each ward is provided with one single and one double bedroom for attendants. At the extreme end of the convalescent ward, on the principal floor nearest the central building, is a reception-room in which patients can see their friends.

"Over the rooms used for kitchen offices is planned an amusement-room, which can be approached under cover from each wing. Attached to the convalescent wards on the men's side, are a library, a writing-room, and a billiard-room; and in a corresponding position on the women's side, a library, a sewing-room, and a gymnasium. The tailor's room from wards on the men's side, and the ironing room from wards on the women's side, can be reached by patients under cover. The kitchen and general service department are provided for, as shown on the plan, in a detached building on a level with the basement floor of the main building, so that a railway may run from the kitchen to the lifts attached to the dining-rooms of the various wards. Bedrooms for the servants are provided near the kitchen department.

"Each wing is connected with the central building by a one-story corridor. The board-room is on the principal floor of the central building, which also contains the reception-room for patients, and the offices for the medical department, and for the steward and matron. The upper stories of the central building are designed for the medical and other offices of the hospital.

"The general character of the elevation is simple, the lines following strictly the necessities of the plan. The material to be used is hard North River brick, with a better quality for face-work. Ohio stone has been chosen for strings and window-heads, with blue-stone introduced sparingly to increase the artistic effect. The basement, where it shows above ground, will be constructed of blue-stone ashler."

In substantial accordance with this plan, three sections of the southern wing have been erected, finished, and furnished, and are now in actual use. The foundation and the basement walls of a fourth and much larger section are laid, and have, for some time, been awaiting the means required to carry them up.

Thus far, this hospital has been built almost entirely without resort to the contract system. That everything in and about it should be solid and durable, commodious and useful, becoming in its aspect and appropriate to its end, has been the constant and not unsuccessful endeavor of the managers.

Ventilation and Water Supply.—In every great building which is to be occupied by many persons, and especially in every great hospital for the wounded, the sick, or the insane, no arrangements surpass in importance those which relate to the supply of air, of water, and of heat. In the construction and appointments of the Hudson River State Hospital, the requirements of ventilation have received careful attention. In the first place, fresh air can always be admitted into every part of the building through a multitude of safely guarded windows. Secondly, a double set of wall-flues, one set with their openings at the floor-line, and in the other set at a point ten feet above it, go up independently of each other till they reach an opening under the roof-ridge. By means of this aperture, which extends the whole length of the hospital, they communicate directly and freely with the external air. This arrangement for the ingress and egress of air is believed to be as effective, to say the least, as any method yet devised in which the change and renewal of the element depend solely on its own automatic movements. But experience has demonstrated that these movements are not, of themselves, sufficient to preserve a fresh and healthy atmosphere in large and populous establishments, and especially in those which from their very nature are subject to many vitiating influences. A great hospital without a *fan* is as uncomfortable as a delicate lady, similarly situated, would be in a highly heated and badly ventilated room. The fan of this hospital, revolving night and day, sends its fresh current to the building through a subterranean tunnel three hundred feet long, and having a sectional area of sixty-four square feet. The air passing into the basement fills to repletion a spacious air-duct which extends through the entire length of the building. From this duct it enters about fifty sheet-iron chambers which open into the air-flues of the apartments and corridors. The air thus brought under ground goes up cool in summer, and when the weather is cold it comes in contact with coils of steam-pipe placed in the iron chambers, and supplied with steam from the boilers which furnish the power. The heating flues open into the corridors of the wards, into the dining, sitting, and bathing rooms, and into the lavatories and water-closets. To keep them from being obstructed by mischievous or careless patients, the apertures are placed about ten feet above the floor. The bedrooms for patients receive their air, whether warmed or otherwise, from the halls through safe openings over the doors and near the foot.

The high and low flues already mentioned, which in their operation remove and change not only the upper, but the lower stratum of air, are found in all the bedrooms, in the sitting-rooms, dining-rooms, bath-roms, lavatories, and, to some extent, in the corridors. In these latter, however, the ventilation is mainly effected through the door-openings just mentioned, the air of the bedrooms being constantly changed through the agency of the high and low ventilating flue which are found in each of them. The effect of this arrangement is an equable temperature throughout.

No registers are used, for the reason that they would impede the air current produced by the fan. But an arrangement by which fresh air from the air-shaft is let directly into the hot-air flue is under the control of the ward attendant, and the supply of heat can thus at once be regulated. The system, as described, has now been for more than two years in actual use, and has proved itself an unqualified success.

The water supply in this hospital is derived from the Hudson River. An efficient engine and steam-pump, placed near the dock, sends an eight-inch stream to the reservoir, a mile and a quarter distant from the river, and two hundred and eighty feet above it. The reservoir, formed partly by excavation and partly by embankment, consists of two basins. The larger basin has a depth of twenty-one feet, and the capacity of the two exceeds three million gallons. The supply-main, which connects the bottom of the larger basin with the service-pipe of the hospital, is a twelve-inch iron pipe nearly two-thirds of a mile in length, with a head at the hospital grade of rather more than one hundred feet. The water, which is unusually pure and sweet, is laid on through every part of the building, and all around it. It supplies the steam-boilers and the laundry, the farm-house and stable, and can be let off when needed for purposes of irrigation. Of this element, so conducive to the safety of the edifice, and so essential to the cleanliness, the comfort, and the health of its inmates, forty thousand gallons are used daily at the hospital, even in its present incipient and incomplete condition. The time will doubtless come when four times this amount will be needed, and the demand will easily be met, so ample and thorough is the provision already made.

An ice-house of six hundred ton capacity has been built just below the margin of the reservoir, and from the clean ice there made is filled without hoisting.

The water-closets are, for the most part, in projections of the building, which give them the advantage of light and air upon three sides. A brick shaft, with a cemented floor, reaches from the basement to the ridge opening in the attic, where it communicates freely with the outward air. This shaft contains the water and the soil pipes, and has, on each floor, a hydrant, a closet with a slop-hopper and a sink, the latter having always hot and cold water for the washing of utensils. Around this shaft are placed in each story the urinals and hoppers. Each hopper has ventilation downward into a vertical pipe, by which the current is then carried to the roof-opening. In an expansion of this pipe, at a short distance up, a small gas jet, constantly burning, makes sure of an ascending air-column, while its light, passing through a bull's eye in front, gives the room at night a sufficient and safe illumination. Every story has its own pipe. Each urinal and hopper is supplied with one of Ivers' self-acting gallon tanks, emptying itself with a drenching stream at intervals, that may be increased or diminished at pleasure. Between the hopper and soil-pipe a stench-trap intervenes, while ventilating pipes extend from the soil-pipes on each floor to the opening in the roof.

The hospital is lighted throughout by rosin gas of excellent quality, made on the premises in Butler's Patent Retort.

All the partitions in this building consist of solid brick walls. Beneath the floor a thick deafening of mortar and furnace slag is laid. The floors are made with narrow strips of oak or Georgia pine, resting on a sub-floor. Two of the parlors have a low panelled wainscot of natural wood. With this exception, the entire finish is severely simple and plain. The amount of combustible material in the building is reduced as nearly as possible to a minimum. Every precaution against fire which a powerful head of water and numerous hydrants judiciously placed can afford, has been taken.

All the water mains and pipes have been securely laid at a depth which frost never reaches. A sewer of ample capacity conveys the refuse water of the hospital to the Hudson River. A large dock for the reception of material was early built upon the river, and a road was made from the dock to the building ground. Another road leads to a quarry on the back side of the hospital tract, from which all of its foundation stone is taken.

The plateau on which the structure stands is about fifteen hundred feet distant from the river, and about one hundred and eighty feet above it. "Its rapid slopes and gravelly formation give every facility for drainage, and promise entire exemption from malarious exhalations. The position of the hospital and of its surroundings is such as to insure the seclusion and quiet so desirable in all establishments intended for the insane. The highway which traverses its low ground is mostly out of sight. Railway trains are *heard* as they rush along its western border, but, with the exception now and then of a transient smoke-wreath, give no token to the *eye*. The river is there, an ever-pleasing spectacle—with its imposing banks, its bright reaches of water, and its almost unceasing exhibition of life and motion. Looking southward, the horizon is walled in by the Fishkill and West Point mountains, while on the north it is bounded by the loftier range of the Catskills."

This hospital was opened for the reception of patients in October, 1871. Since that time 450 patients have been admitted, the largest number under treatment at one time being 202. The twenty-two Eastern counties which have been set apart by statute as the *Hudson River State Hospital District*, are as follows: Suffolk, Queens, Kings, Richmond, New York, Westchester, Rockland, Putnam, Sullivan, Orange, Dutchess, Ulster, Columbia, Greene, Rensselaer, Albany, Saratoga, Washington, Warren, Franklin, Essex, and Clinton. The regulations of the institution restrict the admissions to recent cases of insanity, and exclude epileptics and paralytics.

The present managers of the Hospital are Hon. Abiah W. Palmer, Dr. Cornelius R. Agnew, Hon. Amasa J. Parker, Dr. Edward L. Beadle, General Joseph Howland, Hon. Odell S. Hathaway, Hon. Charles Wheaton, James Roosevelt, Esq., and Dr. Frederick D. Lente. Dr. J. M. Cleaveland is Superintendent; Dr. A. O. Kellogg, Assistant Physician, and Robert Roberts, Esq., Steward.

PRACTICAL POINTS IN THE MEDICAL CARE AND NURSING OF CHILDREN.

VI.—ARTIFCIAL FEEDING.*

By Jerome Walker, M. D., Physician to Sheltering Arms Nursery, Brooklyn.

The practical conclusions on this subject may be summed up as follows:

Natural Feeding.—Under healthy conditions, nursing by mother is a religious duty, which, according to universal experience, is promotive of the health of both mother and child.

Artificial Feeding—Partial or total, depends upon the following conditions and circumstances:

1. *Impediments to Nursing.*—On the part of mother—atrophy of breasts, chaps, excoriations, cracks and fissures of nipples, inflammation. Milk of too rich or too poor a quality, or too much or too little in quantity. On the part of child—harelip, cleft palate, or other incapacity for sucking.

2. *Suspension of Nursing.*—Failing health of mother or child, due to impediments named or to disordered secretions and excretions, pregnancy, menstruation, pus in milk.

3. *Prohibition of Nursing.*—On the part of mother—Scrofula, consumption or cancer, or tendency to these diseases; intemperance, habitual use of opium, syphilis, absence of milk with inability to restore it. On the part of child, irreparable malformations.

4. *Means of increasing quantity and improving condition of Milk.*—Under medical advice, hygiene, generous diet, tonics, warm drinks, ginger and milk, malt liquors, electricity, air-pump, castor oil leaf poultices, and internal use of fluid extract of castor oil leaves.

Mixed nursing is expressed by the name; it consists of partial nursing by the mother, and feeding.

Wet nursing involves the consideration of age, moral and physical condition, habits and residence (city or country), quality, quantity, and age of milk,—on optical, chemical, and microscopical examination, and whether the proposed nurse is also to nurse another child.

Nursing by Animals.—Goats and sheep.

Artificial Food.—1. *Milk.*—Cows', goats', asses', may be given, according to age and condition of child, pure or mixed, in variable proportions, with water, lime-water, soda, salt, sugar, glycerine, cream, gelatine, aromatics, farinaceous flour, nitrogeneous and preserved foods—*warmed;* and by means of sucking-bottles, spoons, and pap cups.

---

* Concluded.—Sanitarian, December, 1873, p. 402.

2. *Substitutes for milk* consist of a great variety of substances, requiring much care in their choice and judgment in their use, while some are worse than useless. All starchy substances—all of the preparations from cereals and tubers—sago, tapioca, arrowroot, rice flour, rizena, tous les mois, salep, corn starch, farina, maizena, and other compounds, should be thoroughly cooked and carefully given.

Besides these, there are many "nitrogeneous" and other prepared foods of miscellaneous character, a catalogue of which would be more likely to confuse than to aid those who have necessity for them. Moreover, since persons who require artificial food for infants have access to medical advisers, who best know the appropriateness of particular kinds of artificial food to the conditions to be fulfilled, we defer to such judgment, rather than risk a discrimination in this connection.

Nursing by the mother is the *only* natural feeding, and it cannot be substituted by any other with safety to the health of either the mother or child, except under the conditions above involved, and dwelt upon more in detail in our first article.* So important is the healthy mother's milk, that "mixed nursing" is to be preferred to wet-nursing. The most appropriate food to be given with nursing has been indicated in preceding articles. In regard to wet-nursing, but little need be added. It is to be resorted to when the mother's milk is not suitable, and when a proper wet-nurse can be obtained, but from the lax condition of morality in these times, and the desire for gain at all hazards, it is a difficult matter to procure a healthy, honest, even-tempered wet-nurse, with plenty and good milk. To the poor it becomes a luxury, and they cannot resort to it, even to save their children's lives. A well-regulated system by which suitable wet-nurses can be procured at reasonable prices is yet to be inaugurated.

Nursing by animals is one of the methods of rearing children, but is little resorted to in this country.

Under the head of "Artificial Feeding" is included everything known as a "substitute." Passing by milk, which is a starting point for all estimates on the value of different articles of food, and has in itself all the elements of nutrition, but which cannot always be used for children on account of the caseine, we are prepared to close our series of articles on Infant Feeding by an examination of the three remaining subdivisions.

Food is generally divided into nitrogeneous or flesh-forming, and carbonaceous or heat-forming, neither term being entirely correct—for the latter will build up tissue, and the former will afford heat under certain circumstances.

The first comprises animal flesh, juices and gelatine, certain vegetables and parts of cereals. They are more easily digested by the child than carbonaceous food, but, from this very fact, are liable to serious objection. Such food is often given in larger quantity than the stomach can digest, simply because the child swallows it.

---

* SANITARIAN for May, p. 63.

The second embraces food chiefly composed of starch. These are farinaceous foods. This second class also includes oil and fat.

The danger of too much reliance on farinaceous food is well brought out in Dr. Dunster's note: "Pure starches like arrow-root, etc., have annually killed their hecatombs of infants, and both people and too many physicians have this yet to learn," etc.

The so-called "prepared foods" with their flaming advertisements and testimonials, oftentimes spurious, and accompanied, as in one instance, by the picture of a wonderful baby "brought up entirely on this and no other food"—all of these originate in a desire to meet the wants of children deprived of mother's milk, and often stand in the way of the mother's duty of nursing.

The country is flooded with them. Some are harmless, many dangerous, and a few useful. The thoughtless endorsement of physicians is sadly to be deplored. A *perfect* substitute for mothers' milk has never yet been made, and I doubt whether it ever will be. An exact analogy in solid and fluid constituents cannot take the place of human milk, with its inherent, unexplainable, life-giving principle.

There has been no systematic analysis, as far as I can ascertain, of foods in this country, but there has been a thorough one made in England.*

Coleman's Corn Flour is entirely rice starch, but this starch is one of the purest and most definite forms of starch.

Sea Moss Farine was Carragheen, not Iceland Moss as stated in advertisements, and was not recommended.

Mayars & Co.'s Semolina, 61 parts starch, is a preparation of wheat. (Wheat contains a larger proportion of nitrogen than other cereals, and hence considered more nutritious.)

Finest Spanish Semolina, 57.5 parts starch, is wheat.

Bullock's Semola, a typical gluten food: gluten 48 parts, starch, etc., 42.

Densham's Farinaceous Food for Infants and Invalids, 69 per cent. starch, rather rich in gluten, is wheat.

Chapman & Co.'s prepared entire wheaten flour: starch, etc., 56 parts, gluten 11.9, finest wheat the basis; represents, to some extent, common brown bread in condensed form.

Hard's Food, starch 70 per cent., particularly rich in gluten, is a preparation of wheat, the starch partially converted into glucose by malt.

Brown & Polson's Patent Corn Flour—starch 86 per cent.—genuine corn starch. Indian corn meal may be ranked with oatmeal in life-sustaining and nutritious qualities.

Kingsford's Oswego Prepared Corn, starch 77.5, is genuine maize starch. Maize is more indigestible than wheat, if not well prepared.

Barry du Barry's Revalenta, starch 57.5, is almost entirely Arabian lentils, and what seems to be barley flour. "Of all foods," says the Report, "this is the most worthless. Lentils are most unpalatable, indigestible and flatulent. The nitrogeneous part is mainly vegetable casein, more indigestible than insoluble animal casein."

---

* Medical Press and Circular, 1872.

Neare's Farinaceous Food, starch 74.5, gluten 12.3, mainly wheat, seems a pure article.

Ridge's Food, starch, etc., 69, gluten 12.3, from pure wheat, is slightly alkaline, is good.

Liebig's Food, starch, 62.5 ; ash rich in phosphates ; is good.

To review—Brown and Polson's corn flower, Coleman's British corn flower, Duryea's Maizena, Kingsford's Oswego prepared corn, are all pure starch preparations—the second rice starch, the rest maize. There are three genuine preparations of glutinous parts of wheat, containing variable proportions of starch, viz., Bullock's Semola, Mayans & Co's Semolina, Keen's Spanish Semolina, forming a group in which nitrogeneous and starch foods are included—all wheat preparations—all supposed to have been rendered more easy of digestion by special processes. Fourth group, similar, except they contain diastase in form of malted barley. Evans' Malt Ext., Heff's Malt Ext., Melling's, Liebig's food, Savory & Moore's food for infants, Sea Moss Farine, and Barry du Barry's Revalenta have no nutritive qualities.

Imperial Granum, a preparation of wheat, is useful ; Chichester's Cereal foods, wheat, oats, and wheat and oats, seem, from experiments made in the Nursery at Randall's Island, to be nearest perfection of any substitute ever presented.

Feeling that the time of the readers of the SANITARIAN has been sufficiently encroached upon, and also having in view for the future a more detailed examination of this whole subject of infant diet, these articles are for the present closed, with the hope that the conclusions arrived at—originally for the writer's own satisfaction—may be of service to others, and that they will invite increased attention to this very important and too much neglected subject.

BOYS, READ THIS.—A gentleman advertised for a boy to assist him in his office, and nearly fifty applicants presented themselves before him. Out of the whole number he selected one and dismissed the rest. "I should like to know," said a friend, "on what ground you selected that boy, who had not a single recommendation." "You are mistaken," said the gentleman, "he has a great many. He wiped his feet when he came in, and closed the door after him, showing that he was careful ; gave up his seat to that lame old man, showing that he was kind and thoughtful ; he took off his cap when he came in, answered my questions promptly and respectfully, showing that he was polite and gentlemanly ; he picked up a book, which I had purposely laid upon the floor, and replaced it on the table, while all the rest stepped over it or shoved it one side ; and he waited quietly for his turn, instead of pushing and crowding, showing that he was honest and orderly. When I talked with him I noticed that his clothes were carefully brushed, his hair in nice order, and his teeth as white as milk ; and when he wrote his name, I noticed that his finger-nails were clean, instead of being tipped with jet like that handsome little fellow in the blue jacket. Don't you call these things letters of recommendation ? I do, and I would give more for what I can tell about a boy by using my eyes ten minutes, than all the letters of recommendation that he can bring me."—*Manufacturer and Builder.*

WARMING AND VENTILATION.

GEO. R. BARKER'S PATENT HEATING AND VENTILATING APPARATUS.

By H. Endemann, Ph. D., New York.

Most of the plans proposed for ventilation lack one very essential point, as they propose to collect two or more branch waste air-flues into one general flue. The fact of the unsatisfactory working of the flues by thus arranging them has been proved and finally settled nearly twenty years ago, when it was ascertained that in such cases it not unfrequently happens that waste air from one room will occasionally enter another room. This will especially then take place when the air only in the main flue is given an upward tendency or motion by warming it, or by the application of other motive power.

The fact that our walls are porous, that windows and doors close never air-tight, explains this conundrum, that air may enter a room through supply and waste air-shaft at the same time sufficiently. The more I have had occasion to examine the methods in use or proposed by various parties, the more I have found that this rule is either entirely or partly disregarded.

The plan of Mr. Geo. R. Barker, of Philadelphia, is, however, entirely free from this objection. Mr. Barker uses no main waste-flue. Every flue is acting only for itself, receiving and discharging the air without any connection with other adjoining waste-flues; and it is for this reason that I consider the plan of Mr. Barker superior to many others proposed.

Every single flue is, till it reaches the room, to be warmed and ventilated by a supply-flue, and thence waste-flue, which is carried up to the roof. On the floor line of the room to be warmed, an iron plate with central circular opening is inserted into the flue, to which the special supply-pipe of sheet iron, terminating in the upper half of the register, is fastened. The lower portion of the register communicates with the flue above. Thus the hot supply-pipe is bound to pass through the under part of the waste-flue, communicating some of its heat to the waste air-flue, the air of which is by such arrangement thus given an upward tendency.

"The apparatus is placed in a single flue, at the floor of the room to be warmed and ventilated.

Fig. 1 shows a section of the plan. The flue is supplied with a partition at some little distance below the register opening, through which the heat from the furnace below is to be delivered. Upon this partition, and communicating directly with the heated air column, is placed a sheet-metal pipe, which terminates in the upper half of the register. Through this the heated air is poured into the room. The lower half of the register is designed for the ventilation;

the design being thus to take advantage of the circulation which would be naturally established, and to draw off the somewhat cooled and vitiated air from below.

FIG. 1.

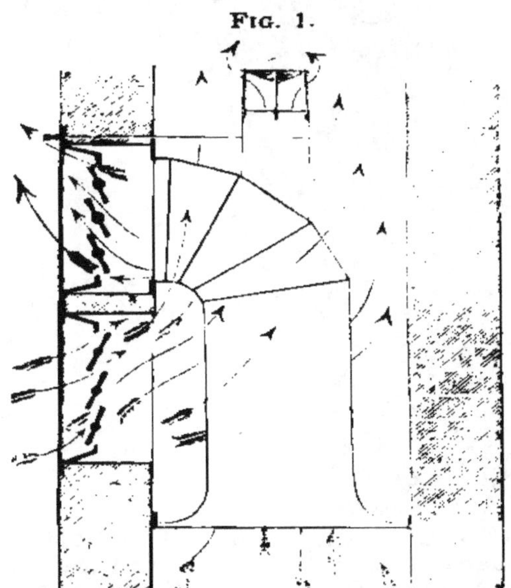

FIG. 2.

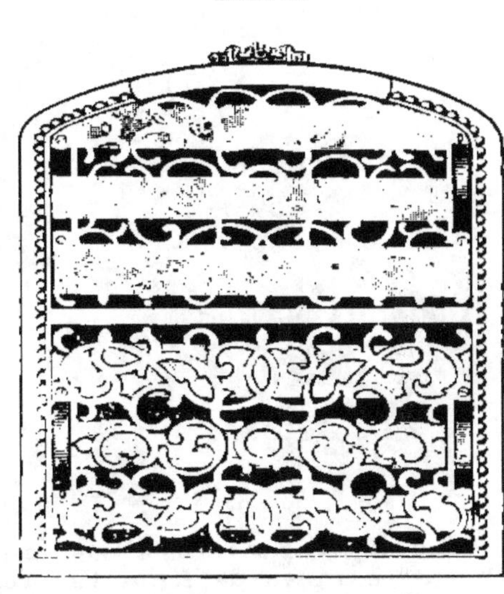

Fig. 2 is a front view of the register face, showing the lateral division separating the heating and ventilating compartments from each other."

The arrangement is very plausible, and I think it is unquestionable that this system could be used to great advantage for the ventilation of houses used as residences; but whether the heat thus imparted to the air of the waste air-flue will be sufficient to cause an adequate activity of the waste air-flues in schools, hospitals or assembly rooms, where *large* volumes of air must be removed, remains to be seen.

The theories of practical men and scientists, who both have done so much to bring ventilation into discredit, will not help us much in deciding such question, as much will depend on the nicety and accuracy with which the proposed work is carried out.

After settling, therefore, on the general principles, we ought to be guided by experience regarding particulars. Experience we can, however, not obtain by general sensations, by testing the atmosphere of a room, packed with persons, with the nose, but only by a series of chemical examinations of the air in rooms before and after the supposed ventilating arrangements are in operation.

Mr. Barker has also tried to apply his system to floor ventilators, as may be seen by the following figures :

FIG. 3.

"Fig. 3 gives a vertical section of the arrangement. The heated air passes upwards from the furnace through the hot-air pipe, C, which is surrounded by a casing, A, extending some distance beneath the floor, leaving an annular space, A A, about the hot-air pipe, which serves as the egress space for the vitiated or cold air."

FIG. 4.

"The register face is also of annular construction, to correspond with the functions of the several parts of the contrivance over which it is placed. (The figure 4 shows its construction.) The openings governing both the ingress and egress passages are controlled by the usual mechanism of an adjustable grating.

The vitiated air which is drawn from the room downward into the annular space A, passes off, in a lateral direction, into a pipe communicating with the ventilating flue."

The circumstances in this case are, however, not so favorable as to insure as good working of the waste air-flue as in his first mentioned combination, the heated waste air being supposed to acquire a downward motion. While this undoubtedly would be true if the fresh air would enter into a hermetically sealed space, it becomes doubtful if we consider the porosity of our building material.

WATER.—In the present state of civilization it appears almost incredible, that an English statesman of the last century imposed a tax on the very first elements provided for our existence—on light and air. Animal life cannot support itself without their free enjoyment; plants are stopped in their development, and are reduced to a sickly and dwarfed condition when deprived of their influence.

The absorption and decomposition of carbonic acid gas can only take place by means of the actinic ray; plants kept in cellars or dark places do not develop a true flower, and are gradually deprived of their beautiful vivid green (cholorophylle). Man, deprived of the beneficial influence of light, loses his strength and energy; looks pale and emaciated; his sleep is restless and disturbed; his digestion and secretions are irregular; his blood is deficient in its essentials, unable to perform its functions, and the seeds of pulmonary or other disease is gradually, but firmly, engrafted into his system.

To future generations, our present mode of taxing the supply of water will be as much cause for just ridicule as Wm. Pitt's tax on windows is to ours. Water is just as essential to our existence as light and air. Ancient Jerusalem, the cities in Assyria, Persia, Egypt, China, and Mexico, had their water supply conveyed from long distances.

In our time, public attention has only been directed to the necessity of an abundant water supply since the repeated visitations of cholera, and the acknowledged fact "that water from springs and wells, contaminated by percolation of sewage, has been the most powerful agent for its diffusion—water is an essential part of our blood and our tissues.

Nature has been lavish in its supply; and there is no earthly reason why the home of the poor should not be as clean, as wholesome, as free from any nuisance or taint, as the mansion of the rich.

Water-meters, valve water-closets, and water-waste-preventers may be quite desirable on the scope of economy; but this economy may jeopardize the health of an entire community. It is criminal to surround the use of such a prime necessity as water with restrictions, rules, and ordinances, when the consequences of such a fatal and illiberal policy can be so plainly demonstrated.

Drains and privies, sinks, and water-closets must be freely and judiciously flushed to avoid the accumulation of organic refuse, or the effluvia will ascend from every opening, every crevice, every hole, and spread disease and misery far and near. It is this false economy which fills our orphan asylums, our poor-houses, our hospitals.

Where the water supply of cities is intrusted to persons who are more careful of party interest than of the welfare of the people; where the best and most abundant gift of Providence is treated as an article of luxury, only accessible to the rich, or doled to the poor, the laws of sanitary science are disregarded, and a heavy responsibility is incurred. Governing is an art. The greatest amount of happiness should be secured to all; and nothing is more essential to the normal bodily and moral condition of men, than an unlimited and unstinted supply of pure fresh water.

NITROUS OXIDE GAS.

By Prof. Faneuil D. Weisse, M. D.

A Paper read before the Medico-Legal Society of New York.

My subject is: "*The Obligations and Responsibility of an Administrator of an Anæsthetic.*"

Its presentation and elucidation was suggested to me by my friend, Dr. Stephen Rogers, after we had served together upon the medical jury, at the Coroner's inquest in the case of Ann O'Shaunnessy. It will be remembered, she died while nitrous oxide was being administered to her as an anæsthetic. The want of appreciation of the obligations and responsibility of an administrator of an anæsthetic, was then made glaringly prominent in the evidence presented to the jury.

From the nature of the organization of this Society, as composed of physicians and lawyers—the latter being less familiar with the fundamental principles of physiology—I will be pardoned, if for their benefit, and also for the fuller exposition of the task before me, portions of what I shall say may, by some, be thought elementary.

The anæsthetics which I propose to consider are those commonly used for the purpose of producing general anæsthesia, viz.: nitrous oxide, sulphuric ether, chloroform and bichloride of methyline. Nitrous oxide, being the one the fatal administration of which suggested this paper, assumes the first rank. I shall endeavor, however, to present the subject matter to bear with the same applicability upon the others.

Dr. E. R. Squibb, in an article on Anæsthetics (read before the State Medical Society of New York, in February, 1871), says: "The condition of perfect anæsthesia is one of the most grave and frightful conditions of life, and by suspending more than half of vitality, it comes so near to death, that it is wonderful to reflect how near the boundary line can be approached, and yet so rarely passed. The issues of life and death are narrowed to but within a few minutes. Add to this the fact that this condition rests with the physician, whether to produce it or not, and it is difficult to understand how its importance can be overestimated." This is a most fitting statement to impress the importance of our subject, and with it I invite your attention.

The obligations of an administrator of anæsthetics refer to the possession by him of a thorough knowledge of: 1st. The physiological play of those functions with which the administration of anæsthetics interferes; 2d. The *modus operandi* of each anæsthetic in the production of anæsthesia; 3d. The warning symptoms, which indicate a jeopardizing of life beyond the limits of easy restoration; 4th. The conditions unfavorable to their safe administration; 5th. The means to be applied to resuscitate a patient.

The functions and physiological conditions interfered with by a state of anæsthesia are as follows, viz. : Respiration, the composition of the blood, its circulation in the capillaries, the presiding influence of the nerve centres over the several functions of the body (more especially the lungs' and heart's action), the contractility of voluntary muscle fibre, and the contraction of the walls of the cavities of the heart.

Respiration: The ultimate objects of this function are :

1st. To introduce, by inspiration into the cells of the lungs, the air containing oxygen ; which oxygen is passed from these through the cell walls and walls of the capillaries of the pulmonary artery (outside of the cells), to reach the colored corpuscles of the blood in the said capillaries, thus oxidizing or arterializing that fluid.

2d. To allow the passage of carbonic acid gas from the serum of the blood, through the same membranous walls into the lung cells, to be exhaled by expiration.

To insure these objects, there must be a free access of a certain amount of available oxygen. I mean, by available, oxygen that can be isolated from its existing combination at the temperature of the body. The proper play of the walls of the thorax and the elasticity of the lung substance. The free flow of blood through the pulmonary arteries and veins.

Composition of the Blood: With respect to the composition of the blood, the elements which interest us are its gases. Venous and arterial blood contains three gases in a state of freedom, viz., oxygen, carbonic acid, and nitrogen. Oxygen predominating in arterial, carbonic acid in venous blood. The nitrogen, being negative in its effects, does not interest us. The oxygen of the blood enters at the lungs, thenceforward it is borne by the blood corpuscles. While flowing in the terminal capillary vessels of the arterial system, it yields up this oxygen to the several tissues, nerves, muscles, etc. It is returned to the blood in the commencing venules of the venous system, after having combined with the carbon element of the tissues, having formed carbonic acid gas, which is held in suspension by the plasma or serum. I desire to lay particular stress upon the location where the carbonic acid, which afterward reaches the blood, is formed. Direct experiments have shown that carbonic acid continues to be formed at the tissues, as long as any available oxygen is present in the blood. Its formation at the tissues may be called parenchymatous, or tissue respirations.

Capillary Circulation: Interference with the capillary circulation is due to carbonic acid gas in the blood ; retained in it, it renders that fluid a poison ; the more so, when the quantity of oxygen is less than twenty-one per cent. The blood, thus altered in quality, no longer flows so freely through the capillaries ; obstruction to circulation commences, and passive congestion supervenes. This state is most dangerous as affecting the pulmonary circulation, because when its capillaries are congested they stem back the blood upon the right ventricle, whose walls become paralyzed from distension. Such are the principal steps leading to so-called asphyxia ; more correctly designated by Dr. Cleveland, of London, as carbonæmia.

Influence of Nerve Centres: This generation of nerve force at the nerve centres depends upon a supply of healthy blood, in order that the determining and regulating influence of these centres should be exerted through the nerves, over the involuntary and voluntary functions of the body. If the vessels of the brain contain blood devoid of oxygen, the necessary chemical reactions evolving the nerve force would be arrested, and the unifying action of the nervous system over the animal organization would be at an end. On the other hand, if the blood in these vessels was overcharged with carbonic acid, it would cause a slackening of the blood current in the capillaries, thus leading to congestion; which condition, as it increased, would produce dizziness, stupor, unconsciousnes, and, if prolonged and marked, death by coma.

The progressive steps in the production of anæsthesia, as it is by poisoning the blood supply these agents paralyze the nervous system, are as follows:

1st. Paralysis of the peripheral sensory nerve fibres.

2d. Of the cerebral hemispheres, by which intellection is impaired and unconsciousness gradually effected.

3d. Of the cerebellum, by which muscular co-ordination is arrested.

4th. Of the spinal cord, which leads to relaxation of voluntary muscles.

5th. Of the medulla oblongata, which presides over the heart and lungs.

This effect is the fatal one to be avoided.

6th. The sympathetic system is affected during the progress of the above effects, but its influence does not become extinct until after all the above-mentioned nerve centres are paralyzed.

Contractility of Muscular Fibre, generally including Cardiac Walls: The contraction of muscular fibre, voluntary as well as involuntary, but more especially voluntary, depends upon the presiding stimulus of the great nervous centres transmitted through the nerves; they will not respond thereto, however, unless the capillaries of the muscle contain properly oxidized blood, free from an excess of carbonic acid.

Blood is incapable in the absence of its chief nutrient constituent —available oxygen—of effecting the necessary play of chemical affinities between it and the muscle cells. Furthermore, the presence of carbonic acid in the blood is a direct poison to the elements of muscle tissue, rendering contraction impossible. It also induces capillary stagnation in the muscle, above described.

It will be remembered that the heart, in its ultimate analysis, is a hollow muscle, divided into four cavities to subserve four special requirements; therefore, what we have said with reference to the influence of deoxidized and carbonized blood upon muscle tissue generally, holds good in every respect with reference to its influence upon the contraction of the cardiac walls, and the induction of capillary stasis in them.

Dr. Squibb has briefly epitomized these above effects, as follows: "The roughly expressed, though perhaps practical, condition essential to anæsthesia is diminished oxidation in the sensorium. It is a kind of partial suffocation or asphyxia, occurring not in the organs of respiration and circulation primarily, but far back of these, in the tissues, where the vital act of oxidation occurs. To diminish this assimilation seems to constitute an anæsthesia ; to prevent it is death from narcosis."

Dr. Anstie says : "Narcosis is a physiological process in which the nervous system is deprived, by the agency of a poisoned blood supply, of its vital characteristics with greater or less rapidity, and which tends to produce general death of the organism by means of such deprivation. . . . . It is a purely paralyzing process."

Special Physiological Action of Nitrous Oxide Gas : As to the modus operandi of each anæsthetic, we have first to consider that of nitrous oxide gas. In this agent we have a chemical compound of one atom of nitrogen and one of oxygen. Its most important properties in our present study are :

1st. That it is not decomposable at the temperature of the body, but requires a much greater heat.

2d. That water will absorb from five-tenths to eight-tenths of its volume.

In order to produce insensibility, by inhaling this gas, a sine qua non is the entire exclusion of air from the air passages. After the administration is commenced, the only available oxygen which the tissues have to depend upon is that then present in the blood, and in the bronchial tubes, etc. Remembering what we previously stated —that carbonic acid is formed by tissue, oxidation, or respiration— we would expect this oxygen to be rapidly consumed. Carbonic acid thus formed, added to that already in the blood, tends to induce carbonæmia. The compound gas, nitrous oxide, alone enters the air passages ; as it is non-decomposable at the animal heat of the body, it does not present available oxygen for the blood corpuscles; thus the blood flowing through the pulmonary capillaries is not oxidized or arterialized. Much of the gas is taken up by the water of the plasma or serum of the blood, while at each expiration a certain amount of it is exhaled. Of itself it is innocuous to the system, and therefore its effects are but negative, viz., by excluding oxygen. Carbonic acid gas continues to be exhaled with the nitrous oxide, and this constituent of the expired gases has been cited as an evidence of decomposition of the nitrous oxide, whose oxygen was therefore said to support respiration. If we consider the ease and rapidity of its anæsthetic effects, and the symptoms of this condition as produced by it, the error of the availability of its oxygen to the corpuscles and subsequent tissue oxidation is made apparent. Nitrous oxide is most rapid in producing anæsthesia, as may be seen by the following data : At seventy-two pulsations of the heart per minute, a complete circulation of the blood is effected by about twenty-seven pulsations, requiring twenty-three seconds; the ratio of inspirations to the heart pulsations is one to four ; hence at seventy-two pulsations, there would be eighteen inspirations, while twenty-seven pulsations, required for the complete blood circuit, would admit of about seven inspirations. It has been observed, that after one full properly taken inspiration of nitrous oxide, dizziness occurs; it only requires from five to seven to anæsthetize. The natural deduction from this would be—the nitrous oxide excludes the normal oxygen of the blood, and its absence is evidenced before a complete circulation of that fluid takes place. The symptoms of nitrous oxide anæsthesia are dizziness, tingling sensation at the surface of the body, as when a limb is said to be asleep, hurried pulsation of the heart and arteries, with diminished and diminishing force, unconsciousness, muscular relaxation, progressive carbonæmia, as manifested by congestions of the venous or carbonized blood at the surface of the body (more especially seen in the dark blueness of the face), and sluggish flow of dark blood during an operation. These conditions, if prolonged, cause the respiratory muscles to stop contracting, while the heart continues to beat feebly for a few moments thereafter. All the above symptoms depend upon poisoned blood supply, due to carbonæmia.

Post-mortem reveals the capillaries congested with venous or carbonized blood, particularly those of the pulmonary circulation; the blood itself is more or less fluid, the walls of the heart are relaxed, the left cavities empty, and the right distended by clots. They are the same as from drowning, hanging, etc.

The following statement made by a would-be ex-cathedra authority: "Nitrous oxide is very efficient as a restorative. It should be given gradually, in moderate quantities, so as not to generate too much carbonic acid. Both it and oxygen are of primary importance in asphyxia. In chemical character and physiological influence they are the direct opposites, and natural antidotes to narcotizing agents and asphyxiated conditions."

These might be passed over as the ideas of an individual writer, but as they present the opinions of a large proportion of the unprofessional administrators of nitrous oxide, I place it opposite the facts above stated without comment.

I feel bounden, as an American physician, to point to this misconception of the chemistry, and the physiological, and therapeutical actions of this gas as an anæsthetic. (Since the reading of this paper, there has appeared in the London *Lancet*, a letter apparently representing American views upon nitrous oxide anæsthesia, in which these same incorrect theories are advanced. In justice to the American medical profession, I take occasion to discard them, and to thereby exculpate ourselves from the semblance by our silence of holding the same.)

Special Physiological Action of Sulphuric Ether: Ether is composed of C_4H_5O.

When administered to produce general anæsthesia, it should be inhaled in the same manner as nitrous oxide, to the entire exclusion of air. In consequence, we induce with it the same conditions and train of symptoms, added to which, we have its special effect upon the tissues of the nervous system, viz.: paralyzing them, according to the degree of local access, by the circulation of the blood. This effect would seem to render it more dangerous than nitrous oxide, but the danger is lessened thereby, because the nerve centres are rapidly affected by the special paralyzing influence of the ether vapor, without necessitating the extreme carbonæmia of nitrous oxide anæsthesia. Furthermore, its special effect enables the inhalation to be suspended from time to time, in order to admit available oxygen. I would not be understood to say that ether is safer than nitrous oxide, but its special effect renders it the more desirable agent for long administrations. The approach of death in fatal cases is the same as with nitrous oxide, expiration stopping before the heart ceases to pulsate.

Special Physiological Action of Chloroform: Chloroform, or the terchloride of formyle, is composed of $CHCl^3$. This is the most powerful and the most dangerous of the anæsthetics. Its greater danger probably depends upon its three atoms of chlorine. While it produces less carbonæmia than the above mentioned agents, its special effect is to so alter the blood corpuscles as to prevent them from assimilating oxygen. This, so to speak, paralysis of the blood corpuscles is not only present at the time of anæsthesia, producing complete deoxidation of the tissues, but the influence upon the corpuscles continues for some time subsequently. This would account not only for the frequent occurrence of the cardiac syncope as a cause of death, but also for the feeble power of the heart, which continues for some time after.

Bichloride of methyline (CH_2Cl_2), which has of late years been considerably used as an anæsthetic, in possessing two atoms of chlorine, participates in the dangers of chloroform, although it has proved itself twice as safe.

What to observe during Anæsthesia: The play of those functions interfered with, should be watched with great solicitude. We should, above all, not allow ourselves to become reckless because of our familiarity with the conditions, after repeated administrations without accident.

The respiratory movements, the pulse, the color of the skin, and of the blood flowing during an operation, the pupils of the eye, should each in turn claim the undiverted attention of him who leads his patient to the very verge of the grave. If danger threatens, the respiratory mechanism will give warning by labored and short inspirations, feeble and long expirations, laryngeal stertor, sudden stoppage of the thoracic movements. A feeble pulse, though it may beat rapidly, tells of the progressively impaired force of the capillary circulation. Arrest of the pulse may occur, dependent not upon capillary stasis, but from arrest of the heart's action, called "cardiac syncope." Chloroform is the only agent which induces this most fatal of all the dangers of anæsthesia.

The occurrence of blueness or lividity of the skin, so common when nitrous oxide is administered, as also the dark hue of any flowing blood, are omens of advancing carbonæmia, which it is our duty to restrict within certain limits. Extreme pallor (from chloroform) indicates impaired action of the heart and warns of approaching cardiac syncope. If the pupils show progressive dilatation, they tell us to admit air, as danger threatens from carbonæmia. An observation with reference to nitrous oxide, made by Dr. Amory, of

Massachusetts, is most important. He tells us: "Never has an animal died unexpectedly; there is a peculiar condition produced by this gas, which, when seen, requires instant relief. Animals, at a certain stage, appear to stop all attempts at respiring, and lie motionless; if not forced to inhale air, they will die." This impresses upon us the importance to watch particularly the respiration, and not to rely too much on the pulse, in anæsthesia. It is an observed fact, that after respiration has stopped in apparent death, the heart continues to pulsate for some time before actual death supervenes.

Of the selection of patients: From what we have so far developed, we would draw the natural inference, that any condition involving imperfect respiration or heart's action, would contra-indicate, or at least add to, the dangers of anæsthesia. Phthisis pulmonalis, cancer of the lung, intra-thoracic tumors, distension of the pleura, compressing the lung, also pleuritic adhesions, impairing their elasticity, are contra-indications.

In the case of Ann O'Shaunnessy, post mortem revealed very marked and extensive pleuritic adhesions of the right lung, which was so congested with carbonized blood as to afford the appearance of the third stage of pneumonia, while the left was free from congestion. This indicated the probable cause of death, as determined by the crippled state of the right lung from the existing adhesions. The morbid conditions of the heart, which would contra-indicate these agents, are dilatations, fatty degenerations, or hypertrophy of the walls, and valvular lesions.

The above states of the respiratory organs would predispose to carbonæmia; the conditions of the heart would render the capillary circulation more susceptible to modification. Cerebral disease, with structural lesions, are cases to avoid, as this organ is rendered thereby more prone to the unbalancing of its functions.

Dangers of Anæsthesia: The dangers which we have to guard against may practically be reduced to two.

1*st*. Failure of respiration from progressive carbonæmia or paralysis of the nerve centre (the medulla oblongata), which presides over this function.

2*d*. Cardiac syncope or arrest of heart's action (chloroform only) from paralysis of the medulla oblongata and want of oxidation of muscle cells of cardiac walls.

In the first instance, while the breathing fails, the heart continues to pulsate. The essential feature, under these circumstances, is arrest of the pulmonary circulation of blood from distension and resultant paralysis of the right ventricle. The indication of treatment is to empty the right heart and restore the respiratory motions of the chest walls.

In the second condition of cardiac syncope occurring from chloroform, we find that while the circulation seems to fail before respiration, the arrest of the heart's pulsation and breathing are almost simultaneous. This failure of the heart, as a primary cause of death, presents to us the most unfavorable conditions for the successful application of restoratives.

Restorative Measures, in case of the Supervention of Symptoms indicating Danger: If any of the warning symptoms enumerated above present, during the administration of either of the anæsthetics under consideration, the administrator should instantly stop the inhalation; place the patient flat upon the back, with the head a little lower than the shoulders, and admit fresh air freely; remove all the clothing from the chest; draw forward the tongue with a pair of forceps and hold it so; dash cold water over the patient's head and shoulders; give several smart slaps over the epigastric region; make pressure with alternate relaxation over the lower part of the sternum; apply ammonia to the nostrils; and introduce a piece of ice into the rectum. All this is accomplished in less time than it takes to tell it. If these measures do not prove successful in inducing respiration, one of two courses is to be pursued, according to the state of the heart. If the heart has stopped simultaneously with the breathing, the phrenic nerves are to be galvanized to induce respiration, effected by "one electrode over the phrenic nerve and the other in the 7th intercostal space," or they may be applied to both phrenic nerves. In either event artificial respiration to accompany the electrization. Artificial respiration may then be resorted to, to assist in the re-establishment of the breathing. On the other hand, if the heart still beats, artificial respiration may be resorted to before galvanism, which latter will probably not be needed, although it should always be tried in conjunction with artificial respiration, if that seems not to be sufficient. Galvanism to the heart and artificial respiration, applied jointly, excite both sides of the heart, and tend to restore the pulmonary circulation. Artificial respiration, which may be performed either by Sylvester's or Howard's method, although the most important means to apply, must not be resorted to injudiciously. It must be remembered that, in inspiration, blood is drawn from the extra thoracic veins into the thoracic, and thence into the right auricle; while, in expiration, blood is withdrawn from the right auricle by the extra thoracic venous trunks in a reverse direction. Artificial respiration should always be commenced by expiration, in order to free the thoracic veins of blood, in the way explained, and to empty the right heart.

In cardiac syncope, galvanism of the phrenic nerves to cause the diaphragm to contract also galvanism of the heart (the right ventricle), affords the most reliable of resuscitation. This is accomplished by "applying the induced current at a point over the right ventricle." It must be borne in mind that, if the heart has ceased pulsating, it is impossible to restore pulmonary circulation without first rousing the heart. One more attempt may be made, viz.: a syringe introduced into a large artery may, by suction, draw out some of the blood, which may be injected back into the artery in a pulsatory or interrupted manner.

This has been found, by experiments upon animals, to revive the action of the heart even one hour and five minutes after death. There is no precedent for using this method in these cases of emergency, but it seems to me that it might be tried as a last resource.

Responsibility: The resonsibitities of an administrator of an anæsthetic agent to a fellow-creature, rests : *1st.* In the selection of patients; *2d.* In the purity of the article administered; *3d.* In the method of administration; *4th.* In the proper attention to the recognition of warning symptoms; *5th.* In having at hand proper means for resuscitation; *6th.* In the timely and efficient application of such means.

1st. From the train of thought we have so far pursued, we can deduce, as a natural conclusion, that an administrator of any anæsthetic should, to a certain extent, be responsible in the selection of his patients. If he is not a physician capable of judging as to the condition of a patient's respiratory organs, heart, and brain, he should require a certificate from the patient's family physician, of fitness to take an anæsthetic. This applies more especially to the administration of nitrous oxide gas, which is almost always administered by non-graduates of medicine or dental surgery.

I conceive that a man administering this gas should be held responsible, by law, for the life of the patient, if he has not required a certificate of fitness from the patient's medical adviser, and it should be discovered by post-mortem, that apparent contra-indicating conditions were present. The reckless manner in which this agent is daily given in our city is but another evidence of the laxity of our laws, in protecting the community from those unqualified to administer remedial agents to the human organism.

2d. For the purity of ether and chloroform, the administrator can hardly be held responsible, as their preparation requires an apparatus only possessed in large laboratories, especially adapted for the purpose. At present there are certain manufactories whose names, by long experience, have been found to be a sufficient guarantee for the purity of the articles which they furnish for the physician's use.

Not so in the instance of nitrous oxide, which is prepared by the administrator, or his assistant (!) The method of obtaining the gas free from all impurities is, in itself, simple and well established. Attention and care will always insure its purity. I regard the administration of gas, in the preparation of which any of the established rules have been neglected, as hazardous; and as such, the administrator should be responsible for its effects.

3d. In the inhalation of the several anæsthetics, the methods differ in certain particulars. With nitrous oxide, air should be entirely excluded, if prompt anæsthesia is desired. With ether the patient's throat and larynx should be accustomed to the vapor, then all air should be excluded. Not so with chloroform, which requires 96½ per cent. of air to be mixed with the chloroform vapor. Such is the mixture as advised by Mr. Clover, the present English authority on chloroform.

If anæsthesia is necessary to be resorted to, especially if the patient's weak condition cannot bear the shock of the operation intended, it is very necessary that its full effect should be induced. It must be remembered that in a partly anæsthetized person, the anæsthetic, if it be chloroform, weakens the power of the heart, and thus the shock of the operation, if pain is felt by the patient, reacts upon the heart, producing fatal syncope more readily than without the anæsthesia. Such a result is not so liable to occur with nitrous oxide or ether; which latter agents have been shown by the sphygmograph (pulse writer) to increase the force of the arterial and cardiac pulsations in the state of properly regulated anæsthesia.

The position of the patient is important, more especially in respect to chloroform anæsthesia. This agent should never be administered in the sitting posture, as the danger of inducing cardiac syncope is much increased thereby. With nitrous oxide and ether, that do not depress the heart, it is not so important.

4th. Above everything, an administrator of anæsthetics should be held responsible for the non-recognition of the warning symptoms above alluded to. His whole attention should be given to the state of his patient's pulse, breathing, pupils, etc. Nor should he think that those participating in the operation for which anæsthesia is induced, share this responsibility with him. He alone is the one looked to to give close attention to the influence of the agent administered. It is true that even chloroform, the most dangerous agent, has only produced one death in 2,873 administrations; ether, one death in 23,204; while nitrous oxide is stated to have been administered 300,000 times with but three deaths imputed to it. One of these occurred two hours after taking the gas, in a patient with advanced phthisis pulmonalis.

The other two cases are the case of Ann O'Shaunnessy, referred to in this paper, and that of a young lady who died in London since the reading of this paper. I do not think that in either of these cases the gas should be regarded as the sole cause of death, but the want of fulfilment of their obligations and responsibilities on the part of the anæsthetizers should bear no small share of the blame.

In spite of these figures, testifying as they do to the comparative safety of this class of therapeutic agents, I think that every administrator should perform his duties, in each instance, with the same care and undivided attention to his patient, as though he expected each succeeding case to be a fatal exception to the overwhelming rule of safety.

5th. We read, in a recent English monograph, that the English anæsthetizer admits his responsibility and his knowledge of the dangers incurred, in the fact that he is furnished with "stimulants—ammonia, the galvanic battery, etc., so that they may be at hand when required."

It may be said, in answer to this, that these preparations are for the admitted dangers of chloroform, but they are at times equally necessary when the safer agents are used.

Every one will admit, who has had any extensive experience with anæsthesia, that, although he may never have had a fatal case, still he has had patients present alarming symptoms, which have yielded to judicious and well-timed restoratives at hand. Every hospital or institution where anæsthetics are frequently administered should be provided with all the necessary means, in case of dangerous symptoms. The galvanic battery should be looked to from time to time to see that it is in order. It is the administrator who should be responsible that such necessary means are present if required. It implies negligence when, in the history of a fatal case of anæsthesia, we read something like the following: "Not having a galvanic battery, it was not applied;" or, "The galvanic battery was used, but it was discovered that it would not work; another battery was sent for, but before it arrived the patient died." So valuable is galvanism in threatened death during the state under consideration, that I think it indeed culpable to find one's self without an agent forethought might have provided. Its application might save a life which we voluntarily put in jeopardy; yet we carelessly and thoughtlessly fail to provide the means of safety which that jeopardizing demands.

6th. Again, every anæsthetizer should know the methods of inducing artificial respiration, not theoretically, but he should have a practical familiarity with the necessary manipulations. He should also know how to apply electricity to the phrenic nerves and right heart.

The proper means of resuscitation at hand, their timely and efficient application is none the less a responsibility. No time is to be lost; life hangs on what is done in two or three revolutions of the second hand. A mistake or omission will be fatal, while coolness and deliberate action, that comes from the mastery of the position by knowledge, will save life.

In presenting this paper, I do not desire to invite the attacks of those who fire off their invective squibs in the columns of our daily papers, to attract the notice of an easily imposed upon community. My sole object will be attained if I succeed in intimidating some of the many who administer anæsthetics, especially nitrous oxide gas. Ignorant alike of obligations and responsibilities, these men quiet their consciences with the reflection that so many have taken it without bad consequences. Had I the power to make and enforce law, I would make a law forbidding the administration of any anæsthetic, except by or in the presence of a regularly graduated doctor of medicine or dental surgeon. The majority of those who are to-day giving nitrous oxide, are mere amateurs (if such a term can be applied), who understand but little of the practice and less of the theory of anæsthesia. They are, therefore, totally unfitted to apply agents to the human body which, even in their safest methods of administration, jeopardize human life by interfering with its most vital functions.

MORT!—The most eminent dealers in wines declare that there is no pure sherry or port in the London market. There is great pertinence in an anecdote of a London dealer, who said to a medical friend, "I will give you a practical hint." Sending to his cellar for a bottle of champagne, he gave his friend a glass, who pronounced it most agreeable and refreshing. "Read that," said the dealer, handing him the cork, and pointing to the inner extremity. He read the startling word *mort!* (death). "That," said the dealer, "is a trade-mark, and where found you may rest assured that no grapes ever contributed to that wine." That trade-mark might, with great propriety, be stamped upon the external extremity of the cork of every wine and beer bottle of the country.—DR. STEPHEN SMITH, *National Temperance Advocate.*

THE AMERICAN ALADDIN.

By Leopold Brandeis, Brooklyn.*

Almost opposite the royal palace a piece of land is lying idle and waste; a shadowy, ill-defined cloud, composed of foul miasma, of poisonous gases, is suspended over it like a huge canopy. The angel of destruction has adopted this vague and gauzy form, and he mixes with the air and enters through doors and windows, through chinks and cracks and crevices, and misery and death are his followers.

The sun had retired to rest, when Aladdin rubbed his lamp, and commanded his servant, the Genius, to build a palace on that waste land in the shortest possible time, and worthy of receiving his beloved, the Princess Badroubboudour. The time of Genii has passed, but we are for ever renewing the wonders of Aladdin's lamp.

Where there are swamps and sunken lots, and stagnant waters today, a few months hence we will find rows of elegant brown-stone dwelling-houses. Carved stone fronts, high and imposing looking stoops, finely railed areas, large plate glass windows, blinds and shutters vividly green, vestibule and tiles in charming combination, captivate the eye. Large and airy parlors, elegant mantels of Italian marble, closets, pantries, speaking-tubes, ranges and heaters, and ever so many more modern improvements lure us on to rent or buy. Accessible as these houses are, by two or three lines of horse-cars, you can reach the ferries or any place in a short time; the builder's advertisement in fact boasts of the unsurpassed location, as combining the advantages of both city and country. You make careful inquiry all around—no case of fever and ague has been known there for many years past. Some one anxious to reduce his rent, some family desirous of securing such superior advantages to their children, perhaps a newly-married couple, all sufficient in themselves, will buy or rent of these seductive dwellings, and form the nucleus for a colony of tenants. As soon as the first excitement of moving in and fitting up is over, just when everything begins to work smoothly and to look comfortable and home-like, some trifling ailment begins to develop itself, and every one is getting anxious and nervous. But a

---

* To the Editor of *The Sanitarian*:

Just as I finished the enclosed article on "The American Aladdin," I received your March number. To my utmost delight, your warning voice speaks there so impressively; the question of drainage is treated there so practically; the defects and needs of our cities are painted there in such lively and glowing colors, that I must consider that article the most complete and exhaustive on the subject ever published. May it find a great many readers, and lead to the improvements so much required for every one's welfare. Yours truly,

L. Brandeis.

Brooklyn, *March* 3, 1874.

slight cold or cough is ascribed to the period of moving in; some difficulty of the digestive organs, to the irregular meals or improper food during that time. The evil appears to increase. The physician is called in and does his best; but one child after another has to be kept home from school; hoarseness and croup, measles and eruptions, infest the house. All possible care is taken, the utmost vigilance and watchfulness exerted to exclude the insidious enemy from the place; but all is in vain. Whence does this unfortunate state of health arise? What produces this chronic condition of preventable disease? Where shall we look for the source of these evils?

The ground on which these houses have been built has not been productive to its owner; year after year he lost the interest on his capital, year after year he had to pay taxes and assessments. Now the speculator will buy these lots of him if he will advance sufficient money for the proposed improvement, and his money will be secured by bond and mortgage.

The American Aladdin, the speculator, makes a contract for the filling up and for the grading of this land; dirt and ashes, garbage and refuse of all kinds is the cheapest and handiest material for the purpose. On this heap of abominations the foundation is laid, the house is reared bright and fresh and showy; provided with all so-called modern improvements as they are, the people are gulled to buy or rent these places often almost before the mortar has set, or the paint is dry.

But the deposit of organic matter, on which the structure rests, remains damp and spongy and fermenting forever. From this compost poisonous exhalations penetrate through every hole, through every opening, through every crack. Emanations, subtle and imperceptible, impregnate the air; noxious sewer gases pervade the entire atmosphere. Under your very feet a continuous bubbling and boiling goes on, as if it was a witch's cauldron; in fact, danger is threatening you and yours from a source so hidden that no human hand could reach or prevent it. This is not a spectre called forth by imagination; these are not the fancies of a diseased mind. Stern reality stares us here in the face; vital statistics furnish their evidence, and every medical man in this broad Union will tell you that localities, as described above, are the hot-bed of disease, the focus where it concentrates, the centre whence it spreads.

Disinfectants are of no avail where the source of the evil can not be destroyed; cleanliness itself cannot battle against dampness, and mould, and corruption. Careful nursing and tonics may be but a temporary expedient to stop the ravages of the destructive enemy, and all our precautions, all our forethought, all our care, cannot lead to any satisfactory result as long as we are occupying any of Aladdin's palaces.

A druggist recently received the following prescription, with a request to make it up: "Fur Kramps: Tinct kamfire, one ounce; tinct lodenum, a little; tinct kyann pepper, two pen'worth; klouform, a little, but not much, as it is a dangerous medicine. Dose, half teaspoonful when the kramps come on."

Editor's Table.

TYPOGRAPHICAL HYGIENE.

234 Broadway, New York, *March* 1, 1874.

Dr. C. R. Agnew: My Dear Sir,—I am sure you will be glad to know that The Sanitarian has reached a degree of success which requires enlargement, by increase of number of pages or change of type. Will you be kind enough to critically examine the enclosed specimens of letter-press, and that which has hitherto been used for The Sanitarian, and recommend to me which one, in your judgment, would be least fatiguing to the eyes, or in any way injurious? Further, please do not confine your examination to these samples, if you think any other better. I wish to adopt the one most consistent with the purpose of The Sanitarian—the preservation of health—and in this respect, of the eyes in particular.

Truly yours, A. N. Bell.

19 East 39th Street, New York, *March* 4, 1874.

Dr. A. N. Bell: My Dear Sir,—Of the specimens of printed pages, I must prefer the more closely printed one. I think that its legibleness is greater. The others seem to be so heavily leaded that the combination of black printed lines and white interspaces does not make a harmonious picture. I believe that the closely printed page, herewith returned, would cause less fatigue for the average reader.

Respectfully yours, C. R. Agnew.

We have accepted Dr. Agnew's choice. The present number contains additional matter over the previous issue equivalent to an increase of twenty-six pages. The reader will not fail to observe an improvement in the quality of the paper also, and in the general make up; and all without any increase of subscription price. It is the result of one year's experience. The Sanitarian has grown upon us; and accepting the necessity of primary and undivided clerical work, we have taken an independent publishing office as being the most promotive of our aims and ends—to make The Sanitarian useful to the people, and to merit their patronage.

QUACK VENTILATION FOR THE PUBLIC SCHOOLS.

The Mayor of New York, in his last annual message, equivocally remarked: "There is no room for doubt that the preceding Board of Education left the school buildings in a very dilapidated condition." Whether his Honor meant to express the dilapidated condition of the school buildings or of the retiring Board, admits of question. For our own part, we are inclined to the opinion that he meant the Board. And, moreover, however well meant his intention to repair the dilapidated condition of the retiring Board by the new appointments, evidence of success is sadly wanting.

So dilapidated, indeed, is the Board of Education, it has taken them a whole year since we first began publishing evidence of school poisoning in New York, under their auspices,* to comprehend the necessity of doing anything to prevent it. Meanwhile, the evidence has been overwhelming from all quarters—from the most credible sanitary inspection and chemical analysis, to the most casual reports in the daily press. At last, with a deliberation which fully justifies the shifting of the Mayor's opinion of their predecessors to themselves, they have moved :—they ask an appropriation of $2,000 to advertise for a specific! They evidently believe that ventilation is obtainable by some whirligig patent contrivance, devised to show which way the air ought to go, but never does,—for the satisfaction of the lookers on and the benefit of the inventor's pocket. The inventors of such machines and those who use them are on the same plane: neither party is sufficiently intelligent on the subject of ventilation to be intrusted with its care.

The Brooklyn Board of Education has also just been aroused from its Rip-Van-Winkle sleep by the report of the Sanitary Superintendent of the Board of Health, who threatens to do for them that which they claim the right of doing for themselves, but which they have hitherto neglected—to have some regard for the healthfulness of their school-houses. They are, at the least, equally dilapidated with their congeners across the river; save only that some of them, and those who from their life pursuits are most excusable and least likely to know anything of hygiene, profess to know all that is worth knowing, and are particularly emphatic in their declarations of self-sufficiency. If, indeed, these gentlemen are as competent as they profess to be for the exercise of their duties, and are withal so criminally negligent, it is high time that they were indicted for children slaughter, for there can be no question that many deaths have occurred in consequence of their neglect. It is surely far more charitable, and we believe more just, to conclude that the execrable condition of the school-buildings of these cities is due to a want of intelligent appreciation on the part of their custodians, than to believe them guilty of so great a crime. These gentlemen, excepting

---

* See THE SANITARIAN for April, 1873.

a small minority, have not been educated either as physicians or philosophers, and there is no reason why they should know much about hygiene or physics.

They know, it is true, something about the variations of temperature, but it is not the trend of their education to apply this knowledge to the ventilation of school-houses. They do not perceive that ventilation is based upon the unimpeded movements of the atmosphere, produced by variations of temperature in the surroundings. And there is no reason, that we are aware of, why they individually should be expected to recognize these or other laws essential to health, any more than it is to be expected of them that they should all be qualified mathematicians, chemists, grammarians, elocutionists, or even master mechanics. And the public has the right to demand of them the ground on which they estimate the health and lives of those committed to their care as of less concern than the choice of mechanics for different portions of school structure, or of teachers in the several departments of education.

Are all who are chosen for these different mechanical avocations, and courses of mental culture, equally competent in all of the other departments of mechanics and learning? A practical inability to perceive the pertinence of this question, on the part of our Boards of Education, is the strongest possible evidence of the exact justice of the Hon. Mayor's opinion of them, of their deplorably "dilapidated condition."

The air of our school-houses, as of other close rooms, only needs to be unhampered to obey the universal law of its nature, to circulate. When shut up in a room, heated and contaminated by respiration, it expands, and if provision is made for fresh air to enter, the foul air, being of less density than the fresh, is displaced, and will escape by any apertures that present themselves, and with especial facility into warmer currents, such as chimney flues, heated shafts and the like. That which remains behind follows the same course. The air of the room being all the while, bulk for bulk, less dense than the outside air, this latter is continually pressing in, to keep up the law of equilibrium established by nature, and the light air is as continually escaping. And thus we should have a continuous circulation. The size and situation of the outlets and inlets should necessarily vary according to the size, crowding, and other circumstances of the room or building, and the relative temperature outside and inside. The greater the difference in these temperatures, if the openings are properly constructed, the brisker the circulation, and the more perfect the ventilation.

In some large buildings, propulsion of the air by means of fans or other machinery is necessary, and for an excellent example of this, the reader is referred to the description under "The Hudson River State Hospital," on other pages.

SCHOOL VACCINATION.

Report of the Board of Education, Elmira, N. Y., 1872–'73 :

This is an unusually exceptional report of a Board of Education in the State of New York, and we sincerely wish that it could be read aloud all over the State, that the other Boards might profit by its faithful observance of law, and conscientious regard for both the mental and physical welfare of schools. The Board of Education of Elmira is the only one in the State, we have reason to believe, that has recognized and faithfully carried out the law requiring the vaccination of school children. Indeed, so generally is this law disregarded, that we very much doubt whether a majority of the Boards of Education throughout the State know of its existence. Boards of Education are *directed and empowered* by it to exclude from the benefits of the common schools, any child or any person who has not been vaccinated, and until such time when said child or person shall become vaccinated. (Chap. 438, Laws 1860.) The Board of Education of Elmira, with regard to this law, and other sanitary duties, elect a Sanitary Superintendent, who is required to visit the schools and ascertain whether the pupils have been vaccinated, and to keep a record of the names and residences of all who are excluded by reason of non-vaccination, and submit the same to the Board at the end of each school term. By the report of the Sanitary Superintendent at the end of the term in October last, we learn that, on his first examination, out of a school population of 5,725, and an average attendance of only 2,697, he found over 200 who had never been vaccinated, besides a considerable number who had been vaccinated imperfectly. These were all immediately excluded until the law was complied with. The whole number suspended for this cause, from the beginning of the term to the summer vacation, was 450 ; and the number of written certificates issued (not including those given by other physicians) was 3,336. At the time of his report, in October, there were not more than six children debarred from the schools on account of non-vaccination, nor was there a single pupil in attendance who was not protected. And Elmira almost wholly escaped the wide-spread epidemic of small-pox of 1873.

THE PUBLIC HEALTH.

Report of the Board of Health, New York, 1872.

Lest our readers may surmise that our chronology is at fault, we assure them that this volume, although due in 1873, is just issued, one year behind time. The volume gives no explanation for the delay.

In a rapid glance at its contents, one looks in vain for the handiwork of collaborators whose names and practical experiences had given zest to previous volumes from this department, and had become familiar to all interested in practical sanitary work; 23 pages of a condensed summary of the labors of the different bureaux of the department afford us but few points for comment.

The reports from the department have led many to expect, at least, such summary results as would show some real advancement in the practical application of sanitary science to the prevention of disease, or amelioration of the causes of the high death-rate of the city. But in this volume we confess disappointment.

The mortality for the year exceeded that of the previous year (1871) by 5,761—the total number of deaths being 32,747, and for want of a better reason, this greatly increased mortality is charged "to the early and intense heat."

Then, why are not the tropical cities depopulated? We turn to page 115 and find that "the mean temperature of the year was 51.46°, *being* 1.28° *lower than that of* 1871, *and* 1.68° *lower than for the previous ten years.* (The italics are ours.) The maximum temperature was 97° on July 2d, the minimum 4° on March 5th and 6th." In the report for 1871 we find "the mortality for that year was 199 less than for 1870," and "the diseases which gave an unusual death-rate were of the contagious class," such as "small-pox and whooping cough." Other reasons must then account for a death-rate of 32.6 per thousand in a city possessing superior sanitary advantages, and a health organization supposed to be, at least, the most efficient of any on this continent. And when we take into consideration that the death-rate for 1871 was 28.6 per thousand, a difference in favor of 1871 of 4 per cent., one naturally inquires as the Frenchman says, "Pour quoi?" We fail to find any explanation, or even attempt at one from any deductions herein given.

This subject, the most important, as it seems to us, regarding the direct effects of good sanitary organization and work, appears to be considered by the Health Board as of the least importance; and no word of warning or suggestion for future sanitary improvements, in order to prevent disease and thus reduce the death-rate, is even hinted at. Again, referring to the report for 1871, we observe this remark: "But if the death-rate of 17 per 1,000 is taken as the standard of a town in which no person dies of a preventable disease, *we have in our own mortality records conclusive evidence of the extent to which the removable causes of death prevail in our midst.*" (The italics are ours.) If, then, the difference between 17 and 32.6—to wit, 15.6

per thousand—is chargeable to "removable cause of death prevailing in our midst," pray why have not some of those causes at least been removed?

There is no complaint of want of funds or limitation of authority in the execution of the health laws; therefore this question, under the circumstances, is not an improper one.

Epidemic cerebro-spinal fever and small-pox, the only diseases which the committee seem to charge with being "preventable causes" of increasing the death-rate, foot up a total of 1,710—a very small show for a total increase of 5,761 over the previous year, 805 of which were by small-pox.

In the records of the Bureau of Sanitary Inspection, and that of Vital Statistics, may be found the real gist and value of the report. Both of these were presided over by gentlemen of acknowledged ability, and to them the Board owes the most of its real practical utility.

We find in a tabulated statement of the amount and kind of service rendered by the Bureau of Sanitary Inspection a total of matters and places inspected, 110,907—giving rise to 26,661 causes of complaint—for each of which a written report was made to the Board. This amount of labor by a corps of 22 inspectors shows a conscientious performance of duty upon their part, and such as we naturally expect from members of the medical profession.

The detailed results of their labors are given in the Appendix and form a large part of the volume, and give, in their details in the nineteen Inspection districts, a very lucid idea of the different sections of the city. Did time and space permit, we would like to illustrate and quote largely from these gentlemen's reports. These individual experiences form invaluable data for the progress and promotion of sanitary science.

The report of the Bureau of Vital Statistics forms the most valuable part of the Appendix, and gives evidence of a master hand in its compilation.

Its various tables and charts are of inestimable value for reference and comparison, and when properly studied afford the experienced sanitarian true indications for the exercise of efficient executive work.

Table xxxi., page 197, exhibits of itself a prolific source of disease, and points a true indication for strenuous and persistent effort upon those charged with the preservation of the public health. It gives 15,750 deaths in 9,375 tenement houses, and when we analyze these the death-rate, in some instances, is truly appalling—*e. g.*, in two houses 24 deaths in one year; one would almost suppose that these were "pest-holes"—and in this connection we cannot but remark that had the amount which the plates cost that illustrate the Epizoötic disease among horses, which we find in the "Appendix," been applied to searching out and removing the cause of the great mortality in these "pest-holes," it would have been better applied. Fifty pages of the Appendix are devoted to a report upon Epizoötic Influenza, which, from all we can see to the contrary, has but a limited bearing upon questions of public human health. It would have been better to have published it separately in pamphlet form, or in some work upon veterinary science.

Second Biennial Report of the State Board of Health of California, 1871, '2, *and* '3.

The title of this volume but poorly expresses its scope of inquiry. The efficient Secretary who did so much in the first place to establish a State Board of Health in California displays his responsibility by a comprehensive repertory of State medicine in general, and deduces therefrom the practical application of the best experiences to his own sphere of duty, which is an exceedingly interesting one. The novel and striking characteristics of California are conspicuously presented, and the relation of health to physical geography instructively exemplified.

Much felicitation is expressed with the mortality of California, and of San Francisco in particular, as compared with other States and cities, but without apparently recognizing the difference in the relative ages of the inhabitants of recently settled regions of country by the most viable inhabitants (the smallest proportions of both the young and the aged), as compared with regions long settled, and retaining the largest proportion of the least viable.

Measured by the proportion of zymotic diseases and consumption to other diseases, California appears in a less favorable light, doubtless due to a well-recognized cause. "Much of the land, especially in the vast tule regions, is of such a nature that probably it can never be effectually drained, and could not be profitably cultivated even if drained. Nevertheless, in careful and thorough drainage lies our only hope of escape from malarial influence."—(p. 54.) Table 1 shows the total mortality, as well as that by the most prevalent diseases in twenty-six localities (p. 54), comprising nearly half the population of the State, with the ratio of deaths per 1,000, from July, 1871, to June, 1872. Population, 261,714; deaths, 4,464—17.1 per 1,000. Of the whole number, 754, or 5.91, were of consumption; 356 of other lung diseases, 309 of diseases of the stomach and bowels, 37 of diphtheria, 24 of scarlatina, and 204 of typho-malarial fevers.

Interesting special reports on Topography, Endemic Dysentery, Intoxicating Liquors, Adulterations of Food, Hygiene of the Teeth,

Sewerage, General Synopsis of a Course of Lectures on Hygiene, and the Health Laws of the State are appended.

Annual Report of the Board of State Charities of Massachusetts, 1874.

The first striking feature of this report is the ratio of increase of the *insane* poor. And that "the ratio which the insane poor bears to the whole number of paupers is constantly growing." In 1864, it was as 1,625 to 6,300; 1872, 1,900 to 5,400; and at present, 2,000 to 5,400. Ten years ago, the ratio being 30 per cent., and at present 40 per cent.

"This change may continue to go on until half the indoor paupers of Massachusetts are lunatics or imbeciles; and yet it does not indicate that lunacy is gaining faster than the general population is growing. It does seem to show that we have checked general pauperism without being able to check that pauperism which springs from insanity." The average number of paupers supported by the State, 6,163, is less by 87, or 1⅓ per cent., than it was ten years ago, while the population of the State has increased 25 per cent. Notwithstanding, as "the State pauper insane are removed from the State at the rate of more than 150 a year, while the settled poor are seldom removed," the conclusion seems to be inevitable, that in Massachusetts, at least, insanity is certainly on the increase.

Infant Mortality is adverted to, apparently, for the correction of "a recent writer," who asserts that "in large cities fully one-half the deaths are of children under five years." In controversion of this statement, as applied to America at least, of 5,888 deaths in Boston, in 1871, 2,395, or 40 per cent only, were of children under five; 1872, 42 per cent.

The percentage of infant deaths to living infants is much less, being in Philadelphia about 25, and in Boston about 24 per cent. for infants under one year old, which is more than double the death-rate under favorable circumstances.

Taken at large, the mortality of infants under one year old ranges from 15 to 25 per cent. of all that are born in a given time.

"The statistics on this subject, vary in different places and in different times, but everywhere this difference exists, and in some cases it is extreme. Thus we are told, on the authority of long experience, that of those nursed by the bottle, in the care of other persons than their mothers, oftentimes only about ten per cent. live to the age of one year, whereas, of the infants who are fed from the bottle in care of their mothers, seventy per cent. live to one year of age. It has also been found that of those nursed at the breast by others than the mother, only twenty-eight per cent. lived, while if nursed by their own mothers, eighty per cent. lived. At the New York Infant Asylum, of those nursed by hired women, twenty-three per cent died; of those nursed by their own mothers, seventeen per cent. died. This fact shows the importance of the maternal relation."

Small-pox.—"The number of cases for 1872, among the State poor alone outside of the State institutions, was reported as 672, but is believed to have exceeded 1,000. For 1873, 971 are already recorded, and it is probable that the number will reach 1,200. It appears that 2,000 State paupers were stricken with the disease. The record shows already 1,633 names, and every town heard from increases the number. The subsidence of the disease appears to be due to a want of material. As an epidemic, it has simply burned itself out." A shocking commentary on our boasted civilization, in view of the long since settled question that small-pox can be wholly prevented. The pecuniary cost of this epidemic alone, in Massachusetts, exceeds half a million of dollars. To have prevented it need not have cost more than twenty-five thousand dollars. But the anguish of the sundered relations necessary to the care of this disease, of the sick and of the dying, has no atonement.

The report altogether is one of unusual frankness and statistical value, and we regret that space will not admit of an extended notice of the State institutions, private charities, and other matters of equal interest.

Annual Report of the Board of Health of Louisiana, 1873.

This report is characterized throughout by a broad comprehension of the duties involved in sanitary administration, and shows corresponding results.

Yellow fever, which, according to its nature, on being once introduced into a congenial climate seems ever prone to reappear, no longer finds in New Orleans a resting place. From beginning to end it is met with a will, and a conscious power to overcome it which should never again be neglected or relinquished. And in view of the terrible prevalence of this disease in other parts of the State, as compared with New Orleans, which used to be considered its nest, the President of the Board does well in recommending legislative action for an extension of sanitary administration over the whole State. "The neglect of sanitary measures and use of disinfectants made the only difference in malignancy between the fever of Shreveport and Memphis, and the fever of New Orleans and Mobile." There were in all in New Orleans 388 cases and 226 deaths.

Small-Pox—1,300 cases, 505 deaths!

"In assigning the responsibility for the prevalence of this preventable disease in the city of New Orleans during the year, it is to be remembered that the law of the State, which gives the Board of Health its powers, and by which its duties are defined, does not mention the subject of vaccination, and provides no means to carry into effect schemes for vaccinating those who require it. The Board of Health, however, furnishes a limited supply of pure, fresh vaccine gratuitously to all physicians of the State who apply for it. It offers gratuitous vaccination at the offices of its Sanitary Inspectors to all who apply, and enforces its ordinance, that no child shall attend the public schools unless protected from small-pox. . . .

"As the best and only preventive of the injuries which small-pox would inflict on this city, I recommend that gratuitous vaccination be offered at every house in the city."

Cholera.—"The first appearance of this disease in the United States in 1873, was at New Orleans." The history of this epidemic has been so abundantly given *au courant* in THE SANITARIAN, that it is not deemed necessary to repeat it. The total number of cases in New Orleans, recapitulated in the report, was 259.—If space permitted we would be glad to notice in detail the various interesting sub-reports on Meteorology, Sewerage, and Drainage, the Chemist's report, etc., all of which show meritorious work.

Total number of interments for the year, 7,505, an excess of the average—due to small-pox, 505; cholera, 359; yellow fever, 126—making from these three unusual causes, 1090.

"Assuming the population to be 200,000, the death-rate will be a little more than 37 per 1,000."

Annual Report of the Board of Health of Baltimore, 1873.

This is a brief report, consists almost wholly of tables. It opens with the felicitation that—

"Excepting the epidemic of small-pox which prevailed during the winter of 1872 and 1873, our city has been absolutely free from epidemic disease, and subtracting the number of deaths resulting from this cause from the whole number throughout the year, it will be shown that our death-rate is below that of any other large city whose reports have been seen by us, and including even this number, we compare favorably with the most favored."

Number of deaths recorded: Of small-pox, 617; of typhoid fever, 225; from consumption, 1,098—from all causes, 7,817. About 27 per 1,000.

Liberal appropriations are recommended for sewerage and drainage, and special attention invited to the chemist's report on the adulteration of milk, with suggestions for its prevention.

Annual Report on the Births, Marriages, and Deaths of Providence for the year 1872. By E. M. SNOW, M. D., Superintendent of Health and City Registrar.

Chiefly a statistical report. Summed up: Births, 2,206; marriages, 1,084; deaths, 1603. Population, estimated at 76,107, giving for the year, of births, 1 in 34.5; marriages, 1 in 35.1; deaths, 1 in 47.47, or of deaths per 1,000, about 30. Chief causes: Consumption, 241; cholera infantum, 151; pneumonia, 98; heart diseases, 92 (!); typhoid fever, 68; old age, 68.

--- ---

INFLUENCE OF ALTITUDE ON HEALTH.

Dictionary of Elevations and Climatic Register of the United States; containing, in addition to elevations, the latitude, mean annual temperature, and the total annual rain-fall of many localities, with a brief introduction on the orographic and other physical peculiarities of North America. By J. M. Toner, M.D. New York: D. Van Nostrand, 1874.

This is one of the very best of Dr. Toner's characteristic compilations, showing an originality of combination of census and other statistics of extensive application to a variety of useful purposes. In this volume, he presents data from a variety of reliable sources, with an introduction and brief comment in regard to the effect of elevation upon different diseases. That yellow fever has, perhaps, never reached a higher elevation in the United States than four hundred and sixty feet, and rarely above Vicksburg (175) and Memphis (262.) The same is the fact in Mexico and the West Indies. As regards pulmonary disease, there appears to be a growing distrust in the curative influence of the sea-shore and the low and damp coast of the tropical islands so extensively patronized in the past. A table presented in the Dictionary, which gives the percentage of deaths to the whole population for the three last decades, and the relative frequency of consumption to total deaths in each of the States and Territories of the United States, as returned in the census of 1860 and 1870, shows that those States, as a general rule, presenting the lowest elevations and greatest area of ponds, lakes, rivers, and wet lands to their whole area, have the largest number of deaths from diseases affecting the various organs. The apprehension that high elevations, because of the lessened barometric pressure, may induce hæmorrhages where the lungs are weakened by disease, has not proved to be well founded. From the testimony of disinterested army officers and other parties, given, not to support any theory, but recorded as interesting facts observed, Dr. Toner is led to surmise that there may be found a region in some part of New Mexico, perhaps as favorable for patients suffering from phthisis, as can be found within the boundaries of the United States.

Current Reports show in:

New York—Prevalence of scarlatina, diphtheria, croup, acute pulmonary affections, and a ratio of deaths from consumption of about 4 per 1,000.

Brooklyn—About the same as New York. From an abstract of the annual records, the Registrar has published the following:

"I feel that a brief summary will not be amiss, and hence make it as general as possible, by stating that there were 10,963 deaths, 5,539 of which occurred among children under the age of five years.

There were reported 5,027 births, and 2,520 marriages, 1,003 still births, 185 deaths among the colored population. The death-rate to one thousand on the basis of the United States Census of 1870, is 27.6, and on the estimated population (435,314) 25.

"The smallest number of deaths to the thousand in any ward, occurred in the Third, where the death-rate was only thirteen to the thousand on the basis of 1870 census, and twelve on the basis of the estimated population. The largest was in the Sixteenth Ward, which was 43 to the thousand, on the basis of the census of 1870, or 40 on the estimated population."

The deaths from consumption number 1,376—12.55 of the whole number.

Small-pox, 118 ; typhoid fever, 103.

Philadelphia,—typhoid fever.

Baltimore,—typhoid fever, scarlatina, and acute pulmonary affections.

Boston,—scarlatina and acute pulmonary affections. Of the total mortality, deaths from consumption average one in about every 5.18.

Chicago,—small-pox.

New Orleans,—small-pox, severely ; deaths for weeks ending, February 8th, 15 ; 15th, 23 ; 22d, 27.

San Francisco,—scarlatina, small-pox, diphtheria, and typhoid fever.

Cleveland,—small-pox, but growing less prevalent.

Cincinnati,—scarlatina.

Indianapolis,—typhoid fever.

Pittsburg,—typhoid fever, scarlet fever, and acute pulmonary affections.

Providence,—scarlatina and typhoid fever. Condensed report for 1873, and comparative for the last six years :

Year.	Population.	Deaths.	Deaths to Population.
1868..............	64,138	1,110	One in 57.78
1869..............	66,522	1,256	One in 52.96
1870..............	68,904	1,263	One in 54.55
1871..............	70,907	1,254	One in 56.54
1872..............	76,107	1,608	One in 47.53
1873..............	78,500	1,719	One in 45.66

The population for the year 1870 is according the national census of that year. The population as given for the other years is estimated from the increase as shown by the census.

Wheeling,—typhoid fever.

THE SANITARIAN.

A MONTHLY JOURNAL.

VOL. II.] MAY, 1874. [NO. 2.

THE RELATIONS OF HYGIENE TO PRACTICAL MEDICINE

Introductory Address to the Class of L. I. College Hospital, March 5, 1874.

By Prof. JARVIS S. WIGHT, M. D.

GENTLEMEN,—In coming to these Halls to pursue the study of your profession, I recommend you to lay aside all ideas of exclusive systems of medicine, for such ideas will lead you from the high aims and objects of your life-work. Bring with you patience, perseverance, industry, and devotion, for you have embarked on a long, a difficult, and a perilous voyage. Cultivate your senses, your judgments, and your hearts, that your education may attain its full vigor and usefulness when coming responsibilities shall rest upon you; and never forget that the highest professional ambition is truth in Science and fidelity in Art. In this way, and under this spirit, you will be better able to comprehend that most abstruse science—*Rational Medicine*, and to master that most difficult art—*Practical Medicine*. And being masters of the Healing Art, you can unveil the principles of Sanitary Science and, by the application of it, exalt your professional work to the highest degree of excellence. And among the multitude of topics that suggest themselves as appropriate to this occasion, I know of none having a more profound interest to the profession and the public than the *Relations of Hygiene to Practical Medicine*.

Hygiene relates to the means of preserving health, and Practical Medicine relates to the cure of disease. One is healing, and the other is prevention. If an ounce of prevention is worth a pound of cure, then Hygiene is of more value than Practical Medicine. Do not understand me to underrate Practical Medicine, for if a man will not allow you to ventilate his house, arrange his dietary, and drain his premises, when he is well, it does not follow that you should not know what to do for him when he gets sick.

First of all, then, let us have the clearest possible conception of the nature of disease; for such conception, and the knowledge that it brings, will throw a flood of light on the subject of Hygiene. And let us rise to this conception by familiar and well-understood terms of comparison.

How, for example, did the dram-drinker get *Stealosis* or *Sclerosis* of the liver? That is, how did his liver become a mass of fat, or how did his liver become hard and "nobby"—like a pile of nutmegs? Alcohol, in one form or another, was the cause, and a "gin-drinker's liver" was the effect—a definitive disease, one that you will often be called upon to treat, and one that you will sometimes have the opportunity to prevent.

Suppose you were to give a man one drop of croton-oil three times a day. It would not be very long before he would fall into a condition of collapse. Now put this collapse side by side with the collapse of cholera, and mark the very great resemblance. Yet one is called a disease and the other is called a poisoning.

Administer Mercury to a healthy man from day to day, and destroy the fibrin, the albumen, and the corpuscles of his blood; give him a sore mouth, and an eruption on his skin. This is called the physiological action of a medicine. It seems to me that this is just as much a disease as syphilis.

Let the heat-ray fall upon the capillaries, and they dilate; let the light-ray fall upon the eye, and the pupil contracts. So opium congests the capillaries and contracts the pupil. The burning sun of summer may strike one down in the midst of life; so may the electric fire from the rain-cloud; so opium, and so, too, may the malignant emanations of a swamp. But malignant malarial fever, as you all know, is called a disease; and can we not apply the term "disease" to "sun-stroke," "lightning-stroke," and "opium-poisoning?"

Eliminate iron from a man's daily food, and his blood is impoverished; deprive an ox of his salt, and he will emaciate; and one who constantly gorges his stomach with beefsteak will have indigestion. In some countries there are people who eat dirt; diarrhœal affections supervene, and the forces of nature literally pull the "dirt-eater" down into the dirt out of which he was made.

One septic poison will cause an eruptive fever, another will cause puerperal fever, another will cause typhus fever, and another will cause typhoid fever. A fever is a disease; but we admit it to be a "poisoning," by saying that a septic poison is the potential cause.

A blow upon the head may cause a "solution of continuity" of the scalp, fracture the skull, and concuss the brain. As the modern physical philosopher would say, the molecular motion of the muscles of the arm is converted into "mass motion," which is again converted into molecular motion in the convolutions of the brain, which receives a *shock*. Inflammation follows with a change of *structure* and *function*.

Disease is, therefore, a departure from the normal structure and the normal function, caused by some disturbing force. I say both function and structure, because, in our present state of knowledge, we divide disease into *organic* and *functional*. Of course, when the structure has undergone change, there is a change of function. And I am perfectly willing to admit, with Trousseau, that every functional disease depends on change of structure. Hence, when our methods of investigation have become perfect, it will, no doubt, be found *that all disease is organic*.

What about the "germ" theory of disease? Let me give you my idea of it. Suppose, for instance, that a student of biology has chosen the yeast plant for his specialty. He discovers the yeast plant, the yeast sporule, the yeast germ. Then he looks through his yeast ideas at the universe. He sees the sun, the moon, the earth and the stars run by fermentation. He sees society develop itself by fermentation; and fermentation presides over our birth, our life, our sickness, and our death. So that if we live or die, it is fermentation. The same thing may be said of the theory of parasitism; the same thing may be said of the proto-plasm theory, and the same thing may also be said of the physical theory of disease. The fact is, we must not put a part for the whole. Disease results from a variety of causes, and the widest generalization gives us the best definition. *Force acts on matter under organization and disturbs its organic relations; hence disease.*

The force that vibrates in the sunbeam; the force that falls in the raindrop; the force that shivers in the falling leaf; the force that ebbs and flows the ocean-tide; the force that the decaying vegetable liberates; the force that builds the oak and fashions the lily; the force that "incepts" the germ of cholera on the Ganges; the force that nature so wonderfully stores up in opium; and the force that is born of Hope, Joy, or Fear, may lay hold of the elements of man's body, and drop them into dust again.

Let me now call your attention to some of the causes that operate to disturb the health of individuals and communities—to such disturbing forces and influences as fall more properly in the province of Hygiene, and which, in our present state of knowledge, are more or less preventable.

One of the most noticeable health-breaking factors is *bad ventilation*. The savage makes poles into a hut, in the form of a truncated cone. He leaves an opening in one side for himself and fresh air to enter. He leaves another opening in the top for the exit of impure air and the smoke of his fire. Our primitive people built chimneys with open fireplaces in their log houses. How simple, how perfect, to warm and to ventilate! But the evolved savage—the citizen—builds his house with four square walls, and leaves a door for the occupant to go in and out. There are windows, to be sure; but the curtains and the blinds bar the entrance of the sunlight. The citizen puts a *seamed* iron box in his cellar, builds a brick box around it, and deadly gases are drawn from the iron box, where the fire burns, into the brick box, whence superheated air rises through registers into the rooms above, carrying sulphurous acid, carbonic oxide, and carbonic acid. And he makes no registers in the side-walls to let out the contaminated air! Go with me into that brown-stone front: You might imagine Dante's inscription written over the door, *Who enters here must leave hope behind.* It may be that a merchant lives there; it may be that a doctor lives there; the suffocating products of combustion and respiration will drive us out in unseemly haste. This is no unfair statement; it is, indeed, too true. The merchant can feel the pulse of Wall street, and the doctor can feel the pulse of his patient, but they never give a moment's thought to the air-pulse that brings from the furnace both heat and death. Our business-men, and doctors, too, go into the country and imitate the savage to gain the luxury of simple and robust health, and I have more than once saved the life of infancy and of age by letting the sunlight into the sick-room, excluding furnace-gas, stopping the leaks of gas-pipes, giving proper nourishment, and throwing medicine to the dogs. And, believe me, you can do the same thing. Do you not know that a candle under a bell-glass will go out in a short time in the products of its own combustion? The *Homo* will just as surely "go out" under like conditions.

The subject of clothing stands by the side of that of ventilation. The clothes we wear constitute a kind of peripatetic house. The birds of the air and the beasts of the field have an annual or a perennial dress. Man puts his dress on and off morning and evening. Why clothe animals and men? To protect, to warm, and to ventilate. What a net-work is made up by the sweat-pores covering the whole body. Occlude absolutely the sweat-pores by disease or with varnish, and death will supervene. You might as well stop digestion as stop cutaneous transpiration.

Textile fabrics of material from nature's loom are experimentally the best for protection, for warming, and for ventilation. By such means we put a kind of artificial lung on the body over the sweat-pores. The textural interspaces contain a "residual air," which is kept nearly at the temperature of the body, and which slowly and evenly warms the constant afflux of cool, fresh air, while the deleterious vapors uniformly go out by diffusion. That is, therefore, the best clothing which best supplements the function of the skin.

I have a word to say in regard to the clothing of the young. And why do I say it? In order that you may be forewarned and equipped for a crusade against a stronghold of ignorance and superstition. I make a plea for the innocent and the helpless who—such of them as survive—will some day be our men and women. Who clothe the young? It is done under the guide of maternity. How is it done? The legs are bare, the arms are naked, the neck and upper part of the chest are exposed, scanty clothing is put on the *body*, and that is all. Why so? Would you believe it? It is done to *harden* the little ones, to give them good constitutions! How cruel, how sad, how touching, and how lamentable may be the result! The mother means this for good. But let her dress herself as she does her infant; let her give it a fair trial; depend on it, the trial will not last long. Will you dissipate on the winter air the warmth that God has provided for developing your child into the full vigor of manhood and womanhood? Will you imitate that poor mother, who gave her newborn infant a daily snow-bath? The gods had compassion on her tender babe and took it away. I will not say that she was guilty of infanticide. I think, however, it is proper to say there has been, during the last few years, some improvement in the clothing of the young.

Some facts of importance may be mentioned about food and drink. The food we eat and the drink we imbibe are transformed into the brawny arm that toils; into the brain that thinks; and into the heart that pulsates. Is it, therefore, an indifferent thing to think of what we shall eat and drink? We have not the mysterious selective power of animals, which, magnet-like, draws them to their proper food. We must, in our experience, choose what is good for us, provided we know. To choose what is good to eat and drink, is a matter of Hygiene. To choose what is not good to eat and drink, is to fall into the hands of Practical Medicine. Chalk in sugar, dough-beans in coffee, sulphuric acid in vinegar, and excrement in tea, are examples of health-breaking factors. For instance, twenty samples of tea were examined recently in London, and only one found pure. The nineteen other samples were sent to the United States, where they will find plenty of purchasers and consumers. Hence, it appears that Hygiene is making progress in England, while, in the United States the prospect is yet good for Practical Medicine. And does it not make some difference who it is that shortens human life? For the tradesman, who intentionally adulterates food, has immunity, fortune, and social position, while the physician or apothecary, who, by accident, makes a mistake, is broken on the social wheel, and ruined.

Out of the question of food grows the chemistry of the kitchen. In the language of modern science, the proper molecular motion is given to food in the fire of the kitchen, and it vibrates in unison with the feelings and wants of the inner man. And, hence, a sound mind vibrates in a sound body. But, whether the molecules vibrate or not, let the kitchen be watched as the doctor watches his patient, as a broker watches the stock market, for eternal vigilance in the kitchen is the price of safety to the individual, the community, and the nation.

The appeal that went up from yellow-fever-stricken Shreveport penetrated to the remotest parts of the Union, and was answered by a shower of gold. The people will give millions for charity, but not one cent for Sanitary Education. Heaps of garbage, filth, mire and slime were rotting and festering in the streets of Shreveport under the rays of a torrid sun, because the people were ignorant of Hygiene. Had they been wise in Sanitary Science, their streets would have been swept and garnished, and Practical Medicine would have been busy with its ordinary routine. Who cares how much employment Hygiene keeps from Practical Medicine? Certainly not the doctor, for, in the hour of peril, the doctor will stand at his post of duty, and if need be, die there. Practical Medicine find fault with Hygiene for a benefaction that is kindred to its own good work! He is no doctor who does not wish for Hygiene a "God-speed."

Hygiene has a wide circle of duties to perform:—The *sewer* of Brooklyn lies under the streets; it is the receptacle of all manner of filth and uncleanliness, and it disgorges its contents through its hundred outlets into the river and bay. Let Victor Hugo describe its contents: "These heaps of garbage at the corners of the stone blocks, these tumbrels of mire jolting through the streets at night, these horrid scavengers' carts, these fetid streams of subterranean slime which the pavement hides from you, do you know what all this is? It is the flowering meadow; it is the green grass; it is marjoram, and thyme, and sage; it is game; it is cattle; it is the satisfied low of huge oxen at evening; it is perfumed hay; it is golden corn; it is bread on your table; it is warm blood in your veins; it is joy; it is health; it is life. Thus wills that mysterious creation which is transformation on earth and transfiguration in heaven."*

From this huge subterranean intestine a diverticulum goes off into almost every house. The kitchen, the dining-room, the parlor, and the bedroom are separated from its pestilential vapors only by an insignificant water-trap, through which disease may come and do its work silently and well.

Do you call this Hygiene? I call it a *sewer*, and sewage, and typhoid fever, and cholera infantum, and "epizootics," and short life, and plague and death. Hygiene preserves health, it prevents disease; it is the daughter of Practical Medicine, and she learned her trade of her mother. Hygiene works at one end of the furrow and Practical Medicine works at the other end. This spurious Hygiene which puts a sewer under the city, is the child of expediency and ignorance. Away with it, and give us the Hygiene that makes twice "blessed" by removing the cause of disease and converting it in the crucible of nature into the elements of life.

Intramural sepulture has been found to be detrimental to health. This is simply a matter of experience. In theory, the same result is obtained. Sepulture now takes place outside of cities; but the city grows—it invades the place of sepulture, hence it is alleged that sepulture is not according to the principles of Hygiene. Why delay the change of "dust to dust and ashes to ashes?" Why wait hundreds of years for the decomposition of the body? Repulsive mummies, putrid flesh, and disagreeable bones are all surely going back to dust again. I do not, at present, undertake to give an opinion on this subject; but they tell us to burn the bodies of the dead—to imitate that which nature does—but what we do, to do quickly. A handful of gray ashes in a sepulchral urn will symbolize the "ashes to ashes and dust to dust," and rivet the links of memory, while the uprising gases from the furnace will symbolize the spirit that's gone. And then of a truth—the dead cannot harm the living.

You will now begin to comprehend the meaning and the value of Hygiene. It teaches us how to use the means of preserving health—that is, it is the science and the art of preventing disease. It teaches us how to bring pure air into our houses, and how to expel impure air; it teaches us how to warm our houses in winter, and keep them cool in summer; it teaches us how to clothe ourselves and our children; it teaches us to buy pure food and cook it scientifically; it teaches us how to enrich the plain that the plain may nourish us; it teaches us how to prevent disease and so prolong human life, and immeasurably increase the sum of human happiness; it teaches us how to dispense with medicines; it teaches us how to add millions to our

* The SANITARIAN, February No., p. 507.

country's wealth, and enhance, apparently, without limit, her material prosperity; and, I have no doubt, that Hygiene will find ways of preventing the unspeakable calamities which flow from the "social evil." It may be that the contaminated, like the lepers of old, will be excluded from society by an impenetrable wall of law and order.

With your permission, gentlemen, I will try to meet an objection that is sometimes urged against Practical Medicine. It is said that patients sometimes acquire an appetite for certain drugs administered to them, and it is alleged, therefore, that such drugs ought not to be given. I answer this objection for two reasons—first, it will illustrate certain relations which may spring up betwixt Practical Medicine and Hygiene; second, I am always glad to remove any unnecessary opprobrium from an honorable profession. Now, I admit at the outset, that drug-eating has followed drug-taking, and that drug-eating is a most deplorable thing; opium-eating and dram-drinking are examples.

Now let us test the validity of the objection. Suppose a friend falls into the water, and is in danger of drowning. You throw him the end of a rope, which he lays hold of, and you extricate him from peril, and save his life. Again, a doctor is called to a patient whose life can only be saved by opium—such cases occur. He gives opium, and saves his patient. Or suppose that the patient is in collapse, and that the doctor bridges over with wine a few anxious and precious hours, and the patient recovers. Are not all these acts commendable? Are they not morally good? Who would refuse to throw the rope, to administer the opium, or to give the wine, even at the risk of there being a little "oil" in it?

Suppose the patient does take to dram-drinking, and destroys his life, would you stop giving wine to save the life of another patient? Or suppose the patient takes to eating opium, and poisons himself, would you withhold opium from one suffering excruciating pain? Or, again, suppose your friend, in a fit of melancholy, should hang himself with the rope that saved his life, would you refuse to drop the end of a rope into the hands of any other man in danger of drowning? I would give a sick man drugs for the same reason that I would tie a bleeding artery—*to save his life.* In health, drugs are un-sanitary; in sickness, healing. They ought not to be given in health, and they ought to be wisely prescribed for the sick.

In the development of society, new facts, new sciences, new arts, and new industries arise; the simple becomes complex, and where one before toiled, two or more now labor. This complexity of development is true of medicine, as a glance at the past will show. Once the priest was the physician. In time the priest confined his attention to religion, and the physician became the medicine-man. Then surgery arose. And, in the mean time, the apothecary began to flourish; and then the dentist came also. And, last of all, but not least, Hygiene comes to work for man's good.

Who shall keep the keepers? Where shall Sanitary Science be taught? And to whom shall it be taught? I will answer this question by and by. In the meantime, let me ask: *Who need sanitary instruction?* In my opinion, the people need it—and the medical profession need it. Let the elements of Hygiene be taught in every common school, in every academy, in every private school, and in every college in the country. The bodies of our youth need the saving grace of cleanliness. And when they grow up they will teach their children the simple and health-saving rules of Hygiene. But where shall we begin to dissipate ignorance? Why, of course, begin with the medical profession, and begin with undergraduates.

It was a damaging thing, when one of the officers of health of New York city gravely informed Judge Whiting that "highjinnicks" meant "a bad smell arising from dirty water,"—damaging both to politics and medicine, but most damaging to the people, whose most important interests were in the hands of ignorant keepers.

But what shall I say of medical schools and Hygiene? If medical schools taught Hygiene *per se*, and insisted upon their graduates being "posted" in the principles of sanitary science, officers of health would at least have the merit of being sanitarians. And yet all the sanitary science that works well has been taught in our medical schools. But the rays of sanitary light are still very diffuse, a few rays coming from each department of medical instruction. Physiology is the science of function; it teaches us that food, drink, air, light, heat, and electricity are needful to the body; it teaches us that osmosis, cohesion, adhesion, and chemism are co-workers to build up our daily life; it teaches us that sensation, thought, volition and motion are manifested through the nerves, and inferentially it teaches us that the abnormal use of our organs eventuates in disease. Hence it follows that the proper use of our different organs constitutes the substance of Hygiene. Chemistry teaches us the atomic, or volumetric, constitution of bodies; it disarticulates the molecules of both organic and inorganic matter; it teaches the student the nature and use of disinfectants; it enables us to turn aside the aggressive forces of deleterious gases and of germinal matters by allowing them to expend their energies on ozone, chlorine, carbolic acid, and sulphurous acid. Chemistry teaches us how to permit the elements to war with each other, that they may have pity on man, who more and more learns how to overcome the elements and convert them into health-giving factors.

Prophylactics constitute the "van-guard" of Therapeutics. A knowledge of prophylactics enables us to interpose a shield against an aggressive morbific force, and thus sometimes to prevent a hand to hand conflict with disease.

The obstetrician is the sanitarian of the cradle and of maternity. He heralds the advent of the "little stranger," and watches over the function that invests the invisible with the form divine. His office, *per se*, is the prevention of disease, and when disease supervenes he is no longer the obstetrician,—but the medical practitioner.

Surgery encounters the sanitary question at every step:—Fresh bleeding surfaces, and wounds healing or sloughing, are so many rich fields for germinal matter to fall on and grow in,—are so many planes where the vital force has been depressed, and has for the time being lost its ability to resist the influence of degrading forces.

The curability of disease bears a constant relation to Hygiene. The poor man with an iron constitution goes down in sickness, when the rich man rises up to health again. Could you see the small unventilated tenement where the poor man lives, and where the sunlight never comes, you would not marvel. And I often think it so strange that men and corporations will continue to use their money in building up such damaging abodes for those who "toil and only toil."

These diffuse sanitary rays make a kind of twilight. And the question is now being asked, would it not be a wise thing to concentrate these scattered rays into one bright beam, coming from a sanitary chair, giving light to the medical profession, who could, in turn, instruct the people. And then the profession of medicine would, indeed, merit the name of being a liberal profession.

The medical schools make a legion of doctors every year; some are qualified, and some are not. The standard of medical examinations is not high enough. Give the diploma to an unqualified man and it becomes cheap. Of course, the qualified cannot place a high value on cheap degrees. The whole thing resolves itself into sound teaching and proper qualification. The wise and proper management of the green-room would lie at the foundation of Sanitary Science, and would constitute the highest "stroke" of Sanitary Art.

What hope is there for Hygiene in this country? Will it succeed? Can it be planted among the people? And will it grow and flourish? In my opinion, Hygiene has a grand future in this country; I will tell you why I think so. The American youth—and especially those who come here to study medicine—have a practical turn of mind; they do not believe much in theories—they believe in the useful first, and after that, the beautiful. It is an acknowledged fact, that our medical men are among the best practitioners in the world; they have more science on the other side of the ocean, but our students are always wanting to know what will cure their patients—and they generally find out, too. Now, I hold that this practical turn of mind is the best kind of soil for the cultivation of sanitary science. Let the seed be planted there—it will take root and grow, and it will be perennial; the seed will be scattered over the length and breadth of the land, and the harvest will abound more and more; the calamities that befell Memphis and Shreveport will not occur again; the beauty and healthfulness of our rivers will not be marred by dead animals, by the refuse of factories, and by sewage; there will be more to live for, and life will be more desirable; there will be less sickness and less need of medicine. Hygiene will be invited to come to our banquets; she will be a perennial guest in our homes; she will be the presiding genius of our hospitals; she will adorn our temples; she will be sculptured in marble and wrought in bronze in our public parks; and she will be raised high above Medicine, and enthroned in the Capitol of the nation with Liberty.

In conclusion, gentlemen, the science of Physiology is more and more emerging from obscurity. Old theories from time to time pass away; new facts are discovered every year, and, of course, a wider generalization. Our studies and researches are bringing us nearer and nearer that *vital constant* which binds together the chemical, the physical, and the physiological, and which underlies gravitation, molecular motion, and *chemism*. The better we know the nature of the "on-going" of the life of the body, the better can we know and understand the action of the *factors* that ceaselessly tend to break down and obliterate the life forces. To turn aside these degrading factors is the province of Hygiene. Give us new information in regard to *structure* and *function;* then follows an improvement in Sanitary Science; an improvement in our knowledge of the physiological action of drugs; and an advancement in the practice of medicine. In fine, it will happen, as in the vineyard of old, that the last shall be first.

Medical Toadyism.—It is a melancholy fact that, among members of a dignified profession, there can be found cropping out, here and there, a disposition to toadyism, which is too marked to escape notice.

Of all varieties of sycophancy this is the worst, because it has more or less effect upon the entire profession, lays before the world a vulnerable and weak side, which serves as a mark for the arrows of ridicule and contempt, and throws discredit upon many who are thoroughly honorable in motive and action, and who regard with disgust the medical toady and his ephemeral acts.

The great and only object of ambition of these "enlightened practitioners" is to "get practice" among the "upper ten thousand," and to this end they worship that elevated and uncertain idol. They are as jubilant, when they can prescribe for a notable or notorious personage, as was "drop and pill Ward" when he obtained royal permission to drive through St. James' Park; or when Chevalier Taylor affixed to his name "ophthalmiator, pontifical, imperial, and royal."

These flattering and clinging doctors often possess a certain amount of shrewdness, in their attention to "great folk," which, for a time, baffles the unobserving in the profession, and even may cloud the vision of those upon whom their assiduities are lavished. Patients often mistake the *real motive* of attention paid, and attribute the same to a heart-felt interest in the case; a desire to be successful, which the perfect toady never feels, though he simulates it to perfection, making him thus an accomplished hypocrite.

If a *successful* toady would you be,
Your first, main study is hypocrisy.
If 'tis too palpable, it will not pass
For virtue true; 't must be like *purer brass*,
Which, when 'tis moulded by *experience* bold,
By *reputation* it may sell for gold.
Therefore, dear toad, tell every mother she,
In her fair daughter, will remembered be;
And every father gladden with the lie,
That in the son, his virtues you descry.
And if, when walking through a splendid street,
Some playful children you should chance to meet,
If *watched by parents thro' the window pane*,
Pat their dear heads; you may a patient gain.

—*New York Journal of Homœopathy.*

THE SEWAGE QUESTION.--THE DRY-EARTH METHOD OF TREATING REFUSE.

By SAMUEL LEAVITT, New York.

Read before the New York Public Health Association, Oct. 23, 1873.

THE EARTH-CLOSET.

This system was introduced into Lancaster, England, by Mr. Garnett, of Guernmore Park.

In 1870, the earth arrangement was taken in hand by the Corporation, its use having been demonstrated. In 1869, there were two hundred privies of this sort in Lancaster. The stools were not covered in detail, but Mr. Garnett's men supplied earth to the pits once a day. No slops entered those pits, and not all the urine. For besides the men's day urine, which here, as elsewhere, would commonly not go into the privies, Mr. Garnett had an arrangement which extended to 170 out 450 families, by which the urine of chamber vessels was kept from the closets. It was collected in large vessels and removed daily. A shilling a quarter was paid to those who would thus keep their urine separate.* At first, the ashes of the town were mixed with earth, but ashes [Bituminous, S. L.] are now discarded, though the street-sweepings are found available. The dried earth is broken up by a steam-turned roller, and is screened so that is it a dry brown powder when used. The report states that as compared with water-closets, as usually kept in similar parts of towns, there is no question that greater cleanliness and less offence are attained by the earth-closets in the poorer neighborhoods of Lancaster.

Again, the death registers show that few or none of the deaths from diarrhœa and typhoid have been in houses provided with earth-closets ; and the medical men of the town agree in stating that since their introduction fever has almost wholly disappeared from parts of the town where it was formerly rife.

Dr. Buchanan thus sums up some of the

ADVANTAGES OF THE EARTH SYSTEM.

1. The earth-closet, intelligibly managed, furnishes a means of disposing of excrement without nuisance, and apparently without detriment to health. 2. In communities the system requires to be

---

*I believe that the time will come when, even in the largest cities, a system of main and branch pipes will be laid for conducting urine to the wharves, where it will be received in barges containing tanks. It would not be such a difficult matter to take it away from each house in close vessels. This outgoing fluid would be worth much more to those who took it away than is the milk which is brought into the city in such quantities.

managed by the authority of the place, and will pay at least the expenses of its management. 3. In the poorer class of houses, *where supervision of any closet arrangement is indispensable*, the adoption of the earth system offers especial advantages. 4. This system does not supersede the necessity for an independent means of removing slops, rain water and soil water. 5. The system might be at once applied to any town of 10,000 inhabitants. 6. As compared with the water-closet, the earth-closet has these advantages : it is cheaper in original cost ; it requires less repair ; it is not injured by frost ; it is not damaged by improper substances being thrown into it ; and it greatly reduces the quantity of water required by each household. 7. The whole agricultural value of the excrement is retained.

In a paper read before the Glasgow Sewage Association, March 30, 1868, E. C. C. Stanford, F. C. S., says: "Water is a mere carrier, and no disinfectant ; its cost also, from the great quantity required, is very considerable. The whole system of sewerage by water carriage is extravagant. It carries the solid and liquid excreta down to our neighbors to rot at their doors, and leaves us a legacy of deadly gases, to remind us that our effort to cheat Nature has signally failed. As applied to even ridding ourselves of the nuisance, it is the finest effort of the 'circumlocution office,' and the best illustration of how not to do it in our generation. Engineers have employed an elephant to do the work of a mouse, and the burly brute has trodden down and laid waste the country."

In another paper before the Glasgow Philosophical Society, Mr. Stanford, says: "Our authorities want, of course, some grand scheme, but they forget that the question is one of minute details. We are assailed by a large army of small nuisances—one at least to every house, and we must attack them one at a time. Attacked in their united strength they will assuredly overcome us."

THE NEW SYSTEM IN AMERICA.

The introduction of the earth-closet into this country is largely due to the labors of George E. Waring, Jr., of Newport, who has written several books on the subject. He thus criticises the popular American systems of treating human excrement: "The water-closet is the chief thing of which women living in the country envy their city cousins the possession. In country houses one of the first steps towards elegance is the erection of an expensive water-closet in the house, provided with a force-pump that is doomed to break the back and the temper of the hired man; a tank and pipes which are pretty sure to be burst by frost every winter ; the annual tax of the plumber's bill; and, worse than all, a receptacle in the garden known as a 'cesspool,' which usually has a private subterranean communication with the well, from which drinking water is taken. The manure is of course lost; it is worse than lost. Too far below the surface to be of use to vegetation, it lies a festering mass, sending its foul and poisonous gases back through the soil-pipe and the kitchen drain into the house; and developing in its putrid fermentation the germs of typhoid fever and dysentery that any film of gravel in the lower soil may carry to the well or the spring. * * * Hence comes typhoid fever, *of which no single case ever occurred in a civilized community without the direct intervention of human agency.* * * Out-of-door privies, those temples of defame and graves of decency, that disfigure almost every country home in America, and raise their suggestive heads above the garden-walks of elegant town-houses, are, I believe, doomed to disappear from off the face of the earth." Mr. Waring quotes as follows from Prof. S. W. Johnson, of Yale College: "The guanoes and fish manures which are brought from a distance or manufactured at a heavy cost for our market gardeners, are in reality paid for, not by them, but by those who purchase their produce in the city markets. The animal who stands at the head of creation requires the richest food and yields to the food producer the richest return. It requires but little art to convert *his excrement into increment*, the conversion may be made extremely profitable. The excreta of a man have been valued in Flanders at $9 per annum, and the Chinese agriculturist will give a day's work for ten gallons of urine."

Writing of the destruction of American soil, Mr. Waring says: "Fortunately it will not continue always. So long as there are virgin soils this side the Pacific, which our people can ravage at will, thoughtless *earth robbers* will move West and 'till' them. But the good time is coming when (as now in China and Japan) men must accept the fact that the soil is not a warehouse to be plundered, only a factory to be worked. The sewers of London wash into the sea the manurial products of 3,000,000 people, to supply whom with food requires the importation of immense quantities of grain and manure. The wheat market of one-half the world is regulated by the demand in England. She draws food from the Black Sea and from California; she uses most of the guano of the Pacific islands; she even ransacks the battle-fields of Europe for human bones, from which to make fresh bones for her people; and in spite of all this her food is scarce and high, and bread riots break out in her towns."

Nearly all the earth-closets in use in this country are modifications of that of Rev. Mr. Moule. The prominent manufacturers are the Hartford Earth-Closet Company and the Wakefield Company. The latter have introduced a large number of their closets into Central Park. Mr. Waring says truly that, "besides the need of this system in smaller towns, there are portions of this city where something of the sort is absolutely necessary. The whole Harlem flat is so low and level, that it will be almost impossible to lay the sewers so high as not to be entered by salt water at high tide."

It has been demonstrated in England that street-sweepings are available for the earth-closet. I believe that it is entirely practicable to use this system for the whole city thus: Let there be a depot-shed in each ward or precinct, to which all the best and driest of the street-sweepings shall be brought and all the ashes. Let the carts dump their loads upon coarse screens, to remove all such refuse as tin and crockery. Let the dirt pass through rollers or stamp mills, and then through revolving screens; and when duly prepared be taken to the earth-closets, and thence to the country. When desired, it can pass several times through the closets. Thus, instead of an expensive removal of street dirt and ashes and night-soil, the city can send these three "nuisances" away in the form of the most valuable known fertilizer.

It is probable that this business will prosper in small towns faster than in cities or isolated abodes. The latter will not take the trouble, and the cities will use water-closets until shamed out of the practice. But individuals will start Dry Earth Companies in towns, as has been done in New Haven, and will soon so demonstrate the merits of the plan that the municipalities will adopt it. The lack of such companies furnishing earth and removing the product, has been the only obstacle to the rapid spread of this great reform. A United States Dry Earth Company should be formed, which would put itself in communication with the coal-dealers throughout the country, who have sheds, screens and carts, and are in the habit of removing ashes. This Company should induce the coal-dealers to sell all the varieties of closets, furnish dry earth, and remove and sell the fertilizer; and they should be guaranteed a fair price for the condensed grades of the latter, at a central depot in New York, when neighboring farmers did not want it. Such an organization would cause the system to spread like wildfire.

The first apparatus patented in this country for such use of earth was the "Excelsior Sanitarian Cover" described below. The patent was dated in 1866. The first Moule commode was imported into this country in 1868. The following testimonials will show the progress of the reform as represented by the Moule, Wakefield, Hartford, etc., closets:

"It is the best means of disposing of night-soil. It is particularly valuable in this city, and in all localities where similar [imperfect] conditions obtain with regard to drainage." J. H. Rauch, Sanitary Supt., Chicago.

"The system of earth-closets at Fort Adams, R. I., appears to have at length settled a question which for twenty years or more has been a source of perplexity, trouble, and expense." J. F. Head, Surgeon U. S. A.

"From ten to twenty earth-closets have been in constant use upon the Brooklyn parks during the last year. We are introducing them in preference to water-closets, even where water supply is already secured and sewers laid." Olmstead, Vaux & Co., Landscape Architects and Superintendents.

One hundred Wakefield closets are now (1873) in use in the Central Park, N. Y.

"As Chairman of the Committee from the Boston Board of Aldermen appointed to assist at the Jubilee Festival, I had occasion to observe the working of the earth-closets, and they appeared an entire success." E. A. White.

"This is one of the cheapest and most useful discoveries of modern times." Mass. Board of Health.

"The most important sanitary discovery of the age." Wm. Lloyd Garrison.

"Whether regard be had to economy, health, or decency, the earth-closet is *facile princeps*." Howard Potter, of Brown Bros.

The following persons give similar testimony in favor of the system: Stephen Smith, M. D., N. Y. Board of Health; R.W. Brady, S. J., President of College of Holy Cross, Worcester, Mass; B. Evans, Supt. State Reform School, Westboro', Mass.; L. D. Wilcoxson, M. D., Conn. State Hospital; J. F. Whiting, Mayor of Rahway, N. J.; W. C. Chapin, Pacific Mills, Lawrence, Mass. The principal Methodist Camp has ordered its universal use on its grounds.

THE EXCELSIOR SANITARY CO.

of New York claim to have issued the first patent for earth-closets in this country, viz., in 1866. However that may be, they have certainly developed some useful inventions. Their best addition to sanitary apparatus seems to be a hollow cover.

The invention consists of a hollow compartment in this lid or cover, for the reception of a suitable deodorizing compound, with openings in the under part, through which, when desired, by turning a handle, the preservative agent is thrown into the chamber-vessel—part before, and part after the vessel has been used, thus bringing the antidote in immediate contact with, and enabling it to overcome, the poison.

Something of this sort is certainly called for, besides the stationary earth-closets, for sick-chambers and many other places where regular closets cannot be used. It is acknowledged by all sanitarians that even the carrying of vessels which emit foul odors and poison the air from the chamber of a patient to empty, is one of the most prolific sources of the spread of cholera. Through a series of complications, such as often befall patents, this useful invention is only now being put on the market. All physicians who have seen it are loud in its praise. It is peculiary adapted to act as a pioneer in this line, because being so small it can be put away in any corner or closet, and kept full of earth ready for sickness, or a rainy day, or a day when the water-closet is broken or frozen. The recent addition of a galvanized iron receptacle—the size of a large slop-jar—with a wooden privy-seat rim, makes it a complete earth-closet. J. G. Collins, Sing Sing Prison, said of this machine: "It is just what is wanted for all our prisons. I cheerfully recommend its introduction into each and every cell of each and every prison." Theodore Dimon, Physician of Auburn Prison, said: "The agent of our prison has determined to have one of your hollow covers attached to each night-pail in every cell of this prison. * * * This will enable us to keep them in use, without cleaning out, for say a week or even longer. The evening march of the working convicts to the pail-ground would be saved, and much exposure to rain and sleet avoided." D. B. McNeil, Inspector of State Prisons, said: "I am satisfied, from experiments made here under my eye, that it is highly valuable and wholly indispensable for purifying the cells of all prisons."

THE GOUX SYSTEM FOR CITIES.

There are a few considerations that make the Goux system especially applicable to this city at present. Perhaps the most important of these is that the company introducing the process here are already running wagons carrying their peculiarly prepared tubs to and from the houses of customers. This does away with the principal obstacle to the use of all these machines. A description of the system will show what are its other advantages. M. Goux's invention reverses the earth-closet system by placing the great bulk of the disinfectant and disintegrating material in the receiving-tub before it is used at all. A layer of any dry absorbent material (preferably earth, ashes, or peat, though sawdust, cut straw, and similar substances seem to answer nearly as well) is placed over the bottom to such a depth that when the mould, which is a close-covered kettle, is placed on it, the upper edge of the mould will be on a level with the upper edge of the tub. Additional absorbent matter is now packed round the mould, so that when it is withdrawn, the vessel, with its packing, shall present a receptacle in the centre the size of the mould. With the absorbing material used there is mixed a small quantity of disinfecting powder—sulphate of iron or green copperas—and there is a simple arrangement placed beneath the seat, whereby every time the closet is used a shower of this disinfecting powder is sprinkled over the vessel and its contents. As soon as the dejections reach the vessel, the fluids are all absorbed by the porous substances on its sides and bottom. The solids are therefore left in a comparatively dry condition, and putrefaction is prevented, while the odor is neutralized by the disinfecting powder. It is claimed that the powder is not needed in out-door closets.

It will be seen that the special advantages of the system are the utilization of the sweepings of houses, stores and factories, for packing, the use of a powerful disinfectant, and the infallible prevention of nuisances, sometimes still contingent upon the use of earth-closets, from neglect or disarrangement of machinery, or failure of earth supply. That which is to negative the most of the natural offensiveness is already in the tub, and will do its work even in the face of intentional neglect or wilful attempt to make mischief.

So much can be honestly said in favor of this system. The claim of its backers, that it supersedes the earth-closet, is not admissible. The latter is nature's true democratic form of governing this important matter. If its product is rather bulky, so much the better; it will stay near and be used upon the soil that furnished the aliment that produced it. Monopolists cannot send it to fertilize distant lands. It may even be considered unfortunate, except so far as city product is concerned, that the dry earth can be used safely, half-a-dozen times, and the fertilizer thus condensed.

The Goux Urinal is a tall cylinder, in which is placed a funnel with a long perforated tube. The cylinder is so packed that the tube reaches to the bottom, while at the same time it is surrounded by absorbing material, mixed with disinfecting powder.

This system has already been introduced largely in Europe, and after a protracted trial made at Aldershot, during 1871, the British War Department, on the recommendation of several sanitary commissioners, specially appointed, has determined to adopt it. Although the contract was made and arrangements prepared for about 4,000 men, yet the service has extended, without difficulty or inconvenience, to about 11,000 or 12,000 men, and no complaints have been made. In 1872, about 1,500 closets were in use every day in Halifax, England, and several large towns and villages in the manufacturing districts were making arrangements to introduce the Goux system.

This is a very important fact, for the Moule system had the start, and as the English are looking very carefully into this matter, it is a proof that they have found the Goux system specially adapted to the use of the rough, careless, slovenly men who usually inhabit barracks, prisons, etc. It is said that there are now about 10,000 Goux closets in use in England.

The *Scientific American* of Jan. 1st, 1872, in an illustrated article on this machine, said :

> This form of earth-closet has been extensively introduced in London, where a corporation, known as the Sanitary Improvement and Manure Manufacturing Company, has been formed, and a large and profitable business inaugurated. The company employs a large number of drays and men, who go around to regular customers, removing the filled tubs and replacing them with others. The town of Halifax, Eng., has also adopted the system, and will soon be entirely fitted. The towns of Bradford and of Wakefield, after a close examination of the results obtained at Halifax, have decided on adopting the system, and the company is in treaty with several other corporations for the same purpose. For hospital purposes the system is excellent.

In the Report of the Medical Officer of the Privy Council of England (1870) appeared the following earlier testimony for the Goux closet : "This system is now somewhat extensively tried at Salford. The ordinary midden-closet can be converted into a Goux pail-closet, at trifling cost, by cleansing out and filling up the midden, and paving the floor beneath the seat. An examination of the amount of nuisance arising from a pail-closet, as compared with the old type of midden-closet in Salford, led us to conclusions largely in favor of the former. In no instance did we find offensive smell from the pail-closet. With proper care they can never give rise to the abominable nuisance which is almost inseparable from the old form of midden."

HOME.—We assert, as a rule, the whole tone of a home depends upon the woman at the head of it—the *average* home ; not the poverty-stricken home, nor the wealthy home. . . . In this *average* home, whether sunshine shall enter the rooms, whether the parlor shall be used and enjoyed, whether the table shall be invitingly spread, whether bright lights and bright fires shall give warmth and cheer on winter nights—whether, in brief, the home shall be an agreeable or a diagreeable place, is usually what the woman determines. Men are powerless in the matter. Some find solace for a dismal home in study, some occupation in business ; some submit with what patience they can ; others are attracted by the cheer of the public-house, and it is specially young men who are apt in consequence to drift away into bad company and bad habits. There are men—and men. Our whole argument refers to individuals among men who succumb to bad influences—not the sex, but a class. —*Appleton's Journal*, Editor's Table, April 11.

THE RIGHTS OF THE INSANE.

By Julius Parigot, M. D., New York.

Read before the Medico-Legal Society of New York, Nov. 27, 1873.

Two very important questions, one of fact and the other of law, are brought into connection with the forced seclusion of insane patients in so-called hospitals or asylums where no medical treatment is employed. In this brief paper it will be attempted to prove that the rights of the insane are in such cases violated, and that the remedy to such an evil lies in the proper amending of the law in order that a legally authentic record would prove the necessity of appropriate medical treatment for each patient.

No one denies at the present time that many vital questions of justice, legislation, social economy, and finance, are involved in the treatment of lunacy. Still, many persons are not aware of the moral obligation devolving upon every citizen to guard the operation of the law under which the seclusion of persons who are insane, and of those who are supposed to be so, takes place, in order to avoid any possible false accusation about the legality of such an act; also to see how the provisions for their care are prepared by boards of trustees or governors; and, finally, to vindicate the rights of those who cannot defend themselves.

What seems to be positively overlooked is the importance and value of medical treatment, as well here in the whole of America as in England and elsewhere. Now, we may read in *The Journal of Mental Science* the following remarks, showing what is going on in England :

> These reports (blue books) show that, on the whole, there is an immense amount of thought, and care, and effort, exercised in the treatment of the insane by all who have to do with them. Year by year the efforts toward a more perfect system of treating and managing them seem steadily to increase in all but one direction. That spasmodic and individual efforts are made in this direction is true, but on the whole the medical treatment of the diseases which are comprised under the term insanity stands still, as compared with the asylum building, general managing, etc. * * * * Three books about a disease with nothing medical in them! Everything that concerns the treatment of those laboring under this disease professedly gone into, and not a word about medicines! Talk of modern skepticism—the reports of the commissioners and reporters in lunacy are the finest examples of medical skepticism extant: for they don't deny, deride, or damn with faint praise—they simply ignore the whole science and its professors. It may be that this will be better in the long run for the medical treatment of insanity, but it is hard to see it if its practical effect is to encourage asylum doctors to ignore the medical aspects of patients, and sink into a state of lethargic indifference to the unsolved problems in brain pathology, diagnosis, and therapeutics, that daily come before them.

The editor, Dr. Maudsley, does not pretend that no scientific progress is attempted or made in public or private asylums. It is admitted that in America we possess many asylums in which men of great merit open and follow new roads to scientific progress. Many institutions might be mentioned in which such efforts are made, and we of the medical profession may congratulate ourselves over the spirit which animates these scientific pioneers. But if we consider only the individual interest of each patient who is immured in an asylum where a positive medical treatment is impossible, and if, with Dr. Maudsley, we sum up the results of a non-therapeutical practice (brought on by the medical skepticism of administrative boards), then we may see the need of amendment of our laws on this subject. Evidently there is a confusion in the given powers and qualifications to serve the people in this matter. No by-laws should exist in opposition to State laws; and if that were so, medical responsibility would have fair play to show what it might do when supplied with everything necessary for its scope and our benefit—the recovery of the patients.*

Not the custody, but the cure of the insane should be the sole object. Such reform of the law, if I am not mistaken, is the *res vestra agitur* of such an association of lawyers and physicians as this. Common efforts would bring at last an immense benefit—namely, that insane patients must be cured, and not be considered, *prima facie*, as beings to be put in custody for their lifetime. Certainly such necessity overshadows all secondary questions of housekeeping details and comfort, though important they are. In general economy, principles must be adopted which infallibly must lead to practical results, as in commercial affairs or in industry. Is it not established that a sufficient capital must be embarked to obtain profitable products? It is the same in our case; an adequate, well-paid staff of physicians would take care of patients, employ all their skill and ingenuity to empty those immense reservoirs of human miseries, and free us of that constantly increasing number of insane, and of the enormous expense we are obliged to bear.

How is it possible that two, three, or even four physicians can take proper care of, and study the particular cases of four hundred, six hundred, or sometimes one thousand patients, shut up in one asylum? We believe that a physician having charge of fifty patients has as many as he can properly take care of, with the view to cure them.

---

* State or chartered institutions should have no more privileges before the law than other institutions for the insane; all should be positively submitted to inspections, either of Commissioners in Lunacy or members of the State Boards of Charities. And any interested party should have free access to the records.

In order to give an idea of what is considered the best general plan of an asylum, we refer to the Medical Register of New York, 1873-74, page 138, in which will be found the so-called advantages of a new *State Asylum*. Amongst numerous *appartements* will be noticed the Steward's and the Matron's, with offices, reception and store rooms; but there will be found no physical and chemical laboratory,—no lecture room,—no clinical wards,—no place for anatomical and pathological researches,—no rooms for scientific collections,—no private apartments for the physician,—no private study. The programme boasts of a better opportunity for classification—"by separating more completely the various classes from the *quiet* to the most *disturbed*." Here, again, clinical instruction is positively denied, or, at least, positively ignored, by both trustees and physicians!

Far from such rational and practical method, what do we see in almost every country? Honorable Boards, meaning well in their own and the generally adopted views, intrusted with legal and administrative powers to do with the insane what they think best, without control. Now, the most moderate and respectful criticism has shown the inefficacy of the means these Boards put in the hands of their physicians ; nay, sometimes such Boards think they must diminish the number of medical officers, lower their dignity, or even not give them any remuneration. It may easily be understood that in such general circumstances, physicians must do their best to please the narrow views of those in whose dependence they are placed ; eventually they will even defend that system, and neglect their duties, as *The Journal of Mental Science* has shown to be the case. We need in this country something higher and more independent. We want a law which everybody must obey and by which the medical profession shall become responsible for its acts. Unfortunately we have a legal mechanism unfit to serve the interest of the people. Even the latest law and the recent act concerning the State Board of Charities and the Commissioner in Lunacy, are full of errors, contradictions, and embarrassments that prevent the aim being reached.

If our asylums are made for the cure, and not for the perpetual custody of patients, why should a law not say so? Why should administrative functions surpass the legal and medical ones?

A responsible head physician, having for principal object science and the medical treatment, ought to have a sufficient and competent staff around him—a staff furnished with the necessary instruments, material and moral, to cure the patients. Anatomical and chemical laboratories and lecture-rooms should be provided and well furnished. We should have less of balls, billiards, and magic-lantern exhibitions as necessary to cut the monotony of asylum life. This chief physician ought also to be intrusted with the power of admitting or rejecting affidavits concerning the mental state of a so-called insane person; and be free (nay, the law ought to command it) to discharge a patient when cured, or sufficiently *compos mentis* to have a trial to resume his position in society. No intervention, either administrative or judiciary, appears here necessary. The responsible physician must be the conscientious expert and judge of such cases, and possess the power to fulfil his mission. If a too-absolute power could be feared, let, then, the superintendent have such jurisdiction only when in council with his medical assistants or his consulting physicians. Such a measure might also serve to curb too free a use of administrative authority on the part of head physicians.

When we consider the important relation of the subjects under consideration, we may wonder that superintendents of asylums are not made (*de jure*) members of the Board of Health of their county. They would complete that Board whose functions embrace as well the conditions of mental as bodily welfare. The Hon. Dorman B. Eaton explained lately at the New York Convention of the American Public Health Association, why a Board of Health determines its own sphere of action, makes the bills by which its own action is legalized, issues summons, sits in judgment, and uses its own officers to carry its decisions into effect. Evidently, the sanction of such power must be the immediate benefit felt by the public at large.

If we inquire into the laws and customs relating to the insane in past and present times, it is very curious to find that, on account of, and in order to prevent, accidents caused by "furiosi," maniacs, etc., measures are taken against them, but that not a single word is to be found in favor of their rights as citizens of a civilized community. Nothing but the oblivion of human rights, or the fear, contempt, and possibly the degradation of the poor patients, can explain such fact. Even in the country of the celebrated Pinel, a curious instance of public neglect of human dignity is found in the text of a law (Aug. 24, 1790) which assimilates the insane to dangerous, wild, rambling animals. It is against that want of feeling, against the absence of principles of justice, that we should urge reform. Let us ask why a law should not protect the life and dignity of the insane? why it should not punish those who violate their rights? *

Let us consider the result of an obligatory legal compulsion for treating the insane medically. A law on the obligatory medical treatment of insane persons confined in public or private asylums, has for its objective basis an inviolable right and a social duty, out of which we may expect, first, the almost certain cure of every patient; secondly, the positive diminution of an evil which attacks principally the moral and educated classes of society; and thirdly, the benefit of the better health (moral and physical) of the community. It is very easy to show why the insane are entitled to the best medical treatment when secluded from their friends.

If, in the interest of society, the insane may be temporarily deprived of their liberty, it is but a preventive measure, just and acceptable in certain conditions, out of which a positive right must be acknowledged, namely, that the law which forcibly isolates or secludes a patient from his friends and family assumes, *ipso facto*, the responsibility of a real and scientific medical treatment. A public convenience or a public right can never include the violation of an individual one, or the non-accomplishment of a duty, such as must be the case if an insane person is secluded in an asylum, unprovided with what is necessary for his or her recovery—in an institution where the number of physicians is quite inadequate to the work to be done. Even were there sufficient medical attendance for ordinary emergencies, we must allow for the peculiar interference of State officers, as the Governor, the Attorney-General, Courts, etc., which, at times, prevents asylum physicians from performing the duties they are paid for, since they are often employed on outside commissions,

---

* Evidently a civil law protecting the insane does not mean an interference with the feelings of love and duty in the family circle. Families are free to go beyond the law, but not to the extent of proscribing the general law, which insures to everyone in his right mind the use of his own property. Such law means the consecration of individual liberty and autonomy, in consequence of which she takes upon herself to care and provide for the patient when himself or his family cannot do it. In one word, the law represents a social obligation which does not prevent, but rather encourages, the moral law of family ties and support.

legal or scientific. The remedy for this evil is obvious; the law should prohibit any judge or lawyer to subpœna an asylum officer to outside cases. Of course, when thus employed, the observation of a patient and his individual treatment are stopped at once, and in such case the remaining officers, having their usual duties also, must neglect the one or the other. Trustees consent to, or are obliged to permit, such irregularities, and the poor abandoned patient (outside of the reach and influence of his friends) is thus deprived of his unquestionable right to treatment which may save him from an incurable issue of his malady.*

An individual treatment so desirable for the patient, substituted to a sort of wholesale enterprise of keeping, would even be profitable to our public charities. The mistake of these economic Boards is patent.

Certainly, nowadays, as far as general treatment goes and material cares are concerned, the insane are better treated than heretofore. They are taken to beautiful institutions, where however, unhappily, economical laws are supreme, and, we might presume to say, irrationally applied, since the only real profit lies in the cure and not the keeping of an inmate. In spite of the desire of many asylum medical officers, no regular individual clinic has yet been established, and, in actual circumstances, it cannot be.

In a practical mode of expression of facts, could not a cure have some relation and reason accounted for as in financial ledgers under the head of credit and debt? If so, the success of treatment could be traced to a scientific disbursement, the conditions of which ought to be prepared and accounted for in really good hospitals. The final question would then be merely as to cost of cures. But what are the results which can reasonably be expected? Calculations have been made and published in the United States upon these questions, in which the pecuniary advantage is not only shown by what it spares by a shorter residence in the hospital, but by the value of the work done during a mean period of active life, compared with that of the same duration as a chronic insane person in a public institution. The proposed scheme is simple, would apparently cost more, but the result *would pay*. The proposed system consists, for recent and acute cases, in a *daily* annotation of the symptoms, and the prescriptions either moral, hygienic, or pharmaceutic. For

---

* The *Annales d'Hygiène Publique et de Médecine Legale* (page 159—1859) make the fullest confession of such fact in France. Unhappily it is the same everywhere. Patients are crammed into large asylums and become incurable because of the fact that they are not individually attended to, in spite of Article XII., Chapter 2, of the French law of the 6th of July, 1838, which says: "Case books shall be kept, in which, once in the month, physicians will note the change effected in the state of each patient." But this article of the law cannot be obeyed. How could a physician, having sometimes 700 patients, do such work every month.

Marcé says in his *Traité des Maladies Mentales* (page 656): Patients are crammed, *without intelligence or morality*, in large asylums, and become incurable for the only reason that they are not treated.

Girard de Cailleux says in his celebrated work, *Etudes pratiques sur les Maladies Nerveuses et Mentales*, that those who dispose forcibly of the person of an insane are bound to furnish them with the means of a cure.

chronic cases, such annotations should be made every week; the whole, being transferred on case-books, would bear the signature of the attending physician, and be certified by that of the medical superintendent. What a change would such a law bring in our asylums! Their reputation benefited, and the patients asking for admittance instead of avoiding them; this fact is of the utmost importance.

There is another side of the question, relating to the necessity of such law. An officially recorded clinic would be the complementary measure of any improvement of a law concerning the legality of an obligatory confinement. First, such mode of legal treatment would be incompatible with any scientific error or a so-called false imprisonment. Now, supposing that reporters of the press could get admission into an asylum, is it not evident that a daily clinic concerning diagnosis and prognosis of a simulated disease would soon establish the truth? Such medical records would contain the whole history of a case. Nothing could escape the investigation of any public officer or that of a friend of patients. Secondly, there would be a guarantee for physicians against false accusations or intrigues often made by diastrephics and maniacs. Thirdly, such records would, from themselves, show the merit and assiduity of the medical staff. The resumé of all these therapeutical cases would be one of the best means for the advancement of science. With such conditions legally established, the experiment for cure might take place as well in an asylum as in free air institutions called *Gheels*.

Under the actual law, appropriate care and treatment are often delayed, to the great injury of the patient. Some persons, disbelieving the urgency that a patient be put immediately in some institution, employ all means to conceal the infirmity of a friend or patient. In other cases, especially those in which there is a perversion of the instincts or of volition, terrible accidents may and do happen on account of delays which the new law would not permit. It has been questioned publicly, to whom, for instance, the privilege of interference is to be intrusted, and by what solemnities the deprivation of liberty is to be accompanied and recorded. The new law would have nothing to do with these so-called difficulties. What is wanted is that the patient be cured, in order that he may become again a member of society. Anybody may honorably assist to that effect. There is no shame in having a friend insane, and it is a duty to render him the service pointed out by the law. Besides, there is no greater solemnity in making a circumstantial and scientific affidavit; the effect on the position of the individual is only felt when the judge makes an order of confinement. Publicity would not be required or feared in such a preliminary proceeding.

In spite of some very rare exceptions, we must say that isolation among relatives is objectionable for all parties concerned. The obligatory medical treatment has other advantages, which cannot be well shown without referring to the actual system. In every free country the deprivation of one's liberty is the greatest restriction which can be placed on a citizen. To some minds, this restrictive measure conveys the idea of personal degradation. It has been inquired if restrictive measures could not be enforced privately in one's own house. There are grave objections to private or secret isolation. First, how will the patient bear it in his own house? It might become a cause of incurability. Secondly, it might be resorted to unnecessarily, and the physician's opinion might not be preponderant. We have the experience of many families whose fireside, although well governed, was the worst place for the patient to be medically treated. Generally, relatives are the worst custodians; for this reason, that they are unable to trace a moral symptom to its real cause. Constant efforts are made to educe, by reasoning, their friend out of his delusions. With the best views and intentions, they aggravate the disease. Besides, there is also a danger for the family. The patient is a point of contamination, especially if the slightest hereditary predisposition exists. For patients who must be kept in isolation, their liberty and the respect of their rights cannot fall within the range of domestic affairs. If one of the members of a family disappears, has the State or the community not the duty of inquiring what has befallen one of its members? The law might admit that, under the supervision of medical officers appointed by judges, such isolation might take place, but the public would soon find out that special institutions are preferable. Again, the interference of the law is as necessary for the interests of the family as it is useful for the patient. On one side, it settles many questions of false delicacy which may injure the patient, and leaves to the family the power to go beyond, but never to fall short of what belongs to the patient. On the other side, the family is not directly responsible; the recovered patient can never be dissatisfied with the proceedings employed for his treatment; he has had the benefit of a really protective law.

Another point of great importance is, as to what such laws should require about the making of medical affidavits or certificates concerning insanity. These legal instruments are of extreme importance. After they establish the probable insanity of a person, and serve to obtain a judicial order for admission into an asylum, their efficacy ceases, and their value must be controlled, admitted, or rejected, by the administrative and medical chief of the asylum—the superintendent. These affidavits, although introductory instruments, should contain all the data of which the asylum officers are absolutely in need. Thus they ought to contain not only the general outlines and a history of the case, with all possible details concerning the patient and his circumstances, but describe the observed indications and symptoms, both moral and physiological. The latter especially must be minutely described, because they are the medical test of the value of such documents. These data are indispensable for the definitive diagnosis made in the asylum. It is easily understood that an individual might simulate with more or less success the moral symptoms, but he could not produce the pathological ones. Medical experts consider generally the coexistence of appreciable signs of a bodily infirmity in co-relation with mental derangement as unequivocal proof. Insanity, like any other disease, has definite forms, recurring through different well-known stages.

In conclusion, I have not the presumption to offer to the Society a perfect scheme. It is simply an idea of what appears to me ought to be discussed, and ultimately perfected. I have no doubt that the above-mentioned evils will be eradicated when a sufficient medical staff, headed by a physician whose responsibility and action should be complete and free, will keep authenticated records of their work and devotion.

TRAPS AND TRAPPING.

By Leopold Brandeis, Brooklyn.

In a previous number of the Sanitarian, some account has been given of traps, and their use and purpose.

The great importance of such appliances has been recognized long before the present era ; even Pompeii has furnished some specimens of ancient stench-traps in a perfect state of preservation. Naturally, their construction is faulty, as there is too much space for the accumulation of refuse, while no provision is made for its removal. The modern trap is constructed on the same principle, but considerably modified. The protection afforded by it depends, to a great extent, on its mode of attachment, and on the general arrangement of the drain and waste-pipes throughout the house.

The usefulness of the drain is conditioned by its line and grade, by its diameter, material, and workmanship.

Horizontal and vertical drains inside of any building must be constructed of a material sufficiently stiff and hard to resist the attacks of sewer rats, and impervious to gases. The joints should be well supported, and carefully caulked. No sharp angles should be introduced, and the descent or grade should be at least ½ inch per foot. The horizontal line of piping in the cellar should be easy of access; a trap of corresponding size, and provided with a tightly fitting cover or lid, for the removal of any accidental obstruction, is required there. Each and every outlet of soil or waste-pipes must be trapped, and these traps ought to be provided with a drain attachment for the removal of filth, without being compelled to cut the pipe or to call a plumber. The usefulness of a trap depends on its shape or depth of bend, and on its freedom from porous places. Its interior surface must be smooth and even, the walls of equal thickness, the bend strong in metal and well curved. The drain attachment should be cast on the trap and consist of soft metal, while the trap screw should be brass, to avoid the corrosion which would result from the contact of two surfaces equally alloyed when continuously exposed to wet. The body of the trap should be sufficiently soft for permitting the formation of a flange to make an air-tight joint to be connected with the waste-pipe. Pure, soft lead will not be affected by the organic acids forming from the refuse and grease passing through it, nor injured by the expansion produced by hot water. The proper size of a trap for a kitchen sink or wash-tub is 2 inches; for a wash-bowl or butler's pantry sink, 1½ inch; for a water-closet, 4 inches. Whether the shape should be single or double S, is best left to the discretion of a competent mechanic. There are two classes of leaden stench-traps in the market; those cast in halves and burned together by means of hydrogen gas are decidedly the best. Any imperfection in the casting may be discovered and mended during the process of manufacture, or the defective part may be thrown aside for re-melting. The seam gives additional support to the walls, and traps of this kind have been tested by very great pressure without permitting any escape of water or gas. It is naturally of the utmost importance that the bend of a trap should always be full of water. In places where the temperature ranges high—viz., near or above a heater—some compensation should be allowed for evaporation. The drain attachment on a perfectly-constructed trap can be opened by the removal of the brass screw; any filth or obstruction may be removed into a pail, the screw re-attached, and some water run in to flush the bend, and to make it clean and wholesome. Where danger from syphoning exists, a small vacuum-valve, costing but a few cents, may be soldered to the trap.

Small, insignificant-looking and cheap as a trap is, nevertheless, we have no appliance in our houses more useful than this trifle, entirely hidden from sight; we have nothing which could afford us greater and more efficient protection against the insidious attacks of effluvia from drains and sewers. We have nothing as durable and as easily kept in repair, or as quickly replaced, as a stench-trap, and all it needs to insure perfect usefulness is common attention and but a small portion of the usual scrupulous cleanliness which distinguishes an American housewife.

Bodily health is a precious boon to rich and poor. If the body is ailing the mind suffers. Pure, uncontaminated air is our first and greatest necessity, and only on this plea can I justify the dry and unæsthetical details of this article, and trust that my apology will be favorably considered.

Laughter as a Medicine.—A short time since, two individuals were lying in one room, very sick, one with brain fever, and the other with an aggravated case of the mumps. They were so low that watchers were needed every night, and it was thought doubtful if the one sick of fever could recover. A gentleman was engaged to watch over night, his duty being to wake the nurse whenever it became necessary to administer medicine. In the course of the night both watcher and nurse fell asleep. The man with the mumps lay watching the clock, and saw that it was time to give the fever patient his potion. He was unable to speak aloud, or to move any portion of his body except his arms, but, seizing a pillow, he managed to strike the watcher in the face with it. Thus suddenly awakened, the watcher sprang from his seat, falling to the floor, and awakened both the nurse and the fever patient. The incident struck the sick man as very ludicrous, and they laughed heartily at it for some fifteen or twenty minutes. When the doctor came in the morning he found his patient vastly improved; said he never knew so sudden a turn for the better, and now both up and well. Who says laughter is not the best of medicines? And this reminds the writer of another case. A gentleman was suffering from an ulceration in the throat, which at length became so swollen that his life was despaired of. His household came to his bedside to bid him farewell. Each individual shook hands with the dying man, and then went away weeping. Last of all came a pet ape, and shaking the man's hand, went away also with its hands over its eyes. It was so ludicrous a sight that the patient was forced to laugh, and laughed so heartily that the ulcer broke, and his life was saved.

HYGIENE OF DWELLINGS.

By CHARLES A. CAMERON, PH. D., M. D., L. K. and Q. C. P., Prof. Hygiene, etc.

The subject of the sanitary condition of dwellings continues to attract the attention of sanitarians, and many interesting books, pamphlets and papers upon it, are constantly being presented to the medical profession and to the public at large. The celebrated Professor of Hygiene, at the University at Munich, Dr. Max Von Pettenkofer, has recently given three popular lectures on Hygiene at Dresden, which have since been published, and also translated* into English.

This work, though written in a purely popular style, yet contains much scientific information which will be new to all, except, perhaps, a very few of the medical men and scientists of this country.

The chapter on ground-air is that which is of most interest to medical men, of whom, we presume, there are few who have not become more or less acquainted with Pettenkofer's researches on the propagation of typhoid fever and cholera by means of underground air.

He remarks that organic matter decays much more rapidly in loose soils than in stiff clays.

The Belgian chemist, Louis Creteur,† had to disinfect the pits which contained the bodies of those slain at and near Sedan.

He found that in the rubble, chalk, and other light soils, the bodies had mouldered away, but they were in a wonderful state of preservation in the heavy adhesive clays.

The more porous the soil is, the more rapidly organic matters decay therein, and the more readily the circulation of air and water proceeds. Such a soil is, therefore, the most abundantly inhabited by the lower forms of life.

Pettenkofer shows that in these loose soils, and, indeed, in the earth generally, there is a large quantity of air usually richer in carbonic acid than the air above the ground, and that the underground air is affected by the currents, temperature, etc. of the above-ground air. A strong wind playing upon the surface of the ground outside a house will sometimes force the gases contained in the ground into the interior of the adjacent houses. In this way, according to Pettenkofer, underground air may be the means of introducing the contagia of certain zymotics into our dwellings:—

"Remarkable testimony as to the permeability of the ground, and of the foundations of our houses, has been given by gas emanations into houses which had no gas laid on. I know cases where persons were poisoned and killed by gas which had to travel for twenty feet under the street, and then through the foundations, cellar-vaults,

---

* The Relations of the Air to the House We Live In and the Clothes We Wear. By Dr. Max Von Pettenkofer. Abridged and translated by Augustus Hess, M. D. London: Trubner, Ludgate Hill, 1873.

† Creteur on the Hygiene of the Battle-Field. 1872.

and flooring of the ground-floor rooms. As these kinds of accidents happened only in winter, they have been brought forward as a proof that the frozen soil did not allow the gas to escape straight upwards, but drove it into the house. I have told you already why I take frozen soil to be not more air-tight than when not frozen.

"In such cases the penetration of gas into the houses is facilitated by the current in the ground-air caused by the house.

"The house being warmer inside than the external air, acts like a heated chimney on its surroundings, and chiefly on the ground upon which it stands and the air therein, which we will call the ground-air.

"The warm air in the chimney is pressed into and up the chimney by the cold air surrounding the same. The chimney cannot act without heat, and the heat is only the means of disturbing the equilibrium of the columns of air inside and outside the chimney. The warm air inside is lighter than the cold air outside, and this being so, the former must float upward through the chimney, just like oil in water. It continues to do so as long as fresh cold air comes into its neighborhood from outside. As soon as we interrupt this arrival, the draught into the chimneys leads to erroneous views, which have many times stopped the progress of the act of heating and ventilating.

"Thus our heated houses ventilate themselves not only through the walls, but also through the ground on which the house stands. If there is any gas or other smelling substance in the surrounding ground-air, they will enter the current of this ventilation.* I have witnessed a case in Munich where not the least smell of gas could be detected in the street, but a great quantity of gas found its way into the ground-floor room of a house where no gas was laid on. In another case, the gas always penetrates into the best-heated room, and produced an illness of its inmates, which was taken for typhoid fever.

"The movement of gas through the ground into the house may give no warning that the ground-air is in continual intercourse with our houses, and may become the introducer of many kinds of lodgers. These lodgers may either be found out, or cause injury at once, like gas; or they may, without betraying their presence in any way, become enemies, or associate themselves with other injurious elements, and increase their activity. The evil resulting therefrom continues till the store of these creatures of the ground-air is consumed. Our senses may remain unaware of noxious things which we take in, in one shape or another, through air, water, or food.

"We took rather a short-sighted view all the while when we believed that the nuisances of our neighbors could only poison the water in our pumps; they can also poison the ground-air for us, and I see more danger in this, as air is more universally present and more movable than water. I should feel quite satisfied if, by my lectures, you were convinced of this important fact, if of none other."

---

* I believe that there is great protection in this respect for houses in England by the system of areas.—TRANSLATOR.

"England has given proof how the public health can be improved by keeping the soil clean through good drainage, abolition of cesspools and abundant water supply.

"It would carry me too far if I were to analyze now to which of these measures the lion's part belongs; I should have to enter upon many controversies which I have no time to fight out in this place. But this is my conviction, which I want to impress upon you, that cleanliness of the soil and diminution of organic processes in the ground of dwelling-houses, are most essential.

"Many have considered these processes, and their effects on the ground-air, to be a mere hypothesis. This view lies now behind us, and facts have been found proving their reality. Stimulated by the investigations of Huxley and Hackel, further researches have followed, and shown that, not only at the greatest depth of the sea, but also in every porous soil, there are everywhere those beginnings of organic life, belonging neither to the animal nor vegetable kingdom—mucous formations, which are called Moneras and Protistes.

"When I wrote my part of the report on the cholera in Bavaria, in 1854, I pointed out already, that the air not less than than the water in the soil, ought to be drawn into the circle of experimental investigations.

"Neither others nor myself acted at once upon my suggestion, and it is only during the last eighteen months that I have examined the ground-air in the rubble-soil of Munich, regularly twice a week, for its varying amount of carbonic acid. The results are surprising, and for the future I shall have to trouble others and myself, not only with ground-water, but also with ground-air.

"The place where the examination of the ground-air of Munich is being carried on is rubble, without any vegetation, and the carbonic acid increases with the distance from the surface. Agricultural chemistry has been aware, for a long time, that a clod of arable earth which is rich in humus, is a source of carbonic acid, but no one expected that, at times, so much carbonic acid should be met with in sterile lime-rubble. A few feet under the surface there is already as much carbonic acid as in the worst ventilated human dwelling-places.

"I have found that the quantity of carbonic acid is smaller at 58 inches than at 156 inches, throughout the year, the months of June and July excepted, when an inverse proportion arises. But then there begins also, in the lower stratum, a considerable increase, so that the upper stratum soon finds itself behind again. This large quantity of carbonic acid in the ground-air of Munich has been far surpassed in Dresden. Examinations have taken place in this town under the authority of the Central Board of Public Health.

"Professor Flick's diary proves that, at least at that spot where his examinations took place, the quantity of carbonic acid was, in winter, already nearly twice as great as in Munich in the month of August. I might become jealous of Dresden, but we must often, in life, put up with being left behind, although we had the first start, and I have no choice left but to resign myself.

"The presence of carbonic acid in the soil, and its periodical motion, are for the present a bare fact. Other places, with different soils, must be examined under varying circumstances, and for longer periods, before an explanation can be attempted."

According to Pettenkofer, the air in our houses becomes unwholesome when the carbonic acid in it, provided it be derived from the respiration of animals, rises from the normal proportion of 4 parts in 10,000 to 1 part in 1,000. The experiments of Dr. Angus Smith and Dr. Hammond have shown that the organic matter in the air, which increases in proportion to the amount of carbonic acid, is by far a more deadly impurity than the gas.

Dr. Alfred Perry, Chemist to the Board of Health of New Orleans, has shown* that not only carbonic acid and ammonia, but also solid and albuminous substances, are evolved during the decomposition of street and gutter filth.

These products "are, for the most part, when breathed in large proportions, fatal to life ; and, in small portions diminish the bodily vigor of persons who are well, and aggravate and prolong diseases which already exist."

According to Dr. Perry, the air of certain parts of the city of New Orleans, when yellow fever prevailed, contained per 1,000,000 cubic metres 110.31 grams of ammonia, and 166.66 grams of albuminoid nitrogen. The latter number, if multiplied by 11, would probably give the actual amount of animal and vegetable matter, chiefly in a putrescent state, floating in the atmosphere of the streets and rooms of New Orleans, and of many other towns too. Whilst on the subject of the hygiene of houses, let us refer to the defective water-closet accommodation which prevails even amidst the middle and lower classes in these countries. In the case of the houses of the well-to-do sections of society, the water-closet is often in a very unsanitary state ; and in the dwellings of the poor the condition of the necessary out-offices is, as a rule, extremely objectionable, both from a moral and sanitary point of view. In the great majority of cases which have come under our notice, the *petits* were in proportion to from 8 to 20 families. A sensible article on the relation which faulty water-closet accommodations bear to the diseases of women, appears in the *Philadelphia Medical Times* for August 23d, 1873. It is contributed by Dr. William Godell. He refers to the defective water-closet accommodation which prevails in the United States many of the diseases which commonly affect women. He advocates the construction of those essential adjuncts to every civilized dwelling in such a manner as would render them warm, dry, and free from draughts and foul air—private and easily accessible water-closets, constructed so as to induce females to use them more regularly than they do at present, because those places are cold, too public, and often too remote.—*The Dublin Journal of Medical Science.*

VIENNA WATER SUPPLY.—Vienna is now supplied with clear spring water, at a temperature of 50° F., brought from the heights of the Sœmmering, a distance of about seventy miles.

---

* Annual Report of the Board of Health, New Orleans, 1872.

THE PRINCIPLES OF VENTILATION:

*Specially Applied to "Car Ventilation and Warming."**

By Lewis W. Leeds, New York.

The peculiarity of *Car Ventilation* is the variableness in the condition with which the cars are surrounded. At one time they are standing in an enclosed depot with the ventilators and doors open, and, notwithstanding, they may be hot, and almost suffocating. Within fifteen minutes thereafter they may be running at the rate of twenty miles an hour against a north-west wind, and ice forming on the windows. Again, in summer, it is often a nice point to determine where the line should be drawn to guard against the accumulation of the personal impurities resulting from a closed car, or to be relieved of such impurities by the opening of windows and ventilators, and covered and choked with cinders and dust.

Probably no three persons accidentally meeting under such circumstances would entirely agree as to the proper amount of heat and air. But the habits of our people are now in a transition state.

There has been so much said lately against the breathing of foul air, that the want of ventilation has become the fashionable scapegrace to which is attributed all the diseases to which we cannot assign other definite cause.

Ventilating contrivances are consequently very abundant, and between the draughts from windows with patent ventilators and the patent stoves, the few passengers who want to enjoy quiet and be let alone, have rather a hard time of it. This is a discouraging picture. But radical improvements in car warming and ventilation are much needed.

Very few comprehend the difference between the effects of the two great principles of warming—*Radiation* and *Convection*. As an illustration of this, the words "Indirect Radiation" are generally used by the heating trade, and by many architects to designate warming by currents of heated air; and they are hard to convince that they are in error.

Nearly all of our present plans of warming are based upon convection. And although *radiation* enters largely into our practice in warming,—nothwithstanding, many persons make use of the term without really comprehending the nature of its meaning. For instance, many persons using an open fire, suppose that the fire warms the air in the room, and that it is the warmed air surrounding them that supplies the heat. It is very difficult for such persons to comprehend that, while sitting in front of the fire, they are frequently surrounded by very cold air, while they at the same time feel hot.

Intelligent persons sometimes express astonishment when I talk of filling the room with air at 50° and still keep the thermometer at

---

* From a paper read before the Master Car Builders' Association, New York, February 19, 1874.

70°. This almost universal ignorance is simply because we have not observed the fundamental principles of natural ventilation. If we commence with the earth itself, and comprehend it as a little speck of solid matter, being hurled with impetuous force through the vast and unlimited space, surrounded by a cold so intense that no means we have can measure it; and the sun, which is so many millions of miles away as to appear but little larger than a man's hat, and that from it comes through the vast space of intense cold this wonderful power of producing heat, the proposition is indeed almost incompresible.

Again: Taking the end of my pencil as representing the size of the earth, a cannon ball would probably require to be some 500 or 600 feet away to represent the relative size and distance of the sun.

One might think the heat which the end of the pencil would get from a red-hot cannon ball placed on Trinity Church steeple, with a strong north-west wind blowing in the opposite direction and the thermometer below zero, would not be of much account; and yet, without making the calculation, we have to use some such illustration as this to convey to the mind the proportion of the sun's heat received by the earth.

Again: Observe the beautiful arrangement made for the distribution of heat to all parts of the earth,—how it revolves; first one side towards the sun, and then the other, as a boy would turn before a bonfire in the street on a cold day.

And there is, besides, the other motion, from end to end, so to speak, giving us the summer and winter. How this heat could pass through so vast a space of intense cold, was one of the problems upon which a great amount of study and research was expended before a satisfactory theory could be advanced.

But the wave theory, so beautifully illustrated and ably advocated by Prof. Tyndall and others, gives such satisfactory explanations, that it is now almost universally accepted as correct.

This theory supposes that the excessive heat of the sun, or the heat of any other body, causes a tremulous motion in the heated body, which agitation is imparted to the atmosphere surrounding it, causing a series of waves, similar to the waves created by throwing a stone into the still water of a pond.

The waves created by the intense heat of the sun continue through the ether which is supposed to fill all space, with little diminution, until they are obstructed by some solid substance. A fair idea of this may be gained by watching the waves from a steamboat over placid water.

Long after the boat has passed, we find waves dashing against the distant shore, and almost as large as when they started from the side of the boat.

Now, the point which we must clearly comprehend is, that the substance or sensation we call heat does not itself pass from the sun to the earth, but that the heat of the sun merely creates these waves, and it is the *stopping* of them, as they come dashing against the earth, that causes the sensation of heat.

This is a difficult point for many persons to comprehend; and yet it is absolutely essential that it should be fully understood and constantly borne in mind, to form a correct theory or to execute intelligently, any method of warming and ventilating.

These ether waves, as before said, are only stopped by solid substances.

Few substances, however, are solid. Glass is not solid in this respect, as these waves pass directly through it ; and ice is not solid, as we find the waves passing through it also. It was a long time before I could clearly comprehend how heat could be passed through a lens of ice, and afterwards be concentrated with sufficient force to ignite a candle.

Now, anything so thin and having so little solidity as the air, offers but little obstruction to the free passage of heat-producing waves, or that which we will now call, as a more simple and comprehensive term, *radiant heat*.

Let us make a distinct and emphatic separation between radiant heat and the warmth we get by currents of heated air coming in immediate contact with our bodies.

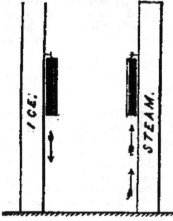

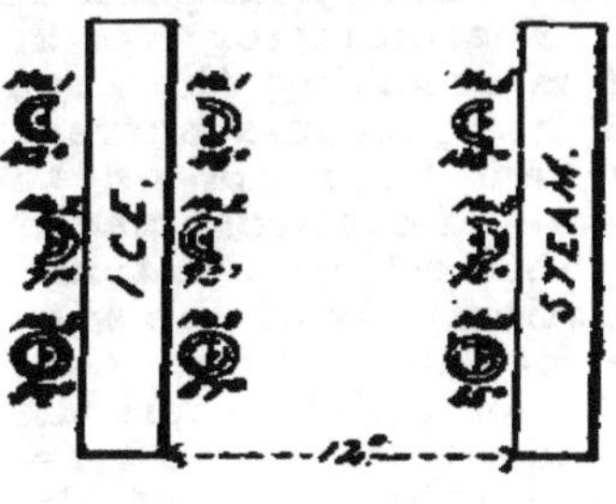

For the purpose of impressing this more forcibly and clearly, I have had this apparatus constructed, and for it I take this occasion to express my obligations and thanks to the enterprising firm of Gillis & Geoghegan.

We have here two boxes or chambers, one holding some ice and salt to produce a cold mixture, and the other filled with steam. These boxes are 18 inches wide and three feet high, and are placed one foot apart. By the smoke you perceive there is a rapid current of air descending along the side of the cold box, and by placing the smoke at the bottom, you will observe there is a rapid ascending current near the vessel filled with steam, which is quite hot.

Now, here is a double current or circulation, such as is constantly occurring all around us, because there are no two things in this room of precisely the same temperature. Nor are the two sides of any one object of the same temperature; consequently this variation of temperature assists greatly in keeping up the constant circulation of the air.

And we might go further, and say that there is scarcely a minute in the whole twenty-four hours in which the air is of the same temperature as any of the solid objects in the room.

I have hung six thermometers on these two surfaces, three on each side. One on each side (Nos. 1 and 6) is in a half-circle double-tube of tin, so arranged as to be exposed to a free circulation of air on all sides; they are shielded entirely from the direct rays of the vessel opposite, but radiated to, or receive the radiant heat from the vessel against which they are placed. Two other thermometers (2 and 5) are hung in a similar vessel, but turned towards, and exposed to the radiation of, the vessel opposite. The other two (3 and 4) are simply hung in a double tube open at both ends for the free circulation of the air, but are protected from the radiation from both of the two opposing forces.

This experiment shows the effect of radiant heat, and that *the thermometer gives no indication of the temperature of the air in which it is placed.*

Here are three well-adjusted and accurate thermometers hanging together and touching each other on each side of the box, and it can scarcely be possible that there is the half of a degree difference in the temperature of the air on the same side; the two sides of course are different.

They have been hanging here some time, and, no doubt, indicate the temperature of the surrounding air. If some gentleman will be kind enough to take these thermometers and read them quickly as they are handed out, and another gentleman will please make a record of the temperatures as they are read, the difference will be manifest.

The experiment at the meeting was not so successfully made as I have since been able to make it, I therefore substitute the mean of seven experiments made, from 11.20 A. M. to 2.45 P. M., February 26th, 1874.

These experiments were made in an open room, there being no enclosure around either the heating or cooling surface. The mean of the external temperature was 35°, temperature of room 67°, and we find a difference of nearly 100° between the two extremes (1 and 6). But the most remarkable circumstance is, that No. 2, hanging against the ice-box, and in the cold current, is 93°, being 20° higher than No. 5, which is 73°, and hanging against the steam surface, and in a current 18° hotter, as indicated by No. 4, which is the air thermometer.

How entirely fallacious, then, is the ordinary thermometer for indicating the temperature of the surrounding air, and how important it is to bear in mind the effects of radiation. Thermometer No. 2, hanging in a current at 67°, indicates 93°—it is receiving the rays of heat from the opposite surface. But No. 5, hanging in a current of 85°, only indicates 73°—it is giving out its heat by radiation to the opposite cold surface. Nos. 1, 2 and 3 were afterwards placed on the outside of the box, and exhibited equally interesting variations. Now, these experiments show a slight exaggeration only of the winter condition of many of our cars. With the feet on a floor, cold enough to freeze water falling on it, the heat in air which enters the lungs at 80° or 90°, and the body, with one side towards and receiving the heat from a red-hot stove, and the other side of the body towards a frosty window, altogether comprehending a variation of simultaneous temperatures, to different portions of the body, of nearly 100°.

Now, I would not be hypercritical, but I sometimes wish I was a master car builder just long enough to introduce some system of warming and ventilating cars that would make such a condition of things as I have described impossible.

These experiments may be repeated by any one, and their correctness verified. Take a box filled with ice and salt to produce a cold surface, and place it near any ordinary steam radiator, or stove, being careful to have the thermometers protected from conducted and radiant heat. The ordinary casing of the common thermometers will not answer. There should be three thicknesses of bright tin, and two or three air spaces, to prevent the heat from being radiated through from one to the other.

It is because we do not fully realize the simple facts as illustrated by these experiments, that we make so little progress in accurate knowledge of ventilating and warming; and it is because the principles are not comprehended, or that so little attention is paid to them that so many blunders and failures are made.

Ventilation is based upon the movements of air at different temperatures, but we cannot get rid of foul air, or supply fresh air in the same manner as we would free a house of foul water or supply it with that which is pure by exact measures, allowing just so many cubic inches for each occupant.

The conditions are entirely different. In studying the movements of the air, if we would compare them with the movements of water, we must imagine ourselves at the bottom of the ocean with the ground underneath us heated as a fire would heat the bottom of a pot. By watching the motion of the water in a glass globe with a fire under it we can form some idea of the constant and immense agitation of the external atmosphere.

Inaccurate, unscientific, and even repulsive as the idea may be to the mathematical mind of the architect, that we should depend in a great measure upon the mere agitation or the mixing up of the fresh and foul air, for our chances of getting pure air, I think, notwithstanding, this is just what we have to submit to. This is what nature teaches us, and although we may be to a certain extent artificial beings, and live in artificial houses, half of a lifetime spent in trying to work in a more precise and accurate manner than Old Madam Nature does, has about worn out my patience in that direction; and I confess that her hurly-burly way of mixing the oxygen, nitrogen, hydrogen and carbonic acid, and all other gases together in one grand mass, and scattering them around promiscuously, is better than any arrangement I have ever been able to devise. The more we study the subject the more evident it becomes that agitation is the natural method of ventilation—it is Nature's great purifier.

Now, if we accept agitation as the true principle of ventilation, we find ourselves far more likely to get our share of pure air by it than by the mathematical cubic-inch programme. Nature does not dole out pure air by the cubic inch, but if unrestrained, supplies every living thing abundantly. She scorns every attempt to measure it, and if we adopt her method of warming, it will be about as easy to supply a hundred cubic feet of cold invigorating air per minute to every individual, as we now find it to be to dole out a pittance of ten cubic feet per minute of warmed, debilitating, nauseating, hot air. I have spent a great deal of time and money in getting up patterns and taking out patents for warming contrivances. But I have done with them. We have been running air-heating to such extremes that I have become perfectly disgusted with it. If we inhale air at the same temperature as the blood, it quickly kills us. Nature never ruins the air for breathing purposes by overheating it—she leaves such miserable business to the managers and warmers of railroad cars, asylums, hospitals, and, not unfrequently, our homes.

The air of a room should always be cooler than the solid objects within it, and the floors, especially, should be warmer than the air above them. This condition creates the desired agitation of the air. It is very seldom that the air of the external atmosphere is as warm as the solid objects at the surface of the earth. When the sun is shining, many of the objects surrounding us are about the temperature of the body; and when the sun shines directly upon us, it is warmer than our bodies, so that we are receiving heat, instead of wasting the vital energies of the body in an overheated atmosphere of a close car or room. The floors and sides of such structures should be about the temperature of our bodies, so that we should not be wasting the valuable heat of our bodies by radiation. With walls and floors warmed to the temperature of our bodies, the air, for breathing, will feel very comfortable at 50°.

It is by this system of warmed floors and warmed walls that the rapid movement of air forms those lovely breezes of our summer evenings, so different from the hurtful draughts of furnace-heated houses.

I had intended to have here a fine model for showing the motions of the air at different temperatures; but, through some unaccountable mistake, it has been sent to the wrong place. It is intended to illustrate that which I venture to call the principle of stratification—where heated air is used for warming; and also, to show the great difficulty of keeping the feet warm and head cool, where the vicious system of overheating all the fresh air is resorted to.

If, in conclusion, you will devise some means of warming the floors of your cars to the temperature of the body, or the temperature caused by ordinary sunshine, you will find three-fourths of your difficulties about ventilation overcome. It will then be easy to have an inlet for diffusing fresh air along the sides of the cars, just above the heads of the passengers, and an outlet through the ridge, to allow of the escape of foul air. We must not forget that when the floor is warmed the air is cooler than the indicated temperature by the thermometer.

If this air is thrown first towards the ceiling, and well diffused, large quantities may be introduced without any person being aware of it, or being in any way inconvenienced by it. I believe, if these principles are carefully studied and borne in mind, we may hope soon to make more rapid progress than hitherto in this important, but as yet little understood, branch of public hygiene.

PETTENKOFER'S THEORY CONCERNING CHOLERA.

Discussion by the New York Public Health Association, Regular Meeting, March 16, 1874.

The discussion was opened by Max Herzog, M. D., who briefly explained Pettenkofer's methods of investigation, his results, and certain practical applications of his conclusions. The Doctor's remarks derived much of their earnestness and force from the fact that the speaker had been a zealous and devoted disciple of Pettenkofer, and had borne a share in the labor of the investigations he described. Briefly stated, Pettenkofer's theories recognize four conditions which must concur before the propagation of cholera is possible. These essential conditions are: First, the introduction of some unrecognized specific germ. He teaches that cholera cannot occur without the importation of the cholera-producing agent. The second essential element is the presence of a porous soil. Pettenkofer believes that those places which have a porous or permeable soil, and those only, are liable to be attacked by epidemic cholera. His third essential condition is the recession of the ground-water, or, in other words, a subsidence of the level at which the soil is saturated with water. He believes that cholera cannot become epidemic unless the cholera-producing material which has been deposited in a porous soil, is exposed to the atmospheric influences which the soil suffers by the recession of the ground-water. Acting on this belief, and observing that the ground-water was at a high level in Munich in 1872, he boldly prophesied immunity from cholera in that year, although many other cities of Europe were threatened and were suffering. In the following year, foreseeing a subsidence of the ground-water, he predicted cholera, and, unfortunately for Munich, his words were verified. His fourth condition depends on personal susceptibility to the poison of cholera. In brief, Pettenkofer's four conditions are, communication, local disposition, timeous disposition, and personal disposition.

In regard to the first and fourth points there was, apparently, no difference of opinion among the gentlemen who took part in the discussion which followed Dr. Herzog's presentation of Pettenkofer's views. The necessity of communication or importation, and the existence of personal susceptibility and insusceptibility were tacitly admitted; but the second and third points excited an animated discussion, in which the following gentlemen took part: Drs. Chandler, Harris, J. C. Peters, S. Hanbury Smith, Janes and Russell, and Mr. Stephenson Towle. The last named gentleman mentioned an observation which he had made in certain portions of New York city where sub-drains had been constructed for the removal of the ground-water. Immediately after the construction of such drains, he had noticed an increase in the number of fever and ague cases, although these untoward occurrences soon ceased, and the district thus drained became more healthy than it was before the introduction of deep drainage. This observation seemed to be an illustration at least of a portion of Pettenkofer's theories. Dr. S. Hanbury Smith mentioned, as a fact of similar import, the ocurrence of a very high freshet which submerged the lower terrace of Cincinnati, shortly before the cholera epidemic of 1849. In the light of Pettenkofer's theory, this freshet might have deposited cholera germs in the porous soil of Cincinnati which became active on the recession of the excess of saturation. Dr. Smith, also, described the offensive condition of the wells of Stockholm, during the epidemic of cholera which he witnessed in that city in 1834. Dr. Peters referred to the occurrence of numerous cases of cholera where the second and third conditions of Pettenkofer were not observed. He was of the opinion that cholera had devastated certain places where the soil was not porous, and that the introduction of cholera germs into the alimentary canal would produce cholera in susceptible persons regardless of the soil on which they lived or the recession of the ground water. He described the absence of "modern improvements" in many of the German cities, and thought that where the porous soil of a populous city was saturated in all directions with excremental matter, the rise and fall of the ground water might be an important element; but in a city like New York, the condition of the soil and the ground water were of third or fourth-rate importance in the problem of preventing cholera.

The drift of the discussion developed the thought that the cholera phenomena observed by Pettenkofer differ in certain prominent features from those which occur in American cities. One of these points of difference was brought out in a dialogue between Drs. Herzog and Russell, the latter being of the opinion that the twelve hundred deaths from cholera in New York in 1866, represented a very serious epidemic, while the former thought that that amount of mortality from cholera was of very little consequence, considering the population and the ordinary annual mortality.

ARMY MEDICAL RANK.

From all parts of the country, wherever two or three medical men are gathered together, comes some expression of opinion regarding the status of the army medical officer, as it is, and as it should be. Resolutions, short but emphatic, and covering all the essential points, show that the profession thoroughly appreciates the question. It is greatly to the honor of the profession that men of first-rate abilities have been found ready to accept positions in the Army, and maintain the dignity of the service; but if that service is to be rendered precarious, and even less desirable than it has been, by inconsiderate legislation, it will certainly be found impossible to keep up the high standard that has hitherto characterized the medical staff of the Army of the United States.—*New York Med. Journal.*

Editor's Table.

THE PUBLIC HEALTH.

NOTE.—The Sewage Question, by Samuel Leavitt, p. 59, is in continuation from p. 513, Vol. I.

Massachusetts.—Fifth Annual Report of the State Board of Health, for the year 1873, pp. 550. This volume is replete with the results of diligent research and investigation into the causes of mortality, which inflict the commonwealth. The first twenty-seven pages are taken up with the *General Report of the Board*, giving a resumé of the work of the year. First of *Small-pox:* The mortality from this disease in 1872 was 1,029, or 70.58 to 100,000 of population of 1870. The mortality for 1873 is not complete, but for the first three months in the year it is believed to have been fully equal to the whole year of 1872. Since April, however, it has rapidly declined, and the last death from it was on Sept. 6th.

Excavations in Clay Lands are emphasized as being especially dangerous to health in regard to brick-making in the town of Medford, where pits below the level of Mystic River and tide water are found to extend over an area of from ten to twenty acres. The particular lands complained of are within four miles of the State House, and measures for effectually draining and grading them are earnestly urged in advance of an encroaching population. For "If anything is proved in sanitary science," remarks the report, "it is the unfitness of undrainable clayey soil for human residence. * * * * Whoever shall occupy dwellings in a sunken territory, whose soil is clay, will sicken and die."

The Sewerage of the Metropolitan District is still very imperfect, dangerous to the public health, and urgently demanding legislative action. "The death-rate of the city proper has, for several years, been so high as to occasion the most serious concern, and in looking for its causes, none are more probable than the imperfect discharge of liquid waste from our sewers, and the rapidly increasing foulness of the shallow estuaries into which they open." *Slaughter-houses* and *noxious and offensive trades* seem to be here, as everywhere else, the most troublesome subject with which officers of health have to contend. The great slaughter-houses of Boston are situated in Miller's River District, in the cities of Cambridge and Somersville, a valley or basin of but few feet above tide-water, bounded on three sides by highlands. Into this basin is collected the rainfall of about twelve hundred acres. In addition to the slaughter-houses herein situated, where 800,000 swine were killed, chiefly in the summer, in 1873, there is an extensive pork-packing house and numerous smaller establishments for boiling meat and fat rendering. There are, besides, in the immediate neighborhood, the usual concomitants—markets, restaurants, etc. The odors from these combined sources are often strong enough to wake persons from sound sleep, in Charleston and Boston, at a distance of two miles from the place of their origin.

"While the Boards of Health of both cities have declared the three swine slaughter-houses to be nuisances, and in various ways have expressed the wish that the State Board of Health should abate them, these establishments have all been enlarged, and their capacity for slaughtering and rendering more than doubled—without permission and without remonstrance."

"The first requisite for such trades, in a sanitary point of view, is complete drainage;" and this being impracticable here, under the circumstances, total removal is insisted upon by the Board, as absolutely necessary for the protection of the public health. The rendering establishments, the Board suggests, can be transferred to one of the islands in the harbor, and slaughtering to a properly-appointed and appropriately-situated abattoir.

The Brighton Abattoir has been in successful operation for six months, beginning in June and going on through the succeeding hot months—slaughtering beeves, sheep, and calves, rendering offal, and drying blood, without giving offence, and with a prospect of continuous satisfaction. But "the price of safety in this respect" is recognized to be "*unremitting vigilance.*"

In this connection, the Hon. Jackson S. Shultz, of New York, gives a very interesting and instructive letter concerning European Abattoirs, which we earnestly commend to all Boards of Health and municipalities throughout the country.

Preventive Medicine, and the Physician of the Future, is the subject of a special essay by Henry J. Bowditch, M. D., Chairman of the Board.

"In this paper there is an attempt to anticipate and to describe the effect which will be produced upon the public mind, and upon the relations which the medical profession will hold towards the community, when preventive medicine, now in its infancy, shall have its full power over the public health.

"As a partial illustration of the subject, the writer attempts to answer the question, 'What, according to our present knowledge, should be the measures inaugurated, and how long should these measures be carried out, in order to prevent, so far as is possible, a human being from falling into consumption, into which, by his hereditary tendencies, he may fall unless the utmost care be taken from birth to beyond middle life to counteract said tendencies?'"

The general topics briefly, but ably, presented in this paper are—residence, nutrition, clothing, bathing, recreation, education, profession and trade; and exercise in its various phases of walking, running, dancing, riding, driving, gymnastics, etc. A paper strictly sanitary in its bearing, and well calculated to promote the importance of Hygiene, both public and domestic.

The Health of the Farmers of Massachussetts, by J. F. A. Adams, M. D.; with a letter on *Some Farm-houses, and Some Mistaken Ways of living in them*, by Mrs. T. F. Plunkett; *Cerebro-Spinal Meningitis in Massachussetts*, in 1873, by J. Baxter Upham, M. D.; *Hospitals*, by George Derby, M. D., Secretary of the Board; *Political Economy of Health*, by Edward Jarvis, M. D.; *School Hygiene*, by Frederick Winsor, M. D.; *The Work of Local Boards of Health*, by Azel Ames, M. D.; *The use of Zincked or Galvanized Iron for the Storage and Conveyance of Drinking-Water*, by W. E. Boardman, M. D., and *The Health of Towns*, a summary "for the most part, contributed by regular correspondents of the Board, in various towns and cities," in response to a circular in which the following questions were asked:

1. "Whether any forms of disease have been specially prevalent.
2. Whether you can discover any cause for such prevalent forms of disease.
3. Whether such causes are, in your opinion, in any degree preventable or removable.
4. Are the Local Health Authorities intelligent, vigilant and efficient?"

To these inquiries there were replies from 154 towns. "More than half of the number are very uncomplimentary to the health authorities. . . . The Boards of Health of most of the cities and towns of Massachussetts have no idea of the responsibility which belongs to their office."

These sub-reports are, without exception, characterized by high appreciation of the sanitary importance of their subjects, and clearness of demonstration in the bearings of the matter treated of on health. We purpose recurring to them again hereafter.

The report, throughout, is characterized by a thorough comprehension of sanitary work, and a high degree of executive skill in securing the services and co-operation of the right men for the right places.

The expenses for the year are summed up to be only $4,347.75. An example of economy, in strict keeping with the inestimable value of the work performed.

Minnesota.—Second Annual Report of the State Board of Health, for the year 1873, pp 98. The "General Report" of the Board occupies a dozen pages in forcibly enunciating the necessity of intelligent Health Boards throughout the State, and cites the spread of Small-pox in 1872, and the prevalence of Typhoid, Remittent, Scarlet Fever, Measles, Scrofulous Diseases and Consumption, generally, as being subject to, and requiring sanitary surveillance only for their total prevention, or, at least, great curtailment. One-fifth of the mortality of the State is attributed to preventable causes; local health organizations and enlarged powers of the State Board are urged as the best means of averting them. Registration is also represented as being inefficient and unreliable. Legislative action is invoked for its correction.

Brief reports, appendices, and inspections on the Inebriate Asylums, State Prisons, Reform and Normal Schools. Typhoid Fever, by D. W. Hand, M. D.; "Remarks on Climate of Minnesota," by Rev. A. B. Paterson, four pages; and a summarized report of six pages on *Health of Towns*, make up the remainder of the Report. We wish we could say of it, *multum in parvo*. Excepting the first dozen pages, it is a very feeble report.

Michigan.—First Annual Report of the Secretary of the State Board of Health, for the year 1873, pp. 101. This Report opens with a copy of the law to establish the State Board of Health, and an account of the organization under it.

"The law providing for the establishment of the State Board of Health took effect July 30th, 1873. This first Annual Report, for the year ending September 30th, 1873, is therefore for a period of only two months." But the prime movers for this organization in Michigan were already ripe for action; there were no vacillating delays or needless waste of time in securing competent and efficient officers.

Executive skill is no less essential in selecting and utilizing labor than in planning work, and this prevailing characteristic of the pioneer State Board of Health of the United States—Massachusetts—is in a fair way of being emulated by that of Michigan. For the immediate future, the following plan of work, and its committal, is eminently suggestive of a fruitful harvest:

1. Epidemic, Endemic, and Contagious Diseases. Zenas E. Bliss, M. D.
2. Sewerage and Drainage. Henry F. Lyster, M. D.
3. Food, Drinks, and Water Supply. Zenas E. Bliss, M. D.
4. Buildings, Public and Private, including Ventilation, Heating, etc. Robert C. Kedzie, M. D.
5. Climate; General and by Season of Year, and as related to Age of Inhabitants. Henry F. Lyster, M. D.
6. Disposal of Excreta and Decomposing Organic Matter. Homer O. Hitchcock, M. D.
7. Poisons, Explosives, Chemicals, Accidents, and Special Sources of Danger to Life and Health. Robert C. Kedzie, M. D.
8. Occupations and Recreations. Rev. Chas. H. Brigham.

9. Education; The Relation of Schools to Health; The Kinds and Methods of Instruction in Use, and Methods to be Proposed. Rev. John S. Goodman.

10. Geology and Topography; Influence on Health of Forest Trees and their Removal, Shade Trees near Dwellings, etc. Rev. Chas. H. Brigham.

11. The Death-Rate as Influenced by Age, Climate, and Social Condition. Rev. John S. Goodman.

12. Legislation in the Interests of Public Health. Robert C. Kedzie, M. D.

13. Finances. Zenas E. Bliss.

Besides this, circulars have been sent to all the physicians of the State, and to the Clerks of all the local Boards of Health, requiring prompt reports of "diseases dangerous to the public health," and statistics.

Three special papers have already been elicited : On *Illuminating Oils*, *Poisonous Paper*, and *The Hygiene of School Buildings*, by Prof. R. C. Kedzie, member of the Board. How to Ventilate School Houses, in our February number, was an abstract of Prof. Kedzie's paper on School Buildings, as, in part, previously presented to the Michigan State Medical Society.

The want of space at present, precludes a corresponding notice of his other papers, which are of the same high order of merit ; but with the executive skill already manifested, and such collaborators as Prof. Kedzie and his associates, as above named, Sanitary Science may well rely upon large acquisitions from the State Board of Health of Michigan.

Dayton.—Seventh Annual Report, for the year 1873, pp. 24 : Total deaths, 694 ; births, 815 ; ratio, respectively, per 1,000, 16.36 and 28.22. Foremost among the deaths stands cholera infantum, 44 per cent. ; diarrhœal diseases, 70 per cent. ; cerebro-spinal meningitis, deaths, 66 ; consumption, 84 ; typhoid fever, 20—average number of deaths from this disease for the last six years, 16⅔. Chief nuisances : slaughter-houses, over-running privy vaults, and soil saturation. The Report is to the point, and the health officers' conclusions, logical.

New Haven.—First Annual Report, pp. 32, 26,—consisting of laws and ordinances: Births, 1,675; marriages, 632; deaths, 1,277. Respective ratios per 1,000, estimating population at 55,000,—30.27, 11.49, 23.23. Registration of births is confessedly imperfect. Deaths from consumption, 151 ; typhoid fever, 55 ; remittent fever, 7 ; cholera infantum, 77 ; diphtheria, 26 ; dysentery, 27 ; scarlet fever, 61.

Nuisance,—only one dwelt upon—"the 'run' from Broad to Water street,......an old arm of the sea, is a springy, marshy swamp, so near the level of the sea that the water is within a few inches of the surface, and the whole section is the receptacle of all that is in its nature filthy and unhealthy."......

CURRENT REPORTS show in :

New York,—ratio of deaths per 1,000, 26.50—prevalence of scarlatina, diphtheria, pneumonia. For the week ending, March 28, small-pox, 6; typhoid fever, 6; consumption, 74.

"The winter mortality has not been as great as in past years, though there has been an excessive fatality from scarlatina and diphtheria. The total number of deaths in the quarter ending March 28th, amounts to 6,534. The number that died in the first three months in the year 1873, was 6,951, or 417 more than in the corresponding period this year. E. HARRIS, M. D., *Registrar*."

Brooklyn,—24. Scarlatina, diphtheria, pneumonia. For the week ending, March 28, deaths from consumption, 21. The unsanitary condition of the public schools continues to excite much attention and general public concern, but little or no progress has been made to improve it.

Philadelphia,—25.83. Week ending March 28, consumption, 51.

Chicago,—34.23. Latest report received March 7th.

St. Louis,—26.18. Four weeks ending March 21, small-pox, 13; typhoid fever, 14.

New Orleans,—March 27 ;—"Notwithstanding our unusually warm weather this spring, we are still having considerable small-pox. Deaths for the week ending March 1st, 16; 8th, 27; 15th, 15; 22d, 25. Otherwise city very healthy. S. C. RUSSELL, M. D., *Secretary*."

Boston,—19.28. Week ending March 21st, consumption, 26; scarlet fever, 8; typhoid fever, 1.

Baltimore,—23.70.

Cleveland,—28.44. Small-pox, week ending March 28th, 7.

Richmond,—Annual Report, 31.86 ; week ending March 28th, 23.22.

Indianapolis,—14.08.

Dayton,—14.65.

Providence,—14.53. Month of March, consumption, 19 ; scarlatina, 17.

"There were 10 deaths in March from *diseases of the heart*, and the number from this cause is constantly large, and has increased greatly within the last few years. Thus there were 100 deaths from diseases of the heart in Providence in 1873; 92 in 1872; 77 in 1871; and 59 in 1870. These figures are so large as to excite attention; but I am satisfied that they are correct. Of the 10 deaths from diseases of the heart during the month of March, 9 were certified by physicians and one by a coroner. Some of the deaths reported are : '*Primary*, rheumatism ; *secondary*, disease of the heart ;' and it is probable that rheumatism is the original cause of a large portion of the deaths from diseases of the heart, though it seldom appears among the causes of death.

"Scarlatina still continues with severity, though the number of decedents from it in March was 6 less than in January, and, in proportion to the length of the month, was 8 less than in February.—E. M. SNOW, M. D., *Supt. and City Registrar*."

—

London,—Week ending Feb. 21st, 21.04 ; small-pox, 2 ; measles, 51 ; scarlatina, 16 ; typhoid fever, 26 ; whooping-cough, 50 ; pneumonia, 110.

Paris,—Week ending Feb. 27th, 20.92; small-pox, 1; measles, 19; scarlatina, 3; typhoid fever, 22; pneumonia, 61.

CHOLERA.—The cholera has broken out afresh at Senong (Feb. 1), 83 deaths having occurred among the troops in three days. In Munich also it still prevails. From the time of its reappearance in that city, Nov. 15 to Jan. 29, there had been 2,733 cases; 1,278 deaths. January 28th and 29th (latest reports), there were 26 cases; 17 deaths.

MEDICAL TOPOGRAPHY OF NEW YORK.

Every citizen of New York, and every individual, whether physician or layman, interested in sanitary science, will welcome the new edition of General Viele's topographical atlas of the city of New York. No dissertation on the necessity of thorough drainage could be more convincing than this graphic delineation of the underground influences of saturation. As a guide and companion to the practitioner in his daily round of visits, this atlas is invaluable. The older editions were in great demand, but the more complete map which is now before us excels the former one, not only in its beautiful execution, but also in extent, as it embraces the newly-annexed territory. If every city in the United States were to have a map of this character, it would be of incalculable benefit, not only in a sanitary point of view, but also as a guide to public improvements. It is folly to ignore existing topographical lines in laying out cities and towns. These natural features seem to rebel against the reckless hand of the would-be improver, and to demand that recognition which is too often denied. Not receiving this, a seeming revenge is taken in future fever nests and saturated spots where disease is ever lurking and where epidemics organize their irresistible forces. Timely wisdom and proper forethought would save all these evil consequences. A thorough knowledge of original topography, and a use of this knowledge in all works of improvement, is the first ncessity —if a city would be healthy. We commend General Viele's atlas to all who are interested in the health and prosperity of New York.

Orders should be addressed to THE SANITARIAN, 234 Broadway, New York.

THE SANITARIAN AND ITS CONTRIBUTORS,—BY DRS. HARRIS AND ALLEN.

NEW YORK, *April* 2, 1874.

DEAR DOCTOR BELL :

Though too busy at hard toil to permit my pen to share in the good work of your contributors, you will allow me to hand in a second year's subscription with my most cordial thanks to the two classes of writers in your journal, who seem to me to have earned the gratitude of society by offering practical suggestions upon subjects that are intimately associated with healthy life and human welfare. I refer to *Sanitary Drainage* and *Infant Nourishment*.

Healthy life is tantamount to social and political prosperity, and it is the sure support of morality and religion. Dr. Walker's papers on Foods would be very useful now in a separate brochure. Like Dr. Routh's admirable little treatise on "Infant Feeding," Dr. Walker's chapters on the *Care and Nourishing of Infants* would save thousands of infants alive, and with vigorous health, if carefully consulted by the persons charged with care in such matters.

Concerning the various papers relating to Sanitary Drainage, I must add the testimony of long and practical observation, and say that I sincerely thank the writers. And concerning the last, by Surgeon Wilson, of the Navy, I must urge the same pen to take up the subject of deep tillage and thorough cropping and culture, in connection with tree culture, as means of natural drainage and of arrest to the development of paludal malaria. The old estates near Harrison's and Haxall's Landings on the James, and of the White House and Yorktown regions, on the Pamunkey and York, and of Port Royal, on the Rappahannock River, illustrate this point as well as the Campagnia did in its best estate, and as they all alike do now in their uncultivated condition.

Dr. Wilson's observations upon the sanitary agency of pine-tree culture is full of instruction. I have witnessed analogous results upon two farms in New Utrecht, L. I., where the farmers drained all their pond-bowls by tapping them at the bottom and letting all water out with the side stratum of coarse gravel under the hard-pans.

Having studied the sanitary relations of undrained lands in every county of this State, I may be able to compare notes with you and Dr. Wilson upon this subject. ELISHA HARRIS, M. D.

LOWELL, MASS., *April* 8, 1874.

DEAR SIR,—I avail myself of the occasion, on receipt of the first number of second volume, to express my appreciation of THE SANITARIAN. I have carefully read it from the first, and, in my opinion, it is eminently adapted to promote the interests of sanitary science in this country. No subject is so important to the welfare of our citizens as a knowledge of Hygiene; and there is no means or agency whatever so convenient and effective to diffuse such information as a live and well-conducted journal. In matters of health, we are far behind our neighbors in Great Britain; and it is high time that all educators, all philanthropists, and especially all members of the medical profession should wake up to this great reform, more important to the interests of our people than any other one thing.

NATHAN ALLEN, M. D.

PERSONAL.

Subscribers who have not yet paid, will confer a favor by prompt remittance. Bear in mind new address, 234 Broadway, New York.

BIBLIOGRAPHY.

U. S. Marine Hospital Service; Annual Report of the Supervising Surgeon, John W. Woodworth, M. D., for 1873. There were treated during the year, 13,529 sick and disabled seamen; 12,697 were sent to hospitals. Average daily number of hospital patients throughout the year, 1,151, at a total cost of $422,502.98, or $1.002 per day for each patient. The process of revision instituted by Dr. Woodworth, under the Act of 1870, is reported to be progressing favorably under the new rules and regulations, and a hopeful prospect is expressed of being able, ere long "to relieve the hospital fund of the burden of supporting malingerers and other impostors, who have succeeded in the past, through lack of medical supervision, in making marine hospitals, to a large extent, mere eleemosynary institutions."

The hospital money collections from seamen during the year, amount to $335,845.95, which is an increase of $12,145.90 over the amount collected in 1872; still believed, however, to be short of the amount really due the fund, owing to the loose construction of the law by many masters of vessels in making their returns. The total expenditures for the year were considerably increased by the prevalence of small-pox—286 cases, with 136 deaths, there having been the year before, 131 cases, with 54 deaths.

The evils of badly constructed hospitals, and the plans suggested for abating them, are worthy of the most attentive consideration. The conclusions of Dr. Woodworth, in this regard, are in complete accord with the best sanitary experiences everywhere at the present time; and the sooner all old monumental hospitals are destroyed, the better for human health. Better none at all, than many such as still obtain.

The *Distribution and Natural History of Yellow Fever*, by J. M. Toner, M. D.; the *Reports on the Yellow Fever for* 1873, by the Medical Officers of the Marine Hospital Service; "*The Sailor and the Service at the Port of New York*," by Heber Smith, M. D., M.H.S., and the "*River Boatman of the Lower Mississippi*," by Erasmuth Smith, M. D., M.H.S., are all valuable papers, germane to the service, and add much interest to the volume.

Catalogue of the Library of the Surgeon-General's Office, U. S. Army.

Royal 8vo, 3 vols., pp. 1,193, 956, and 319. By John S. Billings, M. D. Assistant Surgeon, U. S. Army, in charge of Library.

We deem ourselves highly favored in having received a copy of this inestimable contribution to American medical literature. We learn from it that the Library now (Aug. 15, 1873) contains about 25,000 volumes, and 15,000 single pamphlets, and the present catalogue gives about 50,000 titles exclusive of cross references. Vols. I. and II. give a catalogue of authors. Vol. III., of subjects.

For a work of such magnitude, it is unusually free from blemishes of every kind, and the few that do exist are evidently accidental escapes in proof-reading—*not* errors. And considering the labor involved in the task of proof-reading alone, it has been accomplished with surprising accuracy. Text, paper, type, and binding, all conform to make this work no less a monument of learning, industry, and skill on the part of the author, than of priceless value to the profession.

Schools.—Annual Report of the City Superintendent of the Schools to the Board of Education, of New York, for 1873, pp. 107. The Superintendent's portion of this Report consists of a brief summary of attendance, numbers and grades of pupils and teachers, and a commendation of the suggestions of the Assistant Superintendents in regard to their various departments. It is gratifying to see that some of the Assistant Superintendants have been meritoriously bold enough to speak out in regard to the process of smothering pursued by the Board of Education.

"The By-Laws of the Board of Education require an *average* of but *thirty-five pupils* for each teacher in the Grammar Schools, and this is quite enough, and yet the same By-Laws demand an *average of fifty pupils* for each teacher in the Primary Schools and Departments. When viewed as individual classes of thirty-five and fifty pupils, respectively, these numbers do not seem to be large. But fifty pupils by no means represent the usual size of the primary classes. Probably not more than *one-fifth* of them contain so few as fifty at any time, while nearly *two-fifths* of the classes contain *seventy or more* pupils in each. In consequence of the required *average* attendance of fifty for the entire school year, principals are frequently compelled to make their classes much too large in order to compensate for the small attendance on stormy days, and for absence by sickness, and during the hot days of summer. A required average of *forty* pupils to each teacher, with proper restrictions as to the number of teachers that may be employed, would do much toward relieving the Primary Schools of one of these heavy burdens. Yet full relief can be obtained only by providing more rooms for the classes of the *fourth, fifth* and *sixth* grades, and a reduction also of the average number of children required for each teacher.

In view of the foregoing statements, and your own personal knowledge of these matters, I am sure that it must be painfully evident to you that both the physical and intellectual welfare of thousands of children in our Primary Schools and Departments need immediate provision for smaller classes, more class room, and the means for proper ventilation."—N. A. Calkins, *First Ass't. Superintendent Primary School Department.*

THE SANITARIAN.

A MONTHLY JOURNAL.

VOL. II.] JUNE, 1874. [NO. 3.

DISPOSAL OF THE DEAD.

By GEORGE BAYLES, M. D., New York.

Read before the Public Health Association of New York, April 23, 1874.

Your attention is invited to the consideration of the disposal of the dead in such manner as shall be most in accord with fixed laws; which shall not delay the processes of nature by artificial means to the obvious detriment of the living. It is a subject so peculiarly consistent with the objects of this Association that I, for one, am unwilling to longer delay taking such action as shall determine our sentiments. As Sanitarians, our legitimate approach to a fair investigation of the subject is by the sanitary road. By any other line of approach the obstacles are numerous and very serious. It is, indeed, the true pathway to the right understanding of this subject, and the pregnable side to the subjection of all that is in defiance of and opposed to its scientific aspect. We must appeal to that potent and first law of nature, *self-protection*, and so proclaim it that a wholesome conviction may take root in the popular mind that we are right, and that everything merely ethical and sentimental may yield to sounder views and practices.

Like all great reforms, the first struggle is for recognition. And a reform which contemplates so radical a change in the treatment of the beloved dead is surely a work of time and labor, and depends for success upon an enlightened appreciation of the subject for its general recognition and popular development. Our purpose is to show the evil tendency and pernicious results of entombment and inhumation; and to point out the wiser policy and wholesome results of a different method. But we must take prudent counsel of all the facts as they stand, and be governed in our hygienic campaign accordingly.

The placid, benign, and often spiritualized features of the recent dead constitute a grave protest against the immediate reduction of the deceased body to the dust and ashes to which the Almighty fiat has consigned it. The modern mind is schooled into a fervor of sentimental deference to structural tissues, though they may be sufficiently diseased or disordered to have forfeited their life. There is something that savors of more than superstition in the solemn hush in the presence of the dead, in the super-delicate handling of the corpse by loving survivors under bonds of kindred and friendship. With these manifestations of affection no sympathetic spirit would interfere. Our protest is not against the tribute of love by bereaved and sorrowing friends, nor the manner of its expression; but as the dead body can remain an object of loving caress but a very brief period at the most, our protest is against all that, in our modern times and civilized communities, follows the social leave-taking of the dead.

That which we as physicists and sanitarians know of the changes which follow consignment to the grave, is either not known or only faintly imagined (if even the speculative thought is allowed to intrude upon the mind) by people generally. Let the general mind once grasp the shocking truths, not only of subterranean or subaqueous disintegration of bodily structures and progress towards the redistribution of their ultimate elements, but also the unrestrained expansion or diffusion of these chemically-liberated (and in their transition state often in the highest degree baneful) agents diffused through the earth of our habitation and the water and air which we consume ; let the general mind comprehend the nature of this process in conflict with the life-giving synthetic effects of the ordinary natural chemical changes going on everywhere about us, and designed for our support and welfare: when the public mind does this, it will appreciate our motive and accept our teaching.

Our remaining mission is to point out how nature's certain work can be accelerated, not retarded, and how that work can be divested of all evil. The process involved is not a subject of ordinary thought; it is, on the contrary, rather avoided, and a phantasmal picture of the entombed or interred corpse somehow shrinking into the volume and outline of a simple bony skeleton, is all that is usually comprehended. It would be well, indeed, for the popular imagination to go no farther if it did not involve a tolerance of conditions from which we all suffer, and suffer to a degree that even the scientific investigator has only begun to rightly appreciate. As conservators of the public good, we must protest against any attempt at permanent protection against, or any hinderance of, structural dissolution.

Notwithstanding custom, prejudice, and false education, I have been surprised to find public opinion more easily moulded on this subject than I had been disposed to believe. My conversations with many persons have not been fruitless of effecting reasonable conviction in some that the present method of disposing of the dead is radically defective, both in its sentimental relations and in a sanitary point of view. There is quite an unlooked for leaning towards a more practical, though not the less poetical, discharge of our duties. No available progress can be made in moulding public opinion upon this subject, however, until scientific men are prepared to offer some economical and effectual method, which shall also be decorous and expeditious, for reducing the body to the minimum of material bulk —in a word, to ashes or dust. No means yet advanced and advocated would be of universal adaptability, for the one simple reason, if no other, that they have highly technical features of manipulation that could not ordinarily be commanded, to say nothing of the individual expense and the support of a staff of necrological officers, always on duty. The great problem will be, how to make the reduction at once a funeral ceremonial, rapid in execution, nominal in expense, and commendable to the bereaved. What has rendered the popular mind, in cultivated countries and communities, so receptive and inquiring upon this subject, aside from direct sanitary influences, I do not know. Sanitarians may, perhaps, plume themselves upon being the foster parents of this great new thought, and of its acceptability to reasoning people. But one thing is especially noticeable—popular ideas have insensibly gravitated towards the burning of the dead as the only sure and perfect method.

I suppose just at present neither the theoretical inventor nor the experimental chemist is prepared to offer any better method, but as the combustion process, though not without a very ancient history, has never been perfected, it may not be an idle task to endeavor to devise some other process by which the same end may be accomplished.

The classical student is the one most familiar with incremation. An intimate knowledge of classical literature, were it common, would render the modern mind anxious for the motive and the results of cremation in this generation, and perfectly free from prejudice concerning that fiery method, provided no better one could be found. Burning of the dead was practised by the ancient Greeks and Romans, and is still retained by some Eastern nations. The antiquity of this custom reaches back to a period of history among non-Israelitish nations, contemporaneous with Jair, the eighth judge of Israel. Homer abounds with descriptions of funeral obsequies of this nature. In Central Asia, the practice was doubtless of much more ancient date than history records. Coeval almost with the first instances of this kind in the East was the practice in the Western parts of the world. This custom seems to have originated out of friendship to the deceased, whose ashes were preserved as we preserve a lock of hair, a ring, or a seal which had been the property of a departed friend. Kings were burnt in cloth made of asbestos, that their ashes might be preserved pure from any mixture with the fuel and other matters thrown on the funeral pile. The same method is still observed by the Princes of Tartary. The Greek method was very curious. The intensity of the flame was augmented by the bodies of sheep and slaves, unguents and perfumes, oxen, horses, and dogs, and even prisoners. It was reckoned a great felicity to be quickly reduced to ashes. The curiosities of this custom are quite beyond the bounds of our present purpose, but they are well worth studying, as they serve to show the ideas that animated those who practised it, which were laudable enough, though the methods adopted were crude, heathenish, and abominable. Burning was commonly denied to suicides, and those who had been struck by lightning, under the belief that they had incurred the divine displeasure and summary vengeance, and were utterly outcast from the realms of the gods. Both the

Greeks and the Romans observed the "*Ossilegium*," or gathering of the bones and ashes; also washing, anointing, and depositing them in urns. This ceremony, in all its details, as described by ancient writers, shows how imperfectly the combustion and calcination had been effected. Though the Romans borrowed the custom of cremation from the Greeks, it was not generally practised at Rome till towards the end of the Republic. It had fallen into disuse about the end of the fourth century. The disorders and barbarities which characterized the governments and communal powers during more modern and mediæval times, was doubtless responsible for the discontinuance of this practice. Where there existed no respect for human life, there could scarcely be any respect for the dead. To hustle the dead out of sight, and as quickly as possible out of mind, was the prevailing disposition among the peoples of the world during the dark period of the middle ages. I have little doubt but that a lack of respect for the dead became so general and universal that to shuffle them into a hole in the ground was the legitimate result of this indifference, together with indolence and poverty; still, cremation has a line of succession, as one of the customs of the world. That it was originally done, *i. e.*, in primitive times, to secure the bodies of dead comrades in battle from indignity at the hands of the pursuing or beleaguring enemy; that it was done in later times as a tribute of respect, the ceremony having then a sort of traditional and martial dignity connected with the wars; that in still later times it was done in the belief of its being of great benefit to the departed soul, as well as a great blessing to the living, are legitimate and reasonable conclusions. It was done extensively, and always from good motives, but never perfectly, or in a way to satisfy modern science.

The reaction from that custom, and one that was created at a very remote period in certain parts of the world, was the method of preserving the remains of the dead by embalming. Doubtless the same general ideas and the same motives gave this custom its time-honored popularity. It preserved entire that which cremation preserved only in much diminished and completely altered substance. The embalming custom must of necessity have been the result of modified beliefs concerning the destiny of the dead, and also of much increased knowledge of the arts and sciences. Chemistry and a knowledge of drugs had reached a point in which they were "Applied Sciences." As population increases, under the benign influences of peace and sounder knowledge of the laws of health, the question of the disposal of the dead becomes more and more important. The work of decay begins so soon after death that something must be done, and that quickly. But a small portion of the dead can ever be embalmed, and except in cases where the corpse must be transported a long distance, it is not desirable that it should be. Why should we attempt to fill the country with millions of dead and useless, but, so-called, imperishable bodies? The child may desire to preserve a father's loving face where he can look upon it, but the change it has undergone since the spirit fled renders it no more real than the plaster cast, the marble bust, and much less than the vivid photograph.

For many years, Prof. Reclam, of the Leipsic University, has been engaged in experimenting to discover an economical method of burning the dead. It is not long since Dr. Brunetti, of Padua, tried to burn a human body, but after hours of earnest effort, in which he resorted to a breaking or crumbling of the bones, he was still unable to reduce them to ashes. His failure evidently inspired Prof. Reclam with a purpose to solve this seemingly difficult problem, and the plan whereby he now proposes to accomplish his object is this: Let the body be lowered into a vault of fire-proof stones, and covered by a similar fire-proof roof, with a high chimney extending upwards, to lead off the obnoxious smoke and gases. As soon as the corpse is lowered into the vault, a stream of air raised to the temperature of white heat is turned upon it. Within twenty minutes the whole corpse is consumed, the major part sent up the chimney, a little heap of snow-white ashes remaining to be gathered into an urn or otherwise disposed of. The total cost of the process would be only two or three dollars. The erection of a building suited for the purpose would cost about $15,000. With certain modifications, which the fertile and practical American mind could suggest, this might be a very suitable method of procedure. In a short time there will be hundreds of well considered methods presented to the public whereby the dead may be consumed by heat and reduced to ashes. I can hardly conceive it necessary, therefore, in presenting the subject, to centre all our thoughts and experimental operations upon one method, and that a reduction solely by means of fire.

Has modern chemistry no other resources? Have our electrologists no practical ideas to present, drawn from their magazine of power? Why could there not be a *lithological transformation* of the dead, and a subsequent aqueous or chemical dissolution? Why may there not be a system of thorough *desiccation* and subsequent pulverization? Instead of destroying a corpse by fire, an inventor of Grenoble, France, proposes a method of converting the same into stone: "At the decease of an individual, the body is plunged into a liquid invented by him, and in about five years the individual is turned into stone." So runs the statement. The secret of the petrifaction is known only to the discoverer. But he goes further. He says that "In a thousand years time if persons will only preserve their relations and friends, they will be able to build a house with them, and thus live in residences surrounded by their ancestors." We suggest another application of this process. When the corpse is that of a very distinguished person, and if a statue of the individual is desired in sculpturesque effigy, submit the body to the petrifying process, then have it nickel-plated or electro-plated, with bronze, and set up upon a pedestal, so as to fulfil the function of being a statue.

Aside from this purely eccentric and grotesque idea, this may be a suggestion in the right direction, not for the purpose of preserving the petrified body for any reason whatsoever, but for the purpose of rendering it friable and easily reducible to a powderous dust. In this state it is mouldable, compressible, and, if not to be a treasured relic, is in a condition to mingle readily with the earthy elements of the soil, if scattered upon it. The fatal objection to the Grenoble process is the length of time required to complete the transformation. It becomes little less than actual fossilization.

For the sake of illustrating our idea of a lithological transformation, suppose we were to submit a body to such chemical action as would convert it into one of the compounds of carbon—say, carbonate of calcium, or carbonate of magnesium, or, possibly, one of the hydrated compounds of carbon with calcium or magnesium. Of course, our product, if it were a carbonate of calcium, would bear some relation and resemblance to calc spar, marble, limestone of various kinds, and chalk, also the substance of egg-shells, the shells of mollusks, and (with the addition only of a trace of phosphorus) to the bones of our body. Thus the whole mass of structural tissue would be practically ossified.

To effect this conversion of the body, which, at the outset of the operation, possesses the *carbon* element in sufficient abundance to be capable of almost any definite union, under favorable circumstances, would require immersion in solutions which the experienced chemist would not find it difficult to formulate.

In a body weighing 154 pounds, 110 pounds consist of air and water. Water in any appreciable quantity not becoming a constituent of the *nicro-lithos* of our creation, we appreciate at once the enormous reduction of bulk and weight when the water is disposed of. Therefore, no cognizance need be taken of the water of the body, as a factor requiring special attention, its elimination being inevitable, and all the better, for it would have to be driven off by heat and evaporation if it did not withdraw itself spontaneously. One of the peculiar features of the method is, necessarily, the spontaneous exclusion of the water.

Forty-four pounds of solid matter, then (in a body weighing 154 pounds), is exchanged for 44 pounds of calcareous stone, of so non-compact a nature that it is peculiarly friable, and peculiarly soluble.

Carbon and water (or the elements of water), together with nitrogen, constitute about 98 per cent. of the whole weight of the human body. The nitrogen present weighs about 3¼ pounds in 154, and to this is largely due the usual rapid decomposition.

The suggested process of calcification, or cretafaction, has doubtless special eliminative propensities towards nitrogen, which would be driven off, together with about ten other very common chemical elements, existing in very small quantities, though assisting in the composition of the human body. The elements thus driven off rearrange themselves into ammonia, nitric acid, and other soluble substances, and disperse themselves through the air and fall to the soil for its enrichment. These same nitrates, now poison our drinking water through soakage from the graves, but when diffused first through the air and then cast upon the surface of the soil, are converted by the plant into nutritious food; such is the wonderful power of the vital force to re-arrange the atoms and molecules.

The pith of the whole matter is this: Cannot the dead body, by some chemical process, be metamorphosed into stone, and then reduced to powder, for preservation, like ashes in the funeral urn, or scattered to the winds of heaven to seek its normal starting-point for future morphological transitions?

Let the suggestion meet with the fate it merits. To mitigate the imaginary horrors attendant upon incineration, it may be laudable, in this instance, to let the end justify the means by adopting some method which has not so many unpleasant and really barbarous associations.

I have already mentioned the possibility of utilizing another series of physical changes which may be instituted by the employment of certain means of a definite character: the thorough desiccation of the body and its equally thorough comminution.

The remarkable power of drying is forced upon our attention by many observations and experiences. Most of us have seen the mummified body of the unfortunate victim of Papal Inquisitorial judgment, which was discovered, and taken from its intra-mural grave, in a city of Mexico, at the time the order was issued by President Juarez to examine and break up the religious houses of the country, a few years ago. Indeed, the desiccated corpse of a child was taken from the same sepulchre. Both of these bodies, by the simple process of drying, were reduced to one-twelfth of their original weight, and one quarter of their original bulk. Both were like so much very brittle leather. They would crumble readily by any rudeness of handling, and no mechanical force, of any consequence, would be required to reduce them to powder. The desert sands have buried and desiccated many thousands of unfortunate travellers, as well as their camels.

It is presumed that we have a reliable and unbroken chain of evidence, sufficient in itself to establish the fact that by excluding moisture and guarding against excessive changes of temperature, we can effect desiccation upon *whole* bodies, and that they would continue entire and inoffensive for a length of time which we cannot measure. Note the historical facts relating to bodies found in a state of perfect desiccation after long periods of years.

The admirable train of thought and reasoning upon the "Disposal of the Dead," recently given to the world in a paper by Sir Henry Thompson, is almost conclusive as an argument in favor of the immediate disruption of all integral structure, and the reduction of the body to innocuous atoms after death. By that article I should have been converted to a cremationist had I not been already in possession of a decided bias for the rapid and effectual disposal of the defunct body.

New York was computed, by the Census of 1870, to contain 942,292 persons. I suppose it would be safe to estimate the population of this city and Brooklyn in 1872 at the round figure of 1,500,000 inhabitants. From the last Sanitary Report of the Board of Health of the Health Department of the City of New York, for the year ending April 30, 1873, being the latest published report, I find the mortality of that year, in its totality, 32,647 for New York. The mortality of Brooklyn would be at least one-third as great, so we will certainly be within the mark if we say 10,000, and adding that to the mortality of this city would make a death record for one year of between

42,000 and 43,000 persons within the limits of what is practically one city. Therefore, out of 1,500,000 inhabitants of one large centre of population we commit to the grave in our cemeteries over 42,000 bodies in one year, or at the least 40,000, considering that a few are sent to other parts of the country for interment. The effects of the tardy and really hindered dissolution of such a mass of devitalized matter is terrible to contemplate. Add to all this, the deaths of large animals whose bodies have to be disposed of by processes not as yet rendered free from noxious and baneful emanations, and the sum total of morbid influences is truly fearful. In 1872 there was an epizootic invasion which caused an average mortality among the horses of 89 per week. During the prevalence of the epizootic, the weekly mortality reached as high as 246. For twenty-two weeks it averaged 128 deaths. Then reflect upon the fact that the greatest mortality is during that period of the year when the temperature is very high, the atmosphere dense and sluggish, the ozone and oxygen at their minimum, and human life in cities almost insupportable—with these conditions invariably present, the water and air has to receive by far the largest percentage of noxious and deleterious contributions from the unusually increased mortality. In 1872, the hottest months, July, August, and September, were signalized by no less than 10,025 deaths in New York alone. In one week, ended July 6th, there occurred 1,581 deaths, of which 351 were recorded in a single day, July 2. These figures tell an appalling tale, and open up to our vision horrors which it is high time to dissipate by the beneficent offices of common sense and sanitary science.

There is a temptation, even if we ignore the duty, to look at this matter, under the inspiration of our figures, in the same economical light as that by Sir Henry Thompson. But our argument will gain nothing in force, dignity, and persuasiveness, by an elaborate estimate of the amount of ashes and bone earth, or any other kind of rich fertilizing material, that is withheld from general circulation through natural channels of renovation and re-creation; neither will we excite respectful consideration by calculating the expense that might be saved in the cost of funerals. These things will work out their own recognition by time and the faithful adherence to the one fundamental truth, viz., that the rapid and perfect reduction of the body of the dead to the least possible weight and mass of innocuous matter, is necessary for the comfort and vital welfare of present millions and coming hundreds of millions. Prejudices will long hold out against the dictates of reason and even of practical demonstration.

To those who have decided objections, theological, ethical, or merely sentimental, we have a few words to say. The subject is undergoing discussion in different highly civilized, cultured, and religiously devout countries, and is evidently destined to be forced upon the attention of all. Some of the most obvious objections vanish on a little reflection. The text which condemned Adam's return to the dust is verified by the methods proposed, not less literally than by inhumation, while it must be admitted that to the human sensibilities of the present day, the roundabout way of making the journey seems less repulsive than the really more direct road.

Finally, the question of cremation, or of some equivalent method of disposing of the dead, is not a mere question of preference any more than of prejudice. So to dispose of the dead, as not to vitiate the air by the noxious exhalations and mephitic gases evolved from a reeking, putrefying, mouldering mass of flesh, or not to pollute the water we drink by surreptitious streamlets of venomous juices, streaming and percolating through the soil, until the *potion diabolique* becomes tributary to our springs and fountains, is a duty concerning which there can be no question. We may, with greater impunity, rob the soil of what it has lent to our bodies during their long years of physical integrity and progressive structural development, than we can afford to permit fountains of death to mingle with our fountains of life. We must banish the cemetery and all places of sub-soil interment. We must terminate, by some method characterized by instantaneous promptness, all changes in the corporeal structure, when the life that animated is ended, just as we would extinguish the smouldering wick after the flame has been blown out. This is duty, no less to ourselves than to those who are to come after us. Our cities encroach upon our cemeteries, our villages crowd around and enfold their local graveyards, all hug closely that soddening underground mass of putridity, which becomes cognizant to every sense save that of sight. What we eat and drink, in these localities, becomes tainted with that which has never been allowed to undergo a healthful metamorphosis, and thus to become meat and drink indeed.

Let modern good sense put a period to all avoidable defilement, and make the land sing again, that it enshrouds no longer perpetual death, but is forevermore the womb of life, the well-spring of purity.

Oatmeal, Bone, and Muscle.—Liebig has shown that oatmeal is almost as nutritious as the very best English beef, and that it is richer than wheaten bread in the elements that go to form bone and muscle. Professor Forbes, of Edinburgh, during some twenty years, measured the breadth and height, and also tested the strength of both the arms and loins of the students in the University—a very numerous class, and of various nationalities, drawn to Edinburgh by the fame of his teaching. He found that, in height, breadth of chest and shoulders, and strength of arms and loins, the Belgians were at the bottom of the list ; a little above them, the French ; very much higher, the English ; and highest of all, the Scotch and Scotch-Irish, from Ulster, who, like the natives of Scotland, are fed in their early years with at least one meal a day of good milk and good oatmeal porridge.

Speaking of oatmeal, an exchange remarks that a very good drink is made by putting about two spoonfuls of the meal into a tumbler of water. The Western hunters and trappers consider it the best of drinks, as it is at once nourishing, unstimulating, and satisfying. It is popular in the Brooklyn Navy Yard, two and a half pounds of oatmeal being put into a pail of moderately cool water. It is much better than any of the ordinary mixtures of vinegar and molasses with water, which farmers use in the haying or harvest field.

PROSPECT PARK, BROOKLYN.

When the history of this century shall have been written, it will be found that the subject which more than any other has engrossed the minds of thoughtful men throughout the greater portion of the civilized world, has been the analysis and solution of the problems connected with social life. Among all the enlightened communities of the time, the relations which the different classes of society bear to one another, the personal and social habits of each, their desires and their necessities, will be found to have been among the most fruitful subjects of thought and discussion by philosophers, scientists, divines, and legislators; all having for their object the amelioration of the ills of humanity, and the frustration of evils incident to the aggregation of mankind into large communities.

It will be seen that intelligent discussion has almost invariably been followed by energetic action. Hence, those grand constructions, triumphant monuments to the skill of modern engineering, by which the pure waters of distant lakes and streams are borne through mountains and over valleys to the thirsty denizens of large cities, and dispensed with a free hand to rich and poor alike. Hence, also, the modern system of sewerage, whereby the refuse matter of the population is for the most part carried off in close conduits instead of being exposed to the action of the elements and broad cast as the food for noisome pestilence. Hence, too, the advance in ventilation, disinfection, deodorization, and all the various means by which the air we breathe is freed from contamination, and made fit for its great purpose, the purification of the blood.

We thus come by an intelligent sequence to the introduction of sanitary laws and regulations by which all alike are governed, and by which all are forbidden to do anything which shall endanger the public health. Growing out of these laws has been the discontinuance of intramural burial places, and in their stead, the laying out of rural cemeteries, which, by affectionate hearts and skilful hands, have become spots of inexpressible beauty, where the cypress and the willow are mingled with rare and beautiful flowers, and the signs of death are invested with the emblems of immortality.

It is not a little remarkable, however, in this connection, that extramural burial, now practised by the most enlightened peoples everywhere, is only a return to primitive usage. Both among the Jews and the heathen, in remote ages burial was usually *without the city*. The Athenians, the Smyrnæans, the Lyconians, the Corinthians and the Syracusans all practised extramural burial. The Romans, too, according to the examples of *Numa* and *Servius Tullius*, deposited their dead *without* the city, even before the introduction of the twelve tables, which prohibited both *burning* and *burial* within its precincts. From *Cicero* (De Leg. ii. 22), we learn that of the various modes of disposing of the dead, *inhumation* was probably the most ancient.

Burning, however, is unquestionably of very high antiquity. *Saul* was burnt at Jabesh, and *Asa* was burnt in the bed which he had made for himself, filled with sweet odors and divers kinds of spices. But the *custom* of *burning* and inclosing the remains in urns, grew out of the inhuman treatment of the dead through national animosities. The practice of *embalming* by the Egyptians, was in virtue of a repugnance to exposing the bodies of the dead to animals; they embalmed them, lest after interment they might become the prey of worms. The earliest example of intramural burial we have been able to find, was by the Lacedæmonians, and the practice appears to have grown out of a superstition that the touch of a dead body conveyed pollution. Lycurgus, of Sparta, in an effort to overcome this superstition, introduced the custom of burial within the city. But the *Christians*, from the first, *opposed* it and prohibited it by legal enactments and fines, on the old and reasonable ground that it was detrimental to the health of the living. *Bingham*, in his Antiquities of the Church, has traced the gradual introduction of burying in churches and church-yards, which began in the early part of the eighth century, to the supposed efficacy of consecrated ground, baptized bells and relics; and *Gregory* the Great fostered the practice in order that the relatives and friends, in memory of those whose sepulchres they beheld, might thereby be led to offer up prayers for them. The belief in the efficacy of prayers for the dead, Gregory subsequently caused to be enacted into canon law, and thus the practice of intramural burial by Christians, which Gregory the Great first instituted in Rome, was extended to other places. Then followed the practice of erecting vaults in the chancels and under the altars of churches. And to such an extent was church-yard burial carried, that in the early part of the present century there were many church-yards in London in which the soil had been raised several feet above the level of the adjoining street, by the accumulated remains of mortality. In 1814, Commissioners for improvement in Westminster reported to Parliament that St. Margaret's church-yard could not be used much longer as a burial ground, "*for that it was with the greatest difficulty a vacant place could at any time be found for strangers; that the family graves generally would not admit more than one interment, and that many of them were then too full for the reception of any member of the family to which they belonged.*" *

In 1786, the church-yard of *Saint Innocens*, Paris, situated in one of the most populous quarters of the city, had been made the depository of so many bodies, that, although the area comprised near two acres of ground, yet the soil had been *raised by the accumulation of dead bodies eight or ten feet above the level of the adjoining streets*, and, upon a moderate calculation, more than 600,000 had been buried therein during the last six centuries; *previous to which date* it was already a very ancient burial ground; and, within the last preceding thirty years (before 1786), more than 90,000 corpses had been buried there by the last grave-digger! We might thus pro-

---

*Paris and Fonblanque, Medical Jurisprudence, London, 1823, Vol. 1, p. 93.

ceed to cite many other examples, to inordinate length, of the horrible extent of the practice.

It will suffice to state, that sanitary science has already fought the battle and gained the victory ; and no one who has kept pace with the progress of the contest, or taken the pains to inform himself on the subject, now doubts the danger of proximity to the exhalations and streams proceeding from graveyards. The victory was appropriately signalized by the removal of the mortal remains from the Cemetery of the Innocents, in Paris, above referred to. The shocking stench had been the subject of complaint for many years ; the mephitic fumes had even become visible, at times. Finally, the edict for the removal was issued. The great work was begun in 1785, and it *continued for two years, night and day*, during which time many grand religious ceremonies were performed, in order to reconcile the people to the revolting spectacle. The great symmetrical collection of the emblems of mortality which attracts strangers to the Catacombs of Paris, was arranged, on this occasion, from the bones removed from the famous *Cimetière des Saint Innocens.* Since that time, enlightened populous communities everywhere rival one another in the beauty and attractiveness of rural cemeteries. And thus it is in this, as in many other things difficult of attainment, and where success is at length accomplished and the results determined, cavil is silenced.

Nearly allied to rural cemeteries is the establishment of public parks and pleasure grounds. Long and earnestly have Sanitarians labored to educate the public mind of large cities to the importance of, and necessity for, large open spaces of resort for fresh air and exercise, where all classes may indulge in rational enjoyment ; and, above all, those who, in the absence of such places of resort, are almost totally deprived of every pleasurable excitement. The patience and perseverance of the workers for the promotion of the public health have broken down many barriers, overcome much frivolous and puerile opposition from the wealthy classes—those who ought to have been among the foremost to give countenance and support to the most important of all economies, the economy of human life. But this object, too, may now be considered as attained. The benefit of public breathing places for the multitude, country excursions for poor children, and the like, are now no longer called in question. How different from the times when light was taxed at so much a *pane*, and water, the first necessity to cleanliness and health, was doled out by itinerant venders in stinted measure!

All the foregoing reflections, and many more, have been suggested by the handsome volume which has been presented to us, containing the Reports of the Prospect Park Commission. Familiar with the ground from the outset, and conversant with the contending interests that have pursued the Prospect Park enterprise from its inception, we have watched its progress with a deep and earnest interest in its sanitary relations.

It is now fourteen years since the initiatory steps were taken to secure for the people of Brooklyn the benefits of a large public park.

And although sufficient time may not have elapsed for us to determine the absolute effect it is capable of producing upon the manners and habits of the people at large, yet we may safely discuss its influence upon the public health. Not only in virtue of the purifying process through which the area of the Park itself has passed, in order to fit it for its present stage of development, but also by reason of the silent, yet no less powerful, effect which pure air, clear light, and the repose of nature produce upon all who are subject to their unobstructed influence.

In order to comprehend more clearly what we mean to express by the purifying process of its development, we must recur to the original status of the area now occupied by the Park, or, more precisely speaking, to its original topography.

The entire ridge, or succession of elevations and depressions, which constitute the chief feature of the western portion of Long Island, more especially that portion of it which is embraced within the limits of the city of Brooklyn, and a large part of which now constitutes the Park, had been hitherto regarded as given over, irredeemably, to the miasmatic diseases of various descriptions, which were ever present in that vicinage. The peculiar character of the geological formation seemed to preclude all possibility of a successful system of drainage, either general or local. A series of rounded hills and deep bowl-shaped valleys, composed of an irregular succession of strata of sand, clay, gravel and pebbles, showing little parallelism or uniformity, most of the valleys having no outlet. The heavy rainfall of the region accumulated into large ponds and pools, and there remained in perpetual stagnation, distilling off miasmatic vapors over the whole region. And the saturated clayey subsoil, even where water was not visible, gave increased potency to the always present miasm. The occupation of a portion of this territory for a cemetery, and its subsequent improvement and picturesque appearance, and especially the process of maintaining, by means of steam, a circulation in the water deposits, had a marked effect upon the health of the neighborhood. Still there remained, for several years subsequent to the establishment of Greenwood cemetery in its almost unequalled beauty, the large area now embraced within the limits of the Park, which seemed destined never to be occupied for residences or for any other useful purpose. The construction of the new reservoir upon one of its highest points, brought into stronger relief the general desolation which surrounded it. Everywhere else, stagnant water, saturated soil, the debris of decayed vegetable matter, and the rubbish of advancing street grades, presented a most unsightly aspect—"a desert of the most disagreeable character, rugged, treeless and mutilated." No spot could possibly have been selected which at first sight seemed less adapted by nature or less susceptible of improvement by art as a pleasure resort for the denizens of a great city. Fortunately, however, for the inauspicious undertaking, the Commissioners laying out the Park were wise enough in the beginning to secure the services of an engineer who had not only distinguished himself as the author of the plan for the New York Central Park, but who was also in the front rank of sanitarians on the all-important subject of thorough drainage. Grasping at once with a comprehensive mind this vital point, he devised a plan for the improvement of this area which had for its basis the most complete and thorough system of drainage. He well knew that without it the Park could never be beautiful, and by no possibility could ever be healthful. We allude of course to General Egbert L. Viele, whose elaborate survey and report forms the initial chapter in the handsome volume before us. In reading over that portion of General Viele's report referring to drainage we have been struck with the clear statement of facts therein presented, and the direct manner by which that which at first seemed to be such a difficult problem is readily and clearly solved. And we avail ourselves of the occasion here to state, that unless the other public works now in progress in Brooklyn are constructed with a view to carrying out these same principles in regard to drainage, the inhabitants will lay up for themselves evils which no sanitary regulations or administration can possibly avert, and which will in the end involve pecuniary costs manifold their need at the present time. So far as the Park is concerned we congratulate the Commissioners, their present accomplished engineer, John Y. Culyer, Esq., and the public who have the benefit of it, that the system of drainage so skilfully inaugurated at the beginning has been so successfully carried out. The salubrity of the Park once secured and established beyond peradventure, the coast was clear for the gradual development of those unequalled æsthetic characteristics which justly render it the pride of every citizen and the charm of every stranger.

That the establishment of Prospect Park has had the effect to call forth an increased civic pride there can be no question, and as a consequence, a stronger love for the home circle has been developed; that is to say, a less desire to seek for pleasure or excitement in the larger city on the opposite side of the river. Indeed, all great cities require a distinct centre of attraction, where all classes can meet as it were on common ground. It gives an identity to the citizen and creates a bond of union to the masses. Most of the cities of the old world have such places, and all the large cities of America will ere long be adorned with similar popular features. Unquestionably the primary cause of the pleasure afforded by a large park may be directly traced to the sanitary influences which they almost imperceptibly exert. The denizen of the crowded city lives in a constant state of antagonism with the laws of nature. In his dwelling, his counting-room or his office, the clear light of day is intercepted, and oftentimes nearly excluded, so that gas light is substituted for the light of the sun. The atmosphere is vitiated by want of ventilation. He breathes a tainted air instead of the pure air of heaven. His whole existence is at war with the rules of health. When he escapes from this into the pure atmosphere of a great public park, where nature smiles in all its exquisite beauty, where the green fields, the rustling leaves, the bright flowers, the songs of birds, the limpid water gleaming in the sun, all invite him to a mental repose, where his lungs inhale the pure air, his step becomes elastic with renewed vitality, and his whole being glows with unaccustomed sensations. These are among the sanitary influences of the Park. How much more potent are these influences upon the less favored of our population, who, from the force of circumstances, are compelled to inhabit the crowded tenement, surrounded by poverty and squalor, where all that makes life enjoyable is lost sight of in the long hard struggle for the bare means of existence, where the better feelings of nature are deadened and the higher emotions are stifled in the daily and hourly contact with the darkest and dreariest sight of humanity. The high walls which cupidity to make the most of a small piece of ground has erected on all sides of him, shut out the sunlight from the cramped apartment which he reaches by the narrow staircase and dark passage-way. The air is filled with odors of uncleanliness, and the vulgar din of the innumerable hosts that share with him the vast caravansary are all the sounds that greet his ear. What a change for him is the broad verdant meadow, over which the lofty tree casts its welcome shade, tempting him to recline beneath it. How different the sounds that come to him from the happy groups that line the walks or gather under the trees! How much of the bad instinctively passes from him, and how much of the good he takes in with every breath of that untainted air! Then, too, the happy children that romp unfettered by a care over the broad lawns and through the shady groves, heedless, thoughtless and happy! If the Park were made for children only, it would even then be worth more than all it cost!

There are other impressions deeper and more lasting perhaps than those alone which appeal to the senses, growing out of our large parks. These are the æsthetic influences, no less powerful because they are silent, that are derived from the constant presence of choice works of art, and a familiar contact with beautiful statuary. The neatly trimmed borders, the closely shaven lawns, the cleanly swept walks, the smooth gravel roads, all produce upon the mind that sense of order, that presence of authority, that careful supervision which insensibly awes the most reckless and unruly. One of the most urgent arguments of the opponents of the Park when it was first proposed, and the one most frequently reiterated, was the supposed impossibility to educate the masses into that proper respect for the place which would prevent the exhibition of rowdy vandalism. And yet we now see on all sides the most exquisite parterres of flowers, entirely unmolested by thousands and tens of thousands that daily throng the walks and avenues. Who will say that the public mind is not being educated up by these surroundings to a higher sense of self-respect, and a greater regard for the rights and property of others? Who will deny that the Park is fulfilling a great mission, and infusing into the minds of the masses a profound love of order, a heartfelt sense of the beautiful, and a cordial veneration both for art and nature, which especially in the former must bear its fruit in stimulating the nobler emotions of the soul. The cultivation of a love for nature has been characteristic of the highest type of human development in all ages of the world. Some of the most beautiful gems of thought which have been bequeathed to us by the best minds of antiquity are tributes paid to nature, both in verse and in prose. No writer, ancient or modern, has shown a greater relish for natural beauty than Horace. It is indicated in almost every ode which he has written, and Virgil rivals Horace in this love for nature. Cicero, Pliny, Diocletian, and a host of ancient worthies, have left behind them the warmest testimony of the enobling effects that intercouse with nature has upon the mind. And the highest order of literature which has been produced in modern times is characterized by those glowing tributes to nature, which will ever live in the poems of Wordsworth and our own Bryant, and the essays of Irving. Regarded, therefore, both from a sanitary and an æsthetic point of view, the establishment of large public parks in the vicinity of cities may be classed as among the necessities of modern civilization. They are a blessing both to rich and poor, and a charm to all, affording the highest form of pleasure, both physical and mental; and as they elevate and enoble the better qualities of the minda nd heart, they supplant the baser influences which otherwise lead to vice and crime.

The Age of Man.—The speculations of Dr. A. R. Wallace recently condensed by the *Nation* from an English periodical may well startle even those who have been accustomed to think the Mosaic period was not correct. In fact it says, in Dr. Wallace's reckoning, 6,000 years are but as a day. He reviews the various attempts to determine the antiquity of human remains or works of art, and finds the bronze age in Europe to have been pretty accurately fixed at 3,000 or 4,000 years ago, the stone age of the Swiss lake dwellings at 5,000 or 7,000 years, "and an indefinite anterior period." The burnt brick found sixty feet deep in the Nile alluvium, indicates an antiquity of 20,000 years; another fragment at 72 feet gives 30,000 years. A human skeleton found at a depth of sixteen feet below four hundred buried forests, superposed upon each other, has been calculated by Dr. Dowler to have an antiquity of 50,000 years. But all these estimates pale before those which Kent's cavern at Torquay legitimates. Here the drip of the stalagmite is the chief factor of our computations, giving us an upper floor which divides the relics of the last two or three thousand years from a deposit full of the bones of extinct mammalia and gluttons, indicating an Arctic climate.

Names cut in the stalagmite more than 200 years ago are still legible; in other words, where the stalagmite is twelve feet thick and the drip still very copious, not more than a hundredth of a foot has been deposited in two centuries—a rate of five feet in 100,000 years. Below this, however, we have a thick, much older and more crystalline (*i. e.*, more slowly formed) stalagmite, beneath which again, "in a solid breccia, very different from the cave-earth, undoubted works of art have been found." Mr. Wallace assumes only 100,000 years for the upper floor and about 250,000 for the lower, and add 150,000 for the immediate cave-earth, by which he arrives at the "sum of half a million years that have probably elapsed since human workmanships were buried in the lowest depths of Kent's cavern."

"BERMUDA IN WINTER—A WORD TO INVALIDS."

Just as our last number was going to press, our attention was called to a communication under this title, in a recent number of "*The Sower and Gospel Field,*" calling in question the correctness of an article on the Bermudas published in the "SANITARIAN" for December last. The writer of the communication in "*The Gospel Field*" is a lady, and is evidently in ill health. She characterizes our statements as "false" and "cruel illusions," while she altogether fails to support her own general assertions by any references or particulars. She cannot real'y mean all she says, as for instance, where she asserts that the islands are "always damp with wild tempestuous winds, which chill and enervate the most vigorous." Such boisterous assertions require fuller and more authoritative confirmation, something more precise and certain than the disgust of a sick woman to support them. "Chilly and tempestuous winds," as a general thing, do not enervate. Their rough cordiality tends rather to brace and strengthen. It is the hot air, the baked atmosphere, that induces languor and "enervates the vigorous."

It is very obvious that this invalid went to Bermuda expecting too much, and was "out of sorts" with herself as well as the place. She missed the comforts of home, and was in no mood to discriminate in atmospheres. There were no carpets on the floors, and how was it possible for the air to be balmy? There was nothing nice from Delmonico or Bergman for dinner, and it followed, of course, that "poor humanity suffered useless misery." She had to sit "wrapped in shawls," and under that crowning indignity of woman, it is no wonder she deemed everything horrid and abominable. She was ready to faint for something sweet and dainty, and yet had to "sustain sinking nature" on the unvaried viands that garnished the Bermuda tables. It seems rather an extravagant assertion, notwithstanding all these deprivations, that invalid visitors to Bermuda make a "grave mistake," for which they "pay the penalty of their lives." A strong wind is not certain death, nor do bare floors invariably precipitate patients to an untimely grave, especially in climates where for eight months in the year matting is less comfortable than the uncovered boards. So, too, while the delicacies of the Windsor House in all their successive courses, may more gratefully coax the appetite, there are many men and women who have lived long lives, and drawn out an existence they never knew to be precarious, on the simple fare of the Bermudas. Our fair critic could scarcely have improved the restful hours she found so tedious. Had she properly and profitably "possessed her soul in patience," she would have been more forbearing toward our enterprise, and not said such hard things of the ninth number of our first volume. It would be hard, we are sure, for her to name the invalids who have paid with their lives for the "grave mistake" of going to Bermuda.

She, at least seems to have escaped the extremity of the peril. She should go to Bermuda once more. Notwithstanding her absolute assertions, we can assure her that it is not always a tempest there, and that the bright days are not the rarities she reports them to be. Something a little less acrid, a little more just, seems to be due from her and would be compensating.

Our December article, and one that appeared in *Harper's Magazine*, are referred to together; but so far as any specifications touch us, the writer of the article referred to is mistaken. The paper on the Bermudas, in our December number, was not written in July. It is not clear what difference the month would make in its purpose or character; though some difference seems to be charged or implied. Any greater excuse, or easier explanation, that the warm days may afford for its "false and cruel illusions," must nevertheless be denied to it. Though it pierce the soul of the invalid who thinks so poorly of Bermuda, it is still a stubborn fact that our article was written in *November*, when the nights were quite cool. It is not the fact, either, that the "balmy atmosphere" attributed to the islands exists only in the brain of the writer—that is to say, not if the said writer understands the matter, as he thinks he does. He has lived a great many years in Bermuda, probably more years than the writer of the communication referred to has lived there months or weeks. He got away from the place without dying, and has lived long enough in the more heroic climates of this Continent to outgrow the fresh impressions that sometimes throw a glamor around places we have visited. The balmy atmosphere of the islands lives in his memory as distinctly and certainly as the cedar trees which grow on their hills, and the salt water that fills their bays. It is, moreover, the common testimony of all visitors to the Bermudas, who follow the years and can compare their seasons one with another, that all the credit and advantage of a soft, temperating climate, fairly belong to them.

Our readers will remember that no extravagant claims were advanced for Bermuda in our December article. No undeviating serenity or smoothness was claimed for its exposed latitude. Gales will blow across the Atlantic, and Bermuda cannot get out of their way. The east wind blows everywhere, and an occasional taint infects even Araby the Blest. It was stated that the climate was not deemed favorable for all pulmonary affections; and the summers, it may be added, are long and enervating. But with all drawbacks, it is still certain that Bermuda affords a great and beneficial change, in winter, from this climate, for invalids who have no time or money to spend in going farther to seek a better. It is an extraordinary winter there which does not present more sunshine than cloud, more genial breeze than tempest, more balm than dampness or cold in the atmosphere. The visitor must have experienced a most unfortunate and exceptional season, or must have seen everything with sick and discontented eyes, who can sweepingly denounce the climate of Bermuda, which has proved so hospitable to such numbers of invalids.

One word further as to the health and mortality of Bermuda, of which the writer we refer to has also something to say or insinuate.

In our statements on that point, which is one in which our concern is more immediate, we relied on data carefully collected by Governor Lefroy of Bermuda. These show, as was then stated, that the average death rate for forty-two years, including several years of fever epidemic, and while certain exposed and unacclimated classes formed part of the population, was only twenty-two in the thousand, about the same rate as the death rate of all England. We may now add that this rate compares favorably with the rate throughout the United States. It is ten or twelve per cent. less than that of New York city, and, with few exceptions, there are only small and inland communities that can show a lower rate than that of Bermuda. We append in a note a brief extract from the Report of the Registrar of deaths for the year 1872. This year may be slightly, but only slightly, under the usual yearly average of deaths, and the results are given in an extended as well as tabular form. It will be seen that it confirms all we have said on the subject, and goes far to refute the aspersions of the article which, perhaps at too great length, we have been noticing.

NOTE.—The Registrar General of births, marriages and deaths, of Bermuda, in his report for the year 1872, dated April 17, 1873, says :

"The number of deaths among the civic population in 1872, was 252, viz., 104 whites and 148 colored, and the rates of mortality were 21.37 to 1,000 whites, and 18.68 to 1,000 colored. An increase is shown in the rate of deaths among the whites in 1872, over that of 1871, of 3.39 per 1,000, and a slight decrease among the colored of 0.53 per 1,000. The increased death rate among the whites was distributed generally throughout that class, but I am unable to ascribe it to any special cause. The number of deaths in 1871 among the whites was unusually small, and with the exception of that year, the number in 1872 was smaller than in any preceding year since the commencement of registration. There were 28 military deaths registered, but only 22 are included in the military return."

In the table annexed to the report the total number of deaths, including not only the resident population of nearly thirteen thousand, but also military and official transients, the whole number of deaths for 1872 is 294, the causes whereof are stated as follows, namely : Diseases of digestive system, 60 ; of nervous system, 42 ; of circulatory system, 22 ; of respiratory system, 13 ; of urinary system, 4 ; of cutaneous system, 1 ; tubercular diseases, 31 ; zymotic diseases, 25 ; dropsy, cancer, and other diseases of uncertain or variable seat, 15 ; old age, 18 ; debility, 18 ; still births, 14 ; premature births, 3 ; alcoholism, 2 ; accidents, violence, exposure to cold, 19 ; and causes not specified, 7 ; and the causes of death are stated in accordance with the *Nomenclature of Diseases* published in 1869 under the auspices of the Royal College of Physicians of London.

"TAKING COLD."

By J. R. BLACK, M. D., Newark, Ohio.

Of all the erroneous notions pertaining to the preservation of health, no one is fraught with more mischief than that about taking cold. According to the popular, and I may also say to some extent professional view, taking cold is the greatest disease and death producer in the world. Fully eighty per cent. of those who consult physicians premise by saying, they have taken cold. If a relapse occurs during convalescence, ten to one the blame is laid on the action of cold. "My pain is greater, I must have taken cold; my cough is worse, I must have taken cold; I do not feel as well this morning, I think I have taken cold, but I don't see how," are expressions which the physician hears a dozen times a day. The latter is thereby often led to the reflection that if it were not for death-dealing colds he would have little to do, and convalescence would seldom be interrupted. But if the physician takes the trouble to think a little more upon this subject, he will be convinced that to his own craft is due this stereotyped and never-ending complaint of his patients about taking cold. The sick and their friends nearly always take their cue about disease and its causes from the trusted family doctor; and he accounts very often indeed for an aggravation of the symptoms of those under his charge (the cause of which aggravation by the way, may be, and often is, very difficult to detect) by the easy and satisfying explanation of having taken cold. In this way he gets over the trouble of attempting to make plain to untutored minds what is often a puzzling problem to the most trained intellect, and at the same time shifts the responsibility for the relapse on the uncomplaining and much abused weather. So it is that men and women have been led to regard climatic changes as the greatest enemy to their health; if it were not for them, their health would be next to perfect from the beginning to the end of the year. Thousands of consumptives, especially in the first and second stages of the disease, are firmly of the opinion that if they could only escape the malign influence of one cold after another, their recovery would be assured. To this end precautions of the most thorough character are scrupulously observed, and yet cold after cold is taken; the patient, mother, or nurse knows not how.

To the physician, the taking of cold means the suppression to a greater or smaller degree of the sensible and insensible perspiration, and a temporary diversion of the blood from the capillaries of the surface to some internal part. There is, however, reason to believe that the characteristic effects of what is known as a cold in the head may be unattended with any interference of a proper functional activity of the skin. The respiration of very cold and damp air may produce direct derangement in the action of the lining membrane of the nostrils, throat, and windpipe. More especially is such an effect liable to arise from breathing for hours a very warm, dry, house air, of a temperature of 60° or upwards, and then in less than a second of time, the cold, damp air outside, of a temperature at zero, or even far below it. In my estimation this is the main cause of that exceedingly prevalent complaint, chronic catarrh of the head. The capillaries and follicles of the mucous membrane of the nostrils are every day repeatedly swollen and engorged with blood by highly heated air—so much so as to arrest for a time the usual mucous excretion—and then shrunk and chilled with cold. This sudden and oft-repeated alternation is too much for the vital harmony of the part; it becomes irritated, deranged, and diseased; just as even the tough skin of the hand will become irritated and inflamed by being repeatedly plunged in cold and then in hot water. In primitive times, when houses were more open, and consequently of a temperature more nearly that of the ambient air, such a thing as ozena was almost unknown.

It has long been a familiar fact that cold as a disease-producing agent gives rise to no uniform results. Let a wave of cold air sweep over a continent, and how diverse the results upon the inhabitants? Upon some the result is a cold in the head, upon others an attack of rheumatism, upon others an attack of neuralgia, or of pleurisy, or of ague, or of lung fever, but upon the larger majority the effect is the very opposite of a diseased condition; that is, the cold air braces, tones, and enlivens the whole body. Why such diverse effects, why should an external condition be the source of disease to one and of increased health to another? If cold is *per se* necessarily antagonistic to health and life, why should the larger part of mankind feel better and stronger under its influence? One of the plainest rules of logic is that a cause cannot produce opposite effects, or that putrid pus injected into the blood of two living animals will not produce increased health in one, and disease in the other. The absence of uniformity in the effects of cold upon the body, either in the production of a characteristic disease, or in the presence or absence of this state, indicates that it is not necessarily a cause of disease, and that when it becomes so the effect properly arises from some special abnormal condition of the body. In other words a cold is simply a developer of a diseased condition, which may have been latent or requiring only some favoring condition to burst out into the flame of disease. That this is usually the correct view of cold as a disease-producing agent under all ordinary circumstances may be made plain by reflection upon personal experience even to the most ordinary understanding. When the human body is at its prime—with youth, vigor, purity, and a good constitution on its side, no degree of ordinary exposure to cold gives rise to any unpleasant effects. All the ordinary precautions against colds, coughs, and rheumatic pains may be disregarded and no ill effects ensue. But let the blood become impure, let the body become deranged from any acquired disorder, or let the vigor begin to wane, and the infirmities of age be felt by occasional derangements in some vital part, either from inherited or acquired abuses, and the action of cold will excite more or less disorder of some kind, and the form of this disorder, or the disease which will ensue, will be determined by the kind of pre-existing blood impurity, or the pre-existing fault of the organic processes. If the pre-existing fault be in a deficient excretion of lactic and uric acids by the kidneys and skin, the disease developed by the cold will be rheumatic; if the lungs be at fault, either by acquired or inherited abuses, inflammation will be likely to ensue; or if there be conjoined with the pulmonary fault an impure condition of the blood from the long-continued re-breathing of breathed air, consumption will not unlikely show itself. In no other way can the influence of cold in the development of diverse diseases be accounted for; developing this disease in one, and that disease in another; this disease at one time in a person, and another disease at another time; while at other times and seasons, great and prolonged exposure to cold is harmless.

It follows from these facts and considerations that the secret of avoiding the unpleasant consequences thought to spring wholly from the action of cold upon the body has very little dependence upon exposure, but a great deal upon an impure and weak condition of all the vital processes. In other words, with an average or superior constitution and an intelligent observance of all the laws of health, men and women could not take cold if they wanted to; they might be exposed to the action of cold to a degree equal to the beast of the field, and with like impunity. But in the case of persons with feeble constitutions, and who disregard knowingly or otherwise, and most frequently otherwise, the conditions of healthy existence, no degree of care will prevent the taking of cold, as it is termed. They may live in houses regulated with all the precision of a hot-house—they may cover themselves with the most highly protective clothing the market provides, and yet they will take cold. I do not think the consumptive person lives, or ever will live, even if kept in a temperature absolutely uniform, and clothed in a wholly faultless manner, in whom the well known signs of one cold after another will not be apparent. But, on the other hand, there are those who, like the late Sir Henry Holland, of good constitutions and living in accordance with the laws of health, may travel as he did from the tropics to the arctics again and again, clad only in an ordinary dress coat, and yet scarcely know what it is to have a cold, or sickness of any kind. The truth is, that in order to avoid taking cold from ordinary, or even extraordinary exposure, the vital processes of the body must be made strong enough to rise above the untoward influence of external conditions. If the body is not thus superior, if it is so weak that it can only act harmoniously under the most favorable conditions, a continued state of health is not among the possibilities. No more will a weak body maintain itself without harm amid great external disturbances than will the weak machinery of a steam vessel maintain itself without injury amid a severe storm. The avoidance of elemental disturbances are not possible in the one case any more than in the other, yet it is precisely what persons by the ten thousand are to-day seeking to accomplish in the preservation of their health. The study is not how to make their blood purer, their bodies stronger, but how to dodge the ugly weather.

The conclusion from all this is, that neglecting the conditions upon which strength of constitution and purity of blood depend, and then striving to avoid in a sedulously careful manner the *evil* influence of colds upon the body, is like neglecting the substance for the shadow of health; or more properly, it is like one who starves his body, and then strives to keep quiet in order that his strength shall not be exhausted. Let food be taken, and the exhaustion from exercise will not ensue ; let all the conditions of health be observed, and then the natural changes of the weather will fall harmlessly on the healthy functions of the body.

DISEASE-DESTROYING TREE.—M. Gimbert, who has been long engaged in collecting evidence concerning the Australian tree *Eucalyptus globulus*, the growth of which is surprisingly rapid, attaining, besides, gigantic dimensions, has addressed an interesting communication to the Academy of Sciences. This plant, it now appears, possesses an extraordinary power of destroying miasmatic influence in fever-stricken districts. It has the singular property of absorbing ten times its weight of water from the soil, and of emitting antiseptic camphorous effluvia. When sown in marshy ground it will dry it up in a very short time. The English were the first to try it at the Cape, and within two or three years they completely changed the climatic condition of the unhealthy parts of the colony. A few years later its plantation was undertaken on a large scale in various parts of Algeria. At Pardock, twenty miles from Algiers, a farm situated on the banks of the Hamyze was noted for its extremely pestilential air. In the spring of 1867 about 13,000 of the eucalyptus were planted there. In July of the same year—the time when the fever season used to set in—not a single case occurred ; yet the trees were not more than nine feet high. Since then complete immunity from fever has been maintained. In the neighborhood of Constantine the farm of Ben Machydlin was equally in bad repute. It was covered with marshes both in winter and summer. In five years the whole ground was dried up by 14,000 of these trees, and farmers and children enjoy excellent health. At the factory of the Glue de Constantine, in three years a plantation of eucalyptus has transformed twelve acres of marshy soil into a magnificent park, whence fever has completely disappeared. In the island of Cuba this and all other paludal diseases are fast disappearing from all the unhealthy districts where this tree has been introduced. A station-house at one of the ends of a railway-viaduct in the Department of the Var was so pestilential that the officials could not be kept there longer than a year. Forty of these trees were planted, and it is now as healthy as any other place on the line. We have no information as to whether this beneficent tree will grow in other than hot climates. We hope that experiments will be made to determine this point. It would be a good thing to introduce it on the West Coast of Africa.—*London Med. Times.*

THE VENTILATION OF SCHOOLS.

(*From the Practitioner, London, April*, 1874.)

Our Transantlantic contemporary, the *Sanitarian*, has recently published several instructive articles on "School-house Ventilation." Reading them, and studying the plates with which they are illustrated, the mind is carried back to the early days of sanitary work in this country, when commissions, committees, enthusiastic inquirers, and ingenious inventors, revelled in wondrous diagrams. Who does not call to mind the pictorial sections of public halls, schools, churches, and dwelling-houses then in vogue, in which the distribution of spoiled air was represented by graduated blue tints, which tints have now become almost inseparably connected with our notions of a defiled atmosphere? Then there were the bewildering diagrams of the movements of air in rooms under certain conditions, the direction of the currents being shown by innumerable arrows, launched as it were against "the light militia of the lower sky." It would seem that this tendency to graphic illustration of matters connected with ventilation, and the tendency of mind of which it is the visible sign, still hold their own in the United States.

We presume there must be some climatic peculiarities in the United States which render it necessary that the question of the ventilation of schools there should be mainly a question of artificial means. At any rate, while here the whole tendency has been for several years to trust chiefly to "natural ventilation," so called, all the recent papers that we have received from the United States on school ventilation have shown a preference for systems of artificial ventilation, or dealt with the subject from this point of view as a determined necessity. And it must be confessed that the field thus opened to the ingenuity of inventors has not been idly cultivated. Reading the accounts of the arrangements for ventilation and warming which obtain in some of the schools of Philadelphia and New York, it is a marved to us what the influence must be upon the physical and mental condition of the children, of the artificial atmospheres prepared for them. The subject, from this point of view, is one which might well be commended to the notice of Oliver Wendell Holmes. We should like to have from him a "physico-psychological study," as an advanced French novelist would phrase it, of a young girl (Elsie Zephyr?) brought up under the conditions which appear to exist in these shools. If the different appliances serve their end, the occupants of the class-rooms and collecting rooms must during their occupancy be much in the same condition as delicate morsels in a Norwegian cooking-box. Happily school-hours are limited, and we apprehend that in the United States, as here, human appliances are subject to human fallibility.

What has chiefly contributed to the discredit of artificial systems of ventilation and warming in this country has been the impossibility, in the majority of cases, of obtaining for ordinary purposes that amount of attention to them which was necessary to secure their efficient operation; and in such cases it has been found that ventilation has had to be obtained (if obtained at all) in spite of the system rather than in consequence of it. An apt illustration of this fundamental drawback to artificial systems of ventilation is furnished in the *Sanitarian* for August last. In an article on "School-poisoning in New York" there is a description of the warming and ventilating arrangements of the City School House, which is peculiarly instructive. The class-rooms in this building are arranged to be warmed by furnaces in the basement. The fresh air is intended to be admitted to chambers surrounding the furnaces, and after being warmed there it is passed to the different classes. The inlet and the outlet openings of the class-rooms (both improperly placed) appear, according to the appended diagram, to communicate with the same flue. If this be the case, the upper class-rooms (the building having three stories) would receive, in addition to the warmed fresh air, foul air from the lower class-rooms. Now, on a late examination of these arrangements, it was discovered that the *fresh-air inlet* of one furnace had been *converted into a hencoop*, that one only of the other fresh-air inlets took its air from the external atmosphere and admitted a good supply, and that but one of the evaporating-pans attached to the furnaces had a supply of water, the others being dry and dusty. Moreover, on the reporter ascending to the roof to examine the outlets of the foul-air flues, which were brought together in two louvred cupolas, he discovered that one of these cupolas had been *boarded up for a pigeon-house!* Our own experiences of artificial ventilation of buildings have been much to the same effect as in the above story. They began with a new hospital, built at a time when notions as to artificial ventilation were rampant in this country. The wards were all arranged to be ventilated by a "vacuum system." Shafts communicated with lofty turrets, in which big furnaces were placed. With these shafts were connected other shafts opening on the floors of the different wards. Inlets for fresh air were placed at the upper part of each ward communicating directly with the outer air. The experimental trials of this apparatus were a wondrous success. When the ward doors were closed, the registers of the open fireplaces shut down, the fresh-air inlets opened, and the furnaces of the exhausting-towers lighted, the air rushed up the shafts from the wards with the force of a small gale; and delighted committee-men exhibited to delighted committee-women and visitors the spectacle of strips of paper whipped out of sight by the ascending current and along the shafts, and rejoiced to think that infection and infectious matters could be got rid of with a like facility. When we made acquaintance with the hospital it had only counted a few months' existence; but we lived in it some little time before we came to a knowledge of its wondrous system of ventilation. The only officer who had known the building thoroughly was dead. The ventilating turrets were locked up, and the keys misplaced. The "outlet" openings in the floors of the different wards had been explained to us as *inlet* openings for warm air, but disused because the physicians preferred open fires. Diminutive ward windows, the sashes not reaching within four feet or more of the ceiling, were regarded as blunders, in which efficiency had been sacrificed to architectural effect—these windows having in fact been designed with reference to light alone, and not to ventilation. We lived in the hospital some months, and during that time the system of ventilation was never used, and we were never able to assure ourselves that it had ever been used after patients had been admitted to the hospital. "Sure, sir," exclaimed the senior nurse, "how could we use it, unless we screwed the beds to the floor, and tied the patients to the beds?" At any rate the system was never used in our time, and, what is more, its want was never felt. For notwithstanding small window space, we contrived with this and the fresh-air inlets, and the doors and open fireplaces, to get all the ventilation that was desirable, and, much to the content of the home-committee, to spend on extra beds and patients the considerable cost that would have had to be devoted to the service and feeding of the furnaces, had their use, and the system of flues to which they were attached, been other than an ingenious sham.

With the above-stated experiences before us, and others to the same effect, in reserve we turn, with more admiration of its ingenuity than confidence in its practical working, to the plan for lightning, warming, and ventilating schools by Mr. Lewis W. Leeds of New York, to which was awarded the premium at the late Vienna Exhibition. The drawings represent what Mr. Leeds describes as a "Sunned and Aired School-house" (the *Sanitarian*, December 1873). The plan is restricted to class-rooms without a common room, and each room is so placed as to be disconnected from the others, and to receive a full proportion of sunlight. The principle of warming and ventilation Mr. Leeds seeks to carry into effect is thus stated:—"Nature's great means of purifying the air and supplying it fresh to all living things is AGITATION. The gentle agitation of the air in the schoolroom is of the first importance. This is very naturally and beautifully accomplished by having the floors warmed to 80 or 90°F., and the air above it only 50 or 60°F. This would set the whole air of the room in motion, similar to the water in a pot over the fire." How he proposes to accomplish these ends is shown in two charming diagrams, to which we would refer all interested in the subject, and in which the heat radiates, and the air ascends and descends, and flows in and out just as the delicate arrows show it ought to do, and would do, but for the combined perversity of heat, air, and human nature. Mr. Lewis W. Leeds is, however, one of the few designers who commands our regard and attention in this respect; for he is aware of the obstacles, and gives this caution, that "it is exceedingly difficult to make any plan that shall so cause a constant and uniform motion of the air at all times."

Dr. Ross, the Medical Officer of Health for the St. Giles district of the Metropolis, has recently discussed this subject from what we may term the American point of view.* What he has written upon

* "On the Ventilation of Schools, Hospitals, Law Courts, and other Public Buildings.' Collingridge. 8vo, p. 20.

it deserves an attentive perusal. He comes to the conclusion that the proper ventilation of a schoolroom cannot be secured except by artificial arrangements, and he lays down the principle that "the poisoned air should be carried out of the room as soon as it is breathed." To do this he would have extracting-flues placed on the sides of the room within a few feet of the floor, fresh air being admitted from the level of or near to the ceiling. He gives a drawing of one mode in which his notions might be carried into effect, and offers suggestions for cooling or warming, as the case may be, the incoming fresh air, and even for baking, so as to destroy infectious matters. We disbelieve in the possibility of any such rapid removal of the air fouled by breathing, as Dr. Ross suggests, to say nothing of the mechanical difficulties of regulating for any certain practical use such a nicely adjusted scheme of exhaustion of foul air and supply of fresh air as he recommends. A converse scheme to that of Dr. Ross's was suggested several years ago, in New York, but whether it was ever carried into operation we do not know. In this scheme the proposition was, if we mistake not, to dilute the fouled air as it issued from the mouth. To this end it was suggested either that the seats of the children should have fixed hollow backs, perforated in the rear, so as to deliver finely divided streams of fresh air above the desks behind at the level of the child's mouth; or that each child's desk should have a finely perforated air-chamber upon it fed from the external air.

It is generally forgotten that the difficulty of successfully carrying into ordinary practice schemes of this kind, is, as a rule, in proportion to their ingenuity. If the same amount of trouble were bestowed in teaching school-teachers how to deal, for purposes of ventilation, with the simple arrangements of open fireplaces and common sash-windows, as is given to inventing fanciful methods of warming and ventilation, the objections which attach to those common-place methods would be diminished, at least in this country, to a vanishing point. It would be an easier task to teach school-teachers what it is practicable for them to understand, and what must of necessity be under their supervision, than to teach them complicated and perhaps doubtful systems of warming and ventilation, of which the supervision must be under some less educated person, and which cannot be under their immediate control. The London School Board very wisely contents itself, in its "*Rules to be observed in Planning and Fitting up Schools considered in reference to Schools of large size to be erected in London,*" to limiting the number of scholars in the schoolrooms, and requiring a certain superficial area for each child, with "through ventilation." In practice this has had the excellent result of causing to be applied to school purposes the principles of warming and ventilation which have now been accepted in this country for hospitals. We shall presently return to this subject and describe some of the new schools erected under the School-Board Rules.

DEFECTIVE DRAINAGE.

Remarks on the Health of Ithaca, N. Y., and its Relations to the Drainage of the Cayuga Marshes.

By S. J. Parker, M. D., Ithaca, N. Y.

In the growth of every town and State there is always a point reached where it needs all the appliances for its convenience and sanitary condition that art and experience can give. And that too when its pecuniary ability is least fitted to or prepared to meet them. Such is our own condition. With an University of the noblest proportions, struggling upwards in its ample dimensions, attempting to reach and pass in ten years the growth of centuries, with a sudden inflow of a large population, with the task of remodelling our public schools requiring large expenditure:—with our five railroads, all but one or two built unwisely by the operation of the bonding of towns by the late unfortunate law, that puts us and our posterity in debts, oppressive and wrong; with changes in our dwellings to meet modern taste; with the libraries and other buildings, enlargement of stocks and stores for business; with the advance of the whole cost of material, labor to an extravagant degree,—one and all would seem to make this the last and most unfavorable time for the Committee of Physicians of Ithaca to try still further the burdens that a proper sanitary condition of our town imposes on us. Dr. Potter has prepared his essay on the vaults, water impurities, relations of ventilation, and other kindred topics to public health, with remarks in part on the undrained lands and sewerage of our town. To me lies the sewerage and drainage as affected by the relations of our Lake to the Cayuga marshes.

While any citizen, student of our University, new comer, or old resident of Ithaca, may avoid the diseases of our low lands, it is in vain to deny that we have a powerful and ever to be guarded against miasm. For example, I myself reside in a part of our town absolutely free from intermittent fever. I have never had it; nor have one in ten, or perhaps, not more than one in twenty of my neighbors, and they only by exposure elsewhere; yet my residence is only a few hundred feet from blocks and squares where four-fifths of the residents are liable to ague, and very few wholly escape it. Cornell University is on ground as safe as any in the State of New York, but the cheap rooms for students in Lynn street and other streets near the University are certain to give miasmatic diseases to the careless youths who occupy them. The prevalence of the lighter forms of miasmatic diseases does not increase the death rate of any place as largely as many suppose. Thus, New Orleans is less in its death rate than Boston, Portland, or other Northern cities; notwithstanding, the city is inundated with miasm. Hence, when I say that Ithaca has more than the average Northern miasm, I am not saying that those who come to our town are to expect to die faster or sooner than in any other town. But it is due to the students of the University, and the Faculty and Trustees, that proper means should be used to control the residences of the students, that they shall, as they easily can, be made to avoid miasm; for the death rate of the transient population may be greater than that of the permanent population. Besides, the death rate of the same persons, treated by physicians not accustomed to miasmatic situations, is larger than otherwise, especially if the sickness is developed away from home. We could name, if necessary, some who have died early in miasmatic diseases away from Ithaca, while yet in apparent vigor of flesh and muscle, who probably would not have died under the care of physicians practically familiar with the nature of the disease. And we could also name some residents of Ithaca taken sick elsewhere, who have been pronounced almost or quite moribund, who have been easily relieved by visits of our own physicians; so surely do we learn to control to some extent the influences of miasm, as well as its prevalence. Hence, our duty is all the plainer for doing every thing practicable to destroy this bane of our otherwise delightful town.

The remedy involves the question of the level of Cayuga Lake, or rather of the partially, or at times wholly submerged lands on its borders. For example, a few years ago we had a season, when from the lake to and beyond the repair shop of the Delaware, Lackawanna & Western Railroad, the whole flat was all summer under water, thus submerging in the hot season at least two square miles. As another extreme, during the year 1872, no part of these lands was submerged. The zealous advocate of drainage will exclaim, the year 1872 must have been either better or worse in health than the year of summer flood. Not so. And I am not aware of any remarkable difference, nor have I ever heard that these dissimilar years caused other than slight deflections of our miasmatic lives. That is, our causes of miasm lie so deep that four feet variation of our lake level, does not influence it to such a degree as to make the difference immediately perceptible. And to this fact, the attention of those who are ready to adopt any cheap and partial remedy, is invited. The foundation for the cure of our miasm must be laid by plans deeper and broader than the annual, or even a series of annual changes in the level of the lake, strange as that may appear. For more than forty years I have observed our lake changes and the effects of the resulting miasm. Although, as stated before, I have never had ague nor any malarial fever, as resident of our town, yet I am to-day, so full of malaria that my system often rebels against any further doses of the poison. While, therefore, the malaria of our town is mild in its manifestations as compared with that of many other places, it nevertheless surely causes malarious cachexia with its train of disorders—dyspepsia, neuralgia, rheumatism, and the like, in general prevalence of ill health, for the relief of which, we advocate the lowering of the lake, as it may be the slow but sure means of putting an end to the miasm by the draining and drying of the flat marshy lands which are now subject to inundations. And in this I am in perfect accord with my colleague in this Committee Report, that it is the never ceasing dampness, the constant presence of water in the wet portions of our town, that is the cause of our miasm. At least one-third of our dwellings at present are on lots underlaid by clay, or on clayish sand, but little removed from the permanent water level; and, because of the cheapness of the building lots on these sites, houses are being multiplied and approximating nearer and nearer to the water level. Twenty years ago, we thought three feet above permanent water level too little. Many dwellings are to-day not more than twelve to fifteen inches above the water level, and some are within a spade's depth. And the occupants of these houses, men, women, and children, who are rarely or never well, fail to recognize and deny the cause of their ill-health. Hitherto, Cayuga Lake has presented the most serious difficulties to any plan for our permanent relief; and I believe, that in the discussions now nearly fifty years old, we have ever undervalued them, and ever underrated the foe with whom we struggle. We have sung the Jack Reefs thirty years; we have raised the plaintiff song by Mosquito and Hickory Island bars, and Free Bridge shoal. We have justly blamed those who controlled the canal aqueduct, and demanded that this peril to our health and property be corrected. We have asked State appropriations, and, in a political way, they have been granted and expended; some honestly, others, perhaps, not so. But the magnitude of the undertaking appals any one who looks at the map of the survey made by the Hon. George Geddes, in 1851. The details of this survey show the level from the outlet of Cayuga Lake to Baldwinsville mill dam to be *thirty-eight miles*, with only twelve and a half feet fall, or, a little less than *four inches to the mile!* and this through a crooked channel, liable to the growth of river grasses and weeds, and with an average *depth*, for long distances, *of only a little over three feet*, and a *narrow channel* at that. Were the channel three times as broad, and twice as deep, who would expect a less fall than four inches to the mile? Hence, I am bold to say that, as long as we suppose that we should have adequate relief, even if Jack Reefs, Mosquito bars, and all the other lesser shoals were removed, to-day, we are mistaken. Much as I honor the engineer who gave us this admirable survey, I cannot but regret his indorsement of any plan of relief short of a complete channel through the whole of these thirty-eight to forty miles.

On this question of how we shall relieve our marshes at the head of Cayuga Lake, let us compare the obstacles in our way with those at Havana & Watkins at the head of the Seneca Lake. Seneca Lake is sixty feet higher than the level of Cayuga Lake. The marshes at Havana & Watkins are larger and less above the lake than ours; yet all it requires is to cut the outlet of Seneca Lake deeper by a certain number of feet, the comparatively short distance to near Seneca Falls, and the work is done. No breakwater of your neighbors, and of distant ones, is added to Seneca Lake, to be removed and cared for. On the other hand, to relieve Ithaca and its marshes, we have all the water of the Seneca Lake and Cayuga marshes as well as our own, to provide for in all these thirty-eight miles of Cayuga marshes. Would that were all. Turn to the map of our State, what do we see? There is the whole tide of the Seneca Lake and its floods poured directly into Cayuga Lake, and then comes beyond them the rampant floods of the Clyde River, Canandaigua Lake, Mud Creek, and of whole counties almost to Rochester, all concentrate upon us. Or, in other words, not only have we thirty-eight to forty miles of our own outlet to provide for, but we have all the waters of Crooked, Seneca, Canandaigua Lakes, and Mud Creek, as well as of that ridge of land north of Ontario and Seneca counties, to provide for. No plan that does not provide for all this can relieve us. And here has been our mistake. We have asked Jack's Reef to be cut, and the bar at Mosquito Point, Hickory Island, Bluff and Hand Points to be removed. We ought to ask that the great State of New York not only relieve us, but the thousands of others interested in a tract of one hundred and fifty miles long and three miles wide, including scores of other towns besides our own. We plead that this great nest of miasm, in the midst of the fairest land in our State, be cleansed for the lives and health of citizens of Ontario, Seneca, Schuyler, Wayne, Cayuga, Onondaga, Madison, and Oneida counties—eight of the large central counties of our State.

An examination of the map of New York, beginning this chain of lakes at the westward, will show that Conesus Lake empties into the Genesee River, in the town of Avon; that Hemlock Lake and Honeoye Lake join in an outlet which finds its path to the Genesee River, by the town of Bloomfield, in the lesser town called Rush. We are glad that their swollen waters vex Genesee Falls harmlessly at Rochester rather than swell the reflex tide into our Cayuga Lake. Next eastward, a few miles, is a valley where there should have been a lake eroded by glacial action, but, for some cause, no lake was cut out there in the diluvial or glacial period. Through it flows a stream called Mud Creek; and sluggishly it drains the several towns of Bristol, Bloomfield, Victor, Macedon, Salmira, Marion, and Lyons, where the outlet of Canandaigua Lake joins this Mud Creek, and the name is changed to Clyde River, and its volume flows through saturated swampy lands by the town of Clyde, and thence on to a short distance southwest of Montezuma, where it joins the united river, made by the Crooked, Seneca, and Cayuga Lake outlets. Here it receives the name of Seneca River, and holds it until it reaches the outlet of the Onondaga Lake, at a large area of wet land, near which the outlet of the Oneida Lake joins the now large stream called Oswego River, and thence on, the water from these lakes and swamps flows to the great reservoir of Ontario Lake, over the considerable falls at Fulton and Oswego; having drained imperfectly a vast area of Central New York, and brought dampness, miasm, and ill health to tens of thousands of homes in all this long and marshy tract. True, there are beauties in these lakes, with thousands of acres healthful on their shores. True, there are pleasant farms and towns, but the burden laid on Health Officers, and on the State of New York, is simply enormous, and were it to cost millions of dollars, there are the wisest and best reasons why the work of drainage should be entered on at once with no slack or untiring hand. Again, I repeat, undervalue not the obstacles and the cost of this immense labor.

It would be a comparatively easy task to map out the miasmatic region of our State. Such a map would show a checkered hill and vale near New York city ; a distinct body of the "drained lands" near Florida and New Hampton, in Orange Co., the whole valley of the Hudson and of the Mohawk, are comparatively free, yet requiring, here and there, attention ; the whole northern region from the Adirondacs to Lake Erie, in the same manner mingled sites free, with vast numbers of sites miasmatic, and the southern counties less miasmatic, yet with spots of saturated soil, and, consequently, requiring skill and care. But not until you drive a stake at or near Little Falls, widening over the damp plain to the beautiful city of Utica, does the traveller enter on the great, and the central mass of infested lands. Hence on westward, opens the whole Oneida Lake, Syracuse, Cayuga Marshes, Genesee River, and Lockport to Black Rock, near Buffalo, great undulating plateau, where the miasm is severe. Of course I could speak of this region, as I have so often both by public conveyance seen it, and by my own private carriage leisurely rode through it, crossing the Cayuga marshes by nearly every wagon road, as well as the Syracuse and Oneida Lake region, and that vast plain east of Buffalo, underlaid by the Niagara limestone, and so thoroughly saturated with water. Yet, some day our State authorities must lay their hand on these causes of ill health to its citizens, and immense as is its work, it must be begun and executed, in a manner so broad and complete, that the best informed of us hardly conceive of its magnitude. The loss to the State in fruitful lives, health, and wasted energies, count by millions of dollars in value more than the actual cost would be to remedy the evil and save the lives. I am unable to see any way for accomplishing so vast a labor; a labor large and costly, but it should be accomplished.

That we may form a just judgment of the labor to be done for the good of Ithaca, let us suppose the distance from Baldwinsville to Lyons, where the Canandaigua outlet joins Mud Creek, and the united stream assumes the name of Clyde River, divided into three parts. First, the western part, or from Lyons to the point near Montezuma, where the Clyde River joins the united outlets of the Seneca and Cayuga lakes. In this distance of fifteen to twenty miles (I do not know the exact distance), the Clyde mill dam is to be removed for the benefit of Clyde, and the whole marshy tract west of it for the sake of the local inhabitants. But that concerns us at Ithaca only as we value the prosperity of our State. As citizens of Ithaca, our concern in this district is at two points : 1st, the propriety of completing the Sodus Bay Canal, that the flood water of Mud Creek, Canandaigua Lake, and the whole of that region, may be turned directly into Lake Ontario, allowing only the average of water for the Oswego mill power to go through gates, so that the already vast mill privileges between Syracuse and Oswego be not damaged. This Sodus Bay Canal commences—or rather, leaves the Clyde River—about a half mile west of the village of Clyde; and much work north of this was done by the late Gen. Adams. The depth to be cut through a marshy piece of land was originally but a few feet—six or eight,—not over twelve or fifteen feet (I never knew precisely, though I have been over the ground often). By this cut we should get this advantage—relief from the volume of floods, at times very large, pouring several feet deep over the Clyde dam, in a broad river. This could go by this channel to Sodus Bay, and would relieve us, all the Cayuga country, Syracuse, and the Oneida Lake region.

The second point that interests us is, near the west end of Crusoe Island, where the Clyde River is bent to the southward by this so-called island, which is a moderate elevation of land in the marshes about five miles long and nearly two miles broad. Here we should, for the benefit of Ithaca, embank the Clyde River at the south end of this Island, and cut a channel in the wet marsh, uniting the Clyde River with the outlet of Crusoe Lake, which lies north of the Island. The cut channel would be over two miles long, and the embankment a mile and a quarter near "Armitage's Tavern," as it was a long time called. This would shorten the flow of the waters of the Clyde River between Clyde and Baldwinsville, at least three miles. And what is of more importance to us at Ithaca, it would pour the floods, not on the Cayuga Lake at a point only fifteen or sixteen inches below the low-water level of our lake, but at a place nearly fifty inches below low-water level of the Cayuga. That is, all the floods from the west over sixteen inches high, now use the Cayuga Lake as a reservoir, and fill it up. But by this change any flood less than four feet high, would not affect our lake. And as five feet is the annual average of the western flood of the Canandaigua Lake, Mud Creek, and other sources of floods, we would have at Ithaca only one foot rise in our lake, instead of four feet as we now do. A fact worth more to us at Ithaca than all your Jack Reefs and other expenditures yet made.

So you see that while the labor is large, the results are certain.

But let us pass to the middle or second division of the distance between Lyons and Baldwinsville. What labor is needed there? First, to continue the supposed diversion of our westward neighbor-water from us, would require the Bluff and Hard Point gravel beds, to be cut for two miles, and the Mosquito Bar, and then in a very brief time the already deep and soft mud channel could be opened to Cross Lake. Second, it would require a steam dredge, such as are now at work on the Erie Canal, to dredge the channel from the Cayuga to the bar of Bluff and Hard Point, a comparatively light work. So that while the labor is great enough on this middle section of sixteen miles, yet it is not the main labor or task. The third division is from Cross Lake to Baldwinsville, a distance of ten miles. This has two obstacles. First, the purchase of and removal of the Baldwinsville mill-dam. And the greater one of a bold cut from the straight portion of the river below Jack Reefs to Cross Lake, directly joining the 26th and 31st mile stations of George Geddies' map and survey of 1851, and the distance is about a mile and a half. But it saves the dredging and rock-cutting of four and a half miles of crooked channel, which has already swallowed up several hundred thousand dollars expenditure with but little relief. The next best place is to join the twenty-seventh and the thirtieth mile stations of the survey of 1851, by Hon. George Geddies, leaving the contemptibly small canal artificially cut there, to the south. As this cut of the 26th and 31st mile stations, or the 27th and 30th mile stations, or any other, is rock to be blasted out, it is, in fact, the worst of all the work so far as now recognized. But I have shown, I think, that the labor is immense, and that it needs men at the head of it who are no cowards, nor easily discouraged, but determined to accomplish the vast task, correctly, decidedly and economically.

What are our utmost reasonable capacities of drainage? Several plans suggest themselves. For the relief of Ithaca the removal of the Baldwinsville mill-dam gives us twelve and a half feet. Let this level be cut by way of the channel, to as near a point as possible to deep water in Cross Lake, which has a depth of twenty-five or more feet near the 26th mile station of the 1851 Survey, and then dredge the channel to Mosquito Point and Bar, and we have twenty-five feet fall at Mosquito Point, less the flow fall of the river. Say this is three inches to the mile, which, as the distance is twenty miles or about that, is sixty inches or five feet; this leaves available at Mosquito Bar, twenty feet less the fall between that and Cayuga Lake, which is nearly four and a half feet. Or by this plan, we have roughly, fifteen feet of fall at Mosquito Bar for the drainage of Cayuga Lake and the marshes on and around Crusoe Island to Lyons.

Now, omit the Baldwinsville mill-dam, and you have at Mosquito Bar as before three inches to the mile, or seventeen miles flow, which is four feet three inches less the fall from Cayuga, which is four feet and a half, or only three and a half feet, ins ead of the fifteen feet. Now as the floods average five feet annually, and are often six or seven feet, the plans without the removal of the Baldwinsville dam can never relieve us, for whenever the floods rise, water will be backed on us at Ithaca.

Another plan is connected with the drainage of Onondaga Lake, and the relief of the city of Syracuse and vicin.ty. Onondaga Lake is of no use to Syracuse or the vicinity—it in the end receives the sewerage of the city, and that is all, and it saturates the soil of the flats between it and the city, and sends dampness and miasm to Syracuse itself. By reference to the map, it will be seen Syracuse is exactly in the same condition as we are at Ithaca. All the westward waters disgorge into the Cayuga as a reservoir, and all the waters of the Canandaigua Lake, Mud Creek and Seneca Lake, and our own Cayuga Lake, fall over the Baldwinsville dam twelve and a half feet. *And they do what?* Run not towards Oswego, but directly towards Onondaga Lake, so that we pour all our floods on Syracuse. Hence, the Syracuse basin must be relieved by looking to the channel of the river north of it, or towards Fulton Falls. Were the whole of Onondaga Lake drained, no one would suffer. It should be lowered at least twelve or fifteen feet by cutting the channel deep enough towards Fulton, New York, even if the rock at the top of the high falls there were removed several feet. And to this the citizens of that large city, slumbering over their miasm and soil saturation, will at some future day awake. I have, in imagination, often cut their deep sewers, and cut their obstacles to drainage through the city too often with my eye, beneath the Erie Canal there to be mistaken. I know what I say of the soil saturation of all that region, for I have seen long grass on the streets that could be mown, where now a ceaseless commerce by canal and rail flows on night and day. And I am no stranger there since. But this affects us only as all the fall that can be available by the relief of Onondaga Lake and Syracuse, adds to our fall when the Baldwinsville dam is removed. We clearly have by a thorough plan fifteen feet without the Syracuse drainage. And with it we have five to ten feet more. And hence we see how intimately we go hand in hand with the Onondaga, Oneida and Oswego River drainage. And the final conclusion is, that with the proper use of our full capacity, the whole Cayuga, Onondaga, Oneida, on to Utica, drainage can be fully executed. Feeble plans are not the wisest and best. But the full, comprehensive plan, though it involves a vast system of drainage, is amply sufficient, and when executed, will relieve us of our marshes and throw thousands of fertile acres now submerged, on the market, and improve the sanitary condition of the central counties of the State, where, ever since settlements were made until now, a vast amount of disease has ever prevailed, and still exists, owing to the state of this great tract of not only damp land, but worse, disease-breeding land, with no relief, and with no effort for relief by those who suffer.

We have for Ithaca still another plan. That is, that we ask the State to fill up the marshes at Ithaca, at least six feet;—on the general philosophy of miasm of marshes, cured by filling healthy earth on them. I am convinced that it is often a cheap and effective method of rendering miasm vastly less. But our interest at Ithaca lies in the cheapness of the work. I am told that six hundred thousand dollars would fill the marshes south of our town, and to the line of Fall Creek north of us, leaving the rest of the lake unrelieved. If so, and the State of New York will give us half of that sum, it is a good plan for immediate relief. At least this can be effected. Run two trains of cars over the Athens road, loading at the one hundred acre sand and gravel bank south of Ithaca; load there by steam shovels, and fill on State or Central street, and at twenty thousand dollars a year much could be done. The process would soon make dry lots for new buildings. The filling in of wet lots, *if first properly drained*, is a sanitary measure not to be despised, and in Boston, Brooklyn and Washington, it has been found to be a successful pecuniary speculation in the cash sales of otherwise unmarketable lots.

Finally, a bold, well-known citizen says: "We must demand that a channel be cut through the hills directly for Lake Ontario." It is bold, like all his plans; but it could be done. I question, however, the right to divert a stream away from its natural channel in this manner.

We must awake to our own health. We must rouse the slumbering citizens of other populous neighborhoods to our common interest. We must reach the intelligence of the whole State on this question. Reason, health, and public good are on our side. For our own Ithaca, it is a home to be proud of, except in this one crying evil.

DEVELOPMENT OF INTERMITTENT FEVER AT SING SING, N. Y., BY OBSTRUCTED DRAINS.

By G. J. Fisher, M. D., President of the Medical Society of the State of N. Y.*

I have resided in Sing Sing twenty-three years, during which period the entire population of the village have enjoyed a remarkable immunity from that almost universal disease, intermittent fever; and, indeed, from every form of malarial disease, with two slight exceptions.

In the year 1866 or 1867, a culvert on the Hudson River Railroad was obstructed by dumping rock and sand, which detained a great deal of vegetable and animal matter within an estuary or pond of an acre or more in extent. This resulted in the development of intermittent fever among a number of families living adjacent to this exceedingly impure and stagnant water. Being at the time Assistant Sanitary Inspector for the town of Ossining, I reported this nuisance to the Metropolitan Board of Health; and when the "order" for its abatement was obeyed by the Railroad Company, by reopening the culvert to the free entrance and exit of the tides, it resulted in stamping out the fever and ague. The second exception was first observed three or four years ago, when a considerable number of houses—say over thirty—were erected in the southern end of Spring and State streets. Parallel with, and lying between, those streets, is a valley, which has never been well drained; but of late, the drainage has been so defective as to amount to obstruction; to which must be added the slops, surface drainage, and subsoil, of all these houses, yards, and privies, which has resulted in the development of sufficient malaria to have caused a number of cases of intermittent fever in the immediate neighborhood, where the disease was previously unknown.

Proper drainage would doubtless promptly restore the original salubrity of this locality.

It appears to me that these examples furnish the most positive proof of the direct production of malaria from defective drainage—or, rather, no drainage.

Injury to the health and destruction of the lives of our citizens, where the causes are obvious and preventable, renders a careless and culpably ignorant board of town, village or city officials responsible and, at least in equity, if not in law, actionable for damages as much as a private corporation for like damages to health and life by defective construction of bridges or railway tracks, steam boilers or rickety tenement houses.

---

* In justice to Dr. Fisher, this communication was hastily written in reply to a letter of inquiry in regard to the origin of the disease in question.—Editor.

When will we have laws equal in wisdom and justice with our intelligence and positive knowledge?

In a conversation with Dr. Helm, of this place, concerning the insalubrity arising from malarial exhalations in the valley between State and Spring streets, south of Broad avenue, and by comparing notes, we found that in nearly every house bordering this *apparently* dry valley, cases of Intermittent Fever, Periodical Neuralgia, or Erysipelas, had occurred during the past season. There is no stream whatever running through the valley except during or after heavy rains. The ground is saturated and sodden most of the year. Proper drainage would entirely remedy the evil, but want of concerted action among the property owners, or lack of authority in our village fathers, leaves this very limited local nidus of miasm, or rather this little *generator of malaria*, to poison the neighborhood, and impair the otherwise unexceptionable sanitary reputation of the village of Sing Sing.

A Lady's Nose Saves a Man's Life.—Late on Monday night, says the *St. Louis Democrat*, when the guests of the St. James Hotel had nearly all gone to the land of dreams and happy thoughts, Mrs. ———'s nose was suddenly disturbed by an invisible guest. She could neither see nor touch it, neither could she hear it; but her nose was exceedingly alarmed. She sniffed and sniffed, and then she sniffed again. At first she thought she smelt a rat; then that it was a musk-rat. Next she thought that it must be a Chicago rat. But no, it was even worse than that. She then concluded it must be Judge Busby's 10,000 carcasses come to judgment, and she actually hoisted up the window and looked up and down Fifth street; but, save the silent night, some tottering worshippers of Bacchus, and a few flickering lights in the Southern opposite awaiting, most likely, the arrival of late husbands—she saw nothing there—"and yet all there was she saw." No, it was not that. Nearly overpowered by the "villanous smell," she bethought herself of the dangling bell-rope. Nervously she pulls. Up comes the messenger. He is told to sniff, and report to the office. He does so, and with shrivelled nose hurries away. The office immediately sends up the gas man, who at a single sniff takes in the whole situation. "I'll tell you what it is," said the practical sniffer, "Mr. Beck, of Yulayula, occupies to-night the room next to yours. He has mistaken the gas for burning-fluid, and instead of turning, has blown it out." Sure enough, such proved to be the case. After long and severe pounding at his door, a grunt like that of a Cincinnati gentleman was heard inside, and the nearly suffocated form of Mr. Beck, of Yulayula, snatched from the jaws of the undertaker.

Pins.—A school-boy, being requested to write a composition upon the subject of "Pins," produced the following: "Pins are very useful. They have saved the lives of a great many men, women and children—in fact, whole families." "How so," asked the puzzled teacher. And the boy replied, "Why, by not swallowing them." This matches the story of the other boy, who defined salt as "the stuff that makes potatoes taste bad when you don't put on any.

Editor's Table.

THE PUBLIC HEALTH.

New York.—The proposed State Board and Drainage Acts both failed to pass the Legislature. The Acts for more efficient vaccination in the cities of New York and Brooklyn both passed. The Board of Health of Brooklyn was diluted by the addition of the President of the Board of Aldermen and the President of the Board of Public Works; but at the time of this writing, the Governor has not approved of the Act.

The Health Department of the city has especially signalized progress by the adoption of a resolution for the registration of diseases.

"The death rate, which had risen to 29.15 per 1,000 annual rate, the second week in April, was at 27.90 in the week ending on the 18th inst., and by the reported list of deaths last week (ending April 25), was equal to 23.95 per 1,000.

"The presence and increase of small-pox in several quarters of the city is one of the significant results of the want of an adequate system of continual watchfulness and record that shall duly present to all unvaccinated persons the invitation and facilities to be vaccinated, and thereby protected against the most loathsome contagion. The invasion of the city by vagrant and ignorant persons the past four months has done its share in the propagation of small-pox.

"ELISHA HARRIS, M. D., *Registrar.*"

Deaths reported from small-pox during the week ending May 2, 10; for the four weeks ending with that date, 24. From diphtheria, for the week, 27; four weeks, 103. Typhoid fever, 5; four weeks 17.

Brooklyn.—Bushwick creek and some other soil and excrement-sodden outskirts have been under consideration by the Board of Health. The execrable condition of these situations has been chiefly brought about by the reckless progress of public works. Whether the addition of the President of that Department to the Board of Health will have a salutary effect or not, remains to be seen. But the prospect is not encouraging. Another and no less important subject in its relations to the public health, is the removal of street and house refuse; this seems to have been the ostensible motive for the addition of the two new members to the Board. There is so much room for improvement in these respects, and seeing there is no longer a want of effective power in the Board (assuming the Governor's approval of the Act), as the existing state of things in this regard could scarcely be worse, we hope for improvement.

For the week ending May 2, the total number of deaths was 181, or about 25 per 1,000.

Scarlatina continues predominant, deaths from it for the week ending May 2d, 13; for the four weeks, 51.

The Public Schools.—Annual Report of the Superintendent of Public Instruction of the city of Brooklyn, for the year ending December 31, 1873.—The School Mistress, in History, Prose, and Poetry. An Address,—delivered before the Teachers' Association of Brooklyn, April 17, 1874. By Thomas W. Field, Superintendent of Public Instruction.

In his zeal for the good of the schools, the Superintendent has committed an error of expression so inexcusable to some minds, that it alone has been held up by the local press as the gist of the report. That in regard to mixed classes,—"there are sixty classes of pupils whose average age is greater than fourteen years, in which the young girls are compelled at some portion of the school-day to sit adjacent to or in the same seat with boys and young men of whose antecedents or of whose moral character the teacher can know nothing, or may know much that is degrading. There are long intervals of each day in which the surveillance of the teacher is necessarily withdrawn from the class; there are entire days in which her absence is supplied by one of their own number; during which the intercourse of the sexes is as free and unrestrained as if it were a festival instead of a school."—That this state of things conveys suggestions of evil sufficiently great, without the addition of "sad facts in my possession are testimony which I cannot repudiate," few persons interested in the good repute of the schools of Brooklyn will question. But we should not let this sentiment blind our eyes to other "sad facts" which are the ordinary forerunners and common accompaniments of bad morals:

"More than one hundred and twenty classes have numbers largely excessive of the seating capacity of the room, and far beyond the power of the teacher to give individual attention to any. So monstrous is this over-crowding of the class-rooms in some instances that when the pupils have once assumed their positions, only the front rows are accessible to the teacher without treading upon or removing the intervening scholars. More than thirty young girls have one hundred and twenty to one hundred and eighty pupils committed solely to their inexperience for tuition.

"Ninety teachers have eighty to one hundred and twenty scholars each, and forty-one classes are crowded into dark, and, in some instances, damp basements.

"No excuse can be rational for the long endurance of such violations of sanitary and intellectual law."

Sloth and uncleanliness are logical steps in the road to vice, beginning in foul air; and it ill becomes persons in power who wilfully tolerate physical impurity, to take exception to the expressions of those who simply point out the logical sequences of their own shortcomings. No matter how well provided the system of education may be in the mere abstract, the human mind—and especially in childhood and youth—is dependent on external adaptations, and is bent and moulded by the physical circumstances in which it is placed. When we no longer neglect physical impurity and disorder, we shall withdraw one of the chief causes of moral degradation and vice. For the rest, under all the circumstances, we are more surprised at the degree of excellence than at the shortcomings of the Public Schools of Brooklyn. The heart of the Superintendent is evidently in his work, and although he has unquestionably committed an error of expression, he may have possibly only uttered the truth in an improper place, or at an improper time. He has, evidently with great frankness, given the result of assiduous attention to his duty, and his recommendations in regard to school buildings, curriculum, and classes, are all eminently worthy of the serious attention of the Board of Education.

The School Mistress is an ornate address, creditable to its author, and complimentary to his audience.

The Board of Education has adopted a praiseworthy resolution, requiring physicians' certificates of exemption from danger, of children who have had contagious diseases, before readmission to school. This beginning of sanitary administration should be vigorously prosecuted. The health of the schools should be effectually secured, and vigilantly guarded in every particular.

Staten Island.—The Richmond County Board of Health and Vital Statistics, which was rapidly becoming a successful antagonist of the malarial destroyers of the fair fame of that "Isle of Wight" of America, has met a venomous recoil from the Hydra of disease itself. The enemies of drainage and wholesome cleansing rushed to Albany, demanded and procured the passage of an Act to repeal all Health laws for Staten Island. The Governor wisely hesitates to approve the Act.

The Board was well organized: one Sanitary Commissioner for every town, who, with the County Judge, constituted it for monthly councils, etc., and each Commissioner is *ex-officio* the Sanitary Inspector for his own town. He also acts as a sub-registrar of vital statistics, and the general registration is made at the Central Office by the Clerk of the Board.

Quarantine, Health Officer's Department, May 1, 1874.—Masters of vessels and Pilots will please observe that on and after May 15, all vessels arriving from the following Ports will be boarded and examined from the Hospital Ship in the Lower Bay, viz.: All Ports in the

West Indies, Bermuda, Mexico, the Spanish Main, the East Coast of South America, and the West Coast of Africa.

Also, all vessels from Ports where Cholera or Yellow Fever prevailed at the time of departure, or upon which cases of Cholera or Yellow Fever have occurred during the passage.

Pilots are directed not to leave vessels until boarded by the Health Officer, and to avoid anchoring outward bound vessels at the quarantine anchorage at the Lower Bay. They will also notify masters of vessels that all communications with vessels under or subject to quarantine is strictly interdicted, and that no person is permitted to board or have any intercourse, communication or dealing with their crews or passengers, for any purpose whatever, without a written permit from this department; and no boat or craft will be permitted to invade the quarantine anchorage, either in the Upper or Lower Bay, or to go alongside or hold any communication with vessels subject to or under quarantine.

S. Oakley Vanderpoel,
Health Officer, Port of New York.

In accordance with the above order the Hospital Ship "Illinois" was in due time towed down to her moorings in the Lower Bay.

The Hospital on Dix Island is in excellent order, and the Hoffman Island buildings are, for the first full season, ready for occupancy should vessels arrive with Cholera on board. The U. S. S. Delaware, which was secured temporarily as a place of detention until this Island was completed, has been returned to the Navy Department.

Not much sickness is yet arriving, but many South American ports are infected with yellow fever, and most of the vessels arriving from Pernambuco have had the disease among their crews.

Cholera, as last spring, exists in European towns which are in direct commerce with New York.

The *Health Officer's Station* at Clifton, where it has been permanently established, was occupied for the first time April 1st, and admirably answers its purpose. During the hurried work of examining the numerous arrivals of Spring shipping, there has been abundant proof of the wisdom of selecting this situation.

Minnesota State Board.—The first annual meeting was held in Lansing, at the office of the Secretary of State, April 14 and 15.

Secretary Baker made a detailed report showing the property purchased and issued by the Board, and he also gave a list of articles and books which have been presented to the museum and library of the Board.

President Hitchcock delivered an annual address on the "Entailments of Alcohol," in which he made a scientific and powerful exhibition of the miseries of drunkenness. It would make an admirable campaign document for the Prohibitionists.

Dr. Bliss made a report upon the cases of trichinæ at Port Huron, from facts furnished him by Dr. Northrop of Port Huron. Dr. Bliss was requested to prepare a paper on this subject for the next report of the Board. He also made a verbal report of other cases which occurred in Ionia in 1866.

Dr. Kedzie mentioned a case of the poisoning of a family in Hillsdale County by the use of syrup containing sulphuric acid and sulphate of iron. The Committee on Poisons was requested to prepare a paper on this subject, and other adulterations of food, for publication in the next report of the Board.

A circular has recently been issued by the Board, calling the attention of local Boards of Health to their duties touching diseases dangerous to the public health.

A communication was read from the local Board of Health of Chester township, Eaton County, relative to 37 cases of scarlet fever which had occurred in one-half of this township, when the whole town only contains 165 children. Of the cases mentioned ten resulted in death.

California State Board.—Met at the office of Dr. T. M. Logan, in Sacramento, April 21st. After presentation of their respective commissions, Dr. Gibbons was, on motion, unanimously re-elected President, and Dr. T. M. Logan, also unanimously, Permanent Secretary.

Philadelphia.—Total deaths registered for the week ending May 2d, 267 ; 29 per 1,000. Typhoid fever, 9 ; for the four weeks, 36. We are gratified to know that the excellent pamphlet of "*Special Rules for the Management of Infants during the Hot Season,*" recommended by the Obstetrical Society of Philadelphia, is being generally distributed. It is a highly commendable effort in the right direction.

Chicago.—Total deaths for the week ending April 19, 111 ; 32 per 1,000 (estimating population at 356,000, it being 298,977 in 1870). The high mortality seems not to depend upon any specially prevailing diseases, unless, perhaps, pneumonia, of which there were for the week 15 deaths ; and of the same for the two preceding weeks, 19 ; of small-pox, for three weeks, 7 ; typhoid fever, 9.

Baltimore.—Total deaths for week ending April 27, 132 ; 21.20 per 1,000; estimating population at 284,000. Maryland is to be congratulated on the establishment of a State Board of Health, and one, judged by its organization, wisely chosen. It consists of Drs. N. R. Smith, President ; E. Lloyd Howard, Permanent Secretary ; J. Robert Ward, C. W. Chancellor and Chas. M. Ellis.

Richmond.—Total deaths for week ending May 2d, 26; 25 per1,000.

Norfolk.—Annual report—total deaths for the year 1873, 614 ; 76

less than for the year 1872. From small-pox, 29 ; typhoid fever, 15 ; diarrhœal diseases, 115 ; consumption, 69.

The *State Board of Health of Va.* is again disappointed in its expected appropriation. A bill appropriating $2,000, passed the Senate by the required two-third vote, but on reaching the House of Delegates, out of 76 voters, 27—a little more than one-third—voted against it; unfortunately a number of its friends were temporarily absent. "The failure of the bill is not regarded as a total defeat; on the contrary, its friends look upon the vote as very encouraging, and being almost surely indicative of its passage at the next Session. What will be the action of the Board, we cannot say. But should its present organization be continued, it would be unreasonable for the people or the profession yet to look for any special effort on its part which would require expenditure of money or time."—*Virginia Medical Journal.*

New Jersey has passed an act appointing a Health Commission.

Massachusetts.—Deaths, in sixteen cities and towns, for the week ending April 18th : Boston, 149 ; Worcester, 22 ; Lowell, 19 ; Milford, 5 ; Chelsea, 5; Cambridge, 21 ; Salem, 8; Lawrence, 18 ; Lynn, 12 ; Gloucester, 2 ; Fitchburg, 1 ; Newburyport, 11 ; Somerville, 7 ; Fall River, 22 ; Haverhill, 5 ; Pittsfield, 7. Total, 314. Prevalent diseases—Consumption, 54 ; Pneumonia, 48 ; Scarlet fever, 14. Two deaths from Small-pox, in Fall River.

New Orleans.—Total deaths :

Week ending April 5th	121
" " " 12th	111
" " " 19th	124
" " " 26th	130
	486

Number of Deaths from Small-pox.

Week ending April 5th	23
" " " 12th	18
" " " 19th	15
" " " 26th	23
	79

Number of Deaths from Consumption.

Week ending April 5th	13
" " " 12th	11
" " " 19th	24
" " " 26th	14
	62

S. C. Russell, M. D., *Secretary, &c.*

Pittsburg.—Annual Report for 1873 shows a very creditable category of sanitary work.—"There occurred during the year 3,519 deaths—a weekly average of 67.7; 2,414 occurred in the old City, and 1,105 in the South-Side wards. Deducting those born prematurely, 64; those from causes unknown, 76; and those due to violent causes, 194,—leaves a total of 3,185 deaths from disease.

"Assuming the population to be 133,000" (in 1870 it was but 86,076), "which is the estimate of city officials, the death rate was 26.46 in each 1,000 inhabitants."

There were deaths from—Consumption, 326; Cerebro-spinal fever, 103; Diarrhœal diseases, 476; Small-pox, 25; Typhoid fever, 191. These deaths are abundantly suggestive of much sanitary work yet to be done.

For the month of April, total deaths, 279; Typhoid fever, 5. Estimating the population by the ratio of decade ending 1870, it is now only about 98,000.

Dayton.—For the month of April, total deaths, 62.

Saint Paul.—For the month of April, 44; Typhoid fever, 3.

Pittsfield, Mass., a city of only about 19,000 inhabitants, has an effective Board of Health, consisting of two physicians and a lawyer. The excellent regulations of this Board, with a copy of which we have been favored, we commend to other small cities.

Milwaukee.—Total deaths for the month of April, 155. Small-pox, 2; Typhoid fever, 2.

Wheeling.—Total deaths for the month of April, 28. Typhoid fever, 2.

SUMMER TRAVEL.

The *Herald* of recent date contained an editorial under the query, "Where shall we go for the summer?" which disposes of the great mass of tourists as beyond the scope of its counsel because they seem to know their own business best, and select their own resorts, fully appreciating "the discomforts they will be compelled to endure." But, notwithstanding, advises "*tourists in a small way*" —those who are not posted in the variety of summer travel—"to take a trip through Virginia and North Carolina, or to settle down for the summer among the Pennsylvania Dutch at Ephrata!" Evidently, without any idea in advance of the discomforts the said tourists in a small way themselves may have to endure. But "summer travel acquires a new zest from being out of the beaten track." True, but if Virginia and North Carolina present any inviting summer features except for a stay in the mountains, when the temperature becomes too high for endurance in New York, we acknowledge an inability hitherto to find them. Possibly the *Herald's* advice is based upon the theory of *similia similibus curantur*—a little more heat to cool off with. It would, at least, be delightful to return home under such circumstances to a temperature fitted to restore exhausted nature, and inspire the resolution never to try it again. Under all ordinary circumstances, experience points northwards for relief from excessive heat. The lessons learned from our school-books in this particular are abundantly confirmed. Even one day's travel in the week on the Hudson, if the "tourists in a small way" can do no better, is a good fortifying dose of fresh air for the other six, and the charm about it is, it will stand repetition all summer. And for tourists in a large way, the hotel proprietors all along the Hudson are already astir preparing for the summer harvest. The talk some weeks ago in the height of the panic about lower prices at fashionable places seems to have been only a bid for early boarders—for those who wish to be accommodated for the season in *high* places. The best suits are held in reserve.

Saratoga is making much over the college regatta, in anticipation of an extra lively time during an ordinarily dull week. The proprietors of the leading hotels of Newport, Long Branch, Sharon and Lebanon Springs, Catskill and White Mountains—are all putting their houses in order, in anticipation of a brilliant season.

THE PERILS OF THE SEA.

A little less than a year ago, under the head of *Ocean Travel*, with the "Atlantic" disaster then fresh in memory, we discussed the danger of sacrificing human life to speed of travel. The loss of three ocean steamers recently, and the lesser "accidents" to several others, are terribly suggestive incidents. How much the lengthening of these ships contributed to their loss by rendering them less able to withstand the perils of the sea, we profess to no competent judgment, but the weight of all the evidence produced decidedly tends that way. The object of the process of lengthening to which slow ships of late are commonly subjected, is, however, beyond dispute. Safety, at least, has nothing whatever to do with it; *time*, alone, is the object in view. As to the men who give up their ships in time of peril, they may well be left to the merited contempt of the public, which they deserve. They doubtless possessed the required qualifications. Reckless companies, bent on time as the element to which everything else must be sacrificed, demand reckless masters to accomplish their purpose; and that the masters of such ships, and in such service, should grow timid in the face of danger, is only an exemplification of coördinate qualities. The evil is pervading, but fortunately there are some companies whose appointments hitherto, guaranty some regard for human life.

There are now plying between America and Europe the several ships belonging to the following lines:—From New York to Liverpool, Cunard, National, Williams & Guion, Inman, and White Star; from New York to Glasgow, Anchor and State; from Boston to Liverpool, Cunard; from Portland and Quebec to Liverpool and Glasgow, Allan; from Philadelphia to Liverpool, Pennsylvania; and, in addition, there is the North German Lloyd's from New York to Bremen and from Baltimore to Bremen; the Hamburg-American Packet Company, from New York to Hamburg; the Eagle line, from New York to Hamburg; the General Transatlantic Company, from New York to Havre, and the Red Star line, from Philadelphia to Antwerp. The Cunard line sends two vessels a week from New York and one from Boston, while the Anchor line dispatches three a week from this port. The other lines send a steamer weekly, except the Red Star and State, their vessels leaving fortnightly. The State line is building three new boats, which will enable the Company to dispatch weekly steamers to Glasgow after June 1. By some of these companies the Transatlantic way is mapped out with an accuracy scarcely less deviating than the railway which crosses the continent, so careful are they to avoid accidents; and some of their ships are furnished as *all should be*, with life-rafts, life-preserving mattresses, and all accessible appliances for the safety of passengers. And those which are best furnished in these respects, are almost without exception the best appointed in all other respects—have the most accomplished and trustworthy officers. Tourists will, therefore, always do well to look to the appointments of the ship to which for the time they intrust their lives. If she be lacking in her complement of boats, and is not supplied in all other respects with life-saving appliances and facilities, or if she is not clean—the chances are that she is poorly commanded; that the Company pays little or no regard to a line of travel calculated to avoid collision; that a bee-line and only coal enough to effect it and the greater room for freight, are the chief considerations. From all such, turn away.

THE AMERICAN PUBLIC HEALTH ASSOCIATION.

The leading Reports and papers presented at the two meetings of this Association in the year 1873, are to be immediately published under the title PUBLIC HEALTH. It is to be issued by the well known house of Hurd & Houghton, of the Riverside Press, Cambridge. The price to subscribers is $5. President of the Association, Dr. STEPHEN SMITH, and the Publishers receive subscriptions at 13 Astor Place, New York; pay on delivery of the Volume in June.

AMERICAN DISTRICT TELEGRAPH CO.—The attention of our Brooklyn readers is particularly called to the advertisement of this Company with special reference to summer safety. We recall certain knowledge of its police vigilance on several occasions in discovering unfastened doors and windows, in addition to its *electric* watchman always on post for the immediate call of aid in emergency.

BIBLIOGRAPHY.

YELLOW FEVER.—*Contributions to the Study of Yellow Fever.* A.—The distribution and natural history of yellow fever in the United States, with chart showing elevations of localities where it has appeared from A. D. 1868 to A. D. 1874. B.—The yellow fever epidemic of 1873; Reports from Medical Officers, U. S. Marine Hospital service, with note by the superintending surgeon, John M. Woodworth, M. D.; pamphlet, pp. 51.

Report of the Committee on the Yellow Fever Epidemic of 1873, *at Shreveport, La.* Published by the Howard Association; pamphlet, pp. 23.

Report of the Yellow Fever Epidemic of 1873, Shreveport, La. By Henry Smith, M. D., Medical Examiner to the Louisiana Equitable Life Insurance Co., New Orleans; pamphlet, pp. 12.

Dr. Toner believes with Humboldt and many others, that yellow fever has rarely or never prevailed at an altitude of more than 500 feet above the level of the sea. He illustrates the history of yellow fever in the United States by a carefully prepared chart of all the places and dates of its occurrence.

The report of the Howard Association is another settler to a long settled question by actual observers, that yellow fever is a disease *sui generis*, as different in its nature from malarious diseases, as it ordinarily is in its course and results; that it is like them in nothing save liability to occur in some of the same situations; that it, in short, bears scarcely any more relation to the malarious intermittent of Shreveport, than small-pox does to the malarious intermittent of a Canada swamp. This militates not against the fact, however, that malarious conditions are inviting to, and promotive of the spread of yellow fever, as, indeed, of all other epidemic diseases. We have no disposition to rehearse the criminally inviting conditions of Shreveport at the time the disease was introduced. They are sufficiently well known and recognized, to be a warning for all time to come. That the disease was *carried* there, admits of no question. And that it found abundance of food there, is of as little question. But that—

"Every case of yellow fever is a source of infection, which, in suitable atmospheric conditions develops a poison, which radiates from it as a centre, attacking those first who are more immediately exposed; every case generating the poison until the whole atmosphere of the place is impregnated so that none can breathe it with safety"—

is decidedly at variance with much recorded observation and our own experience. All of the relations for the spread of the disease comprehended in this quotation we believe to be due to, and perfectly consistent with, exposure to like conditions—a living pervading poison, *not* emanating from the person of the sick, but on being once introduced under favorable conditions, as at Shreveport by *fomiles*, is capable of reproduction and dissemination. And, moreover, the citations of the pamphlet before us bear evidence in favor of this view:

"We shall now undertake to prove that our epidemic was imported to us from abroad directly from Havana by the way of New Orleans. It is a *fact* well authenticated that the Bark Valparaiso left Havana on June 16th, and arrived at the quarantine station on June 24th, was detained two days and arrived at the wharf in New Orleans in the 4th district on June 26th. On the 4th of July the mate of the Bark Valparaiso took sick of yellow fever and died July 8th. Fever broke out on the steamers Belle Lee and W. S. Pike which were lying in the neighborhood, and on July 16th, Edward Hymes took sick on board the Belle Lee; on July 29th Thos. Meade, carpenter on W. S. Pike, for twenty days previous to his being taken sick, was taken down with the fever while that boat was lying within 30 yards of the Belle Lee; and again, J. Douglass, who had been employed in loading Bark Valparaiso, was taken sick with the fever on July 29th. This statement has been furnished us through the Board of Health in New Orleans, and is perfectly satisfactory as explaining its introduction into that city. Now upon the breaking out of the fever on the steamers Belle Lee and W. S. Pike, there occurred a general stampede of the waiters, who fled and scattered themselves among the other boats lying in port at the time, and chiefly among the Red River packets, which at that time were regularly plying between New Orleans and this city."

It is highly probable that these fugitives took with them their personal dunnage, wherewith they established new foci in the most susceptible places, until the whole town was thoroughly infected, and all of the inhabitants thereof alike exposed to the pervading poison.

Dr. Smith emphasizes the abominable condition of the town at the time yellow fever was introduced:—

"The overflow of what is known as Silver Lake and other marshy localities, as the spring advances, naturally fills the atmosphere with miasmatic vapors, the source of fevers of every kind. The declivity between the front and rear portion of the city, which, with but trifling engineering skill, could have been culverted and converted into an effectual sewer, became a cesspool for the reception of dead animals of every kind, and a wallowing place for others. Here, too, and at many points within the business section of the city, the offal and garbage were permitted to fester in the sun, and the combined effluvia created a stench absolutely unbearable. In addition, a number of cattle, drowned at the wreck of a steamboat two miles below the city, were hauled on shore, skinned, and their carcasses permitted to rot in the open air."

Other Bibliography—including Exchange Notices—unavoidably crowded out.

THE SANITARIAN.

A MONTHLY JOURNAL.

VOL. II.] JULY, 1874. [NO. 4.

THE WASTE OF LIFE.*

"IT IS HELD IN LAW THAT WHOEVER ACCELERATES DEATH CAUSES IT." (TAYLOR'S MEDICAL JURISPRUDENCE, AMERICAN EDITION, 1861, p. 470.)

Progress in measures for the protection of human life consists in exposing the consequences of their neglect. The fall of a frail structure in Brooklyn a few weeks ago, overwhelming nine or ten men in the ruin, killing three outright, and wounding several others, shocked the whole community. Policemen and coroners rushed to the rescue; his Honor the Mayor, the Health Commissioners, the contractors, and the undertakers vied with one another in their lively sense of the catastrophe. And the action of the Common Council was invoked to prevent the recurrence of such an accident in the future. Such is the natural horror of death when suddenly brought face to face with small motives. Three days later, in the same city, a whole row of half-built houses tumbled down, involving much greater loss to the contractor than in the former case, but as there happened to be nobody in them at the time to be killed, the circumstance attracted but little notice; it was only an unfortunate accident to the contractor—an incident to his occupation. These are fair examples of common occurrences of carelessness in regard to the safety of human life throughout the country. Occasionally one, extraordinary for the number of its victims, happens, such as that of the Mill River disaster, and it is for a time made the theme of pulpit eloquence. Mill dams everywhere are held up as suspicious structures, liable at any time to break away, and demonstrate, to the satisfaction of those who build them, the uncertainty of human life.

It is the same when lengthened steamships founder amid ocean, as in the recent disasters of the French line; or when boilers burst, as in the ferryboat Westfield; or when railroad trains dash headlong to fatal collisions and over embankments. Public indignation is for a time excited. Investigations are undertaken, and lengthy

* An address delivered before the American Medical Association, at Detroit, June 4th, 1874, by A. N. Bell, M. D., Chairman of the Section on State Medicine and Public Hygiene.

publications of that which everybody knew before, that in the construction of such works the protection of human life has received little or no consideration whatever; that the necessity for it has not been imposed as an obligation of the civil authority, nor adequate punishment for its neglect inflicted. But these after all are only the minor degrees of crime in this direction. The danger of imperfect structures to human life is pervading. Palatial dwelling-houses are not unfrequently erected over old burying places, vaults, and cesspools, and within provided with all possible accessories for the retention of the poisonous gases evolved from the soil, in addition to the foul air generated by their occupants. Assembly rooms and theatres are usually no better. And exquisitely finished churches, where mill dams and other death-dealing agencies are made odious, are not uncommonly constructed with so little regard to ventilation as to be dangerous sources of disease. Country dwelling-houses, with beautiful exterior relations of shade trees and verdure, but with neglected graveyard proximities and other death streams beneath and around, with privy vaults, cesspools, and wells all in proximity, are the common nests of typhoid fever all over the country. The indispensable requisites to health—an abundant supply of pure air and pure water—receive but little recognition, and are rarely provided for.

School-houses, public and private, are a disgrace to human nature. Situated, constructed and furnished with utter disregard of the nature of the soil, exposure, air and light, they are in effect systematic institutions appropriated to the nurture of disease and the acceleration of death. With reading lessons recounting the horrible act of the half-civilized nabob of Calcutta more than a century ago, and the no less barbarous act of the captain of the emigrant steamship Londonderry twenty-five years ago, and school physiologies teaching that each individual requires for healthy respiration 2,000 cubic feet of air hourly, notwithstanding these instances and this patent knowledge, examples are not wanting in the public schools of our large cities where the air-space appropriated to each individual is less than fifty cubic feet, and with little or no provision for change. Literally, schools for the growth, culture, and promotion of scrofula and consumption, and the hurdling places of the infections of childhood. Three hundred cubic feet of air-space, with efficient provision for change three times an hour, is the lowest possible estimate which should be allowed. With less than this, the air speedily becomes poisonous, and the active nidus of infection.

Tenement houses are notoriously situated without regard to external relations of soil, air and light; and within, from sub-cellar to garret, curious for their ingenuity as architectural imitations of the bee for space, but wholly devoid of that insect's instinct in regard to cleanliness and ventilation. And, abundant as the city water supply usually is, it is, notwithstanding, supplied in stinted measure to those who most stand in need of it—the poor. The labor of travelling the rickety stairways of tenement houses to a common "standcock" in the lower halls, involves uncleanliness and ill health in a variety of ways. Equivocal vegetables and meats from the most unsavory stalls are scantily washed and improperly cooked. Numerous instalments of clothes are washed in unrenewed water, and the same at the last, is used for bathing the person, scrubbing the floors and stairways. Hence, the tenement house odors which cling so tenaciously to the clothing and persons, as well as to the rooms of the "great unwashed." As a rule, tenement houses are laboratories of poison throughout, and in all their relations to society. Numerous descriptions of them exist in the literature of New York, and possibly some persons may think they are things of the past. But, unfortunately for sanitary science, and to the disgrace of humanity, they are still of the present, and exist in other large cities besides New York. The raid of the sanitary police in New York last year, in view of the expected cholera, discovered thousands of people actually living in holes in the ground, a dozen or more in a huddle, in holes nine or ten feet square, swarming with vermin and rotting with disease. No less than 20,000 of these *troglodytes*, living like moles and bats in the dark, poisoning the atmosphere around, and sucking the life-blood of the people! In the tenement houses of New York, there are many single rooms occupied by from ten to fifteen persons of both sexes, and frequently by several families. There are structures from four to six stories high, divided into hundreds of rooms, crowded with men, women and children, smothering for the want of fresh air, and in dirt and foul odors horrible to contemplate. And there are, not uncommonly, rear buildings to such as these, adding to the stifling condition of the yards, which, with the gutters, are the common filth receptacles for the out-throwings, and the wallowing places of the children; the streets, as filthy as the gutters, for the young girls, and rumholes at every corner for the parents. And these tenement houses are the homes of more than half of the children of New York! In them is carried on the perennial "slaughter of the innocents," of more than two years old and under, in comparison with which the crime of Herod sinks into insignificance!

Such surroundings obtund and destroy human sensibilities. The occupants of such dwelling-places become an easy prey to the sensual excitements of alcohol and other debasing agencies and influences. As people become accustomed to dirt, they cease to recognize its presence and to exert themselves to avoid it; there is no limit to the downward tendency. The same broad road to disease and death is the highway to moral degradation. And that such an institution should breed disease and death; that it should be the hecatomb of children; that it should sustain liquor stalls by the thousand, and supply the ghastly gaiety which flaunts beneath the gaslight and makes night hideous; that it should send the boys who escape the slaughter to State Prison; that the tenement house should do all these things, and more than words can utter, is perfectly consistent with its appointments. And yet, to repeat, more than half the children of New York are born in tenement houses—and New York is called a Christian city! Is the tenement house a Christian institution, or a heathenish? Who is responsible? Is there, indeed *no* responsibility for moral and physical degradation; *no* responsibility for deliberate prevision and business speculation in human life; *no* responsibility because tenement-house property pays better than any other real estate? State Medicine and Public Hygiene! The lesson is yet to be taught in this country that man has no right to poison his neighbor; that to poison the air for his neighbor to breathe is no less criminal than to poison his food or drink; that to smother children in schools and tenement houses, as in other places, is infanticide; that to accelerate the death of any individual is to cause it, and that the crime is homicide.

Savage nations generally practise the belief that there is an advantage in removing that portion of every population which is unable to provide self-subsistence; hence they openly put to death infants, and those who are bowed down with the infirmities of age. The same error prevails among a large class in civilized communities, and those who entertain it argue for a compensating advantage in the removal of a worthless portion of surplus population. But this is an exceedingly superficial view. It is not the surplus, but the valuable portion of life thus thrown away. To whatever extent the duration of life is diminished by noxious agencies, so much productive power is lost, and every community is poor and powerless in the inverse ratio to the average duration of human life. Every death under the age of fifteen years carries with it a positive loss to the community in which the individual has lived, because previous to this age sustenance involves cost—a direct outlay—whilst if the individual is preserved, a productive member of society is added and remuneration rendered. If the probabilities of life in any community are so low as to make the average adult age young, the proportion of widowhood and orphanage is necessarily increased, and the productive members of society proportionately burdened. If a husband dies in the early years of his married life, he leaves as burdens on the world, a widow or children, for whom, in all probability, if he had lived, he would have labored. And thus it is that burdens are created and costs entailed upon the industrious survivors of every community, in direct ratio with a high mortality. The pecuniary costs, therefore, of pernicious influences may be measured by the charges attendant on the duration of life, and the reduction of the period of working ability, and the cost will also include much of the attendant vice and crime, as well as the destitution which comes within the province of pauper support.

These truths tally strangely with the ordinary comprehension of our legislators and Boards of Education, when approached on the subject of measures for the protection of human life. Their philosophy seems to run thus: Every death is a matter of pain and suffering to the immediate circle of the deceased, and is a thing which those more immediately concerned should use every effort to avert, yet it is an undoubted benefit to the community since their is one less consumer of the common stock of public possessions. They seem not to consider that those who die cease to produce, or have not been preserved until the productive period, as well as cease to *consume.* Had Fulton died in his infancy, or Morse before his great invention, the world might long have remained ignorant of the loss sustained by a premature death. Indeed, premature deaths cut right into the centre of commercial prosperity. Early deaths presuppose sickly, feeble lives, at all times incapable of vigorous exertion, and frequently interrupted by periods of disability. The man whose life has not exceeded forty years has had many periods of inability and sickness before its close; and, as a general rule, the short-lived have more years of inability and uselessness than the long-lived, for among healthy men we observe individuals engaged in, and even undertaking great labors in comparative old age. Among such the most prominent merchants and railroad managers of the United States are living examples.

At the outset of my duties as chairman of the Section on State Medicine and Public Hygiene, it became evident to me that any special effort of the Section for the speedy application of the sense of the Association as embodied in the resolutions favoring the establishment of a National Sanitary Bureau, before State Boards of Health become the rule instead of the exception, would be premature, if not, indeed, wholly wasted; or, possibly worse, fraught with success encumbered by political conditions more calculated to hinder than to promote sanitary science. That the labors of the Section might not, therefore, be uselessly spent, I prepared and sent to every member thereof, a circular, calling attention first to the resolutions committed to the Section, and second to *Defective Drainage.*

It is presumed that all intelligent persons are more or less familiar with facts and illustrations demonstrating the utility of, and the necessity for, drainage as a life-saving measure.

The mortality of the United States for 1870 was 492,263. A glance at this tabulated estimate in the Census report will show that about one-half of the total number of deaths were caused by the diseases due for the most part to miasms consequent upon soil saturation and stagnant water. That from consumption alone there were 69,896 deaths. From enteric, intermittent, remittent, and typho-malarial fevers, and cerebro-spinal meningitis, there were 34,521 deaths. Rheumatism, acute pulmonary affections, croup, diphtheria, and many other diseases well known to be largely due to or promoted by the same cause, may, for our present purpose, be left out of the count. Of the 69,896 deaths from consumption, and 34,521 deaths from ordinary miasms, three-quarters of them, at the least, or more than 75,000 lives, might have been saved by drainage. For illustrations of the results of defective drainage, it is more difficult to go amiss than to designate. For its consideration in detail in some of the States, attention is invited to the special reports submitted by the members of the Section representing them.

Since writing up the subject for the city of Brooklyn and county of Kings, for the report on the State of New York, Dr. James Watt, Registrar of Vital Statistics to the Brooklyn Board of Health, has kindly prepared for me a table showing the comparative mortality from consumption in the different wards of the city. Its full value to Brooklyn can be appreciated by those only who are familiar with the city topography, while it illustrates conditions common to all of our large cities.

Take, for example, an old and well-built up ward (the Third), containing a population of 9,984, which is not known to have any soil saturation, its situation being such that the ordinary street grading and sewer culverts effectually drain it. The deaths from consumption in this ward last year were fourteen; or, 1.40 per 1,000 of the population. An adjoining ward (the Sixth), with a population of 28,296, of corresponding large area, however, it being even less densely built up than the former, but about one-half of it subject to soil saturation, had of deaths from consumption, 171, 6.04 per 1,000 of population. Sixty-one of these deaths occurred in hospitals situated in this ward, and were in part from other wards. But after deducting the whole sixty-one, there still remain 4 per 1,000, or nearly three times as many deaths per 1,000 of population from consumption over this area of soil saturation as in the one devoid of it.

Of malarious and zymotic diseases generally, the deaths over the non-saturated soil (of the Third ward) were 2.40 per 1,000 of population. From the same diseases in two soil-saturated wards (Twelfth and Eighteenth) extending over a large area, and for the most part sparsely built up as compared with the non-saturated area, there were 9.86 per 1,000 of population, or nearly four times as many. I might thus go over the whole city and show the influence of soil saturation on the mortality; point out the neglected natural soil saturation in one place, and the carelessly constructed soil saturation in another.

The total number of deaths in Brooklyn last year was 10,968, and not less than one-fourth of them were accelerated by defective drainage. And yet Brooklyn is no exception in this regard. On the contrary, the death-rate of Brooklyn compares favorably with other of our large cities, which is abundantly shown by the following examples: The total annual death-rate of Brooklyn from consumption last year was 3.47 per 1,000 of population (Census of 1870), and on the whole number of deaths the per cent. for consumption was 12.55. In the city of New York, on an estimated population at the present of 1,000,000, there are of deaths from consumption 4.13 per 1,000, and 14.22 per cent. of the total mortality. Boston, 3.96 per 1,000 of population; 13.84 per cent. of total mortality. Philadelphia, 3.05 per 1,000 of population; 13.65 per cent. of total mortality. San Francisco, 2.74 per 1,000 of population; 14.12 per cent. of total mortality. Albany, 3.43 per 1,000 of population; 15.50 per cent. of total mortality. New Orleans (where the benefits of a mild climate opposed to consumption are condoned by defective drainage), 3.96 per 1,000 of population; 13.84 per cent. of total mortality. By States—of the total mortality in the United States, 12.45 was caused by consumption; in New York, 16.17; District of Columbia, 21.19. A concise table of the ratio of the deaths from consumption in every State in the Union may be found in the "Dictionary of Elevations and Climatic Register," by Dr. J. M. Toner. Under approximate temperatures the ratio of mortality from consumption in regard to defective drainage will be found scarcely less deviating than miasmatic fevers.

Wherever misery, disease, and short life predominate, there always exist at man's disposal the means of relief; to find out and apply these means is the exercise of sanitary science.

It becomes our duty as sanitarians to show the authorities that it costs less to have human habitations constructed with regard to the protection of life, with provision for an abundant supply of pure air, water, and light; paved, and cleanly streets; efficient drains and sewers,—than it does to neglect these provisions; that imperfectly constructed houses, mill-dams, steamships, and other human habitations and highways, all fall under the category of neglected measures, accelerating death.

It is not the nature of mankind that evils at war with his well-being should be scattered broadcast, or exist anywhere within the scope of intellectual development. Selfishness and barbarism are noxious agents everywhere, and as such they should be treated, for it is neither the nature nor the habit of the human constitution to become so accustomed to conditions inconsistent with the highest state of human progress as to be unaffected by them. The highest state of human culture furnishes the only standard by which the degree of elevation should be measured; and cleanliness and refinement bear the same relation to each other in the progress of human culture as do filth and moral uncleanness in the degradation of uncivilized communities. The miserable, degraded, and sickly portion of every community is weak, in proportion as the highly-cultivated and healthy portion is strong. To assist the weak in applying such measures for the preservation of life as will protect mankind at large from the injuries which each individual in a narrow-minded selfishness would inflict on his neighbor, is the first and most sacred duty of a paternal government. Contact with well-cleansed streets, and external purity generally, creates a distaste for internal filth and degradation, and there are none so degraded or so impure as not to be benefited and elevated by association with kindness and cleanliness.

It is sometimes remarked by superficial observers that the luxuries of the rich and the miseries of the poor equalize the scale of human happiness by being alike deleterious to health. If we examine into the facts of the case, and ascertain how very small the proportion of deaths is from actual poverty, in this country especially, as compared with the number of deaths from other and preventable causes, and apply the same information to country populations where the proportion of the poor is greater but healthier, we shall find in this circumstance abundant evidence of other causes than povery to account for the excess of mortality.

The worst effect of poverty is that it commonly leads to neglect and filth, and this constitutes an insalubrity which extends to the whole neighborhood. Where large masses of people are congregated together, as in certain quarters of most large cities, it is necessary, in default of systematic State organizations, to have special laws and local regulations. But these are usually efforts to adapt sanitary administration to intolerable conditions; they are ordinarily complicated, expensive, and at times exceedingly harassing. They are established, and their administration undertaken, under the urgency of pressing contemporaneous necessity, subject to the changes of political subserviency. Hence there is a want of co-operative effort —a want of comprehensive executive skill sufficient to control and adjust local interests and prejudices to the demands of public good on the one side, and a want of recognized right and willing acquiescence on the other. Government is unequally administered. Some streets are cleaned and others not; some places are drained, and others more in need of it are left to eke out their poisons. In some instances, street impurities and filth are conveyed from one neighborhood—rich and selfish, perhaps—and deposited in another. They are, for the most part, mere personal regulations, which are always difficult of application and often wholly impracticable for the promotion of health. And they are especially so when recognized as being mere temporary expedients, with no fixed principles. They touch human pride, undermine self-respect, put an end to self-direction, and inspire reckless indifference and opposition. Such personal regulations are, in short, inconsistent with independence and manliness which kindly and paternal culture in every aspect of humanity inculcates and encourages. In all partial and local operations which are not subject to respected authority and fixed care for the public welfare, there must continue to be a waste of effort and of execution; which are not only losses in themselves, but they serve to impede every effort towards general and permanent sanitary improvement by disgusting people with the expense and difficulty attending it.

Efficient and economical sanitary administration depends upon the dignity, qualifications, powers, and responsibilities of the officers who are appointed to execute it. These conditions can be secured in no other way than by legislative action based upon an enlightened comprehension of the economy of human life and the establishment of paternal State authority for its conservation.

Wards.	Population, 18[illegible]	Total No. of De[illegible]	Deaths from Con-sumption.	Per cent. per 1,0[illegible] Population.	Per cent. on tot[illegible] Death-Rate.	Males.	Females.	Males.	Females.	Males.	Females.	Males.	Females.	Males.	Females.	Males.	Females.	Males.	Females.	Males.	Females.	Males.	Females.	Males.	Females.	Deaths in Hospit[illegible]
1	6,476	180	10	1.64	7.69	7	8	2	2	5	1	......	......	......	......	2	1	2	1	2	1	1	......	......	......	...
2	9,117	223	22	2.41	9.86	9	13	2	7	7	6	......	......	......	2	2	4	4	3	3	3	......	1	......	......	...
3	9,984	138	14	1.40	10.37	7	7	4	4	8	3	1	......	......	......	2	1	8	2	......	1	1	2	......	1	...
4	12,087	237	35	2.89	14.76	16	19	8	10	8	9	......	......	......	1	2	3	7	7	7	6	......	2	......	......	...
5	20,490	519	68	3.31	13.01	38	30	12	10	26	20	2	......	......	1	4	6	18	10	12	10	2	3	......	......	...
6	28,296	934	171	6.04	18.84	91	80	31	23	60	57	5	......	2	4	16	13	40	40	21	19	7	4	......	......	61
7	22,312	509	65	2.91	12.57	34	31	14	17	20	14	1	1	1	1	8	4	7	16	11	8	5	1	1	......	...
8	9,592	344	39	4.06	11.80	20	19	10	5	10	14	1	1	1	2	3	4	4	6	7	4	4	2	......	......	...
9	15,279	443	72	4.71	16.21	36	58	11	17	25	19	5	3	3	1	5	6	10	17	11	8	2	1	......	......	...
10	34,592	772	105	3.03	13.60	55	60	26	18	29	31	2	1	2	1	12	17	20	22	18	7	1	2	......	......	..
11	21,243	489	71	3.34	14.70	40	31	16	21	24	10	2	1	1	1	6	7	19	14	11	8	1	......	......	......	11
12	18,302	592	64	3.50	10.81	32	32	6	7	26	25	2	2	......	2	4	8	13	11	13	9	......	......	......	......	...
13	18,711	407	40	2.13	9.82	24	16	20	14	4	2	1	......	......	......	6	8	7	7	8	5	1	1	1	......	...
14	20,649	629	80	3.88	12.71	35	45	15	18	20	27	2	......	1	......	4	12	16	15	8	12	4	5	......	1	...
15	18,406	431	65	3.55	15.08	36	29	20	18	16	11	1	......	2	......	5	5	12	13	13	9	3	2	......	......	...
16	26,438	1,155	135	3.10	11.68	77	58	27	25	50	33	8	8	4	3	17	15	19	19	21	11	5	2	......	......	...
17	17,353	526	43	2.47	8.17	24	19	11	7	13	12	......	......	......	......	3	3	12	8	6	7	3	1	......	......	...
18	11,607	446	59	5.08	13.22	30	29	12	10	18	19	......	......	2	......	6	7	10	9	8	7	4	5	......	1	19
19	16,321	444	45	2.75	10.13	17	28	10	15	7	13	1	2	......	......	5	5	6	9	3	10	2	1	......	1	...
20	19,179	365	44	2.29	12.09	20	24	15	17	5	7	1	1	......	......	5	6	8	8	2	5	4	4	......	......	2
21	27,904	890	92	3.29	10.39	63	39	29	23	24	16	6	3	1	2	8	9	18	16	16	9	3	......	1	......	...
22	11,761	351	37	3.14	10.33	25	12	16	5	9	7	1	......	1	2	8	7	6	1	7	2	1	......	1	......	...
Totals	398,099	10,963	1,376	3.47	12.56	728	650	317	293	409	357	42	23	21	23	133	146	261	254	211	161	54	39	4	4	93

Tabular Statement showing the number of Deaths from Consumption in each Ward, the percentage of Deaths to the 1,000 of the Population, the percentage on the total Death Rate, and the total Death Rate from all causes, including the Deaths in Hospitals.

AIR FOR BABIES.

By JEROME WALKER, M. D., Brooklyn, N. Y.

Two assertions, made in the June No. of the SANITARIAN in an article on "Prospect Park," namely, "that the establishment of large public parks in the vicinity of cities, may be classed as among the necessities of modern civilization," and that "if the park were made for children only, it would even then be worth more than all it cost," should be emphasized.

These "breathing spots," in their tendency to level social arrogance, elevate the æsthetic taste, and to instil into sluggish circulations new life, are to be multiplied, as common sense and hygienic knowledge increases; but, at the same time, conveyance to and from them must be easy, cheap, and safe. This point is brought strongly to mind, as I sit and watch mother after mother, with one or two babies in arms, toiling up the ascent to Prospect Park—the cars full to running over and the day warm, but still mother and baby must see the children's display on "Anniversary Day." Why cannot all this tiring of strength and worry of mind be prevented by a cheap hack-carriage or stage service from some central place (perhaps the City Hall) to the Park, at least on holidays?

It is no easy matter to trundle a baby *in its carriage* for many squares to and from the Park, and then if we add to this all the trundling *in* the Park, and the peculiarity of human nature, not to face towards home until tired out, instead of *reaching* home when tired. In view of such obstacles we need not be surprised at the difficulty so often experienced by physicians in getting mothers to "air the babies in the parks."

We should see to it, as sanitarians, that practical measures are devised in order that children may have the full benefit.

Believing that fresh air could be made of more use to babies in lessening the fearful rate of mortality among them, and that mothers, often used up by household cares and poor health, might have less labor and worry, it occurred to me that some baby-carriage service might be inaugurated at the parks. This, as hitherto tried at some places, has not been found popular from fear of contagion, and perhaps rightly. It has occurred to me that the manufacture and sale of carriage bodies, made of some light material easily portable, and that could be attached to carriage frames, on hire at the Park at a nominal price, would accomplish the object in view. On resorting to Crandall, the "Child's Benefactor," I found a so-called "hammock-carriage," adaptable to the purpose. Mr. Crandall entered heartily into the work, and proposes to have suitable carriage bodies for sale, at a reasonable price, made of various materials, netting, canvas, carpet, etc., light enough to be easily carried in the hand. The frames will be light and durable, can be shut up, and, if need be, arranged to fit into ordinary trunks or into covers made for them.

The practical use of such a baby-carriage can be appreciated by tired mothers, by families boarding, who have no place in which to stow a carriage, and available when in the country during the hot weather.

So much for out-door air. On days when the air is desirable but the ground wet, open the windows, put on baby's hat and cloak, and perambulate the rooms and through the hallways; the exercise will be no less healthful than amusing. Make the most of one of God's best gifts and remedies for health—AIR. The rich often exclude it by costly curtains, adding darkness to the closeness, and so increasing the susceptibility to cold on the slightest exposure. The poor vitiate it by unwholesome living, crowded tenements, and close rooms. Impure air and improper feeding are alike poisonous, doing their work slowly but none the less surely; and the infant, insufficiently supplied with these essential means to health, is to be the future feeble father or mother—*if it lives.*

"I'M ONLY A FLY."—"Dear little lady, do not brush me off again, but listen, and I will tell you something you never heard before."

"What can *you* have to tell, who go buzzing about, walking up and down one's nose, and bothering one so they get cross? Where did you come from, and where do you go in winter?"

"Ah, little lady, you ask many questions in a breath, but I can answer them all. Small as I am, and troublesome as you think me, I have my use, or I would not have been made. I am of the family called horse-fly. Once on a time I had no legs, and was called a maggot, and when in that state I fed on manure and the refuse of your table, and ate up what would have been disagreeable to you if it had not thus been got rid of. When, as a maggot, I had grown to full size, a sort of hard skin covered me all over, and I lay as if dead for a time. By and by, the skin burst, and I came out a perfect fly, having two wings and six legs with which to start on my travels. My head, if you would look at it, has many curious parts in it. In front are the *antennæ*, as they are called—two little horns, useful to me in many ways. If you could *catch* me and look at me through a magnifying glass, you would see a trunk or proboscis, which is quite wonderful and has great strength. I have no jaws to bite with, so when I find a nice lump of sugar, I moisten it a little and then suck it, and that I enjoy as much as some one else I know. I do not need to wear spectacles, for my eyes are large, and are made up of about four thousand tiny pieces. To be sure, I walk, as you say, 'topsy-turvy,' but that is easily done, for I have pads on my legs which cling like the suckers that boys play with. I live through the winter by hiding in some warm corner; but many of my family do not provide for the future, and are overcome by the first frost."

"Mr. Fly, with your wonderful eyes you should see where you are not wanted, and not wake up the baby by walking over her dear little face. If you are so useful, why don't you attend to your business, and not go idling about, for you know idlers are sure to get into mischief?—*Young Catholic.*

TYPHOID FEVER AND SANITARY ADMINISTRATION.*

By JOHN M. FOX, Medical Officer of Health to the Cockermouth Union, &c.

Small-pox may be regarded as a scourge of the past rather than of the present time. The one remedy for it, or provision against it, is universally acknowledged, and a separate national establishment is devoted to its supply.

Cholera is a disease with which happily we are not allowed to become familiar by every-day experience. Its devastations, when it is present among us, are very sad; and may be compared to the havoc of an exceptional interval of war. But during the longer normal periods of peace its name even does not appear in our statistics of public health.

How different is the case with typhoid fever! For it we have no prophylactic provision. Nor is it an obsolete or even an occasional visitant. The following considerations seem to give to this affection an overwhelming interest to sanitary authorities and their officers. Indeed, I would regard it as the test disease of their activity or of their success. Where there is no typhoid fever there is good water, efficient drainage, and a careful inspection of the habits of the poor.

1. To continue the comparison, typhoid fever is a peace disease, being really never absent from us. In the most mysterious and unexpected manner it is ever cropping up amongst rich and poor, the bane both of urban and rural sanitary authorities. A metropolitan water company, or a complicated, well-engineered sewer system affords no exemption; nor, on the other hand, does the country well, or the isolated farm-house. But, as I shall mention by and by, these things ought not so to be. Where typhoid fever occurs (and it never ought to occur) there is sanitary oversight or sanitary neglect, or want of power either in the provisions of the Legislature or the application of those provisions by the local board, to insure plainly-understood sanitary conditions.

2. And yet typhoid fever is far from being a trifling or unimportant disease. The medical officer of the Privy Council, in his annual report (1867) to the Lords of the Privy Council, prepared according to the Public Health Act of 1858, for their presentation to Parliament, states that in round numbers from fifteen to twenty thousand persons are annually slain by typhoid fever alone; and that perhaps twenty times that number, or nearly four hundred thousand of our population, are grievously sickened and endangered by this complaint. Surely this is lamentable enough; but it will appear more so if we remember that—

3. These persons, thus killed, or so long "unable to work," are not the constitutionally cachectic or idiotic, who, in an economical

---

* Public Health, January, 1874.

point of view, might be better spared than others. They are the rank and file of the working army of the nation. Artisans, whose families are often left chargeable to the parish, lawyers, doctors, parsons, statesmen—even royalty itself—all, in their proportion, contribute to make up the disastrous list of deaths and enfeeblements.

4. Nor is typhoid fever in any sense, according to any theory or superstition, a disease which, once in life, a person is supposed to have to "go through." The absurdity is seen at once of undergoing any operation analogous to vaccination as a preventive of typhoid fever. Night soil men are mentioned as being fortified by use against the contagium of typhoid; but an apprenticeship to this occupation is a remedy hardly likely to be tried on a large scale. To undergo an operation, indeed, or to propound a remedy, to make us proof against the influences of dirt seems at variance with the ideas of modern civilization, even if it could ever be practicable.

5. And this brings me to the next consideration, showing the paramount interest which typhoid fever possesses for the sanitarian, namely, that it is directly and positively preventable, and preventable in a way that comes specially under the scope of a sanitary authority. "Tolle causam" is a very ancient medical precept, and it is the only one applicable or necessary in the present case, but not in a manner that comes under the province of the private medical practitioner. His attention is otherwise engaged. But not so the public health officer. It is humiliating, perhaps, to think that the occupation of a sanitary authority should be so much directed to this subject. But if it is a humiliation attached to an inherent and ever operative condition of humanity, is it wise to revolt? This is no sphere for sentiment or æsthetics.

I assert, fearless of contradiction, that the resolute, unremitting, impartial and universal dealing with filth is equivalent to the extirpation of typhoid fever. Is this or is it not a desirable and worthy end? And is it not the function, *primus inter pares*, of a sanitary authority? The Amended Nuisance Removal Act is as old as 1855, and what is it but an explicit enlargement of certain parts of the Local Government Act of 1848, and what is that Act but a consolidation of statutes on this subject dating, perhaps, from the Plague of the seventeenth century?

I repeat, then, that typhoid fever is our present unintermitting scourge in one place or another; that its cause is amongst the fixed and proven facts of sanitary science; and that it is, therefore, the duty of a sanitary authority, under sufficient enactments, ever to be dealing in earnest with this cause. Filth, polluting air or water, or both, is this sole, simple, and removable cause, and the removal of filth in such a way that neither air nor water shall be polluted thereby, means the extinction of typhoid fever. This is as true, and, with present machinery, as practicable as that vaccination, universally applied, signifies the extermination of small-pox. In regard to the present water supply, the maxim must be differently stated, in consequence of past pollutions of soil. Potable water, in accordance with the above axiom, must be brought from a source to which the filth of previous ages or of present drainage has no access. In one word, filth must be removed ; water must be imported.

But is the cause as simple and well-ascertained as stated above? I doubt whether it will be disputed. Buhl and Pettenkofer speak of the height of the sub-soil water as being casually connected with outbreaks of typhoid fever. But Dr. Buchanan has pointed out that this relation is merely one of coincidence and accidental ; the efficient cause being found in the drinking water. Mr. Simon, in his report already quoted, speaks of typhoid fever as "a disease which solely prevails through the pollution of atmosphere and drinking water with excrement." He says also, "the result of an investigation relating to 25 towns, with an aggregate population of 60,000 inhabitants, was to show the exemption which local populations obtain from cholera, typhoid fever, and other endemic bowel affections, in proportion as the local soil, air, and water are kept free from excremental pollution ; a result so confirmatory of much other evidence previously collected of the same etiological question, that henceforth apparently not even the most unwilling witness can deny the relation of the cause and effect in that matter." Dr. Parkes, in his work on Hygiene, 1873, says that "the prevalence of typhoid fever stands in a close relation to the imperfection with which sewage matters are removed;" and speaking of the specific cause of typhoid, he sums up a collection of evidence in these words:— "Fecal effluvia, and fecal impregnation of water, are the channels by which this specific cause reaches the body of a susceptible person."

It will be observed, that the difference of opinion as to the exact nature of the contagium is quite beside and beyond the simple and all-important fact just stated,—all-important, that is in a sanitary point of view,—namely, the essential connection of fecal pollution with the occurrence of every outbreak or single case of typhoid fever. Whether the poisonous emanation has the action of a ferment according to the older notion, or is an independent animal existence of a fungoid or even lower kind, and whether these fungi, or microzmes, live and grow and die in the body, or are merely vehicles of the contagium, these are questions upon which I am not competent to speak. Nor is it necessary for my present purpose. What it is of practical importance to know is, that the detritus of Peyer's glands contains the contagium. This detritus is thrown off in the excrement. The contagium thus passes into the air or into water, and by breathing, air-swallowing, or drinking, is conveyed into the system.

I now come to a very important inquiry connected with the origin of typhoid fever, namely, whether, in a case of fecal pollution of air or water, the presence of evacuations from a typhoid fever patient is necessary in order to produce the specific disease we are considering. It is evident that the medical officer of the Privy Council (see recent reports) and Dr. Parkes incline to the belief that the presence of typhoid evacuations is necessary; though both admit the many difficulties which oppose themselves to such a hypothesis.

I may say at once that this seems to me to be a view quite at issue with a large and increasing multitude of facts. Nor is it as yet supported or demanded by science. For it is admitted that we are in ignorance of the exact nature of the materies contagii in this, or indeed any other kind of contagious fever. If this materies could be demonstrated to us, and shown to be only transmissible in a continuous sequence, as ichor for vaccination, in order to produce its peculiar effects, our assent of course must follow, and our sanitary action must be regulated accordingly. But until this can be done, and until the large mass of cases of simple fecal poisoning begetting typhoid can be otherwise explained than by saying a typhoid stool *must* have been there without our knowing it (which, indeed, is begging, or assuming the very point under dispute), I demand a suspension of judgment in this matter, on the ground both of logic and public safety.

To take a parallel case. It is notorious that scarlatina may be communicated by particles of poisonous material passing into the atmosphere, or even into food, from the skin or throats of persons affected by that disease. But it has not on that account been sought to narrow down the causation of scarlatina to this limit. Yet science is pointing the way to the conviction that there is a specific contagium in scarlet, as in typhoid fever. Both, doubtless, are most surely promoted by direct connection from the known and recognized nidus in each case, the throat and skin in the one, and the mucous lining of the bowels in the other. But it is quite a different theory, and may prove a misleading one, to assume that they have no other origin; and none, I think, would restrict our precautionary measures in regard to the spreading or origin of these two complaints to so narrow an issue. And yet the theory alluded to would logically involve such a result.

In the interest of sanitary work, it is important that the suspension of judgment I plead for should at once be conceded. Indeed, it would be deplorable, if the view became popular, that only typhoid or choleraic discharges were sources of imminent danger. In this way a powerful motive to action would be taken out of our hands. According to the view I am combating, the case would stand thus:—Typhoid stools, if exposed, beget typhoid : ergo, do not expose typhoid stools. On the other hand, our argument should be, filth, if exposed, begets typhoid: ergo, do not expose filth.

The matter was well summed up by Sir William Gull, in a lecture delivered at Guy's Hospital, June, 1872. He says; "There is no scientific theory, but there is a good working theory on the point. The origination of the disease is somehow or other connected with drainage. It has, therefore, been called the filth fever. Hence, to get rid of the filth is to get rid of the fever." These are admirable words, which should be reiterated to, until they are heeded and acted upon by, every sanitary authority in the kingdom.

It is not at variance with this view, to admit that the poison comes to us in the most concentrated form (and perhaps it is a mere question of concentration) in emanations from the discharges of a typhoid patient, and the fearful increase of danger thus arising should also be borne in mind as a motive to action. Sound sanitary advice would therefore assume this form :—Beware of sewage contamination in regard to water ; or sewage exposure in regard to air in any case; but, additionally, because the fatal typhoid contagium may be there, with its enormous power of diffusion, though we may not know it. It is on this account that a single disinfected privy over a stream, or in a court (of which I shall speak again by and by), may be a source of danger. Bearing upon this point, I may just mention how many persons not unfrequently have typhoid fever, and therefore all the power and facility of propagation to others, and do not even suspect the presence of so serious a malady. We have all attended patients who have not gone to bed for the first fortnight, or perhaps during the whole period of an attack. The persistent headache and lassitude, with more or less bowel affection, are often thought to be the entire illness. But though so slight a malaise in one case, it may be the very plague in its offspring.

I have been led to make these remarks upon the causation of typhoid, from the fact that it has been my duty, during the summer and autumn of last year, to investigate several outbreaks of this disease in isolated villages and farm-houses situated in the Cockermouth Union. In some I have been able to trace the origin to the discharges of persons previously affected. But in several, though I have made a special effort to do so, I have failed to discover any history of contagion or importation, or any direct typhoid impregnation. In every case there has been fecal pollution of air or water, but in many fecal pollution of no assured specific character. It is unnecessary to make extracts from my journal, as such cases are familiar, and many are adduced in every work on the subject.

I do, however, propose to furnish brief notes of two or three selected cases, as suggesting the idea that neglected and festering farm-sewage, in close proximity to a dwelling, may be an efficient cause of typhoid fever. As this possible source of danger has not been generally noticed, and is not mentioned by Dr. Parkes in the recent edition of his exhaustive work on Hygiene, I therefore refer to it with diffidence. If it be shown to be untrue, the negative statement will be of some value in clearing the ground in future investigations. But if the observations of others are found to be in harmony with my own, it will be in the interest of a large class of our population, in the rural districts, that the cause I have indicated should receive public attention.

June 16, Dovenby.—Four cases of typhoid fever in one farm-house; one fatal. No history of importation or infection. Privy far away from pump; but liquid manure from farm running down a badly paved yard, and left standing about all round the pump, which supplies drinking water. Directed other water to be used, and well opened. June 26.—The inspector reports: Well opened, and a pipe for overflow so broken as to have been conveying liquid sewage into the well. Not another case in the village before or since.

Nov. 5.—Six cases of typhoid fever at Little Clifton; confined to one farm-house, and adjoining cottage. No other case in the village. No history of importation or infection. Water not polluted. Privy thirty yards from house, and separated by a garden. Cause, supposed to be large collection of liquid manure and washings of cattle excrement in farm-yard, close to the house. I subjoin one paragraph from my report to the Rural Sanitary Authority upon this outbreak: "I have only three observations to make on this part of the subject: one is, that typhoid fever is always associated with absorption into the system of pollution either in air or water as its originating cause; second, that this large, open, animal cesspool, which I have just described, has been shown to be the only source of such pollution applicable in the present case; and third, that upon no point has medical testimony been more unanimous in this neighborhood, than that typhoid fever is remarkably present in farm-houses in this district. In fact it has been mentioned to me as matter for inquiry on my part, as medical officer of health, that from some farms which have been named to me, though healthily situated, and standing apart from towns and town pollutions, typhoid fever is seldom absent. Therefore, taking the former facts in connection with this testimony, I have no difficulty in arriving at the conclusion that the accumulation of liquid and solid manure, in close proximity to a dwelling, is a nuisance injurious to health, and to be dealt with accordingly, being a manifest occasion, as proved in innumerable instances, of the development of that most calamitous of all preventable diseases, typhoid fever. My future practice and advice will be in harmony with the axiom just laid down." I may mention that three of these cases terminated fatally. The above report has been printed by order of the Board.

December 3.—Similar outbreak in farm at Great Clifton. Water pure. Case identical in all respects with above.

I might multiply such cases freely, but the above will suffice.

(To be continued.)

A New Way to Feed Babies.—A recent visitor among the English poor of Bury St. Edmonds relates the following incident: The wife of a laborer, while looking on at a game of "hop-scotch," in which her husband was engaged with other idlers, was describing their way of living. While she was speaking, there came toddling in at the door a splendid specimen of Suffolk infantine humanity, aged about four years, and with limbs like a baby giantess. "There, sir," remarked the old lady, "she don't look much the worse for the lockout, do she?" I replied that she did not, but rather as though a fair amount of the fat of the land fell to her share. "What do you feed her on?" I asked. "'Bacca, sir," replied the old lady with a grin. "Tobacco!" "Well, that's what they say about here. You see, sir, it's this way. She's my gran' young 'un, and her poor mother has seven of 'em, and the father is locked out like the rest; and so a month ago my old man—him as you see making such a donkey of himself a minute ago—he says, says he, 'Old woman, dashed if I can enjoy my pipe, which costs 10½d. a week—half an ounce of threepenny a day'—a cruel hard smoker he's allers been—'I can't enjoy my pipe,' ses my old man, 'and see our Joe's young 'uns wanting a meal; so I'll make over my 'bacca money to help 'em, and put my pipe out till things mend a bit.' And this is the young 'un that gets the benefit of it in milk night and morning."

PROCEEDINGS OF NEW YORK PUBLIC HEALTH ASSOCIATION, MAY 14, 1874.

RÖTHELN (EPIDEMIC ROSEOLA, ROSALIA; GERMAN MEASLES), AS NOW OCCURRING IN NEW YORK CITY.

By J. LEWIS SMITH, M.D.

There is now prevailing is this city a rare eruptive disease which appears to be the rötheln of foreign writers. The first case which I saw was in 71st street, in the middle of December last, and the largest number occurred in February, March, and April, the disease in these months appearing in the thickly settled parts of the city.

I am not aware that there has been anything unusual in the meteorological conditions during the time in which this epidemic has been prevailing. Measles, diphtheria, scarlet fever, and more recently mumps have occurred in isolated cases.

I have statistics of the new disease as it appeared in twenty-one families, examining and treating the cases in eighteen of them. In the remaining three families the symptoms and histories were so fully and clearly described to me that I have not hesitated to accept the cases as genuine. In the twenty-one families there were forty-eight cases.

Premonitory symptoms were absent or mild. In a considerable number of the cases it was not known that the patients were sick until the rash was observed covering the surface. Sometimes children preparing to go to school were observed to have the rash, although they had eaten their meals regularly, and complained of no ailment. In one or two instances they were sent from school because the teachers observed the rash, although they felt well enough to continue their lessons. Others were a little dull or complained of nausea or slight headache from one to three days previously to the occurrence of the eruption. In one case only were there grave premonitory or initial symptoms, namely, in a boy of eight years, who had clonic convulsions.

The rash appeared first either along the back or chest, or upon the face or neck, and, as in measles, it extended downward, not appearing upon the legs till after some hours or on the following day. Its color was most pronounced on the first day, after which it gradually faded, and by the close of the third day disappeared. The hue, especially after the first day, was usually a dusky red. The rash resembled more that of measles than of any other eruptive fever. In one case, a boy of three and a half years, it presented over the trunk very much the scarlatinous appearance. It commonly produced itching; disappeared on pressure, caused a little roughness, as ascertained by carrying the fingers over the surface, and faded without desquamation.

Occurring simultaneously with the dermatitis, there was a mild inflammation of the mucous membrane, covering the buccal, pharyngeal, and nasal surfaces, and of the reflection of this membrane over the eyes and eyelids, namely, the conjunctiva. This gave rise to sore throat, sneezing, sometimes a slight defluxion from the nostrils, suffused, watery, or reddish eyes, and, in certain cases, a puriform secretion collecting at the angles of the eyelids, and more or less usually slight œdema of the lids. In one case, an infant of 23 months, there was so much œdema coming on the second day that it was impossible to examine the eyes. This swelling declined in three or four days.

The febrile movement was ordinarily mild, the pulse in ten uncomplicated cases ranging from 80 to 100, and the temperature from 98¼° to 100°. The appetite was impaired, but not lost; little or no thirst; little or no cough; bowels regular. A common symptom was nausea, and several of the patients vomited. The urine examined in two cases was found normal. The duration of the disease was only three or four days.

The following were the ages of the cases observed by Dr. Smith:

From 8 months to 1 year	2
" 1 year to 2 years	4
" 2 years to 5 "	12
" 5 " " 10 "	23
" 10 " " 15 "	3
" 15 " " 25 "	4
	48

The youngest was, therefore, a nursing infant of 8 months, and the oldest a married woman of 25 years.

Native Contagiousness.—Three of the families were not visited after the first cases occurred, either from their removal or for other reasons, and whether more children were affected is unknown. In three other families there were single children. There remain fifteen families, in twelve of whom the cases were multiple. The disease usually began with one of the older children who was attending school, and after a longer or shorter period, a certain number of days, it appeared in others. The incubative period did not seem to be uniform. In some instances it appeared to be from seven to ten days, and in others from eighteen to twenty-two days, varying, therefore, as in scarlet fever.

Dr. Smith concludes, from his observations, that this disease is a contagious exanthematic fever, allied to measles and scarlet fever, but totally distinct from either. It must be placed in the same category with them. Most cases more closely resemble measles than any other disease, but that there is a specific difference is evident from the fact that those who have had measles are as liable to this malady as those who have not had it. Nineteen at least of the forty-eight cases observed by Dr. Smith had had measles, and some of them only a few months previously. In the Catholic Foundling Asylum, in 68th street, with which Dr. Smith is connected, measles prevailed as an extensive epidemic in February and March, and this was followed by an epidemic of the new disease, which commenced March 25th, and by the first of May had affected about thirty of the children and three nurses. Of these cases a large proportion had had measles.

EPIZOOTIC INFLUENZA; OR, THE SO-CALLED PINK EYE AMONGST HORSES.

By A. LIAUTARD, M. D., Prof. of Veterinary Surgery, New York.

This disease has once more made its appearance amongst the horses of our city, assuming again an epizootic form, like the attacks which we had to witness in the fall of 1872 and 1873.

In the first of these years we remember the epizootic cerebro-spinal meningitis, which proved fatal in so many cases; and in 1873 the catarrhal form came upon us, and spread all over the country, in a form which was mild by itself, easily managed by proper treatment, and serious or fatal only by the complications which followed, and amongst these that of Purpura hæmorrhagica.

This year the influenza which has again given rise to so much unnecessary controversy, has been still milder in its form, its duration, and its extent. It is that which we Veterinarians call Gastric form, Gastro hepatic, Gastro erysipelatous.

The symptomatology of Pink Eye, as the disease is called by horsemen, is always the same. Ushered in almost without prodromes, as in all influenza, the animal is suddenly ill, or in few cases may have been noticed off his food and dull for a day or two. This loss of appetite, which seems to be the first ailment, is very great; it is a perfect disgust for any kind of food, with the exception in few of a relish for fruits and roots. The animal is dull, drowsy, probably very weak, though in many this weakness is absent. The pulse is sometimes full and soft, in others weak, small, and easily compressed—in the first case not more than 48, in the second about 60 to the minute; the mucous membranes generally injected, and in many instances present a yellow saffron tinge. The temperature varies in connection with the condition of the pulse; if this is full, counting about 48 to the minute, the mercury will probably rise to 101°, 102°; but we not infrequently find the temperature run up to 106°, 106½°. The respiration is not altered; the extremities, the eyelids, the abdomen, the sheath in the gelding, will in a few hours become the seat of an œdematous swelling, seldom painful except in the sheath, and retaining the impression of the finger pressed upon it. It is due to that condition of the eyelids, swollen and injected, that the name of Pink Eye is given to the disease. The eyes often become the seat of conjunctivitis; they are partly closed, and more or less muco-purulent discharge is pouring from them.

The bowels are, perhaps, at first very soft—loose, but soon become hard, and severe constipation may be looked for. The mouth is not warm, neither does the tongue present any abnormal condition. On one animal, which was from the first attacked with diarrhœa, there was on the inside of both thighs an eruption of small pimples, which disappeared after about the third day, and was followed by slight desquamation.

In a few cases the series of symptons given was accompanied with mild laryngitis.

There are no sequelæ in this form of influenza. It is the mildest of all influenzas, and the one which gives way the easiest to treatment. I will cite one case, however, that was exceptional: A bay horse, which was affected some six weeks before, and resisted treatment for more than two weeks, when, one day, in visiting him I found on his right hypochondria a hard swelling, somewhat diffuse and painful to the touch. I treated it by external applications of iodine preparations, but it kept increasing; until in the course of three or four days it resulted in abscess. Suppuration was then stimulated, and after a few days, the abscess being opened, about two quarts of the offensive pus was evacuated, and with it a fragment of the prolonged cartilage of one of the false ribs, measuring about two inches in length. The abscess was treated antiseptically afterwards and did well. This is the third case of *Abscess of the Liver* which has come under my observation following this peculiar form of influenza. In every one the abscess was long in forming and maturing. The purulent collection was very large, and the drain upon the system such, that in each case it took a long time for the subject to recuperate.

The series of symptoms belonging to this influenza brings the veterinarian to a very simple mode of treatment: stimulation of the system and especially of the digestive apparatus of the portal circulation. Personal experience justifies me in saying that ordinarily, a few days are more than sufficient to remove all of the difficulties.

If the animal is run down, weak, as indicated by general condition, weak pulse, staggering walk,—the various forms of stimulants are indicated, and as soon as their effect is produced upon the circulation by a change in its character, the treatment should be applied to the digestive apparatus, by a good cathartic, aloes and calomel combined. The same should also be given when the patient is in a plethoric condition, when there is full pulse, etc.

This has been, in almost all my patients, the only treatment followed, and in all, with two or three exceptions, the patients have been able to resume work in five or six days. In fact, I have depended more upon a free action on the bowels than anything else; and it is interesting to notice that, in this form of disease, cathartics have been essential, and without danger; while, in the other form, they are inadmissible except with great caution.

Following this, the vegetable tonics of cinchona and gentian, in the form of tinctures, are useful.

The swellings of the extremities generally disappear without treatment other than hygienic measures, such as frictions, bandages, and exercise. If swelling remains diuretics may be given. Swelling of the sheath sometimes becomes very large, and requires scarifications.

There has been no necessity for public anxiety; no death that I know of has taken place, if the animal has been properly treated. The mortality which was reported as having taken place amongst railroad and stage horses, was due to two causes : first, with the appearance of the influenza, glanders and farcy developed themselves amongst those horses, and their death was attributed to the prevailing epizootic. Second, the treatment followed in these establishments was altogether sedative. In connection with the appearance of glanders and farcy, I think that it might be said that we can attribute it to the influenza of 1873, and its weakening effects upon the system.

I regret not to be able to throw more light upon the causation of the epizootic than last year, when speaking before you of the causes of the one prevailing at that time. But this year, it is interesting to notice that it attacked first a peculiar class of animals. At first the disease was mostly limited to low-bred horses, which are generally badly used and more or less worn out, and all of which are kept in stables where hygienic measures are very deficient; where light and ventilation are imperfect, and in stables situated on low marshy grounds.

Is it contagious? I have taken the discharge running from the eyes of horses, and inoculated the same upon healthy individuals, and have always failed to develop the disease. Still, when it appears in one stable, generally speaking, all the horses kept there take it. In the better kept establishments, in private stables, where hygienic laws are well observed, and where the stock is of a purer breed, the disease has been much milder and limited to a few individuals. If the influence of last year was due to the existence of one species of fungi, it would be interesting to find out if the same would develop this form of disease when introduced into the system of healthy animals.

A Dangerous Paper.—The green paper used to wrap about lozenges, sold in shops, railway cars, and on street corners, has long been suspected to contain arsenic, and with the view of ascertaining the facts by analysis, we recently purchased a roll of lozenges covered with this paper.

A qualitative examination of the paper afforded all the characteristic reactions for arsenic and copper. The wrapper contained twenty square inches of paper. Of this, sixteen were taken for quantitative analysis. The result of the examination showed that this portion contained .1516 grams. or 2.34 grains of metallic arsenic. This is equivalent to 2.94 grains in the whole of the wrapper, a quantity sufficient to destroy life in an adult person. Children in all parts of the country are allowed to purchase the lozenges covered with this poisonous paper, and the rolls are often put into the hands of infants as a plaything. As everything goes into the mouths of young children, it is easy to see that no more dangerous substance can pass into a family than these packages of confectionery. It is quite probable that instances of poisoning have occurred from this cause which have been of a serious or fatal character. There should be laws prohibiting the use of poisonous paper for any purpose.

THE AMERICAN MEDICAL ASSOCIATION.

The recent meeting of the American Medical Association at Detroit may be regarded as a new departure. One year ago at St. Louis, a "*judicial council*" of twenty-one was created "to take cognizance of and decide all questions of an ethical or judicial character that may arise."—Questions of ethics, of rights to membership, representation, and the like which the experience of the Association had abundantly shown were constantly liable to occur. A change in the plan of conducting the work of the Session was also effected by the organization of Permanent Sections: (1.) Practice of Medicine, Materia Medica, and Physiology. (2.) Surgery and Anatomy. (3.) Obstetrics and Diseases of Women and Children. (4.) Medical Jurisprudence, Chemistry, and Psychology. (5.) State Medicine and Public Hygiene. By this prearrangement of the Association, and a well appointed and unusually efficient Committee of Arrangements, there was no time wasted. The chairman of every Section, respectively, was present. Under such auspices, the Association was promptly called to order at 11 o'clock, on Tuesday, 2d ultimo., there being over three hundred members present at the opening.

There was first a happy opening address of welcome, by Dr. William Brodie, Chairman of the Committee of Arrangements:

Detroit, eighteen years ago, when the Association first met there, contained 40,000 inhabitants, now enumerates over 100,000. Her suburbs, then woods and swamps, now resound with the busy hum of the machine, and the axe has yielded to the spade and plough. Brought into existence by the early explorers of our country, and made venerable by the march of time, she possesses the vigor of early manhood, is not behind her more aged sisters of the East, nor cast in the shade by the younger ones of the West.

We boast of Detroit as one of the healthiest cities of the Union, its mortality being only two and one-half per cent. for the year 1873. This happy state of health is not only due to her location on the beautiful Detroit River, but to her complete system of sewerage, over ninety-two miles having been constructed since 1835, at a cost of $1,528,000. Her public school system—the establishment of which on their permanent basis, and of which our citizens are justly proud—was eminently due to the efforts of the late Dr. Pitcher, who was your presiding officer at its meeting in this city in 1855. This system embraces twenty-eight school buildings, at a valuation of $548,000, in which over 12,000 scholars were enrolled for 1873, and education at an actual cost, inclusive of all expenses, of $10.50 per pupil per annum. Her public library deserves mention as one of her most popular institutions, established by the Constitution of the State, managed by the Board of Education, and supported by court fines and penalties. Its total receipts are $74,000; its expenditures $52,000, and its total number of volumes 22,935. Detroit is abundantly supplied with water from the Detroit River. Of its purity Prof. Duffield says: "It is impossible to find river water more free from organic impurities." The daily average supply for 1873 was 8,760,000 gallons, being about ninety gallons, or three barrels, per diem for each inhabitant, at a cost of only $1.74 per annum. The large surplus of water not directly used by the individual, serves to wash the sewers, and adds another reason for the purity of the city and health of her citizens.

Her Police and Fire Departments are unique in the discipline, arrangements and management; while the former protects the person, the latter protects the property from the scourge of fire, and is valued at near $300,0 0. The Detroit Fire Department is in possession of the third self-propelling engine manufactured and in use in the United States, and whose performance will be presented for your observation. Her House of Correction cannot be omitted, and which will be open to your inspection as a model of its kind, and I believe the second in this country that is self-supporting. While punishing crime it reforms the criminal, and returns them to society improved in morals and in health.

The order of business and places of meeting of the several Sections was announced by Dr. Brodie, and the President of the Association, Dr. J. M. Toner, then delivered his address, concisely presenting the present aspect of Medicine in the United States, and its beneficial relations to this Association:

It is not too much to claim that this Association, by the mere moral support it gives in encouraging the formation of local Medical Associations, has done immeasurable good, and added largely to this result. It fully recognizes the unity of the regular profession throughout the United States. At the same time it has erected a standard of medical excellence and ethical *esprit de corps* never before attained in America, and has persistently and publicly held it up for admiration and adoption. It has drawn with distinctness a line that separates the *regular* from the *irregular practitioner*, which will in the future as in the past be firmly maintained. And it is desirable as far as practicable to encourage uniformity in the place and scope of all Medical Societies, which in the sphere of their influence correspond to our civil political divisions; and farther, I think we should continue our efforts to encourage these local medical organizations until every State and county in the United States shall have its Medical Society, holding proper relations with each other and with this body. The Association is now and always has been anxious to bring into its fold the leading physicians from every State, and from every city and village and rural district in the land, and has been soliciting and still invites original papers on any subject that can advance medical science. It has published annually from its organization a volume of contributions and regular and special reports of great value in the different departments of Medicine, on questions of immediate interest in the profession.

It must be apparent to all who are familiar with the history of Medicine or have enjoyed, for a considerable number of years, a position favorable for overlooking the great army at work in the wide field of professional duty throughout the United States, that the concentration of medical thought and the scientific aspirations of the profession of the country, as expressed through this Central Association, are such that, by its unity of action, it exercises more influence now than ever before, or than would be possible without such combined association. This is particularly noticeable in States in which there has been recent legislation affecting the profession and the public health. It is within the observation of all, that while the profession is advancing in knowledge and influence, so is the general intelligence of the people, who are yearly demanding greater protection to their health, and greater skill and ability on the part of physicians in the various branches of Medicine. Education is synonymous with elevation. Knowledge in Medicine, as everywhere else, is power and ability. It is a source of sincere congratulation that our medical educational institutions are rapidly enlarging and perfecting their *curriculums*, and becoming more thorough and efficient in teaching the science of Medicine.

The hope entertained by some physicians of excluding irregular and incompetent practitioners from the profession by legislative enactments and penalties is, I apprehend, in our country not to be realized. The thorough, systematic education, the skill and availability of the services of the regular medical man must instinctively create in the minds of the people an appreciation of his superior claims to their confidence, and thus the profession be a law for its own protection, which must prove stronger and more enduring than the acts of assemblies or ruling of courts.

Its efficiency and influence with the public rest on the amount of its useful scientific and practical professional knowledge. Let us at all times and seasons insist upon increasing these by every means possible. Ignorance and charlatanism should be made odious by contrast.

I wish to call the attention of the profession to the advantages of competitive examinations, whenever appointments are to be made among professional men to medical institutions, as the best mode of securing the most efficient, encouraging the industrial and careful student, and rewarding the really meritorious. We all know that it is not true in fact, whatever may be the theory, that one graduate is just as good and as competent, and no better than another. It is a duty we owe to ourselves and to the public to give our approbation and encouragement to those who by special application and thorough study become eminent in the profession. The man of real ability is usually retiring and without diplomacy, while the shallow pretender is full of tact, and is aggressive and persevering, and therefore, too often for the dignity and the advancement of medical science, intrusted with the management of our public institutions.

Preventive medicine is now attracting the earnest attention of many of the profound thinkers in the profession. Within the personal observation and memory of each of us there have been great advances in the control and prevention of disease. There is much still to be done in this direction. I confidently look forward to the time when epidemics of cholera, yellow fever and small-pox, will be prevented with a certainty just in proportion to the dissemination of knowledge of efficient measures, and the faithfulness with which the means are applied. I think the time is not very far remote when the National Government will feel justified in authorizing a Central Public Health Council of some kind to act as auxiliary and advisory to the different States and Municipal Health Boards and quarantine organizations of the country. The organization of State, County, and City Boards of Health should be encouraged by the medical profession, and authorized by law in every State. It is within the power of such bodies, if properly constituted and filled with intelligent and energetic physicians, who will make sanitary matters a study, to add much to the security of public and private health. Indeed, the organic laws of each State should require every county and city to have such a Board. Their mere existence tends to educate the minds of the people to an observance of hygienic laws. The aggregated experience and reports of such Boards would add greatly to our knowledge of the prevalence of local and epidemic diseases, and their distribution and recurrence throughout the country. The climate in which we live, the pursuits and temperament of our people, and the bubble, rush and enthusiasm which characterize a business life, and its efforts in the new world, are, in part at least, responsible for a numerous class of diseases. In many individuals the stomach and brain are kept in an abnormal state of excitement almost from childhood. The consequence of this strain is manifested in numerous disturbances mental and physical, even in persons who appear to be in good health, as well as the recognized invalid. Cases of obscure and complicated disease are believed to be more numerous proportionally to other sickness with us than with the people of any other country, and diseases of the nervous system are, out of all proportion, more frequently met with among the active business and professional men, and in the well to do class of society, than in other countries. This class of cases, and all the producing causes, deserve to be carefully studied with a view to prevention or cure. There are annually many valuable citizens, statesmen, and professional men carried off suddenly, whose demise in the prime of life and in the midst of their usefulness, is attributable to overworked brains. The question of the influence of localities of different elevations is now, more than at any previous period, engaging the attention of the profession. As population increases in the interior and elevated portions of our country, the number of facts observed bearing on this point will rapidly multiply and be recorded by separate observers and at many different points. Facts thus accumulated will from time to time be digested, and results deduced that will largely assist to solve the problem.

The systematic observations in meteorology that are being made throughout the country, under the direction of the United States Signal Corps and the Smithsonian Institute, promise in their results to be of great value in the study of climatology and the causation of disease. I hope to see that system widely extended and its stations multiplied through the whole country.

The Sections promptly convened at half-past two, and at the same time daily during the meeting.

The Section on Practice of Medicine, Materia Medica, and Physiology, presided over by Dr. N. S. Davis, was well attended, and many papers of interest discussed.

The address of the Chairman before the Association was on the *Progress of Practical Medicine, Materia Medica, and Physiology*, presenting, criticising, and eliminating the true from the false, and emphasizing the characteristics of progress as deduced from and demonstrated by true *learning*, as opposed to mere theoretical reasoning.

The Section on Surgery and Anatomy, presided over by Dr. S. D. Gross, was the most fully attended throughout, and engaged in the most exciting topics of discussion—an undue proportion to a discussion on fractures.

The Chairman's address was on "Syphilis in its Relations to National Health." He took decided grounds, for sanitary reasons, in favor of the regulation of prostitution by law and of medical inspection of prostitutes. It was listened to with profound attention throughout.

The Section on Obstetrics and Diseases of Women and Children, presided over by Dr. F. Parvin, was characterized by the presentation of papers on, and the discussion of, subjects of much importance, and a large attendance.

The address of the Chairman was on *Uterine Hæmorrhage*.

The Section on Medical Jurisprudence, Chemistry, and Psychology, presided over by Dr. A. N. Tally, was at the first sparsely attended, and had but few papers. On the third day a paper on "Emotional Insanity," by the Secretary, Dr. E. Lloyed Howard, and a brief paper on the "Relation of Psychology to Medicine," by the Chairman, were read, and elicited much interest.

No address from the Chairman in consequence of illness.

The Section on State Medicine and Public Hygiene, presided over by Dr. A. N. Bell, and which received most of our attention, was not well attended at the first, but the number and character of papers presented soon attracted attention, and there was from the beginning to the end of its sessions, an increasing interest and attendance. In the absence of the Secretary, Dr. A. B. Stuart, of Minn., Dr. Franklin Staples, from the same State, was elected *pro tem.*

This Section differs from the others in that, besides the election of the Chairman and Secretary of it by the Association, a member is appointed from each State and Territory.

Papers were presented as follows :

Arkansas—D. A. Linthicum : State Medicine, comprehending the consideration of laws in regard to defective drainage and State Hygiene.

California—Dr. T. M. Logan : State Medicine and Public Hygiene.

Iowa—Dr. J. J. M. Angear : Defective Drainage.

Massachusetts—Dr. H. I. Bowditch : On a National Sanitary Bureau and the organization and practical working of the Massachusetts State Board of Health.

Michigan—R. C. Kedzie : 1. A report on the resolutions committed to the Section. 2. A report advocating a National Health Bureau, independent of other branches of the General Government. 3. On the influence of Drainage on Public Health in Michigan.

New Hampshire—Dr. J. W. Parsons : On the Failure to Establish a State Board of Health, and in favor of a National Sanitary Bureau.

Minnesota—Dr. A. B. Stuart: In favor of a National Sanitary Bureau; also on Effects of Defective Drainage.

New Jersey—Dr. E. M. Hunt: On the Want of General Interest and Information Concerning Hygienic Laws.

New York—Dr. A. N. Bell: On Defective Drainage, and opposing the organization of a National Sanitary Bureau at present.

Florida—Dr. Murray: A Medico-topographical Report of Key West, Florida.

Connecticut—Dr. B. H. Catlin: On Defective Drainage.

Virginia—Dr. J. L. Cabell: On Defective Drainage in Virginia as a Cause of Disease.

State Medicine was announced by the Chairman, as the first subject for consideration.

The report of Dr. Bowditch, of Massachusetts, was read. It recommended the establishment of State Boards of Health, and gave a history of the establishment of the Massachusetts Board, which was organized on June 21st, 1869, though the idea was suggested twenty years before. It consisted of seven members, with seven years term of office, one retiring each year, appointed by the Governor and Council. Its members were three of them physicians, and four laymen. The same proportion has since been maintained. The writer thought the admission of the laity was wise, and worked admirably. The Board has power to close up any manufactory or branch of trade obnoxious to health, and has frequently been called on to do so. The courts have sustained them, and granted injunctions at their request. One of the greatest triumphs of the Board was the erection of the Brighton *abattoir*, in place of the many stinking slaughter-houses, which is kept clean by the rules of the Board. Dr. Bowditch was not in favor of the establishment of a National Sanitary Bureau at present, but recommended members to urge the organization of State and local boards of health.

The resolutions referred to the Section for consideration and action this year were read. They (first) declare in favor of the establishment of a National Sanitary Bureau, similar to those of agriculture and education; and (second) request the United States Educational Bureau to extend its scope of inquiry so as to include vital, disease and mortuary statistics, in relation to local and other influences, and to disseminate the information thus obtained.

Portions of a paper by the Secretary of the Section, Dr. A. B. Stuart, were read, favoring a National Sanitary Bureau in the future, but recommending that for the present the Surgeon-General's office be the repository for vital statistics.

Dr. Bell read a portion of his report on the subject, holding that at present the establishment of a National Bureau is not advisable, and urging that work be now directed to the organization of State Boards of Health. There are now only six States which have established Boards of Health, Maryland being the last State to organize such a Board.

Dr. Brown of Waco, Texas, said that a State Medical Board had been organized by the State Association of Texas, and progress was being made toward the establishment of a State Board of Health.

Dr. Cochrane, of Mobile, Ala., spoke at some length. He opposed the present establishment of a National Board of Health, criticised the details of the organization of the Massachusetts Board of Health, and spoke of the history of sanitary legislation in Alabama.

Dr. Kedzie moved the following resolution:

Resolved, That it is expedient at this time to petition Congress for the establishment of a National Sanitary Bureau.

The resolution was discussed at length. Drs. Kedzie, of Michigan; Brown, of Texas; Westmoreland, of Georgia; Pratt, of Michigan; Johnson, of Illinois; Cochrane, of Alabama; Van Demen, of Tennessee; Waterhouse, of Wisconsin; Jones, of Ohio; Baker, of Michigan; and Hitchcock, of Kalamazoo, Michigan, favoring it, and Drs. Thoms, of New York; Howard, of Maryland; Graham, of Illinois; and the President, Dr. Bell, of New York, opposing it, on the ground that it might interfere with the work of establishing State Boards of Health. It was finally adopted.

After some further discussion and suggestions, the following resolution was adopted, to be reported in connection with the one above:

That, with a view to the establishment of a National Sanitary Bureau, it is expedient, at the present time, to press, through State societies and physicians in all the States, upon the Legislatures of our several States, the importance of establishing State Boards of Health.

The second session was devoted to the consideration of

DEFECTIVE DRAINAGE.

Dr. R. C. Kedzie read his report on the effects of drainage in Michigan. He said that the State of Michigan had an unenviable reputation for swamps, and gave an account of the origin and characteristics of them. The United States gave the swamp lands to the State, the proceeds of their sale to be devoted to their drainage and reclamation. Some six million acres were thus given,—by no means all of it, however, being absolutely swamp. A very small amount of the proceeds of the lands, however, has been appropriated to drainage. Dr. Kedzie gave the history of legislation in Michigan for the drainage of swamp lands, and some statistics in regard to the matter. He estimated the amount of swamp lands in the State at four million acres, or about one acre in nine. The estimated amount of ditches dug during the past year is 740,000 rods, or more than 2,300 miles. Probably 20,000 miles of ditches have been dug within ten years. Of the township clerks who reported on the subject, seventy-nine reported the effect of drainage as good, and twenty-nine that no defect was perceived. Dr. Kedzie also read letters from Doctors W. A. Engle, Hartford; J. H. Beech, Coldwater; George Chapman, Hudson; Wm. Brodie, Detroit; L. S. Stearns, Three Rivers; Wm. Parmenter, Vermontville; J. Andrews, Paw Paw; Z. E. Bliss, Grand Rapids; J. P. Smiley, Okemos; O. E. Herrick, Greenville; Wm. Brownell, St. Johns; Geo. E. Rumney, Lansing; J. S. Caulkins, Thornville; A. Nash, Lapeer; Dr. Reeves, East Tawas; W. R. Marsh, Bay City, speaking for Fenton, his former residence, and Dr. E. P. Christian, Wyandotte, physicians of this State, in answer to a circular asking for information in regard to the effects of drainage. The general character of the replies was to the effect that drainage has had a very decided effect in diminishing or modifying malarial disease, some saying, however, that the *immediate* effect of drainage of swamp lands is to increase the amount and severity of malarial disease, owing to the disturbance of decaying matter in draining, but that this is only temporary, and that the permanent effect is excellent. The percentage of malarial disease was reported at 10 to 75 per cent., being largest where there is the greatest proportion of adjacent swamp lands. Some doctors report an increase of other than malarial disease, but Dr. Kedzie explained that this was probably an increase of the *proportion* of such diseases to the total, and not an absolute increase of disease. Some reported that malarial diseases had been reduced to one-half or one-fourth the amount ten years ago. Dr. Reeves, of East Tawas, also reported at length in regard to the climatic effect of the fires in the State in 1871, and earlier fires.

Dr. Bell stated that a report had been submitted by Dr. J. L. Cabell, of Virginia, giving the statistics of drainage in Virginia, collected in the same manner as adopted by Dr. Kedzie, and showing, if possible, a still worse state of affairs than in Michigan—demonstrating that defective drainage is the cause of more than half, if not more than three-quarters, of the mortality in many localities.

Dr. Kedzie spoke of the effect of stagnant water in inducing cerebro-spinal meningitis, and gave an account of the ravages of that and similar diseases in Petersburg, Monroe county, Mich., stating that they were probably caused by mill-dams along the River Raisin. All along the banks of the river up to Adrian, these diseases, attributable to stagnant water, are very prevalent.

Dr. Stuart, of Minnesota, also presented a report on the same topics.

Dr. Bell read a portion of his report upon drainage in New York. In 1830 a medico-topographic State survey was made, which did great good. But even before that year defective drainage was recognized as a chief cause of excessive mortality. The reports of Dr. Joseph M. Smith and Dr. Elisha Harris upon this subject were referred to. A communication by Gen. Egbert L. Viele, severely criticising the arrangements of drainage in New York city, was quoted from. Sewerage, says Gen. Viele, is not drainage, and fails to carry off a large amount of water, which is a fruitful source of pestilence. There is much stagnant water in the upper parts of New York without any outlet, and, though the pools be filled up, the water remains in the earth, the cause of thousands of deaths. Since this communication of Gen. Viele was written, Dr. Bell stated, laws have been passed for deep drainage in New York city.

Dr. Bell added that he had sent circulars for local information in regard to defective drainage to the county medical societies of New York, and that the information thus gained had been published by the Medical Society of the State of New York. He had incorporated this in his report, but would not read it at present.

A medico-topographic report, by Dr. Robert D. Murray, United States Marine Hospital Surgeon at Key West, upon the characteristics of that place, was read.

Dr. Pratt, of Kalamazoo, stated that the three years' drought in his vicinity had resulted in a large proportionate increase in the organic matter in well-water. This had been followed by a large increase of malarial disease among families using well-water, whereas none of the families using the water-works water had been troubled with disease.

Dr. H. A. Johnson, of Chicago, reported verbally in regard to the drainage system of that city and the surrounding country, and also called attention to statistics of disease in Chicago for the year 1872, as tabulated by himself. He stated that there was not one-tenth as much malarial disease as twenty years ago. He also gave facts to show that the death-rate was two or three times greater in wards where the sewerage was not adequate than where the sewerage system was complete.

THE EFFECTS OF ALCOHOL.

The third and last session was devoted to the consideration of the effects of alcohol as embraced in the resolutions of Dr. Horner, referred to the Section a year ago.

Dr. Kedzie read a number of extracts from the paper on alcohol lately read before the Michigan State Board of Health, by Dr. H. O. Hitchcock, of Kalamazoo.

Dr. Morris, of Maryland, said the question of temperance affects the life of our civilization directly, while drainage, ventilation, etc., affect it indirectly, and for that reason he thought preference should be given to it. The Section speaks not for itself or the Association, but for the whole medical profession. He laid it down as a safe rule, based on his own observation and experiments, that a pint of claret or other light wine containing alcohol is the utmost that can be taken by any patient during one day without positive injury to the system. He said it was impossible to make inebriates temperate at once, and he thought it would not be wise to take extreme grounds. The Section should decide the question purely on medical grounds, and not mix it up with any moral questions. He offered a resolution to the effect that the Association appoint a committee to consider the subject of alcoholic stimulants and report at the next annual meeting. After considerable debate the motion was lost.

The resolutions of Dr. Frederick Horner, Jr., of Va., were then taken up and adopted as the sense of the Section.

Resolved, That in view of the alarming prevalence and ill effects of intemperance, with which none are so familiar as members of the medical profession, and which has called forth from English physicians the voice of warning to the people of Great Britain concerning the use of alcoholic beverages, we, as members of the medical profession of the United States, unite in the declaration that we believe that alcohol should be classed with other powerful drugs; that when prescribed medicinally it should be done with conscientious caution and a sense of great responsibility.

Resolved, That we are of the opinion that the use of alcoholic liquors as a beverage is productive of a large amount of physical and mental disease, that it entails diseased appetites and enfeebled constitutions upon offspring, and that it is the cause of a large percentage of the crime and pauperism in our large cities and country.

Resolved, That we would welcome any change in public sentiment that would confine the use of intoxicating liquors to the uses of science, art and medicine.

On motion of Dr. Kedzie the Chairman's address, with other papers, were referred to the Secretary to be prepared for publication. The Chairman asked that he might be allowed to publish his address in his own journal, the SANITARIAN. There was no objection, but on the contrary, several members heartily approved of the proposal. It has been the practice of the Association to consider all papers read before it as private property, and the writer has no right to publish them except as authorized by the Association, but it was the sense of the Section that the subject of public hygiene was of such an exceptional character as to warrant as wide publicity as possible.

Dr. Kedzie offered the following :

Resolved, That the Section recommend to the Association that a committee of three be appointed to report to this Section at the next meeting, on the ventilation of dwellings, school-houses and other public buildings.

The resolution was adopted, and the following members recommended as such committee : R. C. Kedzie, Michigan ; A. B. Stuart, Minnesota ; R. J. O'Sullivan, New York.

Dr. Baker offered the following :

Resolved, That a committee of three be appointed by the Chairman of this Section to draft a bill for the establishment of a National Board of Health, and to confer with Congress as to its adoption.

The resolution was passed, and the following recommended as such committee : H. B. Baker and H. A. Johnson, Illinois ; J. M. Toner, Washington.

Dr. Foster Pratt offered the following :

Resolved, That a committee of three be appointed by the Chairman of this Section to report at the next annual meeting what legislative action, if any, can be taken by Legislatures to enforce by law an examination of all who enter upon the practice of medicine by a State Board of Medical Examiners.

In support of this resolution, Dr. Pratt said the action contemplated did not come strictly under any Section, but, as it related to preservative measures, he thought the Section on Public Health. The plan is already in operation in Kentucky, and something similar in New York.

The motion prevailed by a vote of seven to five. The following were recommended as the committee : Foster Pratt, of Michigan ; S. G. Armour, New York ; D. W. Yandell, Kentucky.

The Secretary then read the minutes of the Section, and they were referred, with the other papers, to the Secretary of the Association, and the Section adjourned *sine die*.

The Chairman's address will be found in full on other pages.

Space will not admit of a fuller report of the proceedings of this interesting Convention.

HOSPITALITY.

No report, however lengthy, can do justice to the hospitality of the people of Detroit, who at every recess and every turn of the Convention stood, as it were, with open hearts and open doors of welcome.

PROCEEDINGS OF THE N. Y. MEDICO-LEGAL SOCIETY, MARCH 26, 1874.

MR. PRINCE'S LUNACY BILL.

The special order of business for the evening being the discussion of Mr. Prince's Bill, now before the Legislature, providing for the care and safe keeping of lunatics, and Dr. Peugnet's paper, entitled "The Medical Jurisprudence of the Stokes Case," the former was taken up first.

The President first gave a history of the bill, and its present status in the Legislature, and then read it as follows :

MR. PRINCE'S LUNACY BILL.

The Governor of the State is authorized to appoint in the City and County of New York not less than ten nor more than fifty, and in every other county not less than five nor more than fifteen, respectable physicians, to be known as Examiners in Lunacy, and to fill vacancies occurring among such Examiners as they occur; and in every case arising in any county, requiring, as provided by law, the certificate of two physicians, to require the confinement or safe-keeping of any person on the ground of lunacy, such certificate shall be required to be signed by two of the Examiners in Lunacy, as appointed, resident in the county in which such case of lunacy is found; and no person shall be received as a lunatic in any asylum, public or private, without such certificate. The appointment of Examiners, as aforesaid, shall be made on the recommendation of the Board of Supervisors, or a majority of the members thereof, of the respective counties. Said Examiners shall hold office during the pleasure of the Governor, and vacancies shall be filled in the same way in which the original appointment was made.

When the bill was first introduced into the Legislature, the Chair continued, I protested against giving such power to the Supervisors. I doubted whether it would not be practically useless at least in this city, to have two experts selected by the Supervisors. Would they not partake, more or less, of political appointments? When the bill was introduced I begged Mr. Prince to give his attention to this subject, and he replied that he felt the force of my suggestion. It was also suggested that as far as this city was concerned, it would probably be better to have the appointments made by the presiding Judge of the Court of Common Pleas, Judge Daly. That suggestion in the last Legislature failed to receive that support which Mr. Prince hoped it would, and considerations of a political nature prevailed.

You have heard from your minutes just read, the action of this Society in regard to this bill. It would probably be unwise to forward that action to Albany at this time. It would be better to consider this matter further, and this bill is now before you for discussion.

J. A. PARIGOT, M. D.—I regard any enactment looking to the care and protection of insane persons as a very important measure. Still, I do not understand how a Board of Supervisors can very well choose a certain number from Physicians, concerning whom they know but little or nothing. I do not favor the idea that such physicians should have the exclusive right to make examinations. How can either the Governor or the Supervisors say whether a physician is capable or not of conducting an examination of this delicate nature? It is necessary for us to say whether we will submit to this power without protest. I, for one, am decidedly opposed to the bill.

Dr. E. C. HARWOOD—The bill as submitted this evening is something almost entirely new to me. I have seen some allusion to it in the papers, but I fail to see its utility. Under the present law, as I understand it, the affidavit of two respectable physicians will suffice to commit a person to an insane asylum, and it seems to me that the insane or the community at large are to derive no special benefits from a bill of this character. The appointment made may partake of a political character, and the party receiving the appointment may have bribes pressed upon him. I do not mean to indict the profession of such a practice, yet there are many members who are not above doing such things, who cannot do so under the present law.

There are a great many cases of insanity where the Commissioner would be entirely unable to form an exact opinion regarding the condition of the patient. There are cases where the question cannot be determined save by a prolonged observation. In such cases the cursory examination, which would in all probability be given by the Examiner in Lunacy, would result in forming a wrong opinion. I have lately had a case myself where a strange physician would have been very much puzzled in making a diagnosis, or in deciding whether it were necessary to send the subject to an asylum or not. It appears to me that the attending or family physician, or one who has had an abundant opportunity to observe the patient, should be called in consultation with the Examiner.

Mr. D. H. RIDDLE—Mr. President, I will say but a few words upon the subject under discussion. The law as it stands now reads somewhat in this way: If any person by reason of lunacy or otherwise becomes fiercely mad, and therefore so far deranged as to endanger his own life or the life or property of others, he may be confined in a suitable place, etc., Then there is a statute which gives authority to the Overseers of the Poor and two Justices of the Peace to commit a person to confinement when he becomes dangerous to himself or to the property and lives of others.

About 20 years subsequently, a law was passed requiring the certificate or affidavit of two respectable physicians to confine a man in a lunatic asylum. The law therefore interposes between the lunatic asylum and the citizen, two respectable physicians.

Now, as the law stands, it is not the condition of insanity which authorizes a physician to confine a man, but he must be dangerously insane; he must be dangerous to his own life, or the life or property of others.

Now I had occasion a few weeks ago to investigate this matter. The case is perfectly familiar to you all; it is of recent occurrence. Two physicians gave an affidavit, and in consequence had a man confined in a lunatic asylum, under the charge of Dr. Parsons, who, in two or three days examined him, and finding him sane (after consultation with the two physicians whose affidavits committed the man), discharged him, as being unfit for a lunatic asylum, although the man was violent and troublesome to his family; yet, after all, it was evident that he was not a fit subject for the asylum. The evidence also showed that the two physicians who gave the affidavit knew very little about the man. One physician, who was the physician to the family, never attended this man, and had never examined him. The other physician was a young man, and had never seen this man more than three or four times. The only ground on which he gave a certificate was the statement made to him by the other physician, and some statements made to him by the family. He stated that he had seen the person eighteen months prior to giving the certificate; he had then seen him on the street, and had seen him running out of a house into the street; first fast, then slowly forward and backward, muttering to himself, and several times he had noticed that he would go out into the street and say, "I will kill them; I will kill them," and other facts of the same character. Now upon these facts, upon what he had thus seen of him, and upon what the family had told him, and what the other physician told him, he goes before a Police Justice, makes an affidavit, and has the man confined.

Well this is a thing which ought to be remedied. There are, of course, physicians who, like Dr. Parsons, take the remedy in their own hands; but there are others who are not so careful. Then you perceive a great wrong, a great injury is done to the citizen. As the law stands now, there is nothing to save a man—nothing at all—from being taken away from his family and friends and being carried away by force and shut up in a lunatic asylum on the affidavits of two physicians who call themselves respectable. These men have only to make an affiidavit and have the man confined. One of the physicians concerned in the case above cited, I doubt very much as to his claim to respectability. His name is not in the New York Medical Register. Under the common law, of course, the physician will take the risk. He will only testify as to the fact of the insanity itself. But the revised statute, as it stands now, imposes a great duty upon the physician. But if the physician be mistaken after the exercise of reasonable care, he is exonerated even if the man is not insane.

Now in England there was a case which I came upon during the course of my investigations; it occurred in 1829. In that case a very distinguished physician had given a certificate, but not upon personal examination; he gave it merely on the statement made to him by the friends of the person. The man was arrested on that certificate and confined. The physician was reprimanded by the Chief Justice, who decided that the examiner cannot be justified by taking the statement of an outside party, and giving a certificate on that ground alone; a personal examination, in addition to information derived from the family and those acquainted with the individual, is required. In other words, it is the duty of the physician to resort to all means of information within his reach.

Some time after that, a new law was passed in England, and I think might be adopted with benefit to some extent in this country. It lays down certain things which the physician must do. He must make a personal examination; must state how many examinations he has made, etc.; and all this must be done within seven days after the person is confined, so that he will not be oppressed by reason of unnecessary confinement. There must be two examiners. Then there are further safeguards thrown around both physician and patient—that if the person who has been committed turns out not to be insane, yet the physician, having done all these things, is protected and cannot be called in question in the courts. Now, I think these provisions are important, and it would be well to adopt them in this State.

With respect to the other branch of the question, I may say a few words; and that is this, Who shall make the appointment of these physicians? I am inclined to think that this is a most difficult part of the problem. I really think that the Supervisors ought not to make the appointment. Certainly, it is far better to leave that to the Governor. The other idea, that appointments should be left to the Chief Justice of the Court of Common Pleas in the city and county of New York, and to certain Justices in other counties, I am inclined to think would be still better than to leave it to the Governor; because they are in the county; they are there, and they are better acquainted with the physicians, and have better opportunities to ascertain their qualifications. And these physicians should be persons versed in matters relating to insanity. I think it should not be as now, that only a diploma is required, but that he should be made to give a certificate of qualification.

I was surprised to find, in this examination which I have made, that young physicians—men who have had very little practice—have given affidavits, and have given more such affidavits, perhaps, than they have had patients.

A man's liberty is a thing of too much importance, it is too grave a matter to be trifled with by making appointments from among those who are incapable of fulfilling the duties necessarily attached to the position of Examiner in Lunacy; and I trust that the subject of this bill will receive that weighty consideration which it demands.

Clark Bell, Esq.—There is an impression that the existing law which enables two physicians to sign an affidavit, is liable to so many abuses and injustices, that it has really thrown some sort of prejudice against the whole business; and it is the object of Mr. Prince's bill to endeavor to remedy what is considered to be an evil. The mere fact that a gentleman has a certificate from a medical college, does not qualify him to pass upon a man's sanity or insanity. I take it, that you, gentlemen, will say that very many of your own profession are not much better qualified to speak upon the sanity or insanity of a person than any one else; and that it is only when he has paid particular attention to this subject, that he is qualified to judge of this subject, and to pass upon the sanity or insanity of a person. Would it not be better to select out of the profession some number of names, and make them directly responsible to the public and profession for the exercise of this particular power, which results in depriving the citizen of his liberty, and which takes him away from his family, friends and property, and virtually places him in prison?

The President then called upon Dr. Parsons, who said: I had

the honor of being consulted in regard to the form of this bill by some gentlemen who were interested in presenting it before the Legislature, so that it is a subject to which I have given some little attention.

Of course it is to be understood that the first great question that engaged our attention was, whether any change at all is necessary; or whether the law, as it now stands, is not good enough.

There are two views that are taken of this subject. The first is, the view taken by the people regarding the liberty of the citizen. It should be duly preserved, and all the rights which the law guarantees him should be zealously guarded. Then, on the other hand, physicians, and more especially superintendents of insane asylums, should be subjected to as little hinderance in the performance of their duty as possible. The reason of this is, that many persons, especially in the higher ranks of life, are extremely sensitive on the subject of having it known that their friends or family are insane. Furthermore, it is of the greatest possible importance that if the person is insane, and requires to be sent to the asylum, he should be sent at the earliest possible moment, and without putting obstructions in the way, or giving undue publicity to the fact of his insanity.

It must be acknowledged that there are occasionally a few persons confined in these asylums who are not insane. This statement I have formerly made, and unfortunately have incurred the opposition of some very estimable men in the profession. But though I may have done injury to the insane and the friends of the insane by expressing such an opinion, still I was under the necessity of urging my own experience to show that the opinion which I had expressed was really true. On the other hand, it must be quoted that the number of those who are admitted to the asylum who are not insane is exceedingly small in proportion to the whole number of those admitted—probably considerably less than one in a hundred. In some asylums where a great deal of care is taken, and particularly in those asylums where members of the higher walks of society are admitted, this is not likely to occur. The case of Mr. Jacobs has just been mentioned; also the case of the *Tribune* reporter. And in this connection it is also well to understand that those physicians who believe that sane persons are sometimes admitted, do not believe, and I myself do not believe, that the certificates are given wilfully, and that they knowingly commit a patient who is not insane.

Admitting, then, that mistakes do occur, the question then arises, whether any greater safeguard will likely be afforded the patient or the community by the appointment of some other set of men than the regular and ordinary practitioner to examine these cases? That question has already been discussed at some length, and part of the conclusions arrived at were in accordance with the views which I hold.

I would be inclined to say that the regular family physician should be one of the parties who should examine the patient, and who should make an affidavit with regard to the fact of his insanity, that he believes him to be insane; and the reasons for this decision to my mind are exceedingly strong.

It is generally acknowledged by the profession that the subject of insanity is not so well understood by themselves as it should be. The great body of the profession are not well instructed in the principles that underlie the investigation of difficult cases of insanity. Now, it is of the utmost importance that the whole body of the profession should interest themselves in this subject; and if it is taken out of the hands of the general practitioner, and placed in the hands of a selected few, their interest certainly will be very much diminished in studying such cases as fall under their notice. Another reason why a general practitioner should be well posted is, that they are required to treat for a certain period of time cases which come under their care. He should be acquainted with the preliminary symptoms of insanity, because they first come under his observation, and we are obliged to gather the early history of the case from him. In the third place, the general practitioner, if he be the family physician, will not only know the general state of health of the person under observation, but he will know something of the hereditary influences. He will know something of the causes which led to the accession of insanity. I would therefore be inclined to recommend that, whatever new regulations were found necessary, the family physician should be one who should join in investigating the case and in making the affi avit.

With regard to the second physician there may be a reasonable question. I am inclined to think, from the study that I have given this subject, that it would be better if the second physician were a recognized expert in the subject of insanity, and appointed by some such authority as would show that he was a real expert, and had a knowledge of the subject, and power to prosecute an investigation of this character in a proper manner. As the law now stands, if I am not very much mistaken, the co-operation of the second physician is of very little importance—very little use. As the law now stands, the family physician does all the labor of the examination—he gives his opinion, and the second physician, at least I have known many such cases, signs the certificate. He has formed his opinion from the statements and opinion of the family physician, who is supposed to know more about the case than any other person. But if the second physician were an expert, if he had the necessary knowledge, and if the necessary responsibility were imposed upon him by his filling some legal status in the matter, and had the necessary powers (I will explain shortly what I mean by this), I really believe many advantages would ensue. 1st. In so far as regards education of the great body of the profession in those principles that underlie the investigation of cases of insanity, it would be a positive advantage to them. Then in the 2d plan, if the consulting physician or expert would point out the proper method of investigation, so that when the next case came under his observation, the general practitioner or family physician would be better prepared to study that case than before. So, too, the interests of the patient and others would be subserved, and the public would be protected. The second physician, instead of falling into the error into which I am sure he does fall in very many cases, would be exceedingly careful during the whole of his examination, and in the making up of his opinion regarding the case. I referred to certain powers which the second physician, the expert, commissioner, examiner, or by whatever name you choose to call him, should have conferred upon him. I refer to the taking of testimony, and of examining and compelling the attendance of witnesses. He ought to have power to place these persons under oath, and take their testimony. And so, too, he ought to have the power to compel the attendance of other witnesses who might know the symptoms of the case, so that he would have it in his power to satisfy himself that he has brought all the evidence possible on both sides of the case.

In conclusion I would say that these are my own individual conclusions. I have not consulted the experts who have looked into the question.

The Chair—I was about to suggest a suspension of the debate on this subject, and take up the paper of Dr. Peugnet, but before doing so, I would be glad to hear from Dr. Brown, of the Bloomingdale Asylum, on the subject.

Dr. Brown—I fail to see the point upon which you have been kind enough to rest any claim from me of an expression of an opinion upon this subject. I have not the honor of being a member of your Society, and have only occasionally attended your meetings. I came to-night to observe how this subject impressed the members of your own profession rather than my own. There is a diversity of opinion existing in your Society, where I supposed a community of feeling would prevail.

The first question in connection with this whole subject which strikes one is as to the necessity of such a bill as Mr. Prince has introduced into the Legislature this year, and previous years. I can understand why he is so sensitive on the subject of forcible incarceration of citizens not insane, and I consider it the province and duty of the Legislature to protect the personal liberty of citizens in every proper manner. But immediately the question arises, whether any ground exists, whether we have any reason to suppose that such protection is necessary to be insured by new laws, and upon that there seems to be a general difference of opinion between the two professions.

Speaking from my own experience, which embraces a residence and service in four different institutions for the insane, and reaching now over a period of twenty-five years of service, I say without hesitation that I am unable to see sufficient reason existing for the enactment of such new law as is proposed. The cases cited as rendering such new law necessary are really very few. A few years ago Dr. Mitchell, of Brooklyn, was unfortunate enough to express an opinion in a case that the man was insane, in conjunction with another physician, and the man was placed in the County Lunatic Asylum of Kings County. He subsequently brought an action for libel. There were three trials; in the first the plaintiff succeeded in obtaining a verdict; but finally the Dr. gained his case on a ruling that he could not be deemed guilty unless an improper motive was proven.

Now, as Dr. Parsons has already said, this question presents itself in the light of what is best for the subject of the disease. And, first of all, is insanity a disease? And if it be a disease, a physical disease; and if it is believed to exist in the individual, who are the proper judges? To be sure, the question, in many instances, becomes complicated with secondary ones in which the law itself is invoked to determine, and the law always refers this matter to a jury of laymen, and considers them competent to judge. But, in the vast majority of cases, they do not reach that point, but must be left to the physicians; and the query arises, who are to be the physicians, or whether the disease is in existence, and what is the treatment necessary? Many believe the question cannot be better determined than by the present law. In my own experience I can recall, certainly, not half a dozen cases where the affidavits have been improperly made; and, therefore, I hold that the reason exists for alteration in the law—in my own mind, and in the minds of many members of the bar.

Another question is, how are these physicians to be paid? Are they to be paid by the Government, by the Board of Supervisors, or in the form of experts?

A vast majority of the insane are poor people; and of these a large majority are what we class as paupers. Most of the city and county asylums are filled with the indigent, and those who fill those institutions are supported at the public expense. I think, if this bill is passed and adopted, in a few years people will appreciate—the counties certainly will appreciate the greatly increased cost and taxes consequent upon such an arrangement as is proposed.

Then there is another thing: The law of New York, to-day, is the most stringent law in the Union upon this very subject of insanity, and there is no other State which requires the sworn affidavit of two physicians. In many States they are satisfied with the certificate or statement of a mere relative. And, within a few years, the State of Rhode Island has made its laws more stringent for the purpose of securing the early treatment of such patients. Mr. Prince states that the bill did not pass last year because physicians of the institution with which I am connected opposed it. It is true that I went to Albany, at the request of a Senator, to state my opinion regarding the probable operation of the law; but it so happened that the committee had decided adversely, and they did not desire any expression of opinion from me, for which I am very glad.

Dr. Brown also said, regarding the attack which had been made upon the Bloomingdale Asylum by a *Tribune* reporter, that the reporter has said in the presence of two governors of the asylum and himself, and he had also documents to the same effect, that the statements made in his paper (the New York *Tribune*) were false, and did the Institution great injustice.

Dr. T. B. M. Cross—It seems to me impossible for a physician, after making but one or two visits, to give an opinion regarding the insanity or sanity of a patient. He of course derives a great deal of information from a physical examination; but he will, perhaps, derive a great deal more from the attending or family physician. There are cases of insanity in which it is very easy to make out a diagnosis; but there are cases, again, which would tax the skill of the most learned expert. It seems to me, that if it be found necessary to alter the law relating to insanity, you could not do better than to permit the family physician to be one of the examiners, in conjunction with one or two other gentlemen who have had experience in insanity,—and the smaller the number of these commissioners the better, because it is very objectionable for families to have a large number of physicians to make examinations in cases of this character.

"THE MEDICAL JURISPRUDENCE OF THE STOKES CASE."

The President stated that he supposed that nearly all remembered that Dr. Peugnet read a paper on the medical jurisprudence of the Stokes case, a few months since, which excited a good deal of interest. Dr. Peugnet divided his monograph into—you observe in the volume. First he made a succinct and careful history of the case of James Fisk, Jr.; then he went into an elaborate description of shock; then he applied his definition to penetrating gun-shot wounds of the abdomen; then he considered the physiological and toxical actions of morphine; and finally, he considered the medical jurisprudence of the Stokes case, and *claimed* that the facts as shown demonstrated scientifically,—1st, that the shooting of Fisk was not done in self-defence, but with premeditation; and, 2d, that the wound in the abdomen was not necessarily fatal, and that the morphine was the immediate cause of death.

To this paper I now invite your attention, and call on Dr. Hammond.

Dr. Hammond—I must confess that I am quite surprised at being distinguished in the manner that I have been this evening, by being called upon to open the discussion of so important a paper as we have before us for consideration, when we have so many learned gentlemen, representing both the legal and medical profession, present with us. I have had a copy of the monograph bestowed upon me, but am sorry to say that I have not had an opportunity to peruse it, consequently I can say but little more than indorse the views of the author in regard to the cause of the death of Colonel James Fisk, Jr. I have felt much interested in Dr. Peugnet's paper; he has made bold assertions, and as I recollect the paper as presented to this body last December, he sustained them in the most scientific manner; by so doing, the medical profession of the world incurred a debt of gratitude to this learned gentleman, which I feel they will not fail to promptly acknowledge. I knew Col. Fisk in my early boyhood; he was the only son of worthy parents, who lived in close proximity to the home of my youth, in the old historic town of Bennington, Vt. On the night of January 6th, 1872, I was with Mr. Fisk's father, who was depressed and overwhelmed with grief, in anticipation of fatal results from the wound his son had received.

I consoled the old gentleman by telling him his son was surrounded by the best medical and surgical talent that our city could boast of, and that I hoped that the means that they would devise for the restoration of their patient would be blessed with success. I could say much in regard to personal observations that I made at the Grand Central Hotel, etc., on this evening, but I know I would not be in order. Therefore I drop the subject relating to personal interest, and return to the one relating to science. We know that

Col. Fisk had received a severe penetrating wound of the abdomen; from the objective signs and symptoms, we might naturally expect death to promptly issue from shock or internal hæmorrhage, but as death did not issue from either of these causes, we would naturally expect recovery, and treat the patient with such anticipation in the case, and if recovery did not issue from proper treatment, the only mode of death we could expect would be the same as occurred in the Richardson and Vallandingham cases—Peritonitis and Septicæmia, and that could not occur short of forty-eight hours or longer.

The sworn testimony rendered on the trial of Edward S. Stokes shows that 3½ gr. of morphia, equivalent to 21 gr. of opium, or 28 doses of morphia were given to Col. Fisk, hypodermically and otherwise, within the space of three and a half hours, and when we come to consider that from ⅛ to ¼ of this drug is the ordinary dose when indicated, and that prudence requires that we should not, under ordinary circumstances, duplicate the minimum or maximum dose until after the lapse of four or six hours; and that the autopsy revealed the fact that Fisk died from neither of the causes I have stated—we must, therefore, in the present light of science, and in all honesty, come to the conclusion that Col. James Fisk, Jr., came to his death from the injudicious administration of morphine (3½ grs., 28 doses having been given within the space of 3½ hours), independent of the wound he received from the bullet that was hurled from the pistol of Stokes. In this case we admit local shock, which paralyzed the absorbent powers of the stomach, and allowed 2 grs. of morphia to remain within it inert, until [illegible] grs. more were given hypodermically, which lighted up a flame that burnt out the life of one of the most noted characters of our continent; the death of Fisk, under these circumstances, is one of the most unfortunate reflections that could fall upon the medical profession of the United States; but, as much as we regret it, it is not without its lessons in science.

No physician of to-day will instruct his student to administer morphia by the stomach in similar cases to this or any case; but the more judicious method of hypodermic administration will be taught and used.

Dr. Charles A. Leale stated that, as the President had called for an expression from him, he should like to mention a fact apparently escaping the observation of those who had made comparative statements in regard to the character of the wound received by the late Mr. Fisk, viz., the size of the missile, which was a pistol ball, weighing only 2¼ drams; while, in those recorded instances cited, where recovery followed intestinal wounds, taken from the records of wars, the perforations were made by much larger missiles, viz., the round leaden ball, the irregular-shaped explosive ball, and the Minnié ball, which must have necessarily produced (other things being equal) more extensive laceration of the walls of the intestines—*ergo*, were much more dangerous wounds. Dr. Leale stated that all who had performed colocentesis well knew, that a small trocar can be passed into the intestines for the exit of flatus; that on withdrawing the instrument, the musculer fibres would contract in such a manner as to completely close the opening; that not the slightest inflammation followed, and that at the necropsy no trace of a wound could be discovered; and this he believes actually oftentimes follows the perforation of a portion of the bowel by small pistol shots; or where larger openings are made, an immediate plastic exudation occurs, sealing the laceration, until circumscribed inflammation and adhesion of surrounding tissues follow, to complete the cure. Again, Mr. Fisk, at the time of his death, was a man in remarkably good health, as was so clearly proved at post-mortem examination; while most of the instances occurring in army life were in soldiers whose constitutions had become very much impaired by chronic diarrhœa, malarial fevers, fatigue, etc.

Dr. R. R. McIlvain—Before I proceed I should like to ask Dr. Peugnet the number of perforations which were made in Fisk's intestines? I am not able to learn that.

Dr. Peugnet, after consulting his monograph, said four of the small intestines, two of the large; six perforations of the intestines, and fourteen of the peritoneum.

Dr. McIlvain—Well, sir, Mr. President, I will state as Dr. Buck stated, that I would not consider it possible for him to recover after receiving an injury of such an extensive character. Such a case could never recover. We have no such case in Christendom or Mohammedanism to demonstrate that he would. There is nothing in the profession to indicate that a man with a number of perforations in the large and small intestines would recover. If it is charged that the physicians killed him, then the man (Stokes) ought not to be incarcerated in prison. He ought to be at large.

Dr. C. S. Wood—I did not have the pleasure of listening to the paper, and have not read the pamphlet as printed, but knowing that this question was coming up I took the liberty of bringing along with me very brief notes of three cases of gunshot wounds of the abdomen, which I will read:

Sacramento, Cal., *Feb.* 16, 1864.

Sir,—Enclosed please find report of a few cases, which, having come under my direct observation and under my care, I transmit with as full particulars as possible, hoping they may be of service, at least in a statistical point of view, and controverting the long-established doctrine that all cases of penetrating gunshot wounds of the abdomen are necessarily fatal; although I agree that an unfortunately large proportion prove to be.

Case 1.—Thomas Murphy, Sergt. 63d Reg. N. Y. V., wounded at battle of Gettysburg. Minnié ball entered left iliac region, passing directly through abdominal cavity, emerging above crest of right ilium, about three inches from the spinal column. Saw him twenty-four hours after receiving the injury; found him very prostrate; feeble pulse; cold, clammy skin; vomiting, etc., with fecal matter escaping from both orifices. He was placed in a comfortable position, with cold water applied to the openings and the free administration of opiates and stimulants, all the while supposing the case would prove fatal in a few hours. Next morning more comfortable; stimulants withdrawn, as some reaction had taken place; beef-tea, with full nourishment, with two grains of opium every two hours, which was almost the only remedy administered during a period of ten days, only that he did not take so large a quantity after about four days. The bowels were not moved until after the ten days had expired, when an enema of oil and turpentine was given, after which he continued to improve as before, until at the expiration of three weeks, when the anterior opening had closed by granulation, and from the posterior one nothing escaped but an occasional flatus, which opening soon united. He had been walking about for the last week; bowels had become regular, and every indication of a perfect recovery.

Case 2.—Daniel Banta, Lieut. 66th Reg., N. Y. V., wounded at battle of Gettysburgh. Minnié ball passed through fleshy part of right arm, just below shoulder, entering chest obliquely and laterally passing across the body, but downwards and backwards, penetrating base of right lung, diaphragm, and intestines in its passage, and emerging on the left side, just below the false ribs and about midway between spinal column and superior ant. spinal process of the ilium; had vomiting and involuntary evacuations, the latter continuing several days; sputa bloody and rust-colored; fecal matter escaping through abdominal orifice; right arm paralyzed from injury of the nerves by the ball, which paralysis has remained to a partial extent for several months. Treatment, perfect quiet, with large doses of opium or morphine, two grains of the former or ¼ of the latter every two hours. This treatment was continued for a period of two weeks, at the end of which time he was able to sit up a little in bed, after which his convalescence continued, although very slowly. Has since returned to his regiment, unable to do any duty, but enjoying a comfortable state of health.

Case 3.—Lewis E. Mosely, private, 61st regiment, New York Volunteers, wounded at the battle of Gettysburg, by ball entering below umbilicus, to the left of the linea alba, passing directly through abdominal cavity, emerging posteriorly on the left of spinal column, accompanied by a profuse discharge of fecal matter from both openings with the peculiar fecal odor; symptoms—great prostration, feeble fluttering pulse; cold, clammy sweat, cold extremities, constant faintings, with all the symptoms of immediate approaching dissolution. Opium and stimulants were freely administered, simply with a view to relieve his sufferings; under their influence he rallied slightly, and on the fourth day a natural fecal evacuation occurred, mixed with both fresh and coagulated blood. Peritonitis did not supervene; the wounds gradually closed by granulation, and on the thirteenth day had sufficiently recovered to be removed to the General Hospital at Baltimore. August 20th, the wounds are entirely closed; the patient is walking about, and considers himself well enough to again resume his duties.

All of which is respectfully submitted.

C. S. Wood, Surgeon, U. S. V.

I simply read these cases, continued Dr. Wood, as matters which may possibly bear on the subjects arising out of the Stokes case, and to show that punctured wounds of the abdomen are not necessarily fatal.

Dr. Peters—There are one or two points which strike me very forcibly when looking over this subject. In the first place, I was surprised to see how little shock there was after Fisk received the wound. He was enabled to walk up stairs. Then he went through the torture of making his will, and had a long talk upon very important business subjects, and was apparently only slightly under the influence of medicines. After he came under treatment I was struck with the rapidity with which he became unconscious after the first dose of morphia was given. I think the hypodermic injections were administered with rather undue rapidity. I am inclined to doubt whether Mr. Fisk would have recovered under any circumstances.

Dr. Alonzo Calkins spoke of the large amounts of opium which the system is able to endure. He has given half grain doses every ten or fifteen minutes, until he had obtained decided action with good results. One case, where a man did not sleep for three days,—the Dr. was determined he should sleep. He therefore gave him opium every ten minutes, until he had given him eight grains in one hour and one-half.

Clark Bell, Esq.—Did he ever wake?

Dr. Calkins—Yes, he did, and in twenty hours, and in a much improved condition.

Mr. Riddle, after a few preliminary remarks, moved that the following be referred to the Executive Committee, which was so ordered.

Conclusions and suggestions from Dr. Peugnet's paper, read before the Medical Legal Society February 27, 1873, entitled Medico-Legal Toxicology:

It would therefore be advisable, in all cases of suspected poisoning, to act upon the presumption that the nature of the poison is unknown, unless the data are clear and unequivocal; for the *ipse dixit* of the medical jurist should have no more weight than circumstantial evidence with the legal chemist, if the latter wishes to base himself on grounds which the *legal acumen* of the counsel, aided by a sound knowledge of medical jurisprudence, will not strike from under him, destroying his reputation as an analytical chemist, leaving him and the debris of his analysis as incongruous a mass as the wall which falls under the blows of a pick.

The medical jurist and chemist of the present day, by becoming votaries and exponents of science, incur an additional responsibility. Every mistake they make is cast up against their science, which is making giant strides towards positivism. Moreover, they cast an unjust, an unmerited reproach on their professional brethren. The medical expert, whether he appears for the prosecution or the defence, owes it to his profession, to his brethren, to testify according to his honest convictions; his answers ought to be categorical if possible. In other words, he should act as *amicus curiæ;* by acting otherwise he prostitutes his profession.

The *ex parte* investigations, such as were conducted in the Wharton-Ketcham trial, ought not to be tolerated in criminal cases. It casts a taint, a suspicion of over zealous partisanship on the proceedings.

Nor should the Coroner's ex parte post-mortem investigation be permitted. Not that I would cast a reflection on any of the gentlemen he might select to conduct the investigation, but the law allows the accused to produce witnesses in his own behalf on every point save this; it is unjust, and might be the cause of a legal murder. Schœppe would never have been convicted on his first trial if the investigation had been conducted in the presence of a sworn expert, representing the interests of the alleged murderer, acting as *amicus curiæ.*

Therefore, as a representative of my profession, I respectfully recommend to the consideration of your Honorable Society, the propriety of petitioning the Legislature to pass a law covering this point, which might be the means of saving an innocent person, and would, *à fortiori*, lead to the conviction of the criminal. In making this appeal to you, I feel that I am advocating the cause of justice, and the cause of humanity, for I am not the only member of my profession who believes that one or more criminals, alleged criminals, have been executed on insufficient medico-legal investigations. Moreover, it would spare us the renewal of such indelible stigmas on the administration of American Criminal Law, as the Schœppe, Wharton-Ketcham, and Wharton-Van Ness trials.

The Society then adjourned.

Editor's Table.

THE PUBLIC HEALTH.

A change of clerical help recently has subjected us to some mistakes in estimating the ratio of mortality, which we hope to avoid in the future. We are aware that the ratio of increase of population in some of our cities since 1870 has been greater than for the last preceding decade, by reason of the war; and, in a few, as in the case of Pittsburg, by the annexation of populous neighborhoods. But, as a rule, we believe the ratio of increase from 1860 to 1870 to be a reliable guide to present populations. Where this is not the case, our health correspondents would confer a favor on us and on each other by accompanying their reports with explanations.

New York—Estimated population, 1,040,000. Deaths, week ending May 30, 484; annual ratio per 1,000, 24.20. From zymotic diseases, total 107; annual ratio per 1,000, 5.20; consumption, 84; diphtheria, 23,—and, apparently, as prevalent in brown stone houses as among the lower order of dwellings. If the well to do are living over defective house drains and untrapped waste pipes, or if there is any other hidden source of blood poisoning, the cause, whatever it may be, should be sought out and the remedy applied without delay. It does not speak well for sanitary research that this disease should be so prevalent, especially at this season of the year. Small-pox, is also, prevailing disgracefully, about twenty-five cases weekly, and eight deaths, for the week ending May 30, extending over various parts of the city. Cases are promptly visited as soon as reported, and vaccination gratuitously offered. But there are many persons so ignorant of the virtues of vaccination as to prefer small-pox. The past experience of the Health Department, and the present prevalence of this disease, very justly stimulates impatience at the delay of Governor Dix in affixing his signature to the vaccination bill, which has been so long awaiting his approval. It is poor economy which counts the cost of preventive measures of such a pestilence. Bad odors still prevail over the eastern portion of the city, and the efficient Assistant Sanitary Superintendent is at present devoting his attention to this nuisance. We trust he will not desist until the cause is found out and effectually abated.

Brooklyn—Estimated population, 450,000. Deaths, week ending June 6, 164; annual ratio per 1000, 18.73. On ratio of increase,

1860-70, 438,338; per 1,000, 19.45. Diphtheria 6; cerebro-spinal meningitis, 1; consumption, 23.

Philadelphia—Estimated population, 775,000. Deaths, week ending June 6, 264; annual ratio per 1,000, 17.71. On ratio of increase 706,170; per 1,000, 19.42. Typhoid fever, 6; Small-pox, 3; consumption, 35.

Chicago—Population 356,000. Deaths, week ending May 16, 103; annual ratio per 1,000, 15.34. Small-pox, 2; Diphtheria, 2; consumption, 13.

Boston—Population, 270,000. Deaths, week ending May 23, 146; annual ratio per 1,000, 28.11. Typhoid fever, 3; cerebro-spinal meningitis, 2; consumption, 36.

New Orleans—Population, 199,000. Deaths, *four* weeks ending May 24, 482; annual ratio per 1,000, 31.48. Small-pox, 74; consumption, 61.

Baltimore—Population, 284,000. Deaths for week ending June 8, 131; annual ratio per 1,000, 24. Typhoid fever, 5; consumption, 14.

San Francisco—Population, 178,000. Deaths for the month of April, 299; annual ratio per 1,000, 20.23. Zymotic diseases, 46; typhus and typhoid fevers, 6; diphtheria, 7; consumption 40.

Pittsburg—Population, 133,000. Due to annexation, besides ratio of increase. Deaths for May, 238; annual ratio per 1,000, 21.47. Typhoid fever, 3; meningitis, 16; consumption, 32.

Charleston—Population, 52,000. Deaths, week ending May 2, 38; annual ratio per 1,000, 38.

Richmond—Population, 65,000. Deaths, week ending June 6, 23; annual ratio per 1,000, 18.40.

Dayton—Population, 34,000. Deaths for May, 52; annual ratio per 1,000, 18.35; consumption, 10.

Paterson—Population, 38,000. Deaths for May, 68; annual ratio per 1,000, 21.47; consumption, 14.

Milwaukee—Population, 80,000. Deaths for May, 162; annual ratio per 1,000, 23.05. Typhoid fever, 4; typhus, 2; diphtheria, 4; consumption 12.

Providence—Population, 75,000. Deaths for May, 163; annual ratio per 1,000, 26. Typhoid fever, 2; diphtheria, 2; consumption 17.

England—Rate of mortality of large towns, for 1873, per 1,000 of population: Portsmouth, 18.04; Norwich, 21.05; Edinburgh, 22; London, 22.05; Sunderland, 22.08; Bristol, 23,01; Nottingham, 23.-02; Hull, 23.09; Leicester, 24.04; Bradford, 24.07; Birmingham, 24.9; Wolverhampton, 25.1; Dublin, 25.07; Oldham, 25.08; Sheffield, 25.08; Leeds, 27.06; Glasgow, 29.01; Salford, 29.03; Manchester, 30.01; Newcastle-upon-Tyne, 30.01.

Paris—Population, 1,851,792. Deaths, week ending April 24, 934; annual ratio per 1,000, 26.22. Typhoid fever, 9; consumption, 178.

BIBLIOGRAPHY.

A Manual of Public Health for the use of Local Authorities, Medical Officers of Health, and others. By W. H. Michael, F. C. S., Barrister-at-Law; W. H. Corfield, M. A., M. D., Oxon.; and J. A. Wanklyn, M. R. C. S. Edited by Ernest Hart. London: Smith, Elder & Co., 1874.

Although this Manual appears to be especially designed for English admistration—adapted to the Local Government Board, and the local boards of health subordinate thereto throughout England—it is, notwithstanding, a Manual on health administration of unusual comprehensiveness of detail, applicable in this country no less than in England.

"Those who are called upon to carry out duties connected with the Public Health Act of 1872, have to deal with subjects involving three separate kinds of knowledge—legal, medical, and chemical . . . Hence the origination of this Manual, in which I have had the advantage of the collaboration of three able and well-known authorities."

The part of the editor has been to arrange and supervise the work; the matter is by the three well-chosen authorities, whose names are given in the title.

Part I. treats of the general scope of sanitary laws, the powers and duties of sanitary officers, and their relation to local authorities, laying special stress on competency to understand the duties imposed, as in all cases essential to efficacious administration. Roads and ways, sewers, water supply, public and private lighting, nuisances, and general surveillance—are all cogently presented in their medico-legal aspects, by one thoroughly versed in the important relations they bear to the main issue, the preservation of health. For the exercise of the functions required under these several titles, much more is required than the mere passport to the practice of medicine—the conventional M. D. *It* conveys little or no knowledge of how to make a differential diagnosis of nuisances, sewers, water supply, soil saturation, and many other subjects of great importance in the etiology of disease and the preservation of health, but not yet included in the college curriculum.

Part II. comprehends the routine practical duties of sanitary officers in relation to refuse matters, water carriage, water supply, epidemic diseases, overcrowding, ventilation, inspection of trades, etc. It is hardly necessary to say that, however strict the laws, definite the rules, or rigid the discipline, sanitary administration is often fraught with great difficulty and great delicacy—requiring extraordinary tact as well as skill for its effectual exercise. People generally, and particularly those who most stand in need of sanitary surveillance, are peculiarly sensitive on the indulgence of conditions and influences in conflict with health; they often regard the inquiries of sanitary officers as intrusions on personal rights; they claim the right even to be sick, if they will, without interference; and even more—to make their neighbors sick, if their neighbors get in the way, or do not stand clear of their own personal indulgences, trades, properties, and maladministrations. But it would be a great mistake to suppose that these characteristics are limited to a class of people in constrained circumstances, bounded by the necessities of a family pig or goat. Far from it. The bare suggestion on the part of a sanitary inspector to a school trustee that disease is caused and accelerated by his inattention; or to a wealthy tenement-house owner that some one has sickened and died in consequence of overcrowding —no matter how mildly these insinuations are made—ten chances to one, the said inspector will be told to attend to his own business; "this is my affair!" And the said inspector, in some cases, may deem himself fortunate if his insinuation has not set in motion a train of influences to supply his place with some one whose chief qualification is political subserviency. Sanitary officers will find many valuable suggestions on delicate subjects to handle in this part of the work, and much information in small compass on the general routine of sanitary work, and the various methods of preventing the spread of epidemic diseases. Water supply, overcrowding and ventilation, and the inspection of trades are treated as leading subjects, and in a way well calculated to be of benefit to health inspectors. There is some unnecessary repetition of Part I. in Part II., which, in a future edition, it would be well to omit.

PART III.—Water, Air, Milk, Butter and Cheese, Flour and Bread, Beer and Wine, Tea, Sugar, and Disinfection are considered *chemically*; their composition under varying circumstances stated, and the knowledge applied to questions of health in a way which makes the information of great value to sanitary officers, not, to our knowledge, so concisely or conveniently stated elsewhere. We heartily commend the book to all sanitary officers and others interested in the promotion of health.

RECEIVED.—*Murray's Observations on Cholera; Gorton's Principles of Hygiene; Education of American Girls; Science of Homœopathy; Autobiography of Edward Wortley Montague; Wondrous Strange; Kate Kennedy; Medical Problems of the Day, etc.*

THE SANITARIAN.

A MONTHLY JOURNAL.

VOL. II.] AUGUST, 1874. [NO. 5

ON THE CONCENTRATION AND SANITARY REGULATION OF THE BUSINESS OF SLAUGHTERING IN CITIES.*

By Stephen Smith, M. D.

One of the first questions which sanitary authorities, newly organized in our cities, have to meet and answer is:—"How can the nuisance created by the ordinary slaughter-house be most effectually abated?" The conclusion which is generally reached is, that a stringent ordinance will remedy the evil, and, accordingly, the opinions and purposes of the Health Authorities are embodied in the form of an ordinance, somewhat as follows:

"That every butcher, leasing or occupying any place, room, or building where any cattle have been, or are killed or dressed, or where any cattle may be kept, and having power and authority so to do, shall cause such place, room, building, stall and their yards and appurtenances to be thoroughly cleansed and purified, and all offal, blood, fat, garbage, refuse, and unwholesome or offensive matter to be therefrom removed, at least once in every twenty-four hours; and shall, also, at all times, keep all wood-work, save floors and counters, in any building, place, or premises aforesaid, thoroughly painted or whitewashed."

But it is found by painful experience that in spite of this declaration the nuisance continues; that, in fact, this carefully worded and high-sounding ordinance proves to be but a tuft of grass thrown at the offenders. It is resolved next to enforce this ordinance by prosecution, or arrest, or by both methods. These proceedings possibly secure *more* care on the part of the butcher, but they do not in any proper sense abate the nuisance. During certain portions of the day the yards are covered with liquid ordure, the walls are bespattered with filth, the drains are choked with refuse matters; and however thorough the cleansing may be, the walls, floors and areas become so saturated that during the remaining portion of the twenty-four hours the whole establishment reeks with foul odors in the summer sun.

After a protracted struggle with this nuisance, stimulated by public censure, it will prove a fortunate circumstance if the health authorities reconsider their action, and adopt a policy more in accordance with the dictates of good sense and of wise sanitary administration.

The slaughter-houses of any city must be placed on the same basis as the markets, so nearly are they related to the public health. The

*Read before the Public Health Association of New York, June 11th, 1874.

business has always been recognized as offensive, and on that account amenable to municipal regulations. But there is a far more important sense in which they should be regarded as subject to special control, viz.: as the medium of food-supply to the people. Considered in their two-fold influence upon the public health, *first*, as sources of filth, and *second*, as liable to furnish impure meats, health authorities should exercise the most rigid supervision in regard to the details of their management. How can such supervision be most advantageously exercised? We answer:—by the concentration of the business in well-appointed abattoirs. These establishments should be so located, constructed and conducted as to secure the utmost degree of cleanliness, and the most direct and complete oversight by sanitary officers. We may thus state the advantages of concentration:—

1. *Facilities would be afforded for the thorough inspection of cattle and meats.* It is of the first importance as a sanitary measure that there should be ample facilities for the intelligent inspection of the cattle to be slaughtered, and of the meats to be exposed for sale in the markets.

The temptation to slaughter diseased cattle in large cities is very great, and the opportunities offered are abundant when the business is entirely unregulated, and free from the surveillance of competent sanitary officers. In every city where no restrictions upon the trade exist, there is a class of men who deal in diseased cattle and meats. In the cattle yards they purchase the sick, lame, or injured stock, and in the markets they select the rejected meats, and then retail this unwholesome refuse of the slaughter-house to the poor.

To guard the people against the imposition of diseased meats, the best regulated foreign cities require the careful inspection by expert officers of every animal brought to market. All obviously diseased cattle are sent to the offal yards, and the suspected are detained in yards or stalls for observation. All the meats offered for sale in the public markets must have a previous inspection. In this manner the people are protected from even the liability of receiving unwholesome meats.

But no sanitary inspection worthy of the slightest confidence can be maintained over the meat supply of our markets while the present scattered, unregulated, and practically unlicensed system of slaughtering is continued. Cattle suffering any and every form of disease may pass unnoticed and unchallenged to any of the slaughter-houses, and the carcass may go thence to the market without hindrance.

The only practicable and indeed possible method of instituting an adequate system of cattle and meat inspection is the concentration of the business in large and well-regulated abattoirs. The very incorporation of butchers in such companies, leads to the expulsion from the business of those irresponsible dealers who live by a sort of contraband trade. But the great sanitary feature of the proposed regulation is the rigid inspection of cattle and meats which may be so successfully carried out.

2. *Abattoirs properly conducted, tend to the purity and preservation of meats.*

Fresh meats afford, during the warm summer months of the year, a fertile soil for the development of the germs which arise from decaying or decomposing matter, vegetable and animal. The germs, are of course, the most abundant where there is the largest amount of organic matter. When implanted on fresh meat, at a proper temperature, they at once begin to develop, and the meat undergoes putrefactive changes. In certain localities, meats cannot be preserved in the summer, except on ice, for even an hour. And it is susceptible of demonstration that meat slaughtered in filthy stalls and exposed to the emanations of unclean yards, areas, drains, etc., quickly takes on putrefaction. If we add to this exposure the filth of the slaughter-houses, the additional exposure to the filth of the street, as the cart is driven to market by the butcher, we have the best conditions that could be devised for furnishing the people of any city with unwholesome meats. That such a meat supply is detrimental to the health of the people, there is no doubt. The effect of inoculating a wound, as a cut on the lip, with meat in this stage of putrefaction, is most dangerous, often resulting in violent inflammation and speedy death.

But in the abattoir, we have these conditions changed. All is scrupulously clean; the air is untainted by decomposing organic matter of any kind; the meats are hung up in a cool dry atmosphere.

3. *The large surface area occupied by the business would be diminished to the least practicable space, and the entire territory occupied could be preserved in a much greater state of cleanliness than that of any one of the single establishments now in use.*

It has been taken for granted by some people that if all the slaughter-houses should be concentrated in one establishment, this single establishment will become as many times more offensive as there are slaughter-houses so concentrated. This view is not only absurd, but practically the reverse is true. If, for the loosely paved yards, the imperfectly drained areas, the absorbent floors, etc., of existing slaughter-houses, widely scattered, we can substitute a single yard with impervious bottom, susceptible of being thoroughly flushed at all times with water—a building with non-absorbent floors, and equally capable of rapid and thorough cleansing, it is apparent that large and filthy areas now reeking with ordure in the summer's sun, and floors saturated with animal matters, would be entirely removed, and the substitute would be a single limited area, at all times kept thoroughly clean, and buildings free from contamination.

4. *Concentration of slaughtering will abate the nuisance of fat-melting, hide-curing, gut-cleaning, and other offensive kinds of work growing out of the business.*

Not the least of the evils arising from the maintenance of numerous slaughter-houses, are those kinds of offensive business, like fat-melting, which are its adjuncts. These trades are carried on by independent operators on their own premises, and always in a most slovenly and negligent manner. The butcher is likely to retain his fat until it becomes putrid, and then it is carried through the streets to the dilapidated fat-melting house where it is rendered with imperfect apparatus; the hides are cured by another small and irresponsible dealer in any old building which he can secure; the entrails, in a state of active putrefaction, are taken by still another dealer through the city to any dilapidated rear building where the workmen can be concealed, and there they are manipulated for days together.

It is frequently urged by those opposed to the abattoir system that there is not sufficient available space in cities for the proper management of the business if it is concentrated. This question has been practically studied recently by Mr. Carl Pfeiffer, sanitary architect with reference to the concentration of the slaughter-houses of New York. From the data which he gives the necessary calculations can be readily made as to the space required for the business of any town. He concludes as follows:

"The space usually allotted to a butcher in most of the slaughter-houses of this city, for killing and hanging cattle, is called a baulk, and occupies a floor space of 10x50 feet, exclusive of yard-room for the temporary storing of the live cattle; for the latter purpose additional space of 15 or 20 square feet is allowed for each animal. One set of butchers in the smaller establishment usually kill and prepare ready for market on an average 25 beeves per day; to kill and dress one bullock ready for market requires 20 to 30 minutes.

A space of 15 feet in width affords ample room for two baulks, and making each baulk 60 feet deep, would give slaughtering and hanging room for 40 cattle per day; add to this a space of 15x40 feet to be used for a pen, in which the cattle are placed previous to being slaughtered, would give room for 40 to 50 cattle. The space usually allowed for this purpose I have found to be from 11 to 15 square feet for each animal. It appears then that in a space of 15x100 feet ample room is afforded for slaughtering, hanging, and yarding 40 cattle. A block of ground 200x400 feet would afford facilities for slaughtering, hanging, and the necessary pen or yard space of 4,000 cattle per day, or nearly three times the capacity that is required by the butchers of this city during any day for the past year.

At the slaughter-house of the Central Stock Yard and Transit Co., at Jersey City, I found that a space of 15 by 80 feet was required for yarding, slaughtering, and hanging 50 cattle per day. The same company in a space of 300 by 400 feet, afford accommodation for the reception, feeding, and watering of 20,000, and the slaughtering and hanging of 5,000 sheep, so that it is safe to assume that in a space of 200 by 300 feet 5,000 sheep can be daily yarded, slaughtered, and hung up, which is more than is required by all of our butchers in this line of business. During the past year the daily average of sheep-slaughtering in this city has been 3,300, so that in the same space sufficient room would be left to do all slaughtering of calves required. This, the sheep and calf slaughtering, is mostly done in the second stories. For hog-slaughtering a space of 1,312 square feet is required for a tub and bench for one set of slaughterers, and 2½ square feet of hanging room for one hog; if the baulks for hogs are made in double tiers, one above the other, then two hogs can be placed in a floor space of 2½ square feet. One set of hog-slaughterers usually kill and dress 200 hogs per hour, and, five hours being their working time, one set of men deliver 1,000 hogs per day, or one-fourth of the number of the entire daily supply furnished by all the butchers. Assuming then a ground space of 200 x 350 feet for a hog slaughtering-house two stories in height, the upper floor to be used for yarding and killing, the lower for dressing, weighing and hanging; the upper floor containing 70,000 square feet, and each hog requiring less than 7 square feet, there would be room for more than 10,000 hogs. Assuming the lower floor to have a central space of 60 by 350 feet, room would be afforded in this for 16 tubs and benches, and 16 set of slaughterers. On each side of this central space would be 70 by 350 feet of hanging room, capable of having 400 baulks; each baulk being 70 feet deep, would afford hanging room for 42 hogs, and the 400 baulks would hold 16,800 hogs, or more than four times as much as required by all the hog-slaughterers of New York.

The above demonstrates that all the slaughtering of cattle, sheep, and calves required by the slaughterers of New York can be done in a building 300x400 feet, and the hog-slaughtering in a building of 200 x300 feet. These buildings could have basements where there would be ample room for the salting of the hides and collecting all offal. A building of 100x100 feet, 8 stories in height, and a basement fitted up with the most approved apparatus would be sufficiently large to admit of the fat-melting and rendering being done for all of the slaughterers' offals. In addition to the meat supplied by the New York butchers, the Central Stock Yard Co. slaughtered at their abattoir at Jersey City for the New York market during the past year, 200,000 cattle, 300,000 sheep, and 600,000 hogs, and from personal observation and survey I have found that this abattoir is worked to less than one-half of its capacity, and could do all the slaughtering to supply the demands of the New York, Brooklyn, and Jersey City markets.

The abattoir also demonstrates that in a large establishment the slaughtering is more readily supervised, and the whole business done more systematically and more cleanly; in fact, so cleanly that nothing offensive is perceptible, owing to the superior sanitary precautions that have been taken in the construction and the constant enforcement of proper regulations, which experience has proved almost impossible to enforce in a large number of small establishments scattered over a great part of the city."

In the light of the preceding discussion we can but conclude that the interests of the public health demand that the business of slaughtering in all our American cities should be concentrated at the most available point for cleanliness and economical management, in one or more abattoirs according to the necessities of the trade. The common slaughter-house is a nuisance against the public health (and public morality) which should be abated wherever it exists.

BOILED HAMMERS.—Old Dr. Twitchell, of Keene, once wanted to blister some one in a farmhouse, far from home. He had nothing with him to do it with. He asked his wife to find him a hammer. The article was brought out, put in a teakettle over the fire, and after the water steamed and bubbled well, he lifted it out and gently touched it to his patient in a half dozen spots, over the seat of pain, with very positive effect. Boiled hammers were, for many years, used in that neighborhood for pleurisy; and every old lady knew nothing was equal to a hammer, and there was a long dispute whether it should be a claw-hammer or not. The yeas finally conquered.

MENTAL CULTURE.*

BY NATHAN ALLEN, M.D., LL.D.

In the advancing knowledge of physiology it has been discovered that all mental culture should be based upon the brain—that education should be pursued in harmony with the laws of life and health, and that where these are violated, the advantages of the former afford poor compensation. Formerly no attention or scarcely any, was paid by school boards and teachers, in the matter of education, to the condition of the body or the development of the brain, and even at the present day very little is paid them, compared with what should be given to those great physical laws which underlie all mental culture. The lives of a multitude of children and youth are sacrificed every year by violating the laws of physiology and hygiene, through mistaken or wrong methods of mental training; besides, the constitution and health of a multitude of others are thus impaired or broken down for life. Nowhere else in society is a radical reform needed more than in our educational systems. Inasmuch as the laws of the body lie at the foundation of all proper culture, they should receive the first consideration. But in educating the boy or girl, from the age of five to fifteen, how little attention is given to the growth and physical changes which necessarily occur at this most important period of life! The age of the child should be considered; the place of schooling, the hours of confinement and recreation, the number and kinds of studies, together with the modes of teaching, should all harmonize with physical laws—especially those of the brain.

The system or mode of treating, in education, all children, as though their *organizations were precisely alike*, is based upon a false and unnatural theory. Great injury, in a variety of ways, results from this wrong treatment; in fact, injuries are thus inflicted upon the sensitive organizations and susceptible minds of young children from which they never recover. That many of our most independent and clear-headed educators themselves express so much dissatisfaction with the working and results of our schools, affords evidence that something is wrong in the present system. As we contemplate the great improvements made in education for the last thirty or forty years, and are surprised that educators were content to tolerate the state of things then existing, so will the next generation, when still greater and more radical changes shall have been introduced, look back with astonishment at this generation, and wonder that it was so well satisfied with its own methods. When our educators become thoroughly convinced that physical development as a part of education is an absolute necessity—that a strict observance of the laws of physiology and hygiene is indispensable to the highest mental culture, then we shall have vital and radical changes in our educational system; then the brain will not be cultivated so much at the expense of the body, neither will the nervous tempera-

* From the Annual Discourse before the Massachusetts Medical Society, June 13, 1874.

ment be so unduly developed in proportion to other parts of the system, now so often bringing on a train of neuralgic diseases which cannot easily be cured, and exposing the individual to the keenest and most intense suffering, which all the advantages of mental culture fail, not unfrequently, to compensate.

The more this whole subject is investigated, the more reason we shall find for making allowances, or some distinction in scholastic discipline, with reference to the differences in organization of children, and for adapting the hours of confinement and recreation, the ventilation and temperature of school-rooms, the number and kinds of studies, the modes of teaching, etc., to the laws of the physical system. But another and still more important change must take place. Some time—may that time be not far distant--there will be a correct and established system of *mental science*, based upon physiological laws; and until this era arrives, the modes and methods of education must remain incomplete and unsatisfactory. The principles of this science, in the very nature of things, must rest upon a correct knowledge of the laws and functions of the brain; and until these are correctly understood and reduced to a general system, all education must be more or less *partial*, *imperfect* and *empirical*. While the old theories of metaphysicians are very generally discarded, they still have practically a powerful influence in directing and shaping our educational systems and institutions. In the selection and arrangement of studies very little attention is paid to the peculiar nature or operations of the various faculties of the mind, or the distinct laws that govern their development and uses. For illustration—instead of educing, drawing out, and training all the mental faculties in their natural order and in harmony, each in proportion to its nature or importance, the memory is almost the only faculty appealed to in every stage of education; and this is so crammed and so stuffed that frequently but little of the knowledge obtained can be used advantageously. Instead of developing the observing faculties by "object teaching," appealing to the senses of sight and hearing, those two great avenues of knowledge, or giving much instruction *orally*, we require the scholar to spend most of his time in studying and poring over *books*, mere *books*. The mind is treated as a kind of general receptacle into which knowledge almost indiscriminately must be poured, yes, forced, without making that knowledge one's own, or creating that self-reliance which is indispensable to its proper use. In this way the brain does not work so naturally or healthily as it ought, and a vast amount of time, labor and expense is wasted—nay, worse than wasted. From this forced and unnatural process there often results not only a want of harmony and complete development of all parts of the brain, but an excessive development of the nervous temperament, and not unfrequently an irritability and morbidness which are hard to bear and difficult to overcome. And not unfrequently it ends in a permanent disease of the brain, or confinement in a lunatic asylum.

When we take a careful survey of the various discussions and diverse theories on this subject, considered metaphysically, and then compare them with the great improvements and discoveries in the physical sciences for the last fifty years bearing upon the same subject, the change or progress looks mainly in one direction, viz., that all true mental science must ultimately be based upon physiology. Here is a great work to be performed, and when accomplished it will constitute one of the greatest, most valuable and most important achievements that was ever wrought in the history of science. A vast amount of positive knowledge has already been accumulated on this subject by various writers, but a great work, by way of analysis, observation and induction, and of further discoveries as to the functions of the brain, remains to be completed. This work must be performed in a great measure by persons profoundly versed in the physical sciences; and no small proportion of it must come from the observations, labors and contributions of medical men.

"Do you Live Over the Shop?"—It has never occurred to any life office to include this among the questions on its proposal paper. Indeed, at first sight there would seemed to be no reason why it should be so included. Fresh air is a good thing, complete change is a good thing also, but these blessings may be purchased too dearly. Going out of town means in the majority of cases sham repose, it means hurrying up the close of business to get away, it means worrying up in the morning to catch the train, it means in many cases far more railway riding than is good for any man, affecting the nervous system, and it is now proved the eye-sight, not only from the temptation to read, but from the mere whizzing past of objects in rapid flight; it means generally more excitement, more nervous agitation, more work for the heart, and higher pressure on life than is consistent with health and longevity. All differs from the calm, placid lives of the business men of the past. Business, it may be answered, is different to what it was in the old days, is more harassing and more trying than what it was. So it is; and, admittedly, the necessity for repose is proportionately greater. The question is whether we have hit upon the right expedient for securing that repose, whether our villas twenty or thirty miles from town, our houses by the sea-side, and our summer holidays, in which we seek rest by scampering over the continent, and woo repose in railway journeys of thousands of miles in length, are the sort of thing to compensate for the extra strain on our energies. Medical men are beginning to agree that they are not, they are beginning to set their faces more and more steadily against our out-of-business expedients, and recognize the fallacy of our pet notion of locking up our cares and anxieties in an iron safe. They know that the active mind only enacts over again the story of the man who fled from the ghost but carried it away with the furniture, that it simply drags at every move a lengthened chain, and that to the physical excitement must often be added the agitation of being away from business. All things considered, then, it becomes a question whether in insurance a distinction should not be drawn between resident and nomadic business men, and whether after all it would be either superfluous or inexpedient to add to the proposal matter—"Do you live over the shop?"—*London Insurance Record.*

Prussia has nearly 400 associations for the improvement of the soil by drainage, irrigation, and the building of dykes.

PROCEEDINGS OF THE N. Y. MEDICO-LEGAL SOCIETY, APRIL 23, 1874.

The President, Clark Bell, Esq., in the Chair.

MORBID IMPULSE.

At a regular stated meeting of the New York Medico-Legal Society, held at the College of Physicians and Surgeons, corner Twenty-third Street and Fourth Avenue, upon the above date, Prof. William A. Hammond, M. D. read a paper entitled, "Morbid Impulse," after which the following discussion ensued:

The President, after congratulating the speaker upon the admirable manner in which the theme had been treated, thus placing the matter before the public through the New York Medico-Legal Society, hoped that a subject of so much importance would draw from both members and others an expression of sentiment worthy of the occasion. He saw before him men who had thoroughly studied morbid impulse, and whose minds were consequently richly imbued with ideas relating to the question: men who had performed no small part in affairs pertaining to insanity, whose opinions had been listened to in courts of justice and elsewhere with that deference to which matured judgment entitled them, whose experience was worthy of consideration and respect. In view of these facts, and also because the plea of morbid impulse had been set up as a strong point in the defense of malefactors, both in this and foreign countries, it ought to receive a full and free discussion. He would therefore call upon Dr. Parsons to open the debate.

Dr. R. L. Parsons—I was not fortunate enough to hear the beginning of the paper just read by Dr. Hammond, but suppose that I have heard the greater portion. The natural history of morbid impulses, as given in the paper, accords as far as I was able to notice, with that given by most writers on the subject, so that little remains to be said on that point.

There are some points, however, that seem to merit further discussion, one of which is the great difference that exists between different individuals in regard to susceptibility to morbid impulses. While the mental organization of some persons is such that whatever impulses they may feel are always entirely within their control, the mental equilibrium of others is so unstable, or their power of self-control is so deficient, that their actions are easily determined by their impulses. In other words, their impulses are liable to become morbid. Of those who show other evidences of insanity nothing need be said. Their general condition is usually such that morbid impulses are to be expected and excused. Morbid impulses are especially liable to occur in epileptics, whether there have been other manifestations of insanity or not. Of this important fact no mention was made in the paper read by Dr. Hammond.

Dr. Hammond—Yes there was. I referred particularly to that.

Dr. Parsons—This must have been before I arrived. There is nothing more then to say on that point; save to corroborate Dr. Hammond's views.

Dr. Hammond—I distinctly excluded cases occurring in epileptics and restricted my cases to those in which there are no other evidences of insanity but morbid impulse.

Dr. Parsons—In those cases in which morbid impulses are the only evidences of insanity, it should be noted that the insane temperament usually exists; that there is a predisposition to insanity, either hereditary, congenital, or acquired. With a predisposition to have morbid impulses there co-exists a diminution of the normal power of self-control. All men have at times an impulse to do things which they ought not to do, but the great majority have the power to resist the impulse. They have the normal power of self-control. Their impulses cannot be considered as *morbid.* If through the influence of disease or of a defect in organization a person have an increased liability to act impulsively, with diminished power of self-control, his morbid impulses may be excusable, either wholly, or in part. His impulses may be such as of themselves to furnish very strong evidences of the existence of insanity.

There is another point to which I will refer; that is the responsibility of a person who has had morbid impulses, and who has subsequently committed an illegal act under the influence of a similar impulse. If I understand Dr. Hammond correctly, he expresses the opinion that if such person did not take proper measures to prevent the commission of the act to which he was impelled, he would in the event of its commission be equally culpable, both morally and legally, as though there had been no morbid impulse. From what I have already said regarding the nature of morbid impulse, I think it will be evident that my own opinion does not quite coincide with that expressed by Dr. Hammond. Since the existence of a morbid impulse is in itself an evidence of mental defect; acts committed under such an impulse must be less culpable than similar acts committed without the influence of a morbid impulse. The fact that the diseased party knew of his impulse to do wrong, would not restore the full measure of his responsibility, for it must be remembered that the existence of morbid impulses implies a diminution of the normal power of self-control of the governing power. If the governing power be diminished the ability to take the preventive measures required must be diminished also. This diminution in *ability* should be taken into account in the administration of the law in such cases.

Reference was made by Dr. Hammond to the influence of habit in rendering normal impulses morbid in character. In this also he is undoubtedly correct. The frequent recurrence of an emotional state may produce such profound and persistent cerebral changes as to cause a well-marked attack of insanity. It should not be inferred, however, that a person who thus becomes insane is fully irresponsible for his insane acts, because he might have controlled his passions or his impulses at a former period, and thus have prevented the final result.

Dr. Meredith Clymer—As Dr. Parsons has remarked, there is little to add in the way of fact or illustration to Dr. Hammond's essay.

The subject of morbid impulse covers a wide field; but as I understand the purpose of the essay, and of this discussion, it is to consider and determine the responsibility of an individual possessed of a dominant depraved idea. This question is a very nice as well as a very important one. It may be said that a great proportion of crime, or at least of vicious acts, is the effect of morbid impulse. That is, there is a condition present in which a strong and dominating desire is felt to do an absurd or unlawful act, and a pleasurable sensation is experienced in doing it, or on its accomplishment. This state may prompt an insignificant or absurd peccadillo, an eccentricity, as well as the highest crimes. It is of moment, therefore, in the aspect which I assume we are looking at the question this evening, that the term morbid impulse should be accurately defined, that we should have a clear notion of what we mean by it, and that it should be discussed strictly within the limits of that definition.

There are, I suspect, few present who at some period or another of their lives have not been under the influence of some dominating idea, which reason forbade, and which it was very difficult to get rid of, or not to put in action. Of this sort is the sudden desire to jump off a height, or to throw one's self into a fast-running stream, or before a coming rail-train, and of like kind is the sudden prompting to say or do something absurd or wrong. Dr. H. R. Bigelow, of the Retreat at Hartford, Conn., in a recent article on "Morbid Impulses" has mentioned an instance of this kind personal to himself. At the funeral of a relative some ludicrous idea excited in him a desire to laugh; he tried for some time to resist it by attempting to call up thoughts appropriate to the occasion. He sat, he says, for awhile on a rack of unrest, the perspiration hanging in drops upon his forehead; but all in vain. Laugh he must or go mad; and laugh he did, just as the corpse was raised by the body-bearers; nor did the impulse seem in any way lessened in power by the horror-stricken faces around him.

I recollect some years ago being at the opera with a musical friend. I noticed that during the performance he took no interest in what was going on; he seemed absent-minded and absorbed in himself. He answered any remark I made to him shortly, and did not seem to wish to be disturbed. His whole behavior was odd, and entirely different from his common conduct at such times. Later in the evening, I asked him what was the cause of his singular behavior. In reply he said, "Did you see that bald-headed man in a seat a few rows in front of us?" I answered that I did. "Well," said my friend, "do you know, from the moment my eyes lighted on that head, that I had an irresistible impulse to smash an egg upon it? I did my best to listen to the music—to get up another train of thought. I would look at the audience, try to follow the music, but to no purpose; my eyes would go back to that bald, shining pate, and the desire to smash an egg upon it was the dominating thought. I could not get rid of it. I am sure if I had had an egg that I should have done the deed." I might mention many other instances of like kind, either within my own experience, or which have been published. You may all remember the case of the clergyman who had to repeat the Lord's prayer in the church service, and who after the sentence, "Our Father who art in Heaven," could not go on until he had said, "and let him stay there."

But we find a class in which the impulse is of a more serious nature; and which incites to the commission of various criminal acts, including self-destruction and homicide. It is claimed for such that they have lost the power of self-control, and are therefore legally irresponsible for their acts. And there lies the gist of this question. The point to be settled, is, whether in any such case there is total loss of self-control; and if admitting that there may be, to ascertain when it happens; when it can be considered as a proper plea in abatement of responsibility. If I understood Dr. Hammond rightly, he excludes from legal responsibility lunatics and epileptics. And yet the general tenor of his essay, it seems to me, is in the contrary direction. While I largely agree with him as to the ability of many, perhaps most persons, to restrain their criminal impulses, and consequently admit their responsibility, still it strikes me that Dr. Hammond's proposition is too general, and its application too unreserved. Dr. Parsons thinks that the degree of punishment should be graded to the degree of ability of the individual to control his acts; thus implying different degrees of the power of controlling impulse. Dr. Hammond would exclude from the benefit of at least mitigating circumstances those who, as Dr. Parsons said, were unquestionably suffering from lessened will-power, and who were, at least at some time, unable to exert a sufficient degree of will to resist an impulse which they knew to be criminal, and which with this knowledge, they may, at another time, have successfully combated.

Dr. Hammond says that he would except from accountability such as were acknowledged to be insane. Now, sir, as to such as are acknowledged to be insane—will the lawyer here always agree to call a person insane whom the practical alienist would unhesitatingly recognize as of unsound mind? There is, it seems to me, an irreconcilable difference between the two professions on fundamental points regarding this subject. Shall we accept the definition of what constitutes insanity, as given by the English judges after the McNaughten case, and which now is the law in England? This authoritative exposition of the rule of law which is to be applied when the plea of insanity is interposed by the defense in criminal cases, is now the law of this State by a recent decision of the Court of Appeals, in the Flanagan case, reported in 52, New York. Our judges are bound by it. Should we be governed by such an ill-founded, and unscientific, and contracted standard, great injustice would be often done. Many persons suffering from a diseased mind will be held accountable for their acts, and punished for them; for in these there may be no delusion present; and they may have full consciousness of the act done, and knowledge of its quality; and yet they have been forced to commit it by, as they believed and felt, a fatal necessity. An individual in such a condition may talk understandingly about the deed before its committal, reason upon, dread the doing of it, have a horror of it, be aware fully of the consequences, and desire to avoid it, have struggled long, and for awhile successfully, against its committal, and yet finally have the will-power overwhelmed by the impulse, and be driven irresistibly to do the act he would avoid if he could. Dr. Hammond does not seem to believe that any impulse is irresistible, even in those of unsound mind; that in every case there is a way to strive against the impulse.

In this view he will, I think, find practical alienists to agree with him. Yet he qualifies the impulse he treats of as morbid; and as it is a mental act, its existence, the acknowledgment of such a mental state, concedes the fact of disease. Now, sir, the law as it now stands in this State as applied to the defense of insanity in criminal cases, will hold persons, as I have just stated, to accountability for their acts, and, as I believe, in many cases, most unwarrantably so, and in direct violation of our statute. We know that epileptics are especially liable to commit acts of violence, of criminal violence, under the effect of sudden and often, perhaps, irresistible impulse. The same may happen in the puerperal state. While Dr. Hammond, as a physician, might recognize the mental unsoundness in those cases, the law of the Court of Appeals in many instances might and would not. If there should be no delusion present, if there was consciousness that the act was wrong, then the judge is obliged to tell the jury that the accused is responsible, and cannot avail himself of the protection of the statute, though every practical alienist would declare him to be suffering from mental disease. Such is the effect of the adoption of the stupid tests of insanity as laid down by the English judges.

I agree with Dr. Hammond that in many, very many instances, it is within the ability of the individual possessed with a dominant depraved idea to control it, or recognizing it that he should place himself where he will be unable to give it effect. It is an evidence of disease, like any other abnormal symptom, and Dr. Hammond by using the prefix "morbid" admits this. But if, failing from ignorance or negligence to do this, the impulse should become absolutely irresistible, I do not see why he should be punished. In such a state he would unquestionably be of unsound mind, the impulse would be an insane one, and such a person in such a state is unquestionably entitled to the protection which the statute gives him when he is a victim of mental disease.

Dr. Abraham Jacobi—I am not a member of this society, neither am I an expert in these matters, and certainly did not expect to speak upon this subject. But if you will permit me to make a few remarks, Mr. President, the first would be that I hardly know what point to discuss. There appeared to me to be, from what I heard of Dr. Hammond's essay, two distinct parts: 1st, the natural history and a complete *exposé* of morbid impulse, and 2d, morbid impulse in connection with the law. If I understand the law correctly, it weighs out a certain amount of punishment for a certain amount of damage done to public morals or to the safety of human society. But in dealing out the law it is understood that the same justice should be considered, the same principle should apply, as in commercial enterprises, in which a certain sum of money is paid for a certain amount of merchandise purchased. I may be incorrect in this, but it has always struck me as justice. If this is true, if the law deals out a certain amount of punishment for certain amount or degree of crime, there must arise a question, and that question is, Whether there is a justification of a criminal act in the existence of impulse, normal or abnormal? When I heard Dr. Hammond's paper it appeared to me that he would arrive at a different conclusion from that at which he did arrive. It appeared to me a paper as of the humanitarian; as a paper of a physiologist it would appeal not so much to the so-called justice as to the greatest possible amount of leniency for all those who have the great misfortune to be subject to a morbid impulse. It appeared to me as if the doctor wanted to explain and by explanation to excuse.

Now the point of view from which I consider this question is in my opinion a correct humanitarian point of view. I am of the opinion that there will be a time in the future when all these things will be taken into consideration, and when our laws will be very different from what they are now. The law of the future will be governed not so much by the principle of the jurist, as of the physician.

As far as the question of morbid impulses goes, we ought to compare them with normal, healthy impulses, in order that we may see in what they differ, or how far they agree. Take, for this purpose, the case of a little child; you place in its hands a doll-baby; he plays with it, examines it, and after examining it a long time externally, he thinks he would like to see what is inside. He takes off the dress, he pulls out its eyes, and after awhile he takes off its head, and thus he proceeds until the doll is destroyed. Now what is this? It is a morbid impulse, with a certain injury done, not to society in this case but to its own object of amusement. This is the beginning of a morbid impulse. It is the formation of or development of a morbid habit, and operates to a great extent as a teaching of that habit; and whatever takes place in the young individual takes place in the grown person afterwards. When we speak of the functions of character or of the brain or intellect, or if we speak of psychical functions, we meet with two kinds. Intellectual functions on the one hand, and emotional functions on the other. When the intellectual functions are not very well developed we have simply idiocy or stupidity, ignorance, etc. When a person is ignorant, stupid, and does harm to himself, he is responsible to himself only, and bears the consequences. When he does harm by his ignorance to society at large, he is made responsible. Now take the same insufficiency of development, on the other side of the question, of the emotional functions. If he does harm to himself he is responsible to himself, that is, he must shoulder the consequences of his doings. If he does harm by reason of insufficiency in his emotional functions, the responsibility is his as long as he harms anybody else. He is morbidly emotional. We know that the more brain there is in an individual the less morbid impulse there should be. Physiologically speaking the less brain the more reflex action. When we remove the brain of an animal and irritate the surface, the reflex action, the involuntary movements will be more powerful than they are in health; also the less the brain is developed the more reflex action on the emotional side. The explanation generally given, that the emotional side is better developed, is more practised.

I should include not the insane alone, whom Dr. Hammond would hold responsible, but I should also include those so-called emotionally insane, the kleptomaniacs and kindred classes of monomania, unless they can be shown distinctly not to be responsible, that is, as having the symptoms of some form of genuine insanity. I have never for a moment been able to believe in temporary insanity. Whenever there is an act committed which is shown to be an insane act, that insane condition must have been encroaching upon the victim as a disease for some time. I do not deny that there are now and then cases of insanity which only exhibit themselves in what are considered to be morbid impulses. These mistakes in diagnosis will sometimes be made: but mistakes are made every day. But I believe it would be much safer to make such a mistake now and then than to run the risks which are occurring every day. Therefore I believe the chapter on insanity and morbid impulse in the books should be modified to a certain extent.

Dr. Hammond—I am glad to see that my friend Dr. Jacobi has taken an *impulse* to join in the sentiments held by myself in this respect, that this morbid impulse occurring in individuals, is liable to spread by suggestive imitation in a very epidemic sort of way. Most of the examples that I have cited went to show that this could be resisted. If we go to work and punish these people, we do a great service to other people. We should not only look at the persons who have morbid impulses, but we should also look to society. I believe in dispensing the greatest good to the greatest number. I would not hesitate at all to hang a man, if he is proved to have committed a murder. If he was fully conscious of an impulse in that direction, and if he had struggled a reasonable length of time against that impulse, he would have conquered. A man who pleads an impulse for the first time, who kills instantaneously, I would not hang, but put under permanant restraint. If not, he may kill others. Now take this case of the man from Arkansas who wrote to me, (and which I refer to in my paper), if he had yielded to that impulse, and killed the child, I would put him under restraint for the rest of his life. And if he had disregarded my advice, and killed his child, I would have gone to Arkansas to help to hang him. This man wrote to me in consequence of having read a report of a debate on insanity, published in the N. Y. *Sun*. He knows full well to what he is subject; he knows that he has an impulse to kill his child. If he does it, he ought to be punished to the full extent. He is not insane. Would you plead moral insanity in his case, and let him go? No! Society has some rights as well as these people with morbid impulses. We know full well the force of example. Every man who commits a crime has an impulse; if he has not he would not do it; and many have impulses and resist them. That should have no more extenuating force with a jury, than the excuse of the man who could not help appropriating another's money. If for self-gratification he commits a crime, he ought to be punished for it. I think there is a great deal of sentimentality displayed in regard to the punishment of people who are of no kind of use to society. I would not hang them all, but would put them out of the way. I am not prepared to say that I am in favor of hanging people. I would put them in charge of Dr. Parsons, and hold them in reserve in the Penitentiary or asylums built for such persons.

As a judge remarked in England, to a poor devil who stole sheep, I am not going to have you hanged for stealing sheep, but that other people may not steal sheep.

Dr. Parsons—It didn't have the desired effect.

Clark Bell, Esq.—The paper of Dr. Hammond is a very able paper, and as suggested by Dr. Jacobi, it discusses the subject in a terse and admirable manner.

Now when a man goes into court and is put upon trial by a jury, upon an indictment, the question of responsibility arises, which Dr. Hammond evidently invites discussion upon: What can be done with him, what measure of responsibility should be attached to a case of morbid impulse? Every man who commits a crime must have had to some extent an impulse, morbid or otherwise, controlling his action. He must have a temptation to induce him to commit the act. Is there a case in this world, or will there ever be any case, where a man conceded not to be insane, conceded to have perfectly healthy actions of mind, capable of understanding and controlling his actions in every respect, knowing the right and wrong of every act, having a full knowledge that he is doing wrong where such a person should not be held responsible? I think not, for these things are questions of law. That is to say, as I understand it, it has been held by the judges of England, and by our own courts, that when the person was fully conscious of the wrongful character of his act, knew that it was wrong, was of normal condition, so as to enable him to correctly understand and distinguish between right and wrong, and had a perfect and free will, if he had chosen to exercise it, but who yielded to a morbid impulse, he should be held responsible. This question of responsibility is the one to which your attention is called.

Now, in the various discussions here on kindred questions, physicians are apt to arrange themselves on one side, with the same difficulties as present themselves here—rather feeling a regret that the existing law might be too severe, and that the paper may not be humanitarian in its character.

If a man has a morbid impulse upon him, so strong that he cannot resist it, there is a question. If a man has an emotion or irresistible impulse to commit a crime against another that he cannot resist, that is a question which I think will stagger the judges, as it did those upon the English Bench. But in the ordinary cases that are presented to the Courts, there is very little question of the guilt of the accused.

Dr. Clymer:—Dr. Hammond has given us several instances within his own experience where, in one at least, there had been previous unsound mind and confinement in an asylum, where the unnatural impulse had been conquered. I would ask him if he would, in a case I will now relate, have employed the same procedure.—A young married woman had exhibited symptoms of insanity for several days, with a strong tendency to self-destruction by throwing herself from a window. One afternoon, sitting with her husband, who had just returned to town, in the absence of the nurse, she complained of the heat of the room, and requested her husband to raise a window at the other end of the room. The window had been fastened down, and while he was fruitlessly trying to raise the sash, she quickly threw open the window nearest her, and flung herself out, and was instantly killed. I would further ask him, if in Dr. Skae's case, mentiond by Dr. Carpenter in his recent work on "Mental Physiology," as a type-case of the homicidal form of impulsive insanity, and which Dr. H. has quoted, whether he would hold such a person responsible? There was no delusion or hallucination; there was a simple abstract idea to kill, taking a specific form, by strangling; there was perfect knowledge of the quality of the act. There was no perversion of ideas, but only an impulse to do what the individual knew to be wrong. If Dr. Hammond should hold her not accountable, the present law of this State would. The practical alienist, in daily intercourse with the insane, meets with such cases constantly, who are as much the victims of mental disease as the most furious maniac, and as little able to control their impulses or their actions.

I do not wish to be understood as advocating the irresponsibility of all such as may have a dominant, depraved or criminal idea. But I do think that we should have some clear notion on the subject, and have some rule, or test of responsibility. I cannot understand yet what class Dr. Hammond would exempt from the consequences of their acts. He has just said he would send such to his friend, Dr. Parsons, to be taken care of, or to some institution proper for their treatment; and that he would hang such, or help to hang them. By the first statement he admits them to be of unsound mind, and by the second, criminal and responsible. As I have said this evening, I largely agree with him in my belief that many cases of morbid impulse can, by proper treatment and discipline, get rid of their depraved ideas, and that in many the dread of certain punishment will hinder its indulgence.

These criminal impulses are often due to imitation. The deterrent effect of a degrading punishment has been most happily shown by the stop which has been put to attempted assaults with firearms on the Queen of Great Britain, since the passage of the flogging act. Since the offence was made a disgraceful one, punishable by whipping, there has been no attempt properly referrable to depraved impulse. In a paper I had the honor to read before this Society several years ago, on "The Legal Responsibility of Epileptics," I related a case then under my observation, in which the ability, in an epileptic boy, to control the morbid impulse was well shown. Where the impulse is unquestionably the offspring of a diseased mind, which prevented the exercise of due volitional power, and where there was strictly no criminal intent, such should be accounted irresponsible. It is, after all, the power to do or to forbear. I own it is a difficult point, often, to decide, but the fact of the difficulty should not compromise a principle or a right, if the latter is properly available. Each case must be decided on its merits, and each should be closely scrutinized.

After a few general remarks by Dr. Hammond, the meeting adjourned.

What Alcohol Will Do.—It may seem strange, but it is nevertheless true, that alcohol, regularly applied to a thrifty farmer's stomach, will remove the boards from the fence, let cattle into his crops, kill his fruit trees, mortgage his farm, and sow his fields with wild oats and thistles. It will take the paint off his building, break the glass out of the windows and fill them with rags. It will take the gloss from his clothes and polish from his manners, subdue his reason, arouse his passions, bring sorrow and disgrace upon his family, and topple him into a drunkard's grave. It will do this to the artisan and the capitalist, the matron and the maiden, as well as to the farmer; for, in its deadly enmity to the human race, alcohol is no respecter of persons.—*The Temperance Worker.*

TYPHOID FEVER AND SANITARY ADMINISTRATION.*

By John M. Fox, Medical Officer of Health to the Cockermouth Union, etc.

(Continued from page 161.)

The conclusion, then, that I would draw is this: that in the present state of our œtiological knowledge we are not justified in supposing that positive typhoid excreta are necessarily to be looked for in an outbreak of typhoid fever; on the other hand, that decomposing excrement of man or animals, allowed to remain exposed to atmospheric influences near a dwelling, may be productive of that disease in a virulent and fatal form. This, I take it, is the "working theory" on the subject, to which our powers and our practice should be made conformable.

If, however, a scientific theory be sought for the views which cases otherwise not easily explained have forced upon me, it may possibly be found in the fact that animals—pigs, notoriously—suffer from typhoid fever; and in the recent researches of physiologists under the direction of the medical department of the Privy Council, M. Villemin, as quoted by Dr. Burton Sanderson, lays claim to an important pathological discovery, namely, that tubercle is a zymotic disease. This suggestion deserves the most careful consideration, and, in relation to the associated diseases of animals, may throw light upon the present inquiry. Thus M. Villemin groups together phthisis, typhoid fever, and farcy, pointing out that their resemblance is not only found in the phenomena observed during life, but in the anatomical changes which, in these diseases, have their principal seat in the lymphatic system. He adds also that bovine phthisis prevails mostly among cattle that are confined and over-crowded, circumstances that point to air-poisoning, and which also favor the hatching of typhoid fever. Dr. Weldenburgh also states, as quoted in the same report, that in rabbits and guinea-pigs inoculated with tubercle, Peyer's patches are found to contain large ulcers. This may be the case in cattle with farcy, or lung disease, or low fever. If so the detritus from these ulcerated patches will find its way into the farm-yard, to be thus exposed, with other excrement, and become an occasion of air or water pollution of a specific character. Here, then, we may have, under favoring condition of the atmosphere, the source of veritable typhoid poisoning. Ground, I conceive, is therefore afforded for the following suggestions.

1. That it may not be amiss for sanitary observers in rural districts to have regard to the health, the housing, and the general condition of animals, in the investigation of obscure outbreaks of typhoid fever in farm premises. 2. To urge physiologists, with the facts previously stated before them, to push the inquiry as to what diseases in animals may be associated in special chemistry, or local lesions, with typhoid fever in the human subject. 3. That of course, in this inquiry, Peyer's patches should be made very particularly the subject of special research.

In conclusion, I have only to state the provisions and powers which

---

*Public Health, January, 1874.

the foregoing consideration of the cause of typhoid fever would indicate as necessary in order to secure successful sanitary administration in regard to this most serious zymotic affection. The maxim seems admirably simple, so simple that the wonder is, that with all our costly sanitary machinery, there should still be so much typhoid fever, as there is so much of its cause, among us. To restate the law in Sir Wm. Gull's words, it is, "to get rid of the filth is to get rid of the fever." Is this an end inconsistent with modern enlightment or modern civilization? Will any one be found to plead for a little prolongation of the era of filth exposure? Will any one, in the face of notorious facts asserted in this paper, be insane enough to urge that a too prompt and vigorous action in this matter can be mischievous? Or can it be believed that our "glorious constitution" is too weak to enforce, or our legislators are possessed of too little sagacity to be able to devise a proper but firm and unbending course of procedure in this matter? If so, our boasted triune authority, in the interest of preservation of the race, is a sad failure, and we might be better provided for under a grand "motherly government." The evil is sufficiently appalling, and the remedy is as strikingly simple and effectual. Let the following considerations be pondered.

1. It may excite a smile if I go back to Moses for the leading principle in this case. The smile however will be repressed, if we consider that the Author of our nature spoke through Moses in the words which I am about to quote. "And thou shalt have a paddle; and it shall be when thou shalt ease thyself abroad, thou thalt dig therewith, and shalt turn back, and cover that which cometh from thee." Whatever havoc modern exegesis may have wrought in regard to old, ill-sustained notions of the chronology of Scripture, it has never, so far as I am aware, found Scripture untrue to nature; and I maintain that the words just cited contain a principle true for humanity in all time, devised by Him who thought better of his own handiwork than modern spiritualists take heed of, and fenced about its preservation in health and vigor, with countless directions and severely penal restrictions. Witness the isolation and the pulling down the very house of the leper. The principle of the removal out of sight of dead organic matter, I maintain that no individual can violate without peril, and no nation can allow to be set aside without national loss and deterioration. Is it beneath a human, Christian Legislature,—not to re-enact the very words, but—to reaffirm the principle of a Divine mandate? The daily offence indeed must daily be shed, and, in modern language it must, in the interest of public well-being be at once removed, hidden, or disinfected.

2. The ultimatum of modern civilization will show us the end to be aimed at in this social difficulty. I have said that Scripture is ever in harmony with nature. What, then, is the method which nature in its highest cultivation has adopted? The answer is unquestioned, the water-closet system; by which, automatically, the excreta are at once hidden and removed far away. This is the resource of wealth and refinement. But what I am anxious to point out, is that in all that concerns public health, whatever arrangement may be necessary for the rich is more urgently necessary for the poor. The rich are scattered,

and have many resources, and an educated instinct in regard to noxious matters. The poor on the other hand are crowded together, have no resources, and have instincts sadly untrained or misguided, or inert about such things. But public health and the ravages of typhoid must ever be kept in view, constraining us never to give up until we have obtained an alteration in the habits and appliances and even sensibilities of the masses of our population in this respect.

3. Do I recommend the water-closet system for universal adoption? By no means. I have already pointed out in this Journal, that, however theoretically perfect, it has many practical disadvantages. But for the poor it is often too costly, and in villages inapplicable.

4. The existing law has already made some movement in this direction, but more apparently with a view to decency than health. By the 51st and 54th sections of the Public Health Act of 1848, extended to the district of every sewer authority, by the 4th section of the Sanitary Amendment Act of 1868, and further extended to the area of every sanitary authority, urban or rural, by the 8th section of the Public Health Act of 1872, it is enacted that no house shall be built without sufficient water-closet, or privy, or earth-closet, (31 & 32 Vic. c. 115, s. 7.) and that such privy shall be kept so as not to be a nuisance. But what can an uncleared privy be but a nuisance, or a small local cesspool for the time being, giving off to the surrounding air all the risk-bearing pollution which it was the object of the Divine precept, and is or should be no less the object of present legislation, to get rid of? In the open privy, void of contrivance of any kind, there is the fatal absence of removal, covering up, or disinfection. Hence the prevalence of smells, and of typhoid fever, and other injurious complaints. A multiplication, according to the requirements of the law, of privies of this kind, may be, and in an epidemic of typhoid is certain to be, only a multiplication of foci of infection.

5. What I contend for is, that the law should go a step further, and render it penal to have a privy so destitute of arrangement that the excrement should be thus uncovered, spreading itself upon, and being washed into, the surrounding soil, and throwing off every moment pestilential, fever-breeding emanations. It should be within the statute to enforce the confinement of the offensive matter, and the disinfection or covering of every daily accession to the contents of the privy. Until this is done, the settled, fixed, and well-proven laws of sanitary science in regard to cholera, typhoid fever, and diarrhœa, find no acknowledgment in the statute-book of our country.

6. This would not be an expensive, a laborious, or irksome task. The dry ash is always at hand for the purpose. I have myself contrived a dust-box and cinder-sifter combined, the use of which involves the daily disinfection of the excreta in the unavoidable act of removing the ashes from the fire, at the same time economizing fuel, and creating a valuable manure. Such a contrivance may be obtained for three shillings and sixpence. But an extension of the requirements of the law would soon produce many economical adaptations of a well-understood principle, which, as I have said, cannot be violated with impunity. It is true that local boards, and vestries, and unions may recommend this

or that system, upon all which the Medical Office of the privy Council has already furnished a report, for the accomplishment of the sanitary treatment of the dejecta of a town or village. But with the *choice* of a system, the permissive nature of the enactment should end. The adoption of *some* system for this purpose should be compulsory upon every town, village and household.

7. It is urged that people will never use the appliance which it may be admitted is desirable. I answer, do people keep their privies so as not to be a nuisance? Let any inspector testify. To what purpose, then, is the statute? It is not a question of facility, but a question of evasion. It is really as easy to cover the dejecta as to keep a privy innocent of injuriousness. The former is, indeed, necessary to the latter. How much more useful and precise would be the report of an inspector! In the former case he would testify to a fact; in the latter he expresses only an opinion. Difficulties will occur in any case, but indefiniteness is a cowardly retreat from them. In so urgent a matter it is desirable that all possible vagueness should be taken from our statute-book. What is the meaning of a privy not being a nuisance? While its contents are uncovered, it is always a nuisance, scattering under no uncommon conditions, already mentioned, the seeds of impoverishing sickness and death. On the other hand, the plan which science demands is clear, precise, and as easily attainable. But what is better, it annihilates diseases of a fæcal origin (so large and fatal a class), and is at once the fulfilment of the law of nature and the law of God.

8. It must never be forgotten that this is not an arbitrary requirement. It is not the whimsical suggestion of delicacy, refinement, or an over-fastidious taste. It is in the interest of, nay, it is essential to, life and health. If it is right, the converse, in being admittedly wrong, is murderous. Let this simple requirement, the daily covering of the excreta, be added to our sanitary enactments, and the habits of the people, unwilling, perhaps at first, will speedily grow up to it. Let Mr. Powell add a definite provision of this kind to his next essay on behalf of our Public Health Law. Sanitary authorities, now multiplied and settling down to work over every acre of England, will be ready to aid its enforcement; and in the recoil of typhoid fever from its baneful pre-eminence among our zymotic complaints, a thankful people will believe that the health and vigor of a nation is a fitting and well-considered aim of an enlightened Parliament.

Cruelty.—"Mother, I am going to die, and when I am no more, I wish the doctor to cut me open, and look at my stomach."

The maternal mind was filled with awful forebodings, and the maternal heart asked what it meant.

"I wish it to be known," he answered, "that I died of starvation."

The small boy is triumphant, and retires to his little bed gorged.

Editor's Table.

THE PUBLIC HEALTH.

Vaccination.—It is with special gratification that we are enabled to announce that since the issue of the July number of THE SANITARIAN, Governor Dix has approved of the act for the prevention of small-pox in New York. Of all the various measures—good (a very few), bad and indifferent which emanated from the recently adjourned legislature of the Empire State, this one is of most interest to the hygienist, and of most value to the public. The new law is entitled—"An Act to secure effective vaccination in the City of New York, and the collection of pure vaccine lymph or virus." By virtue of this act the Board of Health is "empowered to organize a corps of vaccinators within and subject to the control of the Bureau of Sanitary Inspection, to appoint the necessary officers, keep suitable records, collect and preserve pure vaccine lymph or virus," etc. It also authorizes the sale of vaccine lymph or virus whenever the amount collected by the said corps shall exceed the amount required in the proper performance of its duties, the avails of such surplus lymph or virus to be paid to the chamberlain of the city, to be set apart as a distinct fund, and subject to the requisition of the Board in aid of gratuitous vaccination.

This Act affords the Board of Health an excellent opportunity of applying the most effective means of preventive medicine hitherto known to the medical profession, and thereby opens an avenue by which all may escape the fearful ravages of a loathsome disease, a disease which although alike dreaded by the rich and the poor, is at the same time the most easily controlled of all affections which depend upon contagious elements for their propagation. Its tendency is not only to reduce the rate of suffering, sickness, death and bereavement on the one hand or to prevent the remnant of a life being attended with physical suffering and disfigurement on the other; but also to ward off the many other evils which always follow in the wake of a pestilence, especially in a large commercial, manufacturing or laboring community; evils, though of a pecuniary nature, yet deserving careful consideration, and should always be taken into account when estimating the benefit to be derived from the faithful compliance with the requirements of such a law.

In the organization and working of this vaccinating corps, it is important that a proper beginning be made, and that such men be selected

—

and such only, as have already shown, or in some way may show, a peculiar fitness for the duties which will devolve upon them. To be an expert vaccinator, to be able to judge accurately of the quality of a vesicle, to be skillful in the collection of lymph, to be able to judge correctly of the physical condition of the child to be vaccinated, or from whom it is proposed to collect lymph, to be possessed of agreeable manners and good persuasive powers, are all qualities indispensable to him who would become a successful public vaccinator, and when such a person is once installed in office and has shown his fitness for, and faithfulness in the discharge of its incumbent duties, he should never be removed for political reasons, or to make room for personal patronage, as is too common a practice in many of our public departments, although it is gratifying to know that our present Board of Health is uninfluenced by such motives, but will see that public duties of so exalted a character, if faithfully performed, will be duly appreciated and rewarded.

In its efforts to secure infant vaccination throughout the city, the Board of Health will have the advantage to be derived from its own Bureau of Vital Statistics, daily increasing in value as the number of birth reports increases. The vaccination of all reported infants within a reasonable period after birth, can be effected either through the medical attendant or public vaccinator, while the system of house to house vaccination to be inaugurated, with the aid of the various city dispensaries, will probaby reach most of those children whose births have not been reported. Constant effort in this direction will have the effect to prevent the spread of small-pox, and if not to completely eradicate it from the city, to at least confine its operations to a few isolated cases. The benefits to be derived from this work cannot be limited to the large number of lives saved, nor to the still larger amount of physical and mental suffering prevented ; for we must also take into account the amount of labor saved, the prevention of a certain amount of pauperism, more or less of which may always be expected to follow a pestilence, the public expense attending the care of the sick, as most of the inmates of a small-pox hospital are supported at the public expense, and lastly, the uninterrupted prosperity of commercial and business operations, which always receives a severe blow during the prevalence of a pestilence or of an epidemic of any serious nature. When taking these into account, with more remote consequences that might be enumerated, it appears that true economy consists in the faithful application of preventive measures.

To make this law a success, it should have the hearty coöperation of the medical profession and of the public. Physicians should report births promptly, and in all cases, where there is not some good reason for delay, the new-born should be vaccinated at the proper time, and the fact and date of such vaccination reported to the Board of Health, to be recorded with the birth record, which should not be regarded as complete until the fact of vaccination is duly recorded. Physicians throughout the State are deeply interested in the success of this movement, and expect from it to be supplied with reliable lymph for their own use. In this they should not be disappointed, and yet their expectations can hardly be realized without the cheerful coöperation of parents in affording facilities for collecting the material. City and country are equally interested in each other's sanitary condition, as they are in many respects mutually dependent, and should therefore each feel and discharge its obligations to each other; our means of communication and travel, and the necessity of frequent intercourse rendering it impossible to separate these mutual interests. It is a solemn duty devolving upon parents to early secure the successful vaccination of their children, a duty they not only owe to their children and families, but for the neglect of which the public will hold them accountable; for the question of preventing small-pox is not whether the individual or the parent fears its consequences, but whether one has the right to expose the public to a disease so loathsome, and yet so easily prevented; and when parents can be made to feel the weight of this responsibility, an important step will have been gained towards protecting the public from the ravages of small-pox.

Slaughter-houses.—At a recent meeting of the New York Public Health Association, Dr. Stephen Smith, of the Board of Health, presented for consideration the subject of *Concentration and Sanitary Regulation of the Business of Slaughtering in Cities*; to which paper on other pages we invite particular attention. The subject seemed to be exhausted, and the present practices of the butchers shown to be decidedly detrimental to the public health, until Dr. Moreau Morris, late sanitary superintendent, entered a courteous protest against the sweeping measures proposed by Dr. Smith. He had observed great improvements in the methods, buildings and premises of the butchers recently, and no statistics or investigations yet made had satisfied him that sickness and mortality were increased by proximity to the improved slaughter-houses. Experience has shown that the good disposition evinced by those engaged in slaughtering animals made it possible to maintain cleanliness and order, with proper surveillance, in the small slaughter-houses, such as now exist. In his opinion, large slaughter-houses would have difficulty in cooling the meat when hung up. The nuisance caused by rendering arises from the fact that the material rendered is not fresh, and not from the fact that the rendering establishments are small. He doubted whether the concentration of the business would accomplish an improvement in this regard. He thought that the business of slaughtering small stock could be better concentrated than the slaughtering of large animals, and that a number of the smaller houses could be consolidated with advantage. All such establishments should be constructed of non-absorbent material, and situated on water-banks remote from populous places. — Mr. Calvert Vaux inquired whether experience showed any pecuniary advantage in favor of the large slaughtering establishments like the one recently started in Hoboken. — Dr. E. H. Janes was inclined to think that the manager of the Harsimus Company, referred to by Mr. Vaux, considered their investment profitable. — Dr. Stephen Smith said it was impossible to properly control and supervise a business essentially involving so many things and processes liable to emit offensive odors detrimental to the public health, unless the business was more concentrated than at present. It was the difference between watching a square rod and a ten-acre lot. There was a growing tendency to concentration, and he thought the duty of the municipal authorities was to encourage and facilitate this tendency. — Dr. Post had not seen the Harsimus abbattoir, but had inspected the small slaughter-houses on the east side at all hours, and found large, new houses in as good condition as could be expected so far as premises and methods went. The management of these places was all that could be desired, excepting an occasional irregularity in the removal of manure and offal. Many of the larger slaughter-houses were perfect abattoirs of themselves, and their condition was not such as wou'd justify the conclusion that they exert an unfavorable effect on the rate of mortality. — Dr. Smith said that, for the most part, the objections to concentration came, not from the persons and firms engaged in slaughtering, but from the outside parties whose interest lay in securing the rendering of the offal, and the dressing of hides and the treatment of the bones, branches of the business which could be conducted without offense on the premises of a well-equipped abattoir. — Drs. Russell, S. F. Morris, and Bell took part in the discussion, but without expressing decided opinions on this difficult question, in regard to which the Board of Health and the butchers are in conflict. It is a question of great importance, involving much capital on the part of the butchers, and *health* on the part of the public, in the way of which, as a principle, nothing should stand. But the butchers of New York, are, as a class, well informed on the subject, and if it shall be made to appear that slaughtering as at present conducted is detrimental to the public health, they will doubtless willingly submit to whatever sacrifice may be deemed necessary to render it otherwise.

Hydrophobia.—Two or three deaths in New York and Brooklyn

during the last month have been attributed to hydrophobia. June 15, Sanitary Inspector, C. P. Russell, M. D., submitted a summary of "2,407 distinct and authentic cases of *rabies canina*, observed in France, Austria, England and the United States," with such conclusive evidence in favor of its increase by muzzling, that the Board of Health forthwith rescinded all ordinances requiring it. Prof. John C. Dalton has also (June 26) on the request of the Board of Health given the following :—

Directions for the Prevention of Hydrophobia.

I.—A dog that is *sick*, from any cause, should be watched and treated carefully until his recovery.

II.—A dog that is sick and *restless* is an object of suspicion. This is the earliest peculiar symptom of hydrophobia.

III.—A dog that is sick, restless and has a *depraved appetite*, gnawing and swallowing bits of cloth, wood, coal, brick, mortar, or his own dung, is a dangerous animal. He should be at once chained up, and kept in confinement until his condition be clearly ascertained.

IV.—If, in addition to any or all of the foregoing symptoms the dog has *delusion of the senses*, appearing to see or hear imaginary sights or sounds, trying to pass through a closed door, catching at flies in the air when there are none, or searching for something which does not exist, there is great probability that he is, or is becoming hydrophobic. He should be secured and confined without delay.

V.—In case any one is bitten by a dog whose condition is suspicious, the most effective and beneficial mode of treatment is to *cauterize the wound at once* with a stick of silver nitrate, commonly called "lunar caustic." The stick of caustic should be sharpened to a pencil point, introduced quite to the bottom of the wound, and held in contact with every part of the wounded surface, until it is thoroughly cauterized and insensible. This destroys the virus by which the disease would be communicated.

The police force, once familiar with these rules, might be empowered to take and transfer to a place of security any animal presenting suspicious symptoms. To complete the efficiency of the plan, such a place of detention for dogs might be established, under the authority of the Board of Health, to be supervised by a medical or veterinary officer, who should report upon the proper treatment of the animals placed in confinement, and the time when they should be safely returned to their owners.

This action seems to have been rendered necessary on the part of the Board of Health, in order to ward off as far as practicable the effort of certain physicians to create a great excitement on the subject of hydrophobia in order to gain notoriety for superior intelligence on an obscure disease. If there were really any conscientiousness on the part of these mountebanks, and they possessed half the knowledge they pretend to, they would not be backward to use it in disseminating information of the causes and prevention of diseases which kill thousands, where hydrophobia kills one. The aggregate number of deaths in New York, for the week ending July 4th, was 491 :—24 per 1,000. Of this number, 64 were killed by diphtheria ; 48 by scarlet fever ; 25 by measles ; 12 by small-pox ; 3 by typhoid fever, and 2 by cerebro-spinal meningitis. What a pity it is that the Board of Health can not summon to its assistance some of the overflowing energy and humanity of the hydrophobia know-alls, to "*file the teeth*" of these poisons.

Brooklyn, 450,000. Deaths for week ending July 4, 201, excluding 23 still births, 37 more than for week ending June 6; 23.22 per 1,000. Diphtheria 6,—and decreasing; cholera infantum 31. The increase generally, is chiefly due to the effect of heat on the perennial stagnant ponds and saturated soil, which still obtain, notwithstanding the addition of the President of the Board of City Works, and the President of the Board of Aldermen, to the Board of Health;—there is no evidence of an increased efficiency.

Philadelphia, 775,000. Deaths for week ending July 4, 234 : 30 less than for the week ending June 6 ; 15.67 per 1,000.

Chicago, 356,000. Deaths for week ending June 20, 92,—11 less than for week ending May 16; 13.15 per 1000.

New Orleans, 199,000. Deaths for week ending June, 14,172,—44.93 per 1,000. Small-pox 12; 6 less than for the last preceding week, and 8 less than for week ending May 31.

Baltimore, 284.000. Deaths for week ending July 6; 206,—75 more than for week ending June 8; 37.50 per 1,000. The increase seems to have been chiefly due to cholera infantum, of which there were 84 ; and "unknown infantile," 20.

Cincinnati, 239,797. Deaths for week ending July 4, 130; 28.15 per 1,000.

Boston, 270,000. Deaths for week ending June 20, 113 ; 21.76 per 1,000.

Providence.—" You did not do Providence justice last month by reckoning her mortality on the basis of a population of 75,000. There were 151 deaths in Providence during the month of June, or 12 *less* than in the preceding month. Omitting the deaths in the Tenth Ward the number in the city was 131, or 2 *less* than in June, 1873.

The following shows the number of deaths in Providence, exclusive of the Tenth Ward, in each of the first four months of each of the last six years, and also the average for each month in the six preceding the present, from 1868 to 1873 inclusive:

	1874.	1873.	1872.	1871.	1870.	1869.	6 years aver.
January........	131	159	101	92	127	108	108
February	119	123	107	117	100	113	108
March...........	129	145	122	102	104	110	111
1st quarter	379	427	330	311	331	331	327

April	158	151	122	84	106	91	107
May	133	135	125	91	88	76	100
June	131	121	117	88	77	83	92
2d quarter	422	407	364	263	271	250	299
1st 6 mos	801	834	694	574	602	581	626

The above shows the mortality of the city in June as compared with previous months and previous years. But the total mortality in June, including the whole city as it is at present, was 151. The total population of the city by actual census just taken is 99,608; the total mortality in the city including the Tenth Ward, for the first six months of the present year, has been 945. This is equal to an annual mortality of 1,890 or 18.90 in each thousand, or one in 52.7 of the population. This ratio of mortality is extremely small in cities of any size, and very much less than in the larger cities of this country. It is to be remembered also that this is a comparison of actual mortality from a complete record, with an actual population by census. A city with incomplete reports of mortality, and an estimated population, may easily show any desired rate of mortality, however small.

The mortality from scarlatina, in June, was unexpectedly large, the actual number of deaths being greater than ever before known in a single month in the city. In proportion to the population, however, the number of deaths in a single month has several times been greater.

Of the 41 decedents from scarlatina, in June, there were 23 males, 18 females; 40 whites, one colored; 10 of American, 23 of Irish, and 8 of English and Scotch parentage." E. M. Snow, M. D.,

Superintendent of Health and City Registrar.

Lowell, 50,000. Annual report, 1873. Among the noticeable features of the year is the not inconsiderable increase in the number of deaths over former years. There were eleven hundred sixty-one (1,161) deaths, being an increase of one hundred and thirteen, or 10 3–4 per cent. upon the number in 1872. This increase in the death rate does not necessarily indicate that the sanitary condition of the city was worse than in previous years; for without doubt more attention than usual was paid towards keeping the streets and alleys in a healthful condition. The population is yearly increasing and the death rate will keep pace with it. It is estimated that the present population of Lowell is 50,000. Taking this as a basis, one person in every 46.06 died, or 21 in 1,000. Consumption, 207; inflammation of the lungs, 80; typhoid fever, 56.

Richmond, 65,000. Deaths for week ending July 4, 44; 35.20 per 1,000. Diarrhœal diseases, 18, typhoid fever, 3.

Norfolk, about 25,000. Deaths for June, 66,—whites, 31; colored, 35. Typhoid, 1; diarrhœal, 10.

Charleston, 52,000. Deaths for week ending June 13, 37; 36.80 per 1,000. By annual report, for 1873, on population of 1870,

48,956, 1516 deaths; 1 in 32.27. Of whites, population 22,145,—507 deaths; 1 in 43,58. Blacks and colored, population 26,811,—1,009 deaths; 1 in 26.63.

Milwaukee, 80,000. Deaths for June, 138; 20.70 per 1,000.

Toledo, 37,000. Deaths for June, 35; 11.37 per 1,000. The healthiness of Toledo having been called in question recently by a traveller who saw only the "Middle Grounds" swamp, the *Toledo Blade* presents the following comparative statistics, "from official reports for the year 1871.

Toledo,	one death in 73		Baltimore,	one death in 41	
Chicago,	"	" 40	Brooklyn,	"	" 37
St. Louis,	"	" 40	New Orleans,	"	" 19
San Francisco	"	" 45	Buffalo,	"	" 52
Cincinnati,	"	" 55 1-12	Detroit,	"	" 54
New York,	"	" 31	Cleveland,	"	" 42
Philadelphia,	"	" 53			

The average rate in Toledo for the six years ending with 1871, as given by our Board of Health, was one death to 60 6–10 of population, which average is less than the death rate of either of the other twelve cities named above." The same paper of June 25, publishes an excellent address on *State Medicine and Public Hygiene* read before the State Medical Society of Ohio, by Dr. W. W. Jones. The dissemination of such knowledge always reflects beneficially upon the people. And it is a healthy sign in any community to find newspapers, like the *Blade*, alive to the dearest interest of the people, the public health.

Wheeling, 26,000. Deaths for June, 20; 9.23 per 1,000. "A hasty and consequently imperfect enumeration made early last summer by the Board of Education, indicated a population of about 25,300. and 26,000 will certainly be a low estimate for 1873."

S. L. JEPSON, M. D., Health Officer.

Dayton, 34,000. Deaths for month ending June, 46; 16.23 per 1,000.

Pittsburgh, 133,000. Deaths for week ending June 27, 231; 20.84 per 1,000. Scarlet fever 46; consumption, 20; diarrhœal diseases, 18; measles 9; whooping cough, 7; diphtheria, 4.

San Francisco, 178,000. Deaths for *May*, 292; 19.68 per 1,000. Zymotic diseases, 60; typhus and typhoid fevers, 4; consumption, 44,

Richmond, Co. N. Y. Report of the Board of Health for 1873–4, received. It is worthy of more space than we can at present devote to it, and its present consideration is therefore deferred.

Colorado. Experiences of an Invalid :

Cañon City, Col. Ter., April 12, 1874.

Some time has elapsed since I received your last letter. I was then at Colorado Springs.—About 7 weeks ago I came down or over to Cañon and shall spend the spring months here. The natured facilities of Cañon as a winter and spring health resort are undoubtedly unsurpassed by any in the Territory.

Colorado, considered as a resort for invalids with chronic lung disease, is probably unsurpassed by any sections within the scope of civilization. The climate, soil and temperature have been such all winter as to invite one out of doors. The nature of the country and the people prompt to an active outdoor life. I have ridden over 1,000 miles on horseback since the latter part of November, besides a few hundred by carriage. But twice have I been unduly exposed, and neither time did I take cold.

I have had but one cold, and that was taken in a carriage ride on a warm, clear day. I am a very strong advocate of horseflesh as a remedial agent, and shall pursue my present habits for eight months or a year to come. I would not hesitate much in joining a well organized party to go "overland" or (camp-train) to California via "Mexican trail" from Northern New Mexico to Southern California, or via the route of the U. P. and C. P. R. R.

I am expecting my father out here this summer. Should he come I will go by rail to the Pacific coast and remain there some time. I have one, perhaps two uncles in California.

I think that within a few years Colorado will become the greatest sanitarium and the Rocky Mountain country the most frequented pleasure resort in the world. The mountains of Switzerland do not equal it and the Italian atmosphere does not surpass it. The scenery is unsurpassed, mountain, plain and Cañon, valley and gorge seem to have been the handiwork of old nature when in her maddest freaks or most majestic mood.

I consider the Pike's Peak observatory a fine institution, and it has proved much more than its founders intended, *i. e.* however high a man's position in life may be, he is not above corruption. The people out here are a wide-awake, active people. As in Rome the roads indicate a high state of civilization, so here. Betting is the highest endowment of the race, and uniform success carries a man to any position he may wish to attain.

If you wish any sage bushes, cac ti, town or country bonds, alkali, or fine stones, they can be furnished here in abundance.

Let me hear from you soon."—I. M. B.

Foreign.—London, 3,400,701. Deaths for week ending June 6, 1,257; 19.22 per 1000. Typhoid fever, 16; diphtheria, 7. *No small-pox.*

Paris, 1,851,792. Deaths for the week ending June 12, 814; 22.85 per 1000. Typhoid fever, 15. *No small-pox.*

Bermuda. Annual report for 1873.—Whites, 4956; colored, 8035. Of the whites, ratio per 1000, 20.17; of the colored 24.19. Being a decrease among the whites of 1.20 per 1000, and increase of

5.51 among the colored, as compared with 1872. Of Zymotic diseases, 15; 13 of whites, 2 colored. Tubercular diseases, 552; 35 of colored, 17 of whites.

Cholera.—The *Morning Post,* under the date of June 7, publishes: "The cholera has broken out in the Haute-Silesie, prevailing in the coal region with extreme violence."—"Copenhagen, June 6, quarantine was instituted against vessels arriving from Havre lest cholera should be introduced from Denmark.—*Gaz. Hebd.*

Population. We are under obligations to several correspondents for information in regard to population; but we still have a number of reports wanting in this respect, and therefore of much less interest.

The Artist's Holiday.—No persons more than artists are sensible of the unhealthy conditions attending their winter studies and grand exhibitions. A studio filled with rubbish;—debris of old pictures, and new, pictures covered with dust and dusty newspapers which must not be brushed; studies and subjects for study—sometimes shaded with mould and at others with mouldering canvas waiting to be touched up, old drapery and old paper caps—and, nine chances out of ten, old tobacco pipes and "fine cut"—contribute to make up the standing furniture of a successful artist's studio. And then comes opening night. Much time has been spent, and much anxiety felt meanwhile about the hanging of his pictures. The gallery is brilliantly lighted, more gas is turned on than the burners can possibly consume, ventilation is habitually deficient, the greater the crowd the greater the success—and the greater the danger to health. Persons with sound lungs and strong constitutions are endangered thereby, and those with diseased lungs and weak constitutions attend such places at their peril. But just now the artist is free. This is his holiday. Let us follow him up the Hudson. Watching his chance from the deck of one of the noble steamers that almost hourly take in the grand panorama, he at last slyly slips off, stool in hand done up like a walking stick, and pockets full of sketching-tools—and now he is in his glory! Not alone of living, glowing pictures, but the bracing, invigorating air. In his study of his subjects for next winter's labor, he himself becomes a subject, and could you only paint *him* under the shady tree while he sketches the sunshine and shadow twinkling in the boughs before him, you would appreciate the scene to its full, because you would share it with him. You would take in the pure air, you would swell as he does, your pale cheeks would glow, and your whole system would be fortified for a winter's campaign. Even one day in the week in the picture gallery of the Hudson, is better than a thousand in the tents of the heated city.

Trephining.—We are thankful to one and all of our exchanges

who notice us *by name*, who are generous enough to place the names of our contributors over papers which have been first contributed to us, and who add "*From the Sanitarian*," to selections from our pages. But we do not like to be *trephined*. It is a disagreeable and painful operation; a good deal worse than leeching, for the taking of a little blood sometimes is soothing. But trephining—boring a hole in one's skull—is decidedly unpleasant, and drawing the brains out, without so much as saying whose head it is, makes one feel nervous, and bad, Chloroform, under such circumstances, does no good. On the contrary, it rather aggravates the pain.—*e. g.*, "*The Sanitarian*:—We take pleasure in frequently noticing this excellent journal, which is certainly doing a very efficient work in the dissemination of scienific, knowledge upon the subject of public hygiene," etc.—H. R., for July. You take pleasure in it. Of course you do, because in the same number of your notice, under the guise of an editorial, you take a page from *The Sanitarian*, which you palm off as *your* brains! And besides, in the same number you have one of our best cogitations calculated to do us some credit, and lest it should do so, you add at the bottom "*Sel.*"—It is, decidedly. Another of our good things you attribute to somebody else! And another, you adopt with our contributor's name, as if addressed to you, without telling whence you obtained it. A *religious* exchange before us is almost as bad. Administers to *The Sanitarian* a dose of soothing syrup, and straightway confiscates us editorially. We have no faith in that editor's religion. He takes things belonging to other people.

Such things are unhealthy, and should be avoided.

1774—Centennial of Chemistry—1874.

To the Chemists of America.—The year 1774 was rendered memorable by the discovery of oxygen by Joseph Priestly, by researches on Chlorine by Scheele, and important investigations undertaken by Lavoisier, which eventually led to the overthrow of the phlogistic hypothesis; the most important link in the chain having been contributed on the first of August, 1774, by Dr. Priestly.

A re-union of American chemists, for mutual exchange of ideas and observations, would, it is believed, foster a feeling of fraternity among us, and is considered by the undersigned eminently desirable. The approaching centennial affords a fitting occasion for such a gathering. We, therefore, invite the chemists of America to meet at Northumberland, Pennsylvania, where Priestley lies entombed, on the 31st of July, 1874, to celebrate, by appropriate exercises, this memorable epoch in the history of chemistry.

George F. Barker, University of Pennsylvania, Philadelphia, Penn.
Frederick A. P. Barnard, Columbia College, New York.
Charles F. Chandler, School of Mines, Columbia College, New York.
And many others.

Communications should be sent to

H. Carrington Bolton,
Chairman of the General Committee,
School of Mines, Columbia College, New York.

Obituary.

Massachusetts State Board of Health.

Boston, July 1, 1874.

At a regular meeting of the State Board of Health, held this day, it was unanimously voted that the following address of the Chairman, Dr. Henry I. Bowditch, announcing the death and recalling the services of the late Secretary of the Board, Dr. George Derby, be printed in circular form for distribution.

F. W. Draper, M.D.

Secretary pro tempore.

Gentlemen of the State Board of Health:—

A few days since, I warned you of the serious illness of our dear friend and honored Secretary, Dr. George Derby. It is with great sorrow that I have summoned you again in consequence of his death.

Permit me to recall to your notice some of the more salient points in his history, with many of which, you, who have been associated with him in this Board, are already partially or perchance fully acquainted.

Dr. Derby was born in Salem, in 1819; he was the son of John Derby, an eminent merchant of that city.

He took his degree from the Harvard Medical School in 1843. For many years he practised very quietly in Boston, but was little known by the public, or to the profession, until the late war brought to light his latent energy, and his admirable character. During a recent conversation with him, he told me he believed that a love of, and devotion to, music impaired his reputation as a physician and surgeon. I think he judged rightly. Finally, the rebellion broke forth; the first call of President Lincoln upon the patriotism of the country found our friend prompt and determined to do his whole duty. He entered again with praiseworthy zeal into all the work of student life. He took special lessons in practical surgery from our most eminent surgeons, and with more than youthful enthusiasm, studied out the improvements in medicine and surgery that had been brought forward during the many years since his pupilage, from 1838 to 1843. This act marked two of those traits of character which we, his associates on the Board of Health, have seen and admired so much during our intercourse with him: viz., his conscientiousness, and his thoroughness in his dealings with any question. He was unwilling to undertake the care of our patriot soldiers without fitting himself in the most perfect manner for the task. He received from Governor Andrew the commission of surgeon of the 23d Regiment of the Massachusetts Volunteers. He went through the whole war without a furlough, and was always ready to sacrifice himself for the good of the soldiers. He was fearless in presence of danger; performing important operations on the field while under fire, with a perfect coolness and deliberation, when others, superior to him in authority, shrank from the ordeal to which his sense of professional duty summoned him.

Having thus served with a reputation for ability and devotion unsurpassed by any one, he left the army at the final closing of the war, a man comparatively broken down in health, and with the prospect of commencing anew his professional life. For months, by most careful regimen, and the daily use of quinine, he had fought against the insidious encroachments of malarial disease.

When the war closed the reaction took place, in a corresponding depression of his health.

The Government fully appreciating his worth, and desirous of aiding him in his perfect recovery, appointed him to the charge of the National Soldiers' Home, at Augusta, Maine.

After several months' residence there, having partially at least regained his vigor, he resumed practice in Boston. He came back to us a man of noteworthy fame, as a patriot, as an able and full practised surgeon, and a most high-toned gentleman.

Soon after his return he published some papers relating to Hygiene, and he was called to fill the post of surgeon at the City Hospital. He also was made Professor of Hygiene at Harvard College.

During the war, he had married Miss Parsons, a most estimable lady, a lineal descendant of the celebrated Judge Parsons, of the Supreme Court of Massachusetts. She was one of the many ladies of the first families of the State who devoted themselves to the nursing of our sick soldiery, in the hospitals of the Union. That marriage added a charm to his life it had never known before. The pride he took in instilling chivalric ideas of honor into his children was very charming to myself, when admitted occasionally into some of the closest intercourse of private friendship. He was expanding daily, and daily rising in the estimation of his peers in the profession, and with the public.

June 21, 1869, just five years ago, the Legislature passed the Act establishing the State Board of Health.

Ten years previously Dr. Derby had edited the Report to the Legislature relating to the births marriages and deaths in Massachusetts. In the preface to the Report, in 1867, the Secretary of State had used the following language in reference to Dr. Derby, that "during the late war he was four years in active service, with the largest reputation as surgeon."

His publications, as well as his acquired reputation at the State House and abroad, readily pointed him out as the person most fitted, on the score of his manliness, ability and integrity, to be Secretary of the new Board. He, in fact, had no rival.

I need not remind you of all that he has done for us: of the great works he has inaugurated, and successfully carried forward. But none of us, I suspect, even now realize how devoted he has been. We all know how often and how perfectly we trusted him. We felt that the honor of our Board would be always cautiously and firmly sustained. We remember his genial and commanding presence; his indefatigable zeal in everything that was ordered by the Board. We were sure of him, as the most reliable person we could have. How much the present position of the Board, as a motive force in this community, depends on his really wonderful faculty of meeting and of moulding men, we shall never exactly know. For my own part, gentlemen, words would fail me to give you an idea of the debt we owe to him for the present standing of the Board. He guarded our honor with so jealous a care, that sometimes I was inclined to think him unduly cautious, and perhaps too far-reaching in his anticipations of possible evils about to fall upon the Board. These sombre anticipations, I have been of late inclined to think, were owing to ill health. They assumed, sometimes, the appearance of dire forebodings for the safety of the Board, when obliged to run the gauntlet of popular criticism. He could not feel, as I have ever felt, that certainly, in the present condition of the world, if our Board should be for any reason abolished by any legislature, its immediate successor would be compelled, by public opinion, to call another board of similar character, into existence. State, or preventive medicine, has taken so deep a root into the conscience of the English speaking race, that hereafter Boards of Health, or in other words, for the prevention of disease, must forever exist; and they will have more and more weight upon the policy of States and of nations, as well as upon the private habits of individuals.

And now, gentlemen, what is the lesson that rises to us from the life-work of our dear friend and co-laborer in a most noble cause?

Why simply this: let us one and all go on with renewed zeal and with an untiring devotion that shall be worthy of him. Let us make his course our example in our future career. If we do this, I have no fear; for the future of any cause must be bright, provided it be carried forward intelligently and with the single endeavor to do honestly and justly the duty of the hour, as our friend Derby always did his.

God grant his grace to each one of us, and enable all of us to feel, during our future connection with the Board, the beauty of the example left to us by the life of our dead associate!

BIBLIOGRAPHY.

1. *Lessons on Hygiene and Surgery from the Franco-Prussian War. 8vo., pp.* 263.

2. *The Soldier's Manual of Sanitation,* and first help in sickness, and when wounded. Pamphlet, pp. 116. By Charles Alexander Gordon, M. D., C. B., Deputy Inspector General of Hospitals; Ex-member of the Sanitary Commission for Bengal, Late on Special service in the French army, etc. London: Baillière, Tindall & Cox, 1873.

1. The purport of this book is to fill a place indicated by the author, as follows: "Crowds of works on the military aspects of the late great war have appeared during the last two years, and still the cry seems to be, 'they come.' The theme of all is death and destruction *of the enemy.* Tactics, manœuvres, organization, projectiles, arms,—all these, and kindred subjects are discussed from various points of view, lessons being drawn in regard to what should be followed, what avoided, when next armies take the field. In none

of these, however, do we find more than a passing allusion, if so much as that, to the best means of preserving the health and efficiency of the soldier, by whom battles are to be won; for his treatment and management, when struck down in fight, or by the subtle and deadly influence of disease."

This extract is amply suggestive of the purpose of the volume. The potency of practical hygiene to great armies is herein summarized under twenty-three appropriate headings comprehending the education, regimen, and general service of the soldier in peace and war, and never lost sight of as an essential conservative power applicable to all of the varying conditions of a soldier's life. Under the intelligent application of hygiene, military surgery assumes a new aspect.

In time of peace, bodies of men which would otherwise be decimated by fever, are preserved in health; and in time of war, injuries which twenty-five years ago were almost uniformly fatal, are at the present time as uniformly recovered from. But besides the special object of the work as indicated by the title, its principles are of universal application. Everything that is said of military hospitals in regard to plan, space, sunlight, warming, aeration, &c; of the superiority of female nurses in handling of the sick and wounded; alimentation, and most of the details of these several subjects, are no less profitable lessons for civil hospitals and practice, than for military, and eminently worthy of the careful study of all persons who accept the duties and responsib.lities of hospital directors. It is the ablest book of the kind in the English language.

2. The *Manual* by the same author, is a concise abstract of the most useful knowledge for soldiers, "in regard to the best means of preserving their own health, decreasing the risks of sickness, and affording some measure of aid to their comrades when attacked by illness or wounded in battle." We especially recommend the following extract from the brief article on *Beer*. "Taken in large quantities, or during hot weather, it stupefies the person, incapacitates him for work, and renders him liable to illness, either fullness in the head, or *oppression* in the chest. When long indulged in, it deranges digestion, renders the stomach irritable, induces a feeling of sickness and want of appetite for meals, and moreover, tends to cause diseases of the liver and kidneys."

Food: Its varieties, chemical composition, nutritive value, comparative digestibility, physiological functions and uses, preparation, culinary treatment, preservation, adulteration etc.; being the substance of four Cantor Lectures, delivered before the Society for the Encouragement of Arts, Manufactures and Commerce, 1868. By H. Letheby, M. B., M. A., Ph. D. &c., 2d ed. 12 mo. p. 255. London: Baillière, Tindall & Cox.

This is an admirable little book, in no way critical or abstruse. It is well adapted to the popular reader; while it is remarkable for its scope, terse comprehensiveness and scientific accuracy. It treats of the varieties of Food—their chemical composition and nutritive value; comparative digestibility, functions of different foods, etc., and unwholesome and adulterated food.

Sanitary Subjects.—By Richard J. Halton, Licentiate of King and Queens College of Physicians; of the Royal College of physicians, Edinborough; Medical Office of Health, etc., etc. 8vo. pp. 192. London: Baillière, Tindall & Cox.

This book consists of twelve short lectures on sanitary subjects, from a practical point of view, with especial recognition of the propagation of diseases by organic germs. It is a book well adapted to popular reading, and replete with sound knowledge promotive of good health and long life.

The Sewage Question: Comprising a Series of Reports;—being investigations into the condition of the principal sewage farms and sewage works of the Kingdom. From Dr. Letheby's "Notes and Chemical Analysis." Reprint with additions from the "Medical Press and Circular," 12mo. pp. 204. London: Baillière, Tindall & Cox. 1872.

It would be well for every body, in this country at least, interested in the importance of excrement nuisances as factors in disease, to carefully read this volume. It consists of the practical experiences of the various plans and systems hitherto tried, and the observations of a number of the most competent health inspectors and sanitarians of England.

The subject is treated as it deserves to be, as one of the most important sanitary questions of the time. It is indeed, only just now as it were, that the progress of knowledge in the etiology of epidemic diseases, especially, has demonstrated the danger of this source of propagation and the necessity of controlling it. The real question at issue in this relation, is the *protection of human life*, not the "utilization of sewage," the preservation of manure, the raising of vegetables and other insignificant side issues. Treatment and disposal necessarily follow, but these questions should under no circumstances be allowed to usurp the place of the main one, lest attention be diverted from the real source of danger—the poisonous emanations. Every farmer knows the value of excreta to his crops, but very few farmers recognize the danger of contaminating drinking water by privy vaults, manure spreading and irrigation. And the *traders in sewage* ordinarily know not, or if they know, regard not the difference between the mere deodorization and the disinfection of their wares. We would have no restriction in regard to the utilization of sewage; on the contrary, it is of unquestionable and almost untold value. But one restriction—aye, absolute *prohibition*—we would have, that none should be utilized until it is thoroughly divested of dangerous conditions. And by sewage in this relation, we would be understood as including human excreta in every form.

The practice of sewage irrigation in this country, as yet, justifies no conclusions. And "the truth is," elsewhere, "there is a deficiency of precise knowledge on the question at issue. Sewage irrigation as a rule has been carried on in localities where much harm could not arise from it at the worst. Again, it has always been a canon of sewage irrigation that the irrigated lands should be situated in as sparsely populated places as practicable, or removed entirely from inhabited localities.

The evidence pointing to little or no unwholesomeness from sewage irrigation in *England*, has been necessarily largely obtained from sewage-irrigated lands so circumstanced; and although abundantly sufficient to justify sewage irrigation *when thus carried out away from centres of population*, it does not prove more than this. The paucity of evidence one way or the other is shown by the limited number of facts which can be adduced, by their constant repetition, and by the few and insignificant additions which have been made to them of late years.

"The whole subject requires, indeed, to be examined anew, as an independent public health question. This is the kind of work which the Medical Department of the local Government Board is peculiarly well fitted to carry out, and which could be done by it in a manner that would secure fully the confidence of the profession and of the public. That the importance of the questions at issue have not escaped the attention of the Department is manifest from a report now before us, by Dr. Buchanan, on an outbreak of fever supposed to have been connected with the Northampton sewage meadows. This report furnishes important additional evidence to the effect, first, that no unwholesomeness appears to attach to labor on sewage-irrigated land; and, secondly, that there is an occasional source of danger to health from such land which needs to be carefully guarded against, namely: the danger of water in the outflow channel of the irrigated land when an open channel, being mistaken for ordinary brook water and used for drinking. The principles which should guide the action of a sanitary authority in this matter, have been fully and authoritatively set forth in an official paper published by the Medical Department of the Local Government Board, entitled "*Report on certain means of preventing Excrement Nuisances in Towns and Villages.*" This report is based upon a detailed examination of the different arrangements in use for the disposal of excrement in numerous towns and villages.

"It is one thing to determine the best possible modes of sewage disposal and sewage utilization; it is another and very different thing to ascertain the practicable application of such a mode under different conditions of population. . . . It is a fact that water sewerage, though the best mode of sewage disposal known, is inapplicable, as a sole system, in many towns and villages. It is a fact also that sewage irrigation, although it may be the best means of sewage utilization known, is inapplicable in not a few localities. Other modes of sewage disposal are a necessity, and the lesson to be learned from this, in respect to the different other modes in use, is that adopting them, it is incumbent upon local authorities and upon individuals to carry them out in such a way as to avoid nuisance."*

The volume before us containing the reports on various modes in use, we commend as a good starting point for an intelligent comprehension of the subject in its various aspects.

Sanitary Arrangements for Dwellings. By William Eassie, C. E., F.L.S., F. G. S., etc., 12 mo. pp. 188, London: Smith, Elder & Co., 1874. This work accounts of the most ordinary defects in dwelling houses

* *The Practitioner.*—May, October and November, 1873.

and public institutions in respect to drainage, water supply, ventilation, warming and lighting; and suggests effective means of preventing and remedying such defects. The latest improvements in drain-pipes, traps, ventilating, gas-lighting, etc., are illustrated by cuts and lucid explanations. It also treats of *Dampness, Ground air, Cesspools, Earth and Ash-closets, Dust-bins, disinfection*, etc. Familiarity with its contents, and the practical application of its teachings are essential knowledge for the protection of health. It is one of the most useful manuals on sanitary science hitherto published.

Inflammation of the Lungs: Tubercle and Consumption. Twelve Lectures. By Dr. Ludwig Buhl, Prof. of Pathological Anatomy and General Pathology in the University of Munich, etc., etc. Translated from second German edition. By Matthew D. Mann, M.D., and Samuel B. St. John, M.D. 12mo, pp. 161. New York: G. P. Putnam's Sons.

A book of nice pathological distinctions on the different phases of inflammation of the bronchi and lungs; and the nature of tuberculosis and consumption. The latter part of the work, especially, the etiology of tubercle, is worthy of the most attentive consideration. The author's views are radically different from the views generally entertained, while they are maintained by extensive observation and profound pathology. And we very much doubt whether from the time of Laennec to the present, the opinions of any student of tubercle are more worthy of study or more likely to lead to a great advance in the pathology of tubercle than those of Prof. Buhl. The theories of Niemeyer may, in some respects, be regarded as the forerunners of the researches of Buhl, and yet, they are in reality founded upon them. The infection theory of tuberculosis is peculiarly Buhl's, and it is to him more than to any other person the profession is indebted for the newly awakened zeal in the study of this disease. "Ever since I made my debut as a teacher in 1847," he writes, "I have constantly entertained the idea that *miliary tubercle is a disease due to specific absorption and infection.*" * We commend the book as one which no physician who would be "up" in his profession, can afford to be without.

A Conspectus of the Medical Sciences: Comprising Manuals of Anatomy, Physiology, Chemistry, Materia Medica, Practice of Medicine, Surgery, and Obstetrics, for the use of students. By Henry Hartshorn, A.M., M.D. Professor of Hygiene in the University of Pennsylvania, etc. 477 illustrations: large 12 mo. pp., 1024. Philadelphia: Henry C. Lea, 1874.

The second edition of this conspectus for students and manual for practitioners attests the estimation which has been placed upon it; and we doubt not this second enlarged and thoroughly revised edition will win for it still more general use. The progress of medicine in the several departments, during the five years that have elapsed since the first edition was issued, has been carefully summed up and elucidated. The greatest amount in Chemistry, comprising both the old and the new equivalents and formulæ of important substances and reactions, and

* Lecture. X.

thus effecting a plain and accurate transition from the old to the new system. Materia Medica, Practice, Obstetrics and Surgery are characterized by the marked improvements in these several departments during the interval. Altogether as a conspectus of the several departments of which it treats and as a concise review book it is unequalled.

Treatise on Food and Dietetics: Physiologically and Therapeutically considered. By F. W. Pavy, M.D., F.R.S. pp. 600, Philadelphia: Henry C. Lea.

Of the many books published on food recently, this one is the best. The endless discussions indulged in by physiologists and others as to the sources of animal heat, and muscular force and vital energy, are satisfactorily disposed of by the adoption of the physiology of food on the now accepted doctrines of "Conservation of Energy and Correlation of Forces," as applied by Grover in 1842 to the physical world. The use of certain foods because they contain a certain amount of nitrogen or carbon, is shown to be as unreliable, often, as the administration of certain medicines is, from the incompatibility of any two or more as ascertained in the chemical laboratory. The exceptions show the value of the rules. Nitrogenous foods assist in the formation of fat and carbonaceous food in the production of muscular energy, as shown by the experiments of Fick and Wislicenus, corroborated by Frankland, Parkes and Speck. In regard to the elimination of urea as the result of muscular action, the author does not hesitate to declare that the experiments conducted by Flint upon Weston are unsatisfactory. Elimination is influenced by the amount of food ingested.

For achohol some virtue is claimed as an alimentary body. The author's views on this subject coincide with Parkes' and others, that all of the alchohol does not pass from the body, that it acts like a spur in the side of the horse, eliciting force, though not supplying it. Liebig's theories of the action of food are shown to be untenable. And Liebig's extract of beef to be a food, when given in *large quantities*. The chapters on food for corpulency or weak digestion, and preparations for the sickroom, etc., are a fitting conclusion to this excellent volume, fully illustrating the author's teachings that the preservation of health cannot be maintained by fixed rules. As with all sudden departures, Bantingism is shown to have done harm. The book should be in every library.

Milk Analysis. A practical treatise on the examination of milk and its derivatives, cream, butter and cheese.

By J. Alfred Wanklyn, M. R. C. S. pp. 73 New York: D. Van Nostrand.

This little treatise is admirably well adapted to the wants of the analytical chemist; but owing to the expensiveness of the apparatus employed—platinum saucers, etc., of little practical utility to others. The author regards the *lactometer* and *creamometer* as wholly unreliable for the determination of the proportion of the solid constituents; he therefore discards them, and confines himself to analysis as the only reliable means. There is great need of such information as this, and we commend the volume as one well calculated to promote intelligence on a most important subject.

— —

The Science of Homœopathy, or a Critical and Synthetical Exposition of the Doctrines of the Homœopathic School. By Charles J. Hempel, M. D. New York : Bœricke & Tafel.

The fundamental doctrine of Homœopathy in regard to the origin of disease, " is that the vital organism is tainted by a primitive miasm to which Hahnemann applied the name of PSORA." . . This disease is represented as having assumed several forms during the earlier ages of the world, but spreading farther and farther in the shape of a horrible eruption, found at last some alleviation in those means of cleanliness which the Crusaders had brought along with them from the East, such as cotton and linen shirts, which had been unknown in Europe heretofore, and the frequent use of warm baths. These means, together with an increasing refinement and more select nourishment, succeeded, in a couple of centuries, in diminishing the disgusting appearance of psora, so as to reduce the disease toward the end of the fifteenth century to an ordinary eruption, the common ITCH."

At that period of time, the *itch* was the most universally prevalent of all diseases, and this circumstance would seem to have given color to Hahnemann's theory. Moreover, the itch was then as now, when left to itself, a disease which rarely or never gets well. But unfortunately for the stability of his theory—that the itch was an inherent constitutional taint, it was not long afterwards discovered to be wholly an *external* taint, due to a local irritation caused by an *acarus*.

But nothing daunted, our present authority tells us : " The disorders which Hahnemann has enumerated do indeed exist, but not as" (Hahnemann taught), " a consequence of the removal of the itch by local means. The practical disadvantage arising from Hahnemann's erroneous theory concerning the evil consequences of what he considers as a mere suppression of the eruption, consists in the fact that those who swear by the words of the master, entail upon the itch-patient a long period of avoidable distressing and loathsome suffering, which is spared him by those who, following the light obtained by recent investigations, (!) " treat the disease as a local cutaneous disorder, with such local means as are known to be effectual in"—creating (?) by no means, "exterminating the itch mite. Among these the sulphur ointment holds the first rank." This is characteristic of homœopathic progress. And the present " Scientific Idea and Fact of Homœopathy " is summed up in defiance of every principle of science—wholly discarding the known truths of physiology and pathology—reiterating theories based upon the conclusions of Hahnemann, which the author himself acknowledges and shows were based upon false dogmas, while he urges their " perfect accord with the recent discoveries in the realm of physicism, more especially with the great doctrine of the Correlation of Forces," which doctrine he seems to treat as the great homœopathic discovery of modern times, and about which he writes with as much learning as he does about medicine. And in this he is, withal, perfectly consistent. Accepting this book as an authority, homœopathy is eminently progressive. It used to be the case that *infinitesimal doses* was a doctrine in homœopathy no less cardinal than *inherent Psora*, and *similia similibus curantur*. The author claims to have been from the first among the foremost to condemn all exclusiveness regarding doses, and to have contended as he now contends, "that it is every physician's right to prescribe such a dose of the appropriate remedy as in his judgment may seem best calculated to strike down the enemy disease most effectually and quickly." And yet the same author in his preface to Hahnemann's "Chronic Diseases" teaches that "the spiritual force of the homœopathic preparation increases in proportion as the process of trituration is carried up to a higher degree," and condemns "the recklessness with which many homœopathic practitioners use either low or high potencies and administer large or small doses," as "altogether unpardonable and a species of quackery *sui generis*."

Lord of Himself. A Novel, by Francis H. Underwood, pp. 512. Boston: Lea and Shepard.

This new novel fully sustains the expectations of those who were acquainted with the writings of the author in the *Atlantic* and elsewhere. The story is purely a fiction, but Mr. Underwood says every one of its incidents has its foundation and parallel in actual events. The scene is laid in Kentucky when slavery flourished, and the life and manners of the chivalry of that region, the fox hunts, the Christmas festivities, and the hospitalities of the great houses, are graphically described, as are also depicted the evils of the "peculiar institution," which finally terminated in blood. The hero and heroine of the story are Beauchamp Russell and Adelaide Shelburne. The former on arriving at maturity finds the family estates involved, by extravagance and fraud, and without energy and motive to reclaim it, until falling in love with Miss Shelburne he becomes "Lord of Himself," and retrieves his fortune. The incidents of the tale are most excellently wrought out, the characters and conversation being natural to the localities and time, and altogether it is one of the best American novels that has recently appeared, and will undoubtedly meet with a cordial reception from the reading public.

Thurid and other Poems. By G. E. O. Boston: Lee and Shepard, 1874. Three narrative poems that are not poetry. The author understands versification, but has neither sentiment nor imagination, and his plots are stale and commonplace. We hope the friends of the author are pleased with the production, for the general public will surely never penetrate into the secret of these initials.

The book is gotten up in a style worthy of the publishers.

Observations on the Pathology and Treatment of Cholera. By John Murray, M. D., Inspector-General of Hospitals, late of Bengal; pp. 58. New York: G. P. Putnam's Sons. 1874.

This is a commendable contribution by an enlightened observer, towards an end yet in the distance, accepted pathology and treatment of cholera. If all who have the opportunity would follow the example of Dr. Murray, in giving the benefit of their personal observations, that end would not only be promoted, but many lives saved in its prosecution.

Principles of Mental Hygiene. By D. A. Gorton, M. D. pp. 242. Philadelphia: J. B. Lippincott & Co.

The purpose of this book, the author informs us in the preface, is to throw some light upon the intimate connection between the physical conditions and environments of man.

The cosmopolitan nature of man, which is ever subjecting him to new relations, is constantly opening up new phases of changed action upon, and new results to, the human constitution, which will of necessity, in the future, in proportion to our keener appreciation of these results, attract more and more attention to this inviting field of study. Dr. Gorton, as many another before him, has entered it with enthusiasm, and hastens to announce it, in the book before us. He makes no pretence to original research; indeed, he explicitly claims that the best feature of his volume is "the number of quotations introduced from the writings of distinguished savans, past and present." The writings of Quetelet, Ray, Winslow, Guy, Maudsley, Carpenter, Lewes, and the *Bible*, by whomsoever presented, are instructive and profitable reading. And, in so far as Dr. Gorton has quoted from these authors, if the context be taken into consideration, he has aided in the inculcation of wholesome thought and sound philosophy. Our regret is, that he had not studied these works with more diligence—that he had not partaken more freely of this feast of literature on the subject which has captivated him, before he attempted to present it himself in a popular and attractive form. Had he done so, he surely would not have quoted "Graham's Science of Human Life," "The Constitution of Man," by George Combe, and "The Principles of Physiology," by Andrew Combe, as containing "advanced views on the subject," applicable to the present state of physiological and psychological science. Nor would he have made the still worse mistake, on the one hand, of an effort to level the Christian faith with heathen superstitions and speculative philosophy; and, on the other, attempted to elevate the moral status of time-serving political idols by placing them on the same platform with the Saviour of the world. These, and the socialistic tenor of certain quotations in the chapter on Marriage, are serious blemishes to the book. Divested of these blemishes, this book would present many truly commendable qualities, well calculated to promote a popular understanding of an important subject, promotive of both physical and mental hygiene; and we trust that the author will lose no time in re-writing and elaborating the truly meritorious portion of his work, wholly eschewing the objectionable features. *Docendo dicimus.*

The Education of American Girls. Considered in a series of essays. edited by Anna C. Brackett. New York: G. P. Putnam's Sons, 1874; pp. 406. "The Table of Contents," the editor says, "sufficiently indicates the purpose and aim of this book." We think not. The evident purpose and aim of the book is to controvert "Sex in Education," by Dr. E. H. Clarke, which may be learned by an examination of any one of the twelve clever essays by eleven ladies, edited by Miss Brackett. For those who may be induced by this book to read Dr. Clarke's, we advise them to read his first, and then begin Miss Brackett's volume, by first reading Dr. Mary Putnam Jacobi's essay, as she, of all the eleven essayists, best comprehends Dr.

Clarke, from a physiological stand-point. The rest may be read at convenience. Some of them evidently mistake Dr. Clarke's teaching, or they would say less of the equal intellectual capabilities, of which they are, on the whole, a spirited illustration. The whole trend of Dr. Clarke's essay is, education based upon physical organization and sphere of life; each rejecting all comparisons of superiority and inferiority, to be advanced under circumstances the most favorable to the highest culture. These circumstances, Dr. Clarke advocates, should be adapted to the differences in functional organization, and sphere of life. The ladies think not; that the girls being co-equal, are co-enduring, no more liable to the ills that flesh is heir to, by encountering all of the hardships, all of the pressure to which boys may be subjected on the road to fame, than the boys, and that to be thus co-educated, exposed and pushed, is as much the best way for the one as for the other. They rightly claim that co-education is not responsible for the indulgence of errors in dress common to school girls, any more than for defective ventilation, or other surroundings in conflict with health. And on this issue, they have the best of the argument. Besides, the alleged ill results of too much study or too much pushing are quite as common, if not, indeed, more so among boys than girls; and as a mere question of physical endurance, we are inclined to the belief that girls are the superior of boys. But after all, it comes to this: Are women to take care of themselves, fight their own battles, rely upon their own strength and efforts in the battle of life, or to be the companions and helpmeets of men? For those who choose the former, co-education will the better fit them; for the latter, not.

Galvano Therapeutics. Revised report from Trans. Illinois State Med. Society. By David Prince, M. D., of Jacksonville, Ill. Philadelphia: Lindsay & Blackiston. Pamphlet pp. 64. A valuable contribution to Galvano Therapeutics, illustrated by a number of cases, showing the usefulness of the treatment.

Transactions of the Fourth Annual Session of the Medical Society of Virginia, 1873, pp. 120. The most interesting subjects of discussion during the proceedings were chloroform and cerebro-spinal meningitis. Dr. W. W. Parker reported a case of a blacksmith who had in three years taken $3,000 worth of chloroform and fattened fifty pounds. He imagined himself *tricked*. From which delusion he recovered, lived fifteen years afterwards, and died from natural causes. The etiology of cerebro-spinal meningitis was not dwelt upon to much extent, but enough to show the generally accepted belief in its miasmatic origin. The address of the President, Harvey Black, M. D., regarding *Irregular Practitioners and Adulterated Medicines*, sustains "the well-grounded belief" that "medical education furnishes the only presumptive evidence of professional abilities and requirement, and ought to be the only acknowledged right of an individual to the exercise and honors of his profession." For the detection and prevention of adulteration of medicines, and food as well, Dr. Black advocates the organization of a chemical bureau by legislative enactment, with the State Chemist at its head.

The address of Robert S. Hamilton, M. D., on the *Reciprocal Relations of the Medical Profession and Communities*, is an excellent ethical discourse on a subject which needs to be kept constantly before the people.

A supplementary report to the one presented at the third session of the Society, *On the Anatomical, Physiological, and Pathological Differences between the White and Black Races*, by Thos. P. Atkinson, M. D., is a defence, and, in our judgment, a successful one, of the author's previous report, and chiefly in reply to the criticism of the *Boston Medical and Surgical Journal*. The remaining portion of the transactions consists of *Gunshot and other Wounds of the Peritoneum*, by Prof. Hunter McGuire, M. D.; *Intermittent and Remittent Fevers*, by W. A. Gillespie, M. D.; *Nitrate of Amyl as an Antidote to Chloroform*, by W. C. Dabney, M. D.; *Chloroform in Obstetrical Practice*, by A. M. Fauntelroy, M. D.; Committee *Report on Epidemics of Piedmont District*, by Drs. D. A. Langthorne, J. Fauntelroy, and J. C. Green; *Saccharated Pepsin*, by C. W. Thomas, M. D. Report of the *Necrological Committee*, and several reports of cases—all of practical interest.

Transactions of the Medical Society of the District of Columbia, vol. I, No. 1, April 1874, pp. 24. This report seems to come under clause "(*f*.)" of the recommendations of the Committee on Essays to publish "such parts of debates as it may be deemed by this Committee would, if published, be of general interest to the profession at large, or tend to promote the advancement of medical science." It is a condensed abstract of the practical subjects discussed, from July, 1865, to May 15th, 1872. "The Committee recommend that the published Report, or Bulletin, be issued quarterly."

Thirty-first Annual Report of the Managers of the State Lunatic Asylum, Utica, N. Y., for the year 1873. December 1st, 1872. The number of patients remaining in the Asylum, was 535. Admitted during the year 1873, 410. The whole number under treatment during the year was 945. Of this number, there were discharged—recovered, 122; improved, 42; unimproved, 141; not insane, 11; died; 49. Percentage of recoveries, 30. Remained in the Asylum, November 30th, 580. Whole number admitted to the Asylum since its opening, 11,031; recovered, 4,157; improved, 1,670. Percentage of recovered and improved, 53.

"There is high authority for saying that the percentage of recoveries would be far greater if insane patients were subjected to proper treatment during the early stages of disease. The recovery of four-fifths might be reasonably expected, if treated within three months from the first attack; while, if twelve months be suffered to elapse, probably four-fifths may be considered as incurable."

The Report of the Superintendent, Dr. John P. Gray, is characterized throughout by rare executive skill, and devotion to progress in his well-chosen sphere of duty.

Fifty-seventh Annual Report of the state of the Asylum for the Relief of Persons Deprived of the use of their Reason. Philadelphia, 1874.

J. H. Worthington, M. D., Superintendent. Average number of inmates during the year, 85; for the previous twelve months, 69; and for the year ending, third month, 1872, 60. The increase was due to the enlarged accommodations. Discharged during the year—restored, 17; improved, 11; stationary, 6; died, 2. Of the causes of insanity: on an aggregate of 776 cases, *intemperance* is especially emphasized as being the most fruitful. *Warming and Ventilation* is also the subject of some excellent practical remarks by Dr. Worthington; not only in reference to insane asylums, but to other institutions in equal need of automatic arrangements.

The Virginia Medical Monthly, pp. 64, Landon B. Edwards, M. D. editor and proprietor. Subscription, $2.00 per annum, in advance. Single copy, 25 cents. This handsome new journal is characterized by a high order of contributions, and commendable for careful and accomplished editorship.

Detroit Review of Medicine and Pharmacy. This excellent Journal has been enlarged to 64 pages. It is one of the most valuable medical journals in the United States. $3.00 a year. Publishers Detroit Review of Medicine and Pharmacy, 94 Cass street, Detroit.

Autobiography of Edward Wortley Montague, with preface by R. Shelton Mackenzie, LL. D. Philadelphia: T. B. Peterson & Bros. This is one of the most remarkable books that has been given to the public for many years. The author was the only son of Lady Mary Wortley Montague, whose career was, perhaps, one of the most extraordinary of any woman in the annals of England during the last two hundred years. The most celebrated men and women of England, during the reign of George the First, are introduced into this work. There is no flattery of the great, for he tears the mask from the face of vice. The autobiography introduces kings and princes, politicians and poets, men of law and men of letters. In fact it gives life-like portraits of dead men and women: among whom will be found George the Second—Frederick, Prince of Wales—Lady Mary Wortley Montague—Sarah, Duchess of Marlborough—The Earl of Chesterfield—Walpole—Fielding—Colley Cibber—Pope, whose absurd love adventure with Lady Mary is described at length—Howard, Earl of Suffolk—Savage—Lord Lyttelton—Bully Rooke—Lord Scarborough—Molly Segrave—the Duchess of Manchester—Dr. Young—Lady Vane—Lord Patmore and his wife, the Duchess of Leeds—Kitty Hyde, afterwards the Duchess of Queensberry—Lady Betty Molyneux—Lady Fanny Shirley—Windham—Pulteny Lady Bolingbroke—Dodington—Lady Archibald Hamilton—Sir William Yonge—Tom Warrington—Hogarth—Congreve—Gay—Prior—Fox, afterwards the celebrated Lord Holland—Lord Hervey—the Duke of Kingston—Bishop Burnett—Sir Richard Steele—Lady Bella Bentinck—the profligate Duke of Wharton, etc., etc." It is published in one large duodecimo volume of near six hundred pages, bound in morocco cloth, full gilt back, price, $1.75, and is for sale by all booksellers, or copies of it will be sent to any one on their remitting the price to the publishers, T. B. Peterson & Brothers, Philadelphia, in a letter.

Wondrous Strange. A novel, by Mrs. C. J. Newby. Philadelphia: T. B. Peterson & Bros.

This is an unusually lively book. The personages are vividly, sharply and clearly drawn; subtile phases of character are delicately and keenly analyzed, and the incident and narrative is ever fresh, natural and healthful in its tone. It is in all respects equal to the best of its predecessors in the uniform and cheap editions of her works now publishing by Messrs. Peterson & Brothers, and it is a work which is no less attractive by the purity of its tone than by the cleverness with which its characters are drawn and its incidents managed.

Geo. P. Rowell & Co.'s American Newspaper Directory, containing accurate lists of all the Newspapers and Periodicals published in the United States and Territories, and the Dominion of Canada and the British Colonies of North America. New York, Geo. P. Rowell & Co., 1874. The usefulness of this annual is too well known to require an elaborate notice. It will suffice to state that the present handsome volume shows an increase of 493 periodicals over the number exhibited in 1873, the whole number being 7,784. As a book of reference, for advertisers especially, it is indispensable.

The Chicago Journal of Nervous and Mental Diseases, edited by J. S. Jewell, M.D., and H. M. Bannister, M.D., is a handsome and valuable new quarterly, has reached its third issue of unusually valuable current literature on nervous and mental diseases; scarcely less necessary to those whose practice is general, than to those who confine themselves exclusively to this class of diseases. It is in all respects a commendable journal. $4.00 per year; $1.00 per number. Communications may be addressed to the editors, 57 Washington Street, Chicago.

Archives of Electrology and Neurology: A Journal of Electro-Therapeutics and Nervous diseases. Edited by George M. Beard, A. M., M. D. New York: T. L. Clacher.

The first number of this journal has been received, bearing abundant evidence of the fruitfulness of the field it proposes to cultivate. The progress of Electrology and its application to the treatment of many hitherto intractable diseases has won for it the recognition of being a special branch of medical science. And among the foremost of those who have raised it to this plane is Dr. George M. Beard, whose name as editor of a journal devoted to its special cultivation is a sufficient guarantee that the *Archives* will be conducted on scientific principles. The leading papers of the numbers before us are Electrolysis and Croton Chloral, by Julius Althaus, M. D. Nature of Electricity, by Prof. Henry T. Eddy; electrolysis in the treatment of stricture of the uretha by Robert Newman, M.D. New method of treating Malignant Tumors by electrolysing the base, by the editor; and several others of equal value. 145 pp., semi-annual $2.50 a year, in advance; single copies $1.50.

The Unitarian Review and *Religious Magazine.* Rev. C. Lowe, editor. This handsome new monthly has been received, and it bears evidence of substantial interest to the religious community generally, but especially to Unitarians. $5.00 per year. Single numbers, 50 cents. Boston: Leonard C. Bowles.

Dental Cosmos, edited by James W. White, M. D., D. D. S., is among our most welcome exchanges. Always contains something of practical value for the proper care and preservation of the teeth. $2.50 per year. Single copies, 50 cents. Philadelphia: Samuel S. White.

American Journal of Dental Science, edited by F. J. S. Gorgas, M.D., D. D. S., like its congener, *Cosmos*, is fully up to the time in the hygiene of teeth. The more it is read, the less need there will be for that disagreeable filing which makes one shudder to think of. $2.50 per annum. Baltimore: Snowden and Cowman.

American Journal of Pharmacy. Edited by John M. Maisch. It is a pity that this thoroughly useful journal were not better appreciated and patronized by physicians. They may, from it, keep posted on the progress of scientific pharmacy, and benefit much thereby. $3.00 per year. 30 cents a number. Philadelphia: College of Pharmacy.

Peters' Musical Monthly.—Music contributes to health and happiness, and to cultivate a taste for it we know of nothing better than Peters' Monthly. It always contains something fresh and seasonable. New York: $3.00 a year.

The Country Gentleman.—This old stand-by, so well signifying its sphere by its title, is fresh every number in good seed for all agricultural purposes. Farmers and gardeners may as well undertake to do without their implements as this heirloom. Albany. $2.50 per year in advance, or $3.00 if delayed.

The American Turfman is not only a valuable paper in relation to statistics and tables of winning sires, but of much utility to the roadsman and the farmer—to all who would know the best points of the horse. Monthly, $2 per annum; 20 cents a number. New York.

The American Gas Light Journal is a useful paper to all housekeepers; not only contains practical information about gas, its distribution, purity, economy, etc., but collateral information on water, fuel, and the like. New York. $3.00 per year.

The American Builder and Journal of Industrial Art should be patronized for its æsthetical attractions no less than its mechanical advantages. Every number is embellished with elegant illustrations, original and selected, of the best and most economical styles of architecture, both useful and entertaining. New York. $3.00 a year; 30 cents a number.

The National, of Chicago, is one of our most entertaining exchanges; its original matter embraces topics from which all may learn something. Its selections evince excellent judgment and a thorough appreciation of the wants of the better class of the reading public. Price of the "National" is $1.50 per year, which includes a fine steel engraving called "Fun and Frolic." Address The National, 18 Major Block, Chicago, Ill.

THE SANITARIAN.

A MONTHLY JOURNAL.

VOL. II.] SEPTEMBER, 1874. [NO. 6.

SCHOOL DISEASES.

By C. R. AGNEW, M. D., New York.

The observations of Cohn in the schools and University of Breslau, of Kruger in Frankfort-on-the-Main, of Erismann in St. Petersburgh, of Von Hoffman in Wiesbaden, and others abroad, prove most conclusively that one of the bad effects of school and college life is to produce diseases of the eyes. They have shown that near-sightedness increases rapidly in frequency as you go up in the scale of schools from the primaries of the rural districts to the universities. The gravity of this finding may be appreciated when we remember that near-sightedness is a disease, and that it very frequently descends from one generation to another, marked by such organic changes in the eyes as tend to the production of the worst forms of the malady and to blindness. In 1867, Cohn, of Breslau, published the results of the examination of the eyes of 10,060 scholars. 1486 were children in five village schools, 8,574 were scholars in twenty-eight of the schools of Breslau. Twenty of the schools were elementary, two were girls' high schools, two intermediate schools, two where languages and sciences were taught, two gymnasiums. His examinations covered the entire range of school-life. He found that 1,750 of the 10,060 children had defective vision, about 17 per cent. He also examined, without selection, 410 of the 964 students of the Breslau University, and found that not one-third had normal eyes.

His deductions, as condensed in a paper by B. Joy Jeffries, of Boston, are as follows:

1st. That no school was without near-sighted scholars.

2d. That the number varied greatly in the different schools.

3d. That the percentage of cases of defective vision in village schools was comparatively low, one-fourth per cent.

4th. That there were eight times as many cases of defective vision in city schools as in country.

5th. That in the city elementary schools there were four or five times as many cases of defective vision as in village schools.

6th. That there were more cases in the girls' high schools than in the elementary.

7th. That in the city schools there is a steady increase in the number of near-sighted scholars, viz.: Elementary schools, 6.7 per cent. Middle schools, 10.3. Realschule, 19.7. Gymnasiums, 26.2.

8th. In the middle schools one-tenth, in the Realschule one-fifth, and in the gymnasiums one-fourth of the scholars were near-sighted.

9th. The number of near-sighted scholars varied in the different village schools, but was never more than 2.4 per cent., (ranging from 0.8 upward).

10th. In the second middle schools the number of near-sighted scholars scarcely *varied* 3 per cent., in the Realschule scarcely 2 per cent., in the gymnasiums not 4 per cent.

He took measurements of the bodies of the scholars, and made comparative measurements of the school furniture. He examined into the conditions of light and ventilation, and gave it as his opinion that this alarming prevalence of eye disease is due to the prolonged use of the eyes of the young in scrutinizing such small objects as print, and that the bad effect of such work is greatly increased by improperly constructed school furniture. Anticipating the statement that the German schools are not supplied with what we in America call model school furniture, we must say that Cohn measured the model American seats and desks shown at the Paris Exhibition, and found that they were subject to serious objection.

Seats in school-houses should be constructed with an inclination backwards, and backs so modeled as to give support to the spinal column of the scholar, and thus make any prone position of the head too fatiguing to be voluntarily endured. The desks should be standing desks, with light falling upon them over the left shoulder, or from above. Many exercises that now demand pen or pencil should be done at the blackboard, and every effort should be made to vary the position of the body of the scholar all up through those years of its life when the skeleton is growing and the contents of the thoracic and abdominal cavities are taxed to their utmost to maintain the powers of the growing body. The evil influence of prolonged sitting at desks or tables, with the head prone and the thoracic and abdominal cavities constrained, can scarcely be over-estimated.

It is a serious question whether we are not getting what is called education at too exorbitant a price, when the health and usefulness of eyes are impaired or sacrificed. And the mischief that is done to eyes in schools and colleges may safely be taken as an indication of the damage that is inflicted upon other parts of the body. Objectors may, perhaps, say that the appalling statistics obtained by the foreign observers could not be gathered in American schools and colleges. I believe that they might, and I found my belief upon twenty years' work among just the classes of subjects tabulated by Cohn and the other Continental observers. I believe that our system of education, if, indeed, we may be said to have a system, is one of the most damaging in its effects upon the growing bodies of scholars of any in the world. Let any one familiar with hygiene take the pains, as I have, to inquire carefully into the physical effects of curricula of our leading schools and colleges, and he will be compelled to confess that there is the greatest cause for reform. The attention which is paid to gymnastic exercises and other methods of physical culture does not correct the evils. It often happens that those who really need physical exercise most do not get it, or that the exercise is excessive, and does harm to those who engage in it. What we need in our school and college curricula is a diminution of the hours of labor. The working hours too often extend from eight or nine in the morning to ten or eleven at night. The strain thus put upon growing bodies is too great. Some method should be devised by which much that now involves a persistent use of the eyes in confined and unnatural postures of the body could be accomplished through the use of models or photographs, or the blackboard. Much that is now attempted to be taught by badly-printed books might be taught orally or by some form of object lessons. Even if such radical changes could not be accomplished, much might be done towards lessening the evil effects of our present method by shortening the hours devoted to study, by correcting defects in the architecture of class and study rooms, by improving the ventilation, heating, and lighting of school-houses, and by diffusing information among the parents of scholars, so that there may be less in the home-life that is prejudicial to health. And just here we touch the very fountain of the evil. Our schools cannot be much, if any, above the intelligence of their patrons. I do not blame the teachers for the evils in our systems of education. I blame boards of trustees and other school and college boards for not applying the principles that have already been worked out by scientific men. If architects and boards of managers of schools and colleges would apply in the construction and conduct of their institutions of learning even a few of the principles that sanitarians all agree upon, we would at once see a reduction in those forms of disease which are traceable to their present neglect.

School Ventilation.—The defective ventilation of the public schools of New York and Brooklyn, to which we have frequently called public attention, in the Sanitarian, bids fair to continue without any intelligent effort on the part of the Board of Education to remedy it. Several months ago the New York Board of Apportionment placed $10,000 at the disposal of the Board of Education to defray the expenses of determining upon an effective system of ventilation. After advertising for proposals and holding several meetings without eliciting any practical plan, they seem to have let the matter drop, and excuse themselves on the ground of insufficient funds, saying that to carry out any effective system would cost $100,000 or more, which they think the tax-payers would be unwilling to stand. Meanwhile the $10,000 appropriated lies untouched.

The Board in Brooklyn is in like manner doing nothing. School children's lives are evidently estimated to be of little value, by these repective Boards of Education, or they would take some intelligent measures for their protection. Pure air is sufficiently abundant without the necessity of advertising or paying for patent means for admitting it into school-rooms. And if these gentlemen have not the time, inclination, or intelligence sufficient to devote to this purpose, they should lose no time in delegating the duty to some one who has.

PHYSIOLOGY OF INTEMPERANCE.

By A. H. Dana, New York.

In the accomplishment of any great reform there seems to be a necessity for zeal that will not be confined to exact proof. We overlook any error in consideration of the good which is sought. The agitation of the public mind in respect to *temperance* is no exception to the proposition above stated. The time has come, however, when the reformation desired should not depend upon highly colored statements not strictly accordant with scientific analysis, but upon sound practical principles.

It is often reiterated by lecturers on temperance, that there is no nutrition in alcohol—that it furnishes neither alimentation nor heat to the body; which statements are professedly based upon chemical tests; but they are hardly sustainable without considerable modifications. Alcohol does for a short time accelerate the blood circulation, and during that time produces increased vigor; but then follows a relapse—a *devitalizing* process that diminishes animal heat and vigor of body and mind. That it is not assimilated is true so far as this, that it is largely carried off by the kidneys, exhaled by the lungs and exuded from the skin; and it is likely that other fluids of the body pass off to some extent with it. Saliva and the gastric juices appear to be dried up in like manner as by fever.—(*a*)

Again there are medicinal uses of alcohol which are not wholly to be overlooked—as when administered in prostration after the crisis of fever—so also in some acute diseases; and it may be said that deadly poisons are also included in the materia medica and

---

(*a*) Since this article was written Dr. Hammond in an address before the New York Neurological Society (May 4, 1874), has propounded a theory that alcohol *diminishes the destruction of tissue without at the same time lessening the force which would be derived from its continuance.* The latter part of the proposition seems irreconcilable with the antecedent. His own explanation does not relieve the apparent discrepancy.

By the destruction of tissue (he says) force is generated, muscles contract, thoughts are developed, organs secrete and excrete. Food supplies the material for new tissue. Now, as alcohol stops the full tide of this decay, it is very evident that it must furnish the force which is developed under its use.

Again, he says. "that alcohol enters the food and permeates all the tissue is satisfactorily proven." The conclusion of Lallemand and others that alcohol is wholly excreted from the system unaltered he doubts—that if it be sound the action of the alcohol would be limited to the nervous system—but he thinks it now probable that it furnishes the force by entering into combination with the first products of tissue decay whereby they are again assimilated without being again excreted.

It is quite obvious that here is something incongruous, viz., the recombination and utilization of effete matter which has performed its office and in natural course should be excreted.

An intelligent correspondent of the *Tribune* challenges the proof that any portion of the alcohol is assimilated, and asserts that if true, it is susceptible of proof. A derivative of alcohol (which he terms *aldehyde*) would as surely be found if the alcohol was consumed in the body as ashes when coal is consumed in the grate. But nothing of the kind has yet been discovered.

sometimes used with good effect, as Nux Vomica, Prussic acid, Arsenic, etc. This is true, and nothing more is intended than that alcohol has a medicinal action upon disease, which action is seen in the quickening of impeded circulation, thus having the effect to renew for a time impeded vitality.

This action upon the body in a *morbid* state furnishes, however, no evidence of a like salutary influence on *health*--in fact the most efficacious remedies in the treatment of disease would be most hurtful to us in a healthful condition. This is the theory of *Homœopathy*, and seems to be founded upon a sound principle of pathology. It will not however do to deny that what is of use in extreme cases may be in some degree in lighter ailments. What is to be guarded against is becoming subject to a desire for the stimulant when no longer needed, and there certainly is ground of concern that in medical practice whiskey and other intoxicating stimulants are so often prescribed. In consumption and chronic nervous ailments it is not unfrequently done, and the cases are not few of habitual inebriation caused thereby.

According to chemical analysis the constituents of alcohol are carbon, hydrogen and oxygen. *Starch* is composed of the same elements, only in different proportion—so also animal and vegetable *oils*. These substances (*i. e.* starch and the oils) are what is called *calorifacient*. Yet it has been shown that starch alone will not long support animal life, and it may be inferred that *pure oil* would be equally deficient--probably the intermixture of animal fibre is essential, as, in the Arctic regions, the flesh of the walrus or seal. (*a*)

The muscular and glandular tissues of animals are supposed to be supplied by albuminous substances, such as cereal grains and esculent roots ; so also by the flesh of other animals, all of which contain nitrogen and small quantities of sulphur and phosphorus--in addition to carbon, hydrogen and oxygen, the constitutents of starch and oil.

It is questionable how much dependence is to be placed upon the chemical analyses. Arguments derived from elementary constituents seem to be fallacious—proportion is of most account, as is seen in the comparison of oil and starch with alcohol. Bread made from wheat or other cereal grains contains all the elements required for the support of the human system, yet, according to some experiments, has been found not to sustain life for any considerable time without the addition of something else. Flesh is the sole nutriment of carnivorous animals, and, as appears in the case of the Esquimaux, suffices for the support of *human* life.

Passing, however, from these theories, it is incontrovertible that there is a natural combination of substances in the proportion fitted for alimentation. Flesh and bread (of wheat) have each all that is necessary, but let one of the elements be separated, as starch from flour, or oil from flesh, and it will not alone suffice. So alcohol, though derived from substances that in their natural state were nutritious, as *grapes*, *barley*, and the like, loses in the process some

---

(*a*) Which is the sole diet of the hyperboreans.

original element, or is constituted in a different proportion unsuited to nutrition. The effect of mere change of proportion is shown in the combination of nitrogen and oxygen—one of which combinations is the *atmosphere*, an indispensable supporter of animal and vegetable life. Another, varying only in the proportion of the same constituents, is *nitric acid*—one of the most powerful of chemical agents for the destruction of organized substances. The true method of dealing with the subject is by *observation of effects* rather than *deduction from any chemical theory*, the latter is in fact of little more practical use than the hypotheses of *monads* or *atoms* insisted upon by Epicurus—or of the *vortices* maintained by Descartes—is in explanation of the physical constitution of the world.

An argument of chief importance is derived from the *morbid craving* induced by intoxicating drinks. A man that takes a dram to-day will surely want it to-morrow. Those who drink daily are the most punctual in time—in no business engagement are they so exact —not even at meals. Another incident equally marked is the desire of a larger potation, consequent upon successive indulgence, and this, when there is not much self-control ends speedily in drunkenness —or if a man has resolution enough to avoid that extreme he still has a gnawing sensation of uneasiness that unfits him more or less for business. It is almost invariably seen that whoever takes an intoxicating drink daily, becomes a lounger, wasting part of his time in unprofitable talk; generally will be a frequenter of bar-rooms or other like places of resort, and this will grow upon him as he drinks oftener.

Aristotle sets down in the class of intemperate men, not merely those who actually indulge to excess, but those who have a *desire* for such indulgence, and feel a pain for want of it. In the early stage of intemperance there is something exceedingly deceptive. The desire seems not to be very strong ; a man thinks he can easily break off. Nothing is more common than to hear moderate drinkers say they can give up the habit whenever they choose. Let such an one try it and he will find that what he thought was merely voluntary is *a power like that of the many-armed sea monster that fixes a fatal grasp while yet the victim is at a distance and unconscious of the presence of his enemy*.

Again there is a deception in advanced life, a feeling of security in the formation of a new habit. It is not likely (thinks the respectable elderly man) that at my time of life I should fall into excess when I have always heretofore been regular. *Yet nothing is more likely than if indulgence be yielded to at all it will under this false security become excessive*, and the instances are not unfrequent of men who were in early youth exemplary, giving themselves up to unlawful gratifications in later years. Balzac has sharply depicted a proclivity to sensual pleasure between the ages of fifty and sixty, when is often seen an infatuation wholly beyond control. (*a*) This theory applies not merely to the passion of love—whatever may be a man's propensity is apt at that age to break through restraint.

(*a*) *Cæsar Birotteau*.—He exemplifies it in the character of the Notary Roguin, a grave citizen, who, at that age, became infatuated with "la belle Hollandaise" and spent his whole fortune upon her.

Plato rebuked a man for playing at dice, who answered that he was playing only for *a trifle*. But, said Plato, is the *habit* a trifle? Of all habits none are so controlling as indulgence in strong drink. The appetite is constantly increasing, while moral energy is becoming weaker. In the ordinary course there is therefore little hope of reform, and it is rare to see complete recuperation; loss of fortune—pains of disease, misery of his family, do not reclaim the confirmed inebriate. The *fear of such results* may check in some degree the moderate drinker, but in most cases even this is only for a time. His mind becomes clouded, his moral perception impaired, and while he may be conscious of his weakened condition and its cause—still he will seek temporary strength in the fatal expedient of more frequent stimulant.

Exceptional case there are in which the habit is a long time continued without utterly breaking down vigor of mind—the aberration will be sometimes seen, but even in these cases, unless sudden death intervenes, a crisis must inevitably come when reform or imbecility is the alternative.

Conspicuous in the class of victims nobly endowed was Attorney-General Talcot, of New York, one of the most gifted lawyers this country has produced, who died from excess in the very prime of life, and if the veil could be lifted which by a natural feeling of humanity is drawn over the last scene of *great genius ruined*, the lesson from his tragic end would be more impressive than any ever taught by tragedy enacted on the stage. Gen. Root and Silas Wright eminent political leaders (of the same State) reformed in middle life—but too late. The former lingered out the residue of his life in inert misanthropy; the other, shorn of his intellectual force, at least of elasticity, died, not long after his reform, in voluntary seclusion.

Of the living, or those recently deceased, it is more invidious to speak, but who is not familiar with the charge (at first doubted, but at last undenied) against a leading statesman and conspicuous cabinet officer of two successive Presidents. It was a curious but painful matter of observation to mark what should be the ending of his career, which at one time threatened the dishonor of his country.(*a*)

The most interesting subject of inquiry is in respect to the form-

(*a*) I remember well that at the commencement of the administration of President Lincoln, it was much complained by those having occasion to see *Secretary Seward* upon matters of pressing importance, that he was often incapacitated by his habits, especially in the evening. It was wonderful that with such a drawback he was able to keep up with unflagging assiduity his diplomatic correspondence. There is danger even of inviting the supposition that he actually derived vigor from an indulgence generally so destructive of mental power. That there was not a fatal denouement doubtless is largely attributable to the incessant care of him by his family. Still his case was an anomaly, and the solution belongs rather to the physiologist, if the data could be obtained, which probably are now lost.

There was, however, no time during the great national crisis when there was not just occasion to apprehend some fearful result from the Secretary's loss of prudence under the pressure of inebriety. Fortunately his indiscretions were mostly private, and harmful chiefly to himself—much as his occasional predictions of the summary closing up of all our troubles in a judiciously brief period—and his speeches, when "swinging the circle" with his ridiculous chief, President Johnson.

ation of the habit. Reformation after the habit is established is, as before remarked, unusual. The chief good to be accomplished by admonition is to deter the rising generation from exposure to the temptations which have been fatal to so many in the past.

1st. The lowest of all the causes of intemperance is a mere animal propensity, a desire of mere sensuous exhilaration, the stirring up of emotional activity in an organism which is by nature gross and inert. This comes usually by inheritance, in fact it is one of the retributions that by a mysterious Providence is entailed upon the descendants of profligate parents.

The sensualist, whether man or woman, will stamp upon his or her offspring the marks of vice; and especially will intemperance in drink display its baneful influence through several generations. In fact with the increasing power of hereditary proclivity descending from father to son, there would seem to be no hope for a family subject to the consequences of ancestral vice—and so it would be but for counteractions interposed by a like process of nature. There is a warning in the frail constitution which is one of the incidents, and the predisposition to an early death. Greater care is therefore made necessary—yet this is generally insufficient at least during the first generation, to prevent the fatal development in early life of the vice inherited from a depraved ancestor. If there should be physical strength there will be gross indulgence. But whatever the cause may be, whenever there is an inert habit of body without moral refinement, brutish vices are apt to be developed, especially intemperance, and there is ordinarily no cure for this but what nature has provided, viz: the pain of disease—which if unheeded, an early death or a wretched imbecility is the alternative.

2. Another phase of the habit is when misfortune has imposed a hard condition of life upon one accustomed to better things,—or when by hereditary poverty there is a necessity for greater labor than there is capacity to bear. In such cases it is not unfrequent that *a temporary support is sought in stimulants, or inebriation resorted to as a relief from despair.* In these conditions it is obvious the most effectual method to prevent the habit becoming fixed, or if reclaimed, from it after being confirmed—is by respite of the body overtasked with labor, or by solace to the mind crushed with calamity. Many well-meaning people make a great mistake in addressing harsh rebuke to persons of this class. This is only adding to the intolerable weight that already oppresses them; and although there is a low condition of humanity in the inebriate, yet when sorrow or hardship is the cause, there is still a sensibility to kindness—sympathy will do much even unaccompanied by any other gift; but of course the ills of poverty require additional relief. It is reported that in the English factories intemperance is largely prevalent. It is because the operatives are overworked and hopeless of any change for the better. Religious appeal is of little avail without some other aid—or if effectual at all, will be so only as it is addressed to those expecting soon to die. Christian consolation is best administered to sufferers of this class who have been subject to like hardships—*the poor are the best alleviators of the poor.* The general habit of mind induced by poverty and hard

work, is disbelief of divine goodness and distrust of human ostentation of benevolence. Modern civilization has developed charity for the destitute, as is shown by *hospita's, asylums*, and even by our *prisons*,—but the evils to be contended with are also vastly increased by the overcrowding of population—especially in large cities. The barbarous exposure of infants in Sparta and Athens, prevented to some extent the greater inhumanity of leaving the helpless, of whatever age, to die of starvation. Under the Christian dispensation, a cardinal principle of which is care for every human being—and whose influence is wholly opposed to war—a far greater proportion of the born grow up to mature age than in heathen countries—including of course a large number of the sickly, crippled, or otherwise disabled, while the destruction of life by military service or the violence of victorious armies has been diminished. There is therefore a proportionate demand for increased charity, and it is no longer admissible to deem the giving to the poor as merely gratuitous. An obligation should be recognized that prescribes to the rich relief of the necessitous. When this obligation shall have full effect, a great part of the evil of human life will be abated and the vice incident thereto, especially intemperance, be checked. (*a*)

3. Another class of men have a sensitive organism, the usual adjunct of an emotional temperament, or have great intellectual power which constantly overtasks the bodily capacity. The first is the case of genius in poetry, music, and the like—there must be reaction after great *exaltation*—call it *effort* or *inspiration*. There is a collapse—a sense of feebleness—which is unendurable. A stimulant will rouse energy—who will be so rigid as to say there is not some excuse for resorting to such artifical aid? That it is exhaustive and will in the end be fatal to the natural powers of the mind, is well enough known by those who judge by statistics—but no amount of proof will convince one who is in a *syncope* and can get *present* relief even if it be in a mode prohibited by hygienic science.

There is a tradition that Shakespeare died prematurely from the effect of convivial habits; this is not sufficiently proved—in fact we know little of his private life at any period, and more especially after his retirement from the stage.

We may follow this out in men of great intellectual power in other pursuits. An ardent devotion to science is exhaustive. There is no alternative but entire abstinence or habitual and in the end excessive indulgence. Great philosophers have usually been ab-

(*a*) In an address recently delivered by Judge Daly (of New York), he contrasted the conditions of the two classes of society. One surrounded by the comforts and enjoying the amenities of life—the other suffering from hard-handed poverty and privation of all that makes life enjoyable. Trace out the origin of this unequal lot (he said) and it would be found to be intemperance. This I think is putting effect for cause. Misery is a prolific cause of drunkenness. The higher class are more protected from the crushing effect of severe trials; they at all events have greater resources for physical sustentation than the poor. It is not, however, true that even they are exempt from falling into intemperance under such pressure—many poor inebriates are to be seen who have been once in a respectable position, and in such cases some misfortune or stealthy vice has preceded their degradation.

stemious; but they have also been much secluded from the world. (*a*)

The seclusion referred to, was rather privacy—exemption from interruption or intrusion; and it is certain that continuous labor is better endured than irregular efforts.

We know now unmistakably that the great novelist of our own time who enchanted the world by a power that like Shakespeare seemed as if inspired—certainly underived from culture—died prematurely from inebriety at an age but little beyond that of the renowned dramatist. (*b*)

Can it be justly argued from such examples that genius derives any of its inspiration from this self-consuming process, or that in any sense this artificial stimulation of forced effort is a refocalization of mental vigor. This would be unwarranted. On the contrary, the law of nature is that all human excellence is by normal development from a germinal element. The grand conception of the intellect and the splendor of poetic imagery and diction, must come from the mysterious, perhaps heaven-born power of the soul in the exercise of its natural functions. No promethean fire can be brought down in aid of this congenital endowment.

From this source has been derived all that is left to us by human genius. It is only when the natural power has been overtasked that the auxiliary has been thought needful—but whatever has been then produced is only by an enforced effort of nature wasteful of its inherent vigor.

Great thinkers, or men of great intellectual endowment of any kind, brought into public life, have often fallen victims to too great pressure. Mr. Pitt was undoubtedly intemperate, but in an aristocratic style. Sheridan, who deserves a much higher estimate than that of a mere rhetorician, as he has been commonly rated—who was in fact a man of great ability, while he was most affluently gifted with oratory and colloquial wit, became an inebriate. Our own country has furnished memorable instances of the wreck of statesmen.

Who will fail to call to mind as chief in this sad catagory, the great Massachusetts senator—in intellectual power never surpassed—but weak in moral resolution to resist sensual proclivities. There seems to be a tendency in political life to the sin of intemperance.

(*a*) Pythagoras, the patriarch of philosophy, Antiphanes and Zeno, the founders of the Cynic and Stoic sects, and others who were ascetic have been paralleled by great thinkers of later times in severe abstinence—from Copernicus to Comte.

(*b*) Dickens died at the age of 56; Shakespeare at 53. The latter part of the novelist's life, when it was apparent to all who knew him that he was failing under the habit of excessive stimulation, he could not be persuaded into a change, but only increased the quantity of alcoholic beverage as his natural appetite became feebler.

He describes his diet when residing in America in 1868, thus: "I cannot eat to anything like the necessary extent and have established this system At 7 in the morning, in bed, a tumbler of new cream and two tablespoonsful of *rum*; at 12 a *sherry cobbler* and a biscuit; at 3, (dinner-time), a pint of champagne; at five minutes to 8, an egg beaten up with a glass of sherry; between the parts the strongest beef tea that can be made, drank hot; at a quarter past 10, soup and any little drink that I can fancy. I do not eat more than half a pound of solid food in the whole twenty-four hours, if so much."

Our Federal and State Legislatures give testimony to this. The *present* is all—the *future* is uncared for. Douglass almost achieved success in his mad effort to gain the Presidency, but obtained instead a drunkard's grave. (*a*)

Poets and other imaginative writers have been prone to physical stimulants. (*b*) These can not be said strictly to have been overtasked —that is to say not by *continuous* labor—their phase has rather been that of *irregular activity* alternated by *apathetic depression*. If we confine our observation to men not of great celebrity, we shall still find that whoever is overtasked—whether it be by labor too long protracted or by an effort exceeding what his natural power is equal to, will be likely to resort to artificial aid.

4. Lastly, there is a class who are led into intemperance by mere conviviality. Such men are usually endowed with conversational attractiveness, and whether they are guests in a private circle or attend the more sensual entertainment of public dinners, or become the oracles of the club or of the bar-room, the temptation is the same. A reputation is to be maintained; where the spirits flag, artificial aid must be used—at least so thinks the brilliant talker or speech-maker, when he is not in his best mood.

We have touched upon all the predisposing causes of intemperance. The lesson to be deduced is, not so much how to reform (though this should be sought as far as practicable) as how to guard against the evil in its inception.

We conclude with the following aphorisms, which are of general application—perhaps *hygienic* rather than *moral*—but calculated to secure as well efficiency of mind as body—*mens sana in corpore sana*.

1st. Let every man use the powers which God has given him strictly in accordance with their natural scope, and be content with that measure of active efficiency and influence appertaining to these powers in their proper healthful development. To aspire beyond this is to attempt rashly a scheme of life not designed for him, and which if pursued, will be abortive and likely to end in misery and vice.

2d. Avoid all resorts to artificial aid for the purpose of obtaining a *temporary* vigor, either of mind or body. Any thing beyond the natural supply of force by the aliment of healthful food, only reacts and is followed by depression. Especially is this true of alcoholic exhilaration. It may promote convivial wit an hour or two in the

(*a*) It is said that he had reformed before his death; but if so he had already suffered the penalty of excesses by the forfeiture of public respect, which cannot long be maintained against the downward pressure of vulgar vice.

(*b*) Coleridge and De Quincey were life-long sufferers from the use of opium. The most remarkable thing in their history is that they should have retained their faculties so long, under such a baleful influence. How many others there may have been who sank earlier under like habits before attaining such celebrity as to be commemorated for the immolation of their genius, we know not. It is reasonably certain that a few years more of life would have added Byron to the catalogue of wrecks caused by indulgence. *Pope* escaped from dissipation before his powers of mind were fatally impaired, but with shattered health of body. *Swift* continued the habit of too free use of wine against the remonstrance of friends (at least of Pope, who probably expressed the opinion of Arbuthnot and others), and it is a curious inquiry how much this had to do with the great perversion of his mind in later years, and final insanity.

evening, but it makes a dull and ill-natured companion in the morning. For any serious and continuous labor it is as unfit as the running of a horse up hill in order to get greater impetus--a forced effort resulting in a more speedy exhaustion.

THE ALTITUDE AT WHICH MEN CAN LIVE.

There has been a great deal of discussion as to the altitude at which human beings can exist, and Mr. Glaisher himself can tell us as much about it as anybody. In July, 1872, he and Mr. Coxwell ascended in a balloon to the enormous height of 38,000 feet. Previous to the start, Mr. Glashier's pulse stood at 76 beats a minute, Coxwell's at 74. At 17,000 feet the pulse of the former was at 84, that of the latter at 100. At 19,000 feet Glashier's hands and ips were quite blue, but not his face. At 21,000 feet he heard his heart beating, and his breathing became oppressed; at 29,000 he became senseless; notwithstanding which the aeronaut, in the interest of science went up another 8,000 feet, till he could no longer use his hands, and had to pull the strings of the valve with his teeth. Aeronauts who have to make no exertions have of course a great advantage over members of the Alpine Club and those who trust their legs; even at 13,000 feet, these climbers feel very uncomfortable, more so in the Alps, it seems than elsewhere. At the monastery of St. Bernard, 8,117 feet high, the monks become asthmatic, and are compelled frequently to descend into the Valley of the Rhone for—anything but a breath of fresh air; and at the end of ten years service are obliged to give up their high living, and come down to their usual level. At the same time in South America there are towns, such as Potosi, placed as high as the top of Mount Blanc, the inhabitants of which feel no inconvenience. The highest inhabited spot in the world is, however, the Buddhist cloister of Hanle in Thibet, where twenty-one priests live at an altitude of 16,000 feet. The brothers Schlaginsweit, when they explored the glaciers of the Ibi-Gamin in the same country, encamped at 21,000 feet, the highest altitude at which a European ever passed the night. Even at the top of Mount Blanc Professor Tyndall's guides found it very unpleasant to do this, though the Professor himself did not confess to feeling so bad as they. The highest mountain in the world is Mount Everest, (Himalaya), 29,003 feet, and the condor has been seen "winging the blue air" 500 feet higher. The air, by the by, is not "blue" or else, as De Saussure pointed out, "the distant mountains, which are covered with snow, would appear blue also;" its apparent color being due to the reflection of light. What light can do, and does, is marvelous; and not the least is its power of attraction to humanity.—*Chambers' Journal.*

SCIENCE IN LIFE INSURANCE.

The tendency of the times is in the direction of science, which is equivalent to saying that it is in the direction of truth. For the result of science is the evolution of truth, and the overthrow of falsehood. But in this general advance, much that wears a scientific garb and parades a scientific name, is but the assumption, the falsehood of empiricism and ignorance. Old-fogyism, delighting in the name of conservatism, holds hard to the skirts of progress, disguising its plea for retrogression under an ill-founded reverence for the past.

In this struggle of science with empiricism, of progress with retrogression, life insurance has not taken the place it should. Founded upon facts which contain the embryo of one of the noblest sciences of which the world knows, itself adapted in a peculiar manner for developing data for the advancement and perfection of that science, much of its own development has been in an unscientific direction, many of its phases have borne most prominently the marks of empiricism. Narrowness has held control in its affairs where broad-sightedness should have been called into play. Its progress toward actual, scientific accuracy, has in no wise kept pace with the enlargements of its field of operatons.

One may read the principles upon which the Amicable Society of England was founded in 1705, and wonder at the ignorance of all the facts and data which are now deemed essential in the conduct of a life insurance company, or may smile at the simplicity of some of the calculations and formulæ, and yet when we compare the status of the several sciences which have direct or indirect bearings upon life insurance, as they were then and as they are at present, we shall be forced to confess that the scheme was then more nearly abreast of the times than it is now.

There would seem to be a class of men who are afraid of the word "science" in connection with life insurance. They seem to think that science is something essentially impractical, something that theorists may well spend their time over, but which practical men must avoid, or pay the price of their practicalness as the cost of meddling with it. They have failed, or refused, to learn from other departments of the world's industry and progress, that the essentiality of science is practicability, that that is a false and spurious "science" which is not practical.

But if we have this class of men represented in life insurance, we have another class who claim that the scheme is all science, that it is a pure mathematical science. To their mind the science of life insurance is to be found in the sitting at desks all day long, and figuring, figuring, figuring. To their mind the "actuary" is the life insurance company, and the balance of the concern is simply the media through which he works.

A certain department of life insurance has, perhaps, been given up too thoroughly to this class. They have added and subtracted, multiplied and divided, copied and recopied figures, and when this was done, they have subtracted those they had added, added those they had subtracted, divided those they had multiplied, and multiplied those they had divided, all the time imagining that they were very "scientific" and very learned, and were doing a vast amount of good in the world.

But this is not the kind of science which is wanted in life insurance. In the first place, it is but little that the science of mathematics has now to do for the system, and what it has to do will be done only at long intervals and as the result of long and patient research. Yet, if we were to believe these prolific figurers, almost every day, certainly each week, some scientific wonder results from all this figuring. But the truth is, there is nothing original about these things. They are, at the best, simply readaptations of truths and facts long since scientifically determined. They have not even that essential requisite of a scientific fact, usefulness. They are mere fanciful disguises of simple truths or specious falsehoods.

But in another department, and one where scientific research would really develop valuable results, we have not even this show of activity. How much attention do the companies deem it worth while to give to the question of the life and death of human beings? Who thinks of asking why this man dies while that one lives? Who, why one man lives to forty years and another to eighty? Who thinks to wrest from nature the secrets of longevity, and make them of use in the scheme of life insurance?

Yet here are scientific truths, within the grasp of the patient, earnest inquirer, which, once developed, would become indispensable in the scheme of life insurance. Here are facts without which life assurance can never be exactly equitable, truly scientific. Some time they must be developed; if not in the aid of life insurance, then in the unfolding of the civilization and general advancement of the race; and then, gradually, life insurance will be *forced* to avail itself of them, or fall so hopelessly behind the age as to be but a relic of the past.

On the other hand, life insurance has now within its grasp, better than any other branch of industry or development, the data for solving these problems. If she will but reach out and grasp the prize, it is hers. She needs the knowledge which lies unopened before her. Have it she must, sooner or later. The simple question is, will she open it herself now, or will she wait until others get ready to open it for her?—*The Index.*

A Crazy Young Man.—"I'll take a glass of your divine nectar," said a young man in a lager beer saloon the other day. "Vat eest dot?" asked the waiter. "I want a goblet drain of the extract of the somniferous hop." "We ton't gots beem," answered the waiter. "Numskull, bring me a glass of lager." The waiter went to the barkeeper and informed him that a crazy man wanted a glass of beer, but didn't know how to ask for it. "I kess he ton't mooch English speak," said the barkeeper. Most everybody thought the barkeeper was right.

THERMOMETRICAL NOTES IN THE PROSECUTION OF NEW THEORIES OF DISEASE.*

By H. L. Bartlett, M. D., Consulting Surgeon to Kings County Hospital.

This is emphatically the age of positiveness. The "*a priori*" dogma might do for our forefathers, but *now* to believe, we must *see*. This feeling pervades the entire domain of thought. God is only a first great cause, "evolving" other causes. The human soul is but a gaseous emanation of the "pituitory gland," depending for its manifestations entirely upon "molecular metamorphosis." The solid universe is looked upon as an outspread map whereupon to study the "epochs" of by-gone ages and trace the footprints of its extinct inhabitants.

Human history is simply so much data whereby the social scientist fulminates the rise or fall of societies or empires. The circumambient air is so many millions of cubic feet of oxygen and nitrogen, laden with a definite number of "kilograms of ammonia, carbonic acid gas, and other albuminoid emanations, "each and all correctly weighed and measured."

So the human body has been discovered by the modern physicist to be nothing more than a chemical laboratory, where the processes of life can be seen and watched by the aid of thermometric spirometer, æthesiometer, dynamometer, together with the microscope and numerous other scopes, which take within their scope the entire phenomena of life, and hold them up to our astonished vision. Among the "armamentum medicinæ" nothing holds so prominent a place in "positive diagnosis" as the clinical thermometer. What the telescope is to the astronomer, the compass to the mariner, or the microscope to the pathologist, the thermometer is to the physician! We are much indebted to Professor Wunderlick, of Leipsic; Drs. Ringer and Compton, of England; and Seguin, and others, for valuable hints on this important subject, but it seems to me they have been of too general a character to be made available in actual practice. They have informed us of the degree of temperature at which blood of rabbits and guinea-pigs ceases to be vital under the influence of cold, and also the degree of heat they can bear before life is extinct. German patience and industry have tested the blood-heat of all living animals, from the elephant to the microscopic insect, but no German, Russian, Englishman, American, or Frenchman has yet had the boldness to put the genus homo to the same crucial test, and record for the benefit of unborn millions the point above or below zero, which the blood of man may not go and live! This it has been my happy lot to achieve.

This had long been the desire of my heart, when a happy concurrence of circumstances gave me the opportunity.

While passing along the docks of New York one of the hottest days of August last, a woolly-headed, thick-lipped, and sable individual

*Read before Kings County Medical Society, July 21, 1874.

arrested my attention. I found he was a native of Africa, just landed, without means or friends, and evincing great indifference to life.

The idea at once possessed me that here was a fit subject for my experiment. On the plea of some paltry gift I invited him to my office and procured for him a bountiful repast. I then seated him in a chair in my back yard, where the burning rays of the sun concentrated their full force upon his head, and charged him, on pain of my displeasure, not to move.

The sleepiness natural to his race, together with the drowsiness caused by a full meal and the influence of the sun, composed him into a sound slumber, which no sooner did I observe through my rear office window than I immediately proceeded to apply one of Casella's tested thermometers to each axilla, gently fastening the arms in front, so as to keep them in position, and thrusting another into his mouth, which was partly open, and then left him, no doubt, in the full enjoyment of pleasant dreams of his bamboo village under Afric skies.

At the expiration of two hours I examined him, and found life extinct! He had evidently died easy, for his face wore a sunny smile, as if the spirit had indeed been recognized and welcomed in the land of *shades*, whither it had gone. But the *record?* The thermometer registered 112° F! Is it any wonder that in the exultation of the moment I should have exclaimed, as did Pythagoras of old, "Eureka!" "Eureka!" Masonic tradition has it that when that great heathen philosopher made use of the above remarkable and historic expression he had just finished the demonstration of the 47th problem of Euclid, and thereupon sacrificed a hecatomb! But here I had discovered and recorded a fact which should stand as a landmark to the profession through all the ages to come, and place my name among the illustrious benefactors of the race, and at so small a cost!

Having recorded my observation I reported to the police that I had found a man on my premises in a stupid condition—apparently dead—and requested them to remove him to the station-house. The coroner was notified, and a jury of twelve intelligent citizens was impaneled to sit on his body. The unanimous verdict rendered by this learned body was that the man, name unknown, had died from some cause unknown, and that the coroner was at liberty to give his remains to his friends for decent interment. Who was more friendly than I? No one. So thought the coroner, and gave me the body for dissection, charging the county, of course, for the funeral expenses.

The brain I presented the same evening to the Pathological Society, as a specimen of nostalgia. The President remarked that home-sickness was not an unfrequent disease, but that, so far as his memory served him, no specimen of this sort had been presented to the Society since his connection with it, and he thanked me for the pleasure I had afforded the members. Thereupon a most lively interest was manifested in the specimen, and an exhaustive discussion ensued in regard to its pathology. A learned professor remarked that one of the peculiarities of this disease was the development of pigmentary cells or bodies, which in the specimen before him was very marked. (I had not told him that it was the brain of a negro!) Another peculiarity, he said, was a preponderance of the cerebellum over the cerebrum, giving the impulses and passions the mastery over the will and reason; (if he had seen the skull he would have been quite certain).

Dr. Wiseman said that during many years' experience as physician-in-chief of an asylum for the insane, he had seen many specimens of this disease, and all of them were characterized, as this one was, by a large amount of the white or nerve tissue, manifesting itself in life through the emotional faculties. Being somewhat in doubt, after these learned remarks, whether my patient had not, after all, died of home-sickness, and not from too high a temperature of the blood, as I had supposed, I determined to verify my conclusions by further experiments ere I gave my statements publicity. And again good fortune favored me. While on my way home from a professional visit, a man speaking a foreign accent, and meanly clad, stopped me on the street and tried to communicate with me. I beckoned him to follow me to my office, when I found he was a Russian by birth, desperate, and tired of life. I gave him a large potation of whiskey, and motioned him to sit down and rest, which he gladly did; and on the same chair occupied by the African.

He, too, soon fell asleep, and I placed the thermometer as before; impatiently watching the result. At the end of two hours, fifty-nine minutes, and three seconds he ceased to breathe. On examination I found him quite dead. The mercury stood as before, 112° F.! This was conclusive. There could be no longer any doubt that 112° F. was the maximum to which the human blood could go, and this last experiment, no less remarkable than the first, had verified a statement made in Holy Writ, viz.: that "God had made of one blood all the nations of the earth," for the blood of that African must have been identical with the blood of the Caucasian, else why were they alike affected under like circumstances? This point being conclusively determined, the next question for solution was how low could the temperature descend before life should become extinct?

Here, again, fortuitous circumstances favored my investigations. Hardly had I finished the above experiment ere a female came to my office, stating that she and her husband were quite incompatible in their tempers and dispositions. They had been married several years, had no children, and his society had become hateful to her. On further inquiry I found she had an "affinity" in the person of a good-looking undertaker.

Here was my opportunity. She persuaded her husband to seek my advice. I expatiated on the nature of his disease—told him that all his troubles, physical and domestic, came from an overheated brain and blood, and that if he would submit himself to my care and treatment, which at first might seem severe, I had no doubt I could rid him of his misery.

He replied that he would gladly submit to any treatment I advised, as death itself was far preferable to his present condition. I explained to him that I should first endeavor to cool his blood by placing him on a water-bed, under which was a refrigerator constructed for the purpose, and so arranged that a cold atmosphere could be made to envelop both him and the bed; that I should place a thermometer under his arms and mark the temperature of his blood, and when I had succeeded in gaining the point I wished, should treat him thereafter as occasion might require. This explanation was highly satisfactory to him, and it was agreed that we should try the experiment the next day. Accordingly, I repaired to his house, (where everything was in readiness), and reduced his temperature this day to 95° F. As the weather was very warm he found this agreeable, and expressed himself as feeling much better, especially as it seemed to have the additional advantage of cooling his wife's antipathy to him. She was in the secret, and all at once became very loving and tender.

We continued this treatment for one week, and in the mean time the patient was forbidden to be seen out of doors, and the neighbors and friends were made to understand that Mr. ——— was dangerously ill. On the seventh day of the experiment, all things being in readiness, I resolved to reduce the temperature to the minimum. Accordingly, arranging the patient as before, with the exception of having one arm projecting out from the covering, (so as to feel the pulse), I proceeded until his breathing became slow and somewhat labored. Upon removing a part of the covering, so that I could see his face, I found he was in a quiet sleep, perfectly unconscious of all around him, like one under the influence of chloroform. I then replaced the covering and sat down beside the bed, with the fingers of one hand on the pulse and a watch in the other, so as correctly to mark the time when his heart should cease beating. After anxiously waiting two hours and five minutes from the commencement of the experiment the pulse ceased at the wrist, and after the lapse of three minutes more I uncovered the patient and found him quite dead! The thermometer stood at 91° F.! This, I consider, demonstrates the proposition beyond controversy, that a temperature of 91° F., is incompatible with human life. Great care was taken to avoid all sources of error, and in reflecting upon the case I can think of nothing that was omitted in order to make the experiment a success. No post mortem was allowed in this instance, so I was denied the pleasure of presenting any interesting specimens to the learned members of the Pathological Society. I have no doubt, however, that the "immediate" cause of death was congestion of the lungs, and so stated in my "certificate." I may as well state, also, for the encouragement of the younger members of the profession, that the disconsolate widow was so well pleased with the success of my treatment, especially after the discovery, among the papers of the deceased, of a life-insurance policy of $10,000, that, besides paying me liberally for my services, she also presented me with a valuable set of diamond studs, once worn, I presume, by her beloved departed. I accompanied the widow to the funeral as chief-mourner, her "affinity" being obliged to drive the hearse to avoid suspicion, but from April smiles that ever and anon broke through her November tears, especially when said eyes met the sympathetic gaze of the *grave* undertaker.

My professional duties calling me elsewhere I left them to return home together and happy!

The practical results which must flow from these astounding discoveries are too patent to need amplification. Hereafter, when the physician is in doubt, in any given case, as to his prognosis, he has but to consult his thermometer, 112° F., being the maximum, and 91° F., the minimum, compatible with human life, the nearer these two extremes are reached the more danger to life. Hence the following propositions:

1st. No patient will die, with the thermometer normal, no matter what the condition of his respiration, circulation or general symptoms, unless struck by lightning!

2d. No patient can live with the thermometer above or below the extremes above mentioned, unless he be an inhabitant of some other planet than our own.

I would also remark in this connection that when the temperature is inclined to fall below the standard our efforts should be directed to elevate it, and the *direct rays* of the sun, particularly in midsummer, possess a wonderful power in this direction.

While on the other hand, if the heat of the body is inclined upwards, my "*Refrigeratorium*," made exclusively by "Othello & Reindeer," has a most salutary influence in reducing it.

I would also further remark, in reference to the exception, noted in proposition first, that I am having a galvanic battery constructed, of sufficient power to destroy life, and shall embrace the first favorable opportunity of recording the temperature of one moribund from this cause.

(*To be continued.*)

VENTILATION OF SHIPS.—The last official report on the health of the navy shows that men employed in repairing and cleaning ships in the royal dockyards suffer considerably from want of fresh air when engaged in paint work between the double bottoms. Many of these parts of the vessel are reached by crawling on the belly and dragging the body forward by the hands. Staff-Surgeon M'Kenzie Saunders, in medical charge of the Devonport Yard, states that in these corner spaces the supply of air is most scanty; that men have occasionally been hauled out in a state of insensibility by a rope slipped over their feet. Although air-pumps are provided, the men dislike the trouble attending their use, and will frequently continue their work when there is not sufficient air to keep a candle burning. It is satisfactory, however, to know that these men are not kept at work more than three days in the week, but after three or four weeks they usually complain of great lassitude, with headache, having dirty yellow tongues and foul teeth, and experience epigastric pains, constipated bowels, and other symptoms of lead-poisoning, as well as the effects of impure air. These notes by Dr. Saunders go to swell an already formidable array of facts that show the necessity of directing special attention by marine architects to the ventilation of ships.—*Lancet.*

SANITARY NOTES.

Architects are wont to dream of the imaginative elements of their art, forgetful that the substantial and physical lie at the very threshold, and pave the way to the pleasing and graceful. The two conditions are as strictly correlative as the reciprocal action of body and mind. It is a hard matter to learn this, and, as long as confused ideas of the purpose, character, and objects of art prevail, extremely difficult and impossible. So long as art is confounded with wealth, patronage, or fashion, and its followers attach themselves to certain leaders, cliques and even political and religious parties—ay, even ecclesiastical dogmas—as if in truth its very existence and development depended thereupon, it seems folly to tell architects that their most powerful ally is the human body—the simplest wants of a frail humanity.

The whole science of hygiene may be included in the one word Cleanliness. The removal of refuse of all kinds, solid, liquid, and gaseous, is embraced within it, and pure air and water becomes a necessary result of the operation. It is a trite saying, "Nature abhors a vacuum," or, more correctly, it may be said, Nature always *supplies* a vacuum. Whenever we remove foul matter, stagnant water, and superfluous dust, we admit air, and generally far purer air, and water, to take their places.

Cleanliness is a thing that no Act of Parliament will adequately make. Those who are naturally disposed, through laziness or habit, to become uncleanly in their houses, cannot be compulsorily cured by law. We are quite convinced that if cleanliness among certain classes is to be insured, only one course will be effectual, and that is, by avoiding the causes and receptacles of dirt—in other words, the provision of ready means and facilities, or the adoption of self-cleansing contrivances and appliances in the construction of houses. Unless facilities are within immediate use, it is futile to expect the hard-toiled man and wife to keep their dwelling clean ; the laborious part of the operation must be avoided.

Now to aid towards the attainment of cleanliness in a house, the following leading points should be kept in view:

1st. The localization of the receptacles for refuse, &c.
2d. Ready means of removal.
3d. The use of non-absorbent materials in buildings.
4th. Avoidance of receptacles for dirt and dust.
5th. Free ventilation.

Under the first head we may include ashes, dust, slops, soil, &c. Until some more economical system has been adopted by which our dry refuse may be made available as a deodorizing agent, or a portion of it at least converted into fuel, it is desirable to concentrate as much as possible all such refuse, especially in towns. Ash-bins and out-offices are generally noisome adjuncts, and frequently pestilential, from the length of time refuse and vegetable and animal matter are allowed to remain in them before removal. It becomes necessary to devise a means which shall at once afford easy access for getting rid of such refuse, and also its removal as speedily as possible.

We have no hesitation in recommending a plan, we believe original, though one which would effect this object. We should in the first place select the best and most convenient corner of the house (say near the scullery, and outside, if possible; if not in the basement) for the construction of a tank or bin, into which all the ashes, dust and vegetable matter may be shot from the scullery or outer lobby without entailing the trouble of going out of the house, a passage-way or square conduit of concrete, or some impervious material, to be constructed, leading to this closed tank, about eighteen inches square, from the front of the house or from a back approach. Through this tunnel, as it were, and running on wheels, a movable ash-box of block-tin or iron may be made to traverse by lines and pulleys from end to end, accessible only to the dustman, or local board authorities, who could reach it by opening an iron plate or trap outside, leading to a kind of man-hole, where the tackle could be wound round a drum. By this simple means every house could have its refuse removed without the slightest inconvenience from dustmen coming through the house, and often through rooms, causing much trouble to the inmates; and further, no ready excuse could be made for the non-removal of ashes and decaying matter—a very frequent and often well-grounded one. The cost of such a conveyance, the fixed and movable iron ash-box (the latter running on wheels), and the concrete passage would be trifling. The refuse tank, if in the basement, could be readily ventilated from the outside, while the passage would be impervious to all smell, and would be excavated easily under the wooden, paved or asphalt floor. This plan would give to the board or local authorities complete control, at any hour of the morning, over the refuse of every house and street. A similar kind of conduit would be also a ready way of removing the soil of the earth-closet system in towns. In houses on the flat system, an upright shoot would convey all refuse to the movable tank. But the greatest advantage of this method is that it reduces the trouble and labor to a minimum, and thereby becomes a great source of cleanliness. Mr. Blashill, in a paper read at the Architectural Association, the other day, hinted at some of the ways by which a house may be rendered clean. He recommended the use of concrete and asphalt pavements, and tiles for the walls of halls, passages, &c.

These substitutes for wood, porous brick and plaster, are happily getting introduced in some quarters, and we should certainly be glad to see their universal adoption in houses for the laboring classes. For basement floors, subject to dampness, we think a kind of hollow-pot foundation should be used, besides a concrete substratum and filling-in. Skirtings are one fruitful source of dirt, and a harbor for vermin, both in basement and upper floors, and in the majority of dwelling-houses we should make it compulsory to substitute cements, or glazed earthenware slabs. In basements a plain splay or batter to cover floor edges, is all that is required; and we should never tolerate in dwellings for the poor, or even in bedrooms of the better classes, any other sort of moulding than a simple splay. Toruses, ogees and cavettos favor dirt and harbor vermin by the very protect-tion afforded to quirks, and few brushes ever penetrate these crevices of filth. The joints of wood floors are especially open to this objection, and also the angles between floors and skirtings and walls and skirtings. Mere tonguing of joints is only a partial remedy; a stopping of oakum is necessary. All floors should be plugged between the joists, not only to prevent the passage of sound, but as a check to both effluvia and fire. Kamptulicon or linoleum covering for floors may be employed as promotive of cleanliness. Walls should be built hollow in all cases. We do not think with Mr. Blashill that battening is better, as it harbors dust and vermin. We also disagree with him in saying well-burnt brick facing is impervious to damp; our own experience has taught us that the best of bricks set in mortar are absorbent of moisture in wet aspects. As regards the internal coating of walls, nothing is better than plaster or cement; and in the dwellings of the poorer classes we should leave such a facing without papering, as being more conducive to health and cleanliness. Up to a certain height a coating of Parian, or a painted or glazed surface would be beneficial, as it would admit of washing.

Moulded work is a mistake in houses where servants are not kept. Chamfers in all such cases are better and more cleanly, as they throw off instead of harboring dust and dirt.

Mr. Blashill recommends an outside sink placed in the yard; this is better than an inside sink; a still more effective sink would be one placed inside, and provided with a large grating instead of a bell-trap, the waste pipe from which should go directly through the wall, and empty upon a trapped cesspool outside. The sewer air would then rapidly find vent before entering the house, as it now does, by the carelessness of servants, who, to save trouble, often take off the bell-grate so as to allow solid matters to go down, ignorant of the intention of a trap in shutting off sewer gas. We think if all waste and soil pipes could be discharged externally above trapped outlets, so as to allow a continual escape of sewer gas, there would be infinitely less zymotic disease. If such a plan were enforced, instead of carrying the soil-pipe up, as recommended by sanitarians, a constant egress of sewer gas would take place if free ventilation was afforded at every inlet to closets externally to the house. We have discussed this question before in these pages. As to closets, an intercepting lobby is most desired, as in it can be placed a lavatory, and its windows would form an extra ventilator. Projecting water-closets, though unsightly, are to be advocated under the present system of house-drainage. As to the closet apparatus, we think nothing is simpler and cleaner than the stoneware syphon "hopper."

Apropos of ventilation, every house should have ventilating flues carried up from the basement within the chimney projection, opening into each room near the ceiling. This, together with especial fresh air ducts to feed the fires would insure a thorough displacement of the vitiated atmosphere within the house in spite of the apathy or laziness of the inmates.—*Building News.*

THE RELATIONS BETWEEN HUMAN MORTALITY AND THE SEASONS OF THE YEAR.

At the anniversary meeting of the Scottish Meteorological Society, a very valuable paper was read by Dr. Arthur Mitchell, and the Secretary, Mr. Alex. Buchan, giving an account of their investigations on the subject of the influence of the seasons on human mortality at different ages as caused by different diseases. The authors have calculated the weekly average death-rate of London for the past thirty years for thirty-one diseases, together with the averages of temperature, moisture, rain, etc. Considering the weather experienced in the course of the year as made up of several distinct climates differing from each other according to the prevailing temperature and moisture, and their relations to each other, the influence of these climates, characterized respectively by cold, cold and dryness, dryness and heat, heat, heat and moisture, and cold and moisture, on the mortality was pointed out. The weekly mortality from all causes and at all ages shows a large excess above the average from the middle of November to the middle of April, from which it falls to the minimum in the end of May; it then slowly rises, and on the third week of July shoots suddenly up almost to the maximum of the year, at which it remains till the second week of August, and thence falls as rapidly as it rose to a secondary minimum in October. Regarding the summer excess in the death-rate, which is so abrupt in its rise and fall, it was shown that it is wholly due to one section of the population, viz., infants under five years of age, none of the curves for the other ages showing an excess in the death-rate from all causes during the summer months; and it was further shown that the summer excess is due not only to the deaths at one age, but to the deaths from one class of diseases, viz., bowel complaints. The importance of weekly averages in discussing these sudden fluctuations of the death-rate to the changes of the weather was pointedly referred to. Deducting the deaths from bowel complaints from the deaths from all causes, the curve assumes a simple form, viz., an excess in the cold months and a deficiency in the warm months. In other words, the curve of mortality is dictated by the large number of deaths from diseases of the respiratory organs. The curve of mortality in London, has thus an inverse relation to the temperature, rising as the temperature falls, and falling as the temperature rises. On the other hand, in Victoria, Australia, the curves of mortality and temperature are directly related to each other—mortality and temperature rising and falling together. The character of the curve of mortality in Victoria is impressed on it by the deaths of persons below the age of five; and among such young persons the special diseases which determine this influence are diarrhœa and dysentery. This peculiarity arises from its higher mean temperature, 57°·6, as compared with that of London, 50°·0.

In London also during the hottest months of the year the curves of mortality and temperature rise and fall together, whereas in Victoria the curves are throughout the whole year directly related; for though doubtless the deaths from diseases of the respiratory organs fall as the temperature rises, and rise as the temperature falls, yet the number of deaths from these diseases is, owing to the comparatively high winter temperature, never sufficiently large to influence the curve of the whole death-rate. The curves of mortality for bronchitis and pneumonia at different ages, prove that the fluctuation is much less for pneumonia than for bronchitis, and that the excess in both cases of infant mortality is great, but not nearly so great as the infant mortality for diarrhœa. The curves show that the maximum mortality from the different diseases group around certain specific conditions of temperature and moisture combined, the general result of which, as regards the principal diseases, may be thus roughly stated :—

Character of Weather.	Maximum Mortality.
Cold	Bronchitis, pneumonia, asthma, etc.
Cold and dry	Brain-disease, convulsions, whooping-cough
Warm and dry	Suicides, small-pox
Warm and moist	Diarrhœa, dysentery, cholera
Cold and moist	Rheumatism, heart-disease, diptheria, scarlatina, measles, croup.

The deaths from cancer and liver disease show no distinct relation to weather. The period of the year least marked by the occurrence of maximum mortality from any disease, is the warm dry weather which prevails from the middle of May to the end of June. At this season the only maximum is a well-pronounced secondary maximum for measles; and the maxima for suicides and small-pox, which are, however, extended from the middle of April into these months. Convulsions, teething, and atrophy and debility have a secondary maximum in the warm moist weather of July and August. In the United States, where the heat is greater in summer, the secondary maximum for convulsions is more distinctly marked than that of London; and in Victoria the summer maximum is the only one that appears. The contrast offered by certain curves to each other in all points is very striking. Thus the curve for whooping-cough begins to rise above its average in the middle of December, attains its maximum in March and April, and falls to the minimum in September and October, while the curve for scarlatina is exactly the reverse of all this, having its minimum in spring and its maximum in autumn. It was inferred from the general teaching of the curves, that if a curve representing the progress of the death-rate from a particular disease were given for a place whose climate was known, though it might be impossible to name the exact disease, it would be possible to say with a considerable degree of certainty whether, for instance, the nervous system, or the respiratory organs, or the abdominal organs were involved in the disorder which caused the deaths.—*Nature, July* 16, 1874.

UNWHOLESOME MEAT AND HOW TO PREVENT IT.

ABSTRACT OF A PAPER READ AT THE MEETING OF THE AMERICAN SOCIAL SCIENCE ASSOCIATION, 1874.

By George T. Angell,

President of the Massachusetts Society for the Prevention of Cruelty to Animals.

On the 16th of April, 1871, George E. Temple, a Brighton butcher died, as appears from the verdict of the coroner's jury, of "blood poison, inoculated in dressing for market a dead ox, one half of the meat of which was sent into Boston for sale." On the 20th of April a joint special committee of the aldermen and common council of Boston was appointed "to ascertain whether unwholesome meats were sold in that city."

Five months afterwards the report of that committee, containing the official reports and testimony of State cattle commissioners, railroad commissioners, boards of health, and physicians, was published by the city government. By this report and the various official reports and evidence therein cited and contained, as well as by other official reports and evidence more recently published, it appears:

1st. That our Eastern markets, in both cities and towns, are largely supplied with the meats of diseased animals, and to some extent with the meats of animals that have died of disease; 2d, that the eating of these meats produces disease in those who eat them; and 3d, that it is impossible to detect these meats after they have been dressed and put into the stalls.

It is estimated that about six per cent. of cattle, and about nine per cent. of sheep and swine, nearly 600,000 in all, annually die on the passage to market from the west, and a large portion of these are sold in our markets, either as meat, or rendered into cooking lard; while the cattle that get through alive, for the want of food and water, and by reason of the cruelty inflicted upon them, after losing on the average, in transportation, nearly a hundred pounds each in weight, from the most juicy and nutritious parts of the meat, come out of the cars full of fever, and many with bruises, sores, and ulcers; and these, together with smaller animals, to which the loss and suffering is, in proportion, equally great, are all sold in our markets for food.

The Board of Health of Chicago, in February, 1871, reported that "nearly one half the beef, pork, and mutton, offered for sale in that city, was diseased, and unfit for food."

The Cattle Commissioners of New York, in their Report of 1869, say: "It became apparent to the Metropolitan Board of Health, in New York City, that the alarming increase of obstinate and fatal diarrhœa in the metropolitan district, was caused by the use of diseased meats." And they add, that "not only do Western cattle lose a hundred pounds or more per head in transportation, but the tissues of their entire systems are turned into a feeble, disordered, and feverish condition."

The Massachusetts Railroad Commissioners in their Report of 1871, say that these meats endanger the health of our people.

Professor Agassiz says: "Let me call your attention to the dangers arising from the ill-treatment of beef cattle before slaughtering them."

Medical Inspector Hamlin, in his "Notes on the Alimentation of Armies," says: "The flesh of mammalia undergoes great change, by reason of fasting, disturbance of sleep, and long-continued suffering, resulting in its not only becoming worthless, but deleterious."

In 1866 it was found in New York that hogs were killed by feeding upon the blood and entrails of animals diseased by transportation, although they will fatten on the same material taken from healthy animals.

Can these meats be detected in the markets? Professor Cameron, of Dublin, says that "the flesh of oxen in the congestive stage of pleuro-pneumonia cannot be distinguished from that of healthy oxen."

The Board of Health of Chicago, in their Report published in 1871, speaking of the Texas cattle fever, say: "As a general rule, it was found impossible to decide by the appearance of the carcass, after the viscera had been removed, whether it was fit for market or not."

Dr. Derby, of the Massachusetts State Board of Health, says: "There can be no approach to certainty in the recognition of the meat of animals which had been sick at the time of killing, or which have been brought to the slaughter-house dead."

Horace W. Jordan, member of the Brighton Board of Health, also one of the Massachusetts State Cattle Commissioners, testifies before the Boston committee that "when the meat is examined here, it is almost impossible to tell whether the animal was diseased."

And Professor Gamgee states in the Edinburgh "Veterinary Review" of May, 1863, that he has known diseased cattle slaughtered, the beef of which had the appearance of being the best beef that a butcher can show; and yet pigs, dogs, and ferrets died from eating it, and horses died from drinking water into which the blood of one of these animals had run.

From these facts it appears that cruelty to animals avenges itself upon the consumer, and that we shall never be secure against disease from eating poisonous meats until animals are transported without cruelty; as they can be with little loss of weight, greater profit to railroads and everybody concerned, and complete protection to public health.

It is estimated that from sixty to one hundred millions of cattle, sheep, and swine, are killed in this country every year for food; probably more than two hundred thousand a day.

How do they die?

As in that merciful European slaughter-house described by Sir Francis Head, and others; full fed and rested, under the inspection of government officers; in a place kept clean by the constant flow of water, without foreknowledge and without pain; or are they dragged, half-starved and frantic with terror, by a rope, or rope and windlass, into bloody slaughter-houses full of the signs of butchery?

In the light of medical science it makes a difference to the consumer how they die.

Dr. D. D. Slade, Professor of Zoölogy of Harvard University, in a recent lecture before the Massachusetts State Board of Agriculture, says, "the animal to be slaughtered should be conducted to the spot selected, quietly, without the use of goad or club, and everything calculated to alarm should be removed. All slaughtering premises should be kept cleansed from blood, and no carcasses be allowed to hang in view. No animal should be permitted to witness the death of another. Trifling as these measures may appear to the professional butcher, they are of vast importance, not only in view of avoiding cruelty, but as affecting the wholesomeness of meat; there being no question as to the effects of torture, cruelty, and fear upon the secretions, and if upon the secretions, necessarily upon the flesh."

Now please accompany me for a moment, not to one of the more brutal slaughter-houses where the cattle are driven in by men armed with spike poles, where our officers have seen them struck seven blows with the axe before they were knocked down, and where the eyes of cattle are sometimes pricked out that they may be driven in more easily. I will not ask you to go there; but go with me to one of the very best, and kindest, and least offensive, that you may see how these dumb creatures, under the most favorable circumstances, are prepared for your tables. I will simply read you the report of a respectable and reliable gentleman well known to me, and which has been widely published.

"On the 12th of July, 1872," he says, "I went to the slaughter-house of Mr. C. A. Thomas, at Peabody,—it being one of the best in New England,—to witness the mode and conditions of slaughtering.

"The animals were all forcibly drawn by a rope into the room, the floor of which was reeking and slippery with blood and offal, and in full sight of the heads, hearts, livers, and still quivering carcasses of those which had preceded them, which were hanging on the walls, and lying upon the floor around them. The cattle, of course, were wild with fear, and in a condition bordering on frenzy, were knocked down and dressed, and in this state of excitement and heat, growing out of their fears and struggles, were converted into beef.

"The establishment of Mr. Thomas may be regarded as a model one compared with any others in this region. I saw six oxen killed and dressed there, five of which were so badly bruised that to make them look "all right," the butchers pared off great clots of swollen tissue, infused with blood and serum, weighing from a half to several pounds each, and threw them among the offal. Old sores were so neatly cut out, that the unskilled eye would never suspect they had existed. Some of these sore bruises were more than a foot in diameter.

"Cattle at all the slaughter-houses I have visited—at Peabody, Portland, Brighton, New York, and other places—show the same bruised and battered condition."

In confirmation of this permit me to say, that a Fall River butcher told a friend of mine that he was sometimes compelled to cut out of his beef from fifty to seventy-five pounds, diseased by sores caused by transportation; and a Lynn butcher, speaking of animals that die on the cars, said: "We cannot afford to lose them, so we dress them all, and what is not too far gone we put into the stalls."

These are the meats, which, without any inspection whatever, are poured into our markets to supply us with food.

Fishermen, in some parts of Europe, and, I may add, some parts of this country, kill fish with a knife or bludgeon as soon as they are taken from the water, because fish thus killed are found to be better than those which have long gasped and struggled before dying. Professor Slade, in his lecture before the Massachusetts State Board of Agriculture, before referred to, says on this subject, "Various modes of killing fish are practiced. The Dutch, for example destroy life by making a slight longitudinal incision under the tail with a sharp instrument." "On the Rhine, they kill salmon by thrusting a steel needle into their heads." "Fish may be easily killed by striking them a quick, sharp blow with a small stick, on the back of the head, just behind the eyes, or by taking them by the tail and striking the head quickly against any hard substance."

And the Professor continues: "It has been observed that fish which are instantly killed on being taken from the water, are vastly superior in taste and solidity to those which are allowed to die, as is the universal custom with us. And why," he continues, "should not this be the case? Why should we make a distinction between animals that swim, and those that fly or run? No one of us would think of eating beast or bird that died a natural death."

Perhaps, in the light of these authorities, it is well to inquire how the fish brought into our markets are obtained, and how they die.

At the present time nearly all our salt water fish are caught on what are called "trawls," or long ropes, with ten hundred to twelve hundred hooks and lines attached, sunk by stones or heavy weights at either end to the bottom; the fish are caught, of course, near the bottom, and struggle there a considerable time until they die, and then lie dead in the water. Usually the trawls are taken up the same day they are put down, but frequently not until the next day; and sometimes, in bad weather, not for several days. In the mean time they lie dead in the water. I am told by Swampscott fishermen that they sometimes pick over a hundred, and sometimes even a thousand of these fish before they find one they are willing to take home to their families. The rest are sold in our markets, and I may add that hundreds of thousands of young fish of no value, are caught and killed on these trawls, having no time to grow; and because of this, fish are becoming so scarce on our coast that a fisherman cannot now take, on the average, on a trawl, with a thousand or twelve hundred hooks, so many pounds of dead fish, as he used to catch of live ones with a single hook and line.

Other cruelties are inflicted on fish caught alive, in trying to keep them alive. Also on lobsters, in the boiling of which, sometimes while the lower lobsters in the kettle are boiled, the top ones are trying to escape.

For the public health, if for no other reason, these things should be investigated and stopped.

So universal is the law that cruelty to the animal injures the meat, that an eminent English physician, Dr. Carpenter, in a recent letter to the "London Times," assures us that the meats of animals which have been made fat by overfeeding, will sometimes produce gastric diseases in those who eat them. In England it has been found that the flesh of hares chased and worried by dogs, becomes diseased, and soon putrefies. Old hunters tell us they do not like to eat the meat of deer which have been run and worried by dogs, and that they sometimes, when hunting, shoot dogs to prevent their worrying the deer, and so spoiling the meat. The same doctrine applies to game caught and tortured in steel traps. In an essay which took the prize at the New England Agricultural Fair of 1872, I find that the flesh of animals killed when in a state of great excitement, soon putrefies; and that the flesh of animals killed instantly without pain, is found to contain elements indispensable to the easy and complete digestion of the meat (among which is one named "glycogene"), and which elements are almost or entirely wanting in animals that have suffered before dying.

For all these wrongs which I have enumerated, what is the remedy? First better transportation. The Jewish Rabbi goes to our markets and selects what seems a healthy animal. He stands at the slaughter-house while it is slaughtered and dressed. During the process, he carefully examines its internal organs, and if he finds the slightest trace of disease, passes it over to the Christian.

When public opinion shall demand the same inspection of animals, both before and after they are killed, now practiced in continental European cities, and by the Jews, so far as I am informed, everywhere, and the Christian inspector shall stand at our cattle markets, side by side with the Jewish Rabbi, to condemn and cause to be destroyed the meat of every diseased animal, then animals will be brought to our markets without cruelty, and the Christian will eat as good meat as the Jew.

Cattle cars have already been invented and tried with entire success, in which cattle can be carried thousands of miles with food, water, and rest, and arrive in good condition.

When these cars come into general use, railroads will make more money, because one-third to one-half more cars will be required to transport the same number of cattle; dealers will make more money, because (saying nothing of animals that die on the passage) an enormous waste of the best parts of the meat will be saved, and this saving will not only pay the increased charges of transportation, but also leave an immense margin of gain; and consumers getting wholesome meats at one-half to three-fourths the prices they now pay for diseased meats, will buy larger quantities, and so increase the trade. I will also further state:

1. That it is perfectly practicable to supply all animals in transportation with food and water. 2. That the keeping of calves several days without nourishment is entirely inexcusable, for they will readily drink flour mixed with water; and 3, That all animals can be transported on cars properly constructed, with the same speed as men, and the saving in their value will more than pay for their rapid transportation.

How prevent the starving of animals before they are slaughtered, and secure merciful methods of slaughtering them?

We have now at Brighton, Mass., one of the best abattoirs in the world, where every animal can be killed in the most merciful manner; though for want of proper inspection (for which the legislature has been petitioned), animals are killed there with much cruelty.

This abattoir is so constructed that each of the larger animals, after being slaughtered and dressed, may be carried immediately by machinery to another room; all the refuse matter passed through the floor into small metallic wagons, in which it is carried to the rendering-house, and every trace of blood washed off before the next animal is brought in; and calves, sheep, and swine can be killed there without cruelty, by having each brought singly to the slaughter-room, by some one having no blood on his clothing, and stunning it with a single blow of a mallet or hammer, just before, or at the moment it is brought in.

In several of the smaller slaughter-houses of Massachusetts, they now have, for killing cattle, just outside the slaughter-house, box-pens, like a horse's stall, with a door at each end; the animal is driven in and instantly stunned and killed by a single bullet in the head, from a rifle, thrust through an open slide in the front door; the animal is at once hauled into the slaughter-room, leaving no blood in the pen to terrify the succeeding animal, and injure its meat.

By this process it has been found that much time is saved, which, under the systems now generally practiced, is lost in hauling or driving animals into bloody slaughter-houses.

All that is needed is a public opinion which shall require these forms of slaughtering to be generally practiced; and that faithful inspectors shall be stationed at the larger slaughter-houses to see that they are properly carried out, and all animals properly fed and watered up to the time of killing; then the sixty millions, or more, of dumb creatures that are now killed annually in this country for food, will die without pain to themselves, or danger to the consumer.

CAUTION TO WATER DRINKERS.—While travelling recently, our attention was inconveniently called one morning to empty water tanks. But there were others, children especially, who on crawling out of the sleeping bunks were in want of water more than we were—to drink. It was not long however before the cars halted, and the *tanks were filled from a road-side stream*. Of this the thirsty drank. We ventured to suggest to the porter that possibly this water was not wholesome. But the suggestion that "water as *clear* as that," was not clean, to him was absurd. The same suggestion to the conductor, was equally incomprehensible. *It is just such water that collects and holds in solution the poison of typhoid fever, which summer travellers so often take home with them.*

Let it never be forgotten that very few rivers, small ones and rivulets, especially, or wells, are safe sources of water supply, and that many are more dangerous and deadly than loaded fire-arms. The shallow wells of villages and some watering places and other health resorts (!) are among the pests of the country. It is indeed shockingly disgusting in many country places to observe the uniformity with which the cesspool and well are made to stand side by side, as though each was necessary to the other; and to think of the foul, sewerage-reeking soil through which the water percolates to its fetid bed! The practice should not only engage the attention of every health officer in the land, but every person of ordinary intelligence. It is always practicable to provide cities and large towns with good water, but in small villages and country neighborhoods, where houses are few, money scarce, and intelligence scarcer, it is a matter of some difficulty, but it should nevertheless be overcome. Meanwhile, country sojourners and travellers—be wary!

THE POSITION OF WOMAN, WITH SPECIAL REFERENCE TO EDUCATION.

By NATHAN ALLEN, M.D., LL.D.

Abstract of Discourse before Mass. Med. Society, June 13, 1874.

The question might naturally be asked, why discuss the position of woman more than that of man? The answer is obvious: his rights and claims have not been agitated, or attracted the same attention as those of woman.

Within a short period new questions have sprung up for consideration in respect to the rights, the employments and position of woman. While her wrongs in the past are generally admitted, as well as the desirableness of some radical reform, there are certain physiological problems involved in the issue, which should not be overlooked or ignored. If we are not mistaken, there are principles or laws involved, which underlie the very foundations of society. They are not the opinions of individuals or the resolves of public bodies, but the laws of the Almighty implanted in human beings for their highest welfare and happiness. Can these laws be understood—can they be correctly interpreted and properly applied? Most of the discussions upon this subject have been conducted with very little reference to physiological laws. A majority of the parties engaged in them do not seem to consider or realize what effect, if the points at issue are carried to the extent advocated, may be produced on the marriage institution, and the physical welfare of the race. Any changes or agencies that threaten in any way the security and permanency of the family, should be approached with all the care, intelligence and wisdom that are possible. That the marriage and parental relations constitute the groundwork, the main pillars of human society, requires here no argument to prove. The physiological law of *sex* is the corner-stone of these relations, and has, we believe, a far more direct and powerful influence upon organization and character than is generally considered. Inasmuch as woman is so created that her own health is very much affected by this feature in her organization—inasmuch as the physical development of offspring is also very much dependent upon her constitution, these two considerations have an important bearing upon her education, employment and relations to the public. There is a normal and healthy standard for every organ in the human body; and whatever influences tend to change or violate the laws that govern any one of these should be carefully guarded against. Thus in the matter of education it has been very clearly demonstrated by a distinguished member of our profession,* that the boy and the girl cannot be educated just alike. No one but an experienced physician can realize or describe fully the powerful influences which the function of menstru-

* Dr. H. E. Clarke.

ation has upon the health of woman; and this effect, in extent and character, depends much upon the early stages of its development. For the period of some thirty years there is certainly a marked difference in the sexes, which must materially interfere with employments and public duties. Such is the relation, too, of this function to the nervous system, that any derangement or morbidness of action here may affect the disposition and character of the individual.

All writers on physiology agree that too much importance can scarcely be attached to the healthy action of the uterine functions; and when we present the testimony of one writer, it expresses, we believe, the opinion of all. Says Colombat: "The extreme sensibility of the uterus, its physiological importance, its peculiar irritability, and especially its more or less sympathetic connection with other parts of the body, render it a centre of action which in the sex seems in a measure *to domineer over the whole economy*, and form *the principal basis upon which the edifice of the whole organization rests.*"

In settling, then, the points involved in the question of "Woman's Rights," so called, the physiological bearings and tendencies should receive primary consideration. The immediate change produced, however, may not be so noticeable, but in the course of two or three generations its effects become very striking and powerful.

That in the present state of society there is need of some changes or reform looking to the improvement and health of woman, is evident. The very general ill health of American women is often asserted. There should certainly be a reform in the fashion or style of dress; it should harmonize with the laws of the physical system. In the early training of girls the greatest care should be taken to secure the best possible development of the body; and in the whole course of their education, whatever interferes with healthy action or violates physiological laws, should be most scrupulously avoided. As to the higher departments of education and a more extended range of employments, there are substantial reasons and arguments deduced from physiology itself why woman should have these advantages. Let her have the highest culture—physical and mental—consistent with her whole nature. But then, that she should share equally with man in all the strife and competition of business, in the excitement and rivalry connected with political and public life, including suffrage, is physiologically unnatural, abnormal, a violation of the laws of her physical system. In the language of the most distinguished writer on psychology in Great Britain, "she will then have lost her feminine attractions, and probably also her chief feminine functions." One of the cardinal points in attachment between the sexes is, that certain opposite qualities or traits of character attract each other and form the most happy unions. Now if the qualities and traits of character in women are to be assimilated to those of man, what will be its effect upon matrimony and harmony in married life?

In all the situations and pursuits of life the Almighty has established bounds or limitations beyond which woman cannot go without defeating the primary objects of her creation. The reasons are obvious. It gradually changes her organization. By a physiological law of supply and demand, nature, in the case of woman, makes certain drafts monthly upon her constitution. That this law of periodicity be properly observed is indisepensable for good health and the highest development both of the body and mind. Again, if the brain is reflectively exercised too much, the body suffers; so of the brain alone, there cannot be a steady strain upon certain portions of it without impairing the functions of other parts. Maternity is a primary law in her creation. Physiology, pathology, records of health, disease and mortality, establish the fact that this is her NORMAL state. In the observance of this law, certain physical conditions are indispensable; there must be a proper development of those portions of the body concerned in this function; neither can they answer the demands nature makes if kept constantly impoverished.

For illustration: if that portion of the brain whose functions include attachment to the other sex, love of offspring and domestic life—those strong instincts that centre in the family and in the home—is not properly developed or trained, but other portions of the brain, embracing the selfish faculties, are continuously exercised, and strained to their utmost capacity, the result is that it changes organization and character. It tends to undermine the foundation of the marriage and maternal relation, which rests on the purest and most powerful instincts of nature, and transfer it to one of self-interest and convenience. The relation, in fact, is already coming to be viewed more and more in the light of a partnership, as a matter of business and necessity, or, in other words, to be based upon the supremely selfish traits or elements of human nature. That such large numbers of our young married women should be so disinclined to assume the duties of maternity, indicates something wrong. However desirable or important may be the cultivation of any or all the mental faculties, the reason, the judgment, the imagination, and even the conscience and veneration, these alone never bind and cement society permanently in the home and in the family. In such cases children are a burden, confinement at home is irksome, domestic labors and relations are not the most agreeable. What is wanted, and what accords with the order of nature, is a *balance of organization—a harmony of action in all the functions of the brain*—not an excess of the mere animal, nor all intellect nor moral feeling. If a practical test of this law is demanded, what is the testimony of history and the experience of the present age? Let a careful investigation be made as to the productiveness in offspring, and the character of the family relation, of those who have been, or are, supremely devoted to intellectual and business pursuits. How often do we find difficulties and not unfrequently separations between married couples, where both are highly educated and strong minded? And as for offspring, they certainly are not very abundant with this class of people. There may be found exceptions to the last remark, but the facts generally confirm it. It should be stated, that in order to make a fair trial, and witness its full effects, two or three generations must be taken for the comparison. It is this *permanent* result in an intensified form, that makes these changes so important—so fundamental.

It may be said that the argument here employed, as to the position of woman in its relations to marriage and maternity, does not apply to that class who do not assume these relations. But this class composes only a small minority of the whole, and the course pursued by them is an exception to the general law of womanhood. Besides, they cannot change materially the physical functions of their nature without injury to their health, or without affecting, more or less, their character. The remark was made by one of the most distinguished female writers in this country, that the nature of woman was not fully developed without sustaining the relation of wife and mother. How then can the class alluded to, governed by their own consciousness, judge properly and correctly of all the relations referring to the family and domestic life? Can their teachings be safely followed?

Again, what effects would the reforms advocated by many have more directly upon the body itself? In some respects they would tend, undoubtedly, to improve the general health—to increase the muscular power, vigor and strength of the system. In some cases they would decidedly improve the organization, produce more harmony of action in all the organs—a better development of the great laws of life and health. But while they might increase the muscular power and strength, might they not unduly develop the nervous temperament? If there is to be a constant strain upon the muscles and the brain, what will be the effect upon those organs connected with the functions of gestation and lactation? Would it not tend to prevent their proper development and healthy action, by withdrawing from them the nutrition which should go to their support? The better the laws of inheritance are understood, the more directly certain effects may be traced to the physical and mental state of the system at the time of conception and during the period of gestation. Now if all the energies of the body and brain of the woman are to be incessantly taxed, what will be the effect upon offspring? It should be borne in mind that physical and mental habits, when fixed for many years, cannot be easily changed or modified. Then in the matter of furnishing proper nutrition to offspring—which can come from the human breast alone—it is vastly important that the organization should not be so exercised or changed, that this provision cannot be counted upon. The community is suffering seriously from defects of this kind already, without having them increased or aggravated.

ADVICE TO MOTHERS.—Max Adeler, who rather likes to give good sound advice to mothers about their babies, says: "We observed in the papers an item to the effect that a mother in Maryland bit off her child's toe in her sleep. We have so often remonstrated with mothers against the practice of sleeping with their children's toes in their mouths, that we have little sympathy for this woman. Sooner or later the catastrophe is sure to come. No woman should ever sleep with her babe's toe in her mouth, unless she has false teeth which can be removed, or the toe can be wrapped up in sheet-iron."

Editor's Table.

THE PUBLIC HEALTH.

New York, August 6, 1874.—*To the Editor of the Sanitarian*:—The first months of Summer in this city have been more favorable than usual to the public health, the present year. But that charac-

ABSTRACT OF RECORDS IN FIVE WEEKS OF MIDSUMMER, FOR NINE CONSECUTIVE YEARS.

YEARS.	1866.					1867.					1868.				
	1st week	2d "	3d "	4th "	5th "	1st week	2d "	3d "	4th "	5th "	1st week	2d "	3d "	4th "	5th "
Total Deaths..............	493	827	1,362	771	946	472	525	582	677	647	418	614	1,142	781	730
Total of Children under 5 years.	285	478	704	464	424	284	359	394	477	458	233	381	706	548	521
Total by Diarrhœal Diseases..	118	256	453	345	331	67	141	196	267	255	51	176	416	366	348
Mean Temperature..........	79.80	79.67	81.05	75.64	77.27	77.06	72.00	68.00	75.00	73.00	80.00	80.00	88.00	78.00	80.00
Average Humidity...........	66	60	65	77	65.64	65	61	61	64	70	66	68	60	76	69

YEARS.	1869.					1870.					1871.				
	1st week	2d "	3d "	4th "	5th "	1st week	2d "	3d "	4th "	5th "	1st week	2d "	3d "	4th "	5th "
Total Deaths..............	642	726	692	631	591	641	757	1,040	980	681	766	822	640	545	658
Total of Children under 5 years.	417	501	491	427	355	414	493	646	578	436	476	504	403	306	323
Total by Diarrhœal Diseases...	110	212	284	283	224	306	231	327	416	366	227	293	331	252	171
Mean Temperature..........	74.42	70.53	76.27	72.45	75.15	78.27	70.82	70.60	88.31	81.56	76.27	79.48	70.32	69.60	75.52
Average Humidity...........	69	64	62	63	65	60	66	57	54	52	64	63	58	68	70

YEARS.	1872.					1873.					1874.				
	1st week	2d "	3d "	4th "	5th "	1st week	2d "	3d "	4th "	5th "	1st week	2d "	3d "	4th "	5th "
Total Deaths..............	1,591	1,022	894	768	689	683	667	917	908	837	452	640	824	861	751
Total of Children under 5 years.	1,007	705	618	496	407	418	441	658	595	582	238	359	582	590	490
Total by Diarrhœal Diseases....	653	483	423	329	227	206	268	434	408	346	64	162	367	370	305
Mean Temperature..........	86.97	78.83	79.85	74.31	73.64	78.40	71.50	72.80	79.41	78.40	74.30	73.00	75.90	74.80	78.70
Average Humidity...........	75	79.32	81	74	69	69	66	74.7	61.2	68	65	69	59	56	65

teristic of the mortality tables which imparts to them and to the metropolis an unenviable fame, namely that of an excessive infantile death-rate, is not absent this summer, though less conspicuous than in many past years.

The preceding summary of records of total infantile mortality in five consecutive weeks, during a period of nine successive years, presents an important fact in regard to the rise and fluctuations of the death-rate as an invariable sequence of the increase of the summer temperature and hum:dity above 70 degrees Fah., and with the atmosphere at or above 70 per centum of total saturation.

The first conclusion drawn from this extended comparison of experience in nine successive years is that high temperature in this city, when it has continued a few days, is attended by an excessive mortality among children under two years of age, and whenever such intemperature is conjoined with excessive moisture of the atmosphere, the mortality reaches its maximum. The other factors which enter into the general cause of this excessive infant mortality in the various sections of the city and in certain classes of the population are various, but not difficult to understand. The slums of poverty and debased ignorance, and the accumulated evils which overcrowding and tenement-house life imply, present ample causes for all the suddenness and excess of mortality which are recorded in the history of deaths and of the physical wrongs that cause them.

ELISHA HARRIS,
Registrar of Vital Statistics.

Brooklyn, Aug. 7th.—During the month of July Brooklyn suffered a depopulation of 1,339 of its inhabitants. 76 per cent. were children under the age of five years; 487, were due to the ravages of cholera infantum. 80 per cent. of the deaths from this disease occurred in tenement houses in which families are crowded together. Scarlet fever and diphtheria are declining—23 deaths from the former and 21 from the latter. Consumption carried off 106. Small-pox is credited with three deaths. With a population of 450,000, a death-rate of 1,339, per month would give us a death-rate of 35.70 to the thousand of our inhabitants. We must remember that July is the month in which the largest death-rate occurs in Brooklyn.

JAMES WATT,
Registrar of Vital Statistics.

Swill and Sugar-plums.—It is gratifying to know that the Brooklyn Board of Health has finally taken some action in regard to the intolerable nuisances of offal and house garbage. Early in the summer notices were distributed throughout the city, requiring all families to keep wet garbage in separate receptacles, to be called for by the contractors three times a week ; and on the setting in of hot weather, daily. The hot weather came, and instead of the daily calls, to our certain knowledge, the calls were in some cases wholly neglected, and in none have we been able to learn, oftener than twice a week. And in one case with which we are perfectly familiar the call was not made until nine days after the negligence had first been reported at the Health Office, and by it to the Board of City Works. And, finally, when the call was made, it was with a leaky cart, and such as are generally used to add to the filth of the streets by sprinkling them with swill !

Meanwhile, July 30th, with thermometer at 80° and the swill throughout the city particularly savory, at a regular meeting of the Board of Health the following action was taken:

Gen. Jourdan said there were 1,200 orders of the Board either lost or mislaid; they were missing at any rate, and he wanted to know who it was that was responsible for their non-service.

Dr. Conkling stated that the Secretary was now engaged in looking up that matter.

Captain Leich, of the Twelfth Precinct, sent a communication, in which he gave the names of all the people who owned goats, hogs and dogs which were running at large in the Twenty-fourth Ward, with a view to have said parties prosecuted.

The Board, after some consideration, referred the names to counsel, with instructions for him to prosecute said owners.

An important resolution was offered by General Jourdan:

Whereas, Frequent complaints have been made by the press and the people that *terra alba* (which is nothing but plaster-of-Paris or gypsum), glucus, lampblack, glue, tonka bean, tartaric acid, sulphuric acid, analine verdigris, Brunswick green, gamboge, smalt, ultramarine, oil of turpentine, prussic acid, rotten cheese, fusil oil, chrome yellow and other drugs and compounds are largely used in the manufacture of cheap candies ; and

Whereas, The indiscriminate use of such poisonous drugs and compounds is considered deleterious to health ; therefore, be it

Resolved, That the Sanitary Committee, or such officers of the Board as they may direct, do thoroughly investigate and report to the Board as soon as possible, on the mode of and material used in the manufacture of all descriptions of wares and merchandise made or sold by confectioners, in order that children at least may be protected from the evil effects of the dangerous compounds which are sold under the designation of candy.

The matter was referred to the Sanitary Committee.

General Jourdan submitted the following explanation of the uses of the different poisons:

Terra alba, in place of white sugar.

Glucus, in place of gum arabic (consists of a mucilage of starch).

Lampblack and glue, in place of gum arabic and licorice.

Tonka bean, in place of vanilla.

Tartaric and sulphuric acid, in place of lemon.

Analine, a poisonous product of coal tar, in place of cochineal, to color red candies.

Gamboge and chrome yellow, in place of saffron, to color yellow candies.

Smalt, verdigris and Brunswick green, to color blue and green candies.

Oil of turpentine for flavoring; rotten cheese and sulphuric acid to flavor pineapple drops.

But the *swill* was still held in reserve for the favorite contractor who was paid not to do his duty; and another midsummer week, the first in August, was permitted to pass by. August 7th the Board met again, and the physicians of the Board, Drs. Conklin, and Hutchison, by the aid of Hon. J. I. Bergen, President of the Board of Aldermen, finally succeeded in effecting a new contract in spite of the other two commissioners, the President of the Board of City Works and the President of the Board of Police. But the swill is still, *at the end of another week*, only called for *once* a week and by leaky carts. How far this service is essential, or due to the prosecution of the candy interest, evidently considered by certain members of the Board of greater moment, we know not. But we do know that if the swill was thrown into the streets, and the pigs allowed to go at large—the process would be an improvement on that which has hitherto obtained under the auspices of the new Board of Health of Brooklyn.

Philadelphia.—Annual Report, 1873. Measured by its results, this report would leave us to infer that sanitary administration in Philadelphia excels any other large city in the United States. "Taking the actual deaths in our city, 15,224, and making the basis of our calculation on the increase of the population," 750,000, we find the deaths to be one in every 49.26 of the population, or 21.19 per 1,000. The *Medical Times* ludicrously attributes this result to the want of proper sanitary arrangements—the habitual use of open cesspools, the lack of sewage and the villainous open night carts! Verily, these are rare luxuries to boast of. But these are not all. Intramural burial is still practiced in Philadelphia to a surprising extent. "During the year 1873, no less than 3,353 interments took place within the thickly populated districts of the city." The principal nuisances complained of "were full, leaky, and foul privies, and defective water-closets, of which no less than 3,004 were reported. Four hundred and seventy-seven filthy vacant lots, and ponds of stagnant water; 1,602 houses and cellars; 1,299 alleys and courts; 640 bone-boiling and fat rendering establishments, dye-houses, stables, hog pens, manure pits, etc., and 209 other nuisances of various character, are enumerated causes of unsanitary conditions. But "the practice of keeping a large number of cows in dark, crowded and unventilated stables, is unknown in Philadelphia."

"Under the present law, slaughter-houses may be located in any part of the city, provided no nuisance arises from the business." Eighty-two were reported for violating the rules of the Board governing such establishments. On the whole, they are considered among the most prejudicial causes of ill-health, and concentration of the business under properly regulated abattoirs is urged for relief.

The private market-houses are the pride of the city; but the public, are old, deficient and filthy, and frequently reported as nuisances.

Badly constructed streets, worn out and misplaced gutters and curbstones, are common causes of complaint, rendering proper cleansing impracticable. These are all matters of moment of the same kind, differing in degree only from those which the *Medical Times* deems advantageous. But not so the Board of Health, which has evidently exercised its functions with diligence and promptitude. The great advantage of Philadelphia over other cities is *house room*, —AIR. By the census of 1870, the average number of persons to a dwelling in each of fifty of the largest cities of the Union, ranges from 14.72 (New York), to 5.20 (Toledo);—Philadelphia, 6.01, with a population one-third less than New York, has nearly twice as many dwelling-houses, and less than half as many persons dwelling in each. Of the total number of deaths, 45 per cent. were of children under ten years of age. Small-pox, 39; measles, 30; scarlet fever, 319; diphtheria, 110; croup, 200; whooping cough, 97; typhus fever, 31; typhoid fever, 382; erysipelas, 89; dysentery, 81; diarrhœa, 168; cholera morbus, 67; cholera infantumn, 1,114; cerebro-spinal meningitis, 246; tabes mesenterica, 691, and phthisis pulmonalis, 2,292.

Births.—The whole number for the year, including 891 still-births, was 18,702, a decrease of 1,370 from the number in 1872. Thirty-five per 1,000 is assumed as the average, after making due allowance for deficient returns.

Marriages returned—7,891; an increase over 1872, of 395. A ratio to population of 10.5 per 1000. For the week ending Aug. 1st, ult., deaths, 365; typhoid fever, 5; diarrhœal diseases, 102.

New Orleans, 199,000.—Deaths for week ending Aug. 2, 145; congestive fever, 6; malarial, 4; typhoid, 3; remittent, 2; small-pox, 1.

St. Louis, 366,000.—Week ending Aug. 1st, deaths 212; summer complaint, 36; diarrhœa, 8; fever, conjestive, 6; typhoid, typhus and scarlet, each 1; small-pox, 4.

Chicago, 356,000.—Week ending July 18. Deaths, 344; cholera infantum, 158; diarrhœa, 17; small-pox, 2.

Cincinnati, 246,923, (estimated to July, 1873). Annual Report 1873. Total mortality for the year, 5,641 (and 232 still-born), 22.80 per 1000.

Principal Causes of Death, and the percentage to the total mortality in the years 1870, 1871, 1872 *and* 1873.

PRINCIPAL CAUSES OF DEATH.	January.	February.	March.	April.	May.	June.	July.	August	September.	October.	November.	December.	Total.	Percentage to Total Mortality 1873.	Percentage to Total Mortality 1872.	Percentage to Total Mortality 1871.	Percentage to Total Mortality 1870.
Consumption.......	46	68	70	56	64	47	64	46	45	54	49	48	657	11.64	12.04	11.11	14.63
Scarlet fever.......	5	6	3	1	9	10	13	22	31	89	113	108	410	7.26	0.64	0.90	0.40
Pneumonia....	52	23	56	38	17	14	12	18	15	9	17	25	296	5.24	6.43	6.62	7.36
Cerebro-spi'nl men	10	18	31	50	61	27	23	6	02	2	6	3	239	4.23	1.44	0.00	0.00
Cholera infantum..	..	1	2	2	6	93	74	26	21	7	4	2	238	4.21	3.02	2.75	5.17
Cholera...........	..	..	..	..	..	88	84	28	05	2	....	8	207	3.66	0.00	0.00	0.00
Diarrhœa ac & chro	3	2	3	2	3	33	31	41	21	22	3	....	172	3.04	2.69	2.33	2.79
Typhoid fever......	10	7	6	7	7	5	10	12	8	10	35	19	136	2 41	1.[illegible]2	1.64	2.16
Diphtheria.........	9	4	5	3	4	6	4	9	4	8	10	6	72	1.27	1.40	1.24	1 70

The prevailing causes of ill health are stated to be, stagnant ponds, bad sewerage, and swill milk; for the prevention of which legislation is invoked. A special report on cholera is appended, but the subject was so thoroughly discussed by us at the time, and soon after its prevalence, that further notice, at present, is deemed unnecessary.

It will suffice to state that the Health Officer of Cincinnati holds that:

"The manner in which the specific cholera poison reached Cincinnati, and was disseminated through it, can only be a subject of speculation; but it is reasonably certain that the rice-water dejections of patients had nothing whatever to do, either with its introduction or dissemination."

Total births registered, 1,555—not deemed reliable. Marriages, 2,772—one in every 89 of population, and approximately correct. For week ending Aug. 1, deaths 115; typhoid fever, 4; *cholera*, 1; cholera morbus, 1; cholera infantum, 12.

Baltimore, 284,000.—Annual Report for the year ending Oct. 31, 1873.—Deaths, 7,817.—Cerebro-spinal meningitis, 49; cholera infantum, 598; consumption, 1,098; diphtheria, 155; typhoid fever, 235; small-pox, 617; *unknown infantile*, 657. Low-lying lots, the want of proper sewerage, and badly-conducted slaughter-houses, are named as chief causes of insalubrity. The report is on the whole rather meagre, while the large proportion of deaths from the diseases above mentioned are suggestive. For the week ending Aug. 3, deaths, 196—cholera infantum, 70; typhoid fever, 3.

Washington, 150,000.—Week ending Aug. 8.—Deaths, 97—cholera infantum, 20; typhoid fever 1; phthisis, 11.

San Francisco, 178,000.—Month of *June*.—Deaths, 343—typhoid and typhus fevers, 6; phthisis pulmonalis, 45; small-pox, 1.

Providence, 100,000.—Month of July.—Deaths 172—consumption, 22; diarrhœa, 14; scarlatina, 16.

Boston, 270,000.—Week ending July 18, 132; Lowell, 22; Cambridge, 22; Springfield, 17; Lawrence, 14; Fall River, 19. Prevalent diseases, consumption, cholera infantum, pneumonia.

Dayton, 34,000.—For July, 62.—Cholera infantum, 16; acute diarrhœa, 4; consumption, 4. The present condition of Holly water is exciting public concern. By an analysis, recently made by Dr. Jewett, under the auspices of the Board of Health, the organic impurities are such as to compel the Board to withhold its indorsement of its wholesomeness.

Paterson, 38,000.—For July, 79.—Cholera infantum, 16; consumption, 11; diarrhœa, 3; typhoid fever, 3.

Milwaukee, 80,000.—For July, 228.—Cholera infantum, 21; *diarrhœa*, 36; convulsions, 49; consumption, 10.

Richmond, 65,000.—Week ending July 28, 44.—Consumption, 7;

cholera infantum, 3; acute diarrhœa, 4; acute dysentery, 3; typhoid fever, 2.

Norfolk, 25,000.—For July, 90.—Cholera infantum, 10; acute diarrhœa, 16; small-pox, 5; typhoid fever, 2.

Wheeling, 27,000, July 25.—The Board of Education has just completed its annual numeration. I think 27,000 would be a correct figure for our total population. For the six months ending with June, total deaths, 168, against 206 for same period in 1873—12.44 per 1,000. Deaths from cholera infantum, to July 1, 3; same period, 1873, 15.

S. L. Jepson, *Health Officer*.

Charleston, 52,000.—Whites, 25,000, colored 27,000.—Week ending July 27, 57,—whites, 20, colored, 37—cholera infantum, 4; typhoid fever, 1.

Pittsburgh, 33,000,—Month of July, 455: 41,05 per 1,000. Diarrhœal diseases, 165; meningitis, 29; consumption, 25; scarlet fever, 24; Pneumonia, 11; bronchitis, 10; whooping cough, 10; typhoid fever, 7; measles, 6. Deaths from violence, 42.

W. Snively, *Physician to B. of H.*

Michigan State Board, Quarterly Meeting, July 14. *Shadows from the Walls of Death.*—Dr. R. C. Kedsie, from the Committee on Poisons, presented a book of specimens of arsenical wall papers, gathered from various sources, which he had inscribed Shadows from the Walls of Death. In connection with the subject, he cited several cases of poisoning from such papers, and that one sample of the paper presented no less than 1.16 grains of arsenic to the square foot of surface. He also submitted examination of 17 specimens of syrup, only two of which were pure cane syrup. The others were more or less diluted with starch syrup, and contained various proportions of lime, copperas and sulphuric acid.

Dr. Baker submitted evidence concerning 77 cases of unusual sickness; 33 near Dundee, 37 near Petersburg, 2 in the vicinity of Deerfield, and five near Blissfield.

The four villages mentioned are located on the banks of the river Raisin. The water of the river is quite turbid, and at each point there is a mill-dam, and there is an odor arising from the water as it pours over the dams. All along the river in this vicinity are many bayous, which are under water when the river is high, and dry when the river is low. The prevailing diseases of these localities are intermittent and remittent fevers.

The doctor was unable to fix upon any local cause to account for the epidemic. The epidemic had not prevailed in this locality for several years, although isolated cases had appeared during the past year. This epidemic began March 3d at Petersburg, and visited Dundee March 7th. Most of the cases at Dundee occurred in March and April, while nearly all of the cases at Petersburg were in April and May. This village is the site of an old Indian burying-ground, and the present cemetery is within the village limits. An analysis of the best water to be obtained shows it to be contaminated with organic matter and the results of animal decomposition. It might properly be labeled grave-yard juice. The doctor presented a table giving names, sex, age, date of being taken sick, day of death after attack, and day of convalescence after being attacked. Eighteen of these cases occurred in March, twenty-three in April, twenty-eight in May, and five in June. Out of the first half of the cases twenty-nine were males and seven were females, while of the last half only eleven were males and twenty-seven were females. Out of seventy-seven cases twenty-five proved fatal, or 32.46 per cent. of death to cases. Eleven out of twenty-three died on or before the fourth day of the disease, thirteen out of twenty-three on or before the fifth day, sixteen out of twenty-three on or before the sixth day, and nineteen out of twenty-three on or before the seventh day.

The patients generally, before the attack, complained for about twenty-four hours of being tired and lame, of pain in the back of the head and down the spine. It generally began with a chill or cold stage. A few cases were taken as suddenly as if knocked down. Vomiting was a prominent symptom before and after the cold stage. About one half of the cases were rational throughout the attack; but some had violent delirium from the start. There was great tenderness of the body, especially over the deep nerves given off from the spinal column. In many cases the head was thrown back, sometimes to one side, and in some cases the eyes were affected with squint, divergent and convergent. The pupils of the eyes were usually dilated, with loss of power to wink. Copper-colored spots appeared upon the body in many cases.

After careful study of the local conditions actually found in connection with this epidemic, such as those of soil, sewerage, sources of malaria, and general and private sanitary conditions, does not reveal evidence of any influence capable of acting on the human system through the atmosphere, and which appeared to be so different from those in other localities where this disease did not exist as to warrant the belief in its being the cause of this epidemic.

The Secretary read a report, prepared by Dr. Lyster, of Detroit, entitled "Draining for Health," in which he showed that the inhabitants in England and Scotland gain from 20 to 25 per cent. in years, and they suffer less than half the sickness and disability in the well-drained districts. He also showed that the names of the best breeds of cattle, horses, sheep and fowls in the kingdom are taken from these well-drained districts. Dr. Farr, Registrar General, says: "Industry and the army receive their best recruits from the well-drained districts, while they get their worst from the low parts of sickly towns." Dr. Lyster says that wherever drainage of farm lands is found profitable in a pecuniary point of view, in the increase and reliability of crops, it will be advantageous as a hygienic measure to all animal life dwelling upon them.

Morbid Impulse.—Prof. Clymer.

In the proceedings of the "Medico-Legal Society" published in the Aug. No. of The Sanitarian, at page 204, 4th line from bottom.

"In this view he will, I think, find practical alienists to agree with him,"—should read:

"In this view he will, I think, find no practical alienists to agree with him." Meredith Clymer.

St. John's School for Boys.

We take particular pleasure in calling attention to the advertisement of this institution. It is situated in a region of country remarkable for its beauty of scenery and healthfulness, while its internal sanitary regulations are matters of constant care. The appointments of the school throughout, and the general supervision of the Rt. Rev. Frederic D. Huntington, S. T. D., Bishop of the diocese of Central New York, are a sufficient guarantee of the faithful performance of its high purposes.

Columbia Springs.

We are sorry to hear that this delightful resort is just now incommoded for the want of room—that the ever cheerful and happy host is really at his wit's end to know what to do with his welcome guests. The only way is *to extend his term.* The whole of two full months yet remain to reap benefit from Columbia. September and October will not only add new tints to the charming scenery, but the virtues of the water for "rheumatics," especially, will remain unabated; indeed, they will be all the more potent against the return of the winter's *camp pain.* See advertisement.

To the Subscribers of the Popular Journal of Hygiene.

This certifies that we have transferred our claims as Editors and Publishers to the Editor of the Sanitarian, who will supply you with that Journal, instead of the "Popular Journal of Hygiene." All those who have not yet paid their subscription, will please forward the amount ($2.00), to the Editor of the Sanitarian.

It gives us great pleasure to state, that we have been fortunate in making arrangements with a Journal that is superior to any Health Journal published in America, and we feel confident that, at the end of the current year, you will be constrained to renew your subscriptions to the Sanitarian—a Journal that we can recommend in the highest terms, and which cannot fail to give satisfaction.

Williamsport, Pa., Aug. 1, 1874. Helsby & Mays.

BIBLIOGRAPHY.

Lectures on Public Health. Delivered at the Royal College of Surgeons. By E. D. Mapother, M. D., Professor of Hygiene, etc. Second Edition. With numerous Illustrations. 12mo, pp. 664. Dublin: Fannin & Co.; London: Longman, Green & Co. 1867.

Notwithstanding the many excellent books on hygiene, published since the first issue of the work before us, there are none which take its place, and none more applicable to practical sanitary work as applied to great and long-tolerated evils. The introductory lecture, beginning with the status of disease in Dublin, in 1864, draws a picture, which, to English view at that time, was deemed to be in many respects appalling.

The first half-yearly report of the Registrar General's Report for that year, showed a death-rate in Dublin of about 27 for every 1,000 living. Twenty-five years before, it had been estimated at 30 per 1,000; while in the surrounding country it was but 17.

After referring to several gratifying examples of recent sanitary reforms at home, the lecturer referred to America, in contrast, where "unsanitary influences are so rife, that one of the rarest things to be seen is a hale elderly man, and Dr. Nicholl in his recent able and most interesting work, 'Forty Years in America,' confesses to a degeneracy of the Anglo-Saxon type among his countrymen, and attributes it to their unwholesome food, and on the part of the females to injurious habits in respect to clothing and domestic arrangements." Unfortunately, America is farther behind England in sanitary progress now than she was ten years ago. And Dr. Mapother's lectures comprehend the subjects which, above all others, require attention. Diseases due to impure air; water impurities, influences of soil and climate, sanitary architecture, town improvements, sewerage, dwellings of the laboring classes, tenements, prevention of zymotic diseases, and sanitary organization, are illustrative captions of the twenty-four lectures, which, together with a summary of sanitary laws, make up this excellent volume, which no sanitary officer can very well afford to do without.

The Prevention of Artisan's Diseases, by the same author, 1873, is one of a series of Lectures on Public Health, for the benefit of the working people under government auspices, and especially applicable to diseases which ill-regulated trades promote: 1. Those due to the entrance of dirt into the lungs. 2. Those due to slow poisoning. 3. Those which constrained positions or overwork in close rooms engender. The use of a respirator lined with cotton wool, punctilious cleanliness, and commodious and well-ventilated quarters constitute the chief features.

The Presence of Organic Matter in Potable Water Always Deleterious to Health, to which is added the Modern Analysis. By O'Brien Mahoney, L. R. C. P., Ed., etc. Second Edition, 8vo, pp. 112. Dublin: Fannin & Co.; London: Longmans, Green & Co. 1869.

This is a concise book on one of the most important questions of preventive medicine. It is now very generally admitted that one of the most prolific sources of disease is the presence of organic matter in potable water. It is the object of this treatise to give a short but comprehensive view of the subject, and the great advantage to be derived from its study. The tests and processes of Wanklyn, Chapman, Smith, Frankland, Schultze, Nessler, Pettenkofer, Armstrong, Miller, and others, are brought into view, and, altogether, an amount of practical information given on the sources and nature of water impurities, and the means of detecting them, not, to our knowledge, so clearly stated or so readily accessible elsewhere.

Under the Trees. By Samuel Irænius Prime. New York: Harper Bros. 1874.

This is a delightful book, and especially so at this season of the year, by the reading of which, even after vacation is over, one is lead to travel on as it were into new regions, fruitful in new pleasures. "Our Tent Pitched," "The Garden and Gardens," "The Roses," "The Birds," "The Adirondacks," "Memoirs of Italy," "The Last Day of Summer," are sample titles of thirty letters, or rather essays on the beauties of nature and art at home and abroad; seen, enjoyed, and described by a facile pen and a cultivated taste. To quote from these essays would detract from the pleasure of reading them. The rather to all those who cannot now travel with Dr. Prime, but who would renew the pleasures of their own travels, we commend this book. Follow the author from the scenery of the Hudson to the Rhine, from Lake George to the more magnificent Swiss lakes; from the Adirondacks to the mountains of Switzerland. Pursue him into the Alps, and down again; enjoy with him the charms of Naples, the galleries of Florence, the ancient grandeur of Rome—and modern Rome; sunshine ashore and storms at sea;—the whole is one continued round of nature adorned;—a book of rare pleasure.

Hints for Health. Being Two Lectures on the Influence of Air, Water, Food, and Wine on the System. By J. Sherwood Stocker, M. D. 8vo, pp. 47. 1874. London: J. & A. Churchill.

A *library* production and a tolerable literary success. But more likely to do harm than good, in that it endorses and reiterates the trite dogma in regard to the ill effects of *bad* liquors, and the salutary effects of *good*. In other words, it attributes the usual ill effects of the habitual use of alcohol to the bad quality of the article, or the adulterations, and not to the thing itself; and this seems to be the object of the book. It appears not to have fallen under the author's observation that it is very unusual to find any one who habitually uses wine or stronger drinks, who ever confessedly uses any but the "best;" and that it is only when these begin to exercise their ordinary influence that the effects of "bad" liquor become manifest.

Kate Kennedy. A novel, by Mrs. C. J. Newby. Philadelphia: T. Peterson & Bros.

This is the eighth volume of the new, cheap and popular edition of the celebrated novels written by Mrs. C J. Newby, now in course of publication by T. B. Peterson & Brothers, Philadelphia. The London *Athenæum*, in a notice of it, says: "We have read this novel with great pleasure. It is a healthy, sensible and interesting story. The title is sober and scarcely indicates the high order of qualities which are illustrated in the narrative. The readers of "Kate Kennedy" will see for themselves how interesting this matter-of-fact virtue can be made. It is full of incidents and characters which cannot but interest the reader, and is in truth a brilliant and interesting novel." Her novels, "Kate Kennedy," "Wondrous Strange," "Margaret Hamilton," "Right and Left," "Trodden Down," "Only Temper," "Married," "Common Sense," etc., are obtaining a wide-spread popularity. "Kate Kennedy," is issued in a large octavo volume, price fifty cents, and is for sale by all booksellers, or copies will be sent to any one, post-paid, by the publishers, on receipt of price by them.

Principles of Mental Physiology, with their application to the training and discipline of the mind, and the study of its morbid conditions. By William B. Carpenter, M. D., LL. D., etc., etc., 8vo. pp. 737. New York: D. Appleton & Co., 1874.

This is an exceedingly timely book. One which no diligent student of the author's previous works, will fail to see is the consecutive fruit of straight-forward scientific progress. No amount of mere speculative thought or philosophy, has ever served to turn Dr. Carpenter from the most rigid scientific investigation of hastily propounded theories. And after almost half a century's devotion to physiological studies, he practically demonstrates that the true appreciation of mental phenomena is attainable only from a physiological standpoint. Hence this treatise is one of sequence—a result of truths worked out, verified and systematized, as the mere part of a whole. Indeed, the author tells us that it is only "an expansion of the Outline of Psychology contained in the fourth and fifth editions of his 'Principles of Human Physiology,' (1852 and 1855), but omitted from the later editions of that work, to make room for new matter more strictly Physiological." However, "to the character of a system of psychology this treatise makes no pretensions whatever; being simply designed to supplement existing systems of physiology and metaphysics, by dealing with a group of subjects, which, occupying the border ground between the two, have been almost entirely neglected in both."

The work is divided into two parts, general and Special Physiology. Book I, comprehends the general relations between mind and body, followed by the relations of the nervous system generally, and the exercise of its several functions. Book II, treats of memory; common sense; imagination; unconscious cerebration; electro-biology; sleep, dreaming and somnambulism; mesmerism and spiritualism; intoxication and delirium; insanity; influence of mental state on the organic functions; mind and will in nature, and Dr. Ferrier's experimental researches on the brain. Dr. Carpenter has not only placed the medical profession under new obligations to him for this timely treatise, but the public at large; above all teachers, and the heads of families, to whom we particularly commend this work as containing the soundest knowledge of any book hitherto published, for the guide of youth in the study of mental philosophy.

Body and Mind: Inquiry into their Connection and Mutual Influence, especially in reference to Mental Disorders: an enlarged and revised edition. To which are added *Psychological Essays.* By Henry Maudsley, M. D., etc. 12mo. pp. 475. New York: D. Appleton & Co., 1874.

This volume consists of two parts. First, of the free Gulstonian Lectures delivered by Professor Maudsley before the Royal College of Physicians and Surgeons, in 1870, which have become so thoroughly incorporated into the literature of mental pathology as to render a critical review unnecessary.

Of the three lectures forming the first part, the first one brings into view the general Physiology of the Mind—considered in relation to health. The second exhibits some of the more usual forms of degeneracy of the mind, consequent upon disease, and its influence in physical degeneracy from generation to generation. The third treats of the pathology of the mind in general, and points out the relations of morbid states of the body to disordered mental functions.

The lectures are followed by an essay on "Conscience and Organization." An address delivered before the Psychological Section of the British Medical Association in 1872. The object of this essay is to show that conscience is a mere function—a materialistic part of the physical organization ; a mere secretion of the brain. It comprehends a general review of the status of insanity, in its relation to ancient and modern civilizations, and its almost universal heridity.

Part second, consists of four Essays : "Hamlet," "Swedenborg," "The Theory of Vitality," and "The Limits of Philosophical Inquiry." These are reprints, from the *Westminster Review, British and Foreign Medico-Chirurgical Review*, and the *Journal* of *Mental Science.*

These essays are all from a materialistic standpoint, intended to show "how much matter can do without spiritual help." The essays are in every way worthy of the attention they have received as separate contributions to literature in the first place, and of this present more substantial and connected form into a volume.

No one with any pretense to philosophical reading can afford to be unacquainted with Maudsley.

Physiology for Practical Use. Edited by James Hinton, author of Thoughts on Health, etc., with an introduction by E. L. Youmans, 12mo, pp. 507. New York : D. Appleton & Co., 1874.

This is a truly elegant volume in both its internal and external aspects. With no pretense to being a systematic treatise, it nevertheless so clearly comprehends the physiological subjects with which every body ought to become familiar with a view to the preservation of health, that for popular use, it is unquestionably all the more valuable for the omissions. The author claims but a small part in the volume, the mere collating and putting together the papers for republication; most of them having been before published. In their first appearance, however, the author appears to have been the leading spirit in securing the co-operation of a number of professional gentlemen particularly skilled in the several chosen departments, to contribute a series of health-papers to the *People's Magazine.* And these are the papers, carefully revised, and re-arranged into the handsome volume before us, appropriately illustrated with numerous accurate engravings. The essays selected are arranged in chapters : The Brain and its Servants ; the Faculty of Hearing ; the Eye and Light ; the Sense of Taste ; Digestion ; the Bath ; Taking Cold ; Headache ; Ventilation ; the Action of Alcohol ; Occupation and Health, and a dozen more equally interesting subjects of universal importance. The work is almost wholly divested of technicalities, is written in plain, elegant English, with just enough of science to give effect to its salutary teachings. We heartily recommend it for family reading. It will, if observed, prove antidotal to many of the ills that families are heir to.

Electro-Therapeutics : A condensed manual of Medical Electricity. By D. F. Lincoln, M. D., 12mo. pp. 186. Philadelphia : Henry C. Lea. 1874.

This is a very timely book, supplying a real want on the subject of which it treats ; for of the many papers and brochures recently published on electro-therapeutics, they are almost without exception, their respective author's electro-therapeutics, and contribute only to the flood of literature on the subject without dealing with the principles of it, as this book does. And for this we heartily commend it as a well-written, practical work.

Beaten Paths: or a Woman's Vacation. By Ella W. Thompson, 12mo, pp. 274. Boston : Lee & Shepard. 1874.

This is a very interesting book of travel by a pleasant writer, revelling in the delights of new scenes. The author was one of a party of seven women who set out from Boston to *do* Europe, without male attendant, each one of them feeling "that what seven women could not do was not worth doing." How well the other six did their part we are not informed. But we accept this one as a sample traveller, sight-seer, and delineator. To those who have never visited the old renowned capitals of Europe and wish to enjoy them by a description which reads like a novel, we commend this book ; and to those who have seen them, and wish to enjoy them all over again without a second visit, we commend it, for they will see new charms.

Prophetic Voices Concerning America. A Monograph. By Charles Sumner, 12mo, pp. 176. Boston : Lee & Shepard.

This book is a literary monument of a patriot. The monograph of which it is an elaboration, appeared originally in the "Atlantic Monthly ;" and from a note by the author seems to have been prepared with reference to the hundredth birthday of our nation, when "these prophetic voices will be heard, teaching how much of present fame and power was foreseen, also what remains to be accomplished."

Eulogy of Charles Sumner. By Carl Schurz, Boston : Lee & Shepard, 1874.

No admirer of the character of Charles Sumner, will fail to possess himself of this tribute to his memory.

The Conditions of the Conflict.—An oration, delivered before the Medical Society of the County of Kings, Brooklyn, N. Y., Feb. 24, 1874. By Alexander Hutchins, M. D., p. 32.

Dr. Hutchins' orations is an admirable impersonification of the typical physician, as distinguished from the conventional doctor. It is a pity that such a paper is deprived of its usefulness by the restraints of society usage. It is eminently worthy of an extensive circulation, and the "Conditions of the Conflict" between the true and the false are so well put and so readable, that we feel fully warranted in the belief that the public requires the opportunity only, to benefit by it.

Transfusion.—A paper read before the Maine Medical Association. By A. C. Hamlin, M. D. June session, 1874.

We have here presented, in the small space of fourteen pages, seventy-five distinct references, and the opinions of the best men who have written on the subject of *Transfusion*, from its first practice to the present time. Such industry and excerpta constitute the bulwark of true medical progress ; and such papers are of more value to the medical library than whole tomes of visionary theorists.

THE SANITARIAN.

A MONTHLY JOURNAL.

VOL. II.] OCTOBER, 1874. [NO. 7.

THE MANAGEMENT OF SLAUGHTER-HOUSES.

By E. H. JANES, M. D., New York.

Prior to the year 1866, the slaughtering of animals for food as conducted in the city of New York, was carried on without any reference to sanitary regulations, and almost without restriction in regard to the construction and location of buildings devoted to this business. Slaughter-houses were to be seen in various parts of the city, many of these in a dilapidated condition and extremely filthy, the yards badly paved with coarse cobble-stones, the sewerage defective and in many instances entirely wanting, the blood from the slaughtered animals being discharged into the open street gutter, along which it was allowed to flow until it reached a sewer-opening at some street corner, thus rendering the gutter filthy with putrid animal matter, and defiling the atmosphere with offensive and noxious exhalations.

The first movement of importance made by the Metropolitan Board of Health in the Spring of 1866, was the holding of a conference with the butchers, with a view of their ultimate removal to some point either beyond the city limits, or so near the water front as to be no longer a public annoyance, and at the same time to be readily supplied with the best facilities for securing good drainage and cleanliness. It was not however until several years after, that the butchers being repeatedly ordered by the health authorities and after appealing in vain to the courts, finally by degrees yielded, and removed their business from the places hitherto occupied, to their present locations.

The present sanitary code forbids the slaughtering of animals at any place in the city of New York south of 40th street, or between Second and Tenth avenues, which is the first step towards concentrating the business within appropriate limits. There are now in the city fifty-four of these separate establishments, twenty-one of which are situated east of Second avenue, the drainage from which is received by the East River; and thirty-three are west of Tenth avenue, or in a similar proximity to the North River. A few of these are so constructed as to accommodate several butchers each, the building being divided into compartments or "baulks," each occupying a floor space of about ten by fifty feet. These, with a certain amount of yard-room, are rented by individual butchers, either by the year or by the month, the proprietor of the building being always responsible for its sanitary condition. A few of the larger establishments are well-constructed, the floors well and tightly laid, the yards evenly graded and paved, and the arrangements for flushing and sewerage well-arranged. These however are exceptions to the general condition of this class of buildings; for although many of them are comparatively new, they fail to exhibit that degree of sanitary improvement which is required by the sanitary interests of the public; and, I might add, which it is difficult to acquire so long as the business is conducted in detached establishments, and by men whose views of cleanliness and order widely differ.

The present limits of the slaughter-house district on the east side, comprise the area extending from 43d to 47th streets, including both of these streets and the east side of First avenue; and the district on the west side extends from 40th to 47th street west of Tenth avenue, though most of the business on the west side is done on 40th and 41st streets. It is here, near the water front, that the entire hog-slaughtering business is done, with the concomitant business of lard-rendering; the number of hogs killed annually being about 1,200,000. During the warm season every slaughter-house in the city is inspected daily by a sanitary officer, and a careful note made of any neglect in compliance with the requirements of the sanitary code; during the cold weather this duty is performed weekly. This constant surveillance has the effect to considerably modify the nuisance attending this business when conducted in so many separate establishments, and extending over so much area; but it does not accomplish all that is desirable, neither is it by any means a substitute for concentration of the business in large abattoirs. Although as before said, a few of the larger buildings are well constructed and properly located, most of them are deficient in both of these respects, the drainage imperfect, the yards imperfectly paved, allowing filth, blood, and particles of offal to collect among the interstices of the coarse paving stones, or pools of bloody and filthy water to lodge in the various depressions on the surface of the defective pavement. The floors and much of the interior standing work of the building being of wood, readily absorb the animal liquids, and soon become offensive, yielding an odor of decomposing animal matter, while the removal of offal and other portions of the animal not used as food, being the work of different individuals, is never done with that promptness which characterizes the workings of an establishment which is governed by one controlling head. These are evils which attend the present system of slaughtering, notwithstanding the exercise of the most rigid sanitary control; and the question arises whether concentration at the water side would not afford better facilities to conduct the business in an inoffensive manner, as well as more economically. The various branches of business growing out of the slaughtering business, viz.: that of utilizing the various portions of the animal not used as food, all belong to what are recognized as "offensive trades," and would be deprived of very much that is objectionable could the work be done at the same establishment where the animals are slaughtered. At present one person collects the feet to be manufactured into glue; another takes the fat to be rendered; another takes hides, and still another horns, etc., all to be conveyed through the public streets in different directions, to the great annoyance of citizens, to say nothing of the many tripe-boiling, head-picking, and sausage-making establishments which are scattered through certain portions of the city, each contributing its share to impregnate with offensive odors, if not to poison, the atmosphere.

The establishment of one, two, or three large abattoirs, so located as to project over the water, with all of the modern appliances, not only for expediting the work of slaughtering and handling the stock, but for utilizing the refuse, would not only greatly modify the nuisance as it now exists, but would entirely do away with the many other offensive trades which grow out of this, and are located in various portions of the city; and would doubtless prove much more economical than the present system of detached and isolated establishments. These abattoirs should be located, if possible, over the water, so that all waste-fluids and washings can be immediately discharged therein without being dependent on street drain or sewer. The means of flushing should be ample, that absolute cleanliness may at all times be secured; and the floors and posts should be of some non-absorbent material to avoid the offensiveness of the ordinary slaughter-house when saturated with animal liquids and reeking with putrid odors. The atmosphere kept thus pure, the meat will be less liable to suffer from the presence of disease germs, which are always developed from putrid organic matter, and hasten the putrefaction of fresh meats and vegetables. The rendering of the fat and utilizing of animal refuse could all be effected on the premises before the commencement of decomposition, and thus the annoyance arising from this source would be reduced to the minimum.

The abattoir should be so located that animals can be landed on the premises from boat or car, and thus the necessity of driving them through the streets of the city—a most serious evil—be avoided. A competent inspector should be on duty at each abattoir to see that no deceased animals are slaughtered, and that no meat of any improper quality be placed in the market.

The stock-yards and abattoir of Jersey City afford an excellent illustration of the superiority of this system over that of separate establishments. They are located over a small bay, formerly known as Harsimus Cove, and consist of an immense pier, extending from the shore of the cove to the line of the bulk-head, thus having the advantage of the regular flow and ebb of the tide underneath, washing away any particle of filth whether solid or fluid, which may either accidentally or otherwise escape into the water. The abattoir is situated on the end of the pier, and occupies a space of 300x400 feet, while the remainder of the pier is divided into cattle-yards, with the exception of a small part occupied by offices, etc.

The portion devoted to yarding, comprises by far the greater part of the area, and is divided by fences, so constructed as to admit of free ventilation, into smaller yards situated on both sides of a broad carriageway, and all kept scrupulously clean by men whose time is devoted exclusively to this duty. The animals arrive and pass through Jersey City on an elevated railroad, which terminates by an inclined plane on the premises, thus avoiding the necessity of driving through any portion of the city. At the terminus of the railroad is the ferry-landing, from which the freshly slaughtered animal is transported to the New York or Brooklyn market.

That portion of the establishment devoted to slaughtering is well arranged, both in regard to construction and management, so as to meet every sanitary requirement. The floors, being of asphalt, are non-absorbent, and can be flushed at any moment. The several compartments or "baulks" are separated only by iron railing, thus affording every facility for lateral ventilation while the movable skylights and side windows complete the arrangements for upward and cross currents. The work is systematic in every particular. The hides immediately upon being removed from the slaughtered animal, are salted on the premises, and thus placed beyond the danger of putrefaction, while there are complete facilities for the removal of every species of offal, etc., so that at night when the work of the day is completed, not a vestige of animal refuse remains on the premises.

One special advantage of this system is that the sanitary care of the establishment is not left to the individual butchers, but is undertaken by the Abattoir Company, and all under the management of one controlling head, the butchers being restricted to certain hours, during which the work of the day must be finished, that the duty of cleaners may not be interrupted. The advantage of this peculiar feature of the system, cannot fail to be apparent when contrasted with fifty-four separate establishments, each run according to the views of the proprietor, who although willing and anxious to comply with all the sanitary regulations, will continue to fail from the defects of the system under which he labors.

The hog-slaughtering establishment connected with the Harsimus Abattoir is located on the Hackensack River some three or four miles from Jersey City, so far remote from human dwellings as not to be the source of offence or annoyance to any one. As fast as the hogs are slaughtered they are, by an ingenious arrangement of cranes and railways, transferred to well-ventilated cars, where they remain suspended until they reach New York or Brooklyn as the case may be, the track being so arranged that the cars run on the ferry-boat, thus avoiding the necessity of too frequent handling. In this manner I believe that pork can arrive at Washington Market in less time, and in better condition than it can by being packed on heavily laden trucks and transported from 40th or 41st streets through the streets of New York. The same management and discipline are extended to this establishment that are exercised at the Harsimus abattoir; it is here that the fat from both establishments is rendered and the offal utilized; that from Harsimus being transferred by the elevated railroad in tightly covered cars, to which it is removed immediately upon being separated from the animal. The fat is rendered by aid of the more recently approved apparatus, while the blood and offal are in the process of being converted into fertilizers before they are entirely deprived of their animal heat. So complete is the machinery and system by which the more offensive features of the business are conducted, that the odors usually developed by fat-rendering and the utilizing of animal refuse, are hardly perceived a hundred yards from the building.

The economy of the system seems to be established by this experiment. Butchers who do business on a large scale, can rent "baulks" at a lower rate than they can in well-constructed private establishments; while those who kill only occasionally and in small numbers, are invited to make use of the place, the only remuneration required being the feet of the animals.

On the other hand, the company claims the privilege of purchasing the hides and fat from all its tenants, at New York prices. By this latter arrangement, the company is enabled to sustain itself in the enterprise, as the profits growing out of the rendering of fat, the disposal of other portions of the animal not used as food and the conversion of animal refuse into fertilizing agents, go towards making up any deficiency in their remuneration as received for rent.

The result of concentration and intelligent management is such, that one need but compare the two systems to be convinced of the superiority of a well-constructed abattoir conducted on the plan above mentioned, as regards neatness, convenience, public health, and economy.

In the Fifth Annual Report of the State Board of Health of Massachusetts, we have a description of the new abattoir at Brighton, situated about four miles from the centre of Boston, the grounds comprising an area of about fifty acres, bounded on the longest side by Charles River. Although the buildings had not all been completed, the establishment was opened for business on the 17th of June, 1873, and up to January 1st, 1874, we are told that 14,194 cattle, 2,700 calves, and 150,000 sheep had been slaughtered. This abattoir is owned by a corporation known as the "Butchers' Slaughtering and Melting Association," who have established a code of regulations for its management, approved by the State Board of Health. These regulations require the appointment of a managing director, who shall have the entire control of the premises, and see that all the regulations are observed. Persons occupying the premises are required to immediately deposit all portions of the slaughtered animal not used as food through openings in the respective floors to the basement, where there are properly constructed wagons stationed to receive them, which when filled, are removed to the rendering-house, and the contents of each deposited in the appropriate room. No butcher is allowed to sell his hides, fat and tripe to be removed, without notifying the managing director, under whose supervision they are to be removed, he fixing the time of day at which all such material shall be removed, that none shall remain on the premises except such as is to be manufactured there. All hides not disposed of as above, are to be immediately salted on the premises, and fat not so disposed of, is rendered by the corporation. All offal is rendered while fresh, and the scrap of offal and blood is immediately dried, and the fertilizers so produced to be properly packed and stored for sale.

The above is a brief abstract of the regulations established by the corporation. The State Board of Health has made a few additional ones, providing for the disposal of dead and diseased animals, for the immediate treatment of offal and refuse, daily and thorough cleansing of the premises, supply of food and water for the animals; and forbidding the slaughtering of animals not in health, the bringing of animals slaughtered elsewhere, or blood or offal to the premises, or the infliction of injury or unnecessary pain on any animal at the premises of the association.

The rendering-house connected with this establishment is in the centre of the group of buildings, and is supplied with all the necessary machinery. The rendering is done by steam, the vapors from the tanks being passed through a condenser by which the steam is condensed, and the remaining gases are forced into the fire and consumed. This process of rendering is said to give no odor. The gases from the "driers" are treated in the same way. The slaughter-houses, with the exception of the basement story, are built of wood, "and are planned with reference to the individual interests of the butchers and their special modes of doing business." Each is provided with "cooling rooms," where the meat may be kept at a temperature of 40° Fahr. until sent to market. The basement story is of brick, with a concrete floor, and ample drainage. The establishment is well supplied with water and steam power, the former being raised to the fifth story of the rendering house, where, from two immense reservoirs, it is distributed to every portion of the premises. Steam not only runs the machinery but supplies warmth to the several apartments, warm water for cleansing purposes, and as before said, renders the fat, and dries the refuse to an almost odorless fertilizer.

The result of this experiment is, thus far, quite satisfactory to the butchers, to the corporation, and to the Board of Health; and, in the language of the report, it has "fully proved that it is possible to carry on a great slaughtering establishment, without its being offensive either to the workmen in it or the community around it."

In briefly summing up, I would say that the sanitary necessities of a town require its slaughter-houses to be located remote from its centre or its business portions, and if possible by the water-side.

The yards should be so graded and paved that surface drainage from every portion thereof will be freely and readily discharged into the receiving drains, which should be constructed of durable material, with smooth inner surface, that their contents in passing through will meet with the least amount of obstruction from friction.

The buildings should be constructed as far as possible of non-absorbing material, the floors should be strong and perfectly water-tight, and slightly inclined, that drainage may be uninterrupted. A plentiful supply of water is indispensable, and should be freely applied in cleansing the pavements and floors. Offal and manure should be removed daily, and premises thoroughly cleansed as soon as the work of the day is finished. Fences and walls of the buildings, as well as the interior wood-work, should be frequently lime-washed, to which wash should be added a small proportion of carbolic acid.

Concentration of the business of slaughtering in large abattoirs, where all refuse can be utilized at once, and all parts of the animal not used as food can be reduced to inoffensive articles of commerce, would not only facilitate the business, but would promote the sanitary interests of the community.

Finally, whether concentrated or issolated, all establishments of the kind should be under constant sanitary surveillance; absolute cleanliness should be enforced, perfect drainage and sewerage should be maintained, the slaughtering of diseased animals should be prevented and all meats sent to market should have the approval of a competent and conscientious sanitary officer.

UTILIZING SEWAGE.—To the Editor of THE SANITARIAN:—Dear Sir, I use the word "sewage" as applying to both the solid and liquid matter usually consigned, in our carelessness, to our "sewers," although Worcester defines it, after Martin, as "the water flowing in sewers." In fact, this matter is so largely liquid, that the solids are almost wholly lost, and our careless use of water-closets and sink-pipes emptying into drains and sewers, leads usually to the final loss of the invaluable fertilizing quality of the waste matter of the human frame, both solid and fluid, constantly evolved by us all in our waking hours. The instincts of all the higher animals, below man, lead them to bury their waste matter in the soil, and man himself may well take the hint. No better disinfectant or deodorizer exists than loam or dry earth. So Moses meant when he directed the children of Israel to cover what came from them in the ground. Prince Henry, of the Netherlands, in our day, follows the wise Hebrew's rule by providing for the removal of all human waste every twenty-four hours from each home in the city of the Hague to the subsoil of the farms in its neighborhood. His process, or rather that of his chief engineer, I will give in full at another time. Let me devote this letter to a brief sketch of a very simple and perfectly effective disposal of sewage which it has been my good fortune to witness, the two last seasons, at our summer quarters in Scituate, Massachusetts. Our landlord's practice is this: in the fallow spaces of his garden he keeps a hole open of the size of a half barrel, for the chamber-slops, covering it with loam whenever it is full and before it becomes sour, and then opening another; the sink-water is treated in the same way at the end of its spout, and every few days he covers the contents of his privy with sifted ashes. The results are, in the first place, perfectly pure, sweet and wholesome air everywhere about the premises, with a freedom from all effects of malaria which we never knew elsewhere; and, in the next place, a supply of deodorized, fertilizing matter sufficient to yield the two families all our summer vegetables and his own family enough, nearly, for the whole year. He has a small hen-yard to help him, but no pig-stye or stable, and from the hens and the household he obtains, without purchasing a pound, all the guano he requires; and what one wise man does thus well, every one could accomplish also. It is as sensible as it is simple, and we commend it with pleasure through your columns to your readers and through them to the public.

C. T. BARNARD.

Scituate, Mass., Aug. 10, 1874.

CRIMINAL RESPONSIBILITY.*

By Thos. J. Mays, M. D.

Few subjects are of greater importance and more fruitful in correctly modifying our present theories of the innumerable phases of human action, than a study of *criminal responsibility*. Researches in physiology and pathology have forced upon us already a perfect revision of our former ideas of mental action, and still further inquiry will cause, although not without a sharp conflict, a radical change in our present opinions concerning individual responsibility. As man advances intellectually, so will he discard his crude and fallacious reasonings which clung to him as his indispensable hope and safeguard. Witches are no more sacrificed at the stake or hung; maniacs are no longer incarcerated and left to perish for want of proper care and nourishment, criminals who were classed among rational beings, and visited by the stern hand of law, are now known to have been insane and irresponsible, while a wholesale modification of opinion, respecting capital punishment, is taking place at the present time. This revolution of the intellect is, undoubtedly, due to a more proper appreciation of the relation existing between brain and mind. Formerly mind and body were presumed to be separable, could exist independent, the mind only requiring the brain during its terrestrial life, but at present every physiologist is aware of the fallacy of such a doctrine. This notion took its origin at the time when the crude knowledge of nature was confined to priests, and when all the perceptible changes, even in inanimate matter, were attributed to and solved by the supposition of countless supernatural agencies, according to whose caprice man was injured or benefited—punished or rewarded.

In the course of experiment and investigation, man has generalized the appearances of nature, has unveiled their mystery, and referred them to the laws by which they are governed, until now, it is an accepted scientific fact, that all her phenomena, mind not excepted, fall within the sphere of natural laws, and are proper objects for physical investigation. However, until this was accomplished, the scientific world was attacked from all quarters by the ignorant and superstitious, who are always ready to ascribe everything they cannot readily understand, to supernatural causes. Unfortunately, man was the last to be divorced from the supernatural element. Both health and disease were referred to the favor and displeasure of spirits. A man who was deprived of speech or hearing, had a dumb or a deaf devil. If he suffered pains in any portion of his body, it was believed that a witch was inflicting this torture by forcing pins into the corresponding portions of a wax model. The devil was supposed to be omnipotent. There were religious sects, who were

*Read before the Lycoming Co. (Pa.) Medical Society.

required to hawk, sneeze and spit continually, in order to expel the devils which they inhaled. Few ever thought of inquiring into these terrible delusions, as the church denounced all who dared to attempt an investigation.

While this disposition prevailed to refer all diseases to the interposition of demons, rational medicine could hardly be brought into existence ; but as time rolled on and truth and light were developed and diffused by science, these supposed supernatural diseases were assigned to their proper and legitimate sphere, and from thence we date the birth of rational scientific medicine. In the development of anatomy, physiology, and pathology, as indeed in everything else, we see that the more simple and common structures are comprehended previous to those more complicated; hence the brain, the most complex and least understood organ in the body, is the last seat of struggle between the natural and supernatural—between science and demonology.

It is now an admitted fact, by nearly all scientific men, that mind is nothing more or less than brain-function. Dr. Maudsley says : "It must be distinctly laid down that mental action is as surely dependent on the nervous structure, as the function of the liver confessedly is on the hepatic structure." And Professor Claude Bernard says : "Physiology tells us that, except in the difference and the greater complexity of the phenomena, the brain is the organ of intelligence in exactly the same way that the heart is the organ of circulation and the larynx that of the voice." And again, Dr. Carpenter says : "It is one of the best established facts in physiology, although taken very little account of by metaphysicians, that *all* mental action is dependent on a chemical re-action between the blood and the brain."

But on the other hand, a majority of metaphysicians contend that the mind is something altogether independent of the brain, and only uses it as an instrument for its own revelation, and while others are forced to admit that a portion of mind is brain-function, they believe that which they call "free-will" to be altogether extraneous to man, and sufficiently strong to guide and keep him, if he chooses, in the path of rectitude and virtue.

But if every man, as they hold, is endowed with this innate power, why do not all individuals possess it in the same degree? Why is one good and another corrupt? Is it not very evident that a great many fall, while others remain unscathed from the pernicious influences of society? If it does not depend upon some basis which is more or less imperfect in different individuals, why so many different shades of human conduct? And again, if this "free-will" power which does not depend upon a defective material substratum, enables a man to control himself at his own command, why does he not escape the tyranny of his own imperfect organization and become a sinless and perfect being? Surely there is no one who does not desire such a condition of life. And again, if it is free, it must necessarily be uncontrolled and independent. It cannot be the result of a cause, for then it is dependent. It cannot come within the bounds of the physical world, for here everything is the result of the operation of law. In short, can we conceive of anything uncaused, uncontrolled and independent? Yet these properties, if it is free, are essential to its free existence.

Buckle, in his "History of Civilization," discards the idea altogether that human action "depends on some capricious and personal principle, peculiar to each man, as 'free-will,' or the like," on the contrary, he asserts "the great truth that the actions of men being guided by their antecedents, are in reality never inconsistent, but however capricious they may appear, only form part of one vast scheme of universal order, of which we, in the present state of knowledge, can barely see the outline." He further writes, "Indeed the progress of inquiry is becoming so rapid and so earnest that I entertain little doubt that before another century has elapsed the chain of evidence will be complete, and it will be as rare to find an historian who denies the undeviating regularity of the moral world, as it now is to find a philosopher who denies the regularity of the material world." Quetelet, in his "Science of Man," says, "It is curious to see man proudly entitling himself King of Nature, and fancying himself controlling all things by his free-will, yet submitting, unknown to himself, more rigorously than any other being in creation, to the laws he is under subjection to."

The will or volition is the determining agent of the body, it sets free the movements which have been previously organized in the motor nerve centres; depends upon the brain for its basis; is controlled by natural law; and for its proper development and proficiency, training and exercise are as essential as they are to develop any other faculty in the body. All our actions are either instinctive or acquired. The instinctive actions are immediately essential to the maintenance of our lives, and take place from the commencement without any training; they are inherited, and are such as breathing, sucking, etc. But on the other hand there are a great many actions which we learn and after having acquired them thoroughly, perform them as regularly and methodically as we do instinctive actions. This is the case with the acts of walking, writing, speech, &c. We all know how difficult it is to train a child to these actions. Until locomotion is thoroughly accomplished, the child endures a long and painful experience. So a great deal of time and patience is required to bring all the voluntary actions of the body under the guidance of the will.

It is a fact, long ago admitted, that tubercle, syphilis, rheumatism, scrofula and gout may be inherited and transmitted from parent to child, but not until within a recent period was it believed that the brain enters the world with the same imperfections which have long been observed to take place in other organs. If then, all our actions are controlled by immutable and unchanging law, everything the necessary result of a cause, are they who are not responsible for the cause, responsible for the effect? In other words, are those beings who are born into the world with a defective nervous organization and thus inherit a tendency to sin and crime, as responsible for their actions as their more rational fellows? A son inherits a tendency to strong drink, through his whole life he labors under an oppressive and imperfect constitution, and eventually becomes a confirmed drunkard, commits a capital crime, and is accordingly hung. Now, no amount of reasoning can lead us to the preposterous conclusion that there is the faintest shadow of justice in such a procedure—punishing an individual for an act, the effect of a cause for which he was perfectly irresponsible, yet no one will deny that such acts do occur and frequently have occurred hitherto.

The question inevitably follows whether we are not all born with a tendency to sin and how far this annuls the responsibility of every one. This is a point that should be weighed with due consideration; and, on the one hand we know that ante-natal causes and tendencies shape our actions and ends to a greater degree than we perhaps are conscious; but we must not, on the other hand, forget that pernicious and vitiating environments, such as are found in every civilized and uncivilized community, are as potent for evil. In his address before the "National Prison Association," Hon. Horatio Seymour said, "I do not doubt that some men are more prone to vice than others, but, after listening to thousands of prayers for pardon, I can hardly recall a case where I do not feel that I might have fallen as my fellow men have done, if I had been subject to the same demoralizing influences, and pressed by the same temptations. I repeat here what I have said on other occasions—that, after a long experience with men in all conditions of life, after having felt as most men, the harsh injustice springing from the strife and passion of the world, I have learned to think more kindly of the hearts of men, and to think less of their heads." Language like this, coming from such eminent authority, is full of meaning, and cannot fail to carry its weight wherever uttered; yet how much is it at variance with the doctrines and decisions of the courts of law, which hold all men equally responsible, unless smitten by the most consummate aberration of the mind.

We are too prone to stand up and thank God that we are not like these poor men who are blood of our blood, and bone of our bone, who are ourselves, only under different conditions, and the influences which dragged them to ruin may force others to sink to the same level, who do not dream of danger. We love to do this, while at the same time we are guilty of offences, which were committed on similar principles and under like influences. To say that a criminal is responsible for his actions, where he knows that which he does is wrong, and that he could have done differently had he only chosen to do so, is to impute to a defective creature something which we in our better and wiser moments cannot, at least do not, resist, while probably if placed in similar circumstances we would fall side by side with him whom we are so free in condemning. For it must be patent to nearly all, that it is a great wrong and a positive physical injury to overload and abuse our digestive organs, yet where are the precious few who are exempt from this sin? Many who are in this habit will say, and perhaps console themselves, that they have a will power, whereby they can avoid it at their own pleasure, but do not seek to do so; yet this is fatal, for the darkest stained criminal may bring the same plea in self-defence. It is poor evidence that a man possesses much will power, if he never manifests it when demanded for his own health and safety. The true reason that an individual abuses his stomach is not owing to the assertion that he has a will whereby he can control his appetite, but it is on account of his imperfect organization, resulting from inheritance or lack of proper training. This is only one of the many transgressions which we are apt to commit every day, and they pass by unheeded without teaching us the valuable lessson that all our actions are imperfect and that they only develop in proportion to their cultivation, and whenever they receive this properly they will always manifest themselves in the right direction.

It is utterly and glaringly foolish to expect a musician of ordinary skill to perform the different compositions of Liszt, or the sublime symphonies of Beethoven, but it occasions surprise and even condemnation when an individual who was born in crime and poverty, who is deficient in training and education, does not conform to the requirements of social law and order. These are analogous cases as far as capability is concerned, and we can with equal propriety demand as much from the former as from the latter. Whenever the responsibility of an individual is involved, inquiries should be instituted whether and to what extent he is mentally incapable or incapacitated. In the eyes of the law the young members of society are held incapable and irresponsible in proportion to the incompleteness of their development, but it is an indisputable fact that in every country there exist tens of thousands of hopeless vagabonds, usually known as the dangerous classes, who are really so incapacitated that they possess no self-control beyond that of a brute, and are, for the most part, moral infants, if not imbeciles. These persons are the weeds of society, and in truth are men who are in a great degree made and controlled by the pernicious impulses surrounding them. Their condition is the result of causes exciting and predisposing, which to a great degree are preventable, and however often they are subjected to the most rigid prison discipline, the moment their foot is set free, the majority will re-enter their former life of vice and crime.

The majority of criminals are of a very fertile age and naturally propagate their kind at a very rapid rate; and if I had time and ability I might show you how vicious, depraved, and imbecile parents pollute their offspring, to the "third and fourth generation," and how they serve to fill our asylums for the insane to overflowing, and that unless means be instituted to restrain their liberty during the period of fecundity, there must necessarily be an incessant increase in the insane, imbecile and vicious portion of our population.

AN IRISHMAN'S LETTER.—Here is an Irish gentleman's letter to his son in college: "My dear Son: I write to send you two pair of my old breeches, that you may have a new coat made out of them. Also, some new socks which your mother has just knit by cutting down some of mine. Your mother sends you ten dollars without my knowledge, and for fear you may not use it wisely, I have kept back half, and only send you five. Your mother and I are well, except that your sister has got the measles, which we think would spread among the other girls if Tom had not had it before, and he is the only one left. I hope you will do honor to my teachings; if not, you are an ass, and your mother and myself your affectionate parents."

THE PEABODY BUILDINGS, LONDON.

On an irregular site of ground situate on the south side of Stamford street, and approached by Duke street, the Peabody Trustees have erected sixteen blocks of dwellings on the flat system.

Having visited them, we have much pleasure in saying they appear to embrace in a compact form all the conveniences and improvements which experience in this class of dwellings has suggested. The earlier attempts of this kind failed either in paying too little regard to sanitary arrangements, or in a wasteful attempt to make the dwellings too comprehensive. These new buildings are being erected from the designs of Mr. H. A. Darbishire, the architect, by Messrs. Cubitt & Co., the builders.

We will endeavor to convey to our readers the general plan of each block, which is about 70 feet in length by 32 feet wide, and gives accommodation to twenty-one families, or in all 336 families. The entrance is in the centre of the longest side of each block, and leads through a short passage into a central hall about 24 by 8 feet, in which the staircase of stone ascends by single flights to each floor or flat. Each landing is of York stone. Opening from this hall on each level, and at the ends, we get four suites of rooms, or two suites at each end of block, each being lighted from their respective fronts. The living rooms are 14 feet by 11 feet, the bedrooms 9 by 14 feet; as a rule the height of floors is about 8 feet. Laterally or transversely to the staircase or hall we have on one side a single living-room 14 feet, 6 feet by 12 feet, and a small bedroom; and on the other side is an open well-hole or area, which runs from basement to the upper floor of building, where it is covered by the wash-house. This open recess, about 8 or 9 feet square, lights the staircase and forms an important ventilating orifice to each block, and in giving access to the dust receptacle, &c. On either side of this open recess are the sinks and water-closets, the sinks being of slate, and the closets fitted with Lambert's white glazed pans and lifts. The soil-pipes and sink-wastes besides being trapped are carried up to roof as ventilators.

Another important point in the sanitary economy of the building we must notice. Between the stair-flights and adjoining passage a brick shaft 14 inches square, internally rendered in cement, is carried up from basement, where it forms a shoot into the receptacle for refuse, through the roof, where it is covered by slate and terminates as a ventilator in the shape of a small high-pitched covering perforated on each face.

On each floor in the hall a small iron hopper, patented by Cubitt & Co., is let flush into the stone landing, and forms a small plate about 12 by 9 inches, with flush ring. On lifting the upper plate, another plate set at an angle forms a closed hopper, into which the ashes or dust are swept; and after it is charged, the upper plate is let down, and the under plate discharges into the down shaft; thus, it will be observed, a check to the rise of dust or smell is obtained. The refuse being conducted to the basement, is conveyed away by a separate door in the open area. The top ventilator gives free vent to any effluvia that may accumulate or rise from basement, preventing its escape through the valves or doors. In the shaft at each floor vertical doors are provided to clean or sweep the shaft. It will be observed the position of this shaft is central to the block, and forms a kind of stair newel in appearance.

On the upper flat, and floored over the open recess, there is a wash-house with wringing machines, sinks, and coppers, with all necessary taps, &c. On each side of the wash-house, and occupying the extreme right and left, are drying rooms. The waste-water from these will be made to flush the closet soil-pipes, &c. These rooms will be paved with 9-inch tiles. On each floor also, between the water closet and staircase, are coal bunkers with hinged front and top flaps, and shelves over. Each living-room is provided with a high cupboard, the top portion being a meat safe, having a gauze door, the lower portions being used for other purposes.

In the ground floor of each block, and occupying a portion of the open area under a lean-to roof, a bath-room is provided, under which is the dust or refuse receptacle. As the working and efficiency of these establishments depend so much on details, we hope our readers will not deem us tedious in entering into minutiæ. We are quite convinced that after general plan, right modes of finish and proper appliances are all essential. Respecting warming and ventilation, each living-room has a kitchener, and each bedroom a stove Perforated bricks are placed on each side of the windows, about 6 feet high, for the inlet of fresh air, the outer ones being placed a little lower. Over every door-head between the rooms perforated bricks are also inserted ; thus a general current of air is allowed to traverse every floor. The chimney-pieces are of slate. All walls are rendered in Portland cement; woodwork will be stained and varnished. No windows are placed at the ends of blocks. In the centre of roof of each block a large cistern, supplied by meter, is placed, and a constant water supply maintained. One important point of construction we must notice, namely—the joists do not run through the walls, or rest on them ; but are supported on independent corbelling—a very desirable plan.

The blocks externally have no pretensions. The only relief is obtained by flat gauged and rubbed Suffolk white brick arches, and white courses of Beart's perforated bricks, the walls being of white stocks.

Mr. Lumsden is the foreman, and we are indebted to his courtesy for some of the information. A large open space in the centre of the blocks, which are separated by intervals, about 30 feet, is appropriated as a playground. Three of the blocks of these buildings are double.—*Building News.*

Lotion for Fetid Feet.—Permanganate of potash, fifteen parts, distilled water, 1,000 parts. The feet to be washed twice a day with the lotion. They are then to be carefully dried and powdered either with potato starch or lycopodium.

SCHOOLS AND SCHOOL CHILDREN.

No system of instruction is a sound one which does not consider physical health as well as the mental capacity of school children, and provide for the former by good school-houses, well-ordered school-rooms, abundant means of exercise, plentiful ventilation and wholesome light and air; and for their minds, after their bodies are cared for, the necessity is to supply a system of training (not merely a mass of facts) to develop the reasoning faculty, not merely to test the memory or to overload it. There ought to be in every school district capable inspectors to supervise both the actual teaching, with its fitness for the pupils, and their physical condition, so that pupils might be watched and classified and cared for from the outset, and not looked on merely as ciphers or figures in the great indefinite mass. The great defect of our primary schools is that children are dealt with as if they were all of one model and that perfect alike in mind and body; the few who are so stand the strain, but the mass of them either do their mental work at the expense of their physical development, or in a much larger proportion shirk their studies and contrive to grow up strong and idle.

On a former occasion we made mention of the necessity of considering and providing for the health of the body, and especially the risks and dangers inflicted unnecessarily upon the eyes of school children through the lack of proper furniture in the class-rooms and the bad arrangement of desks in relation to the windows. Near-sightedness and weak sight are almost invariably the penalty of ill-arranged school lighting, and in Germany it has been traced out in each separate school-house, so that there was no excuse left for not correcting it. Here a school-house once built and a school once started, there is practically no authority exercised (and sometimes not even employed) to discover and cure faults of construction or errors of instruction. In this respect we want a better and more elastic system of inspection, with power to make every exception that is needed, not as at present, to secure conformity to an arbitrary standard.

The good of the best school books and instruction may all be wasted upon a pupil whose physical condition demands either absolute rest or an entirely different method of motion from that arbitrarily prescribed by our school desks and benches. A fine intellect may be wasted or lost by reason of a physical inability to work to advantage, or to work at all in a bad atmosphere, which to others is a matter of indifference or merely passing inconvenience. The long list of sicknesses peculiar to schools may well be held up as a justification of ignorance, and yet it might be made a useful lesson in physiology, and serve to teach by example alike to parents, pupils and teachers, which of them are preventable and how few are really unavoidable evils. A little instruction of this kind could easily be added to or introduced into existing studies, and if pupils knew a little more of their own physical structure and processes, they would be the better fitted to decide how far they could trust body and mind to carry them on to their various ends in life.

The boy or girl who can give the name of every river and the height of every mountain in Asia, the age of every reigning sovereign in Europe, the date of every battle in America can hardly be as well off for all this burdensome knowledge as one who knows the elements of human physiology and anatomy. who is taught more of the knowledge useful in after life, and can tell how to help himself or another in case of accident or emergency. The boy who is to go into active live, and the girl who is to become head of a household, will have little occasion and and less opportunity to use the greater part of the "crammed" lessons so industriously accumulated during their school years. A fair knowledge of the rules that are at the bottom of all healthful activity, a general acquaintance with anatomy, and a well-grounded taste for natural sciences will all grow into and become a part of their daily lives, and such things are far less likely to make pretentious men or women than that kind of smattering "memorized" facts and dates and words which is too often the penalty of superficial study. The German name "Real School" might suggest the introduction into our own schools of real studies ; of instruction in subjects of absolute knowledge ; of matters that have to do with every-day life and actions of each one of us, instead of some of the learning of the schools, mere abstractions, which are but a poor sort of mental gymnastics, and only serve to train the mind at the expense of its real work in after years for feats of strength and trials of skill that lead to no good now and serve for no end in the future. —*Cincinnati Trade List.*

THE EFFECTS OF WORRY.—That the effects of worry are more to be dreaded than those of simple hard work is evident from noting the classes of persons who suffer most from the effects of mental overstrain. The casebook of the physician shows that it is the speculator, the betting man, the railway manager, the great merchant, the superintendent of large manufacturing or commercial works, who most frequently exhibits the symptoms of cerebral exhaustion. Mental cares accompanied with suppressed emotion, occupations liable to great vicissitudes of fortune, and those which involve the bearing on the mind of a multiplicity of intricate details, eventually break down the lives of the strongest. In estimating what may be called the staying powers of different minds under hard work, it is always necessary to take early training into account. A young man, cast suddenly into a position involving great care and responsibility, will break down in circumstances in which, had he been gradually habituated to the position, he would have performed its duties without difficulty. It is probably for this reason that the professional classes generally suffer less from the effects of overstrain than others. They have a long course of preliminary training, and their work comes on them by degrees; therefore, when it does come in excessive quantity, it finds them prepared for it. Those, on the other hand, who suddenly vault into a position requiring severe mental toil, generally die before their time.—*Chambers' Journal.*

PHYSICAL CULTURE; EXPERIENCES OF AMHERST COLLEGE.

The Department of Physical Education and Hygiene in Amherst College was established by its Trustees in 1860, who believed that, together with the culture of the mental and moral faculties, some special care and instruction was necessary to sustain the bodily powers up to a vigorous and healthy standard.

The most prominent features of this Department are:

First.—*A regularly educated* Physician *has this Department in charge.* It shall be his duty to know the physical condition of every student during term time. He will advise the college as a whole, or any of its members, in matters necessary to the public or individual health; and the student is expected to obey the laws of health just as he should any other of the regulations for college life. If any student is sick or injured so as to need the services of a physician or surgeon, he may be attended by whomsoever he may select. He is required however, to notify the Professor of Hygiene as soon as the second day of sickness, from whom he may receive suitable advice and a proper certificate, or the class officer will refuse him an excuse for his absence.

Second.—Statistics *of the bodily condition of the students are regularly and frequently secured.* Those which have been compiled for the past thirteen years are already interesting. But if carefully gathered for a long series of years, they will be of value to determine the physiological "constants" of the New England college student. From these tables and other information from the best health authorities, means are furnished by which the students may improve in health, and can easily learn whether they are within the bounds of health, and if their development from time to time is normal or otherwise.

Third.—A Gymnasium *with apparatus and regulations to provide safe and suitable physical exercise.*

All the students by classes, in uniform dress, are required to be present at an exercise on four days of the week; and not only is this a required duty, but a prompt attendance upon it, and a faithful discharge of it, forms a part of the college standing of the student.

The attendance upon these exercises during the past year has been nearly 92 (91.7) per cent. of the students, as averaged upon all the exercises of the year, and if from this we deduct a probable 5 per cent. of sickness, we find that the physical exercises are in attendance fully equal to the literary ones. The experience of thirteen years has shown that a required exercise in ordinary hygiene physical training is no more difficult to secure than are requirements in any other departments of college, and is of the highest importance to their physical condition. The training and discipline here are peculiar,—not at all partaking of the quiet order which characterizes a recitation or lecture, for the department was established for the normal and harmonious development of body and mind, and by the law of contrarieties, the closer the mental application, and the more intense its discipline, so will the physical recreation partake the more of abandon and freedom, that might startle the ordinary ideas of a required exercise of college discipline. And while so much order and system is required as will maintain the gymnastic exercises within the bounds of safety, propriety and vigorous recreation, the discipline is by no means of a military character, for the working of this department shows more and more the value of a place and time where the surplus of animal spirits may have safe escape, with the necessarily and properly accompanying moral value.

At the end of the year a prize of $100 is awarded to that class (by the generosity of J. H. Washburn, Secretary of the Home Insurance Company of New York,) which has the most faithfully attended to the exercises of the year, and gives the best exhibition in light gymnastics.

FOURTH.—INSTRUCTION *in human Anatomy, Physiology and Hygiene, and their kindred branches.*

To the Freshmen is given instruction, during their first term, how best to keep their health during student life, as regards their persons, their surroundings and the connection between mind and body.

To the Sophomores, lectures and recitations are heard and given upon human Anatomy and Physiology, illustrated by the skeleton, manikin, drawings, engravings, and classic models, which enlarge and make plain many of the smaller organs of the body.

There is also an optional course of lectures and recitations in Comparative Zoology of the Vertebrates, given the third term of the Senior Year.

Sixty-five students have been on the sick list the past year, or a little more than 21 per cent. of college have been kept from their duties more than ten days on account of illness or accident. This gives a little more than two per cent. of the year as averaged upon all the students, and an average of nearly ten days to each sick student. Four have been on the sick list three times, and seven have twice been on the sick list. March was the month when the largest number (19) were sick, and November when the least (3) were reported. There have been 23 causes or kinds of sickness, (diseases). Of the 79 cases, 30 were of the general character of colds or lung fever, 35 were sick in the winter term, 22 in the fall term, and nine in the summer term.

There have been 429 exercises by classes in the gymnasium. Seniors, 85; Juniors, 104; Sophomores, 122; and Freshmen, 128; (429 in all). The number of spectators at the gymnastic exercises for the year has been 4,246. Of these, 1,092 were ladies. Accurate records have been kept the past year of the number present at each and all of the gymnastic exercises. The percentage present during the year has averaged of the Seniors, 91,600 per cent.; Juniors, 93,500 per cent.; Sophomores, 89,700 per cent.; Freshmen, 91,800 per cent; College average, 91,7 per cent. This record has been necessarily kept in order to help to determine the Washburn prize of $100. The number of students who have raised their rank by the marks given in the department of physical education, 185.

The effect of giving rank in 'the gymnastic exercises, and the establishment of the Washburn prize, cannot be definitely stated, as no full record has been kept till the last year. But during previous years, statistics have been kept for a few weeks at a time, at eight different intervals. If we compare an average of these eight items, with the full list of the past year, there is an increase of 7.080 per cent. in attendance since the department has received a place in college standing, and the endowment of the Washburn prize.

During the month of May, the age of the students by classes was thus averaged :—

Seniors,	22.561 years.
Juniors,	21.751 years.
Sophomores,	20.639 years.
Freshmen,	19,817 years.
College average,	21.192 years.

A Dignified Traveller.—A tall, portly and dignified citizen of the Quaker persuasion, well known in Philadelphia, arrived in New York the other day, and having no baggage but a light travelling satchel, was utterly oblivious to the appeals of the hackmen as he emerged from the railway station.

"Fee—thavono Hotel! Fith Avenoo—goin' ritup! Fith Avenoo?"

Broadbrim stalked right on without a word. Another knight of the whip charged down on him.

"Say Nicholas Hotel? Say Nicholas coach? This way for the Say Nicholas."

No response from the passenger, and not a muscle moved at this appeal. Then there was a rush of half a dozen.

"Kerridge, sir, kerridge? Wanter ride up?"

"Winsur House? Whose goin up to the Winsur?"

"Astor House, sir?"

"Br*ee*voort House? Br*ee*voort?"

"Meatropolitan Hotel? Right down Broadway!"

"'Ere you are! kerridge, sir."

The traveller, looming up like a tenpin among vinegar cruets, and face as placid as a pan of milk, was calmly and silently moving away from the crowd of jarvies, who looked after him with something like amazement, when a sudden thought seemed to strike one, who, running after him, seized hold of one of the handles of his travelling bag with:

"Deaf and Dumb Asylum, sir? Goin' right up."

This was too much. Dignity relaxed into a laugh, and the hack-driver got a fare for a down-town hotel.—*Com. Bul.*

VACCINATION ;—THE COMPARATIVE MERITS OF LYMPH AND THE DRY CRUST.

By John Morris, M. D., Baltimore.

As the public journals announce a new outbreak of small-pox in the city of New York, and as its appearance there is generally a fore-runner of an epidemic throughout the country, it would be well to consider all the causes that lead to its development and the best means to prevent its dissemination.

Our experience of small-pox epidemics is that the German and Irish, vaccinated in the European mode, are principally the sufferers, and though there is a great deal of careless vaccination practised in the United States, we suffer greatly less than the people of Europe from invasions of small-pox.

The great difference that exists in the views and practice of the profession in this country and Europe in regard to the proper plan of vaccination, has not heretofore been a subject of investigation, nor has it excited the interest which, in our judgment, it justly merits. It is time that this matter should receive the attention of the profession ; and our European brethren, in view of the dreadful epidemic which has for the past three or four years ravaged the continent, would do well to make it a subject of inquiry, and see if there be not some defects in their present system of vaccination which may be remedied.

At the outset, it may be premised as a fixed fact that a true vaccination is a certain preventive of variola, and that an outbreak of small-pox can only spring from defective or imperfect vaccination. No medical man of education and experience doubts this proposition. This being admitted, it becomes our duty to see that the fullest extent of protection is secured to the community by the employment of the best and surest means of vaccination.

There are three forms of vaccination at present employed : first, animal vaccination ; that is, with virus taken directly from the heifer. Second, human vaccination, as practised in Europe, in the form of fresh lymph taken from the vaccine vesicle, at an early stage of its development. Third, human vaccination, as practised in the United States ; that is, with virus taken from the dry pustule or crust.

As it is our purpose in this paper to discuss only the question of vaccination by liquid lymph and the dry crust, we shall say nothing in regard to animal vaccination. The thorough examination of its merits and demerits, brought about by the late epidemic of small-pox in Europe, has given every one an opportunity of judging of its efficacy or usefulness, (we may however, remark, *en passant*, that in this country it has gained no new adherents). The two forms of human vaccination, then, are only to be compared and discussed. Our own experience favors the employment of the dry crust, as practised in the United States, for reasons to be adduced.

It is not generally known that there is a very marked difference in the character of the disease produced by the two forms of vaccination, so marked as at once to enforce the most earnest inquiry. The stages of the vaccination are entirely different in the two modes, and the growth of the vesicle and the period of maturation are entirely dissimilar. In vaccination with liquid lymph, the vesicle begins to form on the third or fourth day, and the areola on the fifth or sixth day ; in vaccination with the crust, the vesicle does not commence to form before the seventh or eighth day, and the only evidence to be discovered before that time of the virus having taken is a few small inflammatory points, which make their appearance about the fifth, sixth or seventh day. (The later these points begin to show, the better and more effective is the vaccination.) A careful observation of two vesicles produced by the two methods of innoculation will demonstrate that the pustule produced from the dry crust possesses different elements of action, and yields different physiological results. In vaccination with the dry crust, the vesicle does not begin to form, as already stated, before the seventh or eighth day, when constitutional symptoms first become manifest. These symptoms are more general and better marked, though the local irritation is not greater than in vaccination by lymph. The true characteristic areolar test is always to be discovered when the crust is used, but in the case of lymph, particularly when it is taken from the arm at a very early stage, it is not always to be found, a starved, over-inflamed vesicle taking its place. The maturation, too, of the vesicle is different. In vaccination by lymph, the pustule desiccates and falls off about the fourteenth or fifteenth day, or earlier ; whereas with the crust this does not usually take place before the twentieth or twenty-first day, and then frequently the crust has to be removed by the operation. The cicatrix, too, is different in the two forms, and this is important, for its distinctive marks are always held as a guide to and test of a true vaccination. When the crust is used, we have a deep, cup-like, foveated, indented cicatrix, when lymph is employed, the indentation is superficial, and the other test marks frequently wanting.

Having thus stated the difference observable in the two forms of vaccination, we now proceed to give the reasons for our preference for the dry crust.

1. In vaccinations with the crust, particularly if done by scarification, failures are infrequent, indeed exceptional; whereas with lymph they are exceedingly common, as any one who has read the English medical journals for the past five years cannot have failed to discover.

2. Lymph virus deteriorates more readily and is not so easily kept as the crust. Dry lymph, when used from tubes or points, almost invariably fails. There can be no doubt about the deterioration of lymph. Dr. Short, the Superintendent of the Madras Presidency, in an article in the "Madras Journal of Medical Science," says that this fact is evidenced by the more rapid course of the vesicles and the occurrence of extensive local irritation.

3. Lymph taken from the arm at an early stage of the vaccine dis-

ease, before fever has set in or constitutional symptoms have fully manifested themselves, does not contain those morbific elements necessary to protect the system from variola; whereas in the dry crust these elements are found in an active and concentrated form. If this view be correct, it affords an explanation of the failure of the European system of vaccination. In England they take lymph from the arm before the areola commences to form, indeed frequently as early as the fourth or fifth day. Doctor De Hovell, in a communication to the "Lancet," says the earlier the period the better; and in the instructions published by the Lords of Her Majesty's Privy Council, for the guidance of the profession, we find the following clauses: "7. Take lymph on the day week after vaccination, at the stage when the vesicles are fully formed and plump, but when there is no perceptible commencement of areola." Clause "8. Consider that your lymph ought to be changed, if your cases, at the usual time of inspection, on the day week after vaccination, have not, as a rule, their vesicles entirely free from areola." Here then the old-fashioned, much-prized areola test, to which Jenner himself attached so much importance, is not only ignored but condemned, and a vesicle selected concerning the character of which there can be no certainty. In Paris, the employment of lymph furnished by M. Lanoix, during the late epidemic, proved almost an absolute failure, and even pure animal lynph was unsuccessful in twelve of thirteen cases vaccinated by Doctor Constantine Paul, at Hospital Beaujou.

4. Sequelæ of an unpleasant character frequently follow lymph vaccination; whereas with the crust they are exceptional. In three thousand cases of vaccination by the crust in our own practice, only one single case of local irritation of an unpleasant character occurred. This point is not sufficiently regarded. Evidences of an unhealthy condition of the vaccinefer's system can be readily detected by a careful examination of the growth and maturation of the pustule; but where lymph is taken from the arm at an early day, no such evidences can possibly be diagnosed.

5. Vaccination by lymph does not protect the patient, but necessitates a re-vaccination; whereas a true vaccination by the crust affords thorough protection. In a late number of the "Lancet," the editor says that re-vaccination is urgently necessary; and Mr. Marson reports that in six months, out of 751 cases admitted to the small-pox hospital, 618 or 82 per cent. were in vaccinated persons. We are convinced that no such result could follow in this country. A genuine vaccination here, in our judgement, affords as much protection as variola itself.

The reasons that have been urged against the employment of the crust are very trivial. The theory that blood may be taken up and constitutional diseases propagated by its use, as suggested by Doctor Anstie, is entirely groundless, as is also his view in regard to the danger of pus.

Doctor Blane's arguments in favor of animal vaccination, and the reasons he urges for the use of lymph from the heifer, in preference to human lymph, do not apply to the crust. None of the evils he attributes to human vaccination are to be found in the American mode; but as animal vaccination itself has been in some degree a failure, and has, at times, some unpleasant consequences attendant upon its use, we cannot accept it in lieu of the crust, which has proved so generally serviceable in this country. It may possess advantages over human lymph, but the crust is superior to both.

The history of the late epidemic of small-pox in Baltimore, confirms the truth of these views. Doctor Conrad, the resident physician of the Small-pox Hospital, reports 1,246 cases treated during the years 1871, 1872 and 1873, and, speaking of the remarkable susceptibility of the Germans, says: "No nation on the globe has such rigid laws of cumpulsory vaccination as Germany, no people are so thoroughly vaccinated ; about every one presenting from one to eight, and even sixteen vaccine marks (done in infancy), and yet it is astonishing the number suffering with even dangerous forms of the disease, in some cases unmodified altogether. The fact of so many Germans having marks, apparently of good quality, and yet such grave degrees of variola, led me to make more careful observations of the marks which I found on their arms, as compared with other races and nations. It soon struck my attention that the German cicatrix or cicatrices—for they rarely had less than three—had a less number of foveations, or thimble-like depressions in each mark (while the marks themselves presented a greater display of protection) than was the case with those of the American or African; then again I found but few adult Germans who had been vaccinated since the age of puberty. These two facts alone would account for the excess of disease in the Germans, but for one other fact in comparison. The negro, who had but rarely more than one mark, and that generally imperfect (also done in infancy), *had a less degree of variola than the Germans* with all their vaccine marks. In truth, the observation forced itself upon me that one imperfect mark upon the adult negro (done in childhood) was more protection to him than the very many found on the arm of the German, done at the same age." Dr. Conrad attributes this to a peculiar individual susceptibility in the different races, but in this we are convinced he is in error, and that the difference consists solely in the character of the original vaccination, forasmuch as what he states in regard to the Germans, applies equally to other foreigners vaccinated in the same manner.

One word in conclusion, in regard to the number of punctures or vesicles necessary to protect the patient. In Europe, as we have already seen, three or four are usually made, but with us, one is found to be sufficient. From it we get all the constitutional effect necessary without any undue local irritation. Jenner and his followers made but one puncture, and we are content to abide by the decision and practice of the early fathers.

The New Bonnet Again.—"Wife, do you know that I have got the pneumonia?"

"New monia, indeed! You're the most extravagant man I ever did see—to go and lay out money for such trash when I need a new bonnet so much!"

FURNACES.

By R. C. Kedzie, M. D., Member of the Michigan State Board of Health.

The following correspondence will explain itself:

East Saginaw, Mich., August 3, 1874.

Prof. R. C. Kedzie:

My Dear Sir:—In my study of the furnace matter I have come to the question as to cast iron or wrought. The wrought iron men claim that cast iron leaks deleterious gases through the substance of the iron as well as the joints: while wrought iron leaks at neither, since the seams are riveted as in steam boilers. Now to whom shall I go to settle this matter but to you?

Sincerely yours,

——— —— ———— ————

Lansing, August 8, 1874.

My Dear Major:—Your favor of the 3d inst. is received, asking my opinion in regard to cast or wrought-iron furnaces.

The statement of the wrought-iron men that gases will penetrate and pass through a plate of cast iron, especially when red hot, is correct. The experiments of St. Clair Deville and Troost of Paris, demonstrate this fact. They took a cast-iron stove, the walls of which were one-tenth of an inch thick, enclosed this in a cast-iron cylinder so as to isolate the air around the stove from surrounding air; the stove was heated from low-red to bright-red heat during the experiment, and the air enclosed between the stove and the surrounding envelope withdrawn and analyzed. The results of six experiments showed that this air contained on the average 562 parts of hydrogen and 557 parts of carbonic oxide in 1,000,000 parts of air.

This seems to make a strong case against the cast-iron men. But unfortunately for the wrought-iron men the same thing is true, in a less degree, of wrought iron. Graham has shown that "pure iron is capable of taking up at a low-red heat and holding when cold, 4.15 volumes of carbonic oxide gas." Deville and Troost have showed that wrought iron and even platinum are permeable by gases when heated. It is highly probable that no metal will resist entirely the passage of gases when strongly heated, but this is especially true of iron. By this permeability to carbonic oxide, Graham explains the process of converting soft iron into steel. The experiments of Deville and Troost were undertaken, not to show the objectionable qualities of cast iron for stoves and furnaces, but to show that porcelain should be used instead of iron of any kind for such uses.

The very important fact has been brought to light that while all metals may be permeable by gases at high temperatures, yet at lower temperatures they very effectually resist their passage. One condition of safety is that we should not heat our stoves or furnaces to a high temperature. By increasing the size of the heating surface we may adequately warm the air without any part of the heating surface being heated to such an extent as to allow the passage of gases through the metallic walls. From a false ecomony our furnaces are made small, and then to secure a sufficient degree of warmth in the air the furnace is heated often to a red heat, when they become the source of danger by allowing the passage of the carbonic oxide, the most deadly gas known; and its poisonous effects are shown in the intense headache, the head often feeling as though compressed by a tight iron hoop, languor, oppression of respiration, and general disturbance of nervous functions. But if the heating surface in the furnace is so large that the requisite amount of heat may be secured without raising the temperature of any part of the furnace walls above 500°, this danger may be obviated so far as it prevents the direct passage of this gas through the metallic surface.

It is very necessary that the products of combustion within the furnace should not escape through cracks or joints in the walls of the furnace. For this purpose the castings should be as perfect as possible, and any openings be closed with some indestructible cement. One very important condition for obviating the leakage of the furnace gases into the air chamber is to facilitate the escape of the smoke by an ample smoke-stack and a good draught. The practice of placing a damper between the furnace and the smoke-pipe, and thus regulating the activity of the combustion in the furnace by checking the escape of the furnace gases, is worthy of all condemnation. The same is true of dampers in stove pipes. They tend to throw into inhabited portions of the house the deadly products of combustion which should be allowed the freest escape by the chimney to the open air. The only place where a damper should be used, either in furnace or stove, is where it may regulate the access of air to the fire, and thus check the combustion by shutting off the air to feed the flame. When we interfere to prevent the escape of gases from the furnace, we add a stong force to drive these poisonous materials into the air of our houses, and thus place a club in the hands of death. If we reverse this condition, allowing the freest escape up the chimney while regulating the access of air to the fire, we have the draft of the chimney acting as a force to restrain the escape of gases, either by transpiration through the metal or by leakage at the imperfect joints in furnace or stove.

One fact in favor of cast-iron surface has been generally overlooked, viz.: that it is a better radiator of heat than wrought iron, and consequently will more effectually heat the air passing over its surface than wrought iron at a corresponding temperature.

There has been considerable discussion on the subject of wrought-iron and cast-iron stoves and furnaces in the Eastern States, where anthracite coal is the usual fuel. Where anthracite is used the subject becomes more important, because it is so difficult to completely burn anthracite, i. e., to convert the carbon into carbonic acid instead of carbonic oxide.

Where wood or soft coal is used this subject is of less importance, because it is much easier to completely burn these forms of fuel. While the carbonic acid is injurious, it is very much less dangerous than carbonic oxide. But whatever the kind of fuel, we should seek to secure its complete combustion, and the perfect removal by the chimney of all the products of combustion.—*Lansing Republican.*

ADULTERATED HOUSES.

SOURCES OF DISEASE IN LONDON DWELLING HOUSES—A QUESTION WORTHY OF CONSIDERATION IN NEW YORK.

Most of our disease and a great deal of our crime comes from a single source. Men and women are unhealthy because they live in unwholesome houses; they have recourse to drink partly because the act of getting it takes them out of their houses, and so is in itself attractive, and partly because the physical depression caused by ill-health makes a stimulant of any kind unnaturally grateful; drinking begets drunkenness, and when that stage is reached crime follows in many cases as a matter of course. No one denies this succession of cause and effect; on the contrary, the moral and physical mischief done by unwholesome houses is one of our chief sanitary commonplaces. Yet in no one respect are our sanitary legislation and administration so defective as they are with regard to houses. There are building acts in abundance, and in London, at all events, if the owner of a house wants to make a room lighter by throwing out a bay window or to shelter the inmates from the rain by making a covered way from his door to his garden-gate, he finds that he has to negotiate matters with the local surveyor, and perhaps after all he is not allowed to improve his own property. If, on the other hand, his desires take a negative form, and all he wants to do is to omit some sanitary precaution, he has no difficulty in keeping the surveyor at arm's length. Only the other day for example, it was stated on good authority that many of the newer parts of London, in which the houses have all been built since the existing laws were in force, are without any adequate drainage. Londoners have been burdened with debt and taxation to construct the main drainage works, but the equally important consideration how the drains of each separate house are connected with the main sewers is left to the carelessness or the parsimony of individual builders and landlords. What the state of things is in those parts of the town which are now veneered over with respectability and stucco is well known. The medical officers of health never make a report which does not condemn a number of houses, sometimes whole streets, as unfit for human habitation. They have been doing this for years past, and it would be an interesting subject of inquiry how many of these condemned houses are still inhabited. Occasionally a vestry makes a raid upon some of the worst—or, perhaps, to put it more accurately, upon those among the worst which are not the property of vestrymen—and some faint semblance of a clearance is effected. But the aggregate of unwholesomeness is not, we suspect, much reduced by these intermittent displays of sanitary virtue. And about the better class of houses, as to which doctors and sanitary engineers give such discouraging evidence, nobody troubles himself at all. The sepulchre is newly whitened every three years, according to the stipulation in the lease. But the lease says nothing about the uncleanness within, and that often remains in a state which could hardly be worse if it were really full of dead men's bones.

These evils, and all the consequences which flow from them, will go on unchecked until we have the courage to apply to the sellers of houses the same law which has lately been applied with such good results to the sellers of milk and groceries. The man who sells or lets a house should be held answerable for that house being free from any additions injurious to health. There should be no reserve of foul air in the rooms caused by the want of proper ventilation; there should be no circulation of sewer gases in the basement caused by the absence of proper traps to the drains; there should be no pollution of water caused by the escape-pipe of the cistern running directly into the sewer. These things are no necessary part of a house; they are as much adulterations as alum is of bread, or sand of sugar. There can be no excuse for allowing the sale of houses containing these poisonous matters which would not be equally valid for allowing the sale of articles of food containing poisonous matters. The argument for prohibition is even stronger in the case of adulterated houses than in the case of adulterated food, because prevention happens to be very much easier. The conditions which make a house healthy, are perfectly well understood, and there is no need to wait to put the law into operation until the absence of them has been detected. It would be impossible to examine every article of food before it is exposed for sale, and even if this could be done, adulteration might still be resorted to as soon as the inspector's back was turned. Houses, on the other hand, are not so numerous but that they could be examined before being allowed to come into the market, and when they had once been passed the seller would be under no temptation to tamper with them. If a house is once properly drained and ventilated, the landlord would gain nothing by introducing faults which had been avoided in the first instance. What is wanted is a general building act, specifying certain sanitary requisites, without which no house can be wholesome, and enacting that in future no new house shall be inhabited until it has been warranted to possess them, and that all houses already inhabited shall be provided with them within a certain time after the passing of the act. In the latter case the alterations would be made at the cost of the landlord where the house was let from year to year, because he could at once recoup himself for what he had spent by making a proportionate increase in the rent. Where the house was let on lease the expense would fall either wholly on the tenant or partly on the tenant and partly on the landlord, according to the length of the term, and there should be provisions for determining the tenancy or for prolonging it in consideration of the tenant's willingness or unwillingness to undertake the outlay. There would be no real difficulty in drafting an act which should deal justly with all parties and provide some simple process, such as an appeal to a county court judge, for the settlement of disputed cases.

The only argument that can be alleged against this method of dealing with unwholesome houses is that the adoption of it would increase house rent, and thus bear hardly on the poor. This plea is unsound on several grounds. In the first place it is in part untrue in fact, because, though the alteration of existing houses would involve a certain outlay, the fitting of new houses with proper sanitary appliances need not entail any additional expense. It costs no more to trap the escape pipe of a cistern outside a wall than to trap it inside, but it makes all the difference in the wholesomeness of the water. Secondly, it is by no means certain that the cost would always fall on poor tenants in the shape of higher rents. At least where the owner's profits were large enough to admit of his bearing the expense, competition between landlords would usually avail to keep rents pretty much at their present level, and in the case of the worst class of house property the owner's profits are often very large. Thirdly, and chiefly, the principle has long been established that there are conditions under which human beings cannot be permitted to live, no matter how great may be the saving in point of expense. Cellars are not now allowed to be used as dwellings, and in theory, at least, overcrowding is forbidden. Yet over-crowding and the free use of cellars would tend to reduce rents. In these two cases the legislature has determined that the injury to society caused by the neglect of sanitary laws is greater than the gain to society caused by the cheapening of house-room. All that has here been suggested is that other sanitary laws, which it is equally impossible to neglect without injury, should be enforced for the same reason. It is not proposed that every house should be a miracle of sanitary engineering; all that is required is that a few simple and well-understood sanitary appliances which can never be omitted without great danger to health should be prescribed as indispensable adjuncts to every inhabited house. The law does not allow grocers to sell poisons under the name of spices, and there is just as much need that it should no longer allow builders and landlords to sell fever-traps under the name of houses. The greater because more dangerous adulteration should be forbidden as much as the lesser.—*Pall Mall Gazette.*

Decomposition.—Refuse and waste are the natural enemies to the health of mankind. The products of their decomposition pervade every household. Their offensive odors are charitable warnings to guard against. From the cellar, store-room, pantry, bed-room, sitting-room and parlor; from decaying vegetables, fruits, meats, soiled clothing, old garments, old furniture, refuse of kitchen, mouldy walls, everywhere, a microscopic germ is propagating. It contains in itself the seeds of disease—all that is needed is the proper soil or condition of constitution adapted for its reception. Each germ may find its specific habitat, and hence develop into some specific malady. Typhoid, typhus, cerebro-spinal, relapsing or scarlet fever, measles, small-pox, roseola, cholera or some other form of disease may result.

Cleanliness, pure air, sunlight and pure water are the antidotes. God indicates and provides these in abundance.

He who neglects or rejects these deserves to suffer, as surely he will.

A NEW DEPARTURE IN HYDROPHOBIA.

Proceedings of the New York Lyssomaniaological Society. Prof. Dog-Berry, President in the chair; detailed for publication by Munchausen Curry, M. D., *Cur*-ator to the Hospital St. Bernard. Reported by H. L. Bartlett, M. D.

The President, after congratulating the members upon the interest manifested in the objects of the Society, both within, and more particularly without the profession, and thanking them for the honor conferred upon him in electing him their first presiding officer, said: It may seem to those unacquainted with the object and history of this society, that we are a mere emanation of the dog-days—a fervid canine phantom, dogging the public mind like a sombre ghost, and filling the popular imangination with apprehensions more dire than those excited by the ancient *Cur*-few knell! But so far from this being the case, our theme has been sung in Doggerel from the earliest ages of antiquity; in fact the dog alone, of all the animal tribes, has never been, nor can ever be disassociated from man.

The Dog-star, under the name of Anubis, was an object of *Sirius* worship by the Chaldean Shepherds and Egyptian priests, and the study of its *Cur*vilinear antics was a prominent part of the *Cur*riculum of the Dog Matics and Dog Latins. Anubis was represented with the face of a dog and the body of a man, and its appearance in the heavens gave timely warning of approaching danger; hence the dog became the symbol of *fidelity*! So universal was this worship, that when our venerable patron, the god-like Æsculapius, wanted an emblem to symbolize his care and watchfulness over the destinies of the human race he instinctively, and of necessity, selected the dog. Thus it will be seen that our organization is not a mere *puppet*-show of modern sentimentalism, but is a society made honorable by noble association and hoary with age, being at least as ancient as the Hebrew *Rabbis*. Thus much for its history. What are its aims? We simply propose to institute such measures as shall effectually relieve the public mind from painful apprehensions, while at the same time, we strive to protect our ancient friend from aspersion and undue suffering.

The science of Lyssomania has made gigantic strides since the age of Plato, in fact, has been and is still on a regular dog-trot in the *cursus* of scientific investigation. I myself have recently made some most remarkable discoveries (see N. Y. Tribune) on the pathology of this disease, and notwithstanding some very *cur*lish remarks from some of our dog-eared brethen, I shall continue my investigations and illustrations as heretofore, for the benefit of myself, and the rest of the world. I will not refer to these discoveries in detail for they are already matters of record, but shall content myself with stating the principal Dog-berries therein contained.

Dog. 1. The essence, the "casus morbi" of this *cur*-sor(r)y disease I have named Lyssorhagia, from the fact, that when an animal or person is inoculated with it, it rages throughout the system in a most outrageous way.

Dog. 2. The seat, the "locus morbi" of this dis*cur*sive malady, I have found, after long and patient microscopic research, to be in the "big cells" of the medulla oblongata; from the medulla it oblongates to the optic discs, producing a bewilderment of vision, both in the patient and beholder, and from thence is reflected through every nerve of the poor patient's body, till the *cur*tain falls, leaving nothing but sad reflections to the astonished observer.

Dog. 3. When once the *curse* has made its in*cur*sion into the system, there are no known means of *cure*. Our treatment must therefore be prompt and *incisive*. We must exorcise the poison or the blood will curdle, and death ensue. Hence it follows, that our first duty is to protect society from hydrophobic contamination and *especially the fear of it*. For the accomplishment of this object, many *cur*ious and learned suggestions have been made. Perhaps the first and most natural impulse would be to *cur*tail the entire race of *curs*, thus destroying the disease with its originators. My name might imply that I was in favor of this *appalling undertaking*, but I assure you this is a *grave* mistake. My learned confrère, Dr. Pointer, will I think, con*cur* with me in the opinion that this disease does not originate in the Dog-per-se, but is generated in the caves and dens of the primeval forests, where benign and malign animals "most do congregate" during the long winter nights. Here the conditions of animal life are such, that they are driven to madness, or become rabid through the influence of cold and the want of food. The disease at first attacks the fiercest and most excitable, and they communicate it to others, they in turn to other, till the disease becomes, indeed, a hellish epizootic, raging with devilish fury. When this takes place, the repulsive force of the disorder drives the herd asunder and they start on their work of destruction. The dog, being man's natural vidette, is the first to meet the shock of battle, and of course the first to suffer. So far, therefore, from the canine race being the "primus causa," it is in fact only the connecting link. It may be urged as an objection to this theory, that dogs suffer from the disease which have never come in contact with the epizootic, in its primal form. In answer to this, I would simply ask you to re*cur* to the able and exhaustive paper of Dr. Blood-Hound, in which he gives it as his deliberate opinion, based upon some millions of observations, that the virus of hydrophobia is quite similar to that of syphilis, particularly in one respect, viz., its proneness to take a Rip Van Winkle sleep! Now it is well known that syphilis will not only remain dormant in the system for years, but will extend its baneful influence from generation to generation, extending through centuries of time. The same is undoubtedly true of rabies. The hydrophobic *cur* of to-day, may not have been inoculated with the "original Jacobs," but some of his ancestors have been, and there remains enough of the "original sin" in his blood to cause it to manifest itself upon proper occasion. From these and many other reasons that might be adduced, we may safely conclude, that to rid the world of Lyssomania, it will be necessary not only to extinguish the canine race, including *Canis Major*, itself a *sirius* matter, but we must also remove the prima causa epizootic, which even in the light of modern science is impossible. Our duty, therefore, is prophylactical, and as there are learned members present, who have had large experience in preventive treatment, I shall take the liberty of calling upon some of them.

At the conclusion of the President's address, remarks were made by various members, first:

Dr. Mastiff said: We are advised to file or extract the teeth of dogs as a preventive measure, and though I am aware that no less an authority than Dr. Wolf has advised the practice, still there is the same objection to it that existed against the Frenchman's celebrated "flea powder" viz., "You must first catch and hold the flea!" Besides the "extract" is too largely tinctured with *w(h)ine* and *bark*, and the operation too *rasping* for fastidious nerves.

Dr. Spitz, a celebrated Laplandish practitioner, who happened to be present, said:

The virus of hydrophobia resides alone in the *expectoration*, and hence our treatment must be *expectoratic*. I therefore, advise diminishing the animal's phlegm, even if we destroy the mucus, and for this purpose strychnine or belladonna has been most successful. By permission of the government, some years since I placed congealed blocks of infusion of belladonna and common salt, in all the outlandish places of the Laplandish Empire, where they were accessible to dogs and epizoots, and their natural love for salt induced them to take a sufficient quantity of belladonna to effectually banish this disease from our hospitable shores.

Sir Siberian Blood-hound, a widely known and much respected Russian, also present, said: I have recently been making some very pleasant experiments on the bite of vipers as an anti-hydrophobic. I observed that certain dogs and milkmaids, when bitten by rabid animals, were not affected by the disease. Upon further inquiry, I discovered the remarkable fact, that said dogs and milkmaids, had been previously bitten by vipers, and reasoning *a la* Jenner, I procured a quantity of viper virus and viperized several *curs*. These I subsequently exposed to the bites of animals known to be rabid, but what was my delight, as well as astonishment to find that they not only did not die, but actually fattened and gladdened on this new accession to their blood. I thereupon by permission of the government, tried the experiment upon several hundred convicts, condemned to banishment, with the same happy results. So delighted was the government with the success of these experiments, that it has authorized me to open places, which from Paradisial associations, I have called "viper gardens," at all accessible points throughout the Empire, where the people can avail themselves of this *serpentine* blessing. In fact, I am of the opinion, that the so-called "Serpent" in the garden of Eden, was simply a viper placed there for the purpose of preventing its unsophisticated inhabitants from contracting the epizootic, from the hydrophobic monster, *Cerberus*, who was ever and anon breaking away from his Plutonic master, and playing the devil through the "Elysian Fields." I am also of the opinion, that the vulgarly called "Asp," which the Egyptian

Cleopatra was dandling on her breast, was of the same variety and used for the same purpose, for Mark !—Anthony had evidently made her mad.

Dr. Bull-Dog said, that so far as his observation or researches extended, and they have been neither few nor small, the hydrophobia never originated in the female dog; he therefore advised killing the entire male population and leaving the future care and development of the race entirely to thestrong-minded but pugnacious *Dog Mas.*

Dr. Mongrel remarked, that to his mind, things were a little mixed. He did not see that the dog had anything to do with the question of lyssomania at all. He was called the other day to see a lady of quality, who had been bitten by a pet monkey; as this animal had never bitten her before, she became at once impressed with the idea that he was mad, and insisted on my cauterizing the wound. After trying in vain to allay her fears, I at length acceded to her request, thinking that perhaps this might satisfy her mind. So far from this being the case, she became much more excited than before. She said sharp pains shot up her arm, like electric shocks, and that balls of fire were chasing each other up and down her back and exploding with terrific noise within her head. Soon she commenced gyrating around the room on both feet and yelling and snapping exactly like an enraged monkey. So complete was the counterfeit of her voice, that for a moment I really believed that animal had made his appearance among us. Her face at once lost all its usual expression, and became decidedly Darwinian. She then threw herself upon her hands and feet, jumping from chair to bedstead, and from bedstead to bureau, with the sprightliness of a cat, till in an unexpected moment, she darted through an open window, out upon the roof of an adjoining house, and thence down some friendly chimney *flew*, where she was either cremated or so thoroughly *suited* that she was never heard of more !

Dr. Poodle said—I quite agree with the last speaker. Not long since I was called into the country to see a Scotch groom who had been bitten by an ill-tempered donkey. When I saw him, symptoms of lyssomania were fast developing themselves. Already he had shown his asinine teeth and ears, and while I was looking at him, he began ambling around the enclosure, shouting his infernal "brae" like an ill-omened raven, till, strange to relate, in less than twenty-four hours he was transformed into a perfect *hydrophobic ass !*

Dr. Deer-Hound remarked that these cases reminded him of an epizootic episode in his student's life. He with a German friend, was *stalking* along one of the Alpine passes, when suddenly a pack of hydro-foaming wildcats darted across the path in hot pursuit of an affrighted fox. Quick as thought, the German played his club and dealt one of the pack a stunning blow, and was within an ace of taking him up, when the animal unexpectedly euchred the club with his knavish teeth, thus leaving the poor German to go it alone with his blood-red hand as best he could, and hereby hangs my *feline* tale. Sooner than I can describe the scene, he assumed the raging aspect of a hydro-foaming cat-a-mountain, and mounted high up among the crags, where a *mew* was never seen or heard before or since !

At the conclusion of this cat-o-nine-tail of the *cataminative catastrophe*, the society clo.e.l by gravely chanting the following

DOG-BURIAL DIRGE.

BY

PROF. NEWFOUNDLAND.

Now fades the dread accursed shade
  In deep oblivion's chasm ;
No more need mankind be afraid
  Of ending life in spasm.
The Demon of Saliva quits
  His deadly incubation,
And ceases to engender fits
  Of mad expectoration.

Behold the lyssamanic corse—
  A pathologic shoddy,
To time's disintegrating force
  We here commit the body.
And where uncoffined he is lain,
  The worms will wear them fatter,
For they shall banquet on the slain
  And eat his oblongata.

We come to join in funeral dirge,
  Yet may our souls be jolly ;
For we the cerebellum purge
  Of horror-haunted folly.
The infant as he climbs to drink
  The loved maternal ration,
May now return the lap-dog's wink.
  Without asphyxiation.

No more within the city's streets
  Shall man for pleasure roaming,
Start wildly when perchance he meets
  A canine hydro-foaming ;
Still may not the pedestrian pause
  But calmly tread the flagging,
No more alarmed at Towzer's jaws
  Than at his tail when wagging.

No more shall ragamuffins prance
  At aldermanic dictum,
And lead the dogs a morris-dance,
  Then *pound* each weary victim.
Well may we voice indignant raise
  At such dogmatic fiat,
For if to *catch* the rabies pays
  Contagion must run riot.

Hail ! Newfoundland, as yet unsung
  Where only peace reposes,
Where never yet hath mongrel tongue
  Pronounced death's diagnosis.
Where never are the people led
  By hydrophobic bias,
Where man may pat the canine head
  Without regard to virus.

That land is ours and we shall soon
  On our possessions enter,
And with us bear the priceless boon,
  An unimpaired "nerve-centre."

Now Æsculapius deck thy form
And Hygeia's joy be fuller,
For we have weathered every storm
That threatened our medulla.

Ashes to ashes, dust to dust,
Vail, thou worst of demons,
In Hades' Pantheon thy dread bust,
There meet Delirium Tremens.
Upon thy grave no grass shall leap;
Eternity confess that,
Oblivion only knows thy sleep
And writes thy requiescat.

THE ALCOHOLIC STRENGTH OF VARIOUS BITTERS. — Mr. Henry Vaughan, State Assayer of Rhode Island, has made a chemical examination of thirty-five samples of "bitters," including all the more important ones found in the market. His report to Sheriff Holden gives the following percentages of alcohol in the various samples:

	Per Cent.
Hostetter's Stomach Bitters	43.20
Baker's Stomach Bitters	40.57
Drake's Plantation Bitters	30.24
Sol Fank's Panacea Bitters	37.20
Mishler's Herb Bitters	36.80
Dr. R. F. Hibbard's Wild Cherry Bitters	35.89
Rush's Bitters for the Stomach's "Sake"	34.30
Dr. Fisch's Bitters	32.16
Baker's Orange Grove Bitters	25.70
Speer's Standard Wine Bitters	25.49
Traveler's Peruvian Bitters	22.40
Dr. Clarke's Sherry Wine Bitters	22.40
California Wine Bitters	18.20
Dr. Wheeler's Tonic Sherry Wine Bitters	14.66
Atwood's Quinine Tonic Bitters	40.10
Dr. Holmes' Golden Seal Bitters	34.24
Dr. Job Sweet's Strengthening Bitters	31.41
Webber's Strengthening Bitters	26.87
Flint's Quaker Bitters	22.99
Restorative Bitters	20.54
Luther's Temperance Bitters	16.68
Richardson's Bitters	59.14
Armington's Bitters	33.26
Davis' Bitters	30.50
Colton's Nervine Bitters	29.73
Dr. Warren's Bilious Bitters	29.60
Hartshorn's Bitters	27.35
Atwood's Jaundice Bitters	25.60
Puritan Bitters	25.60
Dr. Langley's Bitters	24.41
Dr. Hoffland's German Bitters	20.85
Oxygenated Bitters	19.28
Walker's Vinegar Bitters	7.50
Dr. Pierce's Bitters	6.36

—*The Laboratory.*

Editor's Table.

THE PUBLIC HEALTH.

New York, Sept. 5, 1874.—*Cause of Disease and Mortality in August.*—In the four weeks ending on the 29th of August, there were 2,699 deaths in the city of New York and its public institutions. The total number of deaths in the previous four weeks was 3,158. The deaths in children under five years of age amounted to 1,644, or 61 per cent. of the total mortality in the month first mentioned. In the last four weeks of July, the number of deaths in children at this age was 2,015, or 63.51 per cent. of the total mortality. The mortality in August was equal to a yearly death-rate of 35.9 in the 1000 inhabitants, the population being estimated at 1,040,000. *Sixty-one per cent.* of the mortality occurred in that portion of the population which is under five years of age, and, until the end of the third week of August, over half of this child-mortality was attributed to diarrhœal diseases. The rate of mortality began to decrease on the 22d of August, when the mean temperature fell to 63° Fahr. The mean temperature for the four weeks was 71–8° Fahr., and the average humidity was equal to about three-fifths of total saturation. It was a remarkably healthful period to all except infants under two years old. The mortality in the classes of population at and over five years of age was equal to a yearly death-rate of 14.84 in the 1,000, annually.

The zymotic diseases are charged with 49.16 per cent. of the deaths, small-pox being charged with 32 deaths; scarlatina with 43; diphtheria with 95, and diarrhœas with 914 (87.63 per cent. infantile). Though in this most health-favoring summer temperature and humidity have, as usual, governed the death-rate, yet there were entire wards and large parts of cleanly, well-built and well-drained districts in which the death-rate has scarcely been affected by the fluctuations of temperature. Sanitary conditions of the localities and classes differ as widely as the death-rates between them in this city.

ELISHA HARRIS, M. D., *Registrar.*

Brooklyn, Aug. 31*st*, 1874.—In compiling the mortality reports for 1872, which have never been published in full, I find some interesting statistics which may be of value to the readers of your journal. I will endeavor to give them to you in as brief a space as possible. The population of the city, by the census of 1870, was 376,099—251,381 native, 144,718 foreign; present population, 450,000. The morta'ity from 1871 to 1873, inclusive, was as follows:

	1871		1872		1873	
Mortality	1871,—10,259.		1872,—12,648.		1873,—10,968.	
Zymotic diseases	" 2,781—27.09	per cent;	" 4,374—34.65	per cent.;	" 3,517—32.07	per cent.
Constitutional diseases	" 2,607—25.45	"	" 2,700—21.34	"	" 2,539—23.15	"
Local diseases	" 3,759—36.57	"	" 4,387—34.66	"	" 3,849—35.09	"
Developmental diseases	" 799— 7.78	"	" 843— 6.70	"	" 751— 6.85	"
Deaths by violence	" 320— 3.11	"	" 389— 2.65	"	" 312— 2.84	"

The increased mortality of 1872 over 1871 is accounted for by the epidemic of small-pox, which killed 737, and by the influence of the high temperature of the year on zymotic diseases generally, and especially on diarrhœal diseases. In one week of excessive high temperature, for example (ending July 6th), the mortality from all causes was 639; cholera infantum, 249; diseases of the nervous system, 146; small-pox, 16. The decrease for 1873 is attributable, in part, at least, to a lower temperature and the non-prevalence of any epidemic.

Deaths for month ending August 31st, 1874, 1,120—29.86 per 1000. Scarlatina, 20; diphtheria, 49; cholera infantum, 275; phthisis pulmonalis, 95; tabes mesenterica, 79; pneumonia, 32. The excess of mortality is particularly marked in those portions of the city characterized by overcrowding and soil saturation.

JAMES WATT, M. D., *Registrar.*

It is evident from the data above given that the death-rate of Brooklyn from preventable diseases is on the increase; and we have no doubt whatever that an accurate record of the present year will make this fact still more evident. Nor is it to be wondered at; for never in the history of the city have sanitary interests been made so completely and odiously subservient to politics—even to the extent of private speculation in disease and death.

We had occasion to publish, in the March number of the SANITARIAN, a description of the progress of public works in Brooklyn,—pointed out the impervious causeways, stagnant ponds and excrement-sodden soil, created by the Board of Public Works, in addition to natural causes, which still remain unabated. Since that time, the president of the Board of Public Works has been made a member of the Board of Health; another member, the president of the Board of Police, is reported to be a chief owner and speculator in these low lands! And these two members somehow manage to be a majority in a board of five for the accomplishment of their purposes. If, as on rare occasion (as recorded in the last number of the SANITARIAN), they appear to be in a minority, so sensitive have they become to other causes of ill health than stagnant ponds and contractors' short-comings, they find no difficulty in apparently blinding the other members of the board with side issues, and, in the end, maintaining their *ground*. The candy dodge was an example of this kind. It succeeded disgracefully in diverting attention, and so gaining time—its only object—and the perpetuation of stagnant ponds, filthy streets, swill, and derelict contractors. The Sanitary Committee, innocent souls, instead of disposing of this deception the moment it was presented, acquiesced in the delay, and went through the farce of making a prolix report on that which they perfectly knew when the resolution was offered, as well as the mover, that they might appear to the public to be doing something. Meanwhile, the stagnant ponds, filthy streets, oozing swill-carts, and pent-up house garbage still obtain,—all biding the summer; eking out their poisons, and, by criminal negligence, adding hundreds to the mortality list. Notwithstanding the Act of June 1st provides:—

"SEC. 3. The said board shall have full and exclusive power and authority over the removal of night soil, and in the removal of dead animals, offal, blood, bones, tainted or impure meats, and in the removal of all the garbage and other refuse matter from said city. Said board is hereby charged with the duty of causing the removal of the same as often as may be necessary, and of keeping the said city clean from all matter or nuisance of a similar kind. The said Board of Health is authorized to make contracts with any responsible person or persons for the removal of said offal, dead animals, night soil, garbage and other refuse matter from the city of Brooklyn, for a period not exceeding five years, and to require and receive bonds in such form and amount as the said Board may approve for the faithful performance by the person or persons aforesaid, to whom such contracts may by the said board be in its discretion awarded, of all and every of the provisions of such contracts, and to cancel and revoke all contracts made by them for the removal of offal, dead animals, night soil, garbage and other refuse matter which may be entered into under this section, as well as all existing contracts for the removal thereof, whenever the contractor shall refuse or neglect to perform any of the stipulations of his contract. To enable said board to carry out the provisions of this section, such sum of money shall be paid by the comptroller of the city, upon bills certified to by the president of said board, and audited by the auditor, as may be necessary; provided, however, that the moneys so to be paid shall not, for the year eighteen hundred and seventy-four, exceed in amount the sum of fifteen thousand dollars."

The controlling members of the board began the exercise of their office by an effort to shirk the law; and, after a month's delay before taking any effective action under it, through the instrumentality of Alderman Ropes, they secured the coöperation of the Board of Aldermen for the time being to help them out. That gentleman, by common consent (on the part of the Board of Health, as well as the Board of Aldermen), moved and secured the adoption of the following:

"*Whereas*, Section three of title twelve of the amended charter renders it *the duty of the Board of Health to exercise full and exclusive power and authority for the removal of garbage from the city*; and whereas the present contracts ordered by the Common Council expire on the 30th of this present month, therefore,

"*Resolved, That the Board of City Works be, and they are hereby, authorized and directed to adopt such measures as they may find necessary for the purpose of continuing the removal of garbage from the city beyond the term of expiration of the present contracts, until such time as the Board of Health shall provide new contracts for the removal of the same.*

"*Resolved,* That the Comptroller be, and he is hereby, directed to transfer from the fund for the cleaning of streets to the fund of the Health Department the sum of $15,000, the Board of Health being authorized by section 3, title 12, of the amended charter, to expend not exceeding said sum during the year 1874 for the removal of garbage, etc., from the city."

The italics are our own.

On this assumption of the Board of Aldermen, the Board of Health bases its excuse for practical manslaughter. The medical members of the board, from the first, allowed themselves to be placed under the feet of men who have no regard whatever for the preservation of human life when placed in conflict with their political aspirations or personal profits; and the only utility of the medical members of the board, and the corps of medical officers attached to it, appears to be the subordinate relation of keeping the records,—which duty, if they will diligently pursue it, tends to the only ultimate public good of the board—the opening of the eyes of the people to the growing unhealthiness of the city under it, and, we trust, to their early perception of the necessity of abolishing this worse than useless organization.

Boston.—Annual Report, but giving an aggregate report on vital statistics from January 4, 1873, to April 25, 1874, a period of nearly *seventeen months,* in which the total number of deaths was 10,372. The distribution of the deaths is given by wards; but nothing is said in regard to the comparative local condition, or relative populations to mortality; hence, the utility of the information given under this head is wholly confined to those who are familiar with the locality, number, and condition of the population of the different wards,—a defect which seems to be due to the want of a proper registration law. Of the total number of deaths, nearly 25 per cent. were of children under the age of one year. The carelessness of infant life in general, and the fatal relations of tenement-houses, bad nourishment, etc., are touched upon with an earnestness worthy of the most serious attention. The charts, illustrating the chapter on vital statistics, are remarkable for their ingenious simplicity and clearness; indeed, they take the place of text. The tables are drawn in squares, numbered on the sides, and the different diseases represented by different colors running perpendicularly from the bottom, so that one can see at a glance the comparative prevalence of consumption, typhoid fever, cholera infantum, etc., during the year.

The conclusion of the epidemic of small-pox, at about the time of the last report, is referred to, and an account given of the expeditious and creditably successful manner in which the epidemic was overcome.

During the period of this report there have been but thirty-one cases, the last one on the 3d of March.

"School-houses, their ventilation, etc.," in Boston, are no exception.

"In many, if not all of our public schools, there are recitation-rooms where too many children are packed in together, and are kept there too long. In one that we know of, whose dimensions are small, from forty to forty-five children are occasionally kept from forty to seventy minutes with closed doors and windows. And this is education! Undoubtedly; for education, as we understand it, comes from the Latin *e* and *duco*, to *lead forth*, or to *draw out*; and if this system does not *draw out* all the life-blood from children, it must be because of their incorrigible stubbornness; it certainly can't be any fault of the system, for 'it is perfect, after its kind.'"

Defective drainage, sinks and drains, are shown to be chief sources of diseases and their abatement intelligently and forcibly urged, as essential to salubrity. The report by J. M. Merick, B. Sc., on the Chemical Analysis of Food, Toilet Articles, etc., subject to adulteration, contains much useful information, and is worthy of extensive circulation.—Deaths in Boston, for week ending August 15, 1874, 220; Worcester, 34; Lowell, 31; Salem, 11; Lynn, 24; Newburyport, 16; Fall River, 46. Prevalent diseases—Cholera infantum, consumption, typhoid fever, diarrhœa and dysentery.

Chicago.—Report for the years 1870, '71, '72, and '73. This is a concise report of 176 pages, which, excepting twenty pages devoted to an account of cholera in Chicago last year, and about as many more devoted to small-pox, is almost wholly made up with tabulated statistics. 1870 gave an average of 140.8 deaths weekly, with a yearly death-rate of 24.4 per thousand of inhabitants; 1871 gave a weekly average of 134.1, with the rate of 21.4 per thousand; 1872, a weekly average of 195.3, with the rate of 27.6 per thousand; 1873, a weekly average of 187.3, with a rate per thousand of 22.3—estimating the population at 400,000.

Of cholera, last year, the total number of fatal cases and cholera morbus, was 116. These occurred, for the most part, in a district of the city characterized by a low sandy soil and poor surface-drainage.

"*The first case occurred on May 24, at 444 Arnold street, in the person of John McFee, a bridge-builder, who had been working near Memphis, and left on account of cholera. When he arrived in Chicago he had diarrhœa, which remained unchecked, and after a week or ten days developed choleraic symptoms and proved fatal.*" [Italics our own.]

"The effect of cleanliness on families and individual cases was marked. Those who observed sanitary laws, attended to the disinfection of stools, and who were prompt in calling a physician, with few exceptions, recovered, and the occurrence of a second case in such families was rare. On the other hand, when the stools were not cared for, and the vomit permitted to remain on the floor, and the bedding (principally feather beds), used without having been properly cleansed, and where no attention was paid to ventilation or personal cleanliness, several cases would generally occur, and, as a rule, prove fatal."

Of small-pox, the number of cases for 1870 "could not be obtained, the total number of deaths for the year was only 15." In 1871, there were 299 cases; 1872, 2,382; 1873, 1,766. . . . "During the month of December, a general vaccination and inspection was ordered." During the while about one in four of the cases reported, died. A lamentable example of tardy action.

Slaughter-houses, tenements, schools, sewerage, streets and alleys, and privies, are all touched upon as being more or less prolific sources of disease, requiring better regulation and constant vigilance.

Mortality for the week ending Aug. 15th (latest received), 304. Prevailing diseases: Cholera infantum, 107; typhoid fever, 10; small-pox, none reported since end of first week in August, 2.

Philadelphia, 775,000.—Week ending August 29th, 288: consumption, 48; cholera infantum, 38; typhoid fever, 12.

Baltimore, 284,000.—Week ending August 31st, 173: Cholera infantum, 22; typhoid fever, 6; consumption, 25.

Cincinnati, 260,000.—Aug. 27th, 1874. I inclose our report for August, to the 26th inst., inclusive: Total mortality, 421, or 1.62 to every 1,000 of inhabitants; under one year of age, 27.55 per cent.; under five years of age, 56 per cent. Principal diseases from which deaths occurred: Cholera infantum, 52; diarrhœa, acute, 14; marasmus, 9; scarlet fever, 42; congestion of brain, 13; sunstroke, 9; consumptiion, 40; pneumonia, 10; old age, 8; convulsions, 28; debility, 10; casualties, 22; diarrhœa, chronic, 9; meningitis, 19; diphtheria, 9.

C. B. Chapman, *Clerk of Board of Health.*

Pittsburg, 136,000.—Sept. 1st, 1874. Deaths for August, 324,—28.60 per 1,000. Diarrhœal diseases, 97; scarlet fever, 24; whooping cough, 16; diphtheria, 8; typhoid fever, 11; consumption, 17; meningitis, 18; respiratory diseases, 8; deaths from violence, 12.

W. Snively, *Physician to B. of H.*

Providence, 100,000.—For August, 209. Diarrhœal diseases, 97; consumption, 33; scarlatina, 20; typhoid fever, 5.

New Orleans, 199,000.—Week ending August 23d, 130. Consumption, 12; fever, congestive, 12; intermittent, 4; remittent, 2; malarial, 2; typhoid, 5; small-pox, 1.

Louisville, 112,000.—Week ending Sept. 5th, 56.

Richmond, 65,000.—Week ending Aug. 29th, 29.

Dayton, 34,000.—For August, 68.

New Haven, 55,000.—For July, 116. Typhoid fever, 7.

Charleston, 52,000.—Week ending Aug. 22d, 37. Whites, 15; colored, 22.

Saint Paul, 25,000 (?)—For August, 78. Cholera infantum, 18; typhoid fever, 4.

Paterson, 38,000.—For August, 83.

Wheeling, 27,000.—For August, 57.

Elmira, population (?)—For August, 30.

FOREIGN.—*Halifax.*—Annual Report of the several departments of the City Government of Halifax, N. S., 1872–3. About one half of this pamphlet of one hundred and twelve pages is taken up with an unusually interesting resumé of house drainage and sewage disposal, by E. H. Keating, City Engineer, with charts illustrating the best systems now used in England. The report throughout evinces such an intelligent comprehension of internal hygiene, as can scarcely fail to be fruitful in good works.

THE AMERICAN PUBLIC HEALTH ASSOCIATION.

301 MOTT ST., NEW YORK, *Sept. 5th*, 1874.

To the Editor of the Sanitarian:

The Annual Meeting of the American Public Health Association will be held in Philadelphia, the second week in November. The session will open at noon on Tuesday, November 10th, at the College of Physicians, and will continue through the two succeeding days.

Reports, papers, and addresses upon the most practical topics in public hygiene, will be presented, and discussions will be opened upon a certain number of questions that most demand attention.

Contributions of experience and study are promised by able gentlemen in different sections of our country. The list of topics as published two years ago, will be largely reported upon, and papers upon several other subjects are promised.

The first volume of transactions and papers is now being printed, and will be issued by Messrs. Hurd & Houghton, of the Riverside Press, under the title, PUBLIC HEALTH. The volume promises to be of much utility, and is creditable to the publishers, as well as to a great number of members of the Association who contributed the papers.

Members and others who offer papers and reports are expected to confine their contributions very closely to *public health* questions, as the Association cannot enter upon general or special matters of social science. It is believed that the strictly public health questions demand exclusive attention, and that they enter so widely upon the domain of physical science, that the ablest cultivators of such knowledge and its uses will be well satisfied to give to their papers the most practical character.

Respectfully, yours,

E. HARRIS, M. D., *Secretary.*

EPISTOLARY.

Dear Editor, enclosed I send
Some verse in metre which I pen'd
A tribute to my darling wife,
The joy and comfort of my life.
It issues from a happy home,
Whose love-knit members seldom roam ;
And if deemed worthy, pray you print,
Your readers *may* find something in't.
If it shall not accepted be
Please send it back by mail to me,
Forbearing criticism unkind.
A postage stamp enclos'd you'll find
Poeta nascitur non fit,
But, gentle friend, pray what of it;
Have you not known men with foot rule
Could measure out whole acres full,
Secundum artem truly done,
But sentiment—fantasy—none ?
I more would say, but inspiration's gone.
I quote what Sprague, with fellow feeling told—
"But not for me, to life's coarse service sold,
" Where thought lies barren, and naught breeds but gold."
Now, having thus my mind—and your's—relieved,
I wish you fortune, if the poem's received.

TO MY WIFE.

(*On our Forty-first Anniversary.*)

Lady, I'll ne'er forget the day,
In other climes, far, far away
Beyond the stormy main, thy name
And beauteous vision o'er me came.

A form majestic, hair of gold,
A face all wreath'd with smiles, that told
Of joyous heart beneath a breast
Where grace and love with beauty rest.

Thine eyes of blue, like sparkling gem—
Protecting arches circling them;
Upholding brow, high, broad and fair,
A crown of beauty, rich and rare.

That vision never can depart,
But evermore possess my heart;
For thou art virtuous and refined,
Thy nature ever good and kind.

E'er since that day thou hast been mine,
My heart went forth and compass'd thine,
Which yielded frankly and confess'd
Of all mankind thou lov'd'st *me* best.

'Tis charming, dearest, to recall
Each happy year of love withal,
And evermore, while life shall last,
May *God's* good grace *renew our past*.

June 25th, 1874. R. H. L.

—

MEDICAL EDUCATION?—Example for 1874. Proof of cause of death. *Attending Physician's Statement on Life Insurance blank.*—* * * * Question. Were you his attending physician before his last sickness; if so how long, and for what diseases? Ans. "Yes since 57–Hyperforax in 1863–Chronick diarhia in 1865–6–7–" Question. State your opinion upon the cause, or manner of death, the attendant disease, and such medical facts as are connected with the case? Ans. "Spasmodic disease of the heart, while sufering under disease of Bronky and Lungs." Question. Was his last illness caused by or aggravated by intemperance or was it the result of any chronic or Constitutional disease? Ans. "Not by intemperance—chronic disease of Bronkium or the Hyperforax as mentioned above." Question. What were the pathological conditions found? Ans. "Great difficulty of breathing and extreme weakness of puls." Signed. ———, M. D.

Example No. 2.—Return of a still-born infant.—To the Bureau of Records. Board of Health. * * * * * Period of Utero-gestation; "about 5 or 6 days." Date of this Birth; "at 8 o'clock P. M. June 20." Sex; "Boy." Cause, &c.; "had constant cough and Prostration of mother." Name of Medical Attendant, —— ——, M. D. Date, June 20th, 1874.

WATER CONTAMINATION.—Just as we are going to press, we have the melancholy echo from Lake Mahopac, of the "caution to water-drinkers," given in our last number. A full account of the criminal carelessness of human life at the Gregory House, Mahopac, will appear in our next issue.

BIBLIOGRAPHY.

Physiology of Man; designed to represent the Existing State of Physiological Science, as applied to the Functions of the Human Body. By Austin Flint, Jr., M. D., Professor of Physiology and Physiological Anatomy in the Bellevue Hospital Medical College, etc., etc. (In five volumes.) Vol. V. Special Senses; Generation. 8vo, pp. 517. New York: D. Appleton & Co. 1874.

This is the concluding volume of Professor Flint's great treatise on Human Physiology, began eleven years ago. The distinguishing feature of this work is, that nothing is taken for granted. The author has thoroughly sifted and weighed the opinions of others, and has held fast only those things which he has found to bear the test of actual experiment and personal observation. Chapter i. treats of the sense of touch, muscular sense and sensibility, the tactile corpuscles, and the venereal sense. Chapter ii. takes up the olfactory nerves, their anatomy and physiology, and their relations to the sense of smelling and tasting. Chapters iii. to vi. are devoted to the optic nerves, the anatomy of the eye, refraction, vision, the functions and mechanism of the iris, the muscles of the eyeball and eyelids, the lachrymal apparatus, etc. Chapters vii. to ix. deal with the auditory nerves and the sense of hearing in all its relations, including the physics of sound, the appreciation of harmony, discord, etc. This necessarily requires a full consideration of the anatomy and physiology of the various parts of the auditory apparatus; x. is devoted to gustation and the nerves of taste, the tongue and its functions, facial paralysis, etc. In chapter xi., the author opens the subject of generation with a general view of the female sexual organs, the ovaries, Fallopian tubes, uterus, and the erectile tissue concerned; xii. treats of the ovum and ovulation, puberty and menstruation, changes in the pregnant uterus, the corpus luteum, etc.; xiii. gives a full account of the male organs of generation, the testicles and their secretion, the glands of the urethra, and the changes in these organs from infancy to old age; xiv. is on fecundation, the part of the male and female in the reproductive process, the entrance and destination of spermatozoids, the influence of the maternal mind on offspring, etc. Chapters xv. to xviii. treat of the segmentation of the vitellus and formation of the membranes and placenta; of the development of the embryon, and the osseous, muscular, cutaneous, and nervous systems; of the development of the alimentary system, the respiratory system, and the face; of the development of the genito-urinary organs in both sexes, and of the circulatory system. The work closes (ch. xix.) with a view of the subject of fœtal life, a consideration of development after birth, maturity, the decay of age, death, and the resolution of the body into its original elements. It is not too much to say of Dr. Flint's complete work, that it stands alone as a comprehensive treatise on human physiology, and that its publication marks an epoch in medical literature.

Hooker's New Physiology; designed as a text-book for Institutions of learning. By Worthington Hooker, M. D., Professor, etc.; revised by J. A. Sewall, M. D., Professor of Natural Sciences, Illinois State Normal University. With questions. 12mo, pp. 376. New York: Sheldon & Co. 1874.

The chief feature of Hooker's Physiology is its simplicity. It differs from other elementary treatises in not being a mere epitome of human physiology, but a physiology adapted to the comprehension of academic students, beginning with the distinction between organic and inorganic matter, and, by an easy ascent from the simplest to the more complex structures and functions, inductively; and with just enough of comparative physiology to illustrate the characteristics of the organization of the human body.

Hygiene is presented in the same manner; illustrations are drawn from the most familiar things, and applied to subjects of the utmost importance. There are no long chapters on favorite topics, or words difficult to understand, but such a simple, succinct and clear presentation of the subject as cannot fail to be interesting to the student, and therefore easy of inculcation. We commend it as one of the best school physiologies with which we are acquainted.

Health and Education. By the Rev. Chas. Kingsley, F. L. S., F. G. S. etc., 12 mo. pp. 411. New York : D. Appleton & Co., 1874.

A book which should be in every household, and the best school teacher's *manual on health* extant. It consists of fifteen practical essays on popular hygiene, by an author who has closely observed and participated in the best of social science reforms in England—sanitary reform for "five-and-thirty years, in town and country," and who here presents, in a style admirable for its simplicity and clearness, the lessons of his observation and experience.

The following extracts from the first chapters on "The Science of Health," indicate both the style and the subject matter of the volume:

"Tens of thousands—who knows it not—lead sedentary and unwholesome lives, stooping, asphyxiated, employing as small a fraction of their bodies as their minds. And all this in dwellings, workshops, what not ?—the influences, the very atmosphere of which, tend not to health, but to unhealth, and to drunkenness as a solace under the feelings of unhealth and depression. And that such a life must tell upon their offspring, and if their offspring grow up under similar circumstances, upon their offspring's offspring, till a whole population may become permanently degraded, who does not know? For who that walks through the by-streets of any great city does not see? * * * * * * Do I say that we ought not to save these people if we can? God forbid. The weakly, the diseased, whether infant or adult, is here on earth; a citizen no more responsible for his own weakness than for his own existence. Society, that is, in plain English, we and our ancestors are responsible for both; and we must fulfil the duty, and keep him in life; and, if we can, heal, strengthen, develop him to the utmost; and make the best of that which fate and our deservings have given us to deal with. * * * We must teach men to mend their own matters, of their own reason and of their own free-will. We must teach them that they are the arbiters of their own destinies; and, to a fearfully great degree, of their children's destinies after them. We must teach them not merely that they ought to be free, but that they are free, whether they know it or not, for good and for evil. And we must do that in this case, by teaching them sound practical science; the science of physiology as applied to health. * * * As to the laws of personal health: enough, and more than enough, is known already, to be applied safely and easily by any adults, however unlearned, to the preservation not only of their own health, but of that of their children."

Essays on Conservative Medicine and Kindred Topics. By Austin Flint, M. D., Prof. of the Principles and Practice of Medicine, etc., etc. 12mo. pp. 214. Philadelphia : Henry C. Lea. 1874.

A collection of several essays contributed at intervals, some years since, to different medical journals, with the object of establishing the recognition of conservatism in the practice of medicine on the same footing as conservatism in surgery; in other words: to promote the more extended application of hygienic measures as therapeutical agents in the treatment of disease. The first one of these essays, entitled "Conservative Medicine" is a periscope of the progress of conservatism in the treatment of disease in modern times, as the general result of scientific researches. "Conservative medicine as applied to Therapeutics;" "Conservative Medicine as applied to Hygiene" and the four essays next following, are all devoted to the elaboration of the principles in the first, and reflect the views of Bigelow and Forbes, of thirty years ago. The concluding essay, "Divine Design as Exemplified in the Natural History of Diseases," is well described by its title, recognizing the Divine institution of disease as a blessing and not a curse. This essay was the substance of an address before the Young Men's Christian Union, in Louisville, Ky., and therefore prepared with especial reference to a non-medical audience. As a whole, although prepared in the first place for medical readers, these essays are for the most part devoid of technical language, and useful reading for laymen as well as physicians.

Alcohol; Its Combinations, Adulterations, and Physical Effects. By Col. J. G. Dudley, New York: For the Author, G. P. Putnam's Sons.

The comprehensive title of this double-leaded pamphlet of 68 pages is misleading. With such a title, "compiled" as the author informs us in the introduction, "from the writings and lectures of the most celebrated chemists, physicians and physiologists of the present age," we would in the first place expect a respectable volume; and in the second place more about the scientific relations of alcohol, and, perhaps less about teetolism as a scientific deduction,—at least, a better and fairer display of the scientific conclusions of *some* of the most celebrated writers on the subject, in regard to its food properties. The author's scripture on alcohol, is wholly confined to teetolism. Had he taken as much pains to search the scientific literature of the *whole* subject as he has to enforce the doctrines of one side only, his work would not only command more respect, but it would be far more likely to promote the object in view. It has been well said by Dr. Mapother, one of the most distinguished writers on health: "Teetotallers ride their hobby to the death."

If they would only confine themselves within reasonable bounds, treat their adversaries with respect, patiently investigate scientific conclusions instead of ostracising all who venture to disagree with them—they would overcome the influence of many scientific men who are unjustly said to encourage intemperance because they find it necessary to combat extreme views.

Epidemic Yellow Fever in Montgomery, Ala., 1873. By R. F. Michel, M.D. Reprint from *Charleston Medical Journal.*—The gist of this paper is the designation of the first *fatal point* in the city,—the circumstances being favorable—poisoned by the arrival of persons from

Pensacola during the prevalence of the disease in that city. "From this point the disease stealthily crept up Commerce, and Court streets, affixing its fatal mark upon many buildings on each side of the way . . giving evidence of the regular advancement of this horrible disease. From these points it radiated in every direction, and our city soon fell a victim to one of the most fatal and extensive epidemics of yellow fever ever experienced by its inhabitants." Alas! will people never learn to meet the arch enemy at the *first fatal point*. Ay, meet and *defeat* him, at the very point of contact. This is an old story; would that it may never be renewed!

Climate and Diseases of the Gulf Coast of the Forida Peninsula, in relation to Pulmonary Tuberculosis. By J. P. Wall, M.D. Reprint from *Charleston Medical Journal*, July, 1874.

A pretty good description of a region of country "about 50 miles or more into the interior, where is found the natural watershed, dividing the peninsula in its length into two nearly equal portions, till the immediate vicinity of the Everglades is reached in the extreme southern portion, from Cedar Keys, 29° 07' to Cape Sable, the extreme point on the main land, in lat. 25° N., a distance of 240 miles." The author gives a formidable account of malarial diseases, and yellow fever, occasionally, in this region, while his data in regard to pulmonary tuberculosis, are insufficient to establish the conclusion "that the interior and western slope of the Florida peninsula is climatically better adapted to those suffering with pulmonary tuberculosis than any other section of the Union."

Syphilis of the Eye. By Henry D. Noyes, M.D. Being chapter viii of "A practical Treatise on the Surgical Diseases of the Genito-Urinary Organs, including Syphilis," by W. H. Van Buren, A. M., M.D, and E. L. Keys, A. M., M.D., New York: D. Appleton & Co., 1874. A chapter of great practical importance to every physician.

Remarks on the Prevalence and Distribution of Fever in Dublin. Illustrated by maps, tables, and diagrams. By Thos. W. Grimshaw, M.D. Dublin: Fannin & Co. Pamphlet, pp. 36, 1872. It is by the study and timely application of the experiences of others that we can most effectually ward off evils which otherwise we are ever liable to incur. Fever nests are built out of the same material everywhere, and in no part of the world is the lesson of Dublin, so lucidly presented in this brochure of Dr. Grimshaw, more necessary to be learned, than by the conservators of public health in our own cities.

Nomenclature of Diseases, prepared for the use of the Medical Officers of the U. S. Marine-Hospital service. By John M. Woodworth, M.D., Supervising Surgeon. Government Print, 1874.

Dr. Woodworth has not only done his service a favor, but conferred an obligation on all compilers of mortality statistics in this country, who have long been in want of such a manual as this; comprehending the English-Latin terminology, and the classification of the nomenclature of diseases, drawn up by a joint committee appointed by the Royal College of Physicians of London, England.

The Sanitary Journal. Devoted to Public Health. Edited by Edward Playter, M. D., Monthly, pp. 32. One dollar per year in advance. Single copy, twenty cents., Toronto.

We welcome the first number of this effort to popularize Sanitary Science. Sanitary Science; Means which shorten life; Effects of Tobacco; Rules for preventing the spread of Contagion, with twice as many equally suggestive editorial headings, indicate a manly grasp of the enemies to human health, and we hope for it a long life and a vigorous contest.

The New York Trade Reporter. All house-keepers as well as all persons engaged in commerce are interested in *trade* as comprehended in this excellent newspaper, which presents a weekly compendium of information essential to the practice of domestic economy, in all its departments. By such information only, can one keep the run of the markets and feel secure in regard to the prices of food, fuel and clothing. Every Saturday, 17 New Church st., $4.00 per year; 10 cents a copy.

The Laboratory. The first number of a 4to periodical of eight pages, edited by James F. Babcock, and published by Wm. W. Bartlet & Co., Boston, at 50 cents per year, has been received. It is a work much needed; undertaking the exposure of the villainous adulterations of food and medicines everywhere distributed in this country as legitimate trade. We sincerely hope for it the very best of encouragement.

Received: The Woman's Temperance Movement; Duty of the Church towards the Present Temperance Movement. New York Temperance Society and Publishing House.

An Introduction to the Study of General Biology. Designed for the use of Schools and Science Classes. By Thomas C. MacGinley. With 124 Illustrations. 12mo, pp. 199. New York: G. P. Putnam's Sons.

Love at First Sight. A Novel. By Captain Henry Curling, author of "The Soldier of Fortune," "The Stolen Child," etc. Philadelphia: Peterson & Brothers.

Transactions of the Medical and Chirurgical Faculty of the State of Maryland. Seventy-fifth Annual Session, Baltimore, 1874.

Transactions of the Michigan State Medical Society, 1874.

Contributions to the Transactions of the Medical Association of the State of Alabama. I. The Yellow Fever Epidemic of 1873. II. The White Blood-Corpuscle. By Jerome Cochrane, M. D., Professor of Public Hygiene and Medical Jurisprudence in the Medical College of Alabama, 1874.

The Relation of Medical Societies to Progress in Science. Inaugural Address of the President of the Medical Society of the County of Kings, N. Y. By Alex. J. C. Skene, M. D., June 16, 1874.

Quarantine; General Principles Affecting its Organization. The transmissibility of Yellow Fever and Cholera in their relation to Quarantine. By S. Oakley Vanderpoel, M. D., Health Officer of the Port of New York.

☞ To Advertisers.—Mr. A. P. Dunlop is authorized to represent The Sanitarian.

THE SANITARIAN.

A MONTHLY JOURNAL.

VOL. II.] NOVEMBER, 1874. [NO. 8.

CARBOLIC ACID; TESTS OF ITS PRESENCE, AND A NEW METHOD FOR ITS QUANTITATIVE ESTIMATION.

By Elwyn Waller, A. M., E. M., New York.

With Remarks by Prof. C. F. Chandler and Others.

Proceedings of the N. Y. Public Health Association, Aug. 13th, 1874.

It is almost unnecessary for me to state the source from which carbolic acid, which has recently assumed such importance, comes, or the mode in which it is prepared.

The coal-tar contains substances which have been grouped as follows:

Bases—Ammonia, methylamine, ethylamine, aniline, quinoline, picolin, toluidine, pyridine, etc.

Acids—Acetic, rosolic, brunolic, phenic, or carbolic, cresylic, phlorylic, etc. The last three are not true acids, but are rather what have been called alcohols. Strictly they belong in a class by themselves—the phenols.

Neutral Substances—Benzine, toluene, cumene, cymene, which are liquid; naphthaline, anthracine, chrysene and pyrene, which are solid.

By distillation at temperatures below 350° to 400° F., the portion called the "light oil" is separated. Steam is passed through this light oil, until all has been carried off that can be thus removed. The distillate consists of what is known as "refined coal tar naphtha." The residue, called "naphtha tailings" is then treated with some fixed alkali in water solution, the oil which separates is removed, the alkaline solution is neutralized with acid, and the oily liquid which separates is run off, and sold as crude carbolic acid, or else refined by fractional distillation for the preparation of purer qualities of that article.

It is of the methods of testing these preparations that I propose to treat. And first as to qualitative tests.

As carbolic acid is often called coal tar creasote, and indeed resembles creasote in many of its properties, it is often necessary to be able to distinguish between the two, for they really are different substances.*

* I may here mention that the formula for carbolic acid is $C_6 H_6 O$ while that for creosote, though not yet definitely ascertained, is believed to be $C_8 H_{10} O_2$.

The simplest method of testing whether one is dealing with creasote or carbolic acid is to test the solubility of the sample in glycerine, which, it is stated, will dissolve the carbolic acid, and will not touch the creasote.

Another test frequently applied is the comparison of the effects on collodion. Creasote does not coagulate collodion, carbolic acid does.

Still another test is that with a splinter of pine wood, by dipping it first in a water solution of the carbolic acid or creasote, and then in concentrated hydrochloric acid. In the course of half an hour the wood assumes a bluish color if carbolic acid was present. At least such is the statement, but some chemists have shown that concentrated hydrochloric acid alone will produce this effect.

The two preceding tests will however probably be sufficient to prove the identity of a sample, should one have occasion to test the point.

A test for carbolic acid, much used at present, consists in adding to the water solution of the substance a little ammonia, then a solution of some hypochlorite and applying heat. If carbolic acid is present, a fine bluish green coloration is produced. The theory of this reaction is that by the action of the ammonia on the carbolic acid aniline is formed, since the same coloration is produced with aniline and a hypochlorite solution alone, without the use of ammonia. This test is said to give the reaction with one part of carbolic acid in 3000. Cresylic acid and thymol are said to give the same reaction.

This test has been used per contra as a test for the presence of ammonia and for that purpose is tolerably delicate.

If nitric acid is added to a solution containing carbolic acid, a yellow coloration is produced, due to the formation of tri-nitro phenic acid (better known as picric acid). One part of carbolic acid in 6,000 may thus be detected, but as nitric acid forms picric acid with various other organic substances of the most varied description, the test cannot be considered as very reliable. The test is best made by warming the water solution of the suspected substance with a few drops of nitric acid. In case either substance is in concentrated form, the action may be too violent to be desirable.

The reduction of metallic salts by carbolic acid has also been made use of, principally with the protonitrate of mercury Hg $(no_3)_2$, but like the preceding, such reduction may be effected by so many other substances besides carbolic acid that not much reliance can be placed upon it. The blood-red coloration of the solution of carbolic acid with protonitrate of mercury containing nitrous acid is stated to be quite characteristic.

This reaction has been proposed as the basis of a quantitative test. Qualitatively it is stated to indicate the presence of one part of carbolic acid in 200,000.

A solution containing carbolic acid when poured upon the surface of concentrated sulphuric acid so that the liquids do not mix, gives rise to the formation of a zone between them, having three different tints, the solution finally becoming red. This test is said to be more characteristic than any of the preceding. One part in 2,000 may be detected by this means. The colors obtained are, however, very delicate, and the liquids should remain in contact for some little time in order to obtain a decided reaction.

Pollacci highly recommends the test with concentrated sulphuric acid and bichromate of potash solution, as being very characteristic for carbolic acid. Concentrated sulphuric acid, and strong bichromate solution are mixed together in a capsule, and a drop of the solution suspected of containing carbolic acid is added. If carbolic acid is present, the solution turns brown. This test is, however, stated to be only applicable to a solution containing pure carbolic acid. With concentrated carbolic acid the reaction is quite violent. The delicacy of this test is stated to be one part in 3,000.

The Euchlorine test* is thus described:

In a five-inch test tube put ten grains powdered chlorate of potash, pour on concentrated hydrochloric acid to the depth of about one inch; allow the evolution of gas to proceed for about one minute. Then dilute with one and a half volumes of water and remove the gas by blowing through a bent tube. Pour in ammonia so as to form a layer on the top. Blow out the chloride of ammonium fumes by means of the bent tube, and add a few drops of the liquid suspected to contain carbolic acid. In the presence of carbolic acid the ammonia layer assumes a rose red, blood red, red brown or dark brown tint, according to the amount of carbolic acid present. One part of carbolic acid in 12,000 gives the reaction. Creasote gives the same reaction.

From the description, the experiment appears to be somewhat hazardous, and I have therefore hesitated about trying it.

The test with sesquichloride of iron is the most common, and much reliance has been placed upon it. It simply consists in adding to the aqueous solution of what is supposed to contain carbolic acid, a few drops of sesquichloride of iron solution.

Carbolic acid, if present, causes the immediate formation of a fine purple coloration. One part in 2,000 may thus be detected. The same colortaion is produced by tannic acid, salicylic compounds and others. The presence of acids or salts interferes with it however.

The bromine water test is another one which is most readily applied. The addition of bromine water to a solution containing carbolic acid gives a whitish, creamy precipitate of tribromphenol which, when but little bromine water has been added, redissolves in the carbolic acid solution. This test will give a reaction with one part of carbolic acid in 43,700 (Landolt) one in 15,500 (Pollacci and Locatelli). The precipitate is soluble in ether, alcohol, bisulphide of carbon and the most of that class of solvents. The homologues of carbolic acid, as cresylic and phlorylic acids, as well as aniline, toluidine, and quinine, chinchonine, morphine, etc., give a similar precipitate. With concentrated sulphuric acid, and bichromate of potash solution the tribromphenol is said to give the brown color already mentioned under that mode of testing for carbolic acid. With sodium amalgam the tribromphenol is converted back again into carbolic acid, which may be recognized by its characteristic odor.

Of quantitative tests for carbolic acid the degree of solubility in water or in alkaline solutions and the sesquichloride of iron tests are usually used. The two first are applied by simply mixing the oil con-

* Am. Jour. Pharm., March, 1873, p. 98.

taining the carbolic acid with water or alkaline solution suffi ient to dissolve it all were it all carbolic acid, and measuring the amount which does not dissolve, subtracting that and calling the remainder carbolic acid. With pure water, as may easily be seen by a simple experiment with a sample of crude carbolic acid, there are practical difficulties in the way, such as the propensity of some of the oil to go to the bottom, while some stays at the top of the water. Beside this the oil sticks to the sides of the vessel, and can scarcely be detached. Acting on Professor Chandler's suggestion, I have shaken the crude acid and water with a measured quantity of olive oil, which collects the portions not carbolic acid, and obviates these difficulties to a considerable extent. The olive oil has no effect on the carbolic acid. The test performed in the same way with the use of a solution of a fixed alkali, instead of pure water, gives somewhat less trouble, but other substances in the tar beside carbolic acid are dissolved by the alkaline solution, as may be seen from the color of such solution.

The objection to both of these tests is that carbolic acid will hold a considerable amount of water, and still mix with the tar, so that the percentages obtained, are often higher than the true percentages of carbolic acid, sometimes by as much as 25 per cent.

The sesquichloride of iron test is good in case one is dealing with solutions containing only pure carbolic acid. As before remarked, the presence of small amounts of various salts, of free acid, or of some of the constituents of the tar interferes with the coloration. The test is performed by comparing the color produced by three drops of sesquichloride of iron in 10 c. c. of the water solution of the sample of carbolic acid, prepared of a certain strength, with the color produced by a corresponding amount of sesquichloride in the same bulk of water containing known amounts of pure carbolic acid. With crude carbolic acid the color obtained has a shade of red even in the most carefully filtered water solutions, and usually fades or alters rapidly, so that an accurate determination by this method is impossible. Moreover, the test cannot be used at all in testing carbolates of lime, and similar preparations.

Taking the precipitation of carbolic acid by bromine as a starting point, I have succeeded in obtaining what I believe to be a reliable method for the determination of the percentages of carbolic acid in the crude samples and in various other preparations. The solutions necessary for the performance of this test are as follows:

No. 1. Ten grammes of pure crystallized carbolic acid are dissolved in one litre of water. This solution serves as the standard with which to compare the results obtained on the sample to be analyzed. I have found by experiment that this solution will keep for at least three or four months, and probably longer, without perceptible alteration.

No. 2. A solution of bromine in water is also prepared by shaking up bromine with water, and allowing the water to stand over it for some time. In practice it is convenient to use two bottles, the one with bromine in the bottom, the other for the solution when it has become sufficiently saturated.

No. 3. A third solution, containing about 150 grammes of alum and 250 c. c. of dilute sulphuric acid (1 : 9 by volume) in one litre, is also prepared. The use of this solution is to cause the ready separation of the bromine precipitate, the excess of acid serving to insure the necessary condition of acidity of the solution, and moreover to hold more alum in solution than it otherwise would. An ordinary water solution of alum does not appear to hold a sufficient amount of the salt to assist materally in the separation of the precipitate.

The analysis is made as follows:

After taking the specific gravity of the sample, 10 c. c. are measured out and run into a litre flask, water added and the mixture shaken, the flask being finally filled up to the mark. After thorough mixing, some of the solution is carefully filtered, and 10 c. c. of the clear water solution is taken and run into a four or six oz. reagent bottle with tight fitting (glass) stopper. 30 c. c. of the alum solution is then placed in the bottle, and in a similar bottle is put the same amount of alum solution, and 10 c. c. of the standard carbolic acid solution. A burette is now filled with the solution of bromine, and from this burette the bromine water is run into the bottle containing 10 c. c. of the standard carbolic acid solution until no more precipitate forms on addition of bromine. The bottle must be shaken after every few c. c. have been added. Toward the end of the reaction the precipitate forms rather slowly, and the bromine, when all the carbolic acid has been saturated, gives a yellow tint to the solution which does not disappear on shaking. 25 to 50 c. c. of bromine water is usually required to precipitate all the carbolic acid. The most convenient standard which may be obtained without much difficulty is about 30 to 35 c. c.

The solution from the sample to be tested is treated in the same way, and the amounts of bromine water required for each respectively are compared, and from this, combined with the specific gravity of the sample, the percentage of carbolic acid may be calculated.*

As the precipitate rises to the top instead of settling to the bottom, it will be found convenient to use a small tube flared at the top in funnel form, in order that the bromine water toward the end of the operation may be introduced into the clear liquid below the precipitate, that it may be seen whether a precipitate forms. The bromine water, when dropped into the tube, should be blown gently into the solution. As the amount of bromine water is small, no inconvenience will be experienced in doing this.

If the solution from the crude sample is not carefully filtered, the precipitate does not separate readily. This difficulty is overcome either by adding a known amount of the standard carbolic acid solution to it, and deducting from the amount of bromine water used, the amount due to the c. c. of standard solution added, or by adding some of the precipitate already obtained to the 10 c. c. of the sample. The only

* *E. g.*, supposing the 10 c. c. of standard required 30 c. c. bromine water, the 10 c. c. of solution from the sample required 17 c. c. and the sp. gr. of the sample was 1.025. The percentage of carbolic acid in the sample would then be

$$100 \times \frac{17}{30} \div 1.025 = 55.28 \text{ per cent.}$$

It is safer to make the test in duplicate. The amount of bromine used should agree within 0.2 c. c.

reliable indication of the saturation of the carbolic acid, the end reaction, as the Germans call it, is the absence of the formation of a precipitate, since with some samples the solution will have a faint yellow tint from the start. This tint, however, does not appear to deepen until all the carbolic acid has been saturated. Vigorous shaking is in all cases necessary to promote the formation of the precipitate.

Cautions.—In running the crude carbolic acid from the 10 c. c. pipette the pipette should be allowed to drip for some time into the litre flask, as otherwise so much of the crude carbolic acid adheres to the sides of the pipette that 10 c. c. is not used, and the results are not correct. In filtering the crude carbolic acid solution the liquid should always about half fill the funnel. If it is allowed to run out, and the oil once comes in contact with the paper, the next addition of solution is almost certain to drive enough of the oil through the paper to cause the bromine precipitate to give trouble by not separating readily.

Water solutions of crude carbolic acid are apt, upon standing, especially when in the light, to turn pinkish or brownish, showing some chemical change, probably the formation of rosolic acid, so that the operations of filtering and testing should be rapidly followed up when once the solution is made. The absence of aniline, toluidine, etc., occurring in the coal tar should be proved before depending on the results, as those bases also give a precipitate with bromine. Usually, however, the mode of preparation of the carbolic acid prevents them from being present, as they are insoluble in alkaline solutions.

I am inclined to believe that cresylic and phlorylic acids, and perhaps some others which might occur in samples of crude carbolic acid, are also precipitated by bromine water, and that in analyzing by this method those substances are reckoned as carbolic acid. What effect they really do have, I have not as yet determined, on account of the difficulty of obtaining those substances pure.

In testing samples of carbolates of lime, etc, 10 grammes of the sample are weighed out and placed in a 250 c. c. flask surrounded by cold water, and dilute sulphuric acid added in excess, water added up to the mark, the whole well mixed, and then filtered, and of this solution 50 c. c. at a time should be used. As the amount of carbolic acid present is usually very small, it is well to add to the 50 c. c. 5 c. c. of standard carbolic acid and to deduct from the amount of bromine water used the amount equivalent to 5 c. c. of the standard. The test is otherwise performed in a similar manner to that before given. The addition of alum solution is unnecessary, the sulphate of lime present serving as a substitute. The calculation of results is made without difficulty.

Other preparations containing carbolic acid, provided they do not contain oxidizable substances as protosulphate of iron, &c., may also be tested by this method with such modifications as may be found necessary.

The bromine water does not of course keep the same standard throughout, but during a morning's work it varies comparatively little. Until the solution gets low in the bottle, every other burette full seldom gives a variation greater than 0.1 to 0.2 c. c. Unless the bromine water is allowed to stand for some little time in the burette the last portions have the same standard as the first. Of course, if allowed to stand long enough, the upper layers will give up their bromine to the surrounding atmosphere, and the standard is not maintained.

Mr. Waller's paper was carefully illustrated and varified by chemical experiments of great interest and beauty. A quantitative analysis of a sample of commercial carbolic acid was made in all its details, in the presence of the Association.

At the conclusion of Mr. Waller's paper, Prof. Chandler called the attention of the Association to the importance of the subject introduced by the paper, saying that the ordinary method of ascertaining the per cent. of carbolic acid has inherent defects which are avoided in the method just presented. As the disinfecting property of a fluid containing carbolic acid depends on the proportion of carbolic acid, it is of practical importance that there should be a reliable method of quantitative analysis. At one time this summer the Health Department of New York saved five or six dollars per day in the purchase of carbolic acid by using the new process for testing the value of the fluids offered for sale.

Dr. Endemann stated that in Mr. Waller's method the carbolic acid is always in excess, and that the precipitate therefore contains mono- and bibromephenol, probably in varying proportions, as well as tribromephenol. He was of the opinion that this would produce discrepancies in the hands of different operators. He suggested a modification of the process by letting the bromine be in excess. That would give a precipitate consisting entirely of tribromephenol, and then the excess of bromine could be determined by a standard solution of protosulphate of iron or protochloride of tin. In reply to Dr. Endemann's remarks, Mr. Waller stated that he had used the new method more than a hundred times and had reason to be satisfied with the results. He had tested the same solution five times with uniform results, and had varied the process by adding the bromine solution sometimes rapidly and at other times gradually, sometimes even allowing half an hour or more to intervene in the midst of the adding of the bromine solution.

Dr. Endemann has since ascertained that the reaction which led him to make the above statement is not due to the carbolic acid, but rather to impurities always present in the not wholly refined article.

Traveling with the Measles.—This advertisement appears in the "London Times:"

Should this meet the eye of the lady who got into the 12:30 train at New-cross station on Friday, May 15th, with two boys, one of whom was evidently just recovering from an illness, she may be pleased to learn that three of the four young ladies who were in the carriage are very ill with the measles, and the health of the fourth is far from what her relations could desire.

It would be difficult to imagine anything more delicate.

"THE SEWAGE QUESTION."

By Charles F. Barnard, Scituate, Mass.

Under this title, Messrs. Longmans, Green & Co., of London, published, in 1867, a work by Frederick Charles Krepp, embracing a general review of all systems and methods hitherto employed in various countries for draining cities and utilizing sewage, treated with reference to public health, and national economy generally; with a full description of Captain Liernur's system for the daily inoffensive removal of fæcal solids, fluids and gases by pneumatic force, combined with an improved method of sewage utilization. The work is dedicated by its author to Prince Henry, of the Netherlands, as the generous and enlightened patron and protector of Captain Liernur's new system. In his preface Mr. Krepp says justly, "The sewage question resolves itself into this: What is the cheapest and most efficient technical process for rendering human excreta useful instead of dangerous." He proposes, therefore, to give in his volume a brief account of all the various systems, drawing his information from the most reliable authorities, both English and foreign, and leaving his readers to form their own conclusions. He adds, "Among the most valuable of these sources of which we have principally availed ourselves, are the writings of Captain Charles T. Liernur, Civil and Military Engineer, who, during a number of years, has professedly had an extensive practice in various branches of engineering on both sides of the Atlantic."

"Among these notes," says Mr. Krepp, "we found a description of a new plan invented by him, called the Pneumatic Sewerage System, which, after a close and conscientious investigation, we herewith submit as, in our opinion, the best solution thus far given to a really difficult problem.

"In this view we are not only countenanced by the approval of eminent engineers and agriculturists, who have, like us, carefully examined the invention, and of several scientific periodicals, giving a critical description of it, but also by His Royal Highness Prince Henry, who, after mature deliberation, recommended it for adoption in the Grand Duchy of Luxemburg; and, further, by the now well-known fact, that the City of the Hague, after having submitted Captain Liernur's plan to a committee of professional inquiry, resolved *at once* to give it a fair, practical trial at the public expense.

"There can be no doubt of the high importance of the subject. Apart from the sanitary conditions involved, it directly bears upon the agricultural development of the country. All mechanical skill and industry, and all commercial enterprise, avail but little in the end, unless we also stimulate the soil to yield the largest crops without impairing its permanent fertility.

"Scientific demonstration and practical experience go far to show, that the best means to obtain such harvests consist in properly utilizing the ashes of the food we consume and the fructifying gases contained therein.

"The removal of human excrements out of cities and towns has always been a question of the highest importance, both from considerations of public health and national economy. It is, however, in later years only that a more serious interest has been excited with regard to city sewerage, owing to three causes:—First, modern civilization, massing the population almost exclusively in cities and large towns; second, chemistry and vegetable physiology, making immense strides in the present century and proving conclusively the surpassing value of human excrement as a fertilizer; and third, our daily experience, teaching us, that the technical means hitherto employed have proved partially or wholly inadequate to meet the requirements in view.

"In many cities, which were thought to be well drained, often at enormous cost—soil, water and air are still contaminated by the decomposition of human excrements, resulting in endemic fevers and deadly epidemics; whilst, on the other hand, our present modes of using sewage matter for agricultural purposes, either yield only poor grass on sandy uninhabitable spots, or render, by their manipulations, human manure so expensive or worthless" (and offensive) "that farmers cannot be induced to apply it on any extensive scale.

"We conclude these general introductory remarks by referring to the fundamental laws of national economy, so lucidly laid down by Professor Thudichum:

"1. The basis of human life, the very root of all society, is the capacity to produce food in such quantities, that a surplus of it may be exchanged for commodities resulting from the labors of other people unable to produce food.

"2. This capacity to produce food must be rendered permanent by a strict observance of the laws of nature regulating vegetable life, the knowledge of which is the basis of agricultural science.

"3. The first and most important of these laws is, that we must return to the soil the mineral ingredients we take from it in gathering our crops. The atmosphere furnishes the nutritive elements, and the soil the minerals, out of which vegetable fibres, vessels and structures containing food are built up. Without these mineral ingredients no harvest can possibly flourish.

"4. These mineral ingredients are continually ejected from human beings and animals in their excrements, by returning which to the soil we furnish it with building materials for new crops, at the same time keeping pure the atmosphere we breathe, and the water we drink, and thus preventing epidemics and" (premature) "death.

"These laws of national economy are based on the sublime laws of nature, and their neglect is invariably followed by national decay. The illustrious Liebig, who has devoted his mighty intellect and talents to the discovery of the laws of vegetable life, raising thereby agricultural chemistry to its present astounding eminence, very justly remarks, that *every law of nature is the ready servant of mankind; beneficent when rightly employed, but destructive when neglected.*

"The removal of excreta out of human habitations may be traced

---

NOTE.—Prof. Thudichum: Grundlagen der öffentlichen Gesundheitspflege in Stadten. Frankfurt, 1865.

to the very first dawn of civilization. An innate abhorrence of matters so very offensive to the senses compels mankind to get rid of them in any way; a natural propensity shared by many animals (the *carnivora*), which scrape their excrements into the ground, and cover them with earth, or otherwise remove them out of their sight and smell. And, if instinct be that by which nature makes known its inviolable laws where reason could not discern them, it is here unmistakably pointed out that the excrements of all *carnivorous* animals at least, including human beings, *should at once be put into the ground.*

"The ancient Hindoos were scrupulously careful and clean in this particular.

"The still more ancient Assyrians, Phœnicians and Egyptians carried off the sewage of their cities by means of drains and canals or open sewers. Phœnicia made asphalt a regular article of commerce for drain-uses, of which she perhaps was the first discoverer.

"We gain a still clearer insight into the customs of the ancient Hebrews by referring to the ordinance of their great legislator: Deut. xxiii. 12, 13: '*Thou shalt have a place also without the camp, whither thou shalt go forth: And thou shalt have a paddle upon thy weapon; and, it shall be, when thou wilt ease thyself abroad, thou shalt dig therewith, and shalt turn back and cover that which cometh from thee.*'"

Moses undoubtedly learned this of the highly civilized Egyptians. With him, however, it was simply a sanitary measure for the cleanliness of the camp and the health of his followers. Asiatic cholera of our day doubtless is due to the neglect of this simple precaution in the crowded caravans of Mahometan pilgrims over the same Arabian sands, and, at the instigation of the late Emperor of the French, an international commission is now laboring to stop the fountain-head of epidemics in the distant East by enforcing this and other sanitary measures in these immense companies.

The original failure of the Egyptians, before and since the era of Moses, to utilize the waste matter of their bodies was largely due to their fortunate possession of 'chemi' or black sediment deposited upon their inter-vales by the annual overflow of the Nile. After entering the promised land the Israelites borrowed, again of their old masters, the system of drains and sewers, and in their days of prosperity added at Jerusalem aqueducts of great cost, still extant in part through the skill and thoroughness of their construction. This water-supply enabled them to flush their drains and convey their temple and city sewage to pits and tanks whence the liquids could be drawn for irrigation and the solids conveyed to the fields as fertilizers. "In this general arrangement," adds our author, "we can trace perhaps the earliest attempts at utilizing sewage."

Mr. Krepp devotes the next one hundred closely printed octavo pages of his work to a full review of all the various modifications of "Sewerage by Water Carriage," as he styles it, in the leading cities or countries of the world of antiquity, the middle ages and our own times, closing with a sketch of the earth-closet system of late introduction.

His conclusion is that both plans, in whatever form they have been tried, are "utter failures," resulting in an almost universal disbelief that the utilization of sewage is at all practicable; and that, in consequence of this, nearly all excrements produced are thrown into rivers, harbors and the sea, or otherwise wasted, the very few cities utilizing their sewage, in some shape or other, forming as yet only a very small minority.

"On the other hand, it has appeared" (*in his review*) "that human excrements have a very high value indeed, containing as they do the very minerals indispensable to the production of the new crops serving for our food, with also certain organic nitrogenous substances, besides greatly assisting in the formation of the nutritive elements of breadstuffs and other vegetables, and evolving certain fertilizing gases, which will largely increase the harvest if only made to penetrate the soil instead of polluting the atmosphere" as also the water we drink and the earth upon which we dwell.

"The best authorities value fæcal matter at 10s. sterling at least as the annual product of an average individual, giving an increased yield of crops worth £1,000,000 for every million inhabitants; a national wealth, which as yet, in most countries, is nearly all wasted or utterly lost.

"We have found that, to make good this enormous loss, guano, bones and other fertilizers are imported, and all sorts of temporary make-shifts employed, involving a continual serious drain of capital and diminution of national wealth. We have noticed besides, that the guano-beds of Peru are nearly exhausted, and have asked ourselves, What is to become of our agriculture when this foreign supply of manure is cut off?

"Again, we have noticed that, in spite of all the capital continually wasted on these poor palliatives, the soil almost everywhere diminishes in fertility, a given number of acres yielding no longer the same produce they did in former times; that this astounding fact is especially striking in the United States of America, a country acting, with regard to her agricultural interests, somewhat like a fast young heir, squandering in a very short time resources intended and sufficient to last him for his whole life.

"We have seen how bountiful the reward, if we obey the divine Laws of Nature, by applying to our agriculture the most valuable mineral or organic substances daily ejected from our bodies, and how severe the punishment if we neglect to do so, and allow fæcal gases, fluids and solids to pollute our atmosphere, infect our soil and poison our wells" and waters.

"We have also traced the connection between these poisonous exhalations and endemic and epidemic diseases of every kind; and the dictates of plain common sense have invariably shown a polluted atmosphere and tainted earth and water to be everywhere the sure forerunners of sickness and death, while our simple faith teaches us that a beneficent Creator never intended pure air, soil and water to injure our health. The laws of Nature, which are His laws, in this connection are so plainly written that they may well be read and understood by all."

Mr. Krepp devotes the remainder of his invaluable volume to a clear and comprehensive account of Captain Liernur's Pneumatic Sewerage System with illustrative woodcuts, which we regret our inability to copy.

The Captain's leading principles are these:

a. Householders and citizens must not on any account be disturbed by sewerage operations; therefore no dwellings are to be entered for that purpose, by night or by day.

b. For most important sanitary reasons all existing cesspools should be suppressed, and the construction of new ones strictly forbidden by law.

c. All fæcal matter must be daily removed, so that no fermentation can take place.

d. No gases whatever must escape during the removal of excrements, in order to avoid all pollution of the atmosphere.

e. No washing or "flushing" by water must be required (or allowed) so that this sewerage arrangement also answers in towns without "water-works," and that privies may not become offensive when water is cut off or wanting.

f. The privy basin (or hopper) must have no valve or contrivance liable to become deranged, and so give offence.

g. No substance of any kind, whether water, earth, lime, ashes, etc., must be used to dilute or change fæcal matters, as this seriously diminishes or even destroys their agricultural value.

h. Excrements must be so arranged for transport that they can, like any other commodity, be sent any distance to lands requiring fertilizers without emitting the least effluvium.

i. When applied to arable soil, no gases whatever must escape, as this will not only cause a loss of most valuable fertilizing elements, but also convert the atmosphere into a medium for diffusing cholera and other diseases.

k. When applied to meadows, fæcal matters must not be spread on the surface, as this will likewise polute the atmosphere, and cause besides cattle diseases.

l. When applied to arable land or meadows, fæcal matters must never come in contact with the roots of plants, as experience has shown this to be hurtful.

m. The whole sewerage question must be so cheap as not to saddle the poor with heavy rates, or burden municipal bodies with unmanageable debts, or cause the cost of collecting excrements to equal or excel their agricultural value.

"The reader will perhaps think that this is rather a formidable array of requirements, and begin to question whether it is really possible to contrive any plan that will fulfill them all."

Let Captain Liernur's plan speak for itself. The main features are: First, small iron air-tight reservoirs placed under the pavement of all principal street-crossings, and connected by small air-tight iron pipes with, say, 100 house-privies each throughout the city. Every pipe has in it a grate or valve of chilled iron, with a very sharp edge where it enters the cellar-wall, and worked by a lever in front and outside of the house. Within the house, on one or more of the floors, are glazed porcelain hoppers, with air-tight seat-covers, so arranged as to let the discharges of the inmates drop directly down the middle of glazed porcelain upright pipes to an iron pipe beneath the cellar floor, and joining the street-pipe where the gate is placed; a ventilating tube also ascends through the roof from the upright pipe, for the removal of any gas accidentally escaping.

Every night a steam engine, partly drawn also by a horse, comes to the reservoirs, with three men in attendance. The engine creates a vacuum, by an air-pump, in each reservoir. Two of the men then pass rapidly by each other to each gate, open it a moment for the house-pipes to shoot with hurricane velocity their contents into the reservoir, and carefully close the gate for the next twenty-four hours.

When the reservoir has relieved all its own houses, its own contents, solid and liquid, and charged with gas, are pumped by steam into a tender attached to the steamer. These tenders, as fast as they are filled, relays of men forward to the railroad yards, and discharge their loads into strong air-tight casks with screw stoppers, to be transported by freight cars the next morning to the waiting farmers who have ordered them. Thus the whole city is relieved every night the year through, without any disturbance of the house occupants or any annoyance to street passengers.

The farmers, upon receiving the casks, place them, bung down, above their deep-soil ploughs, and discharge the contents in furrows made in the fallow stripes of their fields, and the plough closes the earth over the whole as it goes along.

Here the fertilizers lie in the subsoil till another season, gradually discharging their forces, solid, liquid and gaseous, into the ground about them, the kindly chemistry of nature meantime tempering and qualifying them to meet the needs of next year's growing crops.

The level of the Netherlands, it will be remembered, is below high-water mark; "necessity," therefore, may well be styled, "the mother" of Captain Liernur's "invention." The credit and the possibility of his plan he shares with his illustrious pioneers in pneumatics, steam appliances, and agricultural science of our own day. Chemistry, which can now draw the most delicate and charming colors from the disgusting residuum of our gas-works, in his hand wins also, as wonderfully and as surely, our food and our wealth from the least promising and most disagreeable matter with which man has ever had to deal. Perchance its promise and prophecy lurked ages ago in the name *chemi*, which the ancient Egyptians gave to the fertilizing dark sediment left annually by the Nile upon their teeming fields, and "making her desert like the garden of the Lord," to feed their own vast population with bread, and draw neighboring nations "down to Egypt to buy corn."

The "estimate of cost" must close our article. To reach it, Mr. Krepp takes an "illustrative town" of 100,000 inhabitants. "Supposing," he proceeds, "that a privy-closet and a branch pipe were required on an average for every six-and-a-quarter inhabitants, making thus 16,000 closet-fixtures and pipes, with branch pipes of, say, 100 feet in length, then the cost of the whole pneumatic sewerage system may be estimated, with the average prices, at £350,000. This sum includes twelve air-pump engines (two, for repairs), thirty-three premature tenders (three for repairs); sixty horses; four decanting stations, with all fixtures complete; 10,000 barrels, and all the necessary reservoirs and public urinals besides, with pipes, &c., and all labor and superintendence.

"The annual gross receipts, as derived from crops on a sewage farm, if maintained by the city, or by direct sale of manure, for 100,000 inhabitants, at 10s. per head, would be £50,000."

He adds this schedule:

"Interest on £350,000 capital, at 5 per cent.......	£17,500
Current annual expenses	22,500
Expenses	40,000
Receipts as above	50,000
Clear annual surplus	10,000

The moral, social, sanitary and political gains, we believe, would far outweigh the pecuniary.

The plan commends itself for its simplicity, science and efficiency, and will be tried ere long, we trust, in some of our public institutions or great factories, if not in some of our cities or large towns.

"For we have seen," concludes our author—as every intelligent reader of his exhaustive work must, likewise—"that this new plan is in strict accordance with the laws of Nature: hence it is our solemn duty to comply with them, and not to mar any longer such a beautiful design by an irrational treatment of refuse organic matter.

"If we do so, we may rest fully assured that a higher state of Public Health, a development of agriculture hitherto unknown, and a Permanent National Prosperity, will be our ample reward."

Saved Through a Novel.—The following story is told of Alexander Dumas, at a time when he was writing a serial novel for a Paris daily journal: One day the Marquis de P—— called on him. "Dumas," said he, "have you composed the end of the story now being published in the ——?" "Of course." "Does the heroine die at the end?" "Of course—dies of consumption. After such symptoms as I have described, how could she live?" "You must make her live. You must change the catastrophe." "I cannot." "Yes, you must; for on your heroine's life depends my daughter's." "Your daughter's?" "Yes; she has all the various symptoms of consumption which you have described, and watches mournfully for every number of your novel, reading her own fate in that of your heroine. Now if you make your heroine live, my daughter, whose imagination has been very deeply impressed, will live, too. Come! a life to save is a temptaion—" "Not to be resisted." Dumas changed his last chapter. His heroine recovered and was happy. About five years afterward Dumas met the Marquis at a party. "Ah, Dumas!" he exclaimed, "let me introduce you to my daughter; she owes her life to you. There she is." "That fine, handsome woman, who looks like Joan d'Arc?" "Yes. She is married, and has four children." "And my novel has just four editions," said Dumas, "so we are quits."

THE RELATIONS OF SANITARY INSPECTORS TO THE MEDICAL PROFESSION.

By A. B. Judson, M.D., New York;

With Remarks by Drs. Janes, Russell, and others.

Proceedings of the N. Y. Public Health Association, Sept. 10th, 1874.

As a number of the members of this Association are also members of the Corps of Sanitary Inspectors of the Board of Health, it is becoming in us to review the work of that Corps. Ever since 1866 the Corps has consisted of about twenty medical men. Let us inquire into the quality of the work that has been done by them in these eight years, being assured that the members of the medical profession, who were zealous defenders of the right in the long contest which ended triumphantly by the passage of the Health Law, and who take a lively interest in all that pertains to the Board of Health, are not slow to criticise, in a severe but friendly manner, the results of our labors.

It is useless to deny that the great bulk of the work done in the past, and now daily claiming the attention of Inspectors, is not professional work of the highest kind, even if it can be called professional work at all. Our daily, weary, everlasting round of inspections, complaints, and reinspections, unquestionably results in the removal of many causes of disease. It is only necessary to refer to the vast number of structural improvements that have been made in tenement houses, to the countless instances in which premises have been cleansed, and their occupants thus given a better chance to live happily and healthily, and to the incalculable benefits derived from the moral effect of the frequent presence of the sanitary officer, instructing the ignorant and reproving the careless, in order to give generous credit to the corps for noble work done in the cause of sanitary reform. But the question will recur, is this professional work, or is it the best professional work the Corps is capable of?

It is true that much of the work referred to could not be done so efficiently, and some of it could not be done at all, by persons who have not received professional training. In the routine work of an inspector, his knowledge of the subtle nature of the causes of disease leads him to appreciate at their true importance certain conditions which a non-medical officer would rate as of very little or no consequence. Again, the adaptation of a remedy to a nuisance calls into play the mental processes which are habitually performed by the clinical attendant. In both cases, there is a question of diagnosis and what is indicated. And every sanitary inspector knows that there are many cases in which the diagnosis is by no means easy. I have sought counsel in many cases, especially where the origin of dampness in the walls and foundations has been obscure, and on such occasions have repeatedly and gratefully acknowleged the services of an expert or specialist. And again, there is no question that a word of advice or admonition from an inspector, who speaks with the authority of a medical man, goes much further than would the same word from a non-medical man. And again, it should not be forgotten that, when these places were created, there was a possibility that the rush for office would cripple the service, by causing the appointment of men who could not bring the requisite qualifications. When it was conceded that the appointees should be medical men, there was an assurance that responsible men of more or less studious habits would fill the places of those who formerly combined the functions of health-warden and bar-tender.

There are other reasons besides those mentioned for the appointment of professional men on the Corps of Inspectors; but is there not a deepening impression among those familiar with the work of the Corps that much of its labor could be as well, and more economically, done by laymen, and that medically educated men can be more profitably employed in those kinds of sanitary labor for which they are more especially fitted? It would seem that such thoughts must have passed through the minds of the members of the Corps, as they are called on, year after year, to write their annual reports. A perusal of these productions—but I will not occupy the time of the Association in criticism of this long series of reports, written with care and containing the evidences of a vast amount of very useful routine work. It is enough to say that these reports are now-a-days written with a painful consciousness on the part of the writer that the ground has all been gone over repeatedly and that his only hope of distinction is to present the old subjects with an extra rhetorical flourish or a new arrangement of figures in his statistical table of inspections and reinspections. If these reports are a fair exposition of the labors of the Corps of Inspectors, it must be admitted that the profession at large cannot be satisfied with the part which they perform in the eye of the public through their representatives on the Corps. It is reasonable to suppose that the profession looks for something more than mere routine work from a class of men, picked with nice discrimination from its ranks, clothed by law with authority to enter where they will and ask such questions as they please, and relieved by a salary, more or less liberal, from the exactions of private practice.

Let us glance at the volumes of the Annual Reports of the Health Department, and see what share the medical profession of New York, represented by the Sanitary and Assistant Sanitary Inspectors, have taken in the best work of the Board of Health. They have no share in the immense and valuable labors of the Bureau of Vital Statistics. They have no share in the elaborate and, at times, brilliant work of the Chemists of the Board. In 1868 a Report on the Texas Cattle Disease was written by the Registrar of Vital Statistics, and the Inspectors earned a very small share of the credit that was derived from the facts and observations added thereby to physiological and pathological knowledge. The best articles on Small-pox and Vaccination were written in 1868 by the late Dr. Jonas A. Loines, not an officer of the Board; in 1869 by the Sanitary Superintendent; and in 1871 by the Sanitary Committee. The only systematic study of the mortality in tenement houses was undertaken by the late Norris Randal Norton, a clerk in the office of the Sanitary Superintendent, who wrote two elaborate reports on the subject in 1868 and 1869, the subject being continued in 1870 by the Register of Records. The only microscopical examinations of Croton Water were made in 1869 by the late Dr. William B. Lewis, not an officer of the Board. In 1870 a Report on Yellow Fever was prepared by the late Dr. J. C. Nott, temporarily appointed a Special Inspector; in the same year appeared a Report on Relapsing Fever, by a member of the Sanitary Committee, and a Report on Epidemic Cerebro-spinal Meningitis, by the Sanitary Superintendent. In 1871 appeared two elaborate and suggestive articles, by a member of the Sanitary Committee, one on the Movements of the Tenement House Population, which has deeply stirred the owners of real estate on the island; and the other on the Effects of High Temperature on Public Health, which is the first attempt to deal practically with the great problems connected with our phenomenal summer mortality. In 1872 a Report on the Epizoötic of 1872 was prepared by the Sanitary Committee, with the assistance of the Assistant City Sanitary Inspector, and the Consulting Veterinary Surgeon; and a series of cases in which it was suspected that syphilis had been communicated in the rite of circumcision was investigated, and an important and widely-circulated paper on the subject was written by a medical man, not an officer of the Board.

In all these years what special reports bearing evidence of study have been made by members of the Corps of Inspectors? In 1866 one of them described the bad sanitary condition of Washington Market, and in 1867 two of them wrote a report on the Fat Rendering nuisances conducted on the historic ground lying near the foot of West Thirty-eighth street; and in 1868 one of them, temporarily appointed for special duty, presented a new method of resuscitating the drowned; and then the Corps went to sleep so far as special investigations and reports are concerned. In the annual report for 1872, the last volume issued, there are half-a-dozen brief papers by inspectors on special subjects. These papers are not the result of sustained scientific inquiry, but they are deserving of recognition, as an evidence that an effort has been made to encourage the study by the Corps of Inspectors of special subjects connected with public health. The subjects presented are the following: Tobacco and Cigar Manufactories; Manufacturing Establishments where Lead and Arsenic are used; Cellar Habitations; School Buildings; and the City Prison.

In the above review of the work done by the Board of Health on special sanitary subjects, I have tried to compare fairly the work done by the Corps of Inspectors with that done by the Board without their assistance. The result is not very favorable, and, whether the Corps has been actually criticised or not by the profession on this account, there certainly appears to be good ground for dissatisfaction on the part of the profession with their representatives, for failure to produce more tangible evidence of an ability to do work of a higher kind than they have done, and to make some contribution to the scientific knowledge on which depends the usefulness of both the profession and the Health Department.

I have spoken thus freely of the short-comings of the Corps to which

I belong, because I am well aware that the vast amount of routine labor performed, and the fidelity with which it is done, are thoroughly appreciated by those to whom the facts are known. And I beg those members of the profession who are not members of the Corps of Inspectors, who may hear these remarks, not to interpret them as implying a want on the part of the Sanitary Inspectors of industry or desire to take part in labors more dignified and more satisfactory to themselves as professional men than those to which they have been accustomed.

It is just possible that inquiry may be made in regard to the character of the higher order of work which has been mentioned as appropriate for the medically educated Sanitary Inspector. Such an inquiry could hardly be made by any one who has been brought into personal contact with the subjects which occupy the attention of a sanitary officer. Probably there is no calling which brings into play more than that of the medical officer of health a practical knowledge of all the sciences. Almost all the branches of human knowledge are of use to him in his warfare with the enemies of public health. Is it not then appropriate for such an officer, indeed, is it not the duty of such an officer, not only to become familiar with those sciences which are connected with his duties, but to strive to make new applications of the knowledge already acquired, and even to hope, by industry and perseverance, to increase the sum of what is known?

In bringing these remarks to a close, I will briefly mention three or four subjects among the many which await study by the Sanitary Inspector. I do this the more willingly because in this way it will become clearly evident that the medically educated Inspector is peculiarly fitted for just this kind of work.

Among the destructive diseases which invite investigation, Scarlet Fever stands forth with especial prominence on account of its tremendous fatality, and because it belongs to the order of communicable diseases which are believed to be amenable to preventive measures. It is possible that this disease will at some future time be as much under control as small-pox. In view of this possibility is it not the duty of the Corps of Inspectors to make a systematic study of this terrible disease? An early report of every case is made to the Board of Health. With proper instructions a large proportion of these cases could be inspected, and in many cases the mode of communication, always a difficult thing to trace, could be ascertained. By classification and inference it is fair to suppose that from the study of thousands of cases facts of great value are obtainable. I was once sent to ascertain the facts in regard to a fatal case of scarlet fever in the Fourth Ward. I found a father sore with grief at the loss of his daughter. He was a man of local political influence, and believed he had reason to resent the intrusion of a public officer on such a duty. A few kind words convinced him of the propriety and importance of my errand, and the information which was at first rudely refused was freely given. Though blinded with grief he could see that the faithful performance of the duty in which I was engaged might lead to the protection of the families of his fellow-citizens. I believe the profession would appreciate and welcome inspections of this kind made with due regard to professional etiquette, among the families of their patrons, and that they would not only gladly lend assistance in such investigations, but also take professional pride in the work.

Is there a medical practitioner who has not heard anxious inquiries by heads of families in regard to the influence on health of a proximity to ground freshly excavated for the opening of new streets? What more appropriate work for an Inspector than to study this important question in the upper part of this island? Any facts gained or principles established bearing on this question would be hailed with delight by professional men everywhere, and would be of incalculable benefit in the rapidly growing and multiplying cities of the New World.

The subject of ventilation has in the past occupied the attention of some of the best medical minds. But the present state of knowledge on this subject is far from satisfactory. All acknowledge the importance of fresh air; but no one knows the best way to get it into dwelling-houses and assembly rooms. The best plan in use seems to be, to provide each building with as many modes and devices for securing ventilation as the form and materials of the structure and the money of the building committee will allow, and then to leave the occupants to exercise their discretion. Is it not time that some authoritative utterance was heard on this important subject? The Sanitary Inspector who applies himself to this subject, bringing to the task an innate appreciation of the laws of physics, and unfolding by observation and experiment the principles by following which proper ventilation can be secured, would, in my opinion, be doing appropriate work for an inspector, and work which would raise him and his office in the esteem of his professional brethren.

The question of regulating prostitution is one which must sooner or later come before the sanitary authorities of this city. It has already thrown society in England into a tumult of excited discussion. Could an inspector be better employed—could he be more strictly in the line of his duty, both as a professional man and as an officer of the Health Department, than when making observations and records which shall give the Department the mastery of the situation when this question comes up for discussion?

In mentioning the above subjects, I have taken the first that came to mind. The list of important and absorbing questions which present themselves for the attention of the Sanitary Inspector, is almost infinite in its length. Indeed, the fact that these questions are so numerous as to make a choice difficult is probably one reason why the study of them has not been taken up by the Corps.

Discussion being called for, Dr. E. H. Janes stated that the paper was open to criticism. He was of the opinion that the Corps of Inspectors had done more work of a high order than the paper had given them credit for, and that the Corps was entitled to great praise for the part they had taken in the preparatory work which preceded the Reports on the Cattle Disease and the Epizoötic. It was within his knowledge that inspectors had done very good and very early work in the proceedings which led to the abatement of the gas nuisance, and that a contribution made by an Inspector had added materially to the value of a report on vaccination prepared by the Sanitary Committee. He thought that the inspection and abatement of nuisances was sanitary work of a high order, as it was a practical application of preventive medicine.

Dr. C. P. Russell referred to a recent number of the "British Medico-Chirurgical Journal," in which the work of the Inspecting Corps of this city was highly complimented. He stated that the journal in question presented the work of the inspectors of New York as a model of sanitary work, and referred to it as work of a higher order than that performed by officers of similar grade in the health government of other cities. Remarks were also made by Drs. A. N. Bell, P. de Marmon, and A. B. Judson.

Typhoid Fever.—That this disease may be defied in almost every instance by observing proper precautions, there is no doubt at all. All admit that it has its origin in decaying animal or vegetable matter; probably the former, possibly both. This fact was forcibly impressed on our mind during a late trip in the country. In a remarkably healthy neighborhood we found two families quite a distance apart, too, both having several members down with this disease. One glance at the location of each, instantly told why they were thus attacked while their immediate neighbors escaped. The houses in both instances were old and decaying, and stood in such a position that all water which fell near, and all refuse from the houses, flowed directly to them, and were absorbed by the soil underneath. Here the accumulations of years, perhaps, were rotting; both places had a damp, foul smell about them, and the cause of the fever was at once apparent. Farmers are too apt to think that drainage is all well enough for large cities, but of no use about a farmhouse whatever. This is all wrong; and the first desideratum in choosing a location for a dwelling ought to be that there shall be sufficient slope or elevation to secure good drainage. If this is not practicable, then the structure should be placed at a sufficient height from the ground to allow free ventilation beneath; and this should always be left unobstructed; securing the warmth of the building by very tight floors. Another simple precaution of great value is to have the pit or sink, which almost every family has for the reception of refuse matter, so arranged that no foul vapors can escape. This can be arranged by having a double elbow in the pipe leading to it, so that there will be a constant stratum of water in the elbow, to intercept any nauseous or unhealthy gases, as they escape. By allowing no animal or vegetable matter to decay around the house, and by keeping the ground dry by proper drainage, with such other little sanitary precautions as will suggest themselves to the ordinary thinking mind, this dreaded, lingering, prostrating disease might almost be banished from the land.—*Mining and Scientific Press*.

VACCINATION,—LYMPH OR CRUST?

A CRITICISM OF DR. JOHN MORRIS' PAPER ENTITLED "VACCINATION;—THE COMPARATIVE MERITS OF LYMPH AND THE DRY CRUST."

By Frank P. Foster, M. D.,

Director of the Vaccine Department of the New York Dispensary.

Dr. John Morris, of Baltimore, contributes to the October number of The Sanitarian a paper with the title above given, almost every sentence of which seems to me to embody palpable error; error, too, of a sort particularly apt to do harm. If there is any one thing which, above all else, has been striven for by those who have made vaccination a special study, it is to convince their professional brethren of the dangers of precisely those features of practice which Dr. Morris seeks to inculcate.

The key-note of Dr. Morris' contribution is that efficient vaccination can only be accomplished by using the *crust*, and that a vaccination done with *lymph* is delusive and untrustworthy. Dr. Morris certainly deserves the credit of originality in this matter. For, although there is no lack of men who, in their parsimony, have chosen to use cheap crusts rather than expensive lymph, and then have tried to argue themselves into the notion that their conduct was defensible, and although there are others who have often felt compelled to resort to crusts because they were not aware of the length of time that lymph can be kept in a dry state without losing its activity, or because they were not acquainted with the best methods of preserving it, yet certainly no one ever before was so eccentric as to argue publicly in favor of the superior protection obtained by crust vaccination.

Dr. Morris is correct in one thing, namely, that crusts are not used in Europe, and that they are extensively used in this country. To our shame, this must be confessed. I happen to know, however, that every year they are less and less used with us, indeed, a crust vaccination in this city it now quite rare, and the same may be said of most of the other large towns of our country. Physicians begin to recognize that, with our constantly improving postal and telegraphic means of communication, even practitioners in remote parts of the country may receive from the large cities prompt supplies of fresh lymph, so that they are relieved of the necessity of saving up a crust against emergencies. The use of the crust, then, although still too common, is far from being the method most usually followed in America. In proof of this statement I will mention, that during the year 1873 the New York Dispensary distributed 70,302 quill-slips charged with dried lymph, but only 652 crusts; 20,756 of those quill-slips were sent to Dr. Morris' own State, but only 78 crusts. Nearly all of the slips were supplied to Baltimore. The doctor fails, then, to show that American vaccination is distinctively and *par excellence* crust vaccination. His apparent object in making the attempt is to establish a distinction between vaccination here and in Europe, by means of which supposed distinction he accounts for the alleged comparative immunity of Americans from small-pox.

He avers that, in our small-pox epidemics, the Germans and the Irish, "vaccinated in the European mode," are the principal sufferers. He quotes Dr. Conrad, of the Baltimore Small-pox Hospital, to the effect that, in the epidemic of 1871–2–3, in that city, the Germans fared worse from small-pox than did those of other nationalities, and he does not agree with Dr. Conrad in his disposition to impute this fact to "a peculiar individual susceptibility in the different races." Dr. Conrad's figures are not given, so we must seek elsewhere for precise facts. From the last epidemic of small-pox which swept over our country, no more valuable contribution to the literature of the subject has resulted than the able Report of Dr. W. M. Welch, who was in charge of the Municipal Hospital of Philadelphia, which is to be found in the Report of the Board of Health of the City and Port of Philadelphia, for the year 1872. On page 21 of Dr. Welch's Report I find a table from which I condense the following:

	Natural Small-pox.			Post-Vaccinal Small-pox.		
	Cases.	Deaths.	Deaths per cent.	Cases.	Deaths.	Deaths per cent.
Americans........	232	144	62	419	79	18.85
Germans.........	22	13	59	256	34	13.28
Irish.............	31	21	67.74	79	22	27.84
Other Nativity	16	11	68.75	73	12	16.43
Nativity unknown.	6	5	83.33	3	1	33.33

Adducing the confirmatory facts of the previous year in addition, Dr. Welch remarks, "These figures all show a very marked difference in favor of the vaccinations performed in Germany......These two—the use of fresh eighth-day lymph, and the ingrafting upon the arm numerous vesicles—are the peculiarities which characterize the German mode of practising vaccination......We believe that the Germans owe their better protection more to the quality of the virus which they use than to the numerous insertions which they make." Additional facts, confirming those already quoted, will be found on page 70 of Dr. Welch's Report. In regard to the Irish, while their death-rate was the highest of all, from causes of which we are not informed, vaccination seems to have been with them, more than with either the Americans or the Germans, an efficient protection against the *occurrence* of the disease; that is to say, there was a much greater number of cases of *post-vaccinal* small-pox among the Americans and Germans than among the Irish, although the few which occurred in the latter proved fatal in a greater percentage of cases.

According to the Ninth Census, Philadelphia contained in 1870 a population of 674,022, which included 490,398 natives of the United

States, 50,746 Germans, and 96,698 Irish. Among 490,398 Americans, then, there were 419 cases of post-vaccinal small-pox, or 0.08 per cent. of the American-born population; among 50,746 Germans, 256 cases, or 0.50 per cent. of the German population; and among 96,698 Irish, 79 cases, or 0.08 per cent. of the Irish population. Assuming that there was an equal proportion of vaccinated to unvaccinated in each of the three nationalities, the Americans and the Irish were equally well protected against *an attack* of small-pox, and much better protected than the Germans. As regards *mortality*, however, vaccination saved, in proportion, the most lives among the Germans, fewer among the Americans, and fewest of all among the Irish. On the whole, then, I am unable to deduce from these figures any very marked difference in the protection afforded by vaccination to the three nationalities. It has seemed to many good observers, that the change of climate involved in emigration has a particular tendency to impair the protective influence of vaccination. I do not state this as a fact, but it is nevertheless believed to be such by many judicious writers. If so, we should expect our foreign-born population to suffer more than ourselves in an epidemic of small-pox. From the circumstances of their condition in life, too, we should expect them to fall an easier prey to small-pox. That the results, so far as the Philadelphia experience goes, are not, on the whole, more severe upon the Irish and Germans than upon ourselves, seems to me a striking proof of the efficiency of vaccination "in the European mode."

In the great epidemic which raged in both Europe and America, during the period 1870–73, of the three great cities of the United States, New York, Philadelphia, and Boston, New York suffered the least; yet New York contains a far greater proportion of persons of European birth (vaccinated "in the European mode") than either of the others, and, except perhaps Boston, far fewer of her citizens have been vaccinated with the crust. Indeed, for several years past, the use of crusts in public vaccination in this city has been almost unknown.

Facts, then, do not warrant Dr. Morris' statement, that crust vaccination is superior to lymph vaccination as a protective agent. I presume that no one will be disposed to deny that it is *equally* protective except in this respect, that, from its tardiness in exciting the formation of the vesicle, it is not so well fitted to outstrip the variolous infection in cases where vaccination is performed after exposure to small-pox. There are certain objections to the use of the crust—many of them mentioned, indeed, by Dr. Morris, but mentioned only to be overridden by his assertions—which need not now be referred to. The great objection to the crust, however, is, that it so frequently fails to impart the vaccine disease. This statement is at direct variance with what Dr. Morris says, but it certainly expresses the general experience of those who have had most to do with vaccination.

My own experience with crusts, at the New York Dispensary, from the spring of 1866 to the winter of 1871, has not been large, as we never made use of them except when we were unable to get fresh lymph. Under such circumstances, of the primary vaccinations done with crusts, 350 were inspected, resulting in 95 successes and 255 failures—a success of only 27.14 per cent. Since the autumn of 1870 we have used the animal virus almost exclusively, and as we have always been able to get this, we have used no crusts. Up to the beginning of the current year, our success with this lymph was 93.52 per cent. Occasionally a crust yields excellent results. Such was the case with a few of those that we used. Such crusts cannot, however, be distinguished beforehand from those which are inert. Neither typical formation nor known freshness is any guarantee of their possessing energy.

Dr. Morris not only objects to lymph, but he particularly objects to lymph taken from the vesicle before the formation of the areola, which he alludes to as Jenner's "much-prized areola test." Does not Dr. Morris know that the areola, in the opinion of Dr. Jenner and of all subsequent vaccinators, so far as it has been looked upon as a test of anything, has been viewed simply as a test of *systemic infection*, and not at all as a desirable feature of an arm from which lymph is to be taken, but indeed the very reverse? Has he never heard of Jenner's "golden rule?"

To sustain his statement that European is inferior to American vaccination, Dr. Morris says: "Mr. Marson reports that in six months, out of 751 cases admitted to the (London) small-pox hospital, 618 or 82 per cent. were in vaccinated persons. We are convinced that no such result could follow in this country." According to Dr. Welch's Report, above referred to, of 1,137 cases in the Philadelphia Municipal Hospital, 830, or 72.99 per cent., occurred in vaccinated persons. The difference is not startling. Dr. Morris will find that in almost every epidemic the post-vaccinal cases far outnumber those of natural small-pox. At first sight this may seem surprising, but it is easily explained by the fact that, in civilized countries, almost everybody has been vaccinated, therefore, if only a very small percentage of the vaccinated persons were attacked, those who were attacked would still outnumber the non-vaccinated.

As the consideration of animal vaccination is only a side issue in Dr. Morris' paper, I shall notice only his statement, that "in this country it has gained no new adherents." At the present day let us all be thankful for it; no scientific man is an "adherent" of anything. If, however, Dr. Morris means that animal vaccination is not considered trustworthy by a large and respectable portion of the American profession, I would refer him to certain figures in my last Annual Report*, contributed by well-known physicians of Boston, *Baltimore*, and Buffalo; and in particular I would commend to his attention the following extract from a letter dated March 29, 1873, which I received from his townsman Dr. W. T. Jones, the Maryland State vaccine agent: "Enough has been known," says Dr. Jones, "to prove the great superiority of the animal over the humanized lymph. Many persons will not submit to any vaccination unless it be done with the *quills*. The whole profession here, who have used it, pronounce in favor of it."

In conclusion, let me express myself as always eager to do honor to any one who puts on record a well-considered statement of facts, however those facts may tell against received views; but I cannot refrain from saying that Dr. Morris might well have hesitated to publish such *bizarre* doctrines as form the pith of his contribution on such slim data.

* In the Eighty-fourth Annual Report of the Board of Trustees of the New York Dispensary, New York, 1874.

THERMOMETRICAL AND ELECTRICAL NOTES IN THE PROSECUTION OF NEW THEORIES OF DISEASE.*

By H. L. Bartlett, M. D., Consulting Surgeon to Kings County Hospital.

Having demonstrated the limits of animal heat, compatible with human life, I now turned my attention to its causes. To this end, I availed myself of my position as Physician-in-Chief of the Buncombe County General Hospital, and have honestly and impartially tried, as far as it can be done by experimentation, to settle this choleric question. In relating these experiments, I shall present the bare facts, leaving it for other scientists to discover whether I have told the naked truth or not.

As there are, undoubtedly, several causes that tend to elevate the temperature of the body, I determined, in the warmth of my enthusiasm, to test each in turn, and so to begin my experiments with spirit. I selected one of my patients,whose temperature was normal, and placed a thermometer under each axilla, one under each eyelid, one in each ear, and one between each of his fingers and toes, noting each instrument on diagrams, prepared for this purpose, and stationing a trusty assistant at each, to watch and note the probabilities.

I at once administered an ounce of brandy every ten minutes. The first three doses elevated, both the patient and the mercury, one degree each, but what was quite unexpected, when ten ounces had been given, the mercury had fallen 2° F. below normal, thus proving the popular idea correct, viz. : that liquor warms you when cold and cools you when warm. The next day, I placed the patient in the same position, and administered chloroform. At first, the mercury rose as before, but more quickly fell off again below normal. At this point, I resolved upon a bold move, which was nothing less than to paralyze the heart, and depress the temperature to near the minimum, depending upon electricity to revivify the body. Accordingly, I plied the chloroform till the heart ceased beating, and all consciousness had fled! Down, down, went the mercury, till it neared the fatal point, when I suddenly thrust two needles, connected with the poles of a powerful galvanic battery deep into the extremities of the spinal cord, and set the current moving. Soon as thought a slight thrill vibrated along the nerves, the limbs were convulsed, the heart resumed its play, and warmth and life returned. In a short time the patient had so far recovered, as to favor us with a weird German song, at the conclusion of which, he politely drank to our health, in an imaginary cup of lager, and quietly fell asleep, dreaming, no doubt, of his beloved "Faderland!"

I next resolved to try the effect of opium upon the temperature. Having a male assistant, addicted to the inordinate use of this drug, I

---

* Continued from p. 259 (September number).

selected him for my experiment. After having quarantined him for fourteen days, so as to eliminate the opium already in his system, I administered three ounces of McMunn's Elixir, but the effect was so soporific, not to say terrific, that at the expiration of two hours, I began to fear my next duty would be to administer upon his estate!

The temperature was elevated at first, but not to the same extent, nor for as long a period, as in the former experiment. In less than thirty minutes, the heat was below normal, and gradually lessened till, at the end of two hours, it had reached 92° F., with a tendency still downwards. I then applied the galvanic needles as before, and, though it produced convulsive movements of the limbs, still the vital powers seemed to flag. I next resorted to Marshall Hall's method of artificial respiration, together with friction and castigation, but alas! with no better results; the mercury was slowly tending to that point I had already demonstrated to be mortal! No time was to be lost, if I would vindicate the glory of our art. This apparently lifeless body must be resuscitated, or "*Tekel*" would be forever written over the tomb of Physic! Thanks to the science of medicine, Mr. President, our skill was not found wanting. I bethought me, that in an adjoining shed there was a healthy calf, which I kept there for propagating vaccine-virus and for emergencies like the present connected with the public *weal*. With all possible dispatch it was brought, and by means of "Dieulafay's Aspirator" the blood of the calf was sent coursing through the veins of the patient, and "*mirabile dictu*" he lives again! In a short time he was sitting up in bed, and although at first he seemed somewhat *cowed*, by the prospect of *cremation*, he soon regained sufficient vitality to declare, with more energy than elegance, "He would send to grass any bloody calf who should try to *bully* him again!" Concluding he only required plenty of (h)*air* to *ox-id-ize* his blood, I left him to ruminate, no doubt, upon the mysteries of the *Milky Way*. I now turned my attention to the effect of electricity. Among my patients was a bald-headed, wry-visaged pig-headed paralytic; who, during a long sojourn in the Institution, had exhibited more linguistic accomplishments than any person heretofore lisping the English tongue. In fact, he seemed to be a complete phonetic battery, created to demonstrate that law of compensation so often seen in nature, for the activity of all his paralyzed nerves seemed concentrated in his hypoglossal! After some difficulty I placed him in the position above described (for he would voluntarily submit to nothing), and securing one pole of the battery in the great toe of his right boot, and the other to the back of his neck, I ordered my assistants to note the mercury and set the current moving.

Mr. President, the most remarkable phenomena were produced that it has ever been my lot to witness! The mysterious borealis that sometimes illumines the northern pole was as nothing to the scintillations of iridescent light that played majestically around his! Each liliputian hair stood alternately perpendicular, oblique and horizontal, emitting all the while flashes of electric light dazzling to behold. His eyes ejected fire, "like lightning from a summer's cloud." But, his *tongue—his tongue*, Mr. President, was a miracle of motion—a very babel of sounds. Commencing on a low note, he would run the entire gamut without a quaver, or even a semi-quaver, in his crotchety voice. Then he would regale our senses with a grand symphony of all imaginable sounds ever heard on earth, in sea or sky, while at the same time, an inaudible vibration ran along the palsied nerves, the muscles were alternately contracted and relaxed, the joints cracking like the wheels of a superannuated carriage. Then his limbs would be jerked asunder, and as suddenly drawn underneath him again, and he would sit up *à la* Turk. Instantly, he would balance himself on one foot, and twirl himself with the rapidity of thought, his arms flying wildly in mid-air. Then he would stand upon his head, his nether extremities describing every kind of motion known to mathematicians, till, finally, he vaulted into the air with such force and velocity, that the wire severed, and the galvanic current was broken. When he descended, he landed in the middle of the room, his body erect, and glowing with a suffused redness, his arteries throbbing with a vigor and a warmth preternatural, his nostrils distended, his eyes dilated, and brilliant with unwonted fire. In fine, his person had more the look and mien of a being celestial than one of mortal mould. Soon his lips parted, and his tongue moved, but inaudibly, while with eyes directed heavenward, his palsied hands waved us a refrain he could no longer utter!

Owing to the peculiar circumstances of the case, I was not able to record either his impressions or the temperature of his body. The latter must have been very great, however, for the mercury stood 120° F. two hours after death!

I now determined to turn my attention to the effect of food upon the temperature. My experiments in this direction were numerous and varied, but I shall only relate the most extraordinary.

I had in the Institution over which I presided a female nurse, who had grown uselessly *obese* from the number of milk punches and extra dinners she had purloined from the patients under her charge. In fine, she had been there so long that she had imbibed the idea that she was entitled to a fat place. I therefore concluded that it would be no more than an act of simple justice to that public she had so unselfishly served, should I use her *pro bono publico*, even if her bony parts were *de-adiposed* by such proceedings.

I therefore relieved her of all active duties, fitted up a room for her especial accommodation, and told her with all possible gravity and earnestness that I feared her arduous duties had been too much for her delicate constitution, and especially I feared that her solicitude for the sick had deprived her of so much sleep, that I began to entertain serious apprehensions in regard to her future welfare, and deprecated in glowing terms the possible loss of so *weighty* an attaché. I informed her that I feared she was a victim—a self-immolated holocaust to fatty degeneration, and that nothing could possibly save her but an observance of the strictest rules of diet. She replied, "she knew she belonged to a fat generation, but as she did not want to die yet, she would observe any rules I might prescribe." I therefore next day, after noting and recording her temperature, pulse, respiration, weight and general appearance, began by administering a drachm of Cayenne pepper in a pint of saturated infusion of green tea, every hour. The effect was immediately appreciable, beginning with a temperature of 97° F.; at the expiration of the first hour the thermometer had jumped up 2° F., and thus continued to rise until when seven drachms had been given; it had reached the alarming attitude of 111° F., and I had some *scruples* about giving her more. In fact, Mr. President, all my energies had now to be directed in the opposite direction. On closer examination I found her much in the condition of a locomotive overdriven and overheated – only locomotion in her case was impossible, even with the assistance of a *tender*. Her whole body was glowing like a furnace in full blast—not a boreal blast; her face was livid and shone like a phlegmonous carbuncle, (not the precious stone), her eyes glared wildly like an affrighted basilisk, her tongue protruded from her mouth, and exhaled a sickly odor, much resembling the smell of bilge-water when a ship is on fire, and the heaving of her expansive chest and beating of her tumultuous heart were more wonderful to see and hear than the wildest storms of old ocean. Indeed had it not been for the resources of our art, I am confident I should have had then and there a case of spontaneous combustion.

I at once injected 20 grs. of quinine, with an hypodermic syringe, which in a few moments produced the most gratifying results in quieting her heart, and as soon as she could swallow, I gave her half an ounce of Squibbs Fl. ex.-ergot, which demonstrated most conclusively that Dr. Brown-Sequard's theory must be correct, for in less than five minutes there was such a contraction of the striated textures of the body, that she was thrown into the most violent convulsions, and had I not hypodermically injected four drops of amyl, I fear she would have been so far dejected that no human power could have saved her. However, by the use of my Refrigeratorium, I was enabled to cool her body to its natural temperature in about ten days. Alas! her adipose had vanished, and her dried skin hung in ample folds about her emaciated form. She remarked that she felt as though she had been shipwrecked, with ballast and cargo thrown overboard, and she longed for a safe harbor, where she could becalm herself.

Patients dosed with ginger, mustard, Worcestershire sauce and aromatic spirits of ammonia all exhibited nearly the same symptoms as above described.

Having tested the effects of food and medicine, I now determined to try those of muscular motion on the temperature of the body. It was with considerable difficulty that I could at first devise a plan whereby all the causes of animal heat should be excluded. I had already demonstrated that a wonderful amount of muscular motion could be produced by galvanism, but here was the specific influence of electricity upon the nerve centres. I could have given some medicines which would have produced a violent gastralgia, or hypodermically introduced something that would have caused the contraction of every muscle in the body, striated as well as nonstriated, but I feared the consequences. I could have had the patient practice gymnastics, but even in this sort of exercise there is more or less of mental excitement. I finally hit upon the following plan : I floored a room with brick, under which was a furnace, so constructed as to heat it sufficiently warm to make it quite uncomfortable to stand upon, and yet not so hot as to burn the feet, piercing the centre of which was an iron tube about four inches in diameter, also heated. The patient being placed in this room, balanced himself first on one foot and then on the other, till the muscles of the limbs were thoroughly fatigued. For relief he was obliged to climb this tube, the only object in the room to which it was possible for him to cling, and the constant change of position this made necessary, brought into play every muscle of the body, and the amount of caloric so produced was truly remarkable. In fact, the heat of his body became so great at the expiration of one hour and five minutes, viz. : 111° F., that I was not only obliged to remove the patient from the room, but actually had to resort to my Refrigeratorium ! Having thus demonstrated, at least to the entire satisfaction of my patient, the elevating effect of muscular contraction, it was only necessary in order to make my record complete, to ascertain what would be the result of purely mental excitement, in this direction.

This experiment I tried upon one of my assistant physicians. He was a vigorous, florid-complexioned, red-headed man, with a large brain and excitable temperament. Having previously arranged everything for the trial, and prepared as far as might be for any emergency, I invited him into my room and requested him to sit down in a new operating chair I had just purchased. He was ignorant of my design, and, of course, readily complied. I now fastened him into the chair in such a manner that it was impossible for him to move a muscle of his body. I then informed him, with great gravity, that I was exceedingly pained and mortified to learn that he had been so recreant to the high trust and confidence I had reposed in him, that the patients and nurses of the hospital had repeatedly and bitterly complained of his indolence, inhumanity and incompetency, and that I could no longer remain silent. He must now and here answer these charges, or be forever branded a villain ! Thereupon the nurses, some fifty or more in number (previously instructed), filed into the room—each one clamorously accused him of all possible dereliction of duty, and heaped every sort of calumny and abuse upon his devoted head. The effect was truly wonderful. No experiment I had ever tried, not even the administration of capsicum, had increased the temperature half so fast. In less than thirty minutes the thermometer under the axilla stood 111° F., and a differential thermometer, applied to the head, recorded the unprecedented altitude of 113° F. ! This trial showed conclusively, that of all agencies, mental excitement is the most potent in generating animal heat. The question now was, could we save our patient ? I had plunged my thermometer into abscesses, dropsical chests, and abdomens, trephined skulls, incised hernias, Cæsareaned uteri, and lithotomised cysts, but had never seen the mercury take such a flight in living flesh ! To save the life of my assistant would be an act of humanity, but to bring the mercury down successfully from such a height would be worthy of a Harvey ! I thereupon immediately released him from the chair, and assured him that the whole thing was a joke in the interests of science. The nurses, in turn, fell on their knees, and, with tears in their eyes, declared they were not in earnest, and craved his pardon. He comprehended them not, and only gazed at them with a dazed look, like one stunned with a mortal wound. The blood-vessels of the head and neck continued swelling, till his face and very scalp became the color of a freshly boiled lobster, and his hair, like the quills of an enraged porcupine, stood erect, blazing wlth an inextinguishable fire! I at once injected hypodermically, quinea, ergotine and amyl, and gave an ounce of bromide of potassium internally, but all to no purpose. I then resorted to my Refrigeratorium, which only cooled the body, still leaving the cranium as hot as before. In fact, his face and head at this juncture had more the appearance of a young Vesuvius, on the eve of an eruption, than of anything appertaining to humanity.

Not an instant was to be lost, and in the desperation of the moment, I cut open and temporarily tied both carotids, and thus vindicated the glory of our art, and saved the life of my worthy assistant!

Salt in The Seas.—Many people imagine that the ocean water is naturally salt, and will be surprised to know that the salt comes from rocks, and is washed into the sea.

The sea depends on the disintegration of rocks on land for its saltness. It does not originate in oceans and seas. Rains wash it and hold it in solution as particles are liberated by violence, decomposition and gradual action of many natural forces. All streamlets and rivers, therefore, are constantly transporting salt to the sea. If there is more than can be held in solution, then it accumulates in masses at very deep points, which, in the revolution to which matter is subject, may again be a stratum of salt somewhere remote from where the mass was found. Thus the salt mines of Portland, and the vast horizontal beds of pure salt in Texas, as well as that mountain of rock salt in St. Domingo, were collected at the bottom of ancient seas, which are now dry land remote from water.

There are places in Africa where the process of disintegration of salt from rock is regularly going on, but there is not water-power enough to force it onward to the sea. Hence the particles are spread abroad and mixed with the soil. The negroes of Northern Africa having discovered its distribution where there is no water to dissolve in the ground, leach it. In that way they separate the salt. By evaporating the water holding it in solution, an excellent article for domestic purposes is produced. Salt pervades the earth. It exists in the grasses and most vegetable products on which animals feed. In that way they derive enough in most countries to meet the demands of their natures. They require as much as civilized humanity. With them salt is necessary, as with ourselves, for keeping the organs of vision in good condition. Stop the supply, and blindness would ensue.

QUARANTINE.

The following are the conclusions arrived at by the recent International Sanitary Conference, held at Vienna, upon the subject of Maritime Quarantines, after long and animated discussions:

I. Measures to be Taken out of Europe.

With the object of preventing further invasions of cholera in Europe, the conference approves the measures recommended by the Constantinople Conference (1866), particularly the measures of quarantine suggested in the Red Sea and the Caspian Sea. The organization of these measures should be of the most complete description, and such as to satisfy the most rigorous principles of hygiene.

Measures to be Taken in European Ports.

When the cholera has invaded Europe, the conference recommends the subjoined system of medical inspection; but in the case of States which prefer to maintain quarantine, it submits the principles upon which it should be regulated.

(A) *System of Medical Inspection.*

1. There should be established in each port open to commerce a sanitary authority formed of physicians and local representatives, aided by a proper staff. The number of members in each of these different categories will vary according to the importance of the port; but the number should be sufficient to permit of the measures exacted with regard to ships, crews, and passengers being carried out rapidly under all circumstances. The principal officer of the sanitary authority will always be kept informed through official sources of the sanitary state of all ports infected with cholera.

2. Ships arriving from clean (healthy) ports, and which, according to the oath of the captain, have not touched in the course of their voyage at an intermediate suspected port, or communicated directly with a suspected ship, and in which, during the voyage, no actual or suspected case of cholera has occurred, will be admitted to free pratique.

3. Ships arriving from a suspected or infected port, and those coming from unsuspected ports, but which, during the voyage, have had intermediate compromising relations, or on board which suspected cases of, or deaths from cholera may have occurred, will be submitted, on arrival, to a rigorous medical examination, in order to determine the sanitary state of the crew and passengers.

4. If it results, from the medical examination, that no case of sickness, or the corpse of any person dead from cholera exists on board, the ship, with all it contains, will be admitted to free pratique; unless cases of cholera, or of a suspicious nature, have occurred during the voyage, when the ship, the clothing, and the luggage of the crew and

passengers will be submitted first to a thorough disinfection, although both crew and passengers be then free from cholera.

5. If any suspected case of cholera, or death from cholera, be found on board, the sick will be at once removed to a lazaret or to an isolated place provided for the purpose, and the dead will be cast into the sea with customary precautions, or will be buried after fitting disinfection; the passengers and crew will be thoroughly disinfected, and the ship itself will also be disinfected after the removal of the passengers and such portions of the crew as may not be necessary for the disinfection and charge of the vessel. The clothing and luggage of the sick, and also of the healthy passengers, will be subjected, in special premises and under rigorous control of the sanitary authority, to a thorough disinfection. After this disinfection the property of the passengers and crew will be restored to them, and they will be admitted to free pratique.

6. The merchandise landed will be admitted to free pratique, with the exception of rags and other susceptible objects, which will be subjected to thorough disinfection.

(B) *System of Quarantine.—Arrivals from Infected Ports.*

1. Arrivals from infected ports should be submitted to from one to seven full days' observation, according to circumstances.

2. *Suspected Ships.*—If the sanitary authority is satisfied that no case of cholera or of a suspicious nature has occurred on board during the voyage, the duration of observation should be from three to seven days, dating from the time of the medical inspection. If, however, the voyage has lasted at least seven days, the time of observation may be reduced to twenty-four hours, for the examination and disinfection which may be judged necessary. In cases of this category the quarantine of observation may be completed on board if no case of cholera or any suspicious sickness has occurred, and the hygienic condition of the ship be good. In such cases, unlading of the ship is not necessary.

3. *Infected Ships.*—If any case of cholera or of suspicious sickness has occurred during the voyage, or after the arrival, the duration of observation for the healthy should be seven full days, dating from their isolation in a lazaret or other place provided for them. The sick should be landed and subjected to proper treatment in an isolated locality set apart for them, and separated also from the place where the healthy undergo observation. The ship and all objects in it susceptible of retaining infection are to be submitted to a thorough disinfection, after which the persons remaining on board the ship will be subject to seven days' observation.

4. *Arrivals from Suspected Ports.*—Arrivals from suspected ports—that is to say, from ports adjoining and having free communication with a port where cholera exists—should be submitted to observation not exceeding five days in duration, if no suspicious sickness has happened on board.

5. *Various Regulations.*—Ships carrying emigrants and pilgrims, and generally all ships considered peculiarly dangerous to the public health, may, under the conditions previously noted, be subjected to special pre-

cautions to be determined by the sanitary authority of the port of arrival.

6. When the local resources do not permit of the measures herein prescribed being carried out, the infected ship should be sent to the nearest lazaret, after having received such aid as she may need.

7. A ship arriving from an infected port, which has put into an intermediate port, and received there free pratique without having performed quarantine, is to be considered and treated as arriving from an infected port.

8. In cases of simple suspicion, measures of disinfection are not strictly requisite, but they may be carried out if the sanitary authority thinks fit.

9. A port in which cholera prevails epidemically should not carry out quarantine proper so called, but should solely have recourse to measures of disinfection.

(C) *Regulations common to the Two Systems.—Medical Inspection and Quarantine.*

1. The captain, the medical officer, and the officers generally should be required to declare to the sanitary authority all that they know with regard to suspicious sickness among the crew and passengers, subject to penalty in the event of a false declaration or of deliberate concealment. It is to be desired that an international agreement should be come to on this subject.

2. The disinfection either of luggage or of ships will be effected in such manner as the competent authorities of each country may determine.

British Emigrants.—The Emigration Commissioners in Great Britain have recently published some statistics showing the total emigration from the United Kingdom for every year from 1815 to 1872 inclusive. The totals for each period of five years are also given. In the first of these, that is from 1815 to 1819 inclusive, the number of emigrants was 97,799; from 1820 to 1824, 95,030; from 1825 to 1829, 121,084; from 1830 to 1834, 381,956; from 1835 to 1839, 287,358; from 1840 to 1844, 465,577; from 1845 to 1849, 1,029,209; from 1850 to 1854, 1,638,945; from 1855 to 1859, 800,640; from 1860 to 1864, 744,111; from 1865 to 1869, 1,064,983, and during the last three years, 804,588. Thus, in all, 7,561,285 persons have emigrated during the last fifty-eight years from the United Kingdom, of whom 4,905,262 came to the United States, 1,456,647 to the North American colonies, 1,016,526 went to Australia and New Zealand, and 182,850 to other places. It is to be remembered, however, that many of these emigrants were not natives of the United Kingdom. For instance, in 1872 the number of foreigners who emigrated through England was 79,023, or 26.76 per cent. of the whole emigration, and the proportion seems to be annually increasing, while the numbers of English who emigrate do not keep pace with those of most other nationalities.

CONTAMINATED WATER.

LAKE MAHOPAC AND THE GREGORY HOUSE.

By General Egbert L. Viele, C. E.

The facility with which water absorbs impurities makes it the great source of disease, especially in rural districts, where it is so universally exposed to contact with vegetable and animal decomposition.

A timely article in The Sanitarian, for September, called attention to this important subject in terms which should be reiterated every month and every day in the month, until the recklessness of ignorance shall yield to the care and foresight which an intelligent acquaintance with the laws of health cannot fail to produce. It is a good indication of sanitary reform that people are beginning to charge criminality where death is produced by preventable causes; and when the violators of the laws of health shall come to be held to criminal responsibility, and be punished with the same rigor and severity as the transgressors against ordinary statutes, then will begin the true era of sanitary reformation.

A recent occurrence at one of the most attractive and most frequented places of summer resort in the neighborhood of New York, which resulted in several fatal cases of illness, has attracted some notice from the press, and, as it illustrates with particular force the subject of water contamination, should receive careful consideration.

On the night of the thirtieth of June, 1874, a number of the inmates of the Gregory House, at Lake Mahopac, were simultaneously affected with a disturbance of the bowels, accompanied by nausea, and, on the following day, as also on several successive days, a number of others were similarly affected, while many were only slightly disturbed, resulting in several fatal cases of typhoid fever. The cause for this extraordinary state of affairs was sought for in vain.

Lake Mahopac itself and all its surroundings is one of the most salubrious and beautiful spots in America. It has been a favorite place of resort for many years by thousands of people, who have derived incalculable benefit from its pure bracing mountain air, and has been more particularly attractive on account of the remarkable purity of its water, all the numerous hotels being supplied from the Lake, which is one of the principal sources of the Croton water which the city of New York receives through its magnificent aqueduct.

This lake has been called the American Windemere, and certainly there are few spots either in America or Europe which can rival it in natural beauty. Impressed with this fact, a number of gentlemen of taste and capital became, a few years ago, the purchasers of a large portion of the surrounding territory, and also of several of the hotels, with a view to adding to the profuse charms, of which nature had been so lavish, all that art and skill could do to perfect it as a summer residence. The leading features of the expensive and elaborate plan of improvement which was adopted were the sanitary provisions embraced in it. Notwithstanding all this, a fatal disease breaks out, and for some time runs its course, while the cause is a hidden mystery. All the surrounding circumstances seem to preclude the possibility of such a disaster. The place is a purely summer resort. It is especially prepared for this purpose by all the appliances that taste and skill and money can command. No thickly settled neighborhood, or manufactory, or nuisance of any kind exists to vitiate the air in the slightest degree. The immediate grounds of all the hotels are kept scrupulously clean: shady groves, velvet lawns, and parterres of flowers are on every side. In front is the superb lake, with its water clear as crystal. In vain would an observer look for the least cause of disease; yet sickness did occur, and that, too, from a preventable cause. It was discovered, after an elaborate and expensive examination, and the uncovering of water pipes and sewage conduits, to have arisen from a cause so simple, and yet so effective, and so dangerous, while it was at the same time, so hidden and so remote, that nothing but the determined efforts of the proprietor of the hotel, after innumerable failures, succeeded in unveiling it. In less than fifteen minutes the cause was removed: no other case of sickness occurred from that moment, nor can it possibly ever occur again from that source. The circumstances, however, were such as might occur anywhere; and, for that reason are now referred to in detail.

The "Gregory House" is named after a former proprietor, Dr. Gregory. It was purchased, with other property, by the Lake Mahopac Improvement Company, and Dr. Gregory ceased to have any connection with it. The arrangements of sewerage and water supply had been constructed under his supervision, and although not as perfect as they might have been, seemed to have successfully served the purpose for a number of years. The water was conveyed from the lake to the hotel through earthenware pipes into a brick reservoir by gravitation, and as the ground in rear of the hotel is lower than the surface of the lake, the water flows into a hydraulic ram, whence it is forced into the house. The construction of a large extension to the hotel necessitated the use of a small steam engine. and for this purpose another reservoir connected with the first one was built under the building to supply the water for the steam engine. Subsequently to this a steam laundry was constructed, and the new engine did the work of the laundry and the pumping for the house; consequently the use of the smaller engine and *its reservoir* was discontinued. The connection, however, between the two reservoirs was, by a most stupid and criminal blunder, not cut. The new proprietor knew nothing of this connection; it was hidden deeply under ground, and when the continued and copious rains of the last week in June found access to the disused reservoir, already containing impure water, a flow of poisoned water through the former connection took place into the reservoir then in use, and the fatal cases of typhoid fever was the result. Dr. Gregory was certainly reprehensible for not discontinuing the connection between the two reservoirs when one of them was disused, and if it is true that a subsequent proprietor, Ramsay, stated, while the sickness was raging, that he knew the cause but would not divulge it for less than one thousand dollars, he ought to be indicted and punished.

A cause so fatal and yet so easily remedied, so apparently insignificant, and yet so powerful for evil, should attract attention to this case, and induce a most careful examination of all the surroundings of our summer hotels and watering places.

Editor's Table.

THE PUBLIC HEALTH.

New York, Oct. 5, 1874.—*To the Editor of the Sanitarian*:—In no previous summer, during the sixty-eight years in which the records of mortality have been kept in this city, has the general state of the public health been more favorable than during the past three months. The total number of deaths in the thirteen weeks ending on the 26th of September was 8,509. Of this number 5,131, or 69.30 per cent. of the whole, were of children under five years of age, and 3,524 were of infants that had not seen their first birthday; that is, 41.40 per cent. of the total mortality was of the class of nurslings under a year old, and of which a census would probably find about 26,500 living in the city. The number of deaths of children between the ages of two and five years was only 619 in the thirteen weeks. The death-rate in the city during this quarter of the year was equal to 32.72 per 1,000 of the living inhabitants annually.

The total number of deaths in the city in the four weeks ending on the 26th of September was 2,289. Of this number 1,211 were of children under five years of age, and 752 of infants under a year old. The death-rate in the city for the month of September was equal to 28.61 in the 1,000 inhabitants annually. The mortality of children under five years of age was equal to 54.04 per cent. of the whole, but the death-rate in that portion of the inhabitants (88.2 per cent. of the population, or 917,280) who are five years of age and upwards, was only equal to 14.90 in the 1,000 annually. The rate in the children and infants under five years of age (they constituting 11.8 per cent. of the population) was equal to 131.04 per 1,000 of the whole. Zymotic diseases are charged with 989 of the 2,288 deaths in the last month. 39 of these were from small-pox, 54 from scarlatina, 77 from diphtheria, 29 from enteric fever, and 547 from diarrhœal diseases. Only 46 of the deaths by diarrhœal diseases were of persons over twenty-one years of age. There were 306 deaths by phthisis, 166 by pneumonia and bronchitis, 152 by diseases of the brain and nervous system. 381 deaths, or 16.64 per cent. of the whole number for the month, occurred in hospitals and other institutions.

The weather was favorable to health throughout the month of September. The mean temperature for the four weeks ending Sept. 26th, was 70.6° Fahr.; the average humidity was equal to $\frac{7}{100}$ of total saturation; the winds traveled at the mean rate of 115 miles a day, and the total rain-fall was equal to 7.60 inches depth of water. The severe drouth was attended by a largely increased mortality in the undrained portions of the Westchester annexed wards, and the great rain was followed by a decided decrease in mortality in all the densely populated wards. The cleansing of the surface of the city, and the purification of the atmosphere of crowded localities, were signally beneficial to the tenement-house population. The city is free from epidemics, except that diphtheria, which for eleven months has prevailed with unprecedented fatality, still vexes many portions of the city, especially in the district lying between Canal street and the Central Park. E. Harris, M. D., *Registrar*.

Brooklyn, Oct. 7th, 1874.—*To the Editor of the Sanitarian*:—In the last issue of your journal you state that it is evident, from the data given in the reports for the years 1871, 2, and 3, that the death rate from preventable diseases is on the increase. If you will examine carefully the reports for 1872 and '73, you will find that in 1873 the mortality from zymotic causes was $2\frac{1}{4}$ per cent. less than that of 1872, and I have compiled the mortality for the first nine months of this year, and I find that for the same period of last year there were 2,817 deaths due to zymotic influences, and for the first nine months of this year, 2,864, this being a difference of 47 in favor of 1873. But this maybe explained by the following facts: Diphtheria, during 1873, to Oct. 1, caused 166 deaths, while during the same period in 1874 there were 323 deaths assigned to that cause, thus showing a difference from this cause alone of 157 deaths; thus the deaths from zymotic other than diphtheria, is 110 less in nine months of 1874 than corresponding months of 1873. The total mortality for the same period was, in 1873, 8,589 while in 1874 it was 8,288, or 301 less for the present year to date, Sept. 30th; and while our total death-rate is less, we must remember that our population is on the increase of at least 12,000 per annum.

The whole number of deaths from all causes during the month of September, was 980, or 25.11 per thousand; the largest number from any one cause was, from cholera infantum, 122, or 153 less than occurred during the previous month. Phthisis pulmonalis, 120. This is 25 in excess of what occurred last month, and probably due to the sudden changes in the atmosphere; diphtheria, 41; scarlatina, 27; marasmus, 68; pneumonia, 25; typhoid fever, 18; small-pox, 2. The Sixth Ward still continues to furnish the largest death-rate.

Respectfully yours,

J. Watt, M. D., *Registrar.*

We would simply suggest, in reply to Dr. Watt's verification of our statement in the October number of The Sanitarian, "that it is evident from the data given that the death-rate of Brooklyn, from preventable diseases, is on the increase,"—that we include diphtheria among the preventable diseases; and that by excluding typhoid fever, which is also prevailing disgracefully, and on the increase,—the difference, in his point of view, will be still more manifest. Meanwhile, the Board of Health continues to shirk the responsibility of providing an offal dock, and insists upon the contractors providing one for themselves. The Board of Health knows full well that it *alone*, under the law, "has full and exclusive power and authority over the removal of night soil, and in the removal of dead animals, offal, blood, bones, tainted or impure meats," etc., etc., and that without the exercise of the power with which the board is invested, to designate and maintain the right to use a dock for that purpose, the contractors are utterly powerless. The *candy* committee has made a somewhat lengthy report, to the effect that it is not so much the poisonous adulteration, but the excessive indulgence in candy, which impairs digestion and destroys the appetite for plain, wholesome food. There are in the city 341 confectioners, the larger portion of whom manufacture only a quarter or less of their stock. To determine the question who, if any, are making adulterated candy, would involve 10,000 or more analyses. The subject, having answered its purpose, is dropped. And the following is a fair sample of numerous experiences throughout the city:

No. —— Henry St., Brooklyn, Sept. 12th, 1874.—*To the Editor of the Sanitarian*:—Will you please advise me in regard to sanitary matters: I will state my grievances as briefly as possible.

1*st.* About three months ago I had in my house a piece of meat that, during the very warm weather, became unfit to eat the day after I bought it. The cook threw it into the swill barrel, and neglected to inform me that the person who had been calling for garbage had refused to call again. Of course the barrel became extremely offensive, and I went to the police station to ask how I could get rid of it. I was told the only way was to pay somebody to take it. I tried, but found nobody willing. Finally, I hired a cart, sent it beyond the city limits and had it buried.

2*d.* My dog died this summer. I notified the police in Butler St. that I had a dead dog in my house, and was informed that the contractor would be notified. No contractor came, and I disposed of it the best way I could.

3*d*. The house next to mine has been without a tenant since early spring; about two months ago a woman with three children was placed in charge of it. For several days we have perceived a disagreeable smell, and have ascertained that it arises from a defective water-closet in the house referred to. I have, in this instance, applied to the Board of Health, a copy of which I inclose.

What should I do about having garbage and dead dogs removed?

Your old friend and shipmate,

No notice taken. D. L.

New Orleans, Sept. 23*d*, 1874.—Total number of interments for the week ending September 6th, was 87; the week ending September 13th, was 108; the week ending September 20th, was 122. Of this latter number, 24 died of gun-shot wounds, and two have been sent away to be interred elsewhere. Positively, there is no case of yellow fever in the city.

Very respectfully,

S. C. Russell, M. D.,

Sec'y of Board of Health.

Cincinnati, Sept. 28*th*, 1874.—Dear Sir: Our condensed report for September up to the 25th, inclusive, is as follows:

Total mortality, 131.

Under one year of age, 30 per cent.

Under five years of age, 56.64 per cent.

Principal causes from which occurred:

Scarlet fever	32	Dentition	12
Cholera infantum	31	Dysentery	11
Consumption	29	Marasmus	10
Convulsions	20	Congestion of brain	9
Pneumonia	15	Paralysis	8
Diarrhœa	13	Typhoid fever	8

(Population, 260,000.)

Respectfully,

C. B. Chapman,

Clerk, Board of Health.

Pittsburg, Oct. 1*st*, 1874.—Population, 136,000. Deaths, for four weeks, ending Sept. 26th, 290; 25.60 per 1,000. Under one year of age, 29.30 per cent.; under five years of age, 60.35 per cent. Principal causes of death: Diarrhœal diseases, 64; consumption, 25; scarlet fever, 21; hooping cough, 13; typhoid fever, 9; diphtheria, 8; croup, 5; measles, 1; respiratory diseases, 17; meningitis, 13; deaths from violence, 13.

William Snively, M. D.,

Registrar of Vital Statistics.

Philadelphia, 775,000.—Week ending Oct. 3d, 268. Consumption, 38; typhoid fever, 9.

Baltimore, 284,000.—Week ending Oct. 5th, 144. Consumption, 18; cholera infantum, 10; typhoid fever, 5; scarlet fever, 5.

Washington, 150,000.—Week ending Oct. 3d, 57. Consumption, 12; typhoid fever, 3; cholera infantum, 4.

Chicago, 400,000.—Week ending September 26th, 160. Cholera infantum, 44; consumption, 11; typhoid fever, 9; scarlet fever, 3.

St. Louis, 366,000.—Week ending Oct. 3d, 104. Consumption, 8; diarrhœa, 5; dysentery, 5; typhoid fever, 2; small-pox, 6.

Richmond, 65,000.—Week ending Oct. 3d, 23.

Charleston, 52,000.—Week ending Sept. 26th, 40. Consumption, 5; diphtheria, 6; congestive fever, 3.

San Francisco, 178,000.—Month of August, 334. Consumption, 33; typhus and typhoid fevers, 17; scarlatina, 20; small-pox, 3; diarrhœa, 21.

Dayton, 34,000.—Month of September, 25. Consumption, 6; diarrhœa, 3; heart disease, 2; of no other disease more than one.

Louisville, 112,000.—Week ending Oct. 3d, 51. Consumption, 5; cholera infantum, 4.

Buffalo, 130,000.—Month of August, 391. Cholera infantum, 110; consumption, 22; scarlet fever, 68; typhoid fever, 10.

Wheeling, 37,000.—Month of September, 34.

Toledo, 37,000.—Month of September, 65. Consumption, 8; typhoid and typho-malarial, each 2.

Milwaukee, 100,000.—Month o September, 239. Cholera infantum, 28; convulsions, 34; diarrhœa, 83; typhoid fever, 10; typhus, 2; 191 *under five years of age!*

New Haven, 55,000.—Month of September, 98. Consumption, 11; typhoid fever, 5; typhus, 1; cholera infantum, 13; convulsions, 3.

Providence, 100,000.—Month of September, 176. Cholera infantum, 29; consumption, 15; diarrhœa, 11; scarlatina, 12.

"There was nine deaths in September from typhoid fever, or four more than in August. At this season of the year there is usually an increase of typhoid fever, and the attention of the people is called to it. There is less of the disease in the city at present than is usual at this season. It seems to be a disease more prevalent in the country than in the city. While there is often much of the disease in the country portion of the State, and throughout New England, especially in the autumn, it has never, during twenty years at least, been very severe in this city, never approaching an epidemic, or endemic character. Indeed, very many of the cases of typhoid fever in Providence, in the fall of the year, are contracted in the country, and appear on the return of the persons to the city. There are several such cases in the city at the present time."

EDWIN M. SNOW, M. D.,

Superintendent of Health and City Registrar.

Massachusetts.—Sixteen cities and towns for the week ending Sept. 12, 1874: Boston, 195; Worcester, 26; Lowell, 40; Milford,

2 ; Chelsea, 10; Cambridge, 51 ; Salem, 13 ; Lawrence, 19 ; Springfield, 16 ; Lynn, 21 ; Fitchburg, 5 ; Newburyport, 2 ; Somerville, 7; Fall River, 24 ; Haverhill, 4 ; Holyoke, 12. Total, 447.

Prevalent Diseases.—Cholera infantum, 125 ; consumption, 60 ; diarrhœa and dysentery, 36 ; pneumonia, 11 ; typhoid fever, 10.

Cambridge reports five deaths, and Boston four deaths from whooping cough ; none reported elsewhere.

CHAS. F. FOLSOM, M. D.
Secretary of the State Board of Health.

MANAGEMENT OF SLAUGHTER-HOUSES.

PHILADELPHIA, *Sept. 24th*, 1874.

To the Editor of the Sanitarian :

I have been interested by an article on slaughter-houses in the October No. of THE SANITARIAN, in consequence of a movement to erect here, in what is, or shortly will be, the centre of the city, an establishment combining the two at Jersey City and Hackensack, to be under the control of the same parties.

I have been told by gentlemen who have recently visited New York, that the concern at Hackensack is exceedingly offensive to passengers in the cars, and that with a S. W. wind, the odors from it are unpleasant as far as Brooklyn Heights.

As any mistake made here will be exceedingly injurious to the finest quarter of our city for residences, I trust that you will excuse my intruding upon you with a request for any information within your reach upon the subject, and especially as to the experience with respect to the establishment near Jersey City.

Very truly, etc.,
HENRY C. LEA.

NEW YORK, *Sept. 30th*, 1874.

Dr. A. N. Bell, Editor, etc.

In reply to the note from Mr. Lea, of Philadelphia, which you kindly sent me, making some inquiries in regard to the article on the management of slaughter-houses, published in the last number of THE SANITARIAN, I must say that I am most decidedly of the opinion that he has been misinformed concerning the area over which odors are diffused from the establishment on the Hackensack. I have visited the place several times, and on each occasion I have found it inoffensive to the neighborhood. I speak of the rendering and the utilizing of offal and blood ; but we all know that live swine carry with them an odor which is diffusive, persistent, and offensive, and which the parties conducting the abattoir do not pretend to suppress. It must also be acknowledged that all machinery is liable to temporary derangements, and when the object of such machinery is to suppress or destroy offensive odors, any defect in its working will be attended with a proportional failure in the accomplishment of its object. For this reason alone, to say nothing of the nuisance connected with the live stock, I would not like to be understood as recommending the erection of an establishment like the one on the Hackensack; in a location likely to soon become the centre of a city. I think one of its chief merits is its remoteness from human dwellings ; and if some odor should chance to escape during the emptying of a tank, and this should occur while a railway train is passing, the annoyance is but momentary, and I believe reduced to the minimum. In regard to the Harsimus Abattoir, I would say that when crossing at Pavonia ferry I have noticed as I neared the New Jersey side, an odor from the cattle-yards similar to that yielded by every farm yard where live cattle are kept ; but I have never detected any odor that I could recognize as from the slaughtering establishment. I will take this occasion to correct an error in the article referred to. I stated that the cars arriving from the Hackensack, were run on the ferryboat, and taken across the river, whereas the pork is taken across the river on trucks. With the exception of this error, I think the statements will all stand the test of observation.

Truly yours,
E. H. JANES, M. D.,
208 W. 42d St.

COLORADO FOR CONSUMPTION.

COLORADO SPRINGS, *Sept.* 22, 1874.

DEAR SIR :—Yours of the 15th received. My *experience* has fully proven that the climate of Colorado will certainly cure pulmonary troubles in the first stages of observation, just as surely that advanced stages are aggravated. I came here after a severe attack of hæmorrhage, with great prostration, with a severe cough accompanied with expectoration, etc. ; was unable to walk any distance—could perhaps, ride on horseback one-half of a mile. I reached Denver about 15th October. Could see but little change in my condition until after I had been here three or four months. First commenced horseback riding, making one-half mile per day ; continued to increase until my average for a year was at least twenty miles a day. That I made my business, and attended to under any and all circumstances. Rain or snow did not prevent me. Took no medicine but cod liver oil and whiskey, and finally dropped those ; but kept the horse and saddle and spurs, and now I consider myself as well as ever. Three times I have tried to return to Chicago, but each time have had to return to Colorado, and have settled down to the conclusion that it is the best *climate* in the world *for me*. I prefer living East, but consider life here far preferable than to being buried there. Asthma is as certainly cured as people come here. Rheumatism and slow or mountain fevers thrive here, which one would hardly suspect. Persons accustomed to a sedentary life coming here and expecting relief by following the same will be mistaken ; but an active persistent outdoor life will surely tell. An office in the States is just as good for consumptives as one here, but a good riding horse is worth more than the State of New York. Observation fully confirms my experience. More particularly in regard to people staying away from here until the disease is fully seated, then expecting relief from our climate, which they do not receive. You will perceive we are nearly six thousand feet in altitude higher than New York, the atmosphere so rarified that diseased or partly consumed lungs cannot be filled, while a tendency to disease may be overcome. I measure about the chest four inches more than I ever did in my best days. My mother and her sister have been unable for years to do anything on account of lung difficulties. Mother spent a year and a half here with better health than since my recollection, but her trouble seems more like old-fashioned consumption that I have known people to live with for thirty years. I have visited the mountains, but find the altitude too great.

We have a very pleasant town of 2,600 inhabitants. I inclose a view which is a very correct one. We have two hotels here which are as good as can be expected in a town of its size. Over at Manitou, five miles from here, where our mineral springs are located there are three hotels, capable of accommodating from fifty to one hundred and fifty people each. The best route is via Chicago and the Chicago, Burlington and Quincy Railroad to Kansas City, and Kansas Pacific Railroad to Denver, then the Narrow Gauge Railroad to our town. Brother James Phillips has talked strongly of making us a visit this season, and his mother is determined to come if she can find company. We would suggest that you drop James a line to meet you at Binghampton, and come out and make us a visit, look over the country, etc., etc., satisfy yourself in regard to climate, etc.

If any tendency to lung trouble, be careful not to wait until too firmly seated, for I know our climate cannot help such cases. We have hardly a family in our town that does not number among its inmates one invalid. Many come only to hasten disease, others are greatly benefited or completely cured.

Sincerely yours,

F. L. M.

MEETING OF THE AMERICAN PUBLIC HEALTH ASSOCIATION.

The Third Annual Meeting of the *American Public Health Association* will be held in Philadelphia, on the 10th, 11th, and 12th of November, 1874.

The session will open at noon, on Tuesday, the 10th of November, at the Board rooms of the College of Physicians, *on Locust street, N. E. Cor. of Thirteenth street.*

By the courtesy of the Executive Committee we present the following *Provisional Schedule of the Reports, Papers, Discourses and Discussions at the meeting.*

TUESDAY, NOV. 10TH, AT NOON.

Registration of members and others in attendance.

Introductory remarks by the President of the Association.

A paper by Prof. HENRY HARTSHORNE, M. D., of Philadelphia, upon "Causes of Excessive Infant Mortality in Cities."

Paper upon the "Influence of Hereditary Diseases."

"The Health of the People, with Suggestions of Methods of Promotion." By J. R. BLACK, M. D., of Ohio.

"The Health of Tenement Populations, or the Sanitary Wants of Their Dwellings." By EDWARD H. JANES, M. D., of New York.

A Report upon the Death Rate of Towns of Michigan, and comparison of these with DR. FARR'S *Life Tables of Health*—Districts of England. By H. B. BAKER, M. D., Secretary State Board of Health of Michigan.

A Report upon Hospital Construction. By J. S. BILLINGS, M. D., Assistant Surgeon U. S. Army.

A paper upon "Hospital Architecture, and the Perfect Ventilation of Hospital Wards." By CARL PFEIFFER, F. A. I. A.

Conference of Sanitary officers and others upon Methods and experience in the Public Health Service.

DISCOURSES TUESDAY EVENING.

FIRST DISCOURSE, by Rev. SAM'L OSGOOD, D. D.—*The Relations of Health and the Higher Culture.*

SECOND DISCOURSE, by Hon. L. H. STEINER, M. D., of Maryland—*Health a Prerequisite of National Success in Peace and in War.*

THIRD DISCOURSE.—*The Sanitary Relations of Hospitals and the Economy of Perfect Care of the Sick and Hurt.*

WEDNESDAY, NOV. 11TH, 9 A. M.

Business meeting and reception of voluntary papers, etc.

A paper upon the Ground in relation to Diseases. By EDWIN M. HUNT, M.D., President of the Sanitary Commission of New Jersey.

A report upon the deterioration of vegetables and fruits, as connected with their gathering, transportation, storage, and marketing, by S. C. BUSSEY, M.D., of Washington, D. C.

A report upon the sanitary government, vital statistics, and the methods of public health administration in the cities and large towns of North America. By E. HARRIS, M.D., of New York.

A paper upon the question, "Does small-pox become epidemic, or is it spread solely by its own contagious property?" By EDWIN M. SNOW, M.D., Superintendent of Health, Providence, R. I.

A paper upon "Yellow Fever on the Dry Tortugas." By HARVEY E. BROWN, M.D., Surgeon, U. S. Army.

A discourse by Prof. S. D. GROSS, M. D., L.L.D., D.C.L., Oxon.

upon *The Factors of Disease and Death after Injuries, Parturition, and Surgical Operations.*

4 P. M.—A conference upon laws and methods of the public health service of the different cities and States. By officers and members of Boards of Health.

DISCOURSES WEDNESDAY EVENING.

First Discourse, by Prof. Charles A. Chandler, M.D., LL.D.—*Practical Applications of Chemistry in the Public Health Service.*

Second Discourse, by Prof. Edward Orton, President of the Ohio Agricultural College—*Certain Relations of Geology to the Water Supplies of the Country.*

Third Discourse, by Gen. E. L. Viele, C.E.—*Principles and Practices in Drainage and Sewerage in Connection with Water Supplies.*

THURSDAY, NOV. 12TH, 9 A. M.

Business meeting and election of officers and committees.

A paper upon State Medicine as the Basis for the Elevation of the Standard of Medical Education. By Stephen Smith, M.D., of New York.

A Paper upon Syphilitic Contamination and Dyscrasiæ, with reference to public health interests. By Frederick R. Sturgis, M.D., of New York.

A Paper upon Sanitary Relations of Pharmacy to Materia Medica. By J. M. Maisch, Secretary American Pharmaceutical Association.

A paper on Perils of the School Room. By A. N. Bell, M.D., of Brooklyn, N. Y.

A Paper upon "*Hay Fever,*" giving results of original researches, with reference to causation and prevention. By Geo. M. Beard, M.D., of New York.

A Report upon the Sanitary Status of Colorado. By W. R. Whitehead, M. D., of Denver, Col.

A Paper by Hon. Lorin Blodgett, of Washington, D. C.

Voluntary Reports and Papers.

4 P. M.—*Sanitary Conference upon Laws, Methods, and Experience in Public Health Service.*

DISCOURSES THURSDAY EVENING.

First Discourse, by Hon. Dorman B. Eaton, of Washington—*Health Laws and Regulations, and the Interests of State and National Government therein.*

Second Discourse: *The Duty and Resources of the National Government in the Encouragement of Public Health Measures and Sanitary Science.*

President, STEPHEN SMITH, M.D., New York.

First Vice-President, EDWIN M. SNOW, M. D., Rhode Island.

Second Vice-President, C. B. WHITE, M.D., Louisiana.

Secretary, ELISHA HARRIS, M.D., New York.

Treasurer, JOHN H. RAUCH, M.D., Illinois.

Executive Committee—Elected Members—EDWARD JARVIS, M.D., Massachusetts; MORRAU MORRIS, M.D., New York; J. J. WOODWARD, M.D., U.S.A.; S. O. VANDERPOEL, M.D., New York; J. M. TONER, M.D., District of Columbia; A. N. BELL, M.D., New York.

The above schedule embraces only such papers and addresses as are promised. Numerous other reports and papers are expected from members, as well as many voluntary contributions from workers in the field of preventive medicine; and the prospect altogether is that the meeting will be in a high degree successful and profitable. We are also gratified at being able to state that the publishers promise to have the volume of Selected Papers, etc., of the previous meetings ready for delivery on the first day of the session.

BIBLIOGRAPHY.

Introduction to the Study of Biology. Designed for the use of Schools and Science classes. By THOMAS C. MACGINLEY. Illustrated; 12mo., pp. 199. New York: G. P. Putnam's Sons. 1874.

This is one of the excellent "Elementary Science Series," published by Messrs. Putnam, designed to meet the growing demand of academic students for scientific instruction. It begins with the simplest forms of organic life, and traces all growth into typical structures, as centres around which all organic beings may be gathered and compared, and from which true classification may be deduced. Technical terms are explained, and a glossary added, as being essential to future progress. The work is commendable alike to the general reader and the academic student; well calculated to awaken and promote an interest in the subject of which it treats.

Infant Diet. By A. JACOBI, M. D., Clinical Professor of Diseases of Children, etc. Revised, Enlarged and adapted to popular use, by MARY PUTNAM JACOBI, M. D.; 12mo., pp. 119. New York: G. P. Putnam's Sons. 1874.

This manual attests the appreciation of Dr. Jacobi's paper on Infant Diet, which—barring certain exceptions—we commended about a year ago, which exceptions are now made more important in this attempt to adapt them to popular use. We do not, therefore, regard this book as an improvement on Dr. Jacobi's paper, but a detriment to it. Recognizing the danger of alcoholic treatment of disease in non-professional hands generally, and the special liability of nursing mothers to fancied "debilitated" conditions, we do not believe it to be conducive to either good health or good morals to inculcate for "popular use" that "alcoholic stimulants are needed wherever the woman has become debilitated by nursing, and where the secretion of milk threatens to be suspended from this cause, they may directly increase it," (p. 46). For, admitting that circumstances may exist where, from protracted debility, the mother may require alcoholic stimulus, its appropriateness, to the exclusion of other means to the same end, is unquestionably beyond the scope of ordinary *non*-medical minds ; and its "popular use," under such circumstances, fraught with mischief. Scarcely less objectionable is the rule (1) "About Nursing Babies".... "In hot weather—but in the hottest days only—mix a few drops of whiskey with either water or food, the whiskey not to exceed a teaspoonful in twenty-four hours," (p. 118). Were the conditions for the exercise of this rule as certain to be observed as the directions for giving the alcohol, it would possibly be safe. But all practitioners know how much more likely such conditions are to be disregarded, than the administration of the remedy ; that the effect of repeated doses of whiskey in producing quietude, is likely to be interpreted as evidence of its necessity, and its abuse, therefore, almost certain to follow. For the physician, it is a valuable manual, containing many wholesome precepts and giving the clearest description of the physiology of infant digestion of any book we know of ; but the exceptions noticed render it unsafe for "popular use."

Clinical Lectures on Diseases of the Nervous System. By William A. Hamond, M. D., Professor of Diseases of the Mind and Nervous System, etc. Reported and edited by T. M. B. Cross, M. D., Assistant to the Chair of Diseases of the Mind, etc, 8vo, pp, 287. New York : D. Appleton & Co. 1874.

"These lectures were intended especially for the benefit of students ; the chief aim of the author has been to present merely practical views, fully illustrated by cases, with the results derived from treatment, as far as that was possible ; in so doing he has confined himself to a full consideration of the symptoms, the causes, and the treatment of each affection, particularly in their relation to cases." Hence results a thoroughly good, practical book, on a class of diseases common to every practitioner, and not usually sufficiently treated of in systematic works on practical medicine.

Essentials of the Principles and Practice of Medicine. By Henry Hartshorne, A.M., M. D., Professor of Hygiene, etc. 4th edition illustrated ; 12mo, pp. 548. Philadelphia : Henry C. Lea. 1874.

As a hand-book for the busy practitioner, and a review book for the senior student, we believe this work to be unequalled.

The Mother's Hygienic Hand-book. For the Normal Development and Training of Women and Children, and the Treatment of their Diseases with Hygienic Agencies. By R. T. Trall, M. D. 12mo, pp. 186. New York : S. R. Wells. 1874.

A misleading title of a book, wholly unfit for perusal by any other persons than physicians or medical students, and not calculated to be of any benefit to them.

The Building of a Brain. By Edward Clarke, M. D. 12mo, pp. 153. Boston : James R. Osgood & Co. 1874.

An outgrowth of the author's "Sex in Education," a fitting sequel, brought about by an invitation of the National Education Association to Dr. Clarke to prepare a paper on the "Education of Girls."

The essay is divided into three parts—Nature's Working Plans, An Error in Female Building, and a glimpse at English Brain Building. It is in strict keeping with sex in education, demonstrates the necessity of the co-ordinate conservation of all the functions and faculties, and the special errors of female brain-building in consequence of disregarded organic differences. In this Dr. Clarke not only confirms but strengthens and fortifies his conclusions, as before published, by many of the most experienced and competent observers everywhere. And we heartily commend his work as one of the most conclusive and practical efforts for the promotion of the health of American women ever published.

Popular Resorts and How to Reach Them. By JOHN B. BACHELDER, Author of "The Illustrated Tourist," "Gettysburg," etc., etc. 12mo, pp. 186. Boston: John B. Bachelder.

A handsomely bound and elegantly illustrated book, describing most of the fashionable resorts of the country, and how to reach them, but too much of an advertisement. "All is not gold that glitters" is so applicable to the outside appearances of many of our popular resorts that we sincerely trust that the author of this book, who has already announced his edition for 1875, will appreciate the importance of informing the public in regard to certain *internal* arrangements and appliances, and *particularly in regard to water supplies and the protection against contamination.*

Katharine Earle. By ADELINE TRAFTON. Illustrated, 12mo, pp. 253. Boston: Lee & Shepard. 1874.

An interesting story of a very sprightly, but poor and proud girl, who sets an example worthy of following. A delightful book.

Running to Waste. The story of a Tomboy. By GEORGE M. BAKER. 12mo, pp. 245. Boston: Lee & Shepard. 1874.

A rollicking, good-humored story of a girl who grew up to be a very sensible woman in spite of numerous officious obstacles. A worthy example of perseverance and success.

Take a Peep. By PAUL COBDEN. 12mo, pp. 199. Boston: Lee & Shepard. 1874.

A volume of the Beckoning Series. "*Independent*" chicks put into a pretty volume for the convenience of all girls and boys who like good story books. In this they will not be disappointed. Good stories with good morals.

Five Thousand a Year; Clara Lake's Dream; and *The Nobleman's Wife.* Novels. By MRS. HENRY WOOD. Philadelphia: T. B. Peterson & Bros. 1874.

These books all fully sustain Mrs. Wood's fascinating style, so distinguishing a feature of her writings. And to all who delight in reading chaste novels of marvellous and ingeniously constructed plots and unique, but always interesting characters, we commend these books.

Love at First Sight. A Novel. By Captain HENRY CURLING. 8vo, paper, pp. 132. Philadelphia: Peterson & Bros. 1874.

This is a story of English life—of the Curbspine family. It is of intense interest, and cannot well be laid aside when once commenced.

THE SANITARIAN.

A MONTHLY JOURNAL.

VOL. II.] DECEMBER, 1874. [NO. 9.

NEW YORK MEDICO-LEGAL SOCIETY; ITS STATUS AND RELATIONS TO THE SCIENCE OF HEALTH AND KINDRED TOPICS.

Third Inaugural Address, Nov. 27th, 1874.

BY CLARK BELL, ESQ., President.

GENTLEMEN :—It would be impossible for me to conceal from you my high appreciation of the very great honor and distinction which has been conferred upon me by the Medico-Legal Society of New York, in calling me again for the third time into its chief seat, and of that kindness which has marked this act on your part with such unanimity that it will always be remembered and cherished by me with the livliest gratification and gratitude.

In assuming again the responsibilities and duties of your presiding officer, I cannot forbear to thank you all for that great and uniform encouragement and support which has everywhere and on all hands among you been extended to me; which has invested my duties and efforts on your behalf with such a charm, that it has lightened and lessened the labors of my office, and on many occasions rendered them a delight and a pleasure.

Members.

I congratulate you, gentlemen of the society, on the accessions that have been made to the roll of your membership during the year that has just closed.

The present roll of resident or active members of this society now contains 348 names.

The death of Alfred Vogel, of the University of Russia, leaves fourteen names on the roll of your honorary members, with six vacancies; in filling these great care should be observed by this society, as it should be made a position of great distinction and worth.

Your roll of corresponding members now numbers twenty-nine.

I take great pleasure in recommending for honorary membership, MM. Guerard, member of the Academy of Médicine of Paris, France, who was elected president of the Société de Médecine Lègale de

Paris, in December, 1872, and who was one of the original founders of that society, which was organized in February, 1868.

MM. Guerard, has always been an active and conspicuous member of that body, for years before his election to the presidency, a member of its permanent commission, and a physician of distinction in the city of Paris, who has devoted no little of his time to the study and solution of questions involved in the science of medical jurisprudence.

LABORS OF THE YEAR.

During the past year this society has accomplished no little work. The discussions that have occurred at your sessions, and the varied and useful labors in which you have been engaged, have been such as to maintain the high standard you have hitherto established.

One of its most important labors has been the compilation and publication in a bound volume of some of the earlier papers read before this society, with a historical statement of its origin, rise and progress.

This interesting and valuable result has been accomplished under the care, supervision, and labors of a committee of your body, and is just published by J. R. McDivitt, Esq., one of the most enterprising of the law publishers of New York, who furnishes it to members at the wholesale price, under an arrangement originally made with him by this society.

The present volume, which will well repay your purchase and preservation, and which confessedly must enrich the literature of medical jurisprudence, will be followed during the coming year by another and similar one of a like character, which will bring out the papers read before the society that have passed the committee on publication down to about the present time. I esteem this work an important and notable part of the labors of this society, of very great value upon medico-legal questions, thus made accessible to the world, and I particularly commend it to every member of the society, as meriting his countenance, support and encouragement, so that these publications may become a permanent and established feature in the future of this organization. The thanks as well as the material support of members are eminently and properly due to the enterprising publisher, and I can not dismiss this subject from your consideration without also publicly thanking in your name our worthy member, R. S. Guernsey, Esq., who has devoted great pains, time and labor to the successful accomplishment of this very important result.

Library.

I owe you all apologies for great neglect of my duty in not presenting more forcibly and persistently the cause and the merits of your library, which has been duly organized, and started upon a successful basis, since I first had the honor of assuming the chair of this society.

The contributions from members in money and volumes have continued in a way that assures us of the ultimate success of the effort, but are not equal to nor commensurate with the hopes or desires of your president, nor the importance and merits of the enterprise itself.

When gentlemen reflect that so small a sum of money as $5,000 would immediately, and probably within the present year, enable us to purchase nearly every work on these subjects, and aggregate the best library of medical jurisprudence that could be found any where, I am obliged by what I consider my duty to call upon you, gentlemen of the society, to again take into consideration the propriety of raising this sum, either at once or speedily.

If it is thought advisable for any reason not to attempt it all now, let one-half be raised the present, the residue the ensuing year. There are certainly men enough now among our own numbers, who, if they could be induced to make the effort, would at once raise this sum, without an appeal to the two professions outside of our membership.

But so grave is the imperative and immediate necessity for a complete and comprehensive library in this city, which should embrace every known work on medical jurisprudence or its kindred topics, particularly in the English, French, and German tongues, that this society cannot be true to itself or its duties if it neglects to secure the early accomplishment of this very desirable result.

If this society should feel justified in permitting the general public to co-operate with its members in this work, under some arrangement by which every contributor of a bound volume accepted by the society should be entitled to the use of and access to the library, it would probably add a considerable number of works each year to the shelves of the library, if it did not immediately accomplish the desired purpose.

The general resolution originally adopted at the time the library was founded, making it the duty of every member to contribute annually at least one bound volume thereto, has been of very great value and importance in adding to its catalogue.

Quite a considerable number of our members have, with great care and punctuality, attended to the discharge of this duty, whose contributions have been acknowledged from time to time, but your president regrets that he is compelled to report that a large number of members are delinquent in this very important respect.

Allow me, in closing this part of my remarks, to remind members that if this duty was promptly and annually discharged by every member of this society a few years would give us a library on medical jurisprudence alone, second to none in the world, even though no immediate steps were taken at once to secure these volumes by an appeal extraordinary, as at first suggested.

Let every member, then, who has neglected to send the volumes, attend to it at once, and add to a library which has already become quite valuable, and is probably now the best in this country for reference on these subjects.

I append a list of contributions of volumes and money contributed since my last announcement, with the names of the contributors.

Legislation.

The changes that have been made in the laws of this State, during the past year, are of the very gravest character concerning the custody, care and treatment of the insane, and the trials of insane persons, especially where the defense of insanity is interposed.

The prominence that has been given to the discussion of these varied questions in this society has had a large influence upon this legislation, while the labors of a very distinguished gentleman, alienist, and an honorary member of this society, have probably been more immediately instrumental in securing these changes than all other causes combined.

The codification of the statutes of the State, upon this subject, as this legislation was styled, for which we are so much indebted to the services of Professor John Ordronaux, embrace radical and fundamental changes in the whole system, and revolutionized from beginning to end the whole theory and practice in such cases.

The evils that had been charged upon the old system, of the commitment of persons alleged to be lunatics to an asylum, and the wide spread conviction that under the former system gross abuses might have been and were sometimes practiced; were probably causes for an excited public opinion that demanded a change and inclined to one that should throw greater safeguards around the liberty of the citizen, and make it more difficult if not practically impossible to cause the incarceration improperly of any person as an alleged lunatic, who was really of sound mind.

While the practical working of the new law is at first criticised severely by medical men and practitioners, as being almost impracticable and unnecessarily difficult, and doubtful, in cases of insanity, where prompt action is necessary, it may well be claimed that a fair trial of the new plan should be made, with patience, with care, and without feeling, before we condemn it finally and demand its revision or its repeal.

Passing all the multifarious detail of the many changes made by this important statute, it may be well to allude briefly to the radical one in relation to the plea of insanity by or in behalf of persons charged with crime in the criminal courts.

It was a matter of grave concern, in the administration of justice in the courts, for the punishment of offenses, whether the defense of insanity, so often interposed as a plea in defense or justification of alleged crimes, was not undermining public confidence in the administration of justice, by its well-known abuses, and by its being used improperly for the escape and acquittal of well-known criminals, of acknowledged or generally accredited guilt. The very great uncertainty that immediately surrounded a capital case, when this defense was interposed and insisted upon, was well known, and had resulted in a gradual withdrawal of public confidence in the then existing laws upon this subject.

The change made in the new statute strikes at the root of the whole evil.

It practically does away with the defense of insanity, if formally pleaded as a defense to the indictment, or attempts to do so completely.

To guard against the conviction and punishment of insane persons, the old statute is re-enacted and perfected so as to have an investigation into the sanity or insanity of the accused, as a separate and independent proceeding from the trial of the indictment; and thus leave the question of the guilt or innocence of the accused to be tried by itself, if the indictment ever comes to be tried, which in the case of an alleged lunatic must always follow such a preliminary investigation.

I regard it my duty merely to advert to this comprehensive and remarkable change in the law of this State, which is thus put upon trial before the eye of the whole nation. If the workings of this law shall upon trial be on the whole fairly decided to be an improvement upon the old and previously existing systems, it cannot fail to have a very prominent and beneficent effect in initiating similar changes in the laws of other States.

But gentlemen should not be in too great haste, nor impatient of a little delay before arriving at positive opinions, particularly if against the change now inaugurated, until a fair trial and test of its workings can be had.

It is not improbable that before a definite and decisive solution of the question involved can be safely reached, some minor changes, suggested by trial and experience, may be necessary, and the aid of the Legislature invoked to give the proposed plan a perfectly fair trial.

That the important step has been taken, that the new system is now really upon its trial, no matter how much of inquiry or criticism it may excite and awaken, can not but be a source of congratulation to the Medico-Legal Society of New York, nor to the thoughtful men of this society, who have been interested and engaged in the discussions and questions therein involved, and who have taken part in the passage of the new statutes.

Other Societies.

We have received, during the past year, the publications of "La Société Medico-Lègale de Paris," with whom this society is proud and happy to continue on terms of most friendly intercourse, and in correspondence.

The volume, of some 500 pages, issued by our sister society of Paris, being Bulletin, Tome 2, contains records of the years 1870–1872, commencing with the address pronounced by M. Devergie, at the February session of that Society in 1870, on the occasion of his retiring from the Prèsidency, and the Inauguration Address of his successor, M. Bèheir, on the occasion of his accession to that office.

The volume, closing with the election of M. Guerard to the Presidency, in December, 1872, may be called the record of the notable transactions of that society, during the two years of the presidency of M. Bèheir, one of the most distinguished of its members, and an honorary member of this society. This volume, the fruit of its labors, is most valuable, and reflects the very highest credit upon that body. It is a most notable and brilliant monument of the value and importance of that society in the French capital, and to the progress of scientific investigation upon medico-legal questions abroad.

As this work is not yet translated into English, and I am not aware that any other copy has come to our members save the one sent to this society and now in my hands, I trust you will bear with me, while I allude briefly to the general character and work of our sister society in Paris for the period since December, 1872.

The Medico-Legal Society, of Paris, has investigated on various occasions, through a committee of its members duly appointed by the society or its president, interesting questions upon very many subjects, as they have arisen from time to time, in France, either in the civil or criminal courts, or from their own correspondents; some of the most interesting cases of poisoning, of infanticide, of medico-legal discoveries concerning blood, of tattooing, upon the question of identity on a mutilated dead body, many of which have been discussed with great skill and ability, and are therein chronicled.

The work also contains most valuable and interesting papers, reports upon the French law of insanity, and reviews of legal proceedings where medico-legal questions were raised and discussed.

Allow me to quote from the very short, but most excellent address of M. Bèheir, pronounced at his inaugural, a few sentences of which will give you his idea of the duties and position of the Medico-Legal Society of Paris, and which I think will be most pertinent also to the members of the Medico-Legal Society of New York. M. Bèhier says:—I translate but not literally—

"One other cause of the success of our society is certainly the creation of an intelligent, permanent commission ready to respond to all questions submitted to it.

"This is an excellent organization, for it constitutes a perfectly disinterested tribunal upon medical questions in judicial affairs.

"The advice which your permanent commission brings to your knowledge, and frequently to your judgment, is in effect based upon the purely scientific appreciation of the circumstances and the surroundings which constitute the medico-legal question presented for your consideration.

"Neither the influence of the prosecution nor of the defense can intervene here, it can know and will investigate only the absolute, and almost the abstract research after truth, the second term in that device which you have adopted.*

"Gentlemen, this service is not the only one which the organization of this society is call upon to render. It is still useful from another point of view. The constitution of our work in fact unites upon a common field of labor, the medical man, the magistrate and the member of the bar. This is a useful intercourse, and

* "Science—Vèrité—Justice."

one the results of which will be very important. If we see one another more we shall know each other better, and will better appreciate the inherent qualities of each, as well as the peculiar characteristics of each class of our members.

"Sooner or later this community of labor will tend to remove that antagonism which it must be conceded actually exists among the magistrates against the physicians.

"In pursuing our investigations, seeing how we proceed, why we are thus united, and on what labors we rely, the magistrates will give us more of their confidence. They will recognize that the legitimate honest medical man, such as they will always select, is more detached from popular clamor than they are apt to give him credit for; that the conscience which he brings to his mission controls him absolutely; that he desires to thoroughly understand all sciences germane to the question which he examines; they will recognize that it requires tact and system, attention and care to assist in the application of that solid scientific knowledge, which is in fact indispensable. Let us understand better who we are, what we do, what we know, and they will accord more value to our conclusions, and a more benevolent attention.

"They will above all learn, what has not been generally understood by magistrates, that not every physician necessarily understands medico-legal questions; that it requires more than a mere diploma as a doctor of medicine to examine these subjects, that the opinion of physicians should not be seriously opposed to the opinion of an accredited and qualified expert, that it requires special studies to be able to fully understand the questions of forensic medicine, and that certain of these questions necessitate a study and practice of these specialties.

* * * * * * * *

"The labors of our society will serve to enlighten those whose mission it is to apply the law.

"To be frequently united upon a common plane of study, is a circumstance which will tend to smooth away the difficulties I have mentioned. It will also be, in my opinion, an important result if our society unites the two professions, equally independent.

"In the times in which we live, and those to which we tend, if we can unite and close up the ranks of all honest men, we will accomplish a pious and social work.

"In order, gentlemen, to attain this elevated object, the role which our society must play is definitely traced, and closely defined. I have heard it stated in one of our discussions, 'Do not let us place ourselves in opposition to the tribunals; let us take care that our opinions are not rejected, or we lose our authority; let us sacrifice something to success; let us occupy ourselves above all with questions in which our opinions may obtain consideration, and be treated with respect.'

"I am not of that opinion. I believe that our society should investigate in all simplicity, in all conscience, every question that is brought before it, detached from all personal consideration or interest. We must advance courageously without leaning on any other support than that of science and of common sense.

"I know only a few who have for their motto, 'Do well and let people talk,' but I believe that for individuals as well as bodies of men it is the best rule of conduct.

"Truth has its power of evolution, which overcomes all obstacles, whether created by its enemies or its imprudent friends.

"To do well, without looking to the immediate results, will bring honor and credit to our society ; perhaps the time may be long deferred, but premature fruits are not the best ; and only those which are grown in due season, and are the fruit and growth of wisdom, are worthy of our preservation, or will permanently endure."

Bulletin, Tome 3, a work of some two hundred pages, has also been since received, which chronicles the labors of that society, under the presidency of MM. Guerard, from his inauguration in January, 1873 to the 8th of December, 1873, the last meeting of the society in that year.

This volume announces that the Government of France, in a decree, promulgated on the 22d of January, 1874, by the President of the French Republic, has formally recognized that society as established for the public good, and its statutes and regulations as formally approved by the Government of France.

The society has assumed the name of "Société de Médecine Lègale de France," and its constitution, rules and regulations form one of the most important and interesting portions of this volume of its transactions.

The Medico-Legal Society of New York congratulates its sister society of Paris on this fortunate result, which cannot fail to be of signal service and benefit to that society, and must largely increase the sphere of its usefulness.

The papers published in Bulletin, Tome 3, embrace a very interesting class of cases, among which are several relating to murders, infanticides, suicides, and various other crimes.

Among those papers also is an interesting one upon the subject of chloroform as an agent in the commission of crimes, being the report of M. Dolbeau, where the whole subject is ably and critically considered, and was made the subject of discussion in the society at its session of November 10th, 1873.

The views formerly expressed by S. Rogers, M. D., ex-president of this society, upon this subject, are therein quoted and discussed, but the conclusions reached by M. Dolbeau do not entirely agree with those of Dr. Rogers in that class of cases.

The advance made in the French capital in the science of medical jurisprudence, through the agency of this active society, has been decided and gratifying.

It has also been our good fortune to have received the announcement of the organization of a similar society to our own, and upon a like basis, in the city of Cleveland, Ohio.

We have received a copy of its published plan of organization, with officers, constitution, by-laws, etc., and feel an honorable pride in receiving from this young and vigorous society the credit of having inspired its organization for the investigation of the science of medical jurisprudence in that city.

I take great pleasure in recommending that the Cleveland society be furnished with all our publications, and that we should in all ways in our power be glad to aid in its prosperity and success.

I venture to recommend that our new and forthcoming volume be sent in addition to all the sister societies, to the leading libraries abroad and in our own country, and I trust soon to see inaugurated in the city of London, a Society of Medical Jurisprudence which shall occupy, in Great Britain, the position which the Paris society does in France, and our own society in this State and nation. I shall be disappointed if Berlin and Vienna do not shortly inaugurate similar movements in those cities.

The Relation of Science to Medical Jurisprudence.

The advance that science is making in the domain of medical jurisprudence cannot fail to excite your liveliest interest.

Toxicology has become one of the most valuable aids and agents in detecting, convicting and punishing crime, and the extended efforts as chemists of such men as Prof. Doremus, Prof. Chandler, in our country, and Tardieu, Caspar, Mayet, and Devergie abroad, have awakened and encouraged investigations which cannot fail to be of lasting and permanent value to mankind.

When science does intervene now in the cases of detection of poisons by chemical tests she is valuable because, and only when, she is certain. If her voice is to be listened to at all convincingly it must speak with unerring precision. It is either demonstrative or it is valueless. The science of toxicology is as accurate and absolute as mathematics, and when demonstration comes debate ends, doubt ceases, and conviction must follow. We should never regard mere theories as proofs. We may debate them, examine and discuss them in their varied forms and bearings; submit them to tests, fancied, difficult, and even crucial, but, when life, character, liberty or property are at stake, mere theory ceases to be of value. We can only accept the actual, the real, and the unquestionably certain. Science should have an eye of flame clear as the sun, but no heart, no emotion, no fear, no passion. If she points her finger, it should be as the needle to the pole. It must not even vacillate, it must not vibrate, for the result to be accepted as absolute. No leaning of the intellect, no warping of the judgment, no kindling of the heart or affections, no appealing to the passions, the loves or the hates, but cold as the frost, and far reaching and clear as the ether of eternal space. Science leads, if she leads at all, unerringly, unmistakably, and with precision, or she is no safe guide in the domain of medical jurisprudence.

Experts and Expert Testimony.

To speak a language, we must learn it.

No one can practice a trade that has not learned all its deftness and intricacies by study and practice. The hand that has acquired skill and tact, and cunning, for a certain task, has only come to it after long labor and many trials.

So no physician should dare call himself an expert in any branch involved in medical jurisprudence or scientific investigation, until he has studied it to its foundations in its abstract principles, and carefully prepared himself besides by practice and actual contact with it in all its phases, peculiarities, and idiosyncracies, pursuing it into every detail.

It is not enough to know the nature, character, names and antidotes of the various poisons, nor to understand theoretically their varied tests and methods of determination.

Many men of both professions have a very good general knowledge of these theoretically, as learned from books, reading, and observation.

That chemist who, knowing all this, before he attempts to swear, when life and death are in the balance, should have taken all these questions, all these tests, to his laboratory, and worked out one by one every problem for himself, before he is competent to speak with precision to a court or before a jury.

Mere opinions of men are becoming daily less valuable, especially on scientific questions.

The more we attempt to rely or to build upon them the more painfully uncertain do we become of our premises, of our foundations.

The experience of both professions in that class of cases in our courts, when the opinions of medical witnesses only are given, has doubtless been akin to that entertained by the community at large, and helped to shake profoundly the public confidence in them at all.

Counsel submit usually, or frequently in the same case, contrary opinions from medical men, of apparently equal learning, skill and opportunities, upon the same apparent state of facts. For example, in the case of Geo. Francis Train, Drs. Hammond, Clymer and Parsons pronounce him insane, though they have no previous acquaintance with or personal knowledge of him, and base their opinion upon one or two interviews and conversations, while Drs. Finnell, Peugnet, Gardner and others pronounce him sane on similar examinations, and the jury usually balancing the medical testimony, as in that case a panel of the sheriff's jury, having a large experience in such cases, are governed by their own judgment, or the testimony of those acquaintances and friends who are and have been long and intimately acquainted with the party who is the subject of the investigation.

And this case is but a sample of similar evidence in other cases of more or less public prominence.

We must strive to approach nearer by careful study, preparation and skill to certainty. So long as facts only go towards conviction and to formation of opinions merely, these opinions must be accepted with great care, and their weight or importance must be conceded to be of little value.

We do not want opinions, we want certainties. We have nothing but doubts left if we gain as the result of scientific research or inquiry only convictions or opinions.

In the toxological test if the result is not absolutely certain we reject it wholly.

There are more or less bearings and indications in many of the experiments which fall short of certainty, but which are not wholly valueless as evidence, still in such cases we reject all if the result is not absolutely certain.

Let us emulate and establish that standard. It is safer. The teachings of pure science have not merely a charm; they have more; she rewards her devotees; she smiles upon the patient worker, and the truth lies at the bottom of her profoundest depths.

We must then invade and dig and work for the hidden, but we must know, recognize and acknowledge it only when it stands fully revealed. No man, no matter what may be his profession, his apparent standing, or his theoretical or book knowledge, until he has completely mastered the particular subject upon which he is called to testify, as well in its theory as in its practice, is safe to be classified as a competent expert.

Medical jurisprudence, on its medical side especially, is full of specialties.

The medical expert should be a specialist in the widest, broadest, best sense of that term.

The more learned he really is, the more careful, thorough, complete and comprehensive will be his examination of a subject.

His analysis should be fundamental. If we are to deal in opinions only, the opinion of such a witness is valuable; but the more profound the expert the less we shall have of his mere opinions. He will presently deal only in facts. Has he found certainly the truth? Is it certain, absolute, demonstrable? He then can speak, and convincingly. Is he groping in the case, as one in the dark? Does one set of symptoms indicate this, another that?

Is he in doubt, or does he balance facts and weigh them and attempt to offset them, the one against the other? Then we have only doubt; and if opinions are the result, why should they not differ, as men always will differ?

I know, of course, the rule established in our courts, under which, in certain cases, the opinion of experts upon a given statement of facts is permitted to be given; but the whole spirit and philosophy of the law is tending to establish this class of legal evidence on a more solid and substantial basis, and to make it a means of arriving at truth, and to aggregate facts, rather than to cloud and embarrass a case in the mazes and uncertainties of the diverse and contradictory opinions of medical men.

In that remarkably lucid and masterly address delivered by Prof. Tyndall before the British Association of Science, at its recent session, which has awakened so much of interest and discussion on both sides the sea, we find that very learned and brilliant man and thinker, in reviewing the philosophy of Lucretius and his opponents of that and the present time, bringing foremost and prominent into the discussion those grave questions so intimately related to our studies of insanity, diseases of the brain, and mental phenomena, concerning which many members of this society who have given the subject of mental diseases and peculiarities much thought, are at a loss and differ in their conclusions.

Are aberrations of the reason an affair of the material brain? Is mental disease a brain disease? What is the true nature of the soul of man? And what its relation to his physical structure?

In that admirable debate, between the pupil of Lucretius and Bishop Butler, author of the world-renowned "Analogy," these problems, which have puzzled the alienists of our own and past time, are placed by Professor Tyndall in a most masterly way, to investigate whether the mind of man, and his intellectual and reasoning faculties, are a part of his physical being, or whether the body is the mere tenement of the spirit in which it dwells while life remains.

You who have read and studied this paper cannot fail to have noticed how prominent a part this inquiry takes in that remarkable discussion, and to what ends Prof. Tyndall's reasoning might carry these propositions if it be conceded that madness is solely and only the result of a physical disease of the brain, as is claimed by many of our abler alienists. I draw a wide line of demarcation between the actualities of science—between its demonstrable facts—and between the inductions, the theories and the speculations of science.

I have no hesitation whatever in proceeding with the inquiry suggested by Professor Tyndall, to which allusion is given above, by any and all scientific aids, but we must not accept opinions or theories for facts.

Let us pursue the investigations with courage, but with patient persistence, and be prepared to accept results when they are demonstrated only, and when doubt no longer remains.

Is the material and physical brain the instrument of the mind of man? Is it the true seat of reason? Is it a machine—one through or by which the will acts and the faculties develop and exhibit their functions and powers.

Or is it, *per se*, a force, a part of the physical existence of man, in no wise separated or capable of separation from the physical body Is the soul bound to the physical, and does it therefore terminate and end with the sleep of death?

Doubts from a scientific point of view, prove nothing. They are at best but negative testimony, and in a case where something is required to be demonstrated, some fact established, mere negative testimony is of little or no value.

The deductions of science, or the theories depending on such deductions, of which the whole field of scientific and philosophical inquiry is so full at the present moment, must not be mistaken for, nor confused with, its demonstrable facts.

We cannot be too careful in pursuing our investigations in the domain of science; or, in the study of its minor or greater problems, in waiting and hesitating, and in absolutely refusing to accept as truth that which oftentimes seems to be true, or which may be true, or which even is generally conceded to be true.

Indeed mere belief that a certain thing is probably true, or really true, is nothing.

We need not, as has that talented and brilliant professor, attempt to apply the laws and tests of physical science in the domain of the intellect, or of the beliefs and faiths of mankind, for science has little if any thing to do, and can necessarily have little to do with matters of faith or of theology, but we need or should not hesitate from any considerations or fears in following the most thorough, absorbing and careful examinations into all the issues within the domain of medical jurisprudence; for no matter where we find or how we find the real truth, we may not fear to avow or embrace it.

There may be those who fear to pursue these or similar inquiries to their legitimate sequences, through a fear that some result might disturb settled convictions or opinions, but such fears are wholly unworthy, and should not for a moment control any rational or thoughtful mind. I have never for one moment feared the result of any scientific test, examination or trial, upon any of the questions involved in the matters of my own opinions, faith or convictions, and I should not regard the faith, opinion, or the convictions of any man of value, who did fear to submit to any tests that science could really make. A faith that could not stand such a test would be unsafe and unreliable. The great danger is, in accepting those indications or leanings which sometimes appear to be the teachings of science, for scientific facts; and if we examine in this manner and upon these subjects, without great care, we are in danger of being led into the very mazes of doubt, uncertainty and daze in our investigations of medical jurisprudence which Professor Tyndall describes as his own state, in regard toa bstruse metaphysical questions which he has in vain sought to expose to scientific tests and demonstrations.

I cannot better conclude what I have to say upon this subject than to introduce an extract from a letter from M. P. Volpicelli to M. Chevreul, read before the French Academy, and which came to my notice since the above was written, which appears in the Comptes Rendus of August 31, 1874, a translation of which is also given in the October number of the Psychological and Medico-Legal Journal. M. Volpicelli says:—

"We must not forget that the characteristic *truth* in sciences belonging to the dominion of natural philosophy is *demonstration;* and that, unfortunately, in other sciences of this dominion (mathematics alone excepted) the principal facts that constitute them are not connected except by propositions more or less probable, which escape demonstration—the impossibility to pronounce one's self *à priori* on the question of knowing whether a proposition advanced as new is true or erroneous.

"And again there is a distinction, too often forgotten, between exact facts, gathered from experience or observation, and the interpretation given to them—a distinction so well drawn up by a profound genius: *phenomena alone affect our senses, the mind alone discovers the causes*, from which the consequence—the *experimental method à posteriori*, which I have just defined—should only be applied to the *interpretation* which has *led to experiments or exact observations*, for it is undoubtedly this *instigation*, this interpretation, which, if correct, forms *science*.

"It is this *distinction* of facts, *observed to be exact*, and the *interpretation given to them*, which, according to my idea, are not sufficiently known so as to be admitted into the interests of real progress, such as *scientific experiments* and, I may add, the *science of observation*."

Objects, Purposes and Aims.

The Medico-Legal Society, gentlemen, can not, in any sense, be properly called, and should not be regarded as a medical society. It is rather a scientific than a medical society. Composed of gentlemen selected from the body, in the main, of the two great professions of medicine and law, it is not organized for the purpose of taking issues upon any of these questions which excite interest, or divide the medical profession, as such, or which interest only the legal mind, but it essays to discuss and investigate such questions as relate to the science of medical jurisprudence, and to throw light upon the path of the lawyer, court, or jury, in the investigations before legal tribunals, when the aid of the scientific medical expert is needed to explain, to demonstrate, or to enlighten.

As for the physician, this society should aid, encourage, and instruct him in preparing himself for such investigations in the courts, as well as to enlighten him in the multiplied cases now constantly arising where the member of the medical profession is brought into contact with the administration of justice, and to fully explain and define his relations to the laws of the State.

My own idea has been to place this society on the basis and standing of a general scientific society. It is not, and for some time past has not been limited strictly to the two professions of law and medicine. It has been thought advisable to widen it; to embrace eminent chemists, whether medical men or not, for their value upon questions of toxological science and investigation.

It is, as I think, wisely conceded that men who might be called eminent in either science or letters, if interested in the domain of medical jurisprudence, would be a valuable acquisition to this society.

A gentleman of this city, of large intellectual attainments, considerable research, and who devotes his life to scientific and intellectual pursuits, neither a lawyer nor a physician, contributed a paper to this society last season, which was read, and that gentleman, by the unanimous action of the executive committee of this society, passed into the list of its active membership.

I should hail the acquisition of such men a great gain to such an organization as the Medico-Legal Society. Upon this subject, however, I only advance my individual opinions, and so far as I understand them, those of the legal profession in the main. The celebrated M. Devergie, when retiring from the chair of the Medico-Legal Society of Paris, speaking upon this very subject, says : I translate as before :

"In all scientific societies two conditions are usually requisite : homogeneousness in the studies and labors of each of its members ; a simultaneous course, in order to advance that particular branch of scientific study which the society represents.

"Our own has no analogy with its older sisters, save that general and common purpose, the progress of science.

"It differs from them not only in its composition but also in the end which it seeks to accomplish.

"Contrary to usage, its elements are all heterogeneous.

"It represents a fortunate conjunction of law, of medicine, of the veterinary art, and of the sciences of physiology, physics, chemistry, and natural philosophy.

"Forensic medicine is almost a borrowed science. It is not absolutely and by itself self-existent, but appeals to that universality of science on which it stands.

"Nothing is foreign to it ; its progress, like its practice, combines all these elements.

"But it is in its practice that it reveals itself as an art, by the specialty of its interpretations, its diagnosis, its prognosis, and the light by which it makes clear the facts after we have seen them from a distinct point of view."

The Paris society started on a broader, more catholic, and wider platform than we did. In addition to law and medicine, they opened their doors to veterinary surgeons, to all scientists, to physiologists as such, to physicists, pharmacists, chemists, and naturalists.

They place themselves upon the broad standard and basis of a general scientific society, and we shall make a grand forward and upward step when we emulate them in this respect and dismiss forever from our thoughts all questions of the peculiar ethics of either profession, leaving them in full force in societies purely medical for the government of medical men, and societies purely legal for the government of legal gentlemen.

We are of necessity a homogeneous, and in no sense a medical society.

We are united for the investigation of the science of medical jurisprudence, and we should be glad to welcome the light of truth, of reason, or of science, no matter whence it comes, so long as it be truth, real light, and not "science falsely so called."

In one other respect have we not given the same or as much force, prominence or attention as our Paris confrères, especially of late, that is, to the examination by a commission of our members of interesting pending questions of public or private interest in the courts.

The influence of this society in the case of Schoeppe, was doubtless of great benefit to prevent what might have been properly termed a legal murder.

I venture to recommend this very interesting and prominent field for your further labors, advising that same courage, patience and care in the investigations so forcibly recommended by M. Bèheir and which will not only increase the usefulness and importance of your labors, but make them vastly more instrumental in the accomplishment of good and the acquisition of scientific knowledge and research.*

Again thanking you, gentlemen, for the renewed expression of your continued confidence, evidenced by my re-election to this chair, so wholly unexpected and unlooked for by myself, I resume the duties you have so kindly committed to my charge, trusting for the same kindly aid in the future which I have so generously received in the past.

---

* I append an extract from the Statutes of the Medico-Legal Society of France which provides for its permanent commission, which is undoubtedly one of its most important agents :

TITRE IV.

Commission permanente.

ART. 17. Une Commission permanente, composée du Président du Secrétaire génerale et de neuf Membres titulaires, est chargée de recevoir dans l'intervalle, des séances toutes les demandes d'avis motives qui peuvent être addressées à la Societé, et d'y repondre immédiatement s'il y a lieu.

ART. 18. La Commission permanente se réunit selon les besoins et délibère d'urgence dans l'intervalle des séances.

ART. 19. Les décisions de la Commission permanente sont prises à la majorité des Membres présents, elles doivent rèunir au moins quatre voix.

ART. 20. La Commission permanente peut selon la nature des questions à résoudre s'adjoindre un ou plusieurs Membres de la société.

ART. 21. Les décisions de la Commission permanente n'engagent pas la societé; elles lui sont communiquées a la séance suivante.

ART. 22. Les Membres de la Commission permanente sont élus au scrutin, par la societe. La durée de leurs fonctions est de trois ans, et la Commission est renouvelée par tiers tous les ans.

HEALTH AND CULTURE.—We are in danger of becoming a nervous, uncomfortable, discontented, wretched race, unless we use our best thought and effort to bring the highest wisdom, and virtue, and order that are within our reach to bear upon our way of living. Hence the excellence of this American Health Association that now calls us together—where, indeed, I ought to be a learner rather than a teacher, and where I could not presume to open my lips were it not that these learned doctors, who know so much more of the matter than I do, ask me to say something from my own point of view. Instead, then, of invading their territory, and parading my ignorance of the great science and art of medicine, I will be content to stand upon my own ground, and to treat of health and the higher culture as a man who has been a preacher and pastor and general scholar may be supposed to know the subject.

Strictly speaking, health is a part of the higher culture, for body and mind are practically inseparable, and we know nothing of the sound mind apart from sound blood and brain. I am willing, for the present purpose, to take Herbert Spencer's definition of life as the basis of our discussion, and to allow that *life is the continuous adjustment of internal relations to external relations*, if by external relations we comprehend those which are social and religious as well as those which are physical. If life is the continuous adjustment of internal relations to external relations, then healthy life is such adjustment truly and fully carried out, and he is the healthy man who lives in true relations with nature, man, and God.—REV. DR. OSGOOD :—*American Pub. Health Association.* 1874.

CARBONIC ACID AND ITS FATAL EFFECTS.*

By W. H. Thayer, M.D.

The success of a doctrine depends much upon the manner in which it is presented by its advocates; and scientific facts may sometimes fail to receive universal assent, for want of being forcibly put.

The necessity of a thorough ventilation of sick rooms is nothing more than what is taught by every well-informed and thoughtful doctor of medicine. Yet so far are the majority of physicians from putting their ideas on this matter in practice with any considerable degree of consistency, that it cannot be supposed they thoroughly appreciate the premises. I purpose, therefore, to put the subject in another form, to see if it cannot be presented in such a manner as to produce a more decided effect.

I start with the proposition that the most serious impediment to recovery in fatal cases of acute disease is the daily and hourly administration of fatal doses of carbonic acid gas; and the same treatment is the chief cause of the gravity of many cases which, without this poison, would be of mild form.

So little alive to this fact are a very large proportion of medical men that it will require copious and well-authenticated illustrations to convince them. And the difficulty will be rendered still greater by the errors in some of the domestic habits of physicians themselves.

I do not intend to enter into the subject of hygiene in general, or even the management of chronic diseases, but shall confine myself to the fatal or dangerous use of carbonic acid gas, so fearfully common in the treatment of acute disease. Let a person be attacked with no matter what form of acute disease, and in nine houses out of ten the doors and windows will be immediately closed to shut out draughts, and every step taken to retain the air of the room, and avoid any material change. Most houses are now built without open fire-places, and are warmed by stoves, heaters or furnaces, which supply to parlors and bedrooms the air of the dining-room or the cellar. The lungs and the skin of the patient and attendants are constantly exhaling carbonic acid, and the lamps or gaslights are furnishing an additional supply, so that the atmosphere of the room is rapidly charged with it.

Now what is the effect of the inhalation of carbonic acid? The following bit of history will show what it does when inhaled undiluted: In the summer of 1872, a vine-grower, in the eastern part of France, having his vats partly filled with grapes, which had been pressed, and were already in the process of fermentation, had occasion to climb down into one of the vats. He had no sooner reached the bottom than he fell insensible. One of his sons fol-

---

* Read before Med. Society, Co. of Kings, N. Y., Oct. 20, 1874.

lowed immediately to assist his father, but dropped at once beside him, and another person going to their rescue shared their fate. They were with some difficulty all drawn up, but life was extinct. They were asphyxiated before they could save themselves, by the carbonic acid gas which had accumulated in a dense layer over the fermenting grapes.

Similar instances of immediate death from the inhalation of pure carbonic acid gas sometimes occur in wells which have been closely covered for many years, where the gas escaping from the soil slowly accumulates, and, having no current of air to aid its diffusion, gravitates by its weight to the bottom of the well, gradually displacing the atmospheric air. The man who opens the well, and, having put in a ladder, goes down into it, falls insensible before he reaches the bottom.

There are historic instances of slower death by the diluted carbonic acid of a close room filled with people—from that of the famous Black Hole of Calcutta down—which are so familiar to all medical men that they need not be repeated here. There can be no doubt that death in cholera is chiefly due to poisoning by carbonic acid. The blood corpuscles lose their power of taking up oxygen, and as a consequence we find the air of expiration containing oxygen alone, while carbonic acid accumulates in the tissues.

Having seen the effect of undiluted carbonic acid gas upon the healthy system, let us inquire what influence it has upon subjects of acute disease, when diluted to the proportion in which it is commonly found in an ill-ventilated apartment. I will present a very striking instance, taken from a paper on *The Causes of Typhoid Fever in Massachusetts*, published in the Second Annual Report of the State Board of Health of Massachusetts:

"A young butcher, between twenty and thirty years of age, was attacked with typhoid fever. He was a bachelor, and occupied a good-sized chamber, lighted by two windows, and having an open fireplace.

"The fever was mild, with daily febrile exacerbation, hot skin, thirst, slight diarrhœa, and rose spots, with no violent symptoms. There was no indication for drugs. He was bathed two or three times a day with tepid water, and was allowed water freely, iced or not, according to his taste. The covering of his body was regulated by his sensations. A slight wood fire, just enough to insure ventilation, was kept in the fireplace, and one of the windows was raised a little.

"As soon as his family, who lived in the country, heard of his illness, two of them, a maiden aunt and a sister, came to the city to take care of him. They reached his house one afternoon, just after my visit. My patient was, as described above, comfortably sick, with a pulse about eighty, and without delirium. They were frightened to find their relative, who was sick with typhoid fever, so poorly cared for. Guided by their theory of the proper treatment of fever, they proceeded without informing me to reform matters.

"They pinned a blanket over each window so as to exclude the light, and closed the open window; they closed the chimney with a fireboard and set up an 'air tight' stove, in which they made a fire.

In order to mkee him sweat he was packed in blankets, and hot herb-tea was given him.

"When I called the next day, I found his room dark, and filled with a hot and foul atmosphere. The odor was of that offensive sort that sick chambers are too often charged with. But the greatest change was in the sick man, whom I had left so comfortable the day before. He was wrapped in blankets, his skin was dry and very hot, his tongue dry, his lip cracked, his eye wild, his pulse 120, and he was so restless and delirious that it was all his attendants could do to keep him in bed.

"His aunt said she came to nurse her nephew, and had found him with open windows, exposed to noise and currents of air, drinking cold water as freely as he chose, and taking no medicine. These evils she had endeavored to remedy, but in spite of all her efforts he had grown rapidly worse."

The physician states his conversation with the aunt, and his refusal to continue in charge unless everything was restored as it had been on her arrival. The windows were opened, the stove was removed, a fire made in the chimney, and the blankets were taken from the patient. He goes on to say, "I gave the sick man a tumbler of water, which he drank as if he were quenching an internal fire. All this they bore in silence, but when I called for a large tub, and made preparations for a bath, they remonstrated : a bath, and particularly a cold bath would kill him.

"Remonstrances were unavailing, and my patient got a cool affusion by pouring water all over him. He was then put to bed, lightly covered, and soon went to sleep. By night his condition had considerably improved, and on the next day, twenty-four hours later, his fever assumed its previous mild type. His pulse was about 80, and his head tolerably clear. He made a satisfactory convalescence."

The case just related is a fair specimen of a very common malpractice, occurring every day, but escaping notice because the effects of carbonic acid poisoning are not often brought out in so bold relief. The gas existing in a small amount as a component part of the atmosphere, and insidiously accumulating in every inhabited room, we do not easily estimate its effects or the frequency of their occurence, until we undertake its thorough removal ; and it is by cases in which this has been successfully done that we can discover the terrible influence of this poison upon acute diseases. I shall therefore further illustrate it by showing the marked improvement that takes place in acute diseases upon the removal of patients from an atmosphere that is saturated with it. The following cases exhibit the subject in a still more marked manner than the one already cited. They are the most remarkable that ever were published, and ought to be reprinted every ten years, until the whole medical profession has fully assimilated the knowledge they afford. The account about to be given is from a letter of a citizen of Perth Amboy, and statements of Dr. C. McKnight Smith, to Dr. John H. Griscom of New York, in 1852, published in the transactions of the New York Academy of Medicine, and afterwards included in a letter from Dr. Griscom to a select committee of the U. S. Senate, on the causes of the sickness and mortality in emigrant ships, and published in their report in 1854. It is as follows:

"In August, 1837, a number of ships, with emigrant passengers, arrived at Perth Amboy from Liverpool and other ports, on board of some of which ship fever prevailed. There was no hospital or other accommodations in the town, and an arrangement was made to land the sick, and place them in an open wood about a mile and a-half from the town. Rough shanties, floored with boards, and covered with sails, were erected, and thirty-six patients were taken from on board ship, with boats, and carried in wagons to the encampment. Of the thirty-six, twelve were insensible, in the last stage of fever, and not expected to live twenty-four hours.

The day after the landing there was a heavy rain, and the sick were found next morning wet, and their bedding—such as it was—drenched with the rain. The number at the encampment was increased by new patients to eighty-two.

On board the ship, which was cleansed after landing the passengers, four of the crew were taken with typhus, and two of them died. Some of the nurses at the encampment were taken sick, but recovered. All the eighty-two passengers recovered.

Dr. Smith, who attended them, says: "The medical treatment was exceedingly simple, consisting, in the main, of an occasional laxative or enema, vegetable acid and bitters; wine was liberally administered, together with the free use of cold water, buttermilk and animal broths. The four sailors who sickened after the arrival of the vessel were removed to the room of an ordinary dwelling-house; the medical treatment in their case was precisely similar, yet two of them died. My opinion is, that had the eighty-two treated at the encampment been placed in a common hospital, many of them would also have fallen victims." Thus far, Dr. Smith. The main object of my paper is to show that the administration of poisonous doses of carbonic acid gas forms a very prominent part of the usual treatment of acute diseases, and in saying that the treatment of the four sailors was precisely similar to that of the emigrants, the reporter makes a very important error. I contend that this matter of getting rid of the carbonic acid from the atmosphere, which is usually referred to as of secondary importance, should be considered as much a part of the medical treatment as the administration of any article of the materia medica, as it is of much more serious consequence than the use of any one of them.

Two very grave cases of double pneumonia, lately treated, gave convincing evidence of the imperative necessity of ridding the air of the sick room of carbonic acid gas. In both cases I was satisfied that if the amount of carbonic acid which we find in average sick rooms had been added to the atmosphere of the room, the patients would have died, for they could not have borne the addition of any other depressing influence.

The first case was that of a young man, twenty years old, a book-keeper, not robust, and a sufferer from serious dyspepsia for several years past, who, on the night of May 13, 1873, had a rigor followed by fever, which he attributed to exposure in walking in Greenwood Cemetery on the evening before. On the evening of the 13th the characteristic symptoms of pneumonia appeared. I first saw him on the 14th. He was sitting up in bed, unable to lie down from pain in the left hypochondrium ; he coughed much, with expectoration of viscid, rusty sputa ; had bronchial respiration, bronchophony and dullness on percussion over the left back and side, from the middle of scapula to base of chest ; he had no appetite; his tongue had a thick, white pasty coat ; pulse, 130 ; respiration, 44 ; temperature, 103.

In the night of the 16th, hepatization of the right lower lobe took place, with great aggravation of all the symptoms, increased dyspnœa and debility and lividity of the extremities. On the 18th the expectoration consisted of an abundant sanious fluid. Convalescence began on the 20th. On the 21st the returning crepitus was heard in both backs. On the 25th he took solid food.

The case was very grave when the pneumonia became double, and the patient's aspect was so bad on that morning that a neighboring physician, who was called in before I arrived, would not advise any remedies, as he considered him dying and past relief. The lividity of his nails continued very marked for two or three days. But persistent nourishment, active stimulation, free use of carbonate of ammonia, exchanged for the oil of turpentine when the sputa became watery and bloody, quinine, counter-irritation, and the careful and thorough removal of carbonic acid from the air, brought him through. Although the weather was cool, so that we had a fire in the grate, two windows were kept constantly wide open, and an outer door, on the opposite side of the room, much of the time, and a current secured through the room, and across the bed. This was persisted in day and night, and in all weathers, including a cold rain storm ; and of all the agents in his treatment I considered the careful removal of the vitiated air the most important.

In four days from the initiatory chill the second lung was hepatized, in five days more returning crepitus was found, in four more he took solid food, and in five more both lower lobes were found in nearly normal condition.

The other case referred to is that of a lady, 60 years of age, whom I treated in April, 1874, with double pneumonia, followed by diphtheria, involving the entire mouth and pharynx, which latter relapsed and was complicated with acute nephritis, characterized with albuminuria and œdema of lower extremities. Under a series of a affections of so grave a character, a woman of 60 might well be expected to succumb. But she recovered completely—a result which I should not have dared to hope for, had not a good current of air been maintained through her room by means of open windows and doors, day and night, and in all weathers, the temperature being raised by a fire.

In four other cases of simple pneumonia, treated last Spring, the recovery was remarkably rapid under similar circumstances.

I need not multiply instances; but in all acute affections I have always regarded the means employed for a constant and thorough removal of vitiated air from the sick room as the most important of all remedial measures, and in grave cases as giving the patient many additional chances of life.

In support of my own opinion and practice I have an opportunity of adducing the valuable testimony of Dr. C. R. Agnew, in the following letter from him :

"NEW YORK, *Oct.* 14, 1874.

"WM. HENRY THAYER, M. D. :

"*My Dear Doctor*--I must answer briefly and from memory the questions you propound regarding my experience in treating cases of pneumonia in the open air. At the breaking out of the late war I took charge of the State Volunteer Hospital, New York, and had about 120 beds in the north building of the New York Hospital filled with promiscuous cases of those who had become ill *in transitu* from receiving camps to the seat of war. * * * Among the pneumonic cases were several cases of double pneumonia, marked by very distressing, threatening, and intractable dyspnœa. They were treated as I had been taught to treat such cases by Swett, Alonzo Clark, Camman, and my other teachers, but the dyspnœa remained a most distressing symptom, accompanied by exhausting insomnolence. I ventilated the wards as well as I could, and separated the cases as much as possible, but without beneficial result.

"Finally, I adopted the expedient of carrying the patients on litters into the open air and placing them at the south side of the hospital building, where nothing could obstruct the freest circulation of the atmosphere. The litters were all provided with good thick hair mattresses and enough of fleecy blankets to protect the patients. I adjusted to each litter a spirit-lamp and funnel, so that a current of warm air could be made at will to play gently upon the feet of the patient, when his temperature was low or the day unusually cool. I sent an attendant to watch by one or two litters, provided with a parasol, with which to shield the patients occasionally from the sun. I sent the litters out in the early morning, and sometimes kept them out till after dark.

"The effect upon the condition of the patients was invariably favorable—there was marked relief of the dyspnœa within half an hour after the removal from the wards—and I firmly believe that I saved some cases of pneumonia that I otherwise should have lost; this was especially true of some cases of double pneumonia following measles in the adult. I invariably noticed that the recovery was quicker—the resolution went on with astonishing rapidity—and that there was a more vigorous play of the recuperative forces. I had similar experience with fever cases. Indeed I followed the plan of carrying my sickest patients out of doors, and leaving the convalescents to take care of themselves.

"I ought to say that this practice extended through the summer and autumn and well into the winter.

"Ever sincerely yours,

"C. R. AGNEW."

Wherever we have the deadly influence of carbonic acid in the sickroom, we have also an accumulation of organic matters which have been eliminated through the lungs and skin, which are unquestionably a dangerous addition to the air which is to be respired, especially in the case of zymotic diseases. We are not so well acquainted with the toxic properties of these excreta as of the carbonic acid, but for practical purposes it is sufficient to know that the measures which free the atmosphere of one will also get rid of the other. Or if diffusion is not all that is needed to dispose of the organic matter, carbolic acid will accomplish its destruction.

In the treatment of all acute diseases, the advice of Nathan Smith, given fifty years ago, in his admirable essay on "typhus," as to the method of getting rid of the carbonic acid from the atmosphere, is as appropriate as in the cases to which he applied it: "The patient should be kept in a spacious room. His bed should be of straw or husks, especially in the warm season; and it should not be placed in a corner, but brought out into the room. We should contrive to have a current of air pass over the bed by means of doors and windows. It is well to have a fireplace in the room, and in the night, when the air is very still, though the weather should be warm, a small fire kindled, so as to cause a current up chimney, and by that means often to change the atmosphere of the room. In the warm season, the windows should be kept open night and day."

The greatest obstacle to the growth of correct views on this important division of therapeutics is to be found in the faulty construction of houses and contrivances for warming. If we live at home in an atmosphere constantly poisoned by carbonic acid, we are not likely to appreciate fully its effect upon the sick. I trust that the presentation of such very strong illustrations as I have been enabled to offer, may aid in inducing a more earnest attention to the subject.*

One word as to the tendency to the accumulation of carbonic acid in a room. The error often comes from a misapprehension of the means required to get rid of it. Experiments show that it is diffused through the air, and will be found pretty equally throughout any close room, except that it is in its greatest amount near the ceiling in an occupied room, simply because when exhaled it is warmer than the air of the room. Therefore, it is to be removed only by an entire and steady change of the whole atmosphere of the room; which can be accomplished by having a perceptible current through it from side to side, and in no other way. We ought to be convinced of the insufficiency of one open window for getting rid of anything noxious in the air, when we see how long a cloud of tobacco smoke will hang almost motionless in the room when there is an opening on one side only. It should convince us that something more than the mod-

* It is not safe to reason from the well to the sick, to infer that the sick can tolerate an atmosphere that the well are often accustomed to. It is true that thousands of people continue to live, and without serious sickness for a time, in rooms largely charged with carbonic acid gas. In a condition of ordinary vigor the system may resist the deleterious influence for a long time, or become gradually accustomed to a lower vitality, or eventually develop some chronic affection. But the proportion of carbonic acid in the atmosphere that one in ordinary health could bear will be sufficient to aggravate materially the severity of an acute disease.

erate opening of one window is needed to purify the sick room of its poisonous gases.

In the outer air, even in the city streets, the amount of carbonic acid has little variation, and is kept within healthy limits, by the force of currents aiding its diffusion ; but in an occupied room it constantly accumulates, and even with tolerable contrivances for ventilation is found by examination, to exist in an amount far beyond its normal proportion. In the experiments of the late Dr. R. C. Stiles (published in the report of the Metropolitan Board of Health for 1869), on the atmosphere of the public schools of Brooklyn, some of which are regarded by the Board of Education as models in their method of ventilation, the amount of carbonic acid was always in excess, in one school being present in eight times the ordinary amount. The atmosphere of a large proportion of dwelling-houses would not give any more favorable results.

THE HEALTH OF THE PEOPLE.—The glory of a nation is in its strength, not of physical prowess merely, but of that mental depth, breadth, and energy which subordinates the lower instincts and the exterior forces to the will. These two kinds of energy are most intimately correlated, each depending for its highest manifestations upon perfection of organization. The doctrine may now be said to be established, at least among all the deepest and most advanced thinkers, that organization and function are one. The inter-dependence and the inter-action of organic structures and their dependence upon exterior conditions supports rather than invalidates the doctrine. The full significance of these views upon the great questions of human welfare and human development does not seem to be generally realized. So far as mere terrestrial results are concerned, they mean that the biologist must supersede the theologian ; that progress, whether of body or of brain, must be through the culture of organic structure, in all its manifold relations. The popular exclusion of this doctrine in questions of hygiene and of ethics, or the trust reposed in addressing every reformatory effort of this kind to an abstract ethereal entity, either in or above ourselves, is justly chargeable with the terrible indictment of being the main influence by which mankind have been made the most panic-stricken, the most sickly, the most frequently and fearfully deformed, and the most likely to die at an untimely period, and, as malefactors in torment and for the vindication of law, of all animate beings. It has caused many worthy persons to believe that afflictions and sickness are sent, not brought upon ourselves, and that, while it is a binding duty to care for the sick, the deaf, the blind, the maimed, the idiotic and the insane, it is scarcely thought to be obligatory, in a public or personal sense, to prevent through purely mundane instrumentalities, any or all of these evils from ever more afflicting our race. The biologist and sanitarian see the subject in a wholly different light. All animate forms of structure, and all its qualities and variations, are held to be the outcomes, and the outcomes only, of natural and immutable law. When we abide by the law the outcome is good; when we do not it is bad.—DR. J. R. BLACK,—*American Public Health Association*, 1874.

BURNS AND SCALDS.

By John Morris, M.D., Baltimore, Md.

It is very difficult to write a paper on burns and scalds adapted to popular use, and one really intended for physicians and surgeons is scarcely fitted for the numerous lay readers of the "Sanitarian;" and yet there is no subject concerning which the people generally so much require knowledge and proper advice. The introduction of coal oil as an illuminating agent in our times, has been the cause of a vast amount of human suffering, for scarcely a day passes by that some accident from its use is not chronicled in the public journals. The mortuary reports of the city of Baltimore for the years 1872 and 1873 show that no less than fifty-two persons lost their lives from burns. That many of these might have been saved had proper treatment been pursued, we are clearly convinced. The old method of treating burns —the method that has been followed, we may say, for centuries—if not barbarous, was at least the most crude and simple imaginable; bathing with carron oil, that is a mixture of linseed oil and lime water, and soppy applications of the same on cotton constituted the whole armamentarium both of surgeon and layman. Even at this day, this is the course taught by the oldest teachers in the colleges of this country and sanctioned by the medical profession very generally. About fifty years ago, a plan of local stimulation for burns was suggested in place of carron oil by an English gentleman, Doctor Kentish, of Bristol, which for a time was used to a considerable extent. Doctor Kentish recommended the application of spirits of turpentine in a diluted state, to the affected parts. This suggestion met the approbation of Mr. Abernethy, and why it has entirely fallen into disuse we are at a loss to know. Forty years ago Doctor George McClellan, of Jefferson College, characterized carron oil as inert and useless, and Mr. Skey, of Saint Bartholomew's, has more recently expressed the same opinion. In our judgment, however, it is not the mere local application that it is important to consider, but the general management of the sufferer at the time of the accident; and to point out the proper course then to be pursued is more particularly our object at the present moment. What treatment then should be adopted?

Before proceeding to make suggestions on this point, we will say a word concerning the character of burns and the causes of their fatal termination.

Character of Burns.—Surgeons generally speak of burns in three forms of severity: those affecting the skin alone, those affecting the areolar tissue, and those affecting the whole structure of the part. French surgeons go further, and describe six degrees of injury, the sixth being Dupuytren's degree of incineration. The degrees, however, are of very little consequence, so far as treatment is concerned, inasmuch as the danger of a burn does not depend on its severity, but its extent. M. Giraldès tells us that lunatics frequently introduce their heads into stoves, and get their skulls roasted even to the brain substance, and yet recover.

Cause of Death.—Patients die either from shock, exhaustion, or from the effects of nervous reaction. In many instances they die in a few hours, in complete consciousness, no reaction having taken place. Such a case occurred in our practice during the past year. These deaths must be attributed entirely to shock, as they are always free from the coma, congestion, and sometimes the algidity which attend other fatal cases. As this paper is not intended to be a surgical one, but for the guidance of the general reader, we shall devote ourselves to the consideration of the first stage of burns, or that condition immediately following the accident, and the treatment then necessary.

Treatment.—The first step is to remove the clothing from the patient. As rest is all important, this should not be done by the old plan of taking it off piece by piece, but by removing it by a few skilful cuts with a knife or scissors. The patient should then be instantly wrapped in a blanket, or blankets, or large masses of cotton, if at hand, so as to create heat, and thus re-establish the circulation. Patients frequently exhaust themselves by their outcries, and to guard against the depression of nervous force brought about by this cause, anæsthetics should at once be employed. Chloroform or ether should be administered in sufficient quantity to induce partial, or, if necessary, complete unconsciousness. If these agents are not at hand, large doses of opium should be given. This is all important, as the patient must not be allowed to suffer if we wish to conserve the powers of life. The dressing should be made while the patient is in this state. Carron oil, as before stated, is utterly useless, if not injurious. Of all the oils, linseed, in our opinion, is the worst, as it is the soonest to be absorbed by the atmosphere, and become dry. In cases of bad scalds of children, in which a large part of the body is involved, we know no dressing so good as a bran bed, that is a bed of bran, in which the patient may lie, and be entirely covered with a thick investment of the same. This dressing has the advantage of not requiring change, for each day as the moist particles fall off they can be replaced with fresh bran without disturbing the patient. One of the severest cases of scald we ever met recovered by this treatment. A great deal of harm is done to patients by frequent dressings, and any method that obviates this is most desirable. Patients frequently are exposed for hours to the action of the air, suffering unnecessary pain by the old and tedious process of dressing. The air itself does no injury, but the extreme hyperæsthesia of the skin produces a state of nervous tremor which leads to exhaustion. Any one who has seen a case of hydrophobia can readily understand this condition of skin hyperæsthesia.

In burns of the extremities there is no immediate application so serviceable to relieve pain, as hot or cold water, and, strange to say, they act equally well. If the appliances are at hand, the cold bath, as practiced by Hebra, is the best. Those who have visited his wards in Vienna, and seen his treatment of burns by a bed made of straps, in a cold bath, can bear witness to the successful and scientific character of this procedure. For small burns, warm water acts admirably. We have said before, that anæsthetics should be employed in all burns of an extensive character, but, before their effect is allowed to pass off, applications should be made to produce anæsthesia of the parts affected. We have heretofore used for this purpose a solution of Labarraque's chloride of soda, of the strength of an ounce to a pint of water, adding two or three grains of morphia to the solution. This has generally given great relief to the patient, indeed, in a short time destroying all the extreme sensibility. Carbolic acid has been highly recommended as a local anæsthetic, and it may be possible that a solution of it in water, in combination with morphia, might act still better. After a free application of either of these solutions, the parts may be thickly covered with cotton batting. This helps to counterbalance the chilliness, and gives a comparative degree of comfort. In superficial burns of a limited extent, nothing is required but simple cold water dressing. Brandy should not be administered whenever opium or ether can be obtained, as it remotely exercises a depressing influence. Strong hot coffee is the best drink that can possibly be given to counteract nervous exhaustion, or remedy the effects of shock. If brandy is given at all, it should be given with coffee. All earthy applications, such as chalk, calaminaria, etc., should be avoided, as they are not only therepeutically inert, but may interfere with the process of restoration. Local stimulation, such as the application of turpentine, or a solution of nitrate of silver, as practiced at Saint Bartholmew's Hospital, is no doubt proper treatment in the second stage of burns, but as this belongs more especially to the domain of surgery, we forbear to discuss it, as well as the treatment of the after consequences of burns, such as ulceration of the bowels, particularly of Peyer's glands, congestion of the lungs, cicatricial contractions, etc.

In conclusion, we will briefly sum up the recommendations before suggested:—

First. Remove the clothing by cutting it from the body.

Second. Wrap the patient in blankets.

Third. If pain be excessive, administer chloroform, ether, or large doses of opium, and let the necessary dressing be made while the patient is in a state of partial or total insensibility.

Fourth. Produce anæsthesia of the burned or scalded parts by the application of a solution of carbolic acid and morphia. (This solution can be made in almond or olive oil.)

Fifth. After this, wrap the patient in masses of cotton batting.

Sixth. Avoid brandy, and give coffee as a stimulant.

If these simple rules be followed, much suffering may be alleviated, and many a life saved, which otherwise would be lost by the ignorance and mismanagement of attendants.

Building Ground.—We want more of a dry earth system. Perfect underdrainage is the first great need of most cities. Regulations of cellars, and of all other holes below the surface is the next great study. The proper airing of all sub-structure, because of its proximity to the ground, comes in next for consideration. What can we do to sweeten or purify surface-soil already formed is another point. The great question of what to do with all refuse so as to keep it out of city soil is the large and momentous subject which must ever present itself to our attention.—E. M. Hunt, M. D., *American Public Health Association*, 1874.

COMMON DANGERS OF HOUSE-DRAINING.

To the Editor of The Sanitarian:

A valuable article by General Viele, in your interesting journal for November, adds one more powerful illustration to the criminal carelessness and to the reckless neglect with which house-drainage and water supply are changed into an imminent source of danger, instead of contributing to our health and comfort. House-drainage and trapping have been frequently considered in THE SANITARIAN; their important bearing on health and life ripely discussed, and the defects and errors in their construction clearly shown. There can be no doubt that with our progress in recognizing the origin of disease, its classification will be considerably simplified, and that the number of acknowledged zymotic diseases will be largely increased.

The application of science will lead to the most important practical results for the preservation of health, and for the prolongation of human life.

The general principle that "emanations from decomposing animal and vegetable matters" form a subtle, insidious and dangerous poison, is so well established that there is no need of its definition or explanation. But we have to be forever watchful; our sneaky enemy lurks and hides everywhere; every nook, every corner containing even a minute quantity of dust or dirt, every little heap of refuse, every gutter, swamp, or hollow, every house built on filled-in ground, or on swampy soil, every place not kept scrupulously clean and well drained, will generate zymotic, and, under certain conditions, contagious disease. Every crack, crevice or opening of your house-drain or waste pipes, forms but an outlet for the crater under your very feet, throwing out continually its contents of impalpable noxious fumes. Occasionally you will read an article in the morning paper, telling of a mysterious and terrible visitation in a respectable family; some of its members were suddenly carried off by death; others were hardly expected to recover. You may suppose the story to be sensational; but no, it is the fearful, well authenticated truth. The most carefully conducted analysis has not succeeded to trace any poison in food or drink; the post mortem examination shows but traces of inflammation or engorgement of blood-vessels, and no cause is assigned for this isolated and sudden outbreak.

But to the initiated the matter is very plain; the deadly miasma from a drain, from a waste pipe, perhaps from the bath-tub or wash-bowl, next to the sleeping room, has found vent; the cellar may not be perfectly clean, or the trapping of pipes, etc., may not be perfect, or perchance left off altogether for economy's sake. Now this neglect of trapping, or the use of imperfectly constructed and porous traps, is a fruitful source of danger. In addition to the previous and exhaustive articles on "traps and trapping," in your valuable journal, I would only state that traps made of sheet or rolled lead, and soldered on the seams, are poor and dangerous; that each trap must have a drain attachment distinct and separate from its body, and that this drain screw is of as much importance as the trap itself. A kitchen boiler is intended to supply hot water for domestic purposes. The water back of the cooking range and the pipes running to the stories above, are connected with it, while a waste pipe underneath it connects with either the sink waste or the drain in the cellar.

When repairs to the boiler, to the range, or connecting pipes are needed, the sediment cock under the boiler is opened, and the water is allowed to run off. As soon as this is done, the noxious and deadly vapors from waste and soil pipes will ascend and impregnate the atmosphere of the house. The needed repairs are completed, the water from the street pipes is admitted again to boiler and pipes, and it absorbs all the poisonous gas left in them. The air, the water—the food cooked with it—yea, our very walls, clothes, and furniture—are infected, and there remains nothing mysterious to account for the sudden and unforeseen causes of disease or death. The most dangerous enemies to health and life are ignorance and false economy. Every sin or shortcoming against the laws of nature carries its punishment, and those laws have to be studied and carried out to preserve a sound mind in a sound body. LEOPOLD BRANDEIS.

BROOKLYN, *Nov.* 3, 1874.

RELATIONS OF GEOLOGY TO WATER SUPPLY.—The difference between geology and sanitary science was that the geologist studied the water supply as a whole; the sanitarian only as an element of man's health or disease. The springs which issue from the mountain glen were generally very pure. The compounds of soda, iron, lime, or magnesia, were often present in what was supposed to be pure water. Mineral substances held in solution were often factors of disease. There was however, a distinct class of substances of organic origin which many streams took up. These substances were seldom poisonous, as vegetable matter held in solution was much less harmful than when allowed to escape through the air. Animal matter in solution was, however, very poisonous. Cases were cited in which whole families, and sometimes streets of families, were stricken with fever by drinking water impregnated with animal matter. * * There is a great deal of misapprehension in regard to subterranean waters. A little calculation would show that subterraneous streams as popularly imagined were very rare. The porous rocks were the natural filters, and if they were given sufficient time they could change the water of a sewer to sparkling spring water. Yet it should not be supposed that clear water was necessarily pure, any more than cold air is necessarily pure. The conclusion which geology turned over to sanitary science was that drift wells were generally so contaminated as to be prolific sources of evil. Fevers and pestilence were less to be dreaded than those insidious agencies, which lower the tone of the system, and leaves it open to the attacks of disease. In answer to the question, "Where shall we find pure water?" he would answer from wells, from springs, and running streams, but these must be carefully guarded. If wells were rightly located and constructed they would yield pure water.—Prof. EDWARD ORTON, *American Public Health Association*, 1874.

THE STATUS OF SANITARY SCIENCE IN THE UNITED STATES.

An Address before the American Public Health Association, Nov. 10th, 1874.

BY STEPHEN SMITH, M.D., of N. Y., President.

We enter this morning upon the second annual session of this association, and it will not be out of place, in calling it to order, to briefly notice the progress of our work and of sanitary studies, investigations and administration during the past year.

The executive committee has been occupied much of the year in perfecting arrangements for publishing the papers which had accumulated in the hands of the Secretary. It was found, on conferring with publishers, impossible to publish the volume without going outside of the membership of the Association and securing an adequate number of subscribers.

Accordingly a thorough canvass was made, chiefly in New York and Brooklyn, and the result was most favorable. With the number of copies due to members of the association, the requisite number of subscribers was readily obtained, largely from the medical profession.

The task of preparing manuscript for the press by obtaining the revision of authors and careful personal review, and of superintending the printing, has added an incredible amount of labor to the otherwise onerous duties of the secretary.

The fruits of those labors are before you in a volume which in literary and scientific merit and in typographical execution has no superior in sanitary literature.

It will lay the foundation for the permanent prosperity and usefulness of this association, and stimulate into healthy activity all associated efforts in the agitation of those great questions in preventive medicine which underlie national health and prosperity.

The last meeting was rendered painfully interesting by the detailed reports from those cities and towns of the Southwest which had just been frightfully ravaged by two of the most dreaded scourges of the human family.

These reports reminded one of chapters on *Epidemics of the Middle Ages*. It seemed incredible that such scenes of human suffering and death, from any form of pestilential disease, could have occurred in this age of advanced knowledge in methods of prevention, and especially under our observation.

And yet these reports proved that cholera and yellow fever spread through those Southern towns, depopulating houses, districts, and even villages, without other more efficient efforts to control its progress than a stampede of all who could escape. Shreveport and Memphis, especially, have achieved a memorable place in the annals of American sanitary medicine. Favorably situated for defence, they succumbed to these foes without an effort at protection. If but a tithe of the moneys expended in the care of the sick had been previously employed in defensive measures, both of these towns would doubtless have escaped. And what is true of Shreveport and Memphis is equally true of all the towns devastated by these epidemics.

The terrible lessons which these experiences have taught, it has been the aim of this association to gather and record in its annual volume.

The collection of reports from every locality which these pestilences visited, by competent observers, has been a most difficult task, but their value will amply compensate for the labor required.

There was much apprehension at the last meeting that the present year would be marked by a renewal of both cholera and yellow fever in the South and West. But the year has been remarkable rather for the absence of epidemics of every form, and a greatly reduced death rate from ordinary diseases.

During the year 1873, cholera spread very widely over the continent of Europe, commencing in the Eastern districts, but it was at no time nor place nearly as fatal as in our own towns, owing to the timely measures adopted for its prevention. There was the same apprehension of a general prevalence of cholera in Europe during the present season as in this country, but it has not been realized. On a larger retrospect it may be said that the current year has not been marked by the outbreak or prevalence of epidemics in any part of the civilized world.

Cholera and yellow fever, which rarely fail to depopulate some cities of the world in the course of each year, have scarcely been heard from in 1874. Small-pox, after attaining the proportions of a world-wide epidemic in 1872, has again assumed the character of a local pestilence, domesticating itself only in unprotected communities.

A review of the public health reports of the various countries now making periodical returns, and which include the civilized world, shows that the present has been an exceptionally healthy year. Not only has there been no movement on the part of the great epidemics, but the general death rate of the people has been much less than during the preceding year.

The meeting of the International Sanitary Conference at Vienna, on July 1, was an important event in the history of the present year. Representatives were present from England, France, Germany, Denmark, Norway, Sweden, Switzerland, Portugal, Italy, Turkey, Russia, Egypt, Persia, Greece, and many minor governments.

The object of this conference was to consult "on the establishment of uniform quarantine regulations, and the formation of an international commission on pestilential diseases."

Prof. Sigmund, in his opening remarks, very justly said: "The pestilence which in its periodical visitations during more than four decades has snatched away millions of men from countries in the most flourishing civilization, which has a thousand-fold imperilled international intercourse, and which even threatens to advance, was well fitted to induce the governments concerned to enter on a common course of action, in order to frame adequate and generally applicable regulations as to the means of warding it off."

The conclusions to which this conference arrived with much unanimity are of vast importance to the civilized world. It concludes:

1. That Asiatic cholera, susceptible of epidemic extension, is not developed spontaneously except in India, and when it appears in other countries it is invariably by introduction from without.

2. Cholera is transmissible by man, but man is not considered the specific cause apart from the influence of locality.

3. Cholera can be propagated by articles coming from an infected place, which have been used by and belonged to persons afflicted with cholera.

4. Cholera can be propagated by drinks, particularly by water.

In regard to quarantine, the conference adopted conclusions quite at variance with the opinions so long prevalent in Southern Europe.

It recommended only maritime quarantine, and at ports through which passed routes of travel.

The quarantine regulations require personal inspection of persons and cargo, and only such detention as may be necessary to observe the exposed persons for a limited period, and cleanse and disinfect the infected vessel.

The session closed with the recommendation that a permanent international commission be established for the study and prevention of pestilential diseases.

It is humiliating to state that the United States Government was not only not represented in this conference, but there is no evidence that the existence of such a conference was even recognized. And yet the United States has as much real interest in the prevention of cholera, yellow fever, and other pestilential diseases as any European state.

So rapid is the communication between foreign ports and this country than an epidemic of any form in the northern seaport towns of Europe is as immediately threatening to our communities as to those of the States where it is prevailing. The enlightened zeal which civilized and equally semi-civilized States, like Egypt and Persia, exhibit in the effort to protect the people from epidemic pestilences, stands in remarkable contrast with the indifference which our Government manifests, even when these epidemics are ravaging its fairest cities.

An interesting experiment was attempted by the British Social Science Association. At the meeting held in Leeds, in 1871, it arranged for an exhibition of sanitary, educational, and domestic appliances.

The success was so great that the exhibition was repeated the following year at Norwich, during the session of the association.

The result was still more favorable, and an immense number of articles was placed on exhibition.

At the opening of the fair no less than 8,000 persons were in attendance. The amount of useful information in regard to improved domestic appliances gained by the people was most gratifying, and resulted in a large distribution of useful articles. At the recent meeting at Glasgow the exhibition took place, and was a marked success. It may be well for this association to consider the propriety of encouraging similar exhibitions in this country.

The progress of sanitary organization in the United States during the year has not been satisfactory.

Maryland is the only State which organized a State Board of Health, making the seventh now in existence. Bills were introduced into the Legislatures of New York and Pennsylvania, but failed to become laws.

In New Jersey a Commission of Health was appointed to report upon general sanitary questions, and it is believed that a State Board of Health will be organized as a result of the work of this commission. Local Boards of Health have been established very extensively, and there are now, as our correspondence shows, upwards of three hundred such organizations.

It is evident that Boards of Health have somewhat improved in their membership, the medical element becoming stronger as well as more respectable.

There was an effort made during the last session of Congress to obtain sanitary legislation, and the attention which was given to the subjects presented for consideration, and the general interest manifested, gave evidence of the feasibility of securing, at no distant day, such co-operation on the part of the general government as may be needful to perfect sanitary organizations for defence against foreign epidemics, or the control and suppression of domestic pestilences which have a national character and importance.

The Surgeon General was authorized by Congress to investigate the outbreak of the cholera of 1873, by minute personal inquiry, and the report which will emanate from that department will, we believe, be one of the most valuable contributions yet made to the literature of that pestilence. The Senate, by resolution, directed the Secretary of the Treasury to order a thorough study of the yellow fever of 1873, by the medical officers of the Marine Hospital service, and this report will be a valuable collection of all the facts bearing on the origin and spread of that plague.

The interest which Congress has taken in the thorough examination of the outbreak and spread of these great national epidemics, which have so often devastated our most flourishing cities, destroying for the time all commerce, and causing wide-spread ruin, is a most hopeful feature in the progress of sanitary inquiry in this country.

For the first time in the history of the government, the Secretary of the Treasury and the Secretary of War required coöperation of the officers of their respective services with local sanitary authorities in the enforcement of "the quarantine and other restraints established by the health laws of any State," as provided by the laws of 1796. This co-operation of the officers of the general government with local authorities, is a most important and salutary provision in the early legislation of this country, and its enforcement at this time gives renewed indications of the growing interest of the heads of departments in organizing methods of prevention against foreign epidemics.

Sanitary literature has made but little progress during the year in the United States. THE SANITARIAN, edited by Dr. Bell, has very ably sustained our periodical literature, and has done good service in awakening a general interest in sanitary subjects. The reports of the State Boards of Health, with their exhaustive special reports, are invaluable documents to circulate among the people. The reports of local boards have improved during the year, and several will rank as permanent contributions to sanitary science. But we are still obliged to look to Europe, and especially to Germany and England, for that class of works which will lay permanent foundations for the establishment of preventive medicine as a science and an art.

The past year has witnessed the organization of other national bodies not unlike our own, and devoted to the same important objects.

England has its National Sanitary Association, and the leaders of sanitary reform, both in Germany and Russia, have organized national voluntary associations for the promotion of the study of sanitary science and the development of measures necessary to its practical application.

It becomes more and more evident that associations of a voluntary character, like our own, and those of European States, are essential to the healthful progress of the great movement towards thorough and useful sanitary organization. They educate the people, and prepare a public sentiment capable of sustaining any advance the State may make.

The responsibility resting upon these associations is, therefore, of no slight and unimportant nature. As pioneers in investigation and creators of public opinion, they should be capable of bringing to the study and discussion of every object, minds trained to original research, and judgments in capable of being biased or prejudiced by anything but TRUTH.

And of these national organizations of voluntary effort, the American Public Health Association must rank as most important, for it has to cultivate a virgin field, and educate a public sentiment which is at best liable to be unstable. It can rely upon the aid of no intelligent sovereign, as in Europe, but has to trust the sovereign will of a people prompt to receive impressions, but not stable in maintaining a fixed order of things. For this reason our work is peculiar.

We must not only lay broad and deep the foundations of our public health service in the thorough enlightenment of the people, the principles of public and domestic hygiene, but we must educate each coming generation, that a national faith in preventive medicine shall be established which no political or social revolution can disturb, much less destroy. In order to successfully accomplish this great task, we must inquire minutely and accurately into the causes of sickness of every form among all classes of the people, and demonstrate the preventible nature of the maladies which afflict them. We must prove to the laborer, the artisan, the tradesman, the farmer, to the fathers and mothers, and to the children, that *unhealthy homes are of their own creation,* and that small-pox, scarlet fever, diphtheria, measles, whooping cough and the whole brood of domestic diseases are largely of their own cultivation. And these truths must be reiterated until the community is as thoroughly imbued with a knowledge of the causation and prevention of domestic maladies as of the elements of a common education. And much of this work necessarily falls upon voluntary organizations. Our field of work is, therefore, large, and our responsibilities great; but if we labor with an abiding faith in the power of preventive medicine to accomplish the mission which it has proposed, of protecting man from the larger number of the ills which so impair his physical powers, and render his brief and uncertain life miserable, we shall in the end triumph, and lay the foundation of a perfect system of sanitary government.

We meet to-day, in a city whose history has been made famous by men who have contributed largely to the advancement of sanitary knowledge and reform in this country. The wise maxims of Franklin, which appear so often in literature, have become the common heritage of mankind. His inventions and discoveries, all tending to increase the comforts and diminish the wear and tear of man as a social being, illustrate many a page of sanitary literature. Few authors have excelled Rush as a suggestive writer in nearly every branch of hygiene. His works abound with observations and reflections, which we are repeating to-day as new and hitherto unknown. John Jones, whose fame New York shares with Philadelphia, was the inventor and builder of the first pavilion hospital ever devised or constructed. La Roche stands and ever will stand, unrivalled as the historian of the most readed and dangerous pestilence which ever visited our sea-board cities. With the mention of the name of Jewell, we are reminded that there was organized, through his labors, the first convention which had for its object the discussion of quarantine and sanitary subjects. It is not too much to say that to that effort and to that organization this country owes much, if not all, of the present interest in sanitary reform.

The memory of these and other pioneers in the cultivation of preventive medicine in this country, the fruits of whose labors we enjoy, ought to inspire us with renewed zeal in our efforts to extend the bounds of sanitary knowledge, and to secure in every city, village, and township a thoroughly organized and competent public health service.

SANITARY DEFICIENCES.—As American citizens, we boast, and very justly too, of our progress in commerce, agriculture, manufactures, literature, the arts and sciences, and the general diffusion of knowledge among all classes of society, but what have we done as a nation for our sanitary condition, for those things which so vitally concern the public health, the dearest interest of every family in the land? The Government has done nothing; it has not even recognized the necessity of a great Bureau of Health, so essential in a sanitary point of view. Our local boards of health, as they are denominated, are mere shadows, the creatures for the most part of municipal authorities, who farm out our health and our lives to the highest bidder at so much a head. Surely the first, the greatest duty of a nation is to protect the lives of its citizens, by teaching them how to live, how to guard against disease, and how to improve the race. The sanitary condition of a people is intimately associated with its moral and religious welfare. People cannot be good or happy if they are not healthy. The *Bible* declare cleanliness to be next to godliness. Millions of people die every year from preventable diseases. Sensible men no longer ascribe the frightful outbreak of those epidemic diseases which occasionally ravage whole nations, to the wrath of an offended Deity; they know better; they know that they are due, for the most part, to man's ignorance, or man's criminal neglect.—Prof. S. D. GROSS, *American Public Health Association*, 1874.

Editor's Table.

THE PUBLIC HEALTH.

New York, Nov. 18th, 1874.—In the first month of this fourth quarter of the year the city of New York has enjoyed its usual immunity from all forms of epidemic disease except as regards diphtheria. The total number of deaths in the city during the five weeks ending October 31st, was 2,637. The total in the last four weeks of that period was 2,077, the deathrate was equal to 25.95 in the 1,000 annually, the population being estimated at 1,040,000. Of the total number of deaths in these four weeks, 554, or 26.67 per cent. were of infants under a year old; while 948, or 45.64 per cent. of all deaths were of children under five years of age.. Neglect, or failure of suitable nourishment and merely hygienic care may justly be charged with more than half of this infant mortality.

Zymotic diseases were charged with 726 deaths out of the total (2,077,) or 34.95 per cent. of all. Constitutional diseases were charged with 474, or 22.82 per cent. of all. Local diseases (mostly inflammatory,) were charged with 676, or 32.55 per cent. Developmental diseases with 110, 25.30 per cent. and violent causes with 91, or 4.38 per cent. of the total.

The continued prevalence of diphtheria in this city and its decidedly epidemic characteristics, which are now manifested over a region exceeding the area of New York and New Jersey, will worthily demand the most careful study of all physicians. Beginning its epidemic course early in the autumn of 1873 it attained its highest degree of fatality before the beginning of the present year, and thenceforward fluctuated from month to month, with an average of about 25 deaths weekly, until it began to increase again early in October, and on the 15th or 16th of November, reached the greatest degree of fatality ever experienced in this city, causing 20 deaths in those two days, and 66 in the week ending on November 14th. This malady is more prevalent in Paterson and some other towns in New Jersey than in this city, and in that portion of the city of Yonkers lying south of the Nepperhan creek, (a naturally undrained district,) and in portions of Brooklyn, Long Island City, and Jersey City, the endemic not less than the epidemic and the infectious attributes of this disease are conspicuous. In numerous tenement houses and populous blocks of dwellings it may be presumed that th remark of M. Gendron can be justly repeated,—"l'epidemie est l'effet et non la cause de la contagion."

Brooklyn.—To some of the readers of THE SANITARIAN, who also read the Brooklyn *Eagle* and *Union*, it may be necessary to state that THE SANITARIAN is not on unfriendly relations with the Health Department of Brooklyn. On the contrary, it is indebted to the members thereof for many and continuous courtesies, and fully reciprocates the kindly feeling. Boards of Health, Boards of Public Works, Boards of Education, Boards of Charities, etc., comprehend institutions and administrations, which every individual has a right to know the status of, as means of determining the sanitary condition of the community. The sickness and mortality of, and due to such institutions and administrations, are signs of the influences which govern them, in the same way as the sickness and mortality of a family are signs of home influences and surroundings; and it is clearly the duty of the Health Department —as it is of THE SANITARIAN—to keep the people alive to conditions in conflict with health under all circumstances. If the value of health and life in Brooklyn is or has been made secondary to friendship for favored and negligent contractors; to the costs of removing filth from and filling in sunken lots; to political respect, lest the toes of contemporary functionaries be stepped upon; to parsimonious landlords, who prefer that their tenants should die rather than establish sewer connections with privy vaults—if *any* one of these conditions, or others like unto them, exist—the public have a right to know it. The sphere of THE SANITARIAN is to promote everything that is needful for health, and to oppose everything in conflict with it, and it will do this to the full extent of its information and ability, even at the risk of personal offence to certain proprietary and editorial relations of the newspapers to members of the Health Department. But it would be sorry to think so meanly of any member of the Health Department of Brooklyn as to suppose either of the papers in question is justified by them in the pretence of withholding knowledge at the sacrifice of human life, lest its publication injure the reputation of the city for healthfulness. How far this pretence will inspire confidence in the said papers as sentinels of the public welfare, the public itself will judge.

We are gratified to know that, aided by the influence of cool weather, the contractor for the removal of offal has secured a dock and the approval thereof by the Board of Health, and that since the fruit and fresh vegetable season is pretty well over, and the amount of swill and house garbage has ceased to be bulky and offensive, the cartmen call for it with more regularity. There is general complaint, however, on the part of kitchen servants, that the takers are careless and untidy in emptying the buckets.

Lest any of the readers of the *Eagle* or *Union* be led to doubt the result of the unsanitary conditions which have prevailed in Brooklyn, attention is invited to the following correspondence:

NEW YORK, *Nov.* 7, 1874.

To Dr. James Watt, Registrar of Vital Statistics:

DEAR SIR—Will you be kind enough to give me a brief abstract from your records showing the ratio of deaths from zymotic diseases to the deaths from all causes for the last nine or ten months, compared with the same period of time last year and any preceding number of years, at your convenience? Truly yours, A. N. BELL.

DEPARTMENT OF HEALTH, BROOKLYN, *Nov.* 14*th*, 1874.

Dr. A. N. Bell—DEAR SIR:—The excess of mortality from zymotic diseases in Brooklyn, for the last three years, has been due in 1872, to small-pox; 1873, to diarrhœal diseases, and in 1874 to diphtheria. Excepting small-pox, which has been a general epidemic, the total mortality, and the ratio of mortality from zymotic diseases in Brooklyn from January to October, inclusive for three years, has been:

1872, total deaths, 10,855; from zymotic diseases, 3,324; per cent. of zymotic diseases, 32.10
1873, " 9,083; " 2,974; " " 32.74
1874, " 9,209; " 3,124; " " 33.92

Small-pox, 1872, 712; 1873, 118; 1874, 32.

Deaths in October, 842; 22.44 per 1,000,—110 less than in September. Small-pox, 3; scarlatina, 29; diphtheria, 62; dysentery, 21; consumption, 97; marasmus, 52; bronchitis, 16; pneumonia, 57.

JAMES WATT, M.D., *Registrar.*

Yonkers.—A correspondent has sent us a copy of the *Gazette*, containing a report of deaths in the city of Yonkers for the year ending October 31st ult. It appears that the only method of obtaining information in regard to deaths is through the certificates given to undertakers by the attending physicians. How many die, and are buried without certificates, there is no means of knowing. Of births and marriages there is no record.

By the census of 1870 the population was 18,318. Since that time the town has been divided, and the northern portion incorporated into a city, and the southern portion annexed to New York. Estimating the gain in the population about equal to that of the portion annexed to New York, the mortality has been 18 per 1,000; total number of deaths, 323. Scarlet fever, 8; typhoid fever, 14; diarrhœal diseases, 29; cerebro-spinal meningitis, 6; congestive chills, 3; consumption, 55; heart diseases, 13; *pneumonia,* 20; *bronchitis,* 12; *membranous croup,* 8 (5 during last month). The whole are classified: —I. Zymotic diseases, 92; II., constitutional diseases, 86; III., local diseases, 125; IV., developmental diseases, 11, and V., violent deaths, 9.

There is, in this report, an apparent effort to appear formidable instead of accurate. The number and the time of the deaths reported as membranous croup, is very significant of diphtheria, and our correspondent informs us diphtheria now appears to be taking the place of croup. Several other reported causes are in keeping with an evident want of competency or skill, or both. The ratio of deaths from typhoid fever, cerebro-spinal meningitis, congestive chills, and consumption is suggestive of local conditions to which even sensible aldermen should no longer be blind; the Board of Health is composed of aldermen, with the Mayor as president. The sewerage and drainage of the city is very imperfect, and there appears to be no intelligent effort to better it. The water for all domestic purposes is obtained from wells and cisterns in their usual relation to cesspools and privy vaults. Yonkers is sadly in need of a Board of Health with an efficient head.

Philadelphia, 775,000.—Deaths in four weeks ending 31st, 1,023;—per 1,000, 16.8. Consumption, 161; typhoid fever, 42; typhus, 3; scarlet fever, 29; diphtheria, 14.

Baltimore, 284,000.—Deaths in four weeks ending Nov. 2, 539;—per 1,000, 24.6. Consumption, 72; typhoid fever, 19; scarlet fever, 20; diphtheria, 7.

Washington, 150,000.—Deaths in four weeks ending Oct. 31, 280;—per 1,000, 24.2. Consumption, 47; typhoid fever, 7; diphtheria, 1.

St. Louis, 366,000.—Deaths in four weeks ending Oct. 31, 500;—per 1,000, 17.7. Consumption, 52; typhoid fever, 14; scarlet fever, 8; diphtheria, 3.

Chicago, 400,000.—Deaths in four weeks ending Oct. 31, 491;—per 1,000, 15.09. Consumption, 60; typhoid fever, 29; diphtheria, 9; scarlet fever, 6.

San Francisco, 178,000.—Deaths in October, 372;—per 1,000, 25.-75. Consumption, 48; typhus and typhoid fevers, 19; scarlatina, 91; whooping cough, 7; diphtheria, 5; pneumonia, 10; heart diseases, 20; diseases of stomach and bowels, 10.

Cincinnati, 260,000.—"Enclosed please find our report for October to the 26th inst., inclusive—four weeks:

"Total mortality, 354; per 1,000, 17.70; under one year of age, 24.04 per cent.; under five years of age, 44.09 per cent.; over five years of age, 55.91 per cent.

"The principal diseases were: Phthisis, 50; pneumonia, 12; scarlatina, 36; diphtheria, 11; convulsions, 21; heart disease, 11; cholera infantum, 19; inflammation of brain, 10; dysentery, 14; debility, 9; typhoid fever, 13; diarrhœa, 8. Respectfully, etc.,

C. B. CHAPMAN, *Clerk Board of Health.*"

Milwaukee, 100,000.—Deaths in October, 202 (including stillborn, 14);—per 1,000, 24.24; consumption, 13; convulsions, 29; diarrhœa, 25; meningitis, 8; diphtheria, 5; gastric fever, 2; 119 under five years of age.

"The high mortality among children under five years of age that occurred in Milwaukee last month, in proportion to the whole number of deaths during the month, induced us to examine the death rate in a number of American cities, during the month of September, to discover whether Milwaukee was contributing a larger proportion than other cities to the common death roll of the country. It will be remembered that in our monthly report of deaths for September the whole number was given as 239; of this number 190 died under the age of five years; fourteen, however, of this number are reported as being still-born, that is, dead when born; others lived only a few hours. There were only 48 deaths over the age of five, and of these some died of old age. * * * * In nineteen of the principal cities of the Union the death rate of Milwaukee, in the summary of THE SANITARIAN for September, stands as the third highest on the list. Charleston, South Carolina, and Buffalo, New York, alone taking precedence. This high death rate does not by any means indicate insalubrity or unhealthiness of Milwaukee. This can be seen by the very low death rate of adults, those above the age of five years being less than any others of the nineteen cities. * * * The great child mortality was among the poorer class of Germans, and those from the northern and western parts of Europe. Seven-tenths of our population are foreign-born, or the immediate offspring of foreign parents. Foreigners do not have medical attendance for their children until it is too late to benefit them. There is not that proper care in clothing, nursing and food, that this tender period of life requires. We now hope that the free use of our pure Lake water will in the future greatly reduce the death rate among children in Milwaukee. In two weeks more the Water Commissioners will forbid connections with main water pipes until next Spring. All should avail themselves of those two weeks to make the necessary connections and introduce the water into their houses.

"JAMES JOHNSON, M. D., *Health Officer.*"

Pittsburgh, 136,000.—"Five weeks ending October 31, 291, 25.67

per 1,000. Under one year of age, 22.68 per cent.; under five years of age, 49.48 per cent. Principal causes from which death occurred—scarlet fever, 39; respiratory diseases, 22; diarrhœal diseases, 34; diphtheria, 8; enteric fever, 30, violence, 21; consumption, 28.

"W. Snively, M. D., *Registrar.*"

Wheeling, 37,000.—"For October, 29;—per 1,000, 9.4. Diarrhœa, 2; diphtheria 2; pneumonia, 3; whooping cough, 2; scarlet fever, 6; all being in one ward, the southern one of the city. All other causes, one death each. A general tendency to throat diseases.

"Respectfully,

"S. L. Jepson, M. D., *Health Officer.*"

New Haven, 55,000. Month of October, deaths, 86; per 1,000, 18.76. Consumption, 19; typhoid fever, 7.

New Orleans, 199,000.—Deaths in four weeks ending Oct. 25, 530;—per 1,000, 34.6. From most prevalent diseases for three weeks (report for Oct. 4, not received), consumption 50; malarial fever, 15; typhoid, 8; congestive, 22; small-pox, 2.

Richmond, 65,000.—Deaths in four weeks ending Oct. 31, 121—whites, 53, colored, 68;—per 1,000, 24.2. Consumption, 23; typhoid fever, 3.

Dayton, 34,000.—Month of October, 42;—per 1,000, 14.8. Consumption, 6; typhoid fever, 3.

Toledo, 37,000.—Month of October, 52; per 1,000, 16.8. Consumption, 9; typhoid fever, 2.

Charleston, 52,000.—Two weeks, ending Oct. 10 (latest received), 92;—per 1,000, 42.4.

Louisville, 112,000.—Week ending Oct. 31 (only two weekly reports, Oct. 10 and 31, received), 48;—per 1,000, 22.2. Consumption, 7; typhoid fever, 3; diphtheria, 2.

Erie, 26,037.—(Abstract of report in *Erie Dispatch.*) From January 1st, to November 1st, 1874. Total deaths 385;—per 1,000 annually, 19.02. Like Yonkers, the figures are based upon certificates obtainable through the undertakers. Consumption, 39; convulsions, 36; diarrhœa, 48; typhoid fever, 13; *old age*, 33; *teething*, 14; *still born*, 36; unknown, 46; a sufficiently formidable category. The health officer well observes: "If we had a law for the registry of deaths, as in other cities, it would be of great value in a legal point of view. Upon one line of a mortuary book, kept by the city with accuracy, we would find the name, the age, nationality, disease, color of the deceased, with his occupation, ward and street, where he resided—with the name of the physician who attended him in his last illness and the cemetery.

where interred * * * A few of the little ones were found dead on the street, and the coroner held inquests upon their remains. * * * Among the 46 deaths from causes unknown, many of them were infants. Much noise is still made about old-fashioned spills with stench traps, in order to keep the dangerous sewer gases where they belong, and there is abundant room for improvements. * * * History shows that all the leading nations of the world paid particular attention to the sanitary condition of their homes.

"The meeting places of the ancient Egptians, Greeks and Romans were temples as high as the trees of our forests. Now-a-days we find often for hours one thousand people packed together in a low hall, where there is hardly fresh air enough for one hundred, and it is no wonder that the sick headache is raging all over town after the lecture of a great public speaker, or at the time when balls and theatre are in full blast.

"Is it not strange to hear some people complain about the expenses of a small sewer when we remember that 2,500 years ago Tarquinius built the great drain of Rome—the famous Cloaca Maxima—with a diameter of 14 feet, which work is still in existence.

"At some future day the whole length of Millcreek, within the city, will be arched. But before that work is finished the undersigned may figure only in the death list of another sanitary officer."

"Very Respectfully,

"E. W. Germer, *Health Officer*."

Elmira, 21,000.—In October, 27;—per 1,000, 15.4. Consumption, 4; typhoid fever, 3.

Buffalo, 130,000.—In September, (reports a month behind), 296;—per 1,000, 27.3. Cosumption, 22; cholera, infantum, 66; convulsions 18; scarlet fever, 61; typhoid fever, 9; diphtheria, 5.

Providence, 100,000.—In October, 161;—per 1,000, 19.3. Consumption, 19; typhoid fever, 14; scarlet fever, 19.

Boston, 275,000.—In four weeks ending Oct. 24, 583;—per 1,000, 27.5. Consumption 104; typhoid fever, 32; scarlet fever, 10; diphtheria, 6; diarrhœa, 29.

Mortality in Massachusetts.—In 17 cities, and towns for the week ending Oct. 17. Boston, 133; Wooster, 18; Lowell, 24; Milford, 3; Chelsea, 4; Cambridge, 23; Salem, 15; Lawrence, 16; Springfield, 9; Lynn, 7; Gloucester, 3; Fitchburg, 1; Newburyport, 5; Louisville, 15; Fall River, 16; Haverhill, 7; Holyoke, 9.

Sanitary Duties of Army Surgeons—The War Department has issued a general order saying:—"An important part of the duty of a medical officer of the army is the supervision of the hygiene of the post or command to which he is attached and the recommendation of such measures as he may deem necessary to prevent or diminish disease among the troops." The order then specifically defines his duties, which require he shall at least once a month examine and note in the medical history of the post the sanitary condition of the quarters, including all buildings belonging to the post, the character and cooking of the rations, the amount and quality of the water supply, the drainage and the clothing and habits of the men, and make a report thereon in writing to the commanding officer with such recommendations as he may deem proper.

AMERICAN PUBLIC HEALTH ASSOCIATION.

Second Annual Meeting.

The meeting of this newly organized body of sanitary workers last year, in New York, was marked by a popular expression of interest, which, by many, was believed to be dependent upon the special concern which this city has in all questions relating to the public health. The meeting this year in Philadelphia, has clearly proved that the want of popular thought and inquiry concerning these questions is felt in all sections of the United States.

The Philadelphia meeting was conspicuous for the harmony and earnestness evinced by the members in all discussions and expressions of purpose or wishes. The discussion upon hospitals has had no parallel for its thoroughness and fullness in any medical or sanitary congress. The fairness and cogency of the arguments presented by Dr. Wm. Pepper, Dr. Kirkbride, and Dr. Ashurst, in support of a municipal style of construction as well as an educational function of the great civil hospitals, was equalled by the frank and lucid method which Surgeon J. S. Billings, Prof. S. D. Gross and others adopted in support of the pavilion and widely-distributed system of hospitals. In all these and other discussions, even in those upon abattoirs and other mooted subjects, not the slightest asperity or dogmatism was noticeable, but facts, evidence, and the results of the best experience only were presented.

The written papers were of a high order, and more numerous than could be read during the session. The evening discussions and the afternoon discussions constituted important features of this second congress of hygienists. The discourses by Rev. Dr. Osgood, Prof. S. D. Gross, President Orton, General Viele, Senator L. H. Steiner, M. D. and Hon. Dorman B. Eaton, should be published without delay for the use of general readers and the promotion of social science and hygiene.

The second volume of Public Health Papers should now follow closely upon the first volume (of 1873—now in binders' hands,) for the second year's fruit is a natural and bountiful outcome of the first as well as the second year's labor.

For the general status and field of the association, attention is invited to the opening address of the President on preceding pages.—Some of the other addresses and papers will appear in our pages hereafter. *The Perils of the School Room*, in our next.

The following were elected officers for the ensuing year.

President—Joseph M. Toner, M. D., Washington, D. C.

First Vice-President—Edwin M. Snow, M. D., Rhode Island.

Second Vice-President—Prof. Henry Hartshorne, M. D., Philadelphia.

Treasurer—John H. Rauch, M. D., Chicago.

Executive Committee—J. S. Billings, M. D., United States Army, of Washington; Moreau Morris, M. D., New York City; Stephen Smith, M. D., New York City; J. J. Woodward, M. D., United States Army, Washington; J. S. Stuart, M. D., of Baltimore, Md.; and A. N. Bell, M. D., Brooklyn.

Professor Stephen Smith was re-elected President on the first ballot, but declined to serve, on account of the pressure of official and other duties. Dr. Harris, the Secretary, holds over for two more years.

To the County Medical Societies of New York:—

Attention is particularly invited to the following resolution adopted at the last meeting of the State society:—

"That the secretary be instructed to urge upon the county societies the importance of having committees on hygiene in co-operation with the standing committee on hygiene of the State society, and that the investigations of said committees in this regard, on the approval of their respective county societies, be forwarded to the committee on hygiene of the State society in time to be summarized by that committee in their annual report."

While the relations of defective drainage to insalubrity continue to be the most important subject of investigation throughout the State, the standing committee of the State society would by no means limit the field of investigation, but be glad to receive reports on any subject of hygiene within the scope of the county society committees.

Reports of the county society committees are requested to be sent to the chairman of the standing committee of the State society as early as practicable.

A. N. Bell, M.D., Chairman, Brooklyn;	*Committee.*
S. O. Vanderpoel, M.D., Health Officer, Port of N. Y.;	
H. D. Didama, M.D., Syracuse;	
H. W. Dean, M.D., Rochester;	
Wm. C. Wey, M.D., Elmira;	
Stephen Smith, M.D., New York;	
C. R. Agnew, M.D., New York;	

Wm. H. Bailey, M.D., *Sec. N. Y. State Med. Society.*

Albany, *Dec. 1st*, 1874.

Analytical Department.—Interested inquirers will be glad to learn that the Sanitarian has effected arrangements for conducting the analyses of all kinds of waters, articles of food, and chemical products; also for the investigation of chemical processes and consultations on chemical subjects.

Analyses of minerals and assays of ores will also be made at reasonable rates. All letters of inquiry in regard to particular terms, etc., will be promptly answered. Address the Editor of The Sanitarian.

Postage Notice.—Subscribers and exchanges will please meet and excuse any apparent irregularities in regard to the conditional prepayment on this and the next number of The Sanitarian, in view of quarterly requirements for prepayment at the New York Post Office. After January 1st, 1875, all understand, prepayment is required at the office of mailing, and The Sanitarian will be so sent, *without any increase of subscription price.* On some of the journals sent *with* The Sanitarian at club rates, a small extra charge for prepayment will be required.

BIBLIOGRAPHY.

Croup, in its Relation to Tracheotomy. By J. Solis Cohen, M. D. Philadelphia: Lindsay & Blakiston. 1874.

A reprint of an essay read before the Philadelphia County Medical Society, Jan. 14, 1874, referred by that Society to the State Medical Society, and published in its Transactions for the current year. A well-merited appreciation of an unusually meritorious resumé of more than five thousand cases of tracheotomy in croup, performed in various portions of the world, with valuable practical conclusions of use to all practitioners.

The Physicians' Visiting List. 1875. Twenty-fourth year. Philadelphia: Lindsay & Blakiston.

One of the most portable and convenient publications of the kind extant. Physicians at a distance would do well to order it without delay

Clinical Lectures on Various Important Diseases. By NATHAN S. DAVIS, A. M., M. D., Professor of Principles and Practice of Medicine, etc. Second edition. Philadelphia: Henry C. Lea. 1874.

This early issue of a second edition of Prof. Davis' excellent work attests the high appreciation in which it is held. Twenty pages more than the first edition commend it still more heartily to all medical practitioners.

Transactions of the Medical Association of Alabama. 27th Session. 1874. Pp. 421.

This is an unusually valuable society report. Many of its contributions, especially those on the epidemics of yellow fever and cholera in 1873, are worthy of extensive circulation. And the same may be said of the annual address of the president, Job Sobieski Wetherby, M. D., on the sanitary needs of the people of the State, and the related obligations of the medical profession. This address is indeed a fitting sequel to the epidemics of the southwest, last year, which ought to give it much more than a transient significance. "As members of an organization devoted to science and the preservation of life and protection against disease, we must, as a part of our creed, believe :

"That the conditions of perfect health, either public or personal, are seldom or never attained, though attainable ; that the average length of human life may be very much extended, and its physical power greatly augmented ; that in every year in this State thousands of lives are lost that might have been saved ; that tens of thousands of cases of sickness occur, which might have been prevented ; that a vast amount of unnecessarily impaired health and physical debility exists among those not actually confined by sickness ; that these preventable evils require an enormous expenditure and loss of money, and impose on the people unnumbered and immeasurable calamities, pecuniary, social physical, mental and moral, which might be avoided ; that means exist within our reach for their mitigation or removal ; and that measures for prevention will effect infinitely more than remedies for the cure of disease."—A creed which it becomes every true man to believe and promulgate, until every State in the Union shall enact effectual measures for the preservation of the health and life of her children.

The yellow fever epidemic of 1873, by Professor Jerome Cochran, M. D., with statistics of cases and mortality, summarizes the number of deaths from actual records, and approximately, the number of cases and the ratio of mortality. The totals are 16,760 cases, 3,308 deaths ; 10,000 of which cases, and 2,000 deaths are credited to Memphis alone

In Shreveport, 3,000 cases, 789 deaths. The next largest number in New Orleans, and the rest divided among Pensacola, Montgomery, Calvert and Mobile. "No such tremendous mortality was ever heard of before, even in the most malignant epidemics," remarks the essayist, and he seems by implication, at least, to charge this terrible fatality to the use of carbolic acid for disinfecting purposes. "If we accept the statistics of the advocates of carbolic acids disinfection as at all reliable the ratio of the mortality of the cases where carbolic acid has been used is truly appalling. Look at the terrible items as given by the Boards of Health of Mobile and New Orleans. In New Orleans, 1871, the mortality was 47½ per cent. of the cases, 1872, 47 per cent, in 1873, 58 per cent. In Mobile, 1873, the mortality was 47½ per cent. These contrasts fill me with amazement, and I could find no probable explanation until the horrible suspicion flashed upon me that peradventure this unprecedented mortality was the result of the disinfection which had been invoked for the purpose of opposing the progress of the pestilence. But when I saw how utterly worthless were the statistics * * I saw reason to believe that another explanation was possible, and that carbolic acid after all was not so destructive of yellow fever patients as I had supposed. But while I am now satisfied that carbolic acid disinfection has not been the wholesale agent of destruction which the testimony of its friends seemed to prove it to be, I am very far from believing that it is entirely innocent and innocuous. * * * The smell of it is very offensive, and it is very easy for any one who understands the great danger of emesis in yellow fever, and the extreme sensitiveness of the stomachs of yellow fever patients, to understand also how the inhalation of an atmosphere loaded with the fumes of carbolic acid might turn the scales in doubtful cases."

Admitting the great uncertainty in regard to the number of cases, and the much greater certainty in regard to the number of deaths, and, taking in to consideration the comparative populations of New Orleans and Mobile, where most carbolic acid was used, and according to population, where the smallest number of cases of the fever occurred, we are obliged to conclude that Dr. Cochran's criticism on carbolic acid is inconsistent with his facts.

Besides, the "tremendous mortality" which he gives is not unprecedented, as any one may satisfy himself of by referring to La Roche.

The disease found, on first visiting Memphis, Shreveport, and the other places where it prevailed most extensively and fatally, an abundance of intensifying causes of prevalence and fatality long before carbolic acid was thought of. And well would it have been for those places had the people anticipated the visitation of the fever by freely using carbolic acid in advance.

Dr. R. F. Michel's paper on "Epidemic Yellow Fever in Montgomery," is also an instructive one. Traces the fever to the city, and shows that in a city in good condition, and with the free use of carbolic acid and other disinfectants, the mortality was a little over 20 per cent. He also dwells upon *dengue* and its *non*-hæmorrhagic character.

The "Report on Dengue," by Wm. H. Anderson, M.D., gives twenty four years' observation and experience in the treatment of that disease in the city of Mobile and vicinity. It is an autumnal disease, without any tracings in relation to other diseases or peculiarity of season, comes suddenly, runs a speedy course, and rarely or never leaves complications behind; has never known a patient die of it. As to its ever being in any way allied to yellow fever he has never seen a shadow of evidence.

"Cholera in Birmingham," by M. H. Jordan, M. D. The first case "was an able-bodied laborer; had been here about six weeks and had his bedclothes shipped to him from Huntsville a few days before he was taken sick. Cholera was prevailing in Huntsville at that time, and this was the only known means by which he could have taken the disease. No care was taken to disinfect the discharges, which were thrown on the ground in the rear of the house, on the slope of the hill immediately above the branch, which at every rain received the washings from the privies, stables, and outhouses on the north side of it." Five days afterwards a second case occurred, and the disease speedily became epidemic.

The "Cholera in Huntsville," by J. J. Demant, M.D., was also traced; its first case in a family that habitually used water from a well on the brink of a dirty pond, in the vicinity of the Memphis and Charleston Railroad depot.

"The White Blood Corpuscle, in Health and Disease," by Professor J. Cochran, M.D.; State Aid to Hospitals, by Dr. P. Bryce, Superintendent of the Alabama Insane Hospital; Contributions of Physics and Chemistry to Practical Medicine, by T. O. Summers, M. A. S. A; Hæmorrhagic Malarial Fever in Alabama, by E. D. McDaniel, A. M., M. D.; Puerperal Eclampsia, by F. M. Peterson, M. D.; Annual Oration on Cell-Life, the Basis of all Force, both Mental and Physical, by S. D. Seelye, M. D., and several other papers which space will not allow of notice in detail, all show a Society in which its members strive for excellence, and succeed in their several spheres.

THE SANITARIAN.

A MONTHLY JOURNAL.

VOL. II.] JANUARY, 1875. [NO. 10.

THE PERILS OF THE SCHOOL-ROOM.

Read before American Public Health Association, Philadelphia, Nov. 13, 1874.
By A. N. BELL, M. D.

While reflecting on how best to open the discussion of a subject so abundant in detail as the perils of the school-room, came the intelligence of the death of Dr. Francis E. Anstie, one of the brightest ornaments of his profession. His death, as we have since learned, was caused by a wound which he received in a post-mortem examination, while engaged in an investigation which had for its object the discovery of the causes of a fatal school disease, acute idiopathic peritonitis—a disease often found to be due to malaria, which, in this particular instance, was caused by sewer gas. I use the word malaria in this connection in its simplest sense, to signify bad air, but recognize the usua distinction of two kinds of malaria, vegetable and animal.

The diseases common to vegetable malaria, or marshy emanations, are, unfortunately, so well known as not to require special description in this connection. It will suffice to state that they are liable to be greatly modified and aggravated by animal malaria, the kind common to school-rooms.

Animal malaria may be engendered anywhere by the neglect of animal excretions, whether of mankind or of the lower animals. It is especially liable to occur as the result of crowding, darkness, want of ventilation, want of or defective sewerage, and filthy habits, and is subject to intensification by extremes of temperature in crowded apartments. Crowding, or overcrowding, the more common term, is an indefinite expression, and so generally subject to misinterpretation by persons apparently incapable of understanding its true signification, in relation to school-rooms, that its limits require defining. The importance of air space rests upon the absolute necessity of pure air for healthy respiration; but the amount of space required depends upon a variety of circumstances. Hospital conditions, for example, require the largest amount of space, and modern experience has shown that, other things being equal, *no* inclosed space equals plenary exposure. But, for various practical purposes, the limits of space vary from 300 to 4,000 cubic feet—the smallest proportion being the exaction for lodging-house dormitories, and the largest for hospitals—making due allowance in all cases for space occupied by furniture. And *no deviation should be* *made on account of children*, whether in regard to the different members of a family or a school-room. With regard to this point, Mr. John Simon well observes: "It is to be desired that laws and regulations as to overcrowding should not proceed on the assumption that children (to any measurable extent) require less breathing space than adults. Against any such assumption, two facts have been considered—first, that even healthy children, in proportion to their respective bodily weights, are about twice as powerful as adults in deteriorating the air which they breathe; secondly, that the children will almost invariably have certain eruptive and other febrile disorders to pass through, from which adult life is comparatively exempt, and in which the requirement of space is greatly increased. And having regard to these two considerations, I think it best that children and adults should be deemed to require equal allowances of air and ventilation."*

Moreover, it should be observed that the mere space allowance should in no case detract from the absolute necessity of means for renewal, and the smaller the space so much the more certain should be this provision. If 300 cubic feet only be allowed, the air must be changed, at the least, every twenty minutes. To neutralize the deleterious properties of respired air and to replenish it, every person requires 2,000 cubic feet of fresh air hourly, and with less provision than this contamination is sure to follow.

The poisonous effluvia which pervades the atmosphere of close and unventilated rooms is not only re-breathed, but it adheres to all the surroundings; it sticks to the walls and furniture, settles into the drinking cups, into the food utensils, food and drink, permeates the clothing, and attaches to the person. It creates a nidus, which is not only in itself poisonous, perpetually lessening the vital force of all who inhabit it and predisposing to blood poisons of every kind, but it also becomes a hotbed for the planting and propagation of specific poisons, such as small-pox, scarlet fever, measles, whooping cough, diphtheria, and the whole category of epidemic diseases, and a fruitful source of scrofula and consumption. The consideration of these diseases in detail, and their relations to crowded and unventilated places, would comprehend a treatise on the predisposing causes of epidemics. It may be stated in general terms, however, that the specific poisons which perpetuate this class of diseases are kept alive by the conditions common to school-rooms, always exist somewhere, and the history of them all demonstrates alternations of repose and activity, of prevalence in one place and absence in another, of successive invasions of contiguous neighborhoods and succeeding immunities. But the specific morbid poisons, the *seed*, never die; they remain and live on from generation to generation, ever susceptible to enlivening influences, and liable to transmission from place to place, renewing strength by the way, again to become dormant and lie in ambush, awaiting the return of congenial conditions for renewed activity.

The epidemic influences or constitution which some authors are wont to describe as conditions precedent to the activity of epidemic diseases,

* Eighth Report of the Medical Officer of the Privy Council.

and which are believed to be periods of predisposing receptivity of specific poisons, are due in no small degree to the prevailing condition of school-rooms and their congeners. As a rule, the older these conditions—the longer the period of time in which they have been tolerated—the more depressed the vital powers of their occupants, and the greater their predisposing receptivity. Besides, the depressed state of the organism under such conditions is not only predisposing to epidemic diseases, but the liability to and the danger of all diseases is thereby intensified, and vicissitudes of weather, which, under favorable circumstances may be encountered with impunity, under these depressing influences become dangerous perils; and, doubtless, much that is attributed to the season of the year supposed to be predisposing to scarlet fever, measles, whooping cough, diphtheria, and some other common affections of children, is due to the same cause. It is at any rate very remarkable that the beginning of the autumnal school term should be simultaneous with or speedily followed by the sickly term. There is surely something more than a mere coincidence in these relations; they stand much more like cause and effect. The effect of high temperature, in this regard, may seem to imply an exception to these conclusions. Heat has, indeed, received much consideration lately, as a sort of independent cause of disease, and to its influence especially has been attributed the excess of mortality common to infants in hot weather. There is no question that heat exercises a very important influence, but we are fully persuaded that it is so entirely secondary in its relations, even in the heat of summer, as to be among the most preventable of causes. Its influence is mainly due to its effect on organic matter, unventilated apartments and filthy surroundings, and, above all, on the food of infants artificially fed. Evidence is almost wholly wanting on the deleterious effect of summer heat on infants nursed by their mothers, or on older children with healthy surroundings. Its specially dangerous effect is, in short, due to conditions such as are usually present in close school-rooms and tenement-houses. Heat intensifies, but it does not cause the excess of summer mortality, and it frequently has the same effect in overheated school-rooms at other seasons.

Carbonic acid in school-rooms, in some respects, bears similar relations to heat. Dangerous and fatal as it is known to be, when in great excess, its importance, *per se*, is unquestionably very much exaggerated. Naturally it exists in the atmosphere in variable proportions from 2 to 5 volumes in 10,000. But according to Dr. Angus Smith, no discomfort is experienced from the presence of carbonic acid in soda-water manufactories, when the amount is 2 volumes per 1,000, or more than ten times its normal proportion in the atmosphere. And Pettenkofer and Voit, in their experiments with this gas, experienced no discomfort from its presence, even to the extent of five times as much, or 10 volumes per 1,000. Notwithstanding, *respired* air, containing only 1.5 volumes of carbonic acid per 1,000, is well known to cause headache, vertigo, and other painful admonitions of danger. And experience abundantly proves that whenever respired air, or the air of occupied apartments, is found to contain of carbonic acid more than 1 volume per 1,000, such an atmosphere is dangerous to health. It is apparent, therefore, that the ill effects of air which contains only a little more than 1 volume per 1,000 of carbnoic acid, are due to other and more potent poisons. Such air not only contains, besides the excess of carbonic acid, and not unfrequently the more deadly carbonic oxide, dead and decomposing animal matter, and other mephitic gases and exhalations, but it is deficient in its very first life-sustaining property, oxygen.

The average amount of oxygen consumed by a healthy person is half a cubic inch every respiration, which in a day amounts to upwards of 25 cubic feet. And as oxygen constitutes but one-fifth of the volume of the air, a single individual renders not less than one hundred and twenty-five cubic feet of air unfit for respiration, every twenty-four hours, by the mere abstraction of oxygen alone. Meanwhile, there is exhaled by the lungs about 15 cubic feet of carbonic acid, 30 ounces of watery vapor, and an indefinite amount of organic matter, which has been variously estimated at from 10 to 240 grains.

The whole quantity of air actually respired in 24 hours by a healthy person is about 400 cubic feet. This contains, when once passed through the lungs, about five and a-half per cent. of carbonic acid. The proportion of watery vapor depends upon circumstances; as a rule, as much as necessary to saturate it at the temperature of the body: consequently, the amount varies in the inverse proportion of the quantity of moisture the air contained before it was respired. It may be estimated at about 200 cubic feet per hour. 1,000 parts of vapor exhaled from the lungs consists of pure water, 907 parts; carbonic acid, 90 parts, and animal matter, 3 parts. In addition to these, it is well known that other substances introduced into the circulation may be thrown off from the system and increase the danger.

Besides the danger from active and fatal disease from exposure to the conditions which have now been described, all physiologists recognize the influence of depressing agents on the human organization in blunting the sensibilities, obtunding the intellect, promoting stupidity, idiocy and physical deformity. And in this relation at least, the "survival of the fittest" often has a painful significance, not alone confined to the present generation, but, recognizing the accepted law of inheritance, well calculated to shock the sensibilities in anticipation of the future. To discuss in detail the collateral dangers of bad construction, bad furniture, disregard of light, the general want of attention to proper school ages, differential management in regard to sex, physical condition, etc., would extend this paper to an inordinate length. For the discussion of these dangers, it will suffice our present purpose to refer to the papers of Dr. Richard Liebrich and Dr. George Ross, of London, recently published in *Public Health*, a paper by Dr. C. R. Agnew of New York, in *The Sanitarian;* the treatises of Dr. Edward H. Clarke, of Boston, on *Sex in Education* and the *Building of a Brain;* the Report of Dr. Frederick Winsor on *School Hygiene*, in the Report of the State Board of Health of Massachusetts, and other papers recently written on these subjects.

The following abstract of a Report on the Public Schools of Brooklyn, in March last, by the Sanitary Superintendent of the Board of Health, is submitted as an illustration of the conditions which have now been described. I will read only some of the best and some of the worst examples:

"No. 1. Ten rooms to each floor; average attendance 1,004. In one room there were 70 present in 7,560 cubic feet of space—108 cubic feet for each child. At the time of inspection, the second floor had 427 in the grammar department, and the first floor had 708 in the primary department. It was excessively crowded, with not sufficient desk or sitting room.

No. 2. Registered, 334; average, 284. Heated by coal stoves surrounded by metal shields, within two feet of which children were seated in a temperature of 77°, while in other remote parts of the room the temperature was 67°. The windows were open for fresh air, and some children were seated so as to be exposed both to hot stoves and open windows, the former in front, the latter at the side. The outer clothing was hung up in the recitation room.

No. 6. Registered, 983; average, 94 per cent.; 514 in primary department. Ventilators have been provided, but many of them closed and beyond reach, the cords wanting, and practically useless. The heat is introduced directly upon the children. The middle rooms upon the east side of the building are so poorly lighted as to require gas burning at midday. In these rooms the air was very oppressive, and the supply through other occupied rooms.

No. 7. Heated by steam radiators in each room; renewal of air only through doors and windows. One class-room with 32 scholars has 2,250 cubic feet—70 to each scholar.

No. 8. Registered, 600; average, 570. Adjoining buildings so close that the school is deficient in light and circulation of air. The play-room is in the basement, upon which open the privies, from which offensive gases were perceptible. Hot air and registers from steam and radiators. One of the registers is on a level, and just in front of a pupil's desk. Each room was provided with a thermometer. These stood at from 60° to 74° in the different rooms.

No. 9. Average, 1,300; heated by hot air from steam pipes. In one of the rooms there were 126 children, the windows all closed, the ventilating shaft closed, and the hot-air registers open. Each of these children had *fifty cubic* feet of space; the clothing hung up in the room.

No. 12. Average attendance, 745; a one-story frame building, and seems taxed to its utmost capacity to accommodate its ordinary attendance. It is ventilated mainly by windows; although it is provided with a usual number of ventilating shafts, they are not used, and are looked upon as useless. In addition to the large class-rooms, divided by glass partitions, are four small recitation rooms, much overcrowded —one especially, occupied by over thirty pupils, that would not properly accommodate more than fifteen. These smaller rooms have no ventilating appliances besides the windows.

No. 13. Seating capacity, 1,500; average attendance, 1,250; grammar department, 411; primary department, 641; total on day of visit, 1,382. The cubic space on each floor is the same, but primary department contains nearly half the entire attendance.

No. 15. Constructed for 800, has 1,900. Lower floor for primary has 700. Ceilings low, air renewed only through windows. In one room, 2,000 cubic feet; 67 children, 30 *cubic feet* to each child. Playground, 45x36 for 1,000 girls; *less than two square feet for each to recreate in.*

No. 17. Temperature in the several rooms ranged from 58° to 82°. The latter temperature was in a room which had steam pipes, besides the hot air register. In the grammar department the crowding ranged from 95 to 270 cubic feet for each person. In the primary department, from 49 to 152 cubic feet to each child. Special attention is called to the crowded condition of the small rooms on all the floors. In one of the small rooms in the female grammar department, thirty-six girls, 14 years of age and upwards, are confined in 3,430 cubic feet, 95 to each; temperature, 82 degrees; ventilation by a small ventilator near the floor, and by two windows slightly lowered from the top. Another small room in the primary department has fifty children in 2,450 cubic feet of space, 49 to each child. Temperature of room, 59 degrees. The air in all the small rooms, and in all the primary rooms, was quite impure to the senses.

No. 18. 525 children on ground floor; 823 on second floor, with an average of 63 *cubic feet;* on each of the floors above, 400 scholars; in one of the rooms on the ground floor, 32 *cubic feet* for each scholar, and in part over stone flagging. The room is heated by a stove in a corner. Another room, 75x20x6, numbers 150 pupils, and has two openings or windows, about 24x30 inches each; gas burning for light.

No. 19. Wings on each side of the building cut off six class-rooms in the main building from any direct opening upon the external air or light; 960 children on the first floor. The hot air from the register raised the thermometer to 150 *degrees*, and within three feet of this sat a pupil. Says the Inspector, "My last visit to this school was made about the time of closing the afternoon sessions. I cannot describe the condition of the atmosphere; the children seemed completely depressed, and hardly had sufficient energy to leave their places."

No. 20. Average, 763; warmed partly by stoves; not comfortably warm in cold weather; floors very dirty; furnace rooms in a dangerous condition; combustible material scattered about in dangerous proximity to furnaces.

No. 21. Two class-rooms on each side of the stairs; not sufficiently warmed by the hot air registers; the children complain bitterly of the cold. The stairs are narrow and crooked. It would be impossible, in case of fire, for the children to escape from the building without injury and probable loss of life. Main building heated by stoves; 1,045 registered; 621, first floor; 424 on second; the boys' closet unfit to enter.

No. 22. 1,275; overcrowded; insufficiently heated, partly by stoves. The children suffer for want of pure air. One class-room, 12x18, has *one hundred and three* scholars. The floor of the playground is old, worn through, and dangerous; the children at play suffer falls and injuries. The stairs are old, worn, winding, and unsafe; an alarm would cause disaster. Says the Inspector, "Sanitary reasons demand the enlargement of this building. *Seventy-five* to *one hundred* children in a room containing not over 225 square feet!"

No. 23. The small children (900) are on first floor; on second—grammar department—494. The room in the rear extension, 12x20=240 square feet, has 56 scholars—about *four square feet* and *twenty-seven cubic feet* only to each! Closet vaults filthy.

No. 27. Sanitary improvement of the locality necessary. It is the "pig district;" not sewered. Sunken lots and stagnant water are a feature of the district. 1,175 registered; small building heated with stoves; large, with furnaces; closets offensive; no disinfectants used.

No. 29. The arrangement and care of closets are bad; require more water, and should be disinfected. A number of class-rooms without a thermometer; those found ranged from 60° to 64°. An elaborate system of ventilating shafts is supplemented by open windows. 420 in the primary department, and 580 in the other two, illustrating the crowding of the young children; 130 more lives must be sustained in the same cubic space in one instance than in the other. If it is argued their bodies are smaller, and therefore need less room, it may be fairly answered, their bodies are younger, more tender, and so require a purer air. Difficulty is experienced in heating the rooms on the south side in extremely cold weather.

No. 30. In the two rooms at the top of the building 59 and 66 names are on the respective registers. The one room affords *twenty-nine cubic feet*, the *other twenty-four to each scholar!* Warmed by a steam radiator; the top of the windows about on a level with children's heads. A strong draft from the open windows blows upon the children, purifying the atmosphere of the rooms and producing sudden and sharp changes of temperature to children, many of whom are insufficiently clothed. The exposure is unwarrantable, and the rooms should be given up. Vaults not connected with sewer, and not emptied for years; the apartment filthy.

No. 33. Average, 1,400; situated in close proximity to a large group of sunken lots which contain stagnant water, ponded by street grading. Malarial affections prevail to a considerable extent among the children of this school.

No. 34. Direct current of hot air from registers upon children seated near them. Two rooms, 14x18x8½, have 58 and 54 children; one, 9x18, has 56 children; hot air register opens directly into a seat. Open windows admit a draft directly upon the heads of the children. The playground is paved with cobblestones, and several accidents have occurred in consequence.

Primary Schools—No. 1. The space allowed each child varies in the different rooms from 68 to 495 cubic feet; temperature ranged from 64° to 74°; windows open at top. Children seated near hot air registers evidently suffer, and the practice, common to this and other schools, of subjecting them to the violent changes of temperature from proximity to these registers to a remote part of the room is to be condemned.

No. 3. Space afforded each child varies from 42 to 172 cubic feet. In one room are 140 small children; wood stoves heat the rooms, and open windows admit cold air. Temperature in range of seats next to stove was 90°! most remote, 64°.

No. 6. Air oppressive; inadequate ventilators, and windows open. Temperature in some rooms, 50°; in others, 75°. Vaults full and offensive; apartments disgusting; urinals are wooden troughs, without means of flushing, saturated with filth. In this and nearly all the schools, for want of covered passage-ways, the children are exposed to wet and cold in their indoor dress.

No. 7, average 400; stoves for heat; windows only for air; cellar damp, and air stagnant; at times cellar contains water; vaults offensive.

No. 12, average 270; considerable escape of coal-gas from registers; cellars unwholesome; recitation-rooms low; air not sufficiently changed; closets unsewered, and near the recitation-rooms.

No. 13, average, 247; heated by stoves; the middle room not comfortably warm; the yard neither paved nor floored—on the day of inspection—a mud hole; vault full and offensive.

No. 14, average 200; vaults offensive.

No 24, basement of a church, 40x40; lighted and ventilated by four windows; room partly below surface of ground. It is damp; sometimes the water has to be bailed out, and fires made to dry the floor. It is imperfectly warmed, and badly lighted. On foggy days it is necessary to dismiss the school for want of light. There are *four* stoves for *six* rooms. In some of the rooms children are seated within two and three feet of the stove; in others no heat save that which comes from the adjoining rooms. Four hundred and sixty have been registered. Many have been absent from sickness, particularly the younger children. Thermometer ranged from 50° to 95°. *Forty cubic* feet and upwards of air space to each child, according to crowding.

Colored School No. 3, want of drainage of ground beneath the school.

Colored School No. 4, average 70; majority under eight years of age; two rooms; two windows to each room; stove heat; window and doors only afford change of air; 52 cubic feet of air space to each scholar. The Sanitary Inspector states that during his visits to the schools in his district he endeavored to ascertain the amount of sickness in the various departments, and was surprised to learn the number of children unable to attend school on account of contagious diseases. From one class, numbering about sixty, *ten* children were absent, either from *measles* or *scarlatina*, at the time of visit, and one child had just returned to the school after an attack of measles. "I had the curiosity," the Inspector states, "to visit the child's home, which I found to be in a tenement house. The mother informed me the child had been sick with the measles, and when she thought she was well enough she had sent her back. No physician had seen her, nor had any disinfection of the premises been performed. I visited the homes of several children and found much the same condition of things as in the first one visited. With the exception of school No. 15, I ascertained that no physician's certificate was necessary for the re-admission of pupils after absence caused by contagious diseases; that the decision of the proper time for the child's return was left to the discretion of the parents. If this practice was general throughout the schools of the city, I think we should naturally expect an increase in the number of contagious diseases after the June vacation, when the children reassemble for the school term." I have compiled the following statistics from the record of contagious diseases, and the mortality has been kindly furnished me by the Registrar, Dr. Watt:

	Reported Scarlatina.	*Reported* Diphtheria.	*Deaths* Scarlatina.	*Deaths* Diphtheria.	
July, 1873	56	8			Vacation.
Aug. "	50	7			
Sept. "	45	23	8	20	Begin'g Fall T'm
Oct. "	97	60	18	30	"
Nov. "	141	67	26	25	"
Dec. "	192	84	48	96	"
Jan. "	184	81	40	29	"

Total deaths in 1873 from measles, scarlatina and diphtheria, 635. Scarlatina and measles are contagious for an indefinite time (certainly long after the child is able to attend school) I hardly know whether it is a legitimate deduction from these figures that the rapid increase in number of reported cases of scarlatina and diphtheria is due to the spread of the contagion in the schools, but the few cases in July, August and September, and rapid increase in the subsequent months, certainly justify the suspicion that some such element is at work. The absence of many children in the country would partially account for the small number in July and August, but early in September they return to the city, and if material was the only requisite, the number of cases in September would be larger than it is. If the schools are free of contagion, should there not be a sanitary supervision over them? If the Board of Education should report to the Health Office any case of contagious disease occurring in their schools, and a similar report be required from all other schools, this department could have an opportunity of quarantining and disinfecting, and a certificate from the Health Office alone should re-admit to the schools a child convalescent from a contagious disease. It would doubtless occupy the entire time of one inspector, but it will be time and money well expended if these scourges of childhood could in any way be mitigated, and if one life could be saved from the hundreds yearly carried off by measles, scarlatina and diphtheria."

Nearly allied to this condition of the public schools of Brooklyn is the Nursery, a department of the Almshouse for the care of pauper children. The crowded and filthy condition of that institution has very recently powerfully touched the public conscience. With an average number of inmates, the space for each child in the Nursery, without allowance for furniture, is 380 cubic feet. There are attached to it two school-rooms, and these measure, respectively, 117 and 153 cubic feet to each pupil, or five times as much as some of the rooms of the public schools, and are scarcely exceeded by any, either in space or appointments in regard to light and warmth. The object of giving this example is not, by any means, to show that it has not deserved the complaint against it which it has received, but to illustrate the public apathy in regard to other institutions, the schools-rooms for children who are not paupers being at the least equally worthy of public attention.

In an examination of sixteen of the public school-rooms, and, with two or three exceptions, the same as here reported upon, (but when they were less crowded than they are at the present time) and seven private schools in 1869, by the late R. Cresson Styles, M. D., the average proportion of carbonic acid present was 1.64 volume per 1,000, or 3.3 times its normal amount. Two only (and both of these were private schools) were perfectly ventilated; one of the public school-rooms had eight times the normal proportion of carbonic acid present, and more than half of them four times the normal proportion.

It is very far from my purpose to show that the school-rooms of Brooklyn are more perilous than the school-rooms of other cities; indeed, they are not so. In the neighboring city of New York the plan of construction in some of the new buildings is believed to be an improvement over any of the Brooklyn buildings, but, taking them altogether, they are about equally perilous. While engaged in the preparation of this paper, I addressed a note to Dr. R. J. O'Sullivan—for some time sanitary superintendent of the public schools of New York—for special observations. He replied, in part, as follows:

New York, *Nov. 5th*, 1874.

I have practised in one of the most densely populated portions of the city for the past eighteen years, and have been a school officer for several years, and attending and consulting physician of the Eastern Dispensary for upwards of fourteen years, and in the experience I have had in the schools and in the midst of an immense tenement-house population, I have not at any period within the time stated known contagious diseases among school children so prevalent as at the present time. I can merely give you an instance to show how school contagion has contributed to this result: I was called to see a child, six years of age, a few days since, who contracted diphtheria while attending school, and died after a brief illness. Two other cases where defective drainage and ventilation were the predisposing causes also occurred in my practice. The children were aged respectively four and six. They were attacked with diphtheria and scarlet fever, with these results: one recovery and one death. Did time permit, I could go on enumerating cases of a similar character; suffice it to say that there is abundant evidence to show that the present unsanitary condition of our city's schools has contributed in no small degree to the increase of infantile mortality by the great majority of the children living in tenement-houses, in narrow rooms, in close contact with the sick, and carrying contagion through their persons and clothing to the schools. Attending and visiting physicians in dispensary practice will concur in the statement that school contagion has been carried to the homes of the children in various parts of the city. Thus diseases that could be prevented by proper sanitary direction, have, through the negligence of the school authorities, become the means of propagating disease to the entire community. Truly yours, R. J. O'Sullivan, M. D.

Philadelphia, I am sorry to believe, is no better. With an enviable amount of house room for all other purposes, and the banner city of America, for the health of her people, her school-houses, notwithstanding, are a disgraceful exception. The general plan of her school buildings is faulty in the extreme.

Availing myself of the kindness of one of the officers of the Philadelphia school board, I visited one of these buildings a few nights ago, during the school session. And it may here be remarked, as generally applicable that, however necessary night schools may be to meet the convenience of working children and others who cannot attend the day schools, the night schools as a rule are more perilous than the day. The rooms already filled with the mephitic exhalations of the day's service and with no sufficient time for purification—add gas light—an additional means of impurity. The night pupils are, for the most part clad in their working clothes, and many of them from factory life and other occupations which render their persons and clothing unclean.

Of this condition the school I visited on Tuesday night, a few blocks from this hall, is an example. Crowded to the extent of less than 100 cubic feet of air space to each person, in several of the rooms, warmed by radiation from hot-air pipes, without any provision for moisture, and no means for the escape of foul air, an offensive odor pervaded the whole school; and the entire aspect was one of prospective disease and early death. On descending to the cellar, the sickening odor of carbonic acid and oxide was so unbearable as to suggest the propriety of a speedy retreat. The cellar had evidently never been cleansed, or even aerated, since the floors were laid above. And to this hot-bed of disease and death—well stocked with coal, and most likely at the time of storage rendered more certain to evolve its deleterious gases by wetting—every teacher and pupil of this school was exposed. Nor is this, bad as it is, an exceptional case. Indeed the evil is so general, in all of our cities, as to fully justify the conclusion that the examples given are examples of American school-houses generally, and of no particular city. They are a disgrace to our civilization and a shame to our humanity.

Hindrances to Vaccination.—It is of the first importance to uniform success of the practice of vaccination that the vaccinator shall be possessed of a special skill and knowledge of the subject. The physician must have acquired particular practical knowledge and an acquaintance, not only of the true genuine vaccination in all its regular stages, but he must be able to detect the least variation from the normal course at every stage. Vaccinators in Great Britain are required to stand an examination as to their qualifications before receiving an appointment. It is apprehended that great advantage would accrue to the people if the same rule were in existence in the United States.

It is the conviction of not only every medical man, but of every intelligent citizen, that a properly performed and successful vaccination, whether with humanized or animal virus, is as complete a protection against small-pox now as it ever was, and is a more perfect prophylactic than we possess against any other known disease. But it is of the highest importance, and a prerequisite to success, that the vaccinator obtain virus of unquestionable purity. The particular mode of introducing the virus perhaps makes but little difference in the result, provided no undue injury is done to the tissue, and the lymph, or dissolved crusts, are brought in direct contact with the absorbents, although the shape of the resulting vesicle may depend somewhat upon the particular operation. The thumb lancet is the best instrument to use.

Insusceptibility to vaccination is rare. Failure to induce vaccination is more frequently the fault of the virus used, or of the operator. In reference to transmitting diseases in vaccine matter, Marson, who has vaccinated over 50,000 individuals, "has never seen other diseases communicated with vaccine disease, nor does he believe in the popular reports that they are so communicated." Spurious vaccination has been found to pervert or greatly embarrass subsequent successful vaccination. Thus it is necessary to secure good and complete primary vaccination. It is probable that a fruitful cause of insufficient vaccination in the United States originates from the want of quantity rather than defective quality of the vaccine fluid.—*J. M. Toner, M. D., Amer. Public Health Association*, 1874.

ON THE HAND-FEEDING OF INFANTS.

By Eustace Smith, M. D., Lond., Physician to H. M. the King of the Belgians, Physician to the East London Children's Hospital, Assistant Physician to the Victoria Park Hospital for Diseases of the Chest.

I.

There are few subjects of greater interest, or of which it is more important, in a sanitary sense, to possess an accurate knowledge than that which relates to the feeding and nurture of infants. Many mothers are unable to nurse their babies, and there is an increasing dislike to transfer maternal duties to a hireling; consequently the question how best to provide a fitting diet for a being whose digestive powers are feeble and immature, but whose growth and healthy development are dependent upon a suitable supply of nourishment, is one to which it is of the utmost importance to furnish a correct answer.

The mortality among children under the age of twelve months is enormous, and of these deaths a large proportion might be prevented by a wider diffusion of knowledge of one of the least difficult of subjects. The rules for the efficient nourishment of infants are plain and simple, and the application of them, although requiring tact and judgment, is yet not a matter which ought to occasion any extraordinary embarrassment.

The great principle at the bottom of all successful feeding—viz., that an infant is nourished in proportion to his power of digesting the food with which he is supplied, and not in proportion to the quantity of nutritive material which he may be induced to swallow—is so obviously true that an apology might almost seem to be required for stating so self-evident a proposition; but experience shows that this simple truth is one which in practice is constantly lost sight of. That that child thrives best who is most largely fed, and that the more solid the food the greater its nutritive power, are two articles of faith so firmly settled in the minds of many persons, that it is very difficult indeed to persuade them to the contrary. To them wasting in an infant merely suggests a larger supply of more solid food; every cry means hunger, and must be quieted by an additional meal. To take a common case: A child, weakly perhaps to begin with, is filled with a quantity of solid food which he has no power of digesting. His stomach and bowels revolt against the burden imposed upon them, and endeavor to get rid of the offending matter by vomiting and diarrhœa; a gastro-intestinal catarrh is set up, which still further reduces the strength; every meal causes a return of the sickness; the bowels are filled with fermenting matter, which excites violent griping pains, so that the child rests neither night nor day; after a longer or shorter time he sinks worn out by pain and exhaustion, and is then said to have died from "consumption of the bowels."

Cases such as the above are but too common, and must be painfully familiar to every physician who has much experience of the diseases of children. When seen sufficiently early, the treatment of the derangement is simple and the improvement immediate, but it unfortunately often happens, especially among the poorer classes, that application for advice is delayed until the child's strength has been reduced to the lowest point, and all our efforts to remedy the mischief may in such cases prove unavailing.

The disastrous results of ignorant attempts to supply a substitute for human milk have brought the whole practice of hand-feeding into disrepute; but if a food be judiciously selected, with a correct appreciation of infant wants, and an accurate estimate of infant powers of digestion, there is no reason why a child fed artificially, with judgment, should not thrive as well as one suckled naturally at his mother's breast. The food we select for the diet of an infant should be nutritious in itself, but it should also be given in a form in which the child is capable of digesting it, otherwise we may fill him with food without in any way contributing to his nutrition, and actually starve the body while we load the stomach to repletion. No food can be considered suitable to the requirements of the infant unless it not only possess heat-giving and fat-producing properties, but also contains material to supply the waste of the nitrogeneous tissues; therefore a merely starchy substance, such as arrowroot, which enters so largely into the diet of children, especially among the poor, is a very undesirable food for infants, unless given in very small quantities and mixed largely with milk.

The most perfect food for children, the only one, indeed, which can be trusted to supply in itself all the necessary elements of nutrition, in the most digestible form, is milk. In it are contained nitrogeneous matter in the curd, fat in the cream, besides sugar, and the salts which are so essential to perfect nutrition. The milk of different animals varies to a certain extent in the proportion of the several constituents, some containing more curd, others more cream and sugar; but the milk of the cow, which is always readily obtainable, is the one to which recourse is usually had, and when properly prepared this is perfectly efficient for the purpose required. Cow's milk contains a larger proportion of curd and cream, but less sugar, than is found in human milk, and these differences can be immediately remedied by dilution with water and the addition of cane or milk sugar in sufficient quantity to supply the necessary sweetness. But there is another and more important difference between the two fluids which must not be lost sight of. If we take two children, the one fed on cow's milk and water, the other nursed at his mother's breast, and produce vomiting directly after a meal by friction over the abdomen, we notice a remarkable difference in the matters ejected. In the first case we see the curd of the milk coagulated into a firm dense lump, while in the second the curd appears in the form of minute flocculent loosely connected granules. The demands made upon the digestive powers in these two cases is very different, and the experiment explains the difficulty often experienced by infants in digesting cow's milk, however diluted it may be, for the addition of water alone will not hinder the firm clotting of the curd. In order to make such milk perfectly satisfactory as a food for new-born infants, further preparation is required, and there are two ways in which the difficulty may be overcome.

The first method consists in adding an alkali, as lime-water, to the milk. To be of any service, however, the quantity added must be considerable, and one or two teaspoonfuls—the addition usually made to a bottleful of milk and water—is quite insufficient to effect the object desired. Lime-water contains only half a grain of lime to the fluid ounce; of this solution so small a quantity as two teaspoonfuls would be scarcely sufficient even to neutralize the natural acidity of the milk. But it is necessary to do much more than this. Lime-water, no doubt, acts by partially neutralizing the gastric juice—the rennet naturally existing in the child's stomach—so that clotting of the curd is in great part prevented, and the milk passes little changed out of the stomach to be fully digested by the intestinal secretions in the bowels. To attain this object at least a third part of the mixture should consist of lime-water. For a new-born infant two tablespoonfuls of milk may be diluted with an equal quantity of plain filtered water, and then be alkalinized by two tablespoonfuls of lime-water. This mixture, of which only a third part is milk, can be sweetened by the addition of a teaspoonful of milk-sugar. If thought desirable a teaspoonful of cream may be added. The whole is then put into a perfectly clean feeding-bottle, and is heated to a temperature of about 95° Fahr. by steeping the bottle in hot water; when warmed it is ready for use. The proportion of milk can be gradually increased as the child gets older.

There is another plan by which the caseine of cow's milk may be rendered digestible; it is by adding to the milk a small quantity of some thickening substance, such as barley-water, isinglass, or even one of the ordinary farinaceous foods. The action of all of these is the same, and is an entirely mechanical one. The thickening substance separates the particles of curd, so that they cannot run together into a solid lump, but coagulate separately into a multitude of small masses. By this means the curd is made artificially to resemble the naturally light clot of human milk, and is almost as readily digested by the infant.

Although any thickening matter will have the mechanical effect desired of separating the particles of curd, yet it is not immaterial what substance is chosen. The question of the farinaceous feeding of infants is a very important one, for it is to an excess of this diet that so many of their derangements may often be attributed. Owing to a mistaken notion that such foods are peculiarly light and digestible—a notion so widely prevalent that the phrase "food for infants" has become almost synonymous with farinaceous matter—young babies are often fed as soon as they are born with large quantities of corn-flour or arrowroot, mixed sometimes with milk, but often with water alone. Now, starch, of which all the farinæ so largely consist, is digested principally by the saliva, aided by the secretion from the pancreas, which convert the starch into dextrine and grape-sugar previous to absorption. But the amount of saliva formed in the new-born infant is excessively scanty, and it is not until the fourth month that the secretion becomes fully established. Again, according to the experiments of Korowin of St. Petersburg, the pancreatic juice is almost absent in a child of a month old; even in the second month its secretion is very limited, and has little action upon starch. It is only at the end of the third month that its action upon starch becomes sufficiently powerful to furnish material for a quantitative estimation of the sugar formed. Therefore, before the age of three months a farinaceous diet is not to be recommended—is even to be strongly deprecated, unless the starchy substance be given with great caution and in very small quantities. If administered recklessly, as it too often is, the food lies undigested in the bowels, ferments, and sets up a state of acid indigestion, which in so young and feeble a being may lead to the most disastrous consequences. In fact, the deaths of many children under two or three months old can often be attributed to no other cause than a purely functional abdominal derangement, excited and maintained by too liberal feeding with farinaceous foods. There is, however, one form of food which although farinaceous is yet well digested even by young infants, if given in moderate quantities. This is barley water. The starch it contains is small in amount and is held in a state of very fine division. When barley-water is mixed with milk in equal proportions it ensures a fine separation of the curd, and is at the same time a harmless addition to the diet. Isinglass or gelatine, in the proportion of a teaspoonful to the bottleful of milk and water, may also be made use of, and will be found to answer the purpose well.

Farinaceous foods, in general, are, as has been said, injurious to young babies, on account of the deficiency during the first months of life of the secretions necessary for the conversion of the starch into dextrine and grape-sugar—a preliminary process which is indispensable to absorption. If, however, we can make such an addition to the food as will insure the necessary chemical change, farinaceous matter ceases to be injurious. It has been found that by adding to it malt in certain proportions the same change is excited in the starch artificially as is produced naturally by the salivary and pancreatic secretions during the process of digestion. The employment of malt for this purpose was first suggested by Mialhe in a paper read before the French Academy in 1845, and the suggestion was put into practice by Liebig fifteen years later.

"Liebig's Food for Infants" contains wheat flour, malt, and a little carbonate of potash, and has gained a well-deserved celebrity as a food for babies during the first few months of life. The best form with which I am acquainted is that made by Mr. Mellin, under the name of "Mellin's Extract for preparing Liebig's Food for Infants." In this preparation, owing to the careful way in which it is manufactured, the whole of the starch is converted into dextrine and grape-sugar, so that the greater part of the work of digestion is performed before the food reaches the stomach of the child. Mixed with equal parts of milk and water, this food is as perfect a substitute for mother's milk as can be procured, and is readily digested by the youngest infants. It very rarely, indeed, happens that it is found to disagree.

In all cases, then, where a child is brought up by hand, milk should enter largely into his diet, and during the first few months of life he should be fed upon it almost entirely. If he can digest plain milk and water, there is no reason for making any other addition than that of a little milk-sugar, and cream; but in cases where, as often happens, the heavy curd taxes the gastric powers too severely, the milk may be thickened by an equal proportion of thin barley-water, or by adding to each bottleful of milk and water a teaspoonful of isinglass or of "Mellin's Extract."

Having fixed upon the kind of food which is suitable to the child, we must next be careful that it is not given in too large quantities, or that the meals are not repeated too frequently. If the stomach be kept constantly overloaded, even with a digestible diet, the effect is almost as injurious as if the child were fed upon a less digestible food in more reasonable quantities. A healthy infant passes the greater part of his time asleep, waking at intervals to take nourishment. These intervals must not be allowed to be too short, and it is a great mistake to accustom the child to take food whenever he cries. From three to four ounces of liquid will be a sufficient quantity during the first six weeks of life; and of this only a half or even a third part should consist of milk, according to the child's powers of digestion. After such a meal the infant should sleep quietly for at least two hours. Fretfulness and irritability in a very young baby almost always indicate indigestion and flatulence; and if a child cries and whines uneasily, twisting about his body and jerking his limbs, a fresh meal given instantly, although it may quiet him for the moment, will, after a short time, only increase his discomfort. During the first six weeks or two months, two hours will be a sufficient interval between the meals; afterwards this interval can be lengthened, and at the same time a larger quantity may be given at each time of feeding. No more food should be prepared at once than is required for the particular meal. The position of the child as he takes food should be half reclining, as when he is applied to his mother's breast, and the food should be given from a feeding-bottle. When the contents of the bottle are exhausted, the child should not be allowed to continue sucking at an empty vessel, as by this means air is swallowed, which might afterwards be a source of great discomfort. The feeding apparatus must be kept perfectly clean. The bottle should be washed out after each meal in water containing a little soda in solution, and must then lie in cold water until again wanted. It is desirable to have two bottles, which can be used alternately.

At the age of six months farinaceous food may be given in small quantities with safety, if it be desired to do so; and in some cases the addition of a moderate proportion of wheaten flour to the diet is found to be attended with advantage. The best form in which this can be given is the preparation of wheat known as "Chapman's entire wheaten flour." This is superior for the purpose to the ordinary flour, as it contains the inner husk of the wheat finely ground, and is therefore rich in phosphates and in a peculiar body called cerealin, which has the diastatic property of changing starchy matters into dextrine. This flour should be slowly baked in an oven until it crumbles into a light greyish powder. At first no more than one teaspoonful should be given once or twice a day, rubbed up (not boiled) with milk. If there be much constipation fine oatmeal may be used instead of the baked flour.

After the eighth month a little thin mutton or chicken broth or veal tea may be given, carefully freed from all grease. After twelve months the child may begin to take light puddings, well-mashed potatoes with gravy, or the lightly boiled yolk of an egg; but no meat should be allowed until the child be at least sixteen months old. Every new article of food should be given cautiously, and in small quantities at first, and any sign of indigestion should be noted and a return be made at once to a simpler method of feeding.

During all this time the child should be kept scrupulously clean, and his nursery should be well ventilated and not be kept too hot. He should be washed twice a day from head to foot, once with soap. The air of his bedroom should be kept sweet and pure during the day, and at night, if the weather do not allow of an open window, a lamp placed in the fender will insure of a sufficient exchange of air. The child should pass as much of his time as possible out of doors, and while every care is taken to guard his sensitive body against *sudden* changes of temperature, he must not be covered up with too heavy clothing and shut off from every breath of air for fear of his catching cold. A child ought to lie cool at night, and the furniture of his cot, although sufficiently thick to insure necessary warmth, should not be cumbersome, so as to be a burden. If the above directions are carefully carried out—and the mother should herself see that they are attended to—few cases will be found to present any difficulty in their management. Exceptional cases, however, are sometimes met with where special sources of embarrassment may arise. These I propose to consider in a future paper.—*Sanitary Record.*

THE RELATIONS OF TOPOGRAPHY TO HEALTH IN CONNECTION WITH THE PRINCIPLES AND PRACTICE OF DRAINAGE AND SEWERAGE.

An Address delivered by General EGBERT L. VIELE, of New York, before the American Public Health Association, at Philadelphia, November 11th, 1874.

The meeting of this association in the City of Philadelphia recalls the fact that the first Sanitary Congress in America was held in this city May 13, 1857. Previous to that event the barbarous quarantine codes, which time had made venerable, were rigidly enforced. The sick were treated worse than criminals, and the restrictions imposed by ignorance and fear to prevent the spread of disease were not only cruel in themselves, but provoked the very results which were so much dreaded.

In the language of Dr. Jewell, "They advocated antiquated and obsolete doctrines, they embarrassed commerce, oppressed the merchant, imposed severe restrictions on the healthy, inflicted cruelties on the sick, and when rigidly enforced became the ready means of disseminating and entailing disease and death."

The great leader of that congress—a true apostle of sanitary reform —was the illustrious Dr. Wilson Jewell, of Philadelphia—a man of whom any city, any State, or any nation, might be justly proud. How long, how well and faithfully he labored in the cause, his co-workers in the field can bear ample testimony.

His words bore the stamp both of faith and of prophecy when he said: "The work of sanitary reform in our country has commenced in earnest, and my desire and prayer is to be engaged in this work in season and out of season, until I behold the first fruits of our united and persevering exertions displaying its rich influence in the organization of a well-ordered sanitary police, embracing both external and internal hygiene through legislative enactments in all our large cities."

None the less earnest as a champion of sanitary reform was the eminent Dr. John Bell, also of Philadelphia. To him the world is indebted for the most learned and exhaustive treatise on the importance and economy of sanitary measures to cities that ever has been or probably ever will be written. Replete with the wisdom and experience of the past, it will be for all time a guide in the future to the practical sanitarian. And so long as mankind is led by humanity and directed by wisdom to provide measures of protection from pestilence, and relief from disease, so long will the names of Jewell and Bell be honored and revered among men.

The crusade against ignorance on behalf of humanity, so well begun under the auspices of such eminent leaders, has been maintained until the present time, with what results let the diminished death rate of our large cities, and their marked immunity from pestilence, bear witness. Those who have been more or less identified with this cause have come together for counsel and guidance; to exhibit what has been accomplished in the past, and to plan what may be accomplished in the future, by intelligent co-operation.

So far as sanitary engineering is concerned, or that particular department of sanitary science which by virtue of my profession has come under my personal cognizance, I find great reason for congratulation in the progress which has been made both in this country and in Europe. It is true that innumerable obstacles present themselves on every hand. The resistance which is always offered, even by otherwise intelligent minds, to what are regarded as new ideas, would be astonishing if it were not so universal. The capacity of the human mind to reject knowledge is very great, and in nothing does it show itself so obstinately as in those matters where science has to contend with social habits. Every step in this direction is opposed by a great force which might be denominated "the inertia of ignorance," and to overcome it is like removing a mountain.

It has sometimes appeared to me that it required more skill, energy, perseverance, and courage to conduct a sanitary campaign than it does to marshal an army in the field. Ignorance and vice, avarice and greed, politicians and quacks, sordid contractors and corrupt rings, array themselves against progress until experience comes with its terrible lessons to destroy the opposition that no other argument could remove. Hence it is that a convention like the one now in session becomes a great public necessity, for by it important facts are acquired, and through it they are disseminated with the force and power of united action, so essential to success, especially in a case like this, whose magnitude extends to the very limits of human civilization.

Of all the problems embraced within the scope of sanitary science, none are more important or should claim a larger share of attention than those connected with drainage and sewerage. Since, of all the innumerable causes which singly or combined engender preventable disease, the most wide-spread and most certain is the presence of an undue amount of moisture in the soil. When we consider how universal is the presence of water in all created matter forming the larger portion of the great globe itself, and more than three-fourths of all animal and vegetable substance, constituting 795 parts in 1,000 of the blood, 789 parts of the brain, and 756 parts of the muscles; when we consider, also, its amazing power as a solvent, dissolving matter and absorbing its constituent gases with an incomprehensible avidity, when we think of its equally wonderful erosive power, wearing away mountains and plains, and washing the plains into the sea, and recognize it as the prevailing and most potent of all the powers of nature, we cannot wonder at the important part it fills for good and evil in the history of the world. To the action of water is due, to a large extent, the topographical configuration of the earth. The great upheaving forces that elevated the mountain chains were limited in their effects and duration, when compared with the abrading forces of the iceberg, and the erosion of the waters. The latter is unceasing in its activity, destroying and recreating, and were the earth's internal fires to sleep unmoved forever, so long as the dew falls and the clouds form, so long for all time will the surface of the globe undergo constant and increasing change from the action of water. Does it not, then, behoove all men to know well this element of life and death, to study it not only with the microscope as it exists in the dew-drop, and learn its constituents, but to study it and know it in its all-pervading character; in the rivulet, the river and the sea; in its hidden channels through the fissures of the primitive rocks, but above all in the *supersaturated soils which surround them on every side?*

Let us follow it for a moment as it rises in vapor on a summer's day; see it floating upward in fleecy clouds until, in a higher stratum of air, it condenses and gathers into black masses that roll and mingle, while amid quick flashes of electric discharge and reverberating thunder it descends in copious volumes. The parched soil eagerly drinks it. Drooping vegetation revives, and the green earth smiles in beauty from its refreshing influences. Were this to occur only at such times and in such quantities as are alone necessary, man would live in a perpetual paradise; but unfortunately far more water descends upon the earth than is absorbed or required for vegetation. By reason of the physical conformation of the surface a large portion of it passes by the rivers to the sea, but a very large portion is permanently retained in the soil in excess of its requirements. And this portion is the principal source of human misery throughout the world. Man meets it as his great enemy on the threshold of existence. He meets it wherever he goes, in every part of the inhabited and uninhabited earth—in the crowded city, in the secluded hamlet—it follows him like an unseen spectre. Its noisome vapors envelop him like a mantle; they chill the warm blood in his veins; they penetrate into his lungs and disturb all his organs of vitality. When once they gain a foothold in his system, and a burning fever fills his veins with hot blood and his brain with delirium, the crisis of his life has come. Even if he recovers, a power has gone from him, never to return; he rises from his bed like Samson shorn. The old vitality never comes back. I appeal to the medical profession to confirm the truth of this statement. Is there a physician of extended practice in either hemisphere who has not within the last twelve months had under his charge fifty or a hundred cases of sickness, due directly or indirectly to malarial influences? Yet what a strange indifference the great public exhibits upon this subject! But a short time ago the whole British empire was filled with a deep anxiety and expectant sorrow at the severe illness and prospective death of the heir-apparent to the throne—an illness due to a preventable cause arising from imperfect drainage. The destinies of a great nation apparently hung upon this single thread, and the subject became as widely known and discussed as any event of the age, and yet probably not one in a hundred thousand, either in Europe or America, has deemed it necessary to examine the surroundings of his own domicile to see if the like source of disease does not exist at his own door. On the contrary, we have only to look about us to see on every hand individuals constructing edifices, and communities constructing towns and cities, with a reckless disregard of all the warnings of the past, and a reckless indifference to future consequences; in utter violation of those laws and principles upon which depends life itself. Take for illustration the following description of a portion of the city of Salem, from this year's report of the Massachusetts State Board of Health. Speaking of the location of a very large number of cases of typhoid fever, the report states:

"At the foot of Pingree street is a sluggish body of water, fouled by refuse of all descriptions, which taints the air of the neighborhood with its oppressive exhalations. Near this water, on low land, are tenements whose occupants use little precaution to protect themselves from the stench of slops and garbage thrown on the surface of the ground, or from shallow and neglected privies. At high tide the waters find their way along the drain into the cellars of the houses. It surely is not strange that in this neighborhood, during the past year, occurred nineteen cases of typhoid fever. There is a sluggish basin of water lying at the north of Howard street cemetery and the jail (fit proximity). This basin is of triangular form, bounded by Ridge street, the Eastern Railroad, and the land lying back of Northey street. It covers three or more acres of flats. Into it flows the drainage from St. Peter's street, Howard street, Oliver street, Northey street, also the drainage from the gas works. Formerly the coal tar from these works was allowed to flow to waste, but since it has become valuable for coloring purposes, it is retained, and only the ammoniacal liquor is allowed to flow away. So that whereas, formerly, some little antiseptic action was derived from this drainage, now it aggravates the baneful condition of the waters by promoting decomposition. Each spring, with the annual cleaning of gardens, flower-stalks, brush, and all sorts of refuse are emptied along the banks of this basin. On the Northey side there is a low shore, overgrown with sedge-like grass. The only outlet for these waters is by a culvert under the railroad, the emptying of the waters with the ebbing tide is so slow that decomposing animal and vegetable refuse settles among the brush and grasses on the shore and on the flats. Near the gas works, leading from Northey street to the basin, is Woodbury court (a short court with five or six houses on each side). In the two houses immediately bordering the water there have been four cases of typhoid fever this season. Half way up the court have occurred two more, and not far from the head of the court three others, making ten cases in the neighborhood this autumn." In the immediate vicinity there have been twenty-one cases of typhoid fever in all. The report states further that *all this is due to defective drainage*, and that before vigorous measures can be adopted to improve the sanitary condition of the city, the authorities must appreciate the dangers which are imminent.

"*This*," it adds, "*neither they nor the people seem to do.* The nuisance remains the same. although public attention has been repeatedly called to it." All this refers to a locality in one of the oldest, most refined, and wealthy cities in the intelligent State of Massachusetts, of which Boston, the intellectual centre of the United States is the capital, and yet not even the barbarism of Central Africa could exceed this scene of human degradation and filth.

Of the city of Lowell in the same State the report says: "The system of sewerage in Lowell has always been imperfect. In many places there are no sewers at all, in others the pipes are of insufficient capacity or not low enough in position. There has always been great confusion as to their location, owing to the imperfection or absence of maps. Two years ago there occurred here, especially on Marion and Cross streets, an epidemic of typhoid fever. At that time and since then the sewage filled many of the cellars. On investigation a mass of filth was found which filled the entire calibre of the drain-pipe for some distance. This pipe was also found to be too small, and not low enough to create a current." These are not cited as exceptional cases. On the contrary, there is reason to suppose that the same state of things can be found to exist in almost every city and town in the country.

Even here in Philadelphia, which we were led to believe, from the remarks of the courteous chairman of the reception committee, was in an exceptionally healthy condition, are some very unwholesome spots, as the following report of yesterday's meeting of the Board of Health will show:

"The Board of Health, at its meeting yesterday, received a report from the Sanitary Committee, regarding the complaint of a nuisance at Forty-second and Haverford streets, caused by the drainage from a large sewer flowing through the section between the point named and Forty-fourth and Sansom streets. The report says the sewer is the channel of drainage for a populous section of West Philadelphia, in which a number of slaughter-houses are located. Blood and offal from these find their way into this sewer, adding greatly to the offensive character of its contents. This sewage flows sluggishly through the low ground east of the Pennsylvania Hospital for the Insane, thence under Market street, and in a southwesterly direction until it empties into the Mill Creek sewer. The emanations arising therefrom, are sickening in the extreme, and threaten the health of all the neighboring population."

The responsibility for such a condition of things is not always due to ignorance; for, unfortunately, while there are many people in this world who know too little, there are also some who know too much. There are quacks in every profession—quack doctors, quack lawyers, quack soldiers, and quack engineers—men who, having been gifted with an excess of conceit and cunning, use these qualities in the absence of more substantial ones, and succeed, by a pretension to knowledge, in imposing upon credulous people. In all local boards there is generally to be found such a character, who thinks he knows more than any one else. The city of London was for a long time victimized in this way. That city, as we all know, has suffered terribly in the past for want of a proper system of drainage and sewerage. The plague carried off 100,000 people, and this was almost entirely due to defective drainage. For a period of ten years they were struggling to attain a correct and thorough system. A new commission being appointed by Parliament nearly every year, each time just as they were arriving at a practical result, some person, generally a member of the commission, or a particular friend of a Commissioner, would bring forward a plan differing from all the others. This would prevent the adoption of any plan; and so it went on until the matter was placed in the hands of one man, Mr. Bazalgette, who has achieved wonders by simply adopting a comprehensive plan based upon common sense principles.

A practical system of drainage is one the key of which is the topography of the site to be drained, and any attempt to carry out a plan not based upon the topography must necessarily end in failure. When I speak of drainage, I do not include sewerage. Drainage and sewerage are entirely distinct and can seldom be combined, and then only to a limited extent. Drainage is the removal of the surplus water from the soil. Sewerage is the removal of water introduced by means of an artificial water supply, to which is added excrementations and other refuse matter which the force of the water conveys into the sewers. It follows that sewers should be close conduits—to prevent the escape of gases—while drains should be so constructed as to admit of the percolation of water into them from the adjacent soil.

Let us suppose, for example, a site to be selected for a future town or city. The topography of the surface indicates a valley between undulating grassy hills, interspersed with meadows and fields, and dotted here and there with trees. Through the valley runs a limpid brook, sedgy and rocky by turns. In its pure, bright waters the sun is reflected as in a mirror. The beauty of the landscape, the surrounding air, the pleasant sounds and delightful odors, shed on all around a grateful influence. A scene so fair as this should certainly not be despoiled in making it a habitation for man; much less should all these attractive surroundings be converted into health-destroying influences. And yet it is universally the case that the occupation of such a territory by a large number of people seems to be the signal for the exercise of every device that human ingenuity can conceive to destroy its pristine purity. The soil soon becomes saturated with putrescent filth; the stream becomes the receptacle of every kind of refuse, and its sluggish waters are black, and filled with poisonous gases. The natural drainage being interrupted by the grading of the roads and streets, the surrounding soil is soaked with water, and the lives of the people pay the penalty. By what simple means can this be avoided! All that is necessary to do is to make the plan of the town conform, if only in a general way, to the topography of the surface. The streets and avenues, instead of being impediments to drainage, may serve to facilitate it. A system of drainage becomes easy to adopt, and the most universal cause of disease is in a large measure avoided. But even if such a course is not adopted with reference to the original plan, it is nevertheless imperatively necessary that the streams and water-courses should be preserved by underground drains, and also that lateral drains should be constructed to take up the water emanating from perennial springs. If this is not done in the beginning, when it can be done easily and economically, it will have to be done in the end, when the task is surrounded with difficulties, and at an enormous cost, when the safety of the lives of the people demand it, and after the pestilence and the graveyard have demonstrated its absolute necessity. The city of New York affords the most striking example of the errors committed in this respect and evils arising therefrom that can be found on either continent. Probably there is no spot in the world so well adapted for a great commercial entrepot as the island on which New York is built. Surrounded on all sides by wide and deep water channels, having a well-defined water shed, combined with every variety of surface, varying in height from five to 150 feet above high water mark, blessed by a climate of unsurpassed salubrity, it has, nevertheless, been ravaged by cholera and yellow fever, while the utmost vigilance is required to prevent the outbreak and spread of small-pox, diphtheria, and the whole class of low fevers. All this is due in a very large degree to the fact that in laying out the plan upon which the city has been constructed the existence of a vast system of drainage streams was entirely ignored. Miles and miles of running streams, fed by innumerable perennial springs, permeate the original topography in every direction. Over these the streets have been graded, the intervening blocks filled up, and acres of buildings erected, and beneath lies the undrained, saturated soil, giving off its damp, chilling, malarious atmosphere.

It is true that herculean and eminently successful efforts are being made by an energetic and wise Board of Health to remedy all this; but think for one moment of the task before them—the time, labor, skill, and money required to accomplish what might have been so easily done in the beginning. In one small district eighteen miles of underground drains have been laid down within the last three years, at an expense which would have drained the entire city in the commencement. Startling as all this is, every city and town in the United States is following recklessly in the footsteps of New York, and in the end will pay the same penalties. Memphis, in mourning for her decimated population, repeats the sad story.

While this matter of drainage is the first great step for all communities to take, it is none the less necessary to individuals—the residents of the detached villa and farm-house. Wherever and whenever an excavation is made in which to construct a cellar for a house, there necessarily occurs an interruption of the natural drainage of the soil. The underground channels for the percolation of water are intercepted, and must be restored by the construction of a drain below the level of the cellar, and all the surrounding area requires a system of drains connecting with the main outlet. To neglect this is perilous. How many houses constructed after elaborate and well-considered plans, executed under the influences of bright hopes and happy auspices for the future have proved the gateway to death from the neglect of these simple principles? Examine the admirably-designed and graphic charts that illustrate the vital statistics of the last census. The varying shades of crimson tell us that malarial and typhus fevers prevail all over the United States in greater or less intensity, and while knowing that the chief source of this wide-spread calamity is saturated and undrained soil, how painful it is to reflect that the least expensive of all the efforts that man is required to make to secure for himself a healthful and a happy home is the simple draining of the soil! Even for agricultural purposes, draining is the most remunerative of all labor, and experience has shown that draining for agricultural profit has been in many insalubrious districts attended by an immediate diminution in the death rate. In the Dominion of Canada I saw last month the most extensive system of drainage probably ever executed, successfully carried out under the combined action of the Government and individuals. By virtue of an organic law, certain main drains of great extent and capacity are opened by the Government and paid for by a general assessment. Connecting with these are lateral drains opened by the owners of estates at their own expense. Thorough drainage of an extended area is thus secured by a general and uniform system. Those who are directly benefited by it pay the expense, while the public at large obtain immunity from disease. I recommend this wise and beneficent law for general adoption in this country. One word more in reference to domiciliary drainage. We observe throughout this country that on the premises adjoining every isolated or detached residence there are generally three excavations made, one for a cesspool, one for a privy, and another for a well. These are also most generally in near proximity to each other.

The well, of course, is always the deepest, and if the soil is porous, it necessarily receives the leakage from the other two, especially as all three excavations are always faced with stones laid without mortar or cement, precisely in the same manner that drains are constructed to admit the percolation of water through the interstices.

It seems absurd and almost impossible that the receptacle provided for securing a constant supply of pure water should be universally so constructed that every possible opportunity is afforded for destroying the purity of that water; and not only this, but that a plan should be generally adopted for positively insuring the contamination of the water by so constructing the receptacle for refuse matter that the liquid can readily percolate through it into the well. And yet nine-tenths of the homes of our people throughout the land are so arranged. The use of hydraulic cement in these constructions would obviate all this. In addition to which the overflow of the cesspool should be made to pass through charcoal; and, further, dry earth or charcoal deodorization should be constantly used in the privies.

There is one great source of evil through soil saturation, which, although almost universal in extent, has not received that attention which its terrible importance demands. I allude to the construction of mill-dams. The great variety of surface which characterizes not only a large portion of the United States, but that of nearly every State and county and town, naturally results in innumerable valleys, through which flow the waters which make up the river system of our country. The rushing torrents of these rivers and their countless branches are everywhere stopped in their courses and made to furnish the motive power for ten thousand mills and factories. To do this, dams are constructed across the beds of the streams, behind which large bodies of water are accumulated, to be gradually drawn off, as it may be required, to turn the wheels which drive the machinery. The water which is thus dammed back saturates a large amount of soil in every instance. And this is probably the most fruitful source of malaria in the country. In addition to this, the bottoms of the artificial ponds thus formed become a mass of decomposed vegetable matter, to which, by carelessness, much decomposing animal matter is almost invariably added. This deposit is necessarily exposed to the direct action of the rays of the sun each day when the water is drawn down in the working of the mills. The consequence is that in the vicinity of all these mills there are always a large number of cases of typho-malarial fever.

In one instance under my own observation there were at one time 1,200 cases of fever due to this cause, and a physician stated to me that he knew in his own practice of one mill-dam, that did not yield an income of $400, that had caused the death of twenty persons. This great evil extends over our entire country. What is the remedy for it? I would not for a moment propose to interfere with the industrial resources of our land; I would not have a factory stop or a single mill cease to yield its bountiful products. On the contrary, I would increase the number of these necessary adjuncts to an active civilization; I would conserve the latent force of every drop of water that a beneficient Providence sheds upon the earth; but I would do it in such a way that it should be always a blessing and never a curse. I would make every mill-dam throughout the length and breath of the land what it ought to be—a properly-constructed reservoir of pure water, free from all contamination, instead of being a stagnant pond of putrid filth. I would have their form and construction a matter of statute law, as clearly defined as the law against homicide and arson, and the violation of that law followed by criminal punishment.

A very little additional cost in original construction would confine these mill-ponds to a properly defined space, from which all vegetable matter should be carefully removed and the sides protected by walls from contact with vegetation. This would deprive the water entirely of its malarial influences. The sooner our legislators take intelligent action on this matter, the importance of which cannot be exaggerated, the better will it be for them and our country. And let us hope that the time is not far distant when an ignorance of sanitary laws shall debar the aspiring statesman from enjoying the honors of public position. As well might a man attempt to sail a ship who had never before seen the ocean, as for one to attempt to legislate intelligently for the public good who is ignorant of the laws of health.

I have already stated that sewerage is entirely distinct from drainage, it being the essential accompaniment of a water supply, since, without an amply supply of water, no system of sewerage could possibly be maintained; and yet, even with an abundance of water, I confess, with a great deal of mortification for the engineering profession, that the sewerage of nearly all the large towns and cities of the United States is a failure, since everything may be regarded as a failure that does not accomplish the object for which it was intended. Unfortunately, while the profession of an engineer involves a very large amount of responsibility, including in a great measure that of human life, it is surrounded by no legal enactments like the professions of the law and medicine, by which a certain degree of skill is secured in its practice, and it too often occurs that an ignorant and incompetent person assumes the title of engineer or architect, and through personal or political influence becomes charged with duties for which he is entirely unfit. It was long ago said that "fools step in where angels fear to tread."

The problems connected with sewerage are numerous and intricate. They have engaged the earnest thoughts of able minds for many years. Man finds in it a spirit which he himself has raised, and which it is difficult to exorcise. The illustrious Liebig gave to its economic consideration the widest research and most profound philosophy The great cities of London and Paris have labored for centuries to control the vast proportions which it has attained through an enormous and increasing population. Its problems and difficulties multiply with every change of circumstance. A system thoroughly adapted to one locality might be utterly useless in another. But the principal cause of failure arises in most instances from a want of breadth in the original design. It is easy enough to convince people that their particular town or city will one day be a large centre of population; but when it comes to paying for the construction of a main sewer five or six feet in diameter, in anticipation of a large increase in population, while one which is two or three feet in diameter will answer the present purpose, the tax-payers generally decide in favor of the small sewer; so that the engineer is not always responsible. As well might we expect the veins of a child to suffice in capacity for the blood circulation of an adult, as to hope that the system of sewerage which is only sufficient for a small village will answer the purposes of a large city. Any plan of sewerage to be effective must not only be comprehensive in design, but must be based on an anticipated growth of population. The principal points to be considered are:

1. The original configuration of the ground, and natural valleys of drainage.
2. The artificial changes of the natural surface by the grading of streets and avenues.
3. The rainfall, or amount of water discharged from the clouds during the year upon the area to be sewered.
4. The water supply, or amount of water distributed to the inhabitants daily, from the reservoir and water-works.

It will be seen that the surface drainage of graded streets is included in the sewerage system, but this is distinct from the natural drainage through old water courses, from springs, etc.

The imperfections in a system of this kind arise from a want of proper judgment in determining the size, form, and location of the sewers—sometimes from errors, either intentional or accidental, in their construction, and sometimes from want of proper material used. But one of the chief causes of trouble is a want of proper descent to allow a free flow of the sewage. After all, however, the main difficulty is what to do with the enormous accumulation of sewage matter which must result from even the most perfect system. This is the all-important problem which the great cities of the earth are trying to solve. London has endeavored to do it by means of "low, level sewers," and although they have succeeded in purifying the Thames, and thus removing a great source of evil, they have not yet arrived at a satisfactory utilization or disposition of sewage.

The Municipal Council of Paris has, it is stated, adopted a plan for cleansing the Seine, by which the sewage deposited in the river will be directed to the plains of Genevilliers, with what degree of success remains to be determined. Capt. Liernur, a civil and military engineer of Holland, has projected a pneumatic system for the removal of sewage matter, which is now under trial by the City of The Hague. Earth-closets, as a substitute for sewers, are being extensively and successfully used in England and in this country. Of one thing there can be no question. The successful plan which can economically remove, without offense, the refuse matter of cities beyond the precincts, and apply it to the restoration of exhausted soil, will be one of the greatest of blessings. The increasing importance of this subject is more apparent in this country than elsewhere, by reason of the rapid increase in population, and the establishment and growth of new towns, especially in the interior, where difficulties occur that are not experienced along the seaboard. The same stream of water is often the source of water supply and the receptacle of sewage. The consequence resulting therefrom cannot be considered problematical.

For instance, Newark, Hoboken, and Jersey City, in New Jersey, obtain their water supply from the Passaic, while the city of Paterson, a large manufacturing centre, discharges its sewage into the same river at a point higher up the stream than that from which the water for those cities is taken. It is vain to hope that the sewage will be so diffused in running water that it will not contaminate it. Organic matter has always been the readiest means of propagating contagion, and in no way can it be so readily distributed as in water.

There are many minor points connected with this subject which the limited time at my disposal has not permitted me to discuss.

The leading points which have been presented will, it is hoped, stimulate thought and inquiry. The condition of all our cities and towns requires to be carefully examined, especially with reference to improved methods of drainage and sewerage.

The fearful exhibit of the annual mortality, from preventable causes, throughout our otherwise favored land, calls for the active exertions of all intelligent men toward the removal of these causes. Wise counsel and wise legislation are needed. All classes of our people require instruction on this subject. Associations for this object should be formed in every city, town, and hamlet. Public lectures should be delivered, sanitary publications distributed, and the leading principles of sanitary science taught in the schools. Our people, otherwise so intelligent, should not be suffered to remain in ignorance of truths so vital to their welfare. The ignorance of one individual may destroy the health of an entire neighborhood, as the match lighted by a thoughtless child may create an extensive conflagration.

The progress made in sanitary reform during the last decade is a happy augury of what may be accomplished in the future, although the field is large and the laborers few.

Let us not suffer the importance of this great subject to be underrated through ignorance or indifference. The questions involved are of vital moment to every man, woman and child. That the vast majority of men die before their time, is made evident from the fact that so few die of old age; and when we estimate, or rather try to estimate, the sorrow and the misery which must be entailed by reason of the premature loss of the heads of families, not to speak of the desolation which follows the taking away of even one member of a happy domestic circle, the heart sickens at the contemplation, and yet how much of all this sad suffering might be spared by a knowledge of principles so simple that a child can learn them, and the practice of rules so plain that it is criminal to neglect them.

PHYSICAL CULTURE.

By H. L. Bartlett, M. D.

As we descend the stream of time towards man's original source, we find him allied to the beasts of the field, living in rocky caves and dens of the earth, and subsisting on roots and herbs, and the flesh of such animals as his limited skill enabled him to secure. Without knowledge, and almost without the means of defense, man was, at the first, not only at the mercy of wild beasts, but constantly in fear of aggressive attacks from hostile and more numerous tribes of fellow-men; and hence we learn that the earliest peoples of whom we have any record, practised such athletic exercises as were calculated to make them self-reliant and secure in times of peace, and formidable in war.

The Chinese claim to have practised a kind of "Movement Cure" of diseases for more than three thousand years before the Christian era, and although we cannot vouch for the exact age of this system of medical gymnastics, still it is unquestionably very ancient. It was called Cong-Fon, and was practised under the supervision of the priests. Their theory of disease was, that "humid air" was the cause of all the ills that flesh is heir to, and to heat the body and exorcise the vapory demon, they caused the patient to go through all sorts of bodily evolutions in every possible position.

In ancient India the inferior Brahmins practised a similar system, though they taught a somewhat different theory. They believed that respiration had the same influence upon the tissues of the body that fire possesses over the metals, viz.: the power of melting them, and converting them into vapor, hence they not only endeavored to heat the body by violent exercise, but strove to assist the internal fires by deep and forced inspiration.

The ancient Britons, also, under the direction of the Druids, were in the habit of practising certain gyrations and dances in the expectation of driving away evil spirits and diseases, and had from time immemorial cultivated the warlike accomplishments of shooting the bow, swinging the sling, and throwing the spear. Even before their discovery by the Romans, all classes of men were obliged to perfect themselves, in times of peace, in all the then known means of warfare, and so great were their skill and bravery, that they extorted admiration and respect even from imperial Cæsar!

Athletic exercises of a warlike character were also practised by the Hebrews, Persians, Egyptians and Assyrians. In fact, so generally was this the case among the ancients, that Galen declared that "all men were born with a propensity for music and gymnastics."

This was true, not only of the nations of antiquity, but is equally true of the negro tribes of Africa and the Indians of North America, who, we are told by travellers, are in the habit of manipulating and castigating, or flagellating the sick for the cure of nervous diseases.

It was not, however, until the golden age of Greece that athletic sports and games became a subject of national culture. The first historic mention we have of them is given in Homer's immortal story of the Trojan War. When the contending armies were about joining in battle on the ensanguined plains of Ilium—

> "The beauteous Paris came
> In form a god! The panther's speckled hide
> Flowed o'er his armor, with an easy pride;
> His bended bow across his shoulders flung,
> His sword beside him negligently hung;
> Two pointed spears he shook with gallant grace,
> And dared the bravest of the Grecian race."

So, after the obsequies of Patroclus, Achilles instituted the funeral games, in which the Grecian youths joined in chariot races, wrestling, and hurling the javelin.

Pamelius says: "The Grecian youths displayed in war the skill they had acquired in the gymnasium." This, however, could only be said of the Greeks posterior to the Homeric age, for in the earlier periods of her history her warlike sons depended on personal prowess and the experience they obtained in actual combat. Later in her history the Spartans systematized gymnastic exercises and erected gymnasia, and from here they soon spread all over Greece. In fact, in her palmy days, there was no city or considerable town which had not its gymnasium. These buildings were constructed at the public expense, and were celebrated for their magnificence. They were made of the purest Pentelic marble, adorned by the most ornate and stately architecture, decorated by the productions of the most gifted sculptors and painters, and graced with masses of flowers, flowing fountains, ornamented walks and sylvan retreats. In fine, they were so adorned and embellished as to be an embodiment of beauty—an attribute ever worshipped by the Greek, whether displayed in nature or art. As they were built at the public expense, so was the attendance of the youth upon their instruction compulsory. The Greek education commenced at the age of seven years, and consisted of music, grammar (which included poetry, rhetoric, and oratory), and gymnastic exercises, these last occupying more time and receiving more attention from the students than the study of music and grammar combined.

The gymnasium was under the general supervision of what was called the gymnasiarch, and the exercises were of a three-fold character, viz.: military, medical, and athletic, each department being under the personal care of teachers appointed for this work, assisted by numerous menials.

The medical department was under the direction of trained physicians, and was designed more particularly for the sick and infirm, though they also gave directions in regard to the care of the athletæ. As, however, the Greeks were eminently a military people, the exercises of the gymnasium partook largely of a military character. Hence the instituting of Olympic, Pythian, Nemean and Isthmian games.

During their continuance there was a general suspension of hostilities throughout Greece. In them patrician and plebeian alike joined in combat, only excepting the illegitimate and ignoble. Even the women were expected to take part in them, and in some of the States a woman could not be married until she had proved her prowess in a public exhibition of her skill! In fact, the Spartans taught that it was right and proper for female slaves to stay at home and ply the distaff, and perform menial labor; but Spartan mothers must be made of sterner stuff. Consequently, the girls received nearly the same attention as the boys.

The gymnasia were generally built just without the city, and those at Capua and Rascuna were particularly resorted to by the athletæ, as the air of those cities was considered more salubrious and stimulating. The exercises of the gymnasium were almost wholly performed in the open air. We have said that the Greek education consisted of music and grammar, combined with physical exercises. Indeed, their motto was: "Mens sana corpore sano."—"A sound mind in a sound body." Within the spacious amphitheatres of the gymnasiums the solemn funeral rites of the dead were performed; here philosophers and sages met to discuss important questions, and to instruct their pupils; here poets came to recite their epics, and here the divine arts of music and oratory were cultivated and exhibited as they never have been since in the history of the human race; here came gaily decked matrons and beauteous maidens to behold the athletæ, and cheer the victors with their presence and glad acclaims!

Among the principal institutions of this kind were the Lyceum, where Aristotle taught his scholars while walking, hence the Peripatetics; the Academia, made illustrious by the philosophy of Plato, and the Cynosorges, or School of the Cynics.

The object of the Greek education was threefold, viz.: to develop personal beauty and strength, to foster a love of knowledge as known in their day, and above all, to cultivate in the youth a love and respect for their country, and a worship of honor and renown.

Though the victors in the sacred games were only crowned with olive or laurel, still, to celebrate their fame, the most gifted poets invoked the Muses, and the most august personages vied with each other to do them reverence. They were received in the forum by the highest magnates, and allowed to sit in the senate chamber beside the grave senators. They were also exempt from taxation, and their names given to the year. No wonder that a people educated in such a school should have exhibited those qualities of courage and personal daring which have ever made this nation so famous in the history of the world! No wonder the Persian officer exclaimed to his commander: "Heavens! against what men are you leading us? Insensible to interest, they combat only for glory!"

Among the ancients the Greeks stood unrivalled in deeds of arms, and among the moderns no poetry equals in sweetness and pathos that once sung by the "Hellenic Bard," while the ravishing beauty of their Venus, and the fine proportions of their Hercules are still unequalled specimens of high art.

Thus it would seem that it holds true with nations as with individuals, that the highest mental achievements are attainable only by those nations or individuals who have the most perfect physical development.

When the cohorts of Greece had succumbed to the legions of Rome, the gymnasium was transplanted into Italy, and as the latter were a gayer and a more luxurious people than the former, their public institutions were made to conform to their national character.

With the Greeks the bath was only an accessory to the gymnasium, while with the Roman it was made to contribute to his enjoyment and pleasure; and so the gymnasium became the Therma. These were erected in every principal city of the empire, both at home and abroad. They were on a grander scale and more magnificent than even the gymnasium.

If the marble were no purer, nor the architecture more noble, still they were of larger proportions and more lavishly adorned. Within the great hall were the statues of Hercules, Hygeia, and Esculapius, the gods to whom they were dedicated. Adorning the frescoed walls were the productions of their most celebrated painters, and the floors were tessellated with the most beautiful and costly mosaics, while gems of art, trophies of conquest, and curious relics, met the gaze at every turn.

Here the gay Romans congregated to witness the gladiatorial shows, to enjoy the baths, to listen to their orators, poets, and musicians, and to refresh themselves in the public restaurants.

The luxurious Roman wooed the Graces rather than the Muses, and cultivated those arts which ministered to a sensuous though elegant taste, more than to great intellectual endowments.

The national characteristics of the two nations just cited, evidenced the influence and results of two distinct systems of education.

The Greeks worshipped beauty, and were, according to all accounts, physically the most perfect race that has ever lived; while the Roman education tended to foster a love of martial renown, and a stoical indifference to privation and pain. The gymnasium was the home of poets and philosophers. The Therma the school of gladiators and warriors. Such was the influence of physical culture on these two great nations of antiquity. With the disappearance of these two nations, the gymnasia and Therma also disappeared as physical educators, at least so far as nations were concerned, but after the lapse of centuries, when the chivalric age had succeeded the classic, there were developed other physical causes as potent to form national character as those already enumerated.

In this age, the love of physical beauty had given place to the worship of the spiritual Madonna, and the joust and tournament took the place of the classic games.

The holy wars and knightly entertainments developed an amount of strength and endurance hardly to be believed in our effeminate age. The coat of mail, the helmet and battle-axe of an ancient Templar would bear a modern gymnast to the earth. These causes were not only powerful means of physical culture, but they also educated the people, and taught them the power of associated thought and effort.

They filled the mind with a love of romance and adventure, which in after years culminated in such glorious results, in the discovery and peopling a new world.

This brings us to what may properly be called the scientific period of the gymnasium, a period in the world's history when the general diffusion of books through the discovery of the printing press, made the possession of knowledge the heritage of the people. A period when the discovery of the means of modern warfare no longer required the display of so great physical powers, in order to perpetuate national supremacy, but on the contrary when a nation's glory depended more on its advancement in the arts and sciences, and the general diffusion of knowledge—an epoch in the world's history when *brain* took the place of *muscle!* In fact the tendency now was, to ignore the wants of the body, in the eager race for knowledge, and there was eminent danger of filling the civilized world with a race of dyspeptics. Fortunately human anatomy and physiology had kept pace with other departments of science, and through the instrumentality of the medical faculty, ever conservators of public health, and the influence of public educators, the wants of the physical man were not neglected.

Conspicuous among the names of those who did much to renew interest in this subject, was Peter Henry Ling, born at Smaland, Sweden, November 15, 1766. Ling seems to have been an adventurer in his younger days, serving in the Swedish navy, and subsequently travelling quite extensively over Germany, France, and England, becoming familiar with those languages. He also made himself acquainted with the literature of the gymnasium as practised by the ancients, and studied anatomy and physiology, so far as they related to the movements of the human body. He at once saw that the great defect in the ancient system was, that it simply gave strength to the already strong, and that without regard to physiological law. He, therefore, conceived the idea of exercising the sick or infirm with passive motion, or motion produced by a second person, and invented a large number of appliances for this purpose. This was a great advance, and though at first he met with many rebuffs, still he succeeded by this enthusiasm and perseverance in pursuading the Swedish government to adopt his plan in the State Military Schools, and in 1814 the Central Academy of Gymnastics was instituted at Stockholm.

The results of this system were so satisfactory that they were also adopted in a modified form by the governments of Prussia and Germany, France and England, and national military schools for gymnastic exercises were established by those respective governments, at Berlin in 1847, at Vincennes in 1852, and at Aldhurst in 1861. Besides these government institutions, there are in Europe alone more than thirty so-called "movement cures," where Ling's system is practised. He taught that every change of attitude of the body altered the relative position of the internal organs, and consequently influenced more or less their functions; that every movement of the body was the expression of an *idea* of the mind, and that everything which developed the body or any part thereof, necessarily developed the brain, and per contra. In fine, he tried as far as was possible, with the light he had, to regulate gymnastic exercises according to scientific principles, and gave many valuable rules for the proper care of the sick.

While Ling was at work in Sweden, other influences were operating in other countries calculated to develop physical strength.

In England, especially, renewed interest had been excited in what were called the "manly sports," viz., boxing, wrestling, cricket, and boat races, and these were not only encouraged and patronized by the lower classes of society, but by the faculties of the great universities, and by the nobility, and so general has the belief in the truth of the Greek axiom become among educators, both in this country and in Europe, that the students in the universities and colleges are encouraged to join in all manly sports, and the results of these contests are heralded all over the land, and excite an interest second only to that produced by the victors of the ancient games. I think we may say without exaggeration, that the results of recent contests have excited more comment, and the names of the champions are more familiar to the popular ears than are the names or deeds of the greatest generals or philosophers of the age!

I do not consider this a matter of regret, for it demonstrates the fact that the public, at least, have recognized the validity of the statement, that great mental attainments, as a rule, go hand in hand with a good physical development. This truth has been abundantly proved in the past history of nations as well as of individuals.

In the early history of the Greeks, they educated their sons almost exclusively for military purposes, but in the later periods of Grecian dominion their arms were effeminated by luxury and vice. The same may be said of the Romans. While Rome's glory was in the ascendant, her sons willingly submitted to all sorts of privations and hardships, but when her irresistible legions had no further kingdoms to conquer, they listlessly beheld the gladiatorial shows and their own decadence.

Carthage and Spain are no exceptions to this rule, and the late war between France and Germany demonstrated the difference between a nation full of mental vigor and physical strength, and one puffed up with egotism, and the foundations of whose national life had been sapped by immorality and vice; and England to-day, is an example of a nation in a transition stage between past greatness and future effeminacy and decay.

We are too young a nation to draw a conclusion from; and yet, even here we see the effects of physical causes upon our national character. So long as our vast prairies need cultivating, and our trackless forests need clearing—so long as our mines want working, and our vast commercial interests demand developing, there is no fear of our national decadence; but the time will come in the future, when we, too, as a nation, shall feel the stagnation in our national life caused by wealth and vice.

Dr. Beddoe declares in his paper on the stature and bulk of man in the British Isles, "That those nations have shown the most intellectual strength who have exhibited the most physical stamina;" and he further says: "Those nations which have attained the highest physical development have also been the most exalted morally." This is equally true of individuals. Dr. Morgan, than whom no man has had better opportunities for observation, says: "It is a curious fact that the victors of the Oxford and Cambridge boat races also bore off the highest academic honors, and these same men succeeded best in after life." This is also the almost universal testimony of those qualified to speak in this country.

The importance of this remark will be better appreciated when we remember that physical qualities are much more likely to be transmitted to posterity than mental or intellectual ones; hence it is that those most conspicuous in commercial, civil or military life, are men more indebted to their progenitors for a sound and robust constitution than for illustrious pedigree. Knowledge we must acquire, but a sound or feeble physical constitution we inherit from our parents.

THE MIASM OF THE PONTINE MARSHES.—Mr. Balestra, in a series of investigations upon the nature and origin of the miasma of the Pontine marshes, found the stagnant waters filled with organisms of various species, and among them one in particular, which was abundant in proportion to the degree of putrefaction in the water. This is a small alga, which floats on the surface of the water, and presents the appearance of drops of oil. At a low temperature these germinate very slowly; but during the warm weather, and when exposed to the air, they reproduce very rapidly. The author, finding that the addition of a small quantity of arsenious acid, or sulphate of soda, or, still better, of the neutral sulphate of quinine, destroyed the vitality of this plant, infers that the miasma of the marshes is due to its existence and propagation; and that the well-known agency of these medicaments in curing fever depends upon their chemical action upon the plant which causes it, especially as its spores are found to be disseminated everywhere through the atmosphere. The plant is not developed in a dry season, although it makes its appearance in great quantity during moderately rainy weather, occurring in a warm season. The non-occurrence of the fever in the winter, according to the author, is due less to the cold, which prevents the vegetation of the plant, or retards the decomposition of organic substances, than to the abundance of the rain which covers the places where these spores exist, their dissemination into the atmosphere being thereby prevented, and only facilitated by the drying up of the soil, which allows the spores to float readily.—*Nature.*

SANITARY POETRY.—Health Officer Dr. Germer recently received an unsigned postal-card containing the following doggerel. As it is anonymous, we omit the name of the place complained of:

Dear doctor, pray come take a smell,
On —— street, rear of —— hotel;
The kitchen yard, where odors foul,
Would dim the optics of an owl,
Perched nightly high upon his roost,
In wisdom wrapped, serene, forsooth;
His plaintive hoot and dismal cry,
Would note the essence of the stye;
And call for Germer. Vere vas he?
De bresedent ov de Sanitaree. —*Erie Dispatch.*

Editor's Table.

THE PUBLIC HEALTH.

New York, Dec. 10th, 1874.—The total number of deaths in the four weeks ending Nov. 28, in the city of New York, was 2,130. Zymotic diseases were charged with 672 deaths; constitutional, 438; local, 802; developmental, 132; violent causes, 86.

The death rate for the four weeks was equivalent to 26.62 in the 1,000 inhabitants, annually. The infant mortality was at its minimum for the year—451 deaths, or 21.17 per cent. of the total mortality, were of infants under a year old; 901, or 42.30 per cent. of the total, were of children under 5 pears of age. Old age evinced its feebleness and its readiness to loose the silver cord of life, as the wintry cold began. There died from various causes 145 persons who were 70 years of age and upwards, in the month. The sudden deaths in this class of decedents were chiefly from apoplexy, diseases of the heart, or the lungs. Diarrhœal diseases are charged with 100 deaths in the month; bronchitis and pneumonia caused 289 deaths; enteric fever, 37; diphtheria, 236, and small-pox, 73 deaths. The course of diphtheria continues to be marked by a decided preference for those districts of the city in which the ground is most defectively drained and the surface most unclean; yet this disease is widely distributed and has been marked by numerous instances of special malignancy in particular families and dwellings. Its persistence as an epidemic in the Twentieth and Nineteenth wards, and its passover of the region between Fulton and Grand streets, are among the instructive facts in its prevalence.

The practical value of sanitary cleansing and ventilation of dwellings, school-rooms and all places of public assembling, needs to be tested to the utmost in New York, and other cities and towns where diphtheria is prevailing. The family physician can now do good service in giving timely suggestions and aid to prevent needless causes which contribute to the prevalence and persistence of this malady. Though it is decreasing in this city, it is increasing in many other places westward and southward. The same is true of small-pox, which has awakened fresh attention to the duty of vaccination. The almost instant control and extinction of small-pox at the State Asylum for deaf mutes in this city, has proved anew that the true defence against this enemy of asylums and children everywhere must be sought at the *point of the lancet* with ample charges of *fresh vaccinia.*

The annexed memorandum shows what advice and action have been recommended by the Sanitary Committee of the Board of Health in this city to aid physicians and families in securing the observance of precautionary hygienic measures against acknowledged causes of diphtheria. The distribution of several thousand copies of this memorandum has been directed by the Board of Health.

ELISHA HARRIS, *Registrar of Vital Statistics.*

Extract of Memorandum on Diphtheria, issued by the Board of Health of New York.

PREDISPOSING CONDITIONS—The person.—Diphtheria attacks by preference children between the ages of one and ten years, the greatest mortality being in the second, third, and fourth years; children of feeble constitution, and those weakened by previous sickness, and those suffering from catarrh, croup, and other forms of throat affections.

Social relations.—All classes are liable to diphtheria where it is prevailing, but those suffer most severely who live in low, wet grounds; in houses with imperfect drains, or surrounded by offensive matters, as privies, decaying animal and vegetable refuse; in damp rooms, as cellars; in overcrowded and unventilated apartments.

Seasons.—Diphtheria is not affected by either heat or cold, drought or rain.

PRECAUTIONS—(*a*) The dwelling or apartment.—Cleanliness in and around the dwelling and pure air in living and sleeping rooms are of the utmost importance wherever any contagious disease is prevailing, as cleanliness tends both to prevent and mitigate it. Every kind and source of filth around and in the house should be thoroughly removed; cellars and foul areas should be cleaned and disinfected; drains should be put in perfect repair; dirty walls and ceilings should be lime-washed, and every occupied room should be thoroughly ventilated. Apartments which have been occupied by persons sick with diphtheria should be cleansed with disinfectants—ceilings lime-washed and wood-work painted, the carpets, bedclothes, upholstered furniture, etc., exposed many days to fresh air and the sunlight (all articles which may be boiled or subjected to high degrees of heat should be thus disinfected); such rooms should be exposed to currents of fresh air for at least one week before re-occupation.

(*b*) Well children.—When diphtheria is prevailing no child should be allowed to kiss strange children, nor those suffering from sore throat (the disgusting custom of compelling children to kiss every visitor is a well contrived method of propagating other graver diseases than diphtheria); nor should it sleep with or be confined to rooms occupied by, or use articles, as toys, taken in the mouth; handkerchiefs, etc., belonging to children having sore throat, croup, or catarrh. If the weather is cold, the child should be warmly clad with flannels.

(*c*) When diphtheria is in the house or in the family the well children should be scrupulously kept apart from the sick in dry, well-aired rooms, and every possible source of infection through the air, by personal contact with the sick, and by articles used about them or in their rooms, should be rigidly guarded. Every attack of sore throat, croup and catarrh should be at once attended to. The feeble should have invigorating food and treatment.

(*d*) Sick children.—The sick should be rigidly isolated in well-aired (the air being entirely changed at least hourly), unlighted rooms, the outflow of air being as far as possible through the external windows by depressing the upper and elevating the lower sash, or a chimney heated by a fire in an open fire-place: all discharges from the mouth and nose should be received into vessels containing disinfectants, as solutions of carbolic acid or sulphate of zinc, or upon cloths which are immediately burned or, if not burned, thoroughly boiled or placed under a disinfecting fluid.

Brooklyn.—Population, 450,000. Deaths during the month of November, 846; annual ratio per 1,000, 22.44. 243 deaths were of the zymotic class, or 28.86 per cent. on total death rate for the month. Small-pox, 6; diphtheria, 90; croup, 48; typhoid fever, 14; consumption, 105; pneumonia, 66; bronchitis, 28.

Philadelphia, 775,000. Four weeks ending Dec. 5th, 1,095; annual ratio per 1,000, 18.35. Consumption, 178; typhoid fever, 35; diphtheria, 32; scarlet fever, 51.

Chicago, 400,000.—Four weeks ending Nov. 21st, 402; annual ratio per 1,000, 10.5. Consumption, 45; typhoid fever, 25; diphtheria, 10.

St. Louis, 366,000. Four weeks ending Nov. 28th, 506; annual ratio per 1,000, 17.97. Consumption, 40; diphtheria, 7; typhoid fever, 14; small-pox, 94; scarlet fever, 21.

Baltimore, 284,000. Four weeks ending Nov. 30th, 558; annual ratio per 1,000, 25.54. Consumption, 68; diphtheria, 17; typhoid fever, 20; scarlet fever, 38.

Boston, 275,000. Four weeks ending Nov. 21st, 547; annual ratio per 1,000, 25.85. Consumption, 94; typhoid fever, 16; diphtheria, 9; scarlet fever, 15.

Cincinnati, 260,000. Four weeks ending Nov. 28th, 398; annual ratio per 1,000, 19.09. Consumption, 48; typhoid fever, 21; diphtheria, 6; scarlet fever, 32.

New Orleans, 199,000. Four weeks ending Nov. 29th, 527; annual ratio per 1,000, 34.42. Consumption, 66; typhoid fever, 7; malarial fever, 13; yellow fever, 2; diphtheria, 14; small-pox, 10.

San Francisco.—For fiscal year ending June 30, 1874, Mr. Langley, in the recently-issued City Directory, computes the population of San Francisco to be 200,770, which will give a mortality rate equal to about 2 per cent. of the population—a slight increase over the previous year. If, however, we exclude the Chinese (estimated at 14,500) in this calculation, we have results which may be better appreciated in tabular form, as follows—the facts as to population being derived from the Directory and the late School Census:

	POPULATION.	DEATHS.	RATE PER 1000
Chinese over 17 years of age	13,214	435	32.9
All others over 17 years of age	127,004	1,943	15.3
Chinese under 17 years of age	1,286	30	23.3
All others under 17 years of age	59,266	1,625	27.4
All others under 5 years of age	21,171	1,310	61.9
All others over 5 years of age	165,099	2,238	13.5
Total Chinese	14,500	465	32.1
All others	186,270	3,548	19.6
Total	200,770	4,013	20.3

A notable feature of the year has been a very large increase of zymotic diseases, mainly from scarlatina, which occasioned more than one-third of the mortality of its class. The proportion of deaths from zymotic diseases, including the Chinese, has been 23 per cent.; excluding the Chinese, 25½ per cent. Small-pox, 48; scarlatina, 387; measles, 6; diphtheria, 38; croup, 28; whooping-cough, 32; typhus fever, 6; typhoid fever, 80; consumption, 566. The Health Officer claims for San Francisco an unusual exemption from pulmonary diseases, as compared with other cities, and makes this comparison:

NUMBER OF DEATHS TO EACH 10,000 INHABITANTS.	San Francisco, 1873.	New York, 1872.	Philadelphia, 1873.	Brooklyn, 1873.	Chicago, 1873.	Boston, 1872.	Cincinnati, 1873.	New Orleans, 1873.	Buffalo, 1873.	Providence, 1873.	Liverpool, 1872.	Birmingham, 1873.
From Consumption	25	43	31	31	16	43	26	42	11½	30	32	23½
Pneumonia, Bronchitis and other lung diseases	14	31	18	26	18	28	12	26	10	18	45	43
Total	39	77	49	57	34	71	38	68	21½	48	77	66½
Per cent. of total to all Deaths	22.2	23.5	23.6	22.0	11.4	21.9	15.3	19.1	17.2	22.1	28.4	26.2

But it should be borne in mind that all of these cities have their worst class, which especially swells the ratio, and if the "Chinese" were excluded from the computation in each of the others given, San Francisco would not, probably, exhibit less than an average number.

For the small infantile mortality San Francisco is especially remarkable, being the same as Providence, and only second to New Orleans, which has the smallest ratio to total mortality (exclusive of Chinese)—37 per cent.

Since the last Annual Report over four miles of sewers have been constructed, there being now a total of 66 miles in the city, and at least as much more required—foul water in the streets being among the chief nuisances. The Report is altogether notable for its conciseness and clearness.

Washington, 150,000. For month of November, 266; annual ratio per 1,000, whites (110,000), 14.74; colored (40,000), 39.3. 24.5 per cent. of the entire mortality was from zymotic diseases. Consumption, 40; pneumonia, 17.

Buffalo, 130,000. For month of November, 233; annual ratio per 1,000, 21.50. Consumption, 25; scarlet fever, 65; typhoid fever, 8; diphtheria, 3; croup, 10.

Louisville, 112,000. Two weeks ending Nov. 21st, 99; annual ratio per 1,000, 22.98.

Milwaukee, 100,000. For month of November, 139; annual ratio per 1,000, 16.68. Typhus fever, 15; consumption, 8; diphtheria, 7.

Providence, 100,000. Month of November, 151; annual ratio per 1,000, 18.12. Consumption, 21—5 American, 16 foreign parentage; typhoid fever, 7; scarlatina, 16; pneumonia, 12.

Richmond, 65,000. Month of November, 100; whites, 53; colored, 47; annual ratio per 1,000, 18.46. Consumption, 17; typhoid fever, 3; diphtheria, 2.

New Haven, 55,000. Month of November, 63; annual ratio per 1,000, 13.74. Consumption, 21; typhoid fever, 5; pneumonia, 5.

Wheeling, 37,000. Month of November, 37; annual ratio per 1,000, 16.44. Scarlet fever, 8; consumption, 3; typhoid fever, 1; diphtheria, 1.

Toledo, 37,000. Month of November, 39; annual ratio per 1,000, 12.64; typhoid fever, 3; typhus, 1; diphtheria, 3.

Dayton, 34,000. Month of November, 34; annual ratio per 1,000, 12.

Elmira, 21,000. Month of November, 29; annual ratio per 1,000 16.57. Diphtheria, 2.

Massachusetts.—Deaths in sixteen cities and towns for the week ending Nov. 14th: Boston, 143; Worcester, 17; Lowell, 23; Milford, 1; Chelsea, 4; Cambridge, 24; Salem, 6; Lawrence, 11; Springfield, 7;

Lynn, 2; Gloucester, 3; Taunton, 6; Newburyport, 5; Somerville, 10; Fall River, 19; Holyoke, 6. Total, 287.

Prevalent Diseases: Consumption, 52; pneumonia, 32; scarlet fever, 18; typhoid fever, 13; croup, 10; diphtheria, 5.

CHAS. F. FOLSOM, M.D., *Sec. of the State Board of Health.*

ABATTOIRS.—Philadelphia is rightly much exercised on account of the projected *Schuylkill Drove-yard and Abattoir* by the Pennsylvania Railroad Company. The place fixed upon for the proposed structure, is on the western shore of the bend in the Schuylhill, a short distance below the Fairmount Dam, where the depth of water in the river averages only about ten feet, and where on account of its proximity to the dam there is very little current, as the amount of water discharged over the dam is small. The thickly populated portion of the city begins on the eastern and opposite bank of the river, which is at this point, only about 400 feet wide. The western bank of the river, especially, is shelving, and for a considerable length marshy. In the event of pollution, therefore, a large portion of the city would be sure to suffer.

The following expression by the American Public Health Association, at its recent meeting, on the subject of Abattoirs in general, is eminently worthy of attention. The subject was introduced by Professor Henry Hartshorne, as follows:

Resolved, That for a city, properly arranged and conducted abattoirs, subject to municipal regulations, are preferable to a number of private slaughter-houses located in different parts of a city.

That the best practicable management of large abattoirs with cattle and hog yards cannot be depended upon at all times to prevent their drainage from contaminating water and the atmosphere in their vicinity.

Therefore such establishments should be located as far as practicable from the centres of population, and, if possible, upon tide-water.

After presenting these resolutions, Dr. Hartshorne propounded several questions to Dr. Rauch, of Chicago, who, as Health Officer of that city, has made himself familiar with the subject. These, with his replies, are as follows:—

First. Can the disposal and utilization of refuse be made invariably perfect (as a matter of experience) as regards water and air?

A. No. Occasionally atmospheric conditions obtain, especially at night, when it is impossible to conduct, as far as my experience goes, the disposal and utilization of refuse without offence. This is sometimes observed near the establishment, and sometimes remote. Generally speaking, however, under favorable atmospheric conditions, these processes can be carried on without being offensive or injurious to health, provided the scientific appliances for rendering, drying, and the disposition of the gases arising therefrom are strictly and carefully maintained, under vigilant police supervision.

Second. How far may the odor of such an establishment, including cattle-yard be detected with certainty?

A. The odor of establishments of this character can be detected at varying distances, dependent upon temperature, condition of atmosphere, and wind. Have recognized them in a marked degree at a distance of ten miles. The odor of the cattle yards, under like conditions of atmosphere, temperature, and wind, have been detected at a distance of one mile.

Third. From what is known, can the drainage of an abattoir be safely allowed to enter a fresh-water stream flowing through a town?

A. Not as a general rule. It depends upon the amount of the drainage into, the quantity of water in, and the rapidity of the current of the stream. Under all circumstances it is important that this drainage should enter streams below the limits of a town or city.

Fourth. What effect has been observed upon property values and settlement near an abattoir?

A. As a necessary consequence they will diminish the value of property for residences. People generally keep at respectful distances from such establishments.

After some further discussion, the resolutions were unanimously adopted.

ANALYTICAL DEPARTMENT.—In connection with notice given in last number, that THE SANITARIAN has effected arrangements for having analyses of all kinds of waters, articles of food, etc., etc., made with accuracy and dispatch, correspondents are informed in regard to samples:

Waters required for qualitative analysis, not less than one gallon; waters required for quantitative analysis, from five to 15 gallons.

Ores, minerals, &c., samples as large as practicable, distinctly labelled.

Food articles, in quantities depending upon their nature, one pound, or more.

Vessels containing samples should be perfectly clean.

Inquiries promptly answered by addressing the Editor of THE SANITARIAN.

BIBLIOGRAPHY.

Public Health. Edited by DR. ABBOTTS SMITH. London: Statham & Co., 32 Fetter Lane. New York: A. N. Bell, M.D., Editor of THE SANITARIAN, 234 Broadway.

In a recent number, *Public Health* recurs to the pleasing coincidence of the almost simultaneous appearance of that journal in London, and THE SANITARIAN in New York, a little less than two years ago. It has been with singular pleasure during the while that we have frequently drawn upon the bountiful pages of our able contemporary for the best experiences of English sanitary science.

Among the able papers in recent numbers of, and common to *Public Health*, are the following:

A Visit to a Kindergarten. By J. B. BUDJETT, M.D. *The Manufacture of Gas; The Liernur Sewerage System in Holland,* by DR. L. G. EDGELING; *Enteric Fever arising from Water Contamination,* by E. R. MORGAN, M.R.C.S.; *The Influence of Social and Sanitary Conditions on Religion,* by HENRY W. ACLAND, F.R.S.; *Wooden Hospitals: Their Advantages from a Sanitary Point of View,* by JOHN DAY, M.D.

These papers are eminently worthy of the most extensive reading, and are well placed in this justly popular and widely circulated journal.

The Sanitary Record. A Journal of Public Health. Every Saturday, London: Smith, Elder & Co.

We begin in this number of THE SANITARIAN the republication of a series of papers "On the Hand-Feeding of Infants," by EUSTACE SMITH, M.D., from *The Sanitary Record.* This is a *Weekly* sanitary *newspaper*, giving the current news and reports of the proceedings of sanitary officers, and occasional leaders on important questions in State medicine and public hygiene as they arise; and numbers among its contributors some of the foremost men in sanitary science.

Medical Use of Alcohol, and Stimulants for Women. By JAMES EDMUNDS, M.D. 8vo., pp. 96. New York: National Temperance Society and Publication House.

A common sense expression of sound conclusions, by a thoroughly competent observer and medical practitioner of large experience. A book which should be read by everybody who would be informed on the real nature of alcohol, and who would be fortified against the sophisms of apologists for its use.

The Breath, and the diseases which give it a fe tid odor. By JOSEPH W. HOWE, M.D. 8vo., pp. 108. New York: D. Appleton & Co.

A concise epitome of large practical experience in the treatment of the diseases of the air passages, on a subject which has not hitherto received the attention it deserves. The subject is treated from a thoroughly scientific standpoint, taking account of its causes, and symptomatic relations; and the application of appropriate treatment.

The Drift of Medical Philosophy. By D. A. Gorton, M. D. An Essay; pp. 70. Philadelphia: Lippincott & Co., 1875.

A good representation but far from being a vindication of that kind of philosophy which would make man an irresponsible being—a criminal on account of his peculiar organization or hereditary vices—and murder, theft, and arson, symptoms of disease. The author confesses himself to be a specificist in the treatment of disease, in accordance with "a true law of therapeutics—*similia similibus curantur,*" but he has failed to show any treatment of such diseases superior to that which time-honored custom sanctions as being best for the well being of every community, however disagreeable it may be for the patient.

The Illustrated Annual Register of Rural Affairs for 1875. Albany: Luther Tucker & Son.

An excellent manual for gardeners, fruit growers, and farmers; containing designs for fences, trellises, hothouses, stables, etc., of much practical utility.

Microscopical Examinations of certain Waters submitted to Jabez Hogg; and a *Chemical Analysis,* by Dugald Campbell. With Introductory Notes by Samuel Collett Homersham, London.

A pamphlet of twenty-seven pages, clearly comprehending a subject of great magnitude; the respective characters of surface and subterranean waters, illustrating the important difference in the wholesomeness of impounded water, obtained from lakes, rivers and streams, and deep spring or subterranean water. "It cannot be too widely known that uncontaminated deep spring or subterranean water . . . is found free from all living vegetable or animal productions, and from all putrescible organic matter." . . Of "uniform normal temperature, being at the source of the average of the climate for the year, which in this country differs but little, being about 50°. At all times clear, colorless, bright, well aerated, holding in solution seven to eight cubic inches of air per gallon, and it is wholesome, pleasant and fresh to the taste.

"On the other hand, river, stream, flood, and surface waters impounded in lakes and ponds, have a normal temperature near the freezing point in winter, and often as high as 70° in summer. These waters, even after careful filtration, are frequently and unavoidably delivered to consumers discolored and repulsive to the sight when seen in large bulk, . . although in this respect they may pass muster when seen in small quantity, as in a tumbler. Even careful filtration through the best filters does not separate or free the waters from decaying organic matter held in solution, from urine, from minute living animal organisms that feed and grow on impure contents of waters, and which so rapidly increase and multiply therein, more especially when the water is comparatively warm, as in summer and autumn, seasons of the year when it is most abundantly drunk."

The subject is an exceedingly important one, and in England especially it seems to be attracting deserved attention; many large provincial towns having within the last few years abandoned the use of river and other surface waters for domestic use, and taken their supply from subterranean sources.

Winter Homes for Invalids. By JOSEPH P. HOWE, M.D. 12mo., pp. 205. New York: G. P. Putnam's Sons, 1875.

This is an interesting volume to invalids in search of winter resorts. It treats of California, Florida, Colorado, Georgia, the Carolinas, Kentucky, the West Indies, the Bermudas, the Sandwich Islands, the Mediterranean, Florence and Rome, the Italian Lakes and "Cold Climates, for Consumptives." The differences in these places suitable to the various conditions and experiences of invalids, are all briefly but clearly stated, and altogether the work is one of much practical utility.

The Exhibition Drama. Comprising Drama, Comedy, and Farce, together with Dramatic and Musical entertainments, for private theatricals, Home Representations, Holiday and School Exhibitions. By GEORGE M. BAKER. 12mo., pp. 248. Boston: Lee & Shepard; New York: Lee, Shepard & Dillingham, 1875.

This is a delightfully entertaining book for young people, of "The Amateur Drama Series." It comprises eight exhibitions, the last one, A Christmas Carol, arranged as an entertainment from Dickens' Christmas story.

The tableaux are well illustrated, easily represented and well adapted to the varying wants of occasional exhibitions for the school, parlor or Sunday-school.

Ivanhoe. By Sir Walter Scott. Philadelphia: Peterson & Brothers. Peterson's cheap edition for the million, of the Waverley Novels.

Ivanhoe, by Sir Walter Scott, the first volume of an entire new edition of the Waverley Novels, now in course of publication. Each book will be printed from plain, clear type, double column, and each work will be issued complete in one large octavo volume, with a *new illustrated cover on each book*, and be complete in twenty-six volumes, at twenty-five cents each, or five dollars for the complete set, and single volumes or complete sets will be sent post-paid everywhere on receipt of price by the publishers. This will be the cheapest as well as the only complete edition of the Waverley Novels published in this country, as it will contain all the author's notes, as well as all his last corrections and additions. The volume now ready, "Ivanhoe," contains a portrait of Sir Walter Scott, engraved on steel from Newton's original picture, painted at Abbotsford, being the last portrait Scott sat for, which of itself is worth the price of the volume.

The Smuggler's Ghost. By Mrs. Henry Wood. Philadelphia: T. B. Peterson & Bros.

The Smuggler's Ghost," is a new book from the pen of Mrs. Henry Wood, the author of "East Lynne," and it will form a delightful addition to the reading of any lover of a fascinating, powerfully written romance. Mrs. Wood, though a prolific writter, is ever fresh and pleasing. There is an endless variety which is as surprising as it is agreeable to her readers. Her earlier books have taken the public by storm, and we predict for "The Smuggler's Ghost" a great popularity and a large sale. Large octavo volume, paper cover, price twenty-five cents, and is for sale by all booksellers, or copies will be sent per mail, post-paid, to any one, on their remitting the price to the publishers.

The Runaway Match. By Mrs. Henry Wood.

"The Runaway Match" is from the fertile pen of Mrs. Henry Wood, and it will undoubtedly command a large share of attention from the novel-reading commuuity. "The Runaway Match" sustains the previous efforts of this accomplished writer, and will prove an acceptable addition to her already extensive literary labors. It is issued in one octavo volume, paper cover, price twenty-five cents, and is for sale by all booksellers, or copies will be sent to any one, post-paid, on remitting price to the publishers.

Transactions of the Michigan State Medical Society; Series II., vol. vi., pp. 83, 1874.

The annual address by Dr. Edward W. Jenks, President, admirably sets forth the true dignity of the profession, and the benefit of society organizations for the common good. "The times in which we live, the increasing facilities for obtaining knowledge, the rapid progress being made in every department of life that calls into action the human intellect, seems to permit of no useful place in the world for 'stationary men.' To stand up for the profession, to maintain its dignity and honor, implies working in it and for it."

A resolution was adopted and a committee appointed with a view to such legislation as will effectually protect the profession from the pretensions of quackery by *registration* and *examination;* the examination to be confined to such subjects, purely medical, as all medical sects are agreed upon.

The papers read before the society were cases of Malignant Tumors of the Jaws, by T. A. McGraw, M.D.; Observations on Opthalmology, by Eugene Smith, M.D.; Tumor of Cerebellum, by J. M. Snook, M.D.; Report on University Medical Department, by Drs. Pratt, Brownell, Barnum, and Hitchcock; Improved Method of abstracting Cataract, by Geo. E. Frothingham, M.D.; Memorial of Dr. Zena Pitcher, by Drs. Stuart and Brodie; Report on Ventilation of Dwellings of the Poor, by R. C. Kedzie, M. D.; and Cephalic Tumor, by J. C. Wilson, M.D. While these papers and reports are all characterized by the care and research common to this society, Dr. Kedzie's paper on the Ventilation of Dwellings of the Poor, is worthy of special attention on account of its extensive practical utility for the preservation of health at little cost. The adaptation of a foul air flue to a stove a little different from the plan of Dr. Kedzie, we have ourselves frequently directed the application of, and witnessed the good results. Our plan has been, to simply have a "jacket" put on the stove pipe; an additional pipe a few inches larger than the smoke pipe proceeding from and nearly up to the stove, with a perforated collar round the smoke pipe of corresponding size with the outer pipe to hold the end in position. This outer pipe to follow the smoke pipe its whole length, short or long, into the chimney flue, and at its entry of the flue held off from the smoke pipe, as at the end near the stove, by another perforated collar, so as to admit of the current passing through it (outside of the smoke pipe all round) into the chimney. At the upper end—assuming that the pipe ascends and perforates the chimney near the top of the room, have slots cut in the outer pipe for the lighter foul air near the ceiling to enter, also;—the two virtually constitute the foul air flue, run up with chimneys in some first-class houses, with registers at both the top and bottom of the room.

Dr. Kedzie improves upon this by having the "*jacket*" divided by a vertical diaphragm, passing from opposite sides of the smoke pipe till it intersects with the outer pipe, and thus making two shafts, one to carry off the foul air, and the other being kept closed and separate from communication with the foul air shaft, to pass down behind or under the stove, and thence through the walls of the building to the external air, so that pure fresh air may freely enter it. Let this also have openings in it at the end near the place of entering the chimney. It is plain that the fresh air will be drawn into and warmed by the smoke pipe, and in this way fresh air not only, but fresh air, *warmed*, will be constantly drawn in to supply the place of the foul air as constantly expelled.

Medico-Legal Papers. Papers read before the Medico-Legal Society, of New York, from its Organization. First Series. 552 pp., 8vo. New York: McDIVITT, CAMPBELL & Co. 1874.

Rarely have we had presented to our consideration a Society work of more practical utility than this volume. Besides a brief *Introduction*, giving an account of the Society, and an *Appendix*, giving the Constitution and By-Laws, it comprehends twenty-four papers on Medico-Legal questions—not by any means confined to the mere professional interest of the two professions which constitute the Society, but of extensive practical utility to the public. Papers on the management of the Insane; Inebriate Asylums; the Sale of Poisons; Considerations upon Alcoholism; The Moral and Criminal Responsibility of Inebriates; The Influence of Epilepsy upon Criminal Responsibility; Hereditary Influences, and others of like value, and almost without exception, papers of profound research and thorough study make up the volume.

The publishers deserve well, not only of the medical and legal professions, but of the public, for the good work they have done in bringing out this volume, and we are glad to learn that if their action meets with anything like the encouragement it deserves, a *Second Series* will speedily follow.

Annual Report of the Surgeon General, U. S. Army, 1874.

During the five years just ended the average losses of the army by deaths and discharges for disability have been 47 per 1,000 of strength for the white troops, and 52 per 1,000 for the colored. In both classes the mortality from wounds, accidents, and injuries has been as high as 5 per 1,000, or five times as great as the death-rate from such causes in the British Army serving in the United Kingdom. Such "wounds, accidents and injuries," refer chiefly to homicides, suicides, and accidental drowning, and of these the quinquennial average shows among the white troops 83 homicides, 63 suicides, and 100 drowning casualties per 100,000 of mean strength, and among the colored troops 254 homicides, 26 suicides, and 29 drownings per 100,000.

Of the comparative physical and moral stamina of white and colored troops—we learn that among the former during the past year the average number constantly on sick report was 46 per 1,000 of mean strength, the death rate being 13 per 1,000, while among the latter the sick ratio was 52 per 1,000 and the mortality 15 per 1,000.

An account is given of the vast and important work performed in connection with the Army Medical Museum, which now comprises one of the most valuable scientific collections in the world, and appropriations are solicited for the publication of a descriptive catalogue thereof, and of additional copies of the "Medical and Surgical History of the War."

"The act recognizing the staff corps of the army, approved June 23, 1874, while allowing appointments of assistant surgeons in the army, cuts off two of the five lieutenant-colonels and ten of the sixty majors, thus preventing any promotion for several years to come. This is much to be regretted, as it places the officers of the medical corps below those of all the other staff corps and of the line of the army as regards promotion, which is felt by them as a hardship and injustice, the results of which cannot fail to be injurious to the best interests of the service."

It is no wonder that in view of such a state of facts, the number of candidates for the medical staff of the army is so small that *fifty-six vacancies* now exist in the grade of assistant surgeon.

The medical corps of the army, in its relative sphere of duty, is not only unexcelled, but scarcely equalled by any other corps. And this glaring injustice of withholding rank and retarding promotion is no less calculated to discourage the ardor which has hitherto characterized it than to present, as really appears, an insurmountable obstacle to competent accessions.

To be *graded* below one's fellows in both rank and emoluments is a prospect little calculated to induce accomplished candidates, and the sooner this state of things is clearly appreciated and acted upon by the powers that be, the better for the best interests of the army and the country.

Transactions of Medical and Chirurgical Faculty of the State of Maryland. Pp. 199. 75th Annual Session. Baltimore, Maryland, 1874.

The Faculty is organized into six working sections—on Surgery; Practice and Obstetrics; Materia Medica; Pharmacy and Chemistry; Hygiene, Meteorology, etc., Anatomy, Physiology and Pathology, and Psychology and Medical Jurisprudence. The routine business of the Session is followed by an admirable address, the Annual Oration, on the Character of the Model Physician, by Hon. Lewis H. Steiner, M. D. Next follow the Reports of the Sections, all carefully divested of redundancy and to the point, and besides these, voluntary papers and communications—on the Pathology of Inebriety, by Joseph Parish, M. D; Hypodermic Injection of Ergot in Post Partem Hæmorrhage, by P. C. Williams, M. D.; Significance of Præsystolic Murmur, by Frank Donaldson, M. D.; Leukaemia, by Henry R. Noel, M. D; Case of Multiple Fracture, by McLane Tiffany, M. D.; Reform in Medical Education, by C. W. Chancellor, M. D.; Small-pox, by J. S. Conrad, M. D.; Connection between Excessive Nerve and Brain Worry and Bodily Disease, with Pathology and Treatment of Cancers, Tumors, etc., etc., by J. J. Caldwell, M. D.

Transactions of the New Hampshire Medical Society. 84th Anniversary. 128 pp. 1874.

By the Annual Address of the President, Dr. John L. Swett, the Society is shown to be one of general prosperity. There are no discords, and, as measured by the lively interest manifested in professional education, and in Dartmouth in particular, the members fully appreciate the advantage of their own best welfare when they do most to advance the general welfare of the community. Equally manifest is this disposition in the President's address in regard to intemperance:

"So long as the plea remained undisputed, that alcohol furnished elements for respiration and the evolution of animal heat, and that, by diminishing atomic changes in the tissues, it acted indirectly, at least, as food, an effectual argument was in possession of its advocates; and from these false premises many conclusions were drawn, which seemed to be in favor of its virtues, and obtained a strong hold upon the popular mind. Not alone was it claimed to be a supporter of respiration and a preventive of waste in the animal economy, but it was said to impart a strength to the body, and to increase the powers of the mind; that it was a protector against cold, and guarded the system when exposed to heat; that it was a promoter of digestion, and secured exemption from ordinary disease, and in times of pestilence was all but sovereign. So deeply are these impressions rooted in communities, and so much have they been fostered by the silence, if not dignified by the approval, of some of our own profession, that when an opinion is expressed adverse to the benefits of alcohol, it meets with but little credence, and is too often regarded as the utterance of the mere temperance man.

"But the time has arrived when the light of science shines brightly upon this part of the question, and it has already been demonstrated by the most patient and careful chemical analysis, conducted by such men as Boecker, Prout, Percy, Perrin, Smith and others, that alcohol furnishes none of the elements either of respiration or nutrition, and that, consequently, the hypothesis on which all other claims rest is proved to be fallacious."

The address throughout is notable for its thorough comprehensiveness and cogency.

The oration, by Dr. S. M. Dinsmoor, discusses *quackery*, dwelling principally upon that phase of it which is "too much *inside* our own ranks," due for the most part to too great a desire to please patrons, together with some strong allusions to winking at, if not abetting abortions; and the use of alcohol. The other important papers are: Tuberculosis, by C. P. Frost. M.D.; Changes in our Climate, and their effects upon disease, by John Randolph Ham, M.D.; and several reports of important cases—all of much practical value.

Transactions of the Medical Society of the State of Pennsylvania. Twenty-fifth Annual Session, 1874. Philadelphia.

The plan of working of this society affords an excellent model for other State Medical Societies, comprehending a schedule of topics for county society reports on medical topography and the relation of diseases generally to local conditions and meteorological influences. The volume before us comprehends the reports of twenty counties, giving much practical information in regard to the causes of epidemics which ought to be available towards obtaining State sanitary administration, and such legislative action as will promote the saving of human life.

Transactions of the American Medical Association. Vol. 25, 1874.

This volume, in its careful and thorough report of all that was done at Detroit, bears testimony to the faithful labor of the various secretaries of sections, and especially to that of the Permanent Secretary, Dr. Atkinson, and the publishing committee. The notice given of the proceedings soon after the meeting adjourned, in the July number of The Sanitarian, renders an extended notice at present unnecessary.

Transactions of the Medical Society of the District of Columbia. Quarterly, Oct., 1874.

Reports of cases of herniotomy, spontaneous rupture of the aorta, biliary calculi, cancer, and corea.

Toner Lecture, No. 3, on Strain and Overaction of the Heart. By J. M. Da Costa, M. D., Professor of Practice of Medicine in Jefferson Medical College. May 14, 1874.

A very timely and able paper, related to physical exertion and popular sports. Dr. Da Costa's researches in this direction are of great value to medical practitioners for the early detection of functional and organic heart affections, ere they cease to be amenable to treatment.

THE SANITARIAN.

A MONTHLY JOURNAL.

VOL. II.] FEBRUARY, 1875. [NO. 11.

BUILDING GROUND IN ITS RELATIONS TO HEALTH.

Read before the American Public Health Association, Philadelphia, 1874.

By EZRA M. HUNT, M.D., New Jersey.

The condition of the ground has very much to do with all questions of health. The character of the soil, the degree to which it can dispose of all that comes in contact with it—whether in the form of gases, of animal or vegetable decay, of pure and impure liquids,—all have intrinsic and vital bearings upon human health. The making of the earth a place fit for the healthful habitation of man, is a part of the problem which creative skill has considered. We need to become aware of the constant activities and adjustments taking place to this end. These are not accidental or incidental, but involved, as if the chief things intended to be conserved. Where natural transformations are in nowise interfered with by art, it is wonderful to see how processes involving productions inimical to health are so conducted as to be entirely consistent with vigorous existence. While decomposition is the rule, evil therefrom under natural conditions is the exception. While, for instance, enough carbonic acid is produced each day to kill all the inhabitants of the earth, yet it is so well managed as not to interfere with the health of man or animal.

But the very moment a spot comes to be builded upon, it is by necessity placed in abnormal conditions. The building clears the ground of that herbage which had no unimportant sanitary office in appropriating the products of decay. It covers it from sunlight and sun-heat, and necessarily makes its condition as to moisture quite different. It interferes with the range of winds, and modifies the immediate thermometric and hygrometric conditions of the atmosphere. It throws the rain-fall into streams upon the ground around its sides, instead of allowing it to diffuse itself in drops. In winter it causes accumulations of snow and ice. It alters the course of water, making, it may be, the cellar, the well, the cistern, the cesspool, the privy vault and the sewer parts of its underground drainage. In a word, it alters the whole relation of the ground occupied and of its immediate surroundings. Besides all this, the necessities of habitation create filth, garbage and dust, and refuse of various kinds, which are conveniently added to the soil just where it cannot use them.

Pettenkofer says of the city of Munich, that about ninety per cent. of its excretions go into the ground. It is thus easy to see the varied conditions interposed by human dwelling-places, and how these conditions are magnified by the multiplication of buildings and the crowding of inmates. The great sanitation of nature is suspended, and factors of insalubrity introduced to a degree that arrests our most careful attention. If cities are ulcers on the body politic, they are not less anti-health combinations against the body physical. It is no small or unimportant thing to have removed the grass that sucks up the miasm, shaded the ground from sunlight, changed the laws of its moisture, altered its water-courses, and interfered directly with the forces which elaborated health. It is as easy to make destructive sanitary changes as to make destructive physical or chemical changes. The one or the other may depend upon only slight variations of atomic proportions. In chemistry, the equivalents of calomel and corrosive sublimate differ but little; so a single interrupted change may determine whether we shall have prophylactic or destructive agencies. Cotton wool and glycerine are very harmless substances; but a slight chemical variation, in which no important change has taken place in outward aspect, makes of the one gun-cotton, and of the other nitro-glycerine. The change is so little, and the deadliness so great, that chemistry itself stands in wonder and speaks of their fatality as accidental, and calls them "substitution products." We know not but that similar derangements in nature's methods of disposing of the products of decay in the ground make those fortuitous combinations which we call choleraic or zymotic, and cause these to break forth into the fearful explosions of fatal disease. Changes thus actually made are interruptions to the equilibrium and compensations which nature has established, and as such are fraught with danger to human health.

Consider what a complex thing the ground is.—We are so apt to look upon it as a mere succession of strata to hold us up, that we forget its complicated structure. It has in it not mere mineralogy, but it is made of fire and air and water as well as earth. The sun causes in the earth a diurnal wave of heat in our climate of about four feet in depth, varied somewhat by soils and seasons. As this recedes by night, there is circulation of heat beneath the surface;—the line of uniformity of temperature is from fifty-seven to ninety-nine feet below the surface (Forbes). This one fact shows the range of heat which circulates above the earth. When the sunshine strikes upon it, it acquires a much higher temperature than the surrounding air. The difference is sometimes so great as to make near the ground on a very hot day, a refraction sufficient to cause indistinctness. When we remember how much moisture and evaporation depend upon relative temperature, and how much all these bear on health, we get some idea of the hygienic condition of the ground. The house may stand over it, the pavement may cover it, and stone and concrete seem to make it a basis for travel; but from it is evolving an influence on temperature, which penetrates and affects all the animals that dwell upon it. Since the warmth of the earth, radiating and being extracted at night into the colder atmosphere, causes the dew, this is but one of the registers of the relation between the ground and the air above. The heat and moisture of the ground, and the temperature of atmosphere above it, are unavoidably relative; and it is just as sensible to talk of changing ground, as of changing air for health. "In the interior of substances, as well as in air, a stream of radiant heat is constantly passing and repassing in all directions." Heat, as a form of motion, has its activities in the earth as well as above it. Temperature affects chemical affinity, and so has to do with combinations and decompositions. As many decaying substances have little chemical stability, mephitic gasses are easily produced. "Even the laws of gaseous radiation have," as Balfour Stewart expresses it, "lately become of great practical importance."

A city interferes with the constant effort of heat after equilibrium of temperature, as recognized in the theory of exchanges. The whole subject of thermo-dynamics has intimate relation to the ground.

Besides, its temperature has to do with thermo-elective inversion and with electric conductivity. So marked is the influence of the ground that meteorological investigations keep clear of the surface. The British Association has a committee on underground temperature. When we come to see the abnormal condition in which the ground is placed in regard to heat, and remember its indispensable office in dealing with air and water beneath the surface, we cannot but come to feel still more the sanitary significance of the study. Indeed medical men need to remember that earth sanitation has to do with great questions of physical science, and so is a department of physics to be studied technically as such.

Next, the ground is largely made up of air. We are familiar with the fact that into a pail of soil we may pour part of a pail of water and yet not have an overflow. But we forget that all this space between particles of soil when not displaced by water in the ground is occupied by underground atmosphere.

Not only do loose soils contain air but all the softer rocks and the frozen ground. An animal will keep alive for days in a space surrounded on all sides by what we call air-tight ground, by reason of the air it obtains from the ground itself. You may compact it with heavy rollers, but still that invisible spirit of air is running hither and thither, beside each particle never meant to be stagnant but doing great sanitary work. In its circulation it is meant to oxidize and hydrocarbonate animal and vegetable decay so as to make it innocuous, and great volumes of carbonic acid are handed over to vegetable life. *Questions of ventilation are not all above-ground.* It is in constant interchange with the surface air or else confined and fouled in its impeded underground circulation. Bad air stagnated in the ground is hurtful in all that constitutes insalubrity by interfering with normal and healthful affinities. Even the rain as it passes through the atmosphere becomes aerated and carries into the soil more oxygen than air itself to oxidize organic matter, if only the spaces are not already filled with stagnant water or foul air.

It is believed that one of the causes of the prevalence of such fevers as typhus and typhoid in the winter is that the great inner heat of houses causes the currents of air from the surrounding ground to set towards them, under the general law of currents as affected by heat. So the basement and the house suck up the ground air contaminated by its wrong conditions, and the local heat causes it to penetrate more than in the summer. Gas and the air of cesspools have thus been perceptible in houses not supplied with them, and where the situation was not near. Often in cities foul gases instead of being consumed are discharged by pipes into sewers and underground connections. This may relieve the atmosphere from the nauseous outgush, but too often sends them to mingle with the underground air to be discharged in diluted but nevertheless harmful quantities into the houses.

If the soil air is polluted by sewage, or only by the interruption of those processes which nature has instituted for purifying it, we are sharers in that contaminated air. There are some systems of ventilation which actually serve to draw in, not only cellar but polluted ground air, and send it circulating through our houses. If bed-ridden sickness is not caused there is yet that lowering of vital vigor which makes invalidity. The want of tone of system of which those complain who are confined to houses, is often in part owing to the impure ground-air which finds its way into their breathing atmosphere.

It is but recently that attention has been drawn to the fact that carbonic acid may be rapidly produced in such a way in the ground, where the natural ability of the soil to dispose of it has been superseded, as to cause it to be suddenly imparted in large quantities to the upper air.

On this whole subject of ground ventilation we have much yet to learn. The drain-pipe is not only useful to rid the ground of surplus water, but also as an artery for air. It has pneumatic as well as aquatic importance. Nay more; in closely compacted cities a system of underground pneumatic tubing would greatly aid the purity of soil and help to compensate for some of the interference with heat and air which a city interposes. Air is the great disinfectant, and its freer circulation underneath cities needs to be secured upon a plan. Both the drying and the cleansing of the soil depend upon this as upon no other agency.

The fact of water in the ground is more apparent than that of air, but still its relations thereto are underrated in its sanitary bearings. There is a depth varying with soil and locality at which the ground water is in general intended to fill up the spaces between earth particles. But in several feet of the ground nearest to the surface it is intended that the soil should have both air and water in circulation. Between these and heat there is a co-relation and conservation which is conducted as wonderfully and as scientifically below ground as above it. The surface, like the human skin, is but the plane of contact, while within is incessant motion. This condition of relations is necessary for the carrying forward of changes which, when uninterrupted, tend healthward, but which, when suspended, contaminate the ground. There is a vis medicatrix naturæ in the earth as well as in man which is dependent upon the uninterrupted play of natural forces. The effect of stagnant water is to cause the decomposed vegetable and animal matter in the soil to accumulate. This is illustrated by the fact that the occurrence of stagnant water is necessary to the production of peat. Organic, and especially agricultural chemistry, is tracing these changes in their wonderful adaptations to growth. The conditions of temperature of air, and of liquids, are self-regulating to a surprising degree where art does not intervene. But to this end there must be air and heat and water circulation. Even those myriad organisms from bacteria upward, which science is revealing, are instituted methods for disposing of organic material, but it is only amid the activities of air and water circulation that their existence occurs. The capacity of the ground for air is already shown, and by expelling the air from dried earth, or in other words, by pouring into it water, we find its capacity for water. Such ground as we are familiar with will thus take in 50 per cent. in volume of water, and even marble will hold four per cent.

That which we call dry ground has still much moisture in it. When we are treating of the ground we have therefore intimately to do with vital questions as to water. Says Moreau Morris, recently sanitary superintendent of New York City: "Medical and sanitary science and experience forbid the erection of dwellings upon an undrained soil. Heat and capillary attraction bring to the surface that moisture and dampness which should have been removed by sanitary engineering. The result is malarial fevers, consumption, suffering and death as punishments for neglecting applications afforded by the light of science."

It is not enough in building a city to preserve in full all natural water courses. Even the perfection of field-drainage will not suffice. You are about permanently to cover the ground, so as to add to its dampness and in various ways interfere with its natural changes. The readiest and most indispensable way of compensating for radical alterations you are making, is by the multiplication of underground tubes. I know not but that ere long, with the precision of a mathematical result, we shall be able to state how much sunlight, sun-heat, radiation, evaporation, etc., we have shut out in a solid square of buildings, and how many square feet of new pathway underground is required in compensation.

But heat and air and water, as they circulate beneath us, and form parts of the ground, are not only important in themselves, but they enable the organic and inorganic substances of the ground to undergo their disintegrations and reparations.

The water is the menstruum circulating through the soil by which vital or destructive changes are carried on.

So air and heat are lending their aid, and the earth itself using them as instruments, has its own constituent particles in process of change.

All these are wonderful when studied in their conservative sanitary tendencies, and wonderful also in the evil which may result from interrupted processes.

Grandly and gloriously does nature provide for all that relates to this underground world as to its organic and inorganic material, its air, its heat, its water, its animal life, so far as health is concerned, if only its surface and the world above are left to the uninterrupted play of natural provisions. It gives off its superfluous carbonic acid to plants, or stores away its heat for fuel. Field and forest, air and sky, are in happy correspondence. The culture of the earth is itself in the direction of natural appropriation, and so when rightly conducted aids the healthful activities of nature. Ground, then, is not a mere passive stone-like thing. We need to know that in a hygienic point of view it is only by the working of manifold chemistries and philosophies carried on and out, by definite plans, that it makes itself habitable and healthful. It is a foundation made up of fire and air and earth and water and inner life, the salubrious condition of which is dependent on its being left to the uninterrupted play of those forces by which heat and air enter it with unimpeded facility, by which water has easy access and uninterrupted outflow.

And now in bold contrast we must recur to the fact that a habitation or city is an artificial construction which in its chiefest characteristics interferes with all these natural conditions of ground. It is the interposing of a great separation between the forces above and beneath. It cannot suspend relations, but it can and does fearfully complicate them. It interposes hazardous hindrances or limitations to changes which are hygienically necessary. The ground, when it evolves unhealthy decompositions, also evolves its enormous vegetation to dispose of them. The city does not prevent the decomposition, but does away with the natural process of disposing of it.

The ground, when by its trees or herbage it shuts out sun-heat, has its millions of leaves to absorb noxious material, and even uses its woods and its herbage to regulate temperature. The city has no full compensation. It has also its natural well-distributed rain-fall and water-courses. The city quite deranges all these. We need by careful thought over that which goes on in the natural ground, and its indispensable relations to health, to recognize what an unwholesome fact a city is. But besides complicating interruptions it adds enormously to the sources of contamination. It creates occasion for the manifolding of natural conditions and processes, and then suspends them. Weigh with large scales, in full and fair estimate, what is done and is needed to be done in the unbuilded earth by the forces of nature, and how far a house, and towns, and cities interpose hindrances. Weigh with larger scales the immense factors of sanitary evil in all the excretions incident to living, so much of which falls to the ground.

The more we investigate the more we come to know the enormity of the contrasts and interferences which the building of houses introduces. Wherever we thus mass men, art has interposed unsanitary conditions which art must rectify. Having informed ourselves of the nature of the ground, and what in its natural state it does to elaborate health, we must see how far we can abate the evil of the circumstances we have necessarily introduced. How far can we restore natural conditions by artificial appliances?

As we furnish new sources of evil in new vegetable decompositions, animal excretions, garbage, sewage, dirt, foul gases, and filth in manifold forms, how shall we reduce all these to their minimum and best provide for their removal?

With these cardinal facts as to the ground in its natural state, and with an appreciation of the complicating circumstances introduced, we go first of all to the sanitary engineer and ask what is the state of the ground under our buildings as to its air, its moisture, its heat, its proportions of decayed or decayable matter? If too much water, how best shall we draw it off, and so give access to air to correct dampness and foulness? The basements and the sub-cellars must be closely questioned. Which is the better, a house without cellar or basement, located on a water-soaked soil, or one whose cellar is nearly full of water, but with room for a stratum of ventilated air between?

Is it not best to secure the water supply for other than drinking purposes from local wells in order to aid in the drying of the soil? What is the best system of drainage? How far can we thus aid or restore and supplement natural conditions, and by giving air and heat free entrance enable the ground to dispose of its matter in a healthful way? Where dampness exists how much can be done by cemented floors and sides below ground? How much good or ill by artificial heat? How shall sewage be conducted through ground so as not to contaminate it, and water so as not to add to dampness? Shall the streets or yards be protected by pavement or covered with trees, grass, and foliage so far as possible? What evils arise from city dust, and how far is street sprinkling advisable? Shall intra-mural interments be allowed at all?

How shall width and direction of streets, and heights of buildings, and proximity of rear buildings, be best regulated to secure needed sunshine? How shall structures be painted so as to favor a healthy temperature? How shall streets be paved so as least to interfere with right changes in the ground? In repairing pavements, should any absorbent or disinfectant be used? How shall the water from buildings and the general rain-fall be best disposed of? How shall garbage and all animal excreta be kept out of the ground, since foul ground-air will foul the atmosphere? How shall miasm—mother of fevers springing from the ground, and at home now in cities—be detected and prevented?—for it, too, is a subtle result of unnatural combination. What are the relations of drainage, sewerage, and all under tubing? May not all cities study the laws of "pipe-laying" above ground less, and below ground more, with advantage? These, and such as these, are among the manifold vital questions which sanitary science has to ask in reference to the ground. The great problem in every habitation, and especially in every city, is to make up for the evils which dwelling in ceiled houses entails, and by compensatory methods to place the soil in as good condition for health as it would be if not thus occupied.

In inspecting the unhealthy locality about Second avenue and Seventy-sixth street, New York, although the ground had been raised, a cause for a uniformly excessive death rate was found in the obstruction of a natural water-course, and the substitution of drains and sewers at too high a level.

In another case, sickness in a fine row of buildings was found to depend upon the fact that the underground received the foul drainage of two or three squares. It is easy for one part of a city, or even for the sub-cellar of one or more houses, to become the cesspool for a neighborhood, by some little error or circumstance that turns the outfall in that direction. We are constantly finding out, more and more, how much sickness depends upon invisible ground conditions which the sanitary engineer must remedy, or which the city fathers above ground must prevent, if they desire to keep themselves or their children out of it. Whole groups of zymotic diseases are traceable to ground conditions. Rheumatism and all pulmonary affections are vastly dependent upon ground moisture. Foul air, foul water, and foul decompositions come from the ground, and must be attended to in the ground, and also prevented from getting there. There is a climatology of the ground as well as of the atmosphere, and air, rain and temperature are its great regulators.

Although a city is a complex problem in a sanitary way, it is solvable. Science is not as far behind as is the municipality in its application. With the ground, especially, we know what to do, if only the command was given.

Many an experiment is now full-fledged experience; and we can say we know. We must look down as well as up and around. If these foundations are polluted, in vain we work on the surface and in upper air. A proper ground base is what we want for human habitations more than any sanitary want of the age. If to-day our association, instead of a walk amid the beautiful streets of the cleanest of American cities, could walk out for sanitary service between the sub-soil and the surface soil, wonderful revelations would be opened up to our view. There would be found deposits of filth where least suspected, defective sewers, soil overladen with decompositions, stagnant water and stagnant air, connections between cesspools and sink wells and houses where now unknown; stenches more varied than Coleridge found in the city of Cologne, and unsanitary conditions enough to alarm and awaken the inhabitants that people the surface.

Could we at one lift take up four feet depth of city soil, with its undue moisture, its overladen decomposition, its unfriendly germinations, and all its altered conditions due to its city covering, and compare it with an equal surface upon some elevated plane in the open country, we would at once detect causes quite sufficient to account for manifold differences in sickness and mortality. Independent of the interruption of natural purifying forces which a city introduces, could we get together the amount of filth which, in one way or another—solid, liquid, or aeriform,—finds its way into city ground, we would be shocked at the enormous tonnage. We would not wonder that chemists and sanitarians have come to speak of some soils as zymotic, and others as "typhoid, ripe."

Within forty miles of this place is a city of 25,000 inhabitants as to which reliable reports made to me, say: "It has no system of sewerage. Garbage is thrown into back alleys, or in rear of lots, to take care of itself. House closets are drained into cesspools and ground near the buildings. The solid contents of privy vaults are removed at long intervals, and the liquid portions soak into the soil. The Board of Health has held no meetings for a long time, generally awaiting some great nuisance, or the actual invasion of an epidemic. It has no system of vital statistics, no certificates of causes of death, and so no actual record as to its insalubrity. All that we know of it is, that it is a good place for medical practitioners, and that they recognize a ground condition in many parts which is most deplorable." Large cities are not the only ones which suffer. We can find in country towns and villages ground which any New York inspector would report a nuisance. Damp ground, wet cellars, decaying vegetables, garbage, well and cesspool and privy too near each other, occur in many small places. We are aware that soil itself, when it has a chance to act on the dry earth system, will, where not subjected to constant and excessive contamination, purify itself to some degree; but yet, from wrong conditions about the ground of houses, about the drinking water as affected thereby, we see many evil results. To preserve porosity to ground beneath and near dwellings, is among the most important of sanitary efforts. This merely means to give air free access to soil by preventing stagnant water. The indispensable disinfectant below ground as well as above, is air, the circulation of which in the soil depends upon temperature, and this on light and heat as applied to the surface. The carbon is provided for vegetable life and other purposes, but when we come to deprive the soil of plants and substitute animals, we cause it to be unappropriated by the one, or harmfully appropriated by the other. Where, as in some parts, made soils are composed of an over accumulation of decaying matters, or of foul material removed from streets, the building of houses over it may conceal, but cannot destroy the contamination. More or less of the foul air must find its way out of the soil and endanger the health of those living upon it. Some claim that concrete and cement and stone shut up the soil so as to prevent or moderate the evil, but experiments show that air and moisture still continue their interchange. While coarser filth can be more easily gathered from such a surface, and flushing and cleansing more easily conducted, the air of the soil beneath still has active relations to the atmosphere above. By this perpetual motion of air and water in soil, and by the laws of diffusion and capillary attraction, nature is busy maintaining an equilibrium of healthful compensations, which is embarrassed by human tenements, but fortunately not altogether suspended.

There is indeed need that each dwelling and building be recognized as of itself instituting some unsanitary relationship in the soil about, and as such it is subject to treatment.

As all our smaller cities and towns depend on local wells for water supply, foul ground involves foul drinking water, and so the necessities of a clean soil are still further magnified.

We have thus sought to make prominent a consideration of ground as related to dwellings, and to attract attention to the interruptions of natural laws conservative of health which they interpose, and to the additional contamination with which they afflict the soil. Having found out how important for health it is that these ground changes should go on, and that soil and air and heat and water should have their proper relations, we are better prepared to seek how to reduce this interference to its minimum or to compensate for it by other methods.

Having found what a serious thing it is to add bad material from above to ground whose purifying power we have already embarrassed by structures of art, we can all the more feel how diligent we must be in preventing the debris of human dwellings to add to the evil.

The engineer, the chemist, the microscopist, the physician, the architect, the sanitarian, have already been able to establish facts and record the needs, and sanitary legislation has much to do in reducing the results to practice. If we have increased the ground water by covering it from heat and light, we must, by special drainage and outflow, give greater facilities for its subsidence. If we have shut out the air, we must thus make room for it, and keep the ground air pure both by circulation and by not multiplying materials for decay.

Having interfered with some of the natural ability of soil to dispose of decomposition, we must not overspread it as if we were top-dressing a meadow or enriching a wheat-field. With intelligent recognition of the facilities of self-correction and health equilibrium which we have embarrassed by our buildings and pavements, we must by art compensate therefor, and as far as possible prevent all abnormal conditions. Every advance in sanitary science is showing how much disease is the penalty of transgression of nature's laws, and how much of the penalty accrues from wrong telluric conditions. The voice of spilled lives cries from the ground. We want more of a dry earth system beneath and around our dwellings, more of pure circulating air in the underground flow, more of an uncontaminated surface soil. The air we breathe, the aliments we take, the clothes we wear, the ground we live on, these are the sanitary corner-stone of upbuilding life. Not the least is a ground whose earth, and air, and heat, and moisture, and cleanliness, fit it for the tread of the great masses of population.

Perfect under-drainage under the definite skill of engineers, is the first great need of most cities. Regulation of cellars and of all other holes below the surface, is the next great study. It would be found that the mere filling up of a cavity does not dry it, and that drains underground will not carry water or refuse up hill any better than they do on the surface. The proper airing of all substructure, because of its proximity to ground, comes in next for consideration.

What we can do to sweeten or purify surface soil already fouled, is another point.

Then the great question of what to do with all refuse so as to keep it out of city soil, is the large and momentous subject which must ever present itself to our attention. Surely in the unnatural state in which building itself has placed it, it has enough to do without adding one iota of this burden.

Enough if we feel the momentous interests involved in ground purity. Enough if we can arouse each other to a closer study of these fundamental and vital interests, and at the same time convince the citizen and move municipal authorities to more careful thought and more intelligent action. We must get the homes of the people on better foundation than damp water-soaked, air-polluted, filth-burthened ground. While at work upon the surface, abating all influences inimical to health, we must not let the covered earth, because concealed by dwellings, escape our searching ken. We must see to it that its soil particles are not overladen with vegetable or animal decay, that its fountains of moisture are not impeded in their flow, or saturated with impurities, that air has free circulation through all its spaces, that its regulative ability, as to temperature, is not unduly complicated. Thus starting with a healthy and a health-imparting ground, we are on a right basis, and are prepared to upbuild as on good foundations that grand system of sanitary science whose object is the prolonging of life, the preservation of health, and the conservation of human happiness.

Car Ventilation.—A party of railroad and scientific men made a special trip between Boston and Springfield, Mass., recently, for the purpose of testing a new mode of car ventilation. The arrangement is an application of the fan system.

Upon the centre of the axletree of one of the trucks is securely fastened a driving pulley 22½ inches in diameter; from the driving pulley runs a small triangular belt, 1½ inches wide, over another pulley 4½ inches in diameter, attached to a fan made of galvanized sheet-iron upon a steel shaft. This constitutes the mechanical adjustment for putting in motion the required supply of air. Ordinary car-wheels are 33 inches in diameter or 8.64 feet in circumference; hence in passing over a mile of track the wheels make 611 revolutions, and the size of the pulleys being as one to five, the fan revolves 3,055 times; that is, when the train moves at, say, one-third of a mile per minute, or twenty miles per hour, the fan revolves at about 1,000 per minute, or 1,500 at thirty miles per hour. To conduct the air which has been put in motion by the centrifugal force of the fan, to the top of the car, and to distribute it evenly, the fan is surrounded by an elongated sheathing of wood, which may be seen under the car, and which is continued by a tin conducting tube through the closet to the distributing pipes, which in turn emit the air into the car. This sheathing being air-tight, the fan is, so to speak, hermetically sealed, and none of the outside air can get to it or feed it except that which passes through the air-chamber. Now, since all the air which finds its way into the air-chamber must pass through the fine screens, which are inserted in place of the window glass, the dust and cinders must be left outside the car. The experiment was very satisfactory. A small quantity of cologne was placed in the air-chamber, and the odor was immediately perceived in every part of the car. The same effect was observed when smoke was made in the air-chamber, which found its way at once in a uniform diffusion in the car. The air was then shut off, and the car was filled with a dense cloud of smoke; upon admitting air the smoke was principally removed in three minutes, and in six minutes the car was entirely clear. Notwithstanding the large amount of air taken into the car, there was no dust from the roadbed nor cinders from the engine.

PHYSICAL CULTURE.

INFLUENCE OF EXERCISE UPON THE ORGANS OF THE BODY.

BY H. L. BARTLETT, M D.

It is a law of our being, that use imparts strength, and produces growth, in all our bodily organs, hence we possess within ourselves the means of our own development.

This may as truthfully be said of the mental faculties as of our bodily organs, and so intimate are the relations of the different parts of our system, that we cannot increase or diminish the capabilities of any particular faculty or organ, without affecting the powers of the whole.

The accident of birth is indeed independent of our volition, but the extent to which our minds may be cultivated, or the powers of the body developed, depends upon education.

One fact, at least, is well established, viz.: that the mind is *only* developed and the body *only* attains its greatest perfection by use.

When we speak of exercise, we mean the *enforced* use of the voluntary muscles, the primary effect of such use is upon the muscles themselves, producing first a destruction of tissue, thereby generating a certain amount of heat, and at the same time causing an acceleration of the blood in the inter-muscular veins, which in turn brings back renewed nourishment to replace the molecules destroyed, and not only so, but this destruction seems to create an aptitude for consumption in excess of the amount lost, and so the muscle actually grows in contractibility and volume.

Whether muscles grow by the development of new fibres, or the enlargement of old ones, is not well settled by physiologists.

Probably, however, they increase by both processes, and the blood-vessels supplying them proportionally enlarge.

This is not only true of the muscles brought into play in any given motion, but the effect is equally felt by their antagonists, so that we cannot enlarge one set of muscles without correspondingly increasing the size of those opposed to them, and thus the perfect symmetry of the body is preserved.

The second effect of violent muscular exercise is upon the circulation and respiration. In a state of repose, the bulk of the blood is in the veins, and as soon as pressure is made upon them by the contraction of the muscles, their contents are hurried on to the right chamber of the heart, and from these to the lungs, and so back to the heart again, to be distributed throughout the system.

It is found by observation that the effect of "training," or the persistent use of gymnastic exercises, is to enlarge the heart and lungs both in size and capacity. Archibald McClaren, Superintendent of the Oxford gymnasium, and author of "Physical Education," says: "One of the army officers sent to me to be instructed in gymnastics gained five inches in girth around the chest in less than three months."

That this growth is not explained by the mere enlargement of the pectoral muscles, is proved by the increased volume of air which the lungs are enabled to expire, as is demonstrated by the spirometer, and *post mortems* abundantly show an increased capacity as well as size in the heart and large blood vessels.

The lungs increase both in length and breadth, forcing the ribs outward, and the diaphragm downwards.

It is for this reason that athletes and gymnasts are enabled to make prolonged and violent exertions without getting out of wind. The capacity of the heart and central arteries being enlarged, they can accommodate more blood. Their contractile power being increased by this new demand upon them, they are enabled to send on the current through the lungs with increased velocity, and thus by their greater capacity are able to oxygenize the blood as fast as it is supplied to them, and so no congestion takes place, and no inconvenience is felt.

The normal capacity of the lungs of an adult male is about two hundred (200) cubic inches. It is computed that an enlargement of three inches around the chest gives an increase of fifty cubic inches of lung capacity. In how many cases of lung diseases would this fifty cubic inches make the difference of life or death to the patient? The average body of the adult male contains about eighteen pounds of blood. The average heart has a capacity of three ounces, so that to change the entire volume of blood in the body, the heart must make ninety-six beats, which it does in less than a minute and a half.

In athletes, however, the capacity of the heart is much more than this. So that when one makes a violent exertion, that organ is not overwhelmed by the sudden influx of blood.

It is also computed that a healthy heart can exert a power equal to 13 lbs. at every beat; and in very muscular persons, this is probably largely exceeded.

The mere statement of these facts demonstrates what an advantage this physiological increase in the size and power of the heart gives one in the emergencies of life, to say nothing of the ability to make great and prolonged exertions!

How many persons have succumbed to disease, or fallen by the way, when unexpectedly called upon to make some unusual effort, for the want of this heart power!

In my own practice, I have lately had a case which illustrates this remark: a young person, apparently in robust health, was taken sick with a mild fever, and when seemingly convalescent, suddenly and unexpectedly died. On making the *post mortem*, I found that the septum between the ventricles of the heart had given way in consequence of fatty degeneration, and hence the fatal result.

The death of the late Mayor of the city of New York was also a case in point. A slight, unusual exertion, overtaxed the circulation, and death ensued. Nor is it to be wondered at that the heart gives way when its labors are so largely increased by some powerful effort, or as a consequence of febrile action, when we remember that a mere change in the posture of the body alters the pulse in a marked degree.

Dr. Guy found the average pulse of a healthy male, in a recumbent posture, to be 66 per minute; while sitting, it was 71, and standing, 81, and how often—as the result of febrile excitement—it will run up to the fearful altitude of 140 or 150 in the same time!

Thus we see that physical exercise not only enlarges and strengthens the voluntary muscles, but also develops those that are involuntary, and increases the capacity of the blood-vessels and lungs. Not only so, but it quickens all the bodily functions and stimulates all the excretions.

Dr. Edward Morgan (Oxford) states that when a person is violently exercising, the lungs eliminate three times the amount of carbonic acid gas that they do when in repose.

The secretions of the kidneys and bowels are largely increased by exercise, and its effect is still more marked on the cutaneous respiration.

In the light of these facts, exercise becomes literally nature's great physic, eliminating from the system the effete and poisonous matter which have lived their little span of life, and only wait to be carried, in funeral procession, out into oblivion!

If the latest theory be true, that the seat of volition and sensation is identical with the centre of thought, it follows, as a physiological law, that the highest intellectual attainment is only possible where the physical powers are of the first order.

All human experience proves that exercise is a necessity of our being. Plato declared that "moderate exercise produced a good habit of the body," and Prof. Parkes has given it as his opinion that "a healthy man ought to take exercise equal to a daily walk of nine miles."

In the young the muscles yearn for exercise, and the restlessness of youth is but an expression of this want.

In the report of the medical department of the British army for the years 1857 and 1858, it is stated that "the mortality in the army is as much due to the monotonous and inactive life of the soldiers as to their vicious habits and practices." The same report further says: "Among causes of death in the infantry, want of exercise and labor is a large one." For this reason most of the great governments of the earth, ours excepted, have created gymnasia wherever they have had extensive barracks for soldiers, so that they might obtain abundant exercise when not engaged in active campaigns. It is a well-known physiological fact that the excessive accumulation of fat is a sign of bodily decay, and there are many cases on record where the muscular tissue has disappeared from want of use, and its place been supplied by fat, so that the limbs could not be voluntarily moved, even when the volition existed. The process of decay by fatty degeneration is much more rapid than decay by atrophy; hence, persons who live to an advanced age are always thin.

"One of the first objects of training" is to get rid of all superincumbent adipose, and the best way to do this is by exercise. Exercise therefore not only assists in purifying the blood of all effete substances and hastening the supply to the tissues of healthful pabulum, but also of relieving the body of all superfluous matters which tend to obstruct or clog its movements.

Rational exercise not only develops and strengthens the body, but it has a chastening and subduing influence upon the mind, promoting serenity, and producing sleep. Diana was the goddess of chastity, and was represented by the ancients as a huntress, because they held that of all occupations hunting was best calculated to free the mind from impure thoughts, and excite in it a love for the good and the true.

The restlessness of a mind diseased is best relieved and subdued by exercise. So natural is this feeling that the insane at once resort to it, when laboring under great mental excitement, and those having charge of them, both among the ancients and in modern times, have had recourse to and encourage it—not only as a means of diversion, but of cure in most nervous disorders.

FLORIDA FOR INVALIDS.—If a perfectly equable climate, where a soothing warmth and moisture combined prevail, be desirable for consumptives, it can be found nowhere in the Southern States save in south-eastern Florida. The number of persons whom I saw during my journey, who had migrated to the eastern or southern sections of the State many years before, " more than half dead with consumption," and who are now robust and vigorous, was sufficient to convince me of the great benefit derived from a residence there. Physicians all agree that the conditions necessary to insure life to the consumptive are admirably provided in the climatic resources of the peninsula. That great numbers of invalids find the localities along the St. John's river, and even on the coast, distressing to them, is said by some physicians to be due to the fact that those invalids go there after disease has become too deeply-seated. The European medical men are beginning to send many patients to Florida, cautioning them where to go. It would seem impossible for the most delicate invalid to be injured by a residence anywhere on the eastern or south-eastern coast from St. Augustine down. For those who from various causes find that each successive northern winter,—with its constantly shifting temperature and its trying winds, which even the healthy characterize as " deadly," —saps their vitality more and more, Florida may be safely recommended as a home, winter and summer. For the healthy, and those seeking pleasure, it will become a winter paradise ; for the ailing it is a refuge and strength ; for those severely invalided its results depend entirely upon choice of location and the progress which the disease has already made. The perfection of the Florida winter climate is said to be obtained at Miami, near Key Biscayne bay, on the Miami river. There, among the cocoanuts and the mangroves, invalids may certainly count on laying a new hold upon life.—*Edward King, in Scribner's for November.*

THE ENIGMAS OF LIFE.*

By A. H. Dana, New York.

What I have to say upon the old questions that have hitherto baffled speculative inquiry, will be in the nature of suggestions to be added to the countless hypotheses already accumulated, rather than positive solution.

I. *The rapid transition of the physical organism of man from birth to maturity, and then to decay.* We must assume that nothing is wrought in the creative economy without a purpose. What beneficial purpose can be learned by inquiry into the incidents and results of this transitional existence? According to the doctrine that the present state is a preparation for another and an advanced state, there should be progression through the entirety of this life. How then can be explained the decline soon following maturity, and the collapsing in old age into disability? If it was mere physical weakness, without corresponding decay of mental vigor, we might suppose the process to be a mere sloughing off of the exterior,—like the exumenation† of the worm, and the putting forth the butterfly. But in the later years of advanced age, vigor of mind in general subsides with that of the body, sometimes merging into utter imbecility. From the commencement of the decline there is no further apparent progress in mental development that might be supposed to be available in a future life. There is, indeed, a retrospection over the past,—a dwelling upon the incidents of the years that have gone by,—or upon thoughts and plans that during that period have occupied the mind; and from such review may result a more impartial estimate of the real value of what we have sought after, and more particularly of our own intrinsic character. But, oftener, prejudices and errors that have been the outgrowth from unfavorable circumstances in life, or from natural wrong proclivities, become confirmed in later years. There is less of vigor then to resist what deliberate judgment disapproves; and the check interposed in the active part of a man's life by the counter pressure of opposing interests and passions of other men, is withdrawn in proportion to the isolation by infirmity from such collision.

Again, if the process of decline is in any sense prep rative for another state, it would still be limited to the comparatively small number who go through the entire succession of changes—adolescence, maturity, decay. But what is to be thought of the vastly greater proportion of those who are cut off before maturity? What of the moiety of the human race which in civilized communities die under the age of five years?

Finally, when we consider the marvellous structure of the human organism,—its intricate interior network of nerves, arteries, capillary

---

* This article was written before I had seen the publication of similar title by Mr. Gregg. But, though the general subject is alike, the topics and scope of discussion are diverse. I have referred in notes to some of the divergencies.

† *Exumenation*, stripping off the skin.

tubes,—the unexplained, perhaps inexplicable flow of blood to and from every part, in conduits, diminishing from the *great aorta* to the minutest ramifications, under the propulsion of the alternate *systole* and *diastole* of the heart,—the varied apparatus appropriated to the organs of sense, especially the eye and ear,—the mysterious endowment of the brain and its medullary co-agencies, whereby impressions are transmitted to it from the outer sense, and the still more amazing intercommunication between the soul and its material environment through a semi-material agency;—when we consider all this, and the various other marvels which physiologists have in later times brought to our knowledge, would it not seem as if this chiefest work of creation should be destined to a duration proportioned to the exquisite completeness of its mechanism? Yet we are confronted by the swift transition from developed maturity to entire annihilation of bodily functions,—the body itself being then laid away in the earth to decompose into its original elements. No part of it is ever to be used again. Its whole purpose has apparently been accomplished. When to this is added that by far the greater part of the human race do not attain complete development, when further progress is thus arrested, and disintegration ensues; and that of those who reach maturity, comparatively few have allotted to them a protraction of life thereafter sufficient for the accomplishment of any end justly corresponding with the capability of this sensorial organism—we inquire in vain for a solution that shall wholly relieve our perplexity. The whole subject appears to be shrouded in mystery.

II. *Pain of body—for what salutary purpose was it intended.*— Allow the limited class of cases in which pain may be deemed *premonitory* or *prophylactic*—a warning against more dangerous impending harm; allow also the instances in which impaired health is restored by means of reiterated admonitions of pain consequent upon transgression of sanitary laws, and conceding in these a precautionary or remedial use, what are we to think of pain when it becomes inveterate by the ascendency of disease, and so remains until the close of life? Is it a satisfactory answer to say that this is intended as a warning that should put us on our guard against the incipient causes of disease? But how often is that inception from a naturally feeble organism, or from hereditary predisposition, or from an environment of pestilential elements, or from involuntary subjection to an uncongenial climate, or other unfavorable conditions.

Or, again, is it more satisfactory to suppose that we are in this life in a *perpetual probation*, and that pain is an element of such probation? But, to make this an entirely rational solution, there should be some correspondence between the pain and the cause of its infliction. If it was always meted in exact proportion to wrong doing, if the wicked suffered penalty from which the righteous were exempt, or if the penalty was measured by the extent of the transgression, there would then be apparent a law resting upon a salutary or at least a comprehensible basis. Such, however, is not the uniform tenor of human life. So far as respects what in a worldly view is deemed desirable—success in attaining the objects of general pursuit—it has ever been observed that men who are unrestrained by strict principles of right, accomplish it in largest proportion. Such is the general course in the pursuit of political power, and the like is seen in the conditions of private life, the accumulation of wealth, social position, etc. True it is that many and striking instances of retribution for wrong doing are also seen, yet perhaps not preponderant over the instances of suffering by those who have done no wrong, or not such as relatively deserved the suffering. In the latter category are to be included not merely the wrong done directly to good men by the devices of the evil-minded, and the penalty suffered by the innocent through prejudice or mistake, but also the evils entailed by hereditary descent, or accidents of early association. Thus the offspring of a profligate parent undergoes the life-long penalty of pain of body, and children born in poverty are predestined to bear privation from which the best moral qualities do not exempt them save in exceptional cases.

Or if even it should be conceded that upon the whole a good life *tends* more to insure real happiness than a bad one, which is the postulate of Bishop Butler, and admitting the force of his argument that this may be a better discipline than it virtue was always and immediately rewarded, and vice as surely and speedily punished, there still remains the unquestionable fact that the larger proportion of mankind are cut off too early in life to derive an instructive lesson from their own experience or from their limited observation of life in general. There is also the additional fact that the supposed tendency of virtue and vice is not so marked, even as observed by the wisest men, as to furnish in itself a motive of much influence on the great mass of mankind, certainly not a sufficient motive for the resistance of the powerful incentives to evil by which they are environed. On the contrary the general deduction by thoughtful men in every age has been that human life, regarded merely in its present earthly relations, is subject to a preponderance of evil, at all events to this extent, that its continuance is not to be desired, as expressed in the saying which Aristotle quoted and approved, "that it would have been best not to have been born, and next to that, it was best to die." We have thus a second enigma which has perpetually tasked human speculation to solve.

III. *A kindred inquiry and of like difficulty is the meaning and purpose of the apparent suffering which is the lot of all brute races, and of some of these largely in excess of what is endured by man.* Look at the countless myriads of holocausts daily sacrificed for the use of man, in which a vast amount of suffering is involved by the want even of that measure of humanity which would be feasible in this slaughter to lighten the pain of the victims. Again, look at the cruelty exercised upon beasts of draft or burden by brutish men. But still harder is the lot of wild but harmless animals, who are the prey of fiercer and stronger carnivora. What a vast field of violent destruction is there in the forests and prairies of the North and the jungles of the tropics—everywhere entire races of animals that subsist by the devouring of other races—from the polar bear and the wolf of the prairie to the lion and tiger of Africa and Asia. It has been argued in extenuation that the process of destruction is speedy—that the life of the victim is quickly extinguished by the carnivorous enemy—and this is called a kind providence. I doubt if this is uniformly true. Beasts of prey may indulge in a luxury which human carnivora have found attractive.*

Again, animals which are preyed upon sometimes escape in a mutilated condition. The antelope or giraffe is often pierced by the arrow or spear of the African hunter, and may carry with him the barbed missile fixed in his flesh, and suffering agony therefrom, but powerless to remove it. The elephant killed by the European hunter not unfrequently shows previous wounds made by the rifle bullet, which had been long festering. So the tendons of the hind leg are sometimes cut by the agile Hamran, whereby the huge animal is disabled from motion; but unless both legs are thus cut he may linger till death ensues by starvation or loss of blood, or become a prey to the lion and hyena that are watching his exhaustion.

Wherefore are the subject races thus doomed? No auxiliary purpose of probation can be predicated of them, unless upon the hypothesis that they have a future existence. But even this fails of an entire solution. There is no apparent correspondence or necessary connection between the present suffering and the future equivalent, or in other words, there is nothing probationary in the present suffering, as it can lead to no result without a change of organism. To suppose that there shall be a gratuitous award in another life that shall be a compensation for the misery suffered in this, would be meaningless, if the one is not the proper sequence of or in some concatenation with the other.†

IV. *Pauperism.*—So uniform is the encroachment of every people upon the necessaries of life—the saying of Christ, "The poor ye have always with you," has constant verification under every condition of national life. When a people is impoverished by tyrannical power, whether of foreign rulers or of indigenous despotism, the proportion of the very poor is of course larger, but under the best form of government and the amplest prosperity in industry and trade, there is, and ever must be, a class who are unprovided with what may be deemed neces-

---

* We have the testimony of *Bruce* and *Parkyns*, both of high repute as travellers, that the Abyssinian has a special relish for the raw flesh of animals, cut off before life is extinct, and that it was formerly the practice at feasts to serve slices from the living cow, the poor creature being thus subjected to a lingering death while the savage feast continued.

† The theory of *Descartes*, that the lower animals are automatic, exhibiting actions like those of conscious beings, but in fact without sensation, would, if it had any basis, relieve the question we have discussed from all difficulty. But that theory has until recently been with general unanimity regarded as wholly visionary and baseless. Professor *Huxley* has, in a late address delivered before the British Scientific Association (Aug. 25, 1874), attempted to give some color to the assumption; but the tests which he referred to in support of it apply equally to rational as to irrational creatures, and inasmuch as *we have the consciousness of pain*, his argument fails to show the absence of pain in the brute. His conclusion, however, though he declares a strong partiality for the doctrine of *Descartes*, is that "probably the lower animals, though they may not possess that sort of consciousness which we have ourselves, yet have it in a form proportional to the comparative development of the organ of that consciousness, and foreshadow, more or less dimly, those feelings which we possess ourselves." This, he thinks, would involve comparatively less suffering of the brute, and that it would be safer to adopt it than the more congenial hypothesis that the lower animals are altogether insensible.

saries, or in other words, who are dependent to some extent upon charitable aid for the common comforts of life. This class is the first to suffer in times of scarcity; famine, of course, reaches beyond to the less destitute. But the question we have to do with is the incessant, irrepressible advance of population beyond the regular means of subsistence. In China, where there is a more uniform level of the mass of population than in any other country, there is such accumulated aggregation of the people that the subsistence of a large proportion is stinted in the extremest degree, their diet having been reduced to a grade very little above that of lower animals. Corresponding with this is the grade of humanity which is also reduced to a sensuous nature from which the moral element is almost wholly excluded.

In England, on the other hand, where has been developed the largest freedom, political and religious, of which there is a precedent in civilized states (with the exception of our own, which, however, is but an offshoot from that), while there has been, perhaps, the greatest intelligence and highest degree of comfort ever enjoyed, yet it has been limited to one class. Another and far more numerous class is seen in direct juxtaposition and contrast with the first,—struggling for bare subsistence, depressed into cheerless poverty and sequent ignorance. Such are the manufacturing operatives of England and the peasantry of Ireland.

No adequate counteraction has yet been found for this excess of population over the means of living, or rather for the deficient ability of the many to avoid being straightened for subsistence. Political economists have speculated in vain. The self-restraining proposition of *Mill* (that is, the voluntary renunciation of marriage or of its incident the propagation of children), which he announces as a finality, —the last and only effectual remedy—is in fact utterly powerless. Self-restraint, as was amply proved by *Malthus*, is most inoperative in the very class by whom it is most needed.

This inequality being thus by necessity to be regarded as an inevitable condition of humanity, another hypothesis has been propounded, which, recognizing the actual condition, and assuming that it is irremediable, asserts that the whole course of human experience *has reference only to the advancement of the race, without regard to individuals.* In other words, the theory is, that the process of natural selection, by which improvement is wrought in plants and lower animals—the weak being displaced by the strong—the inferior being gradually extinguished, applies also to human progress, that civilization means the advancement of a few at the expense of the many—that great achievement in war, science or art, is for the benefit of a privileged class, that social happiness is the peculium of a select number, the *αριςτοι*, and wretchedness the inheritance of the vastly more numerous *proletaries, serfs, and slaves.**

---

* *Gregg* insists that the law of natural selection would have been sufficient to prevent over-population, and to have secured the progressive advancement of the race, had it not been counteracted by certain elements of civilization. That is to say, that the strong would have overpowered the weak, and propagated

This cheerless view of human life is wholly antagonistic to the Scripture doctrine, by which we are taught that the *individual* is every thing, and the *race* nothing, except as embracing the aggregation of individuals. Nor is our natural instinct and rational deduction less decided against such hypothesis. The mere fact that every individual of the race is endowed with faculties susceptible of an expansion of power to an undefined extent, and having functions that reach far beyond the present environment, enforces an inevitable belief that such endowment was not without a purpose; and that it would be derogatory to divine wisdom to suppose such purpose limited to the contingences of the present brief existence. Still more derogatory would be the assumption that *one* is trampled down and crushed out, merely to make way for *another*, or is subjected to a life of misery, only in subservience to the enjoyment of another.

V. *What is to be concluded upon this review.*—Are we left to a chilling negation of the active faith which is the essential element of all human progress, to frail conjecture, to mere hypothesis without trust or hope? The question is not to be answered by counter hypotheses, or by other conjectures. We are to seek for logical deductions from established facts. The following course of argument will, I think, lay the groundwork of a more satisfactory belief, or, at least, like the finger-post, indicate the right direction for inquiry.

1. The wisdom and power displayed in the creation of man, and the marvellous completeness of his structure, demonstrate that such creation was a deliberate plan; and again, that there could not possibly have been a mistake. What was intended must have been accomplished. The creative power was adequate to do what was undertaken.* Nor can it be supposed that there was defect of knowledge. All the consequences of this introduction of a new power superior to

---

only those like themselves. But civilization extends protection to the weak, and encourages propogation of their likes; and by a reversal of the proper order of nature, these are even more prolific than the better class. The rich have no occasion for apprehension as to the support of their offspring, even if they should be weak in body; and the very poor are reckless of consequences, propagating without forecast large families, that must struggle with the like hardships that have been borne by the progenitors.

* Mr. Gregg denies that we are warranted in assuming *omnipotence* as an attribute of the Supreme Being. It is, he says, incomprehensible how infinite love and illimitable power should have created such a world as this, but that we have no authority for the belief that there is unlimited power. Compared with that of man, the power of God may be said to be immeasurable, but not therefore infinite. That we are to conceive of him as *conditioned*—hampered, it may be, by the attributes of the material on which he had to operate, bound, probably, by laws inherent in the nature of that material.

This reasoning presupposes the eternity of matter—in other words, that the Creator had to take it as already existing, and to use it subject to laws which he could not reverse.

Tyndall, though not in express terms avowing his belief in the eternity of matter, yet maintains that there is inherent in it *a potency adequate to the production of every form of life;* which potency is contained in the primitive elements called *atoms*, in the language of Democritus and Epicurus. These atoms or molecules he supposes to act by a law of their own, and the other proposition seems not remote, viz., that this law is irreversible. (*Address before British Sci. Ass., Aug.*, 1874.)

any pre-existing among the works of creation must have been forecasted through the vast future, and duly weighed.

2. There being then in the mind of the Creator a prevision of the entire course of human history at the time of the creation, it follows by necessity that the design had in view was worthy of his wisdom, but that to understand that design there must be a like knowledge of such history, either by prophetic vision or by actual fulfilment. The former sort of knowledge, even in the most inspired of our race, has been fragmentary and of trivial extent compared to the measureless entirety. The latter has been infinitesimally brief as compared with the entire future of man. It is not necessary in this connection to take into account the immortality of the soul. The mere earthly continuity of the human race in its successive generations, is projected into the vast perspective beyond finite calculation. Six thousand years of existence, involved as that existence is through that entire period in anomalies—seemingly irreconcilable contradictions—in wickedness and misery, confusion and uncertainty, determines nothing against omniscient judgment. The entire experience of the past may be but as the faint and indistinct coruscation before the dawn.

3. Again Bishop Butler argues well that we see on every hand evidence that the creation of which we have knowledge, or rather with which we are immediately environed, is but a part of a greater system, with which we are connected in some way now unknown. What seems to us inconsistent may have consistency in its relation to the entirety. Even the apparent failure of the human organism to accomplish in this life what may be attained by the possible expansion of powers with which it is gifted in its double nature, the *physical* and *psychical*, and the unexplained waste of that marvellous organism by its early disintegration, may have a solution in an unexpected way. It may perhaps be in some development like what has been suggested by psychologists, viz., the existence of an intermediate nature called by them *nerve spirit*, which it is assumed retains the lineaments of the present visible corporeity and carries with it at death all the sensuous functions which have appertained to this outward form.

This, indeed, it may be objected, is resorting to hypothesis which we have proposed to waive. But it is not necessary to assume this or any other hypothesis as absolutely true. The argument is that an explanation may be supposed which would solve the enigma. Concede that it may not in reality be the true explanation, yet if there can be any within the range even of conjecture, we may justly assume that some solution, whether it be that or some other, can be found. It is, in fact, an inevitable presumption from the wisdom and power of the Creator. There can be no greater presumption of anything in the future than that human existence will be developed as part of a plan that in its entirety is consistent in all its parts.

Nor does this mode of reasoning subvert the previous argument in respect to individuality. That argument rests upon the *apparent display of purpose as to individuals.* The unexplained phenomena involved in individual life, we may justly argue, will have a rational exposition in their relations with other incidents of cosmical life. Nor does this necessarily involve the sacrifice of one being for the advancement of another, if such a result could by any possibility be avoided by Divine wisdom. But any such inevitable restriction or disability cannot be proved.

4. The foregoing presentation is in conformity with the Scripture doctrine, which is that in all men, even the most debased, there are elements of a better nature; a susceptibility by an appeal to which there can be restoration to purity, as if by a re-leaven, or excrementative rejection of the effete, which appeal is made to every individual man by the awakening power revealed in religious experience. The image or likeness of God, in which man is said to have been originally created, though much defaced, is not wholly obliterated. The vilest of men were called to repentance by Christ and his apostles, and converts were made even among those who were outcasts from society. They did not, it is true, answer questions growing out of the conflictions or contradictions of human life. "Did this man sin, or his parents, that he was born blind?" was a question that touched upon one of the great perplexities of human speculation, viz., of suffering by the innocent for the misconduct of others, and particularly the hereditary descent of maladies of mind or body. The answer was to the effect that the blindness was not a penalty for sin, but a dispensation of God for a wise purpose.* But on the other hand, nothing is more clearly taught in the Scriptures than the individuality of man in the sight of God, as in the case of the beggar Lazarus, carried to Abraham's bosom† a parable illustrating the personal care of God over the most humble and down-trodden of the race; the prodigal restored to his place in the family on his penitent return from the lowest profligacy;‡ the woman who anointed the feet of Jesus, of whom he said, "Her sins, which are many, are forgiven, for she loved much." § Notice also the denunciation of the self-righteous Pharisees—"The publicans and harlots shall go into the kingdom before you." ‖

If such, then, is the regard which God has for the lowest in the scale of humanity, will His providence fail in any of the exigencies of life? Will the sufferings of any of His creatures be unmarked, if not even a sparrow fall to the ground without his notice? (Mat. 10, xxiv.) And if a cup of cold water given to one of the *little ones* shall not be without reward (Mat. 10, xlii), and "If any shall offend one of such *little ones*, it were better that a millstone were hanged about his neck, and that he were drowned in the depths of the sea" (Mat. 18, vi.), how can it be that God himself will not extend to these least of His children a supervision and protection? Shall we not rather have faith that all things shall work for the good of His creatures? All the incidents of

---

* "Neither hath this man sinned, nor his parents; but that the word of God might be made manifest in him." (Mat. 9, ii.) Of the same purport was the answer as to the Galileans, sacrificed by Pilate—"Suppose ye that these were sinners above all the Galileans, because they suffered such things? I tell you nay; but except ye repent, ye shall all likewise perish."

† Luke 16, xxii.

‡ Luke, ch. 15.

§ Luke, ch. 7.

‖ Mat. 21, xxxi.

life are under the direction of God, and are connected with the future. There can be no mere chance; no intermission of Divine oversight; all that we call *casualties*, all that we now deem misfortunes and miseries, belong to the regular procession of events, and will of course not be allowed to conflict with the purpose of the Creator as affecting every individual soul.*

PREVENTING SMOKE.—The atmosphere of our large towns, where people live by hundreds of thousands all the year round, is not yet guarded against needless pollution by smoke zealously as it ought to be. Greater exertions are due than have yet been made toward maintaining and improving salubrity. Smoke occurs when fresh coal is thrown suddenly, in too large quantities at once, on a hot fire. By extreme care a fireman may throw coal into the furnace so gradually as to make very little smoke; but mechanical arrangements for introducing constantly and uniformly the new supply of fresh coal have been devised, and several of these have been such as to reduce the smoke emitted to almost nothing.

I have seen in the neighborhood of Glasgow, at Thornliebank, one method which is applied to about thirty ordinary 40 horse-power boilers, in which upwards of 100 tons of coal are daily burned, and from the chimneys of which not more smoke is emitted than from many a kitchen fire. This method is under the patent of Messrs. Vickers, of Liverpool, and it seems to work very well. It was introduced at a time when coal was exceedingly high in price, as much to effect economy in fuel as to prevent smoke; and although the first cost was somewhat about £130 per boiler, the proprietor considers himself to be already more than repaid for his outlay, as a saving of fully 12 per cent. in the fuel consumed was effected. At the same works I have also seen in operation the method of Messrs.. Haworth & Hosfall, of Tormorden, which has, I am told, in certain circumstances, some advantages over the other. In this, as in the other, the coal is fed uniformly by mechanical arrangements. The mechanism is different in the two cases, but the result in the motion communicated to the coal is very much alike. The bed of coal, which is gradually supplied in front, is caused to travel along the bars towards the inner end of the furnace, and the combustion proceeds in a very uniform manner in conditions highly favorable to economy of fuel, and without the emission of almost any visible smoke.—Prof. JAMES THOMPSON, C.E., LL.D.—*Address before the British Association.*

---

* There is a touching pathos in the words—"Come unto me, all ye that labor and are heavy laden, and I will give you rest." (Mat. 11, xxviii,) A sympathy for human suffering is expressed—a sympathy more intense than we can realize—and which extends to every individual sufferer. We find here nothing of the heart-chilling speculation that regards men only as a race, a select part of which is to be elevated by the pain and destruction of the rest. A fitting commentary on these words is furnished by the exhortation of the apostle: "Therefore, let all them who suffer according to the will of God commit the keeping of their souls unto Him in well doing, as unto a faithful Creator." (1 Pet., 4, xix.) All may rest in the assurance that God will not forget any of His creatures, but will fulfil all that is implied in the capacities and susceptibilities with which He has endowed them. Yet this, of course, must be subject to the condition that we hold such assurance "in well doing."

ON SOME DIFFICULTIES CONNECTED WITH HAND-FEEDING OF INFANTS.

By EUSTACE SMITH, M. D., London, Physician to H. M. the King of the Belgians, Physician to the East London Children's Hospital, Assistant-Physician to the Victoria Park Hospital for Diseases of the Chest.

In a previous paper (see SANITARIAN, Vol. II., p. 444) a short sketch was given of the principles upon which the hand-feeding of infants should be conducted, and some plain rules were laid down, attention to which, in a large majority of cases, will insure a successful result.

Cases, however, occasionally happen where special difficulties are met with. We sometimes find that cow's milk, however carefully it may be prepared and administered, cannot be digested. Soon after being swallowed it ferments, and either excites vomiting or produces great flatulence and discomfort, while the general nutrition of the child becomes slowly impaired. Whenever this occurs we should be careful to satisfy ourselves that the fault really lies in the milk, and not in any recklessness in feeding or neglect of cleanliness in the feeding apparatus. Milk put into a sour bottle soon begins to ferment, and therefore especial care should be taken that the bottle is thoroughly washed out immediately after the meal; and before it is again used the absence of sourness should be carefully tested by the sense of smell. Attention should also be paid to the time of feeding and to the quantity given at each meal.

The incapacity for digesting ordinary cow's milk may be a natural peculiarity of the child, but it is more often a merely temporary infirmity. In the former case no amount of preparation seems capable of rendering the milk digestible. So long as it is being taken the child wastes slowly, he is restless and uneasy by day, and excessively fretful by night, and appears to be tormented constantly by abdominal pain. In such cases, if there are objections to a wet-nurse, recourse must be had to the milk of some other animal, and preference should be given to a milk which contains a smaller proportion of casein than is found in the milk of the cow, such as goats' or asses' milk. Either of these will do, and will often agree well, especially if a third or fourth part of barley-water be added; or a teaspoonful of Mellin's patent extract may be dissolved in either of these milks diluted with an equal part of water. Goat's milk has the strong flavor peculiar to the animal, but this is often not objected to by infants; besides, it may be removed to a certain extent by boiling. Asses' milk is sometimes found to have slight laxative properties, but in this case, also, boiling the milk will often remove this disadvantage. A milk which is very useful for weakly infants and others who cannot digest ordinary milk, is obtained by milking the cow after the usual daily supply has been withdrawn. The residuum thus obtained goes in some parts of the country by the name of "strippings." It is very rich in cream but comparatively poor in curd. One part of this diluted with two parts of water will in almost all cases agree well; or one part of plain water may be replaced by barley-water if there appears to be any difficulty in digesting the casein.

It is in cases such as these, too, that condensed milk is so often successful. Condensed milk is merely cow's milk deprived of a considerable proportion of its water, and sweetened, in order that it may keep better, with cane sugar. This milk, given freely diluted, will often agree when fresh cow's milk cannot be borne. At first the strength used should be in the proportion of one teaspoonful of the milk to a teacupful of warm water.

The difficulty in digesting curd is not always limited to the casein of cow's milk: it is sometimes found in a child nursed at the breast, even when suckled by its mother. Such a case lately came under my own notice in a child of seven months old—a little boy—who had been suffering for some weeks from severe abdominal pains. He was excessively peevish and fretful, and at night would wake up with a scream, and twist about his body, evidently under the influence of severe griping pain. His bowels were very confined, and the motions consisted of hard round light-colored lumps. The child's nutrition had begun to suffer, for although he looked well his flesh was becoming soft and flabby. He was reared entirely by the breast, and his mother was a very healthy young lady, with a plentiful supply of milk. Aperients had been found to relieve the child for a time, but the symptoms always returned very shortly afterwards. Whenever the breast was stopped for a few days he immediately improved, but relapsed again directly suckling was resumed. The child was evidently suffering through his inability to digest the curd of his mother's milk, and it became a matter of great importance to enable him to do so, otherwise he would have to be weaned and fed in a different way. The mother had herself, by taking saline and other medicines, and by making many modifications in her diet under medical advice, endeavored to alter the quality of the milk, but without success.

Several methods of remedying the evil were tried. The intervals between the times of suckling were increased, so as to give a longer period for digestion, but this change had no effect whatever.

Alternate meals of barley-water were then given from a bottle. By this means the quantity of milk taken by the child in the course of the day was diminished, and the interval between the times of taking the breast was still further increased. No improvement, however, followed the alteration; the griping pains still continued, and the constant fretfulness of the child was most distressing to its mother.

The plan was at last adopted of giving the child barley-water from a bottle immediately before he took the breast, in the hope that by this means the milk might be diluted directly it reached the stomach. This method succeeded perfectly, and the child had no further unpleasant symptoms.

Milk—even human milk—often becomes indigestible, not because it is too rich in curd, but because the child is suffering from some gastric derangement which has temporarily reduced its digestive power. In such cases the mother is sometimes recommended to wean the child, from the mistaken notion that her milk is not suited to the baby. Such a gastric derangement may even date from the time of birth, and so long as it continues may occasion great perplexity, as no food will agree until the disorder is removed.

A. B., a fine child aged eight weeks, was stated to have been persistently sick after food ever since its birth. He had been suckling for the first seven weeks, but invariably vomited the milk shortly after taking the breast. A week before I saw the child he had been weaned—to his mother's great regret—by order of the medical attendant, and had been fed upon condensed milk diluted in the proportion of a teaspoonful to the half-tumbler of water. This, however, he vomited, as he had done the breast milk. He was stated to smell sour occasionally, and when he vomited the ejected matters were discharged with considerable force, but without any retching. The bowels also were loose, and the motions consisted principally of undigested milk. The child looked pretty well, but had a slight yellowish tint of the skin. He was losing flesh fast.

In this case the cause of the indigestion was evidently catarrh of the stomach, which dated from the time of birth. It was explained to the mother that her milk was not unsuited to the child, but that it disagreed temporarily, as did all other food, on account of the condition of the digestive organs. She was recommended to begin nursing again immediately, but as her milk had partially disappeared, the breast was limited to two meals a day, and a supplementary diet composed of one teaspoonful of Mellin's extract dissolved in one part of "strippings" and two of water was ordered every two hours. At the same time suitable measures were taken to improve the condition of the digestive organs. Under this treatment the vomiting soon ceased, the gastric derangement quickly subsided, and as the secretion of milk returned in considerable quantity, the child after a short time required little food in addition to that furnished by his mother.

The two preceding cases will illustrate the difficulty often experienced in rearing children even when nursed at the mother's breast. They have been also introduced as affording a proof that there is no specific quality in human milk rendering it especially appropriate to the diet of a young child other than that of holding its curd in a form in which it is most easy of digestion by the infant. If this quality be absent, or if from some temporary derangement the digestive power of the child be reduced, the effect is the same whether he be fed from the breast or from a feeding-bottle. In either case he soon shows all the signs of labored digestion, and unless some change be quickly made his nutrition becomes seriously impaired. The occurrence of gastric catarrh is the principal difficulty to be contended with in the hand-feeding of infants. If a food be continued after it has begun to disagree, a catarrah of the delicate mucous membrane is almost invariably set up. When this derangement is once established a change in the diet will not be necessarily followed by improvement, as the tendency to the fermentation of food, which is one of the chief characteristics of the disorder—owing to a large increase in the alkaline mucous secretion—still remains, and is encouraged by every additional quantity of fermentable matter which may be swallowed. A sour smell from the child's mouth is a certain sign that this fermenting process is in existence, and measures should at once be taken to put a stop to so injurious a condition. A reduction in the quantity of milk is often an essential step in such treatment; and if the case be a severe one, and the fermenting process active, it may be necessary for a day or two entirely to exclude milk from the diet. Its place must be taken by mixtures of whey and barley-water in equal parts; freshly-made veal broth (half a pound of meat to the pint) and barley-water (equal parts); or Mellin's extract dissolved in whey, thickened with a little isinglass or gelatine, or in barley-water.

Barley-water is very useful in these cases, for it supplies the necessary *consistence* to the food. A child may refuse a liquid if it be made too thin. Infants who turn away from "Mellin's Extract" dissolved in whey alone, will often take it eagerly when a certain proportion of barley-water, or of gelatine, is added to the mixture. A food, to be taken readily by babies, must possess a suitable consistence.

After a day or two, and when all signs of fermentation have ceased, the milk may be returned to, but it should be given cautiously at first, and in small quantities, and the first symptom of discomfort is a sign that the quantity must be reduced.

Hand-feeding differs from suckling by requiring rather more attention on the part of the nurse, and some tact in accurately adapting the quality of the food to the powers and requirements of the baby. To be thoroughly successful there are two points which it is important to bear continually in mind:—The first is the one which was so strongly insisted on in a former paper: viz., that we should be careful to provide the infant with a diet which not only contains in itself all the elements necessary to nutrition, but which also presents them in a form in which the child is able with perfect ease to digest and assimilate them. The second point to be remembered is that the digestive organs of an infant are excessively delicate and liable to be deranged by apparently trifling causes. His digestive power, therefore, is subject to frequent variations corresponding accurately to his state of health, and a diet which is appropriate one day may be unsuitable the next. Unusual irritability and fretfulness, abdominal discomfort and griping pains, vomiting or diarrhœa—any of these symptoms clearly indicates that the digestive powers are for the time below par, and that some modification in the diet is required.

If attention be paid to the directions given in this and a previous paper, the successful rearing of an infant "by hand" will be found to be no very difficult matter. It requires, it is true, intelligence and tact, but above all it requires *vigilance*. With proper care, and with ordinary knowledge of the requirements and capabilities of a young child—such knowledge, in fact, as it is the object of these papers to supply—a mother may adopt the practice of hand-feeding with full confidence in a satisfactory result.—*The Sanitary Record.*

DIPHTHERIA.

PROCEEDINGS OF THE PUBLIC HEALTH ASSOCIATION OF NEW YORK.

A regular meeting of the Public Health Association of New York, was held Dec. 10, 1874, at the lecture-room of Prof. Charles F. Chandler, at the School of Mines, on 49th street, between Madison and Fourth avenues, to take into consideration the present prevalence of Diphtheria. The large room was more than filled, and this first meeting of the association held at the School of Mines, demonstrated not only the interest felt by the medical profession in the objects and methods of the association, but also the perfect adaptation of this beautiful lecture-room to all the ordinary purposes of scientific illustration and demonstration.

The president, Prof. Charles F. Chandler, LL.D., occupied the chair. On recommendation of the Executive Committee, the following persons were unanimously elected active members: Jerome Walker, M D., James C. Bayles, Esq., J. E. Comfort, M.D., and Paul F. Munde, M.D. The first paper of the evening was on:

THE CAUSES AND NATURE OF DIPHTHERIA, WITH A REVIEW OF THE BACTERIAN THEORY.

By J. Lewis Smith, M. D.

Dr. Smith spoke substantially as follows: Since the death of Bretonneau, some twenty-five years ago, it has been abundantly proved that diphtheria is communicable otherwise than by innoculation, for the result of numerous chemical and microscopic investigations has been to nearly demonstrate that the disease is contagious by contact with the patient, through exhalations from the surface and through his breath. And it is thought that the cause of diphtheria has been found in the existence upon the diseased parts in the diphtheritic cases, of small vegetable parasites, which are endowed with life and motion, and which have been designated *bacteria*. These parasites increase in number as the disease increases in intensity, and if diphtheritic inflammation attacks any surface which is covered by the parasites, which cause certain other diseases, such as catarrh, the parasites diminish and disappear, as though deprived of the required nutriment. And on the other hand, when diphtheria disappears, other vegetable forms may succeed. The grayish-white spots which appear upon inflamed surfaces at the beginning of diphtheria, are entirely composed of these bacteria, which have come in contact with the mucous membrane, and have adhered to it, and which, unless prevented, will multiply rapidly, and then by burrowing through the tissues, will infect the whole system. The reason why diphtheria primarily and chiefly affects the surfaces of the nose and throat is that the air which contains the germs of the bacteria constantly passes over these surfaces. The important conclusion to be deduced from these facts is that diphtheria is entirely local in its commencement, and is amenable to local measures. This bacterian theory, thus established by microscopical investigations, receives some support in clinical observations from the fact that diphtheria prevails most in localities which are favorable to the development of low forms of animal and vegetable life, such as filthy and crowded apartments, along streets and alleys, and along low grounds where vegetable and animal refuse collects. Additional confirmation of the bacterian theory was found in the fact that diphtheria begins in one spot, and then may be easily treated and cured, and that it is only in a subsequent stage that it infects the whole system, and becomes a generally dangerous disease. But the speaker thought there was another factor in the propagation of diphtheria, which the advocates of the bacterian system had too much overlooked, namely, a predisposing condition of the system. This, he thought, was shown by the fact that sometimes bacteria may be found in the air of localities where diphtheria has not occurred, and in such numbers as to force the belief that they had frequently passed over the fauces in the inspired air. Bacteria are sometimes, too, found in the mouth in perfectly well persons, and sometimes, when breathed, they cause no inflammation in the lungs. These considerations, and other minor ones noticed by the speaker in clinical experience, justified, he thought, the opinion that diphtheria is, in certain cases, a constitutional malady in its circumstances, while in other cases, if not in most, it is primarily local, and only subsequently constitutional. In conclusion the speaker said that diphtheria had scarcely been absent from New York for a single season during the last ten or fifteen years; the primary form predominating during diphtheritic epidemics, and the secondary form in the intervals and during epidemics of scarlet fever and measles, it being a peculiarity of diphtheria that instead of being incompatible with other morbid processes it is likely to engraft itself upon them. He thought the disease in question might fairly be called epidemic in this city. Diphtheritic inflammation attacks by preference such inflamed surfaces as are deprived of their covering of skin, and in this he found an explanation of the frequent complicati on of scarlatina and measles by diphtheria. For in those eruptive diseases an inflammation is already established upon the fauces which affords a nest in which the bacteria, or diphtheritic virus, might lodge and develop. Then, alluding to the anti-hygienic conditions which produce diphtheria, the speaker said that when it appeared in New York in 1857 and 1858, after an absence of more than fifty years, some of the first and most severe cases seen by himself occurred in the upper part of the city, along the old water-courses, where, in consequence of street grading, water was stagnant, and impregnated with decaying animal and vegetable matter. In fifteen years' treatment of diphtheria, the speaker said, he had not observed an instance in which it appeared to be communicated from house to house by the clothing, as is sometimes the case with scarlet fever and measles. When it spreads from house to house, or even from room to room in the same house, it is almost always carried by the visits of persons having diphtheritic inflammation. The area of contagiousness of diphtheria is therefore confined to the room in which the patient resides.

A brief discussion of some of the pathological points advanced in the paper of Dr. Smith followed, in which Prof. Edward Curtis and Dr.

Louis Elsberg took part; and Prof. Chandler exhibited, by means of a powerful magic lantern, numerous photographic representations of the microscopical appearances of bacteria.

A brief and suggestive paper was then read by Dr. George Bayles, on "*The Public Sanitary Control of Diphtheria.*" This was followed by:—

FACTS IN THE HISTORY OF DIPHTHERIA IN THIS CITY AND COUNTRY.

By ELISHA HARRIS, M.D.

That diphtheria is not a new disease, and that its recent modes of prevalence are not new or in any manner unusual, is clearly proved by the medical writings of the best observers of disease. While in Europe the records of this malady extend back to the very dawning of scientific medicine, and through the last four centuries its fatal prevalence has been vividly described under various names, and its persistence and fatality have been entered in the historical records of numerous places over a vast range, from the Mediterranean to the North Sea, the history of diphtheria as the "putrid sore throat," the "malignant angina," the "angina suffocativa," etc., has been written in New York and various places in America from early colonial times.

As it is not important to our present instruction that we should search and recite the old records, we may as well proceed at once to the experience of the present generation of medical men, who have been enabled to describe this malady under the appellation we now give to it—diphtheria. Dr. Craik's description of the sudden and fatal instance of this disorder in the case of Gen. Washington in 1798; the account given by Dr. Jacob Ogden of the prevalence of it in the vicinity of New York in the middle decades of the last century, and Dr. Samuel Bard's recitals of his study of the "suffocative angina," as it prevailed in the City and Colony of New York in the sixth decade of that century—now upward of 100 years ago—will always be referred to with quite as great satisfaction as respects accuracy and clearness of definition as we can derive from the descriptions of "putrid sore throat," the "malignant cynanche," or the "black tongue," of which alarming descriptions and alarming examples occurred in many places some thirty years ago.

The first fatal case of diphtheria, certified and registered by this name in the city of New York, occurred in the practice of Dr. William Maxwell, a most trustworthy diagnostician, on the 20th of February, 1850. The second and third cases occurred on the 25th, the fourth was registered nearly a fortnight later, and before the end of the year fifty-three deaths by this disease had been recorded in the city. But this disease had actually been prevailing, in a mild way, and was recognized all through the summer and autumn of 1858, and the winter of 1859. Dr. Abraham Jacobi had found that five of the forty-five patients suffering from a peculiar throat affection, etc., at the German Dispensary, in the children's department, were cases of diphtheria, and before the end of 1859, there had been 112 cases recognized at that institution, and during the year 1859, there were eighty-eight more of these cases.

Dr. Whittlesey, on Randall's Island, had a few cases among his 500 nursery children during that time, and recalled a few instances of this malady which had supervened upon measles, and those were instances of diphtheritic ophthalmia. The supervening disease killed the patients, but they appear in mortality returns as cases of measles.

This city and its vicinity suffered thus lightly until near the end of 1859, when all, or nearly all, family and dispensary physicians noticed and commented upon the presence of diphtheritic symptoms, and the specks and patches of the characteristic deposits in the mouth and fauces; yet, up to the close of 1860, the certified causes of death continued to exhibit evidences of hesitation and much confusion in the diagnosis of this disease. Croup, scarlatinous angina, and numerous other kinds of angina were certified by physicians who had not become familiar with this disease or posted themselves in regard to its history and characteristics. But in January, 1860, diphtheria became very prevalent, and was widely distributed over the city, and fourteen deaths from it were registered in the Bureau of Vital Statistics. The malady was not only epidemic, but exceedingly malignant in certain localities and particular dwellings. The abstract of the mortality which has occurred from this disease presents ample proof that from the beginning of the year 1860 to the end of 1864 diphtheria had become a dangerous enemy to life in our city.

During the two years, 1858–'59, when this disease was gaining its new foothold in the city of New York, it had more quickly become epidemic in numerous smaller cities. It appeared in the city of Albany early in the spring of 1858, and in that half of the city which is situated south of State street it almost decimated the children between two and seven years of age. There were upward of 2,000 cases of the disease recognized in the whole city during the first ten months of its prevalence, and there were in that period 179 deaths from it recorded.

During all that period this malady made no mark in the city of Troy—only seven miles distant, and virtually a suburb—in which the local and domestic conditions of the population seemed far less propitious than those in Albany. But the infection had not yet become planted there. Its prevalence had almost ceased in the former before it commenced in the latter city.

During the years 1860 and 1861, diphtheria prevailed as a local epidemic—often only as a neighborhood and house epidemic—in hundreds of populous towns, from New York to Nebraska, and from Maine to Alabama. Regarded, usually, as an epidemic that depended upon atmospheric causes—the doctrine of fatalism too often—this malady struck down one and another of the noblest physicians, and hundreds upon hundreds of child visitors by its infectious quality—its communicable poison—in the sick-room. The death of the esteemed Dr. Frick, in Baltimore, who was brought down only twenty-four hours after a special exposure to a malignant case, and died upon the seventh day after that exposure, showed to the profession in all Maryland that the disease must be regarded and sanitarily treated as being, in a certain and most important way, infectious. But until the wide-spread suffering from it in 1860, 1861, and 1862 had nearly ceased, there was but little heed given to the essential sanitary duties, the local circumstances, and prophylactic measures by which this destroyer of life may be held in check.

The actual number of deaths charged to this disease in New York in the year 1874, as registered at this date, is 1,665; 514 in excess of the number in 1873.

The course marked by this disease in the different wards of the city in 1873, and thus far in 1874, is instructive.—

The Twentieth Ward, for example, has from the first been the most unfortunate district. The Sixteenth, next south, nearer the tide-level, has suffered much; the Nineteeth, on grounds even higher than those of the Twentieth Ward, has experienced more than its quota of this malady. The house epidemics of diphtheria have been most marked in the districts in which the most fatal general distribution of it has been experienced. The occurrence of four fatal cases in an esteemed and well-provided family in West Thirty-eighth street, near Eighth avenue, last Spring, and the death of four children in a single apartment on Eleventh avenue, near Fortieth street, in twenty-four hours, a few days ago, are sad instances of the excessive malignancy of diphtheria in the localities in which it is most persistent and wide-spread. This has been witnessed in many cities and villages. It is a fact which should aid in the discovery of the chief local and geographical factors of the malady. It points to the earth, and emanations from grounds, or from local nuisances, yet the most we find, hitherto, points to faulty conditions of the surface and under drainage, and to the emanations from such grounds, and, as seems true in numerous instances, to the presence of ammoniacal gases. The Twentieth Ward of our city suffers excessively from these combined causes. The epidemic district in Albany in 1858 and 1859 suffered largely from like local circumstances, and so we might quote hundreds of similar instances. But these local, and probably aggravating or fostering conditions in districts, streets, and particularly tenements, do not produce the disease.

It is a noticeable fact that since the improved sewerage and pavement of the district south of Houston, the Bowery and Market street have suffered but lightly during the past two years, though the First, Fifth, and a portion of the Seventh Wards have had quite a wide diffusion of the disease.

PRACTICAL CONCLUSIONS.

1. If diphtheria has gained a foothold in any city or populous neighborhood, it selects certain localities in which its persistence is specially marked, and its persistence, as shown by repeated outbreaks or continued prevalence, seems to hold an important relation to certain conditions of soil, drainage, and sanitary wants of dwellings, which admit of preventive measures.

2. The extension of the disease from one individual to another, and to entire households or families, and from family to family, and from place to place, are facts so well proved in the history of the disease that the entire separation of the sick from the well, at least of children

sick with this disease from all others, should be regarded as a first-rate sanitary duty.

3. That the immediate sanitary as well as perfect medical care of every family exposed to it seems to be a duty required by every consideration of humanity and public health.

4. That a complete and exact record of diphtheria as it prevails in any locality is a duty of much importance to society, and that for the purpose of promoting the successful discharge of this duty to society and the medical profession, the Public Health Association of the city of New York respectfully submits the following resolution as embodying its view upon the subject:

Resolved, That every Board of Health, every county and city medical society, and every practitioner of medicine in the State of New York, is most respectfully urged to cause a correct record to be prepared concerning the beginning, progress, local, domestic, and hygienic conditions under which this disease appears, progresses, and is brought under any degree of sanitary treatment.

Dr. Walter De Forest Day then exhibited and described a carefully prepared map of the city of New York, showing the direction of the old water-courses, which traversed the island before the ground was covered with pavements and dwellings, and the exact location by street and number of all the deaths which had been caused in the city by diphtheria from October 1, 1874, to date.

THE MYSTIFICATION OF QUACKS.

"Good Doctor Alcon, I am come to crave
Your counsel, to advise me of my health;
For I suppose, in truth, I am not well;
Methinks I should be sick, but cannot tell!
Something there is amiss that troubles me,
For which I would take physic willingly."
"Welcome, fair nymph! Come, let me try your pulse.
I cannot blame you hold yourself not well.
'Something amiss!'" quoth he; "here's all amiss!
The whole fabric of yourself distempered is;
The systole and diastole of your pulse
Do show your passion's most hysterical.
It seems you have not careful been
To observe the prophylactic regimen
Of your own body; so that we must now
Descend into the therapeutical,
That so we may prevent the syndrome
Of symptoms, and may afterwards apply
Some analeptical alexipharmacum
That may be proper for your malady."—*Selected.*

Editor's Table.

THE PUBLIC HEALTH.

New York, January 6th, 1875.—The total number of deaths in the five weeks ending January 2d, 1875, was 2,730, and 2,146 of this number occurred in the four weeks that ended on the 26th of December. The death-rate began to increase in a very decided way at the close of the second week in December, and it still continues above the mean rate of the year 1873, the increased mortality during the last two weeks of December, and the first days of the new year, was in persons of advanced age or in those enfeebled by chronic diseases. *Zymotic* diseases during the five weeks were charged with 824 of the 2,730 deaths which occurred in that period; constitutional diseases were charged with 575; local, 1,051; developmental, 171; and violent causes 109.

The death-rate for the five weeks was equivalent to 27.29 per 1,000 inhabitants annually. There were 587 deaths of infants under 1 year old, and 1,156 of children under 5 years. The number of deaths of persons 70 years of age and upwards was 183, or 6.70 per cent. of the total mortality. Phthisis pulmonalis caused 434 deaths, or 15.90 per centum of the total mortality; bronchitis and pneumonia 421, or 15.42 per centum, enteric fever, 31; puerperal diseases, 38; small-pox, 155 deaths, of which 74 were in Small-pox Hospital; diphtheria 251, or 9.19 per centum of the total mortality. There has been a steady decrease in the number of fatal cases of diphtheria since the middle of December, but the regions of its chief fatality continue unchanged, as mentioned in the last number of THE SANITARIAN. It is now a noticeable fact that the principal family physicians in this city give minute attention to the sanitary precautions by which the progress and fatality of this malady are diminished.

The total number of deaths during the year 1874 in this city was 28,727. The death-rate, estimated upon a total population of 1,040,000 was 27.62 per 1,000 of the living inhabitants. Of this total mortality 13,719, or 47.75 per cent. of the deaths were of children under 5 years of age. The estimated number of living births is 35,000. As 11.8 per cent. of the population of the city are under 5 years of age, the rate of mortality in that class of children is 111.8 per annum in every 1,000 of them. That portion of the city inhabitants 5 years of age and upwards to oldest ages, suffered a death-rate of only 16.36 per 1,000 of their estimated number.

The city of New York has a high birth-rate, now estimated as being equal to from 33 to 34 in the 1,000 inhabitants. From this newly-born portion of the population death claims an enormous deduction by causes which depend more largely upon the defective nourishment and unhygienic domestic circumstances of these tender lives than upon all other causes combined. While this excessive waste of infantine life has scarcely been rebuked by the public health measures which have for several years been reducing the prevalence of the preventable diseases in all classes except young children, human life in its most active and useful ages, namely from 20 to 60 years, in both sexes, has been acquiring increased security.

ELISHA HARRIS, M. D., *Registrar.*

Brooklyn, January 9th, 1875.—The total number of deaths in the city of Brooklyn—with a population of 450,000 inhabitants—during the month of December, 1874, was 916, or 24.40 per 1000; small-pox, 15; scarlatina, 57; diphtheria, 103; croup, 55; typhus fever, 4; marasmus, 18; consumption, 106; bronchitis, 48; pneumonia, 72.

Mortality for the year 1874,—11,011 ; 24.46 per 1000.

Zymotic diseases	3,684;	33.49	per cent.
Constitutional	2,285;	20.07	"
Local	3,872;	35.11	"
Developmental	867;	7.88	"
Violence	303;	2.75	"
Consumption	1,267;	11.45	"
Pneumonia	744;	6.76	"
Bronchitis	285;	2.59	"
Nervous system	1,231;	11.19	"
Circulatory system	397;	3.60	"

Small-pox, 53; measles, 90; scarlet fever, 479; diphtheria, 580; croup, 318; whooping cough, 130; cholera infantum, 968; diarrhœal diseases, 1,370.

J. WATT, M.D., *Registrar of Vital Statistics.*

The Board is at present much exercised in regard to the garbage nuisance to householders throughout the city, and evidently sees in this neglect, on the part of contractors, one cause at least of the continued prevalence of zymotic diseases, and particularly of diphtheria.

An abstract of a report by the Sanitary Committee has been published by the Board for general distribution, and, in part, is as follows:—

"*December* 23, 1874.

"Diphtheria, in all years, is a disease of certain localities in Brooklyn; but in the present year it has spread over new districts and has become *epidemic*. * * * The occurrence of diphtheria in a house should lead to an immediate inspection of all possible sources of contagion: *within the house;* trace to its source every foul smell, whether from obstructed or leaking soil-pipes, from water-closets and waste-pipes, imperfectly trapped or defective at the joints; from cellar-air tainted by forgotten and decomposing "rubbish," or by the exhalations of a lot filled in with ashes mixed with garbage and street-sweepings; or from apartments filthy, over-crowded and ill-ventilated: *in the yard;* remove all filth and decomposing substances, clean and disinfect foul-smelling privies, cesspools and cisterns: clean and fill disused cesspools and old privies; these latter are very numerous in this city and an especial source of danger. * * * * Prevent the children from attending schools that are over crowded, over-heated, and unventilated, and whence they return with pallid faces and aching heads. Purify the air of the home and rectify defects of drainage, etc.

Diphtheria frequently begins in a mild form, and may pursue its course without serious illness; therefore, for the safety of schools and families, every child suffering from an attack of sore-throat, cough or catarrh, should receive the attention of a physician without delay."—J. T. CONKLING, *President*.

The following resolution was adopted by the Board at a meeting held October 29, 1874:

"*Resolved*, That the Sanitary Committee of this Board be and are hereby requested to inquire into the present condition of the garbage service in Brooklyn, and to report the facts, and to make such recommendations to the Board as the Committee may find necessary."

At a meeting of the Board, January 7th, the Sanitary Committee reported:

Evidence on file in the office of the Board of Health, shows that the contractors for the collection and removal of dead animals, garbage, night soil, etc., have not and are not now doing their duty in accordance with the contract they have entered into with the Board of Health. They do not, as required by specification two, call regularly at all dwellings and all other buildings, and remove promptly and in as cleanly a manner as possible, all kitchen and other garbage that may be offered either on the sidewalk or in the front area or under the front stoop. On the contrary, as a general rule, they take only such garbage from the houses at which they call as is placed on the sidewalk for the coming of the garbage carts. They do not always, as required by specification three, give due and adequate notice by the ringing of a bell at a regular hour through every street, lane or building, to the occupants of all buildings that they are about to approach for the removal of kitchen and other garbage, and they have neglected generally to comply with the contract, especially as it relates to the collecting and removing of kitchen garbage. * * * * The organic refuse of cities must be removed promptly, for it decomposes rapidly and soon becomes an intolerable nuisance. Fortunately the cold weather is now upon us, and decomposition has not taken place very rapidly, but we are liable to be placed in the same position in midsummer; indeed the city has heretofore had this experience with the garbage contractors in the hottest weather, and the dead animals have been left in the streets, and the garbage in our houses, to decompose and fill the air with pestilential miasma, and the city has been compelled in the emergency to employ other contractors at an enormous expense to remove the offensive material. * * * Let us profit by the lessons of the past and determine at this favorable season of the year the best method of avoiding the difficulties heretofore experienced by ourselves and our predecessors in causing the removal of the refuse of our city. . . J. C. HUTCHISON, *Chairman.*

In view of the above report of the Registrar of Vital Statistics and the large ratio of mortality from zymotic diseases for the year 1874, and the final proposed action by the Board of Health, attention is recalled to the declarations of THE SANITARIAN for several months back, to the increase of zymotic diseases, and the general prevalence of unsanitary conditions to which certain of the Brooklyn newspapers were purblind.

Philadelphia, 775,000. Four weeks ending January 2, 1,147; annual ratio per 1,000, 19.20; diphtheria, 32; consumption, 192; pneumonia, 63; typhoid fever, 41; typhus, 3; scarlet fever, 65.

Chicago, 400,000. Four weeks ending December 19th, 411; annual ratio per 1,000, 13.35. Consumption, 5[illegible]; pneumonia, 30; typhoid fever, 19; diphtheria, 9. .

St. Louis, 366,000. *Three* weeks ending December 26th, 397; annual ratio per 1,000, 18.79. Consumption, 42; pneumonia, 37; diphtheria, 7: typhoid fever, 7; small-pox, 61; scarlet fever, 13.

Baltimore, 284,000. Four weeks ending January 4th, 456; annual ratio per 1,000, 20.87. . Consumption, 68; pneumonia, 41; scarlet fever, 50; typhoid fever, 12; diphtheria, 9.

Annual Report for year ending October 31st, 1874. A concise and lucid report, setting forth the chief evils in conflict with health in Baltimore, to be: "the opening of privy vaults, and the nightly transportation of their contents through the streets of the city," and especially during hot weather; the tolerance of slaughtering-houses within the city limits, and defective machinery for the removal of garbage. The abatement of these evils is vehemently urged on the evidence of the best experiences everywhere. "No epidemic or contagious disease has prevailed," and the only excessive mortality particularly designated is that of cholera infantum during the hot months, and attributable in a great degree to the opening of privy vaults; and consumption, which is attributed to the large number of "persons resorting here from other States, hoping to find a climate more congenial to their health, as well as those from other parts of this State seeking medical aid, and who remain until their disease is terminated by death."

Total number of deaths for the year, 7,401; ratio per 1,000, 19.27. Cholera infantum, 766; consumption, 1,036;—both, certainly, in very large proportion. Typhoid fever, 244; scarlet fever, 174; diphtheria, 102; dysentery, 70.

The reports of the General Superintendent of Streets and the resident physician of the Marine Hospital, both show efficient service, and the latter, especially, a success and economy of management worthy of emulation, notwithstanding certain portions of the establishment seem to be in a bad condition. Number of vessels boarded at Quarantine during the year, 917; quarantined, 12; patients treated in Marine Hospital, 11; (yellow fever, 4; varioloid, 3; remittent fever, 2; and of typhus and intermittent, each 1). Amount of money received for quarantine fees and from patients treated, $4,688.26; total hospital expenses, $11,499.47.

Boston, 275,000. Four weeks ending Dec. 27th, 596; annual ratio per 1,000, 28.17. Consumption, 95; pneumonia, 63; typhoid fever, 16; diphtheria, 10.

Cincinnati, 260,000. Four weeks ending Dec. 26th, 526; annual ratio per 1,000, 26.30. Consumption, 57; diphtheria, 8; typhoid fever, 26; scarlet fever, 31.

New Orleans, 199,000. Three weeks ending Dec. 20th, 388; annual ratio per 1,000, 35.59. Consumption, 44; small-pox, 9; diphtheria, 6; pneumonia, 26.

San Francisco, 201,000. Month of November, 314; annual ratio per 1,000, 18.79. Consumption, 39; pneumonia, 17; typhus and typhoid fevers, 12; diphtheria, 5; scarlet fever, 11.

Washington, 150,000. Four weeks ending Jan. 2, 263; annual ratio per 1,000—whites (110,000), 16.09; colored (40,000), 39; total ratio per 1,000, 22.88. Consumption, 49; pneumonia, 47.

Third Annual Report, ending Sept. 30th, 1874.—In comparison with the preceding annual reports, this is distinguished by marked progress in sanitary work and results.

"The total number of deaths reported for the year ending Sept. 30th, 1874, is 2,637—17.58 per 1,000 of the entire population of the District. Of this number, the very small proportion of deaths from zymotic diseases (653) indicates the successful efforts of the Board of Health in diminishing the causes which give rise to this class of maladies, proving at the same time that they are completely under the control of preventive sanitary measures, vigorously enforced. In proportion to the means supplied and the energy intelligently expended in the abatement of nuisances injurious to health will this class of fatal maladies gravitate toward its minimum of production and fatality."

The Health Officer calls special attention to a class of houses into which the poor are crowded, of which 389 have been condemned, and urges that stringent laws be enacted for their abatement. Many stagnant-water lots have been filled, and great benefit accrued therefrom, but the marshy banks of the Potomac are a continued source of malarial poison, calling for increased powers and active measures.

Defective plumbing, and the evil consequences arising therefrom, have received attention, and regulations are urged to remedy the evil.

Well-regulated abattoirs, distant from the city, are urged by both precept and example, as an essential regulation for the promotion of health to all populous communities.

Much benefit is attributed to the excellent regulations for the removal of night soil by the "Odorless Excavating Apparatus Company," and the great utility of the process warmly commended. Several of the Public Buildings, and notably the Treasury Department of the Pension Bureau, are represented to be sadly in conflict with the health of their occupants, in regard to space, defective ventilation and temperature. The importance of food inspection is dwelt upon, and new enactments and appropriations asked for, for its prosecution.

Correspondence with various foreign health authorities is published with the Secretary's report, adding much to its interest, besides showing the pains taken to elicit practical information from all sources.

Pittsburgh, 137,000. Month ending Dec. 31st, 253, 22.16 per 1,000. Under one year of age, 27.27 per cent. Under five years of age, 48.61 per cent.

Infectious Diseases.

	NUMBER OF CASES REPORTED.	NUMBER OF DEATHS.
Scarlet fever	81	30
Typhoid fever	72	25
Diphtheria	20	4
Measles	10	2
Cerebro-spinal fever	2	1
Varioloid	4	..
Small-pox	1	..
Chicken-pox	1	..
Total cases reported	191	Total deaths, 62

All cases not reported, as some of the leading physicians in the city object to reporting their cases.

W. Snively, *Registrar.*

Milwaukee, 100,000. Month of December, 163; annual ratio per 1,000, 19.66. Consumption, 18; convulsions, 25; diphtheria, 4.

Providence, 100,000. Month of December, 170; annual ratio per 1,000, 20.4. Consumption, 25; pneumonia, 13; typhoid fever, 11; scarlet fever, 28.

Annual Report for 1874: Total deaths, 1,983. Ratio per 1,000, 19.83; to population, 1 in 50.23. Consumption, 269; typhoid fever, 59; diphtheria, 20; pneumonia, 124.

The population, number of deaths, and proportion of deaths to population in Providence, in each of the last seven years, have been as follows :

YEAR.	POPULATION.	DEATHS.	DEATHS TO POPULATION.
1868..................	64,138	1,110	One in 57.78
1869..................	66,523	1,256	One in 52.96
1870..................	68,904	1,263	One in 54.55
1871..................	72,800	1,254	One in 58.05
1872..................	76,696	1,603	One in 47.84
1873..................	80,592	1,719	One in 46.88
1874..................	99,608	1,983	One in 50.23

Deducting the Tenth Ward in 1874, and the number of deaths would be 1,659, or one in 50.02 of the population. The population given above for 1870 and 1874, is according to census. For the other years it is estimated.

EDWIN M. SNOW, M. D.,
Supt. of Health and City Registrar.

Richmond, 65,000. Two weeks ending January 2d, 61 ; whites, 25 ; colored, 36 ; annual ratio per 1,000, 24.40. Consumption, 10 ; diphtheria, 1 ; typhoid fever, 1 ; pneumonia, 7.

New Haven, 60,000. For month of December, 74 ; annual ratio per 1,000, 14.81. Consumption, 12 ; typhoid fever, 5 ; typho-malarial fever, 1 ; small-pox, 1.

Charleston, 52,000. Four weeks ending Dec. 12th, 135 ; whites, 54; colored, 81 ; annual ratio per 1,000, 31.82. Consumption, 11 ; diphtheria, 18 ;

Toledo, 50,000. For month of December, 35 ; annual ratio per 1,000, 11.34. Consumption, 7 ; pneumonia, 3.

Total number of deaths for 1874, 600 ; population estimated at 50,000 ; ratio per 1,000, 12. S. W. SKINNER, *Health Officer.*

Dayton, 34,000. For month of December, 33 ; annual ratio per 1,000, 11.64.

Total deaths for 1874, 479 ; ratio per 1,000, 9.21.

Total births, 972 ; ratio per 1,000, 18.69.

Galveston.—Annual Report : Estimating the population of the city at 34,000, according to the late census our ratio of mortality is but 16 19.34 for each 1,000.

The past year has been one of universal healthfulness, no disease having assumed the character and proportions of an epidemic.

Not a single case of yellow fever has occurred in the city, and not one has been imported into the harbor of Galveston, notwithstanding there has been a constant commercial intercourse with the West Indies by means of the Morgan line of steamers and by sailing vessels owned by Mr. C. H. Ruff. These vessels, during the years 1873 and 1874, have made, under my observation during the quarantine season, forty-two trips hence to Havana and returned, and not one single case of yellow fever has occurred, and yet the yellow fever was never worse in Havana than during the year 1873, and prevailed to an ordinary extent during 1874.

When it is recollected that the crews belonging to these vessels were not permitted to go ashore, except in Havana, and that when there it is presumed they indulged in every variety of excess and exposure incident to their avocations and character, I think it wonderful that not one of them contracted yellow fever.

I know of no reason for the exemption they enjoyed, except the sanitary conditions they are submitted to on board, the uniform cleanliness of the vessels employed, and the willing co-operation of the owners in every measure of prevention I suggested.

GEO. W. PEETE, M. D, *Health Physician.*

Elmira, 21,000. Month of December, 15; annual ratio per 1,000, 8.57.

ANALYTICAL AND FOOD DEPARTMENT.

Persons wishing articles noticed or analysed, under this department, are requested to forward specimens, and all letters of inquiry in regard to terms, etc., to the Editor of THE SANITARIAN.

"CRUSHED WHITE WHEAT."—In answer to many inquiries in regard to crushed white wheat, recently advertised in THE SANITARIAN, the article known as such is the product of the Atlantic Flour Mills, Brooklyn (Messrs. F. E. Smith & Co.), one of the most complete and perfect establishments in the country. While the proprietors of these mills turn out immense quantities of the finest grades of flour, they are notwithstanding alive to certain conditions not fulfilled by flour in its ordinary aspect; and acting upon the well-known fact that the most highly refined flour is divested of some of its most valuable nutritive elements, they determined to manufacture a coarse flour from the most choice qualities of wheat, for the special benefit, not only of dyspeptics and other invalids, to whom it is particularly well suited, but for all who "prefer to get the most for their money." The process of manufacturing the "*crushed white wheat*" consists in "thoroughly softening the grain in every part. The hard crust containing the *gluten* or *nitrogeneous elements* is put into proper condition to cook *quickly* and *uniformly* with the soft and crumbly portion of the centre, being the *carbonaceous* portion.' The wheat used is of the CHOICEST kind, raised in the best wheat-growing sections of the United States. It is first thoroughly cleaned and purified from all extraneous admixture, by the most complete and severe mechanical contrivances, and prepared in such a manner that *all of the elements of the grain are preserved.* The *iron* and *silex* are preserved in the outer or true bran; in this portion of the berry also lies the greatest amount of waste, which is a natural stimulant, and greatly assists nature in keeping the bowels and digestive organs in proper and healthful action.

Excepting for those who have particularly irritable digestive organs, this is certainly one of the most wholesome preparations of wheat ever produced.

Best Preparations for Leather.—Any chemist able to produce best preparations of any kind for leather will please state to undersigned particulars, with price, cements, polish dressings, burnishing-inks, etc., desired. Address: "Leather Manufacturer, care Ed. Sanitarian."

The Abattoir Question in Philadelphia continues to absorb the attention of all who have the health of the city at heart, and we regret that our space was too much preoccupied to make room for the excellent paper of Dr. Rauch on the subject, in the present number. It will appear in our next. Meanwhile we hope for the success of the citizens of Philadelphia in opposing the selfish interest of the railroad company, and trust that the result of the contest may be the establishment of an abattoir in an unobjectionable place.

American Surgery and Hospitals.—In the month of November Dr. John Erie Erichsen, F.R.C.S., gave an address at University College Hospital, London, upon his impressions of America, and we have his address now before us in a recent number of the *Lancet*. The doctor made a professional tour of our country, and appears to have seen the leading surgeons and hospitals here. His impressions are creditable to our people and their physicians and surgeons, and to his kindness and intelligence. He thinks that the profession ranks higher here than in England, as compared with the legal and the clerical professions, which there receive so much government patronage. He is pleased to see that our surgeons follow the footsteps of their great English progenitors, and also study the manuals and journals of the English schools. He regrets that so little is required of students of medicine in advance, and that no preliminary examination is exacted, while the course of study is shorter than in England.[1] Yet he likes the large method of instruction here, which allows sometimes a thousand students, as in New York, to witness important operations in hospital clinical theatres. He is surprised and delighted by our hospitals, alike by their munificent endowments and their admirable structure. He calls the Roosevelt Hospital in New York without exception the most complete medical charity in every respect that he had ever seen in a hospital, the construction of which reflects the greatest credit upon its designers. The architect, Carl Pfeiffer, has his share of this praise. Our surgeons of this city are named with high respect among their brethren, and this is the list of foremost names in the profession. "It would be needless to name to you such men as that Nestor of American surgery, Gross, or Pancoast, of Philadelphia; or Van Buren, Wood, Parker, or Sayre, of New York; Bigelow or Hodges, of Boston; Smith or Johnston, of Baltimore." He ends with advising English medical students to go to America and visit the great hospitals and schools in the cities of the United States.

Big Invention.—Lloyd, the famous map man, who made all the maps for General Grant and the Union army, certificates of which he published, has just invented a way of getting a relief plate from steel so as to print Lloyd's Map of the American Continent—showing from ocean to ocean—on one entire sheet of bank-note paper, 40x50 inches large, on a lightning press, and colored, sized and varnished for the wall so as to stand washing, and mailing anywhere in the world for 25 cents, or unvarnished for 10 cents. This map shows the whole United States and Territories in a group, from surveys to 1875, with a million places on it, such as towns, cities, villages, mountains, lakes, rivers, streams, gold mines, railway stations, etc. This map should be in every house. Send 25 cents to the Lloyd Map Company, Philadelphia, and you will get a copy by return mail.

The American Newspaper Directory is an epitome of newspaper history. It is also regarded as an official register of circulations. This feature requires the closest scrutiny to prevent it from leading to abuses. The plan adopted by the publishers of the Directory, to secure correct and trustworthy reports, is rigid in its requirements and adhered to with impartiality. Successful publishers, who have something to gain by a comparison, are generally prompt, not only to send reports in conformity but give Messrs. George P. Rowell & Co. such information as enables them to weed out unsubstantiated statements of pretenders in journalism. The popularity of the book, and the general confidence in its accuracy and good faith, are attested by the immense body of advertisements it receives.

BIBLIOGRAPHY.

Longevity, Biometry;—The Measure or Span of Life—answering the questions, Am I probably long or short-lived? Can I myself know the indications? An Exposition of the Laws of Life or Life-time, Exhibited in Family Inheritance and Personal Indications of Longevity. By T. S. Lambert, M.D., LL.D. Second edition. New York: Wm. Wood & Co.

This is a concise work, containing much useful information on the conditions generally which serve to individualize every person, and make each one, as regards his viability, a law unto himself. The author is the well-known President of the American Popular Life Insurance Company, and he has embodied in this work the principles which are being elaborated more and more by Maudsley, Allen, and other writers on the laws of inheritance, by which the probabilities of health and life may be approximately measured.

"As a law of family inheritance, it is expected that a child will be affected by diseases similar to those of its parents; as a rule, a boy by those of the mother, a girl by those of the father. Shall they not from each equally inherit health, vigor, and longevity, if possessed? * * 'Visiting the iniquity of the fathers upon the children unto the third and fourth generations,' is a part of one of the Commandments, also indicating that the virtues of the fathers shall bless their children. Therefore, the expression from the Commandment has a double application. * * * * * * * * * * * *

"Every one has noticed that nearly all the members of some families die aged, while those of others are gone before what would be called the middle age of the former. It is a common and correct remark, that 'some are as old at forty as others are at sixty;' the latter will, in fact, be more likely to live twenty years than the former. The years a person has lived, is by no means the most important element for judging how many he may probably live. Nor is present health of much more consequence; since it is often the case that families are very vigorous and healthy while they live, yet are not long-lived. They inherit healthy but short lives. Notice the Laplanders. Observe the citizens of Zurich, Switzerland, very healthy, but seldom reaching the age of sixty; while members of one Italian family living in their midst since the sixteenth century, reach the age of eighty or ninety. The Welsh are the longest-lived people in Europe. The Scotch are longer-lived than the English, and the Irish shorter-lived; yet they are all healthy as a people.

"On the other hand, some who do not have robust health are noticed to live long; it is said that they attain old age because they take such excellent care of themselves. Yet, though it is not denied that the care is useful, it will be usually found that they had at least one probably long-lived parent, and thus inherited longevity from one side if not from both; for though it is often the case that those die young who have long-lived ancestry, it is very seldom that any person lives to be more than a year or two older than any of his ancestors,—parents, grandparents, etc."

It is upon the conclusions submitted in this work that the practice of the American Popular Life Insurance Company is based, which is to rate every applicant according to probable length of life—"deducing it from his ancestry, constitution, habits, vocation, residence, intelligence, instincts, health, age, and whatever else, if else there be, which can affect the potentialities of life;" *grading* and *rating* life according to quality and conditions, as in fire and marine insurance, giving the best grades the benefit of the lowest cost of premiums.

Experimentation on Animals as a means of Knowledge in Physiology, Pathology and Practical Medicine. By J. C. Dalton, M. D. Professor of Physiology, etc. New York: F. W. Christern, 1875.

A timely little book on the necessity, character, and results of physiological experiments and studies on living animals. It is an answer in advance to the annual effort of Mr. Bergh to procure legal prohibition of physiological studies necessary for the advancement of science and the promotion of human health and life. Mr. Bergh in his enthusiasm to protect the brute from needless pain, seems to make no exception, either in kind, manner or object of using the brute creation for the benefit of mankind.

Professor Dalton shows that the charge of inhumanity against experimental physiologists is unfounded. That "the exhibition of pain in an experimental laboratory is an exceptional occurrence." That the experiments are performed "under anæsthesia, when the animal is as completely unconscious of what is going on as the human patient while suffering an amputation." Rare instances only arise where the sensibility of a particular part is the special subject of investigation, but even in these, the pain inflicted is "small in amount, and momentary in duration."

To the sentimental objection to the destruction of animal life, Dr. Dalton justly remarks that this is as fully justified for the preservation of human health and the relief of human sickness as is the slaughter of "cattle for their beef and hides, musk deer for their perfume, the cochineal insect for its carmine, and Spanish flies for the materials of a blister." The necessity for experimentation on living animals rests on the self-evident proposition that the medical sciences "have to do with the phenomena of life, and there is no way of learning what the vital phenomena are, except by examining them while life is going on."

An appendix presenting the testimony of the medical profession as to the necessity of experimentation on animals closes an argument which, as it is avowedly intended for the educated public rather than for medical readers, we commend to the attention of all who are inclined to take part in the controversy forced upon popular notice by Mr. Bergh, and especially of the legislators before whom he argues his *ex parte* statement of the case.

Electricity for Nervous Diseases. By Dr. Friedrich Fieber. Translated from the German by George M. Schweig, M. D. New York: G. P. Putnam's Sons.

An admirable manual of sixty-one pages only, giving the practical gist of the benefits conferred on mankind by the therapeutical use of electricity. To all who would know the conditions best suited to, and the best means of applying electricity in the treatment of disease, this manual is commended.

Contributions to the Annals of Medical Progress and Medical Education in the United States before and during the War of Independence. By Joseph M. Toner, M.D. Washington: Government Print, 1874.

This publication is no less creditable to the Bureau of Education, under whose auspices it is published, than to the author. With his usual industry the author seems to have ransacked every source of information directly or indirectly bearing on his subject, and has not only collated brief memoirs of all the earlier physicians and surgeons of any note, but given a concise review of professional progress under colonial rule, the rise of hospitals and schools of physic, the course of legislation relating to medicine and hygiene, with many quaint mementoes of the olden time. Although small in bulk, this brochure bears evidence of more painstaking research than many a more pretentious volume, and affords an entertaining picture of one phase of life among our forefathers.

Caleb Krinkle. A story of American life. By CHARLES CARLETON COFFIN. "Carleton." Boston: Lee and Shepard, 1875.

An entertaining story of friendship, beginning in school life, which, under refining influences, ripens into life-long attachment and mutual benefit, so as to completely absorb the attention of the reader throughout; and the book closes with the wish of the reader that there was more of it.

Medical Society of New Jersey. Transactions 1874. 108th Anniversary. 270 pp.

After the usual routine minutes of a delightfully harmonious session, follows a happy address by the President, Dr. T. J. Thomason, on *Medical Truthfulness*; it discusses the temptations and trials of the everyday life of physicians, and inculcates the most wholesome truths for habitual guidance. The "Obstetrical Forceps," is the subject of an essay by Dr. John V. Schenck, wherein he urges a more extended use of the forceps to shorten the pains of labor, without risking, as is too often the case, the mischievous consequences of tedious labors. *Affections of the Eye from Small-Pox.* By Dr. CHARLES T. KIPP, is an excellent practical paper, which, in view of the continued prevalence of small-pox, should be widely circulated.

By the Report of the Standing Committee, "the general health of the State has been good during the year; in many portions of the State unusually so." In Camden County there were "a few obstinate cases of remittent fever......passing into a typhoid state. Enteric fever...... remarkably on the increase. Hudson County has been visited by...... intermittent, remittent, and typho-malarial fevers......In Monmouth County, in addition to an extreme epidemic of whooping-cough, there occurred during the winter an epidemic of diphtheria of the most malignant and fatal character......Dysentery and cholera morbus in adults is noticed as an endemic in Perrineville, as also cholera infantum and less severe forms of bowel affections......In Sussex County cerebro-spinal meningitis is noticed as occurring last spring in a mild form."

The detail of this summary of the Standing Committee is given in the reports of district societies, which show much interest and much excellent society work.

Vaccination. A Report on, by E. L. GRIFFIN, M.D. Fon-du-Lac, Wis. Reprint from State Society Transactions. An excellent contribution to the literature of the subject.

Municipal Law and its Relations to the Constitution of Man. By R. S. GUERNSEY, of the New York Bar. (Reprint from Archives of Electrology and Neurology.)

An exceedingly interesting brochure on a subject worthy of more attention than it has hitherto received.

Archives of Dermatology. Quarterly, Vol. 1. No. 1, pp. 96. Edited by L. D. BUCKLEY, A.M. M.D. New York; G. P. Putnam's Sons. Oct., 1874.

Dr. Buckley brings to his own exteneive experience a score of collaborators in this important field of medical practice. And this "sample copy" leaves no room to doubt that the field will be cultivated with both ability and assiduity. The contents are divided into original communications, society transactions, clinical records, digests of literature, bibliography, and miscellany.

The New York School Journal, begins its new volume and new year with pleasing assurances of the prosperity which it deserves. New paper, typographically perfect, and handsomely illustrated with engravings of the New York Normal College, old King's College, and the present Columbia College building, with a full page cut, "Kept In," a picture of a Dutch school at recess time, which explains itself. Descriptive articles, attached to the illustrations; much miscellaneous school news, and other news. "The School Room," a department for school children; an entertaining serial, and other interesting matter, merit the attention and patronage of all who are interested in the progress of education,—and who is not?

Vick's Floral Guide for 1875—the January number—is a useful as well as beautiful illustrated catalogue of flowers and vegetables, the seeds of which are on sale by the proprietor. It consists of over 100 pages, 500 engravings, 500 descriptions of flowers and vegetables, with directions for culture. The Floral Guide may be obtained by sending 25 cents to Mr. James Vick, Rochester, N. Y.

Field, Lawn, and Garden. A Journal of Rural Affairs and Choice Reading.

Truly so. Rarely have we seen a more tasteful and instructive family journal on subjects interesting to every household. Monthly, $2 a year; 20 cents a number. W. B. Davis & Co., Madison, Wis.

The Nursery, a monthly magazine for youngest readers, is *the toy* of toys for the little ones. Every number is illustrated with object lessons of beautiful pictures, and just such pretty stories with good morals as children delight to learn and profit by. $1.50 per year, in advance. Boston: 36 Bromfield street. John L. Shorey.

Received.—*Fifth Registration Report of Michigan.* Vital Statistics. 1871.

Proceedings of the Sixth Annual Session of the American Philosophical Association. Hartford. 1874.

Valedictory Address, delivered by Thos. M. Logan, M. D., Professor of Hygiene; Commencement Exercises of the Medical Department of the University of California, San Francisco, Oct. 29, 1874.

Relation of Boards of Health to Intemperance. A Paper Read Before the National Convention of Health Boards, Washington. 1874.

An Account of the Epidemic of Cholera in Kentucky, 1873. By Ely McClellan, M. D., U. S. Army. Reprint from Vol. I., Public Health Papers. 1874.

Puerperal Diseases—The Means Employed at the Preston Retreat for their Prevention and Treatment. By Wm. Goodell, M. D., Physician in charge. From Obstetrical Journal, 1874.

Disinfection and Disinfectants. By Elwyn Waller, A. M., E. M. Reprint from Public Health Papers. 1874.

Application of an Instrument for Relief of Deafness Caused by Adhesions of the Oscicula of the Tympanum. By Howard Pinkney, M.D. Reprint from New York Medical Journal. 1874.

THE SANITARIAN.

A MONTHLY JOURNAL.

VOL. II.] MARCH, 1875. [NO. 12.

VENTILATION FOR HEALTH.

By JOSEPH WILSON, M. D., Medical Director U. S. N.

Seeing many of my friends needlessly dying of marsh fevers, I formerly wrote an Essay on Drainage for Health, with the hope of thus saving some lives. (SANITARIAN, Vol. II, No. 1.) The farmers seem to understand pretty well the influence of stagnant water in destroying their wheat crop ; but that their own health and lives depend on the same thing, is a fact by no means so familiar to them.

But there are other influences besides malaria, capable of impairing the healthful influence of the air we breathe. We need not describe the Black Hole of Calcutta,* as this barbarity is notorious enough. But the same thing, with little variation, is constantly repeated in the last half of the nineteenth century, in what are called Coolie ships,—American and English, French and Spanish, as they traverse the Pacific Ocean.

In these cases, it is commonly supposed, even among well educated people, that the deadly influence is carbonic anhydrite (carbonic acid gas), or the want of oxygen in the confined space; but this opinion is easily disproved. We are familiar with cases of poisoning by carbonic anhydrite, and it produces no such symptoms. The Dogs' Grotto near Naples, has its floor covered with the gas, deep enough to kill a dog without interfering with a man standing upright; but when the dog is removed in time for resuscitation, he recovers without further harm. Many persons have lost their lives by incautiously descending into a well in which the atmospheric oxygen had been partially replaced by carbonic anhydrite,—and many more have been saved by withdrawing them from such situations in time for resuscitation. Similar accidents are common enough among the workmen of breweries, who are exposed to all degrees of this contamination, without special influence on health, unless the proportion of gas be such as to produce asphyxia.

About twenty years ago, Professor W. A. Hammond instituted a

* On the evening of the 15th of June, 1756,—146 persons were shut up in a room twenty feet square, and but 23 were alive next morning. A similar incident occurred after the battle of Austerlitz.

small Hole of Calcutta for the purpose of studying this subject. A mouse placed under a bell-glass, with chemical agents to remove the carbonic acid as fast as formed, died about as soon as when no such agents were present; but when the organic matter was thus removed, leaving the carbonic acid to accumulate, the mouse lived much longer, —remained a long time, apparently suffering but little inconvenience. Oh, cruel Dr. Hammond!

There is another black affair in history, which though reasonably familiar, needs ventilation at the present time. In the early part of the last century, the Circuit Courts of Oxford, England, became quite celebrated for blackness, and were more terrible to judges and juries than even to the criminals. Lawyers and witnesses, sheriffs and tipstaves all alike died by the score; and through boarding-houses and taverns the pestilence several times spread throughout the community.

These Black Assizes were the subject of investigation and Report by a Parliamentary Committee in 1730,—from which it appears that the pestilence was not peculiar to Oxford :—"Chief Baron Penyelly, holding Circuit Court in Somerset County, died suddenly, together with his retainers and attendants, including the sheriffs and many others, poisoned by the stench of the prisoners brought before the court for trial."

This was typhus fever—a most terrific, contagious pestilence—caused by the crowding and want of ventilation of the prisons, as at that time arranged.

Some of our county prisons are probably rather "black" in this way at the present time. We have nearly forty States, and an average of perhaps forty county prisons in each State—sixteen hundred county prisons. These may not be all well arranged and well managed; and, in fact, the crowded condition of the Philadelphia County Prison was constantly the subject of remonstrance by the visiting physician for several years, and typhus fever cases were occasionally reported. This crowding has lately (1873) been mitigated by the building of a House of Correction for convicts sentenced to short terms of imprisonment.

The typhus pestilence was very destructive on board emigrant ships, and at the New York Quarantine station, till it was checked by Congressional legislation, March 3, 1855. Some of the tenement-houses in New York City are very destructive of human life by this pestilence just now, the banner houses in this respect, showing a report of twenty-four deaths per annum from each house. The residents of these houses ride in the city passenger cars, and everybody riding in their company runs some risk of such fate as befell Baron Penyelly. Should those who ride in such company be quarantined—prevented from visiting healthy rural districts? The ladies should be careful when they go shopping, for the young men who sell ribbons often patronize these cars.

Varnish and gilding are sometimes the cause of death. In order to add to the splendor of a religious pageant, a child was varnished and gilded over the entire surface of his body, and he died in a few hours, before it was possible to divest him of his fatal finery. This matter has since been studied by means of experiments on animals. If the surface of the body be covered with varnish, death always takes place, generally in a few hours, the promptness of death being somewhat proportioned to the completeness of the coating. A rabbit generally dies if even the fourth part of his body is covered. A closely-fitting suit of caoutchouc clothing produces similar results. (*Famcault*, Comptes Rend, vi., 1838; xvi., 1843.) Those cruel Frenchmen!

We have now briefly alluded to the action of several deadly poisons which are produced by the human body, even in health, and which are to be removed by ventilation:

(*a*) First—Carbonic anhydrite (carbonic acid gas), which kills the dog in the cave,—the man in the brewery vat. Perhaps this substance is not so poisonous, after all; Prof. Hammond has shown that it hardly kills a mouse, and a drink of cool Seltzer water (carbonic acid water) is rather refreshing. Immersion into carbonic anhydrite, like immersion in water, is fatal, by excluding atmospheric air from the lungs, thus producing death by asphyxia. Unless it be present in sufficient quantity to produce asphyxia, no great harm seems to result.

(*b*) Second—The real deadly material of the Black Hole seems to be an organic poison exhaled from the lungs and skin, under ordinary circumstances of health. We have no name for this poison; we know that it is very deadly, and in the open air it is so rapidly removed or diluted as to leave us no evidence of its existence. It seems that the human constitution may be trained to tolerate this poison, somewhat concentrated. We have information from the proceedings of a court-martial in 1870 that a man confined for punishment actually lived fifteen consecutive days in a closet about thirty inches square and seven feet high, "canvas tacked over the cracks to make it tight!" This man had but little more air space than the average of the prisoners of the Black Hole, and I talked with him a year afterwards. He suffered very much at first, and "they had to take him out." He did not know the "ceremonies of the place," and when he recovered, and they were going to put him back, he resisted, broke loose and ran away. He was soon caught, and instructed that he could stand it better without his clothes, so he was returned to the closet naked. He was twice on deck to the mast, and, with these exceptions, he was not out of the closet, not even to take his bread and water, or to go to the privy; he had a wooden bucket, which was emptied twice a day, sometimes oftener. This man was of weak intellect—almost imbecile—and after a good washing, so far as I could learn, he was in as good health as ever.

(*c*) The more immediate cause of death in the case of the gilded boy and varnished rabits, is still a puzzle to physiologists. We know very little about the excrementitious matters discharged from the skin, except the carbonic anhydrite and water, which certainly the lungs and kidneys might discharge without trouble. "The experimental facts, however, would indicate that the skin possesses important functions with which we are entirely unacquainted." (*Flint*, Physiology of Man.) The experiments demonstrate the necessity of the free action of the skin in its relations with the atmosphere, whether the function be the elimination of poisonous excretions, or some other vital reaction.

(*d*) The jail-fever poison, the "stench" that killed Baron Penyelly and his associates, is much more important than any of the others in its actual destruction of human life; and fortunately it is now so well understood that typhus fever is as preventable as drowning. The inhabitants of jails, large tenement-houses, emigrant ships on long voyages, etc., are liable to be much crowded, without opportunity to keep their clothing, especially underclothing, reasonably clean. The excretions of the body, the insensible perspiration remaining in this soiled clothing, undergoes decay, thus resulting in the Black Assize stench—the typhus fever miasm. Thus originates this contagious pestilence, the most deadly known. It killed the judges and lawyers and sheriffs of the Oxford and Somerset Assizes; it killed a large portion of the people of London, in an epidemic about once in every twenty years, driving crowds of others to encamp in distant fields, till the great fire of 1666; it now kills many people in the tenement-houses of the large cities every year, and the Western merchants carry it in their clothing to their homes, thus starting epidemics occasionally in distant cities.

All the above-mentioned poisons emanate more or less directly from the bodies of healthy men. The other contagious pestilences which have afflicted the world, are caused by poisonous miasms emanating from the bodies of diseased persons—erysipelas and pyæmia, measles and puerperal fever, cholera and scarlet fever, diphtheria and small-pox, whooping-cough and mumps; and all these may be in great degree prevented, always mitigated, by attention to ventilation.

Wind, the atmosphere naturally in motion, is the great power of ventilation for health; and our principal duty is to prevent needless interference with this great force of nature. We must spend part of the time in the open air; we should allow the wind occasionally to blow through our houses and under them; we should not be varnished nor gilded, nor should we wear close-fitting caoutchouc or patent-leather clothing. Bed-clothing should be spread out to air with windows open part of the day, so that articles damp with perspiration need not be covered up in making up the beds. The soiled clothing of healthy people, if kept in close bundles and closets, without washing, is dangerously infectious with the typhus miasm; and Lind informs us (Diseases of Europeans in Warm Climates), that the washerwomen taking bundles of clothes from recently arrived ships, died in considerable numbers, and carried abroad the contagion, until they adopted the habit of "first spreading them abroad to air."

In discussing various arrangements for ventilation, it is necessary to bear in mind some familiar properties of the atmosphere, generally forgotten, or not understood by the partisans of special contrivances. The atmosphere, mechanically, is simply a *gas*—a perfectly elastic fluid; it expands when heated, becoming lighter, bulk for bulk, in proportion to this expansion; and hence warm air floats to the top of cooler air, as oil floats on water. The law of *diffusion of gases*, expresses a truth, but this diffusion is so slow that practically it may be omitted in our calculations, where circulation comes into account. The *condition of heat* in gases is similarly slow and insignificant. The atmosphere of a room, and its walls, are mainly warmed by *radiation* and the introduction of warm air. Air once breathed is warmed in the lungs to about 35° C. (95 F.), and that which carries off the insensible perspiration is similarly warmed by the surface of the body. Bearing these mechanical principles in mind, we are prepared for the study of the subject of ventilation practically.

The simplest movement of the atmosphere occurs where there is a living animal in a close apartment, without any aperture at all, such as the mouse under a bell-glass. Each breath of the creature sends a portion of warm and foul air to the top, displacing cooler and purer air, till the entire atmosphere is vitiated, and the animal dies. If the animal were at the top, his atmosphere being the first spoiled, he would die the sooner.

A slight modification of this arrangement is a small opening at the side, as in the Calcutta barbarism. In this case the vitiated air, reaching the ceiling and pressing for escape at the small opening, meets such resistance that it escapes but slowly, and probably with an interrupted flow, such as we observe when we empty a bottle of water by inverting it. Those sitting or lying on the floor of the Black Hole, fared better than those who, attempting to stand, breathed the foul air above.

The navy sweat-box—an outrageous invention of the last half of the nineteenth century—was not quite so bad, though it was on the berth deck of the ship—a place no better ventilated than a good cellar to begin with. This contrivance was of wood, not very neatly fitted, so that there were cracks at the bottom and top of the door; and thus there was an accidental provision for a continuous ventilation current, —the purer air entering below, while the foul air pressing upward escaped by a steady stream through the upper crack. There were usually some auger holes in the door by way of perfecting the ventilation. I once actually counted thirteen such holes, three-eighths of an inch in diameter—aggregate area equal to one round hole of one inch and thirty-five hundredths (1.35). I am not aware of any recorded death from the use of this invention, and it has departed. May we never see the like again!

Enough of these thrilling horrors have been alluded to, to prove the necessity of earnestness in the study of ventilation for health. The ventilation of ships has been carefully studied; and Congressional legislation based on such study has put a stop to the importation of the typhus pestilence into the port of New York. All that is peculiar to the situation is plainly discussed in a short chapter of my Report on Naval Hygiene (published by the Navy Department in 1870).

The smallest sea-going vessels, whose apartments are without any opening except the hatch of entrance, are well ventilated without special care; the vitiated air escapes upward through the hatch, unless there is unusual energy and perseverance in keeping the hatch closed.

Large ships have similar convenience for ventilation in the large open hatches, so that in cool weather they would be sufficiently ventilated but for the partitions necessary for closets and store-rooms. Partitions separating cargo, should be of open-slat-work; but when separating cargo from inhabited apartments, they should be made tight—caulked and pitched, so as to give independent ventilation. In warm climates, even in the warm weather of cool climates, there is occasionally need of other arrangements. The external temperature may be nearly as high as that of the human body, 35° C. (95° F.); so that respired air, being no warmer, will not ascend, and we must seek for some other force than the necessarily high temperature of respired air. If there is wind, it may be directed down a hatch by a wind-sail, or ventilation flues with cowls may be used, and air-ports opened in the sides of the ship, to ventilate like open windows. But if the vessel is much crowded it can not be otherwise than very uncomfortable in warm weather; and, whether warm or not, it is always dangerous in case of excessive crowding, especially with careless dirtiness and helplessness. A bag of soiled clothing may start a deadly typhus epidemic at any time, like the jail fever of the Black Assizes. The less accessible parts of a ship, in very warm weather, notwithstanding much care, occasionally become offensive and dangerous. The machine which I have always found effective in such emergencies is a simple rotary fan, very much like the farmer's fan for winnowing grain. It should have the circular part about four feet in diameter, with cog-wheel or pulley gearing to increase velocity four-fold. A boy turns the crank fifty revolutions a minute, thus driving the wings of the fan more than thirty-seven thousand feet an hour (37,800)—seven miles; so that an hour of this work—light work for a boy—with a fan of apertures a foot square, is sufficient to change the entire atmosphere of a thousand-ton ship. I find it necessary to drive the fan at about this rate; if it runs slower, the air is not carried along by the wings; if faster, there is force wasted in giving the needless increase of velocity. A canvas hose conducts the air to or from an apartment. A half-hour of this work, every calm evening, is a great means of safety in regions of yellow fever. There is no disadvantage in having a larger fan, except the inconvenience of carrying it about; a smaller fan is inefficient unless it is geared for greater velocity.

(*To be continued.*)

The Law of Fatigue.—Haughton, in his "Animal Mechanics," thus states the law of fatigue: When the same muscle, or group of muscles, is kept in constant action until fatigue sets in, the total work done, multiplied by the rate of work, is constant. Suppose a man, walking at his ordinary pace, does not become tired until he has gone thirty miles. If he walks twice as fast, then by this law he would be exhausted at the end of fifteen miles, having done only half the work in a quarter of the time; if he walks three times as fast, he will be tired at the end of ten miles, having done one-third of the work in one-ninth of the time; and so on, the total work varying as the square root of the time necessary to produce fatigue.

Where the rate of work is very rapid, as in a boat race, it is of course impossible to keep it up for any great length of time. The actual amount of work is thus illustrated by Dr. Haughton: "A good idea," says he, "may be formed of the rate in which the muscles give out work in a boat race, by comparing this work with the average daily work of a laborer. In many kinds of labor there are four hundred foot-tons of work accomplished in ten hours. The oarsman performs in one minute the one hundredth part of his day's labor, and if he could continue to work at the same rate, he would finish his day's task in one hour and forty minutes, instead of the customary ten hours. The work done, therefore, in rowing one knot in seven minutes is, while it lasts, performed at a rate equal to six times that of the hard-worked laborer."—*The Galaxy.*

STATE BOARDS OF HEALTH.

PLAN OF AN ACT TO ESTABLISH STATE BOARDS OF HEALTH, AND TO ASSIGN CERTAIN DUTIES TO LOCAL BOARDS OF HEALTH.

Prepared by a Special Committee, and approved by the Executive Committee of the American Public Health Association, and ordered to be printed.

SEC. 1.—That the Governor, by and with the advice and consent of the Senate or Council, shall appoint six persons, three of whom shall always be physicians, who, with the Attorney-General of the State, shall constitute the State Board of Health. Of the six persons first appointed; two shall serve for two years, two for four years, and two for six years, from the first day of April next following their confirmation, and the Governor shall hereafter biennially appoint, by and with the advice and consent of the Senate, two members of said State Board of Health, to hold their offices for six years from the first day of April next following their confirmation. Any vacancy in said Board occurring during the recess of the Legislature shall be filled by the Governor until the next regular session of the same.

SEC. 2.—That the State Board of Health shall meet at least once in every three months, and as much oftener as they may deem proper, their first meeting being held within two weeks after the first of April in each year, and four members shall always constitute a quorum for business. No member of the Board shall receive any compensation, but the actual travelling and other expenses of the members while engaged in the duties of the Board shall be allowed and paid out of the appropriation made for its support. They shall select, annually, one member of the Board as President, and shall appoint a suitable person, who shall be a physician, to be their permanent Secretary and executive officer, who shall hold his office so long as he shall faithfully discharge the duties thereof, but who may be removed for cause at any meeting of the Board, a majority of the members voting therefor.

SEC. 3.—That the Secretary shall keep a record of the acts and proceedings of the Board, perform and superintend the work prescribed in this act, and such other duties as the Board may order under their general direction, and shall receive an annual salary of   , which shall be paid him in the same manner as the salaries of other State officers are paid, and such necessary expenses as the Comptroller of the Treasury shall audit, on the presentation of an itemized account, with vouchers annexed and the certificate of the Board, shall be allowed him.

SEC. 4.—That the said State Board of Health shall take cognizance of the interests of health and life among the people of this State; they shall make sanitary investigations, and inquire respecting the causes of disease, and especially of epidemics, the sources of mortality and the effects of localities, employments, conditions, ingesta, habits, and other circumstances upon the public health, and they shall collect such information in respect of these matters as may be useful in the discharge of their duties and contribute to the promotion of health and the security of life in the State; they shall cause to be made, by their Secretary or by a Committee of the Board, regular inspections at such times as they may deem best, and special inspections, whenever directed by the Governor or the Legislature, of all public hospitals, prisons, asylums, or other public institutions, in regard to the location, drainage, water-supply, disposal of excreta, heating and ventilation, and other circumstances in any way affecting the health of their inmates, and shall also suggest such remedies as they may consider suitable for the removal of all conditions detrimental to health in the said institutions in writing, to the officers thereof.

Sec. 5.—That the said board shall cause all proper sanitary information in its possession to be promptly forwarded to the local health authorities of any city, village, town or county in the State which may request the same, adding thereto such useful suggestions as the experience of said Board may supply. And it is also hereby made the duty of said local health authorities to supply the like information and suggestions of said State Board of Health, together with a copy of all their reports and other publications. And said Board of Health is authorized to require reports and information (at such times and of such facts, and generally of such nature and extent, relating to the safety of life and promotion of health as its by-laws or rules may provide), from all public dispensaries, hospitals, asylums, infirmaries, prisons and schools, and from the managers, principals and officers thereof; and from all other public institutions, their officers and managers, and from the proprietors, managers, lessees and occupants of all places of public resort in the State; but such reports and information shall only be required concerning matters or particulars in respect of which it may in its opinion need information for the proper discharge of its duties. Said Board shall, when requested by public authorities, or when they deem it best, advise officers of the State, county or local government in regard to sanitary drainage and the location, drainage, ventilation and sanitary provisions of any public institution, building, or public place.

Sec. 6.—That it shall be the duty of the State Board to give all information that may be reasonably requested, concerning any threatened danger to the public health, to the local health officers, and all other sanitary authorities in the State, who shall give the like information to said Board; and said Board and said officers and said sanitary authorities shall, so far as legal and practicable, co-operate together to prevent the spread of disease, and for the protection of life and the promotion of health, within the sphere of their respective duties.

Sec. 7.—That said Board may, from time to time, engage suitable persons to render sanitary service and to make or supervise practical and scientific investigations and examinations requiring expert skill, and to prepare plans and reports relative thereto. And it is hereby made the duty of all boards, officers and agents having the control, charge or custody of any public structure, work, ground or erection, or of any plan, description, outlines, drawings or charts thereof, or relating thereto, made, kept or controlled under any public authority, to permit and facilitate the examination and inspection, and the making of copies of the same by any officer or person by said Board authorized; and the members of said Board, and such other officer or person as may at any time be by said Board authorized, may, without fee or hindrance, enter, examine and survey all such grounds, erections, vehicles, structures, apartments, buildings and places.

SEC. 8.—That it shall be the duty of the State Board of Health to have the general supervision of the State system of registration of births, marriages and deaths. Said Board shall prepare the necessary methods and forms for obtaining and preserving such records, and to insure the faithful registration of the same in the several counties and in the central bureau of vital statistics at the capital of the State. The said Board of Health shall recommend such forms and amendments of law as shall be deemed to be necessary for the thorough organization and efficiency of the registration of vital statistics throughout the State. The Secretary of said Board of Health shall be the superintendent of registration of vital statistics. As supervised by the said Board, the clerical duties and safe-keeping of the bureau of vital statistics thus created shall be provided for by the comptroller of the State, who shall also provide and furnish such apartments and stationery as said Board shall require in the discharge of its duties.

SEC. 9.—That the said Board, on or before the first day of January in each year, shall make a report in writing to the Governor, upon the vital statistics and the sanitary condition and prospects of the State, which report shall also set forth the action of said Board, and of its officers and agents, and the names thereof for the past year; and shall contain a full statement of their acts, investigations, and discoveries, with such suggestions for further legislative action or other precautions as they may deem proper for the better protection of life and health. This report shall also contain a detailed statement of the moneys expended by said Board, and the manner of their expenditure during the year for which it is made; but the total amount paid for the expenses of this Board, including the salary and expenses of the Secretary, shall not exceed   , which amount is hereby annually appropriated for this purpose, to be paid by the Treasurer, on the Comptroller's warrant, in such sums as the certificate of the Board, with proper vouchers annexed, may certify from time to time.

SEC. 10.—That this act shall take effect from the date of its passage; and that all acts, or parts of acts, inconsistent herewith be, and the same are, hereby repealed.

NOTE.—At the organization of the American Public Health Association a standing committee upon State and Local Sanitary Organization was formed; and its first report is now published. At the last annual meeting a special committee—Hon. Dr. L. H. Steiner, a State Senator of Md., Chairman—was appointed to draw up, and submit for consideration of the executive committee, the outline of an Act for creating a State Board of Health. The foregoing draft of the required outline of an Act was submitted by Senator STEINER's special committee, on the 27th of January, at a meeting of the executive committee, and the following action was taken thereon:—

Resolved: That Dr. STEINER's report on the draft of an act to create State Boards of Health is adopted as a satisfactory report.

Resolved: That a copy of the said report be forwarded to the executive and legislative authorities of all the States, together with a recommendation that health officers be appointed or Boards of Health be organized in all counties, towns, and cities throughout the several States, to co-operate with the said State Boards.

The following remarks by the special committee correctly set forth the purpose of the special committee to which was referred the preparation of a draft of an Act for the establishment of State Boards of Health:

"This outline of *An act to establish a State Board of Health, and to assign certain duties to Local Boards of Health*, has been prepared after a careful examination of the field to be occupied by such a Board, and a thorough study of the peculiarities of the acts already passed by those States that are already supplied with such Boards. As the *enacting language* of almost every State differs, they have employed none, leaving that to be supplied in each State in accordance with its constitutional requirements or time-honored usage. In regard to the constitution of the Board, it may be desirable in some States, as New York for instance, to include in the *personnel* of the Board such officers as the Comptroller and State Engineer, and in others, to reduce the number to four appointments by the Governor. These are, however, matters to be decided by each State for itself. They do not affect the other sections of the Act which have to do with the definition of the duties of the Board." L. H. Steiner, *Chairman*.

This project of law is respectfully submitted to you, Sir, as directed by the Association, in the earnest hope that the important subject to which it relates may receive the attention which it deserves in your State, and that this effort to secure some degree of harmonious and effective methods of sanitary administration may receive your aid and encouragement.

With the highest respect,
Yours, on behalf of the Association,
Elisha Harris, M.D., *Secretary*.

58 Bible House, Astor Place, New York.

Cure for Discontent.—An English country gentleman became tired of his house, and determined to sell it. He instructed an auctioneer, famous for his descriptive powers, to advertise it in the papers for private sale, but to conceal the location, telling persons to apply at his office. In a few days the gentleman happened to see the advertisement, was pleased with the account of the place, showed it to his wife, and the two concluded it was just what they wanted, and that they would secure it at once. So he went to the office of the auctioneer and told him the place he had advertised was such a one as he desired, and he would purchase it. The auctioneer burst into a laugh, and told him that that was the description of his own house, where he was then living. He read the advertisement again, pondered over the "grassy slopes," "beautiful vistas," "smooth lawn," etc., and broke out, "Is it possible? Well, make out my bill for advertising and expenses, for I wouldn't sell the place now for three times what it cost me."—*Building News*.

BRAIN CULTURE IN RELATION TO THE SCHOOL-ROOM.

By A. N. Bell, M. D.

Read, by invitation, before the Department of Superintendence of the National Teachers' Association, Washington, Jan. 27th, 1875.

Education is a primary necessity of man. It is by education that the organs of the body acquire accuracy in their movements. The senses of sight, hearing, taste and smell all *learn* to act. And the earliest charm of infant life is to observe the progress of the education of the senses; to watch the study of a toy; to see the hands holding it at various distances, turning its different sides to view, tasting it, shaking it, and finally, when a little older, breaking it to see whence comes the noise. Who that has watched this process has not learned the first accomplishment of a teacher—to promote the education of the senses by the association of physical exercise, amusement and study? The passage from infancy to childhood is but an imperceptible step, marked by the continued expression of new experiences. Everything excites new impressions; everything must be examined with due deliberation—no hurry, no pressure, no fatigue. And during the while—aye, even during the whole period of waking hours—there is incessant motion. Nature has implanted in the young of all animals a pleasure in exercise, muscular action being not only necessary for strengthening the muscles, but also the bones to which they are attached. The actions of crying and laughing, the deep inspirations of sobbing and joy, both alike tend to develop and strengthen the lungs; and the active exercise of the lungs promotes and develops the action of the heart, which with increasing vigor sends the blood to every part of the body. In all this the brain participates to an extraordinary degree, requiring that the young mind be exercised with the utmost care. By experience and habit the child acquires judgment, learns to compare one movement with another, to direct its organs to special objects, to produce this or that action, to take this or that attitude for the accomplishment of its purposes; and all the subsequent capacity of the brain will greatly depend upon the care with which it is cultured during the period of growth. Imagination, perception and memory, faculties which are always preceded and determined by the sensations, are all the subjects of education, enlarged and extended in proportion as new excitements and impressions call them forth and give them application.

"Glancing broadly at the whole range of psycho-physical phenomena," observes Dr. Tuke, "it is clear that it would be taking a very contracted view of the relation between mind and body if we did not include in this relationship a reference to the inseparable *nexus* existing between the two, arising out of the fact that the organ of the mind is but the outgrowth and ultimate development of the tissues and organs of which the body itself is composed; that it not only unites them in one bond, but is in truth a microcosm of the whole."*

---

* Influence of Mind upon the Body, in Health and Disease. By Daniel Hack Tuke, M. D., M. R. C. P. p. 23. Philadelphia: 1873.

Of all parts of the human body, the brain is the last to gain maturity. According to Owen, "the brain has advanced to near its term of size at about ten years, but it does not usually obtain its full development till between twenty and thirty years of age."* While the brain has not usually more than *one-fortieth* of the weight of the body, it receives about *one-fifth* of the whole volume of the blood. It is scarcely necessary to state, in this connection, that every organ and tissue of the body is nourished by the blood, and that upon the supply of it and the *condition* of it, nutrition and development, for weal or for woe, depend.

During the period of growth there is not only the development of new parts, but, in the brain especially, a change of structure going on until that degree of perfection has been attained which is necessary to the exercise of all the functions. Hence this period is characterized by extraordinary functional activity in every part of the body.

It is this which makes the demand of food so much greater during the period of growth than in after years. Not, however, that the larger proportion of food in demand is wholly required as new material applied to actual increase, for that bears a very small proportion to the amount which is required for constant renewal which the increase involves; but the extraordinary functional activity in disposing of it, and the corresponding necessity for replacing the waste in the building-up and perfecting the structure according to the original plan. For it is characteristic of every living thing to follow out a certain inherent type or pattern, subject, of course, in some degree to modification under the influence of external conditions, or when these are aggravated, to acute disease and death; but such circumstances do not effect a permanent change in the original design. During the period of growth and change of structure the modifying influence of external conditions is most strongly marked. The constitution of the individual adapts itself to the circumstances, and becomes fixed for the life-time. So that if a child of originally healthy constitution be subject for a considerable length of time to such injurious physical conditions as produce a tendency to disease, unless the conditions are speedily changed, the effect is to establish a constitutional weakness or disease, not only during the life of the individual, but it may be a *diathesis* with hereditary qualities for several generations. For when the modification of the individual is once fixed in the growing brain it becomes part of the general fabric; the different organs adapt themselves to the change, and the condition is maintained by nutritive substitution. On the other hand, constitutional vices contracted during the period of growth may be gradually overcome in the progress of new generations; and, by a continued subjection to healthy surroundings, the normal type regained. It is apparent, therefore, that the changes of growth and structure are all effected by, and through the circulation of the blood; its condition depends upon the air we breathe.

Air, everybody knows, is the absolute necessity of every living thing. It is the very first element of our bodily tissues, and

* Anatomy of Vertebrates. By Richard Owen, F. R. S. Vol. III. p. 144. London: 1868.

breathing affords three-quarters of the nourishment of our bodies; and the other quarter, which we obtain in the form of solid and fluid aliment, is also in great part composed of oxygen, nitrogen, and carbonic acid,—the elements of the atmosphere. Chemically, the air consists of a mixture of two kinds of gases,—oxygen or *vital air*, and nitrogen, in the proportion, by volume, of one-fifth of the former to four-fifths of the latter; and besides these, carbonic acid, or *fixed air*, which exists in the free atmosphere in the proportion of about four parts to ten thousand.

In the small proportion in which carbonic acid exists in the free atmosphere, it produces no evil effects; but in larger quantities it is not only dangerous, but frequently fatal. Being heavier than the other gases of the atmosphere, it is usually found in excess in low or confined places, such as mines, grottoes, and wells, and in the holds and steerages of ships, and in unventilated apartments generally. Under all such circumstances it is more or less dangerous to life.

The bad air at the surface of close rooms is carbonic oxid, the product, usually, of burning gas and bad arrangements for warming. This being the lightest of the deleterious gases in close rooms, rises to the surface.*

Pure oxygen will sustain life but a short time, owing to its stimulating qualities; it requires dilution, which seems to be the purpose of nitrogen, which cannot sustain life at all, and alone is deadly from its negative qualities. Carbonic acid, pure, is not respirable. If an attempt be made to inhale it, the glottis closes and prevents it from entering the lungs. When diluted with twice as much or more of air, it ceases to produce that effect upon the glottis, and is permitted to enter the lungs and the blood, and acts as a narcotic poison directly upon the brain. It is not possible to state how large a proportion of this gas may be present in the air without danger; it doubtless differs with different individuals. By experiments on animals it has been shown that an atmosphere containing five per cent. of carbonic acid is fatal in about thirty minutes.

Facts abundantly prove that respired air, or the air of occupied apartments containing of carbonic acid more than one volume per 1000, is dangerous to health. Such air contains, besides the excess of carbonic acid, not infrequently, the more deadly carbonic oxid, dead and decomposing animal matter and other mephitic gases and exhalations arising from defective sewerage or vaults, but it is besides deficient in its very first life-sustaining property, oxygen.

The average amount of oxygen consumed by a healthy individual is half a cubic inch to every respiration, which in a day amounts to upwards of twenty-five cubic feet. And as oxygen constitutes but one-fifth of the volume of the atmosphere, a single individual renders one hundred and twenty-five cubic feet of air unfit for respiration every twenty-four hours, by the abstraction of oxygen alone. Meanwhile, there is exhaled by the lungs about fifteen cubic feet of carbonic acid,

---

* Specific gravity: oxygen (unit), 1000; atmospheric air, in the aggregate 1105.63; nitrogen, 971.37; carbonic acid, 1524.5; carbonic oxid, 971.2.—*Graham.*

thirty ounces of watery vapor, and an indefinite amount of organic matter, variously estimated at from 10 to 240 grains. The whole quantity of air actually respired in twenty-four hours by a healthy person is about 400 cubic feet. This contains, when once passed through the lungs, about five and a half per cent. of carbonic acid, or *more than one hundred times as much as it did when it entered them.*

It is plain, therefore, that in order to reduce respired air to the same standard of purity it had before it was respired, and to keep it so, the supply of fresh air must be at the least equal to one hundred times the volume of that which is thrown out, and upon this condition rests the importance of air space—the space required depending upon circumstances.

For various practical purposes the limits of space may vary from 300 to 4,000 cubic feet--the smallest proportion being the exaction for lodging-houses, and the largest for hospitals--making the allowance in all cases for space occupied by furniture. And no deviation whatever should be made on account of children, whether in regard to the different members of a family or a school-room. The smaller the space the greater the necessity of, and the larger the opening required for the admission of fresh air. If two or three hundred cubic feet only be allowed to the individual, the air must be changed every fifteen or twenty minutes, provision for which necessitates a draught, and in cold weather, great waste of heat; hence it is evident that the danger of "taking cold" in a small room, if it is kept ventilated, is much greater than it is in a large one. To reduce the gaseous components of respired air to their natural proportions and to neutralize its deleterious qualities, every person requires from 2,000 to 2,500 cubic feet of fresh air every hour. To admit this amount of fresh air into a room is not so difficult as persons generally suppose. It has been calculated that with ordinary exposure, an open space equal to five inches in the square, will admit the passage of 2,000 cubic feet of air hourly; this of course implies that there should be an equal amount of open space for the escape of the air displaced. If, therefore, an ordinary window of three feet wide be open about an inch and a half at the top, and there be a chimney flue in the room, the purpose is accomplished. Or the same by two windows on opposite sides of the room; or, it may be by crevices equal to this space about a door, in co-operation with one window. The multiplication of persons, it is plain, requires a corresponding multiplication of means.

In the aeration of the blood, the organs of circulation and respiration are both no less essential to the maintenance of life than they are to each other. Their combined functions constitute the only means of admitting air into the body. And these functions must co-operate and be maintained without intermission for one single minute, from birth until death. And yet they have rest; the heart reposes about one-fourth of its time, and the lungs about one-third; but the periods of repose are too short to allow of any escape from a dangerous atmosphere. The amount of blood in the human body constitutes about one-eighth of its entire weight, but it is variable within certain limits, depending upon the time and amount of food taken. Air is drawn in by the lungs through the windpipe or trachea, which divides and subdivides into numerous smaller tubes leading to the air cells, which in the aggregate constitute the lungs, situated, one on each side of the chest, and the heart between. The number of the air cells has been estimated at seventeen millions, presenting a surface, if spread out, equal to about 22,000 square inches, or thirty times the surface of the whole body. The lining membrane of the air cells attenuated to the thinness of a cobweb, is the medium by which the air communicates with the blood. But the air in the lungs is not wholly changed with every breath. It cannot suddenly penetrate the membrane which separates it from actual contact with the blood, and effect the required change in a moment. On the contrary, the air cells are constantly full, the quantity contained being from 20 to 30 cubic inches, and of this the amount changed with each breath is only about one-tenth. Each fresh supply mixes with that which remains, and the change goes on incessantly, while that which is breathed out, although about the same in quantity, is, as already shown, very different in its properties. If the walls of an air cell be examined with a microscope, it will be found to be covered with a network of exceedingly small blood-vessels, called capillaries, but much finer than hairs; and so closely packed together that the interspaces between are smaller than the vessels. These little vessels are the communicating extremities of larger ones, beginning and ending in the heart. At every beat of the heart blood is sent into the pulmonary artery, and through it into the capillaries, where it is brought into contact with the lining membrane of the air cells and through it exposed to the air, thence it returns again to the heart by the continuation of the capillaries into the pulmonary veins. It is calculated that at each pulsation of the heart not less than $\frac{1}{17}$ lb. of all the blood in the body passes into the lungs; three times every minute the whole mass of blood is passed through the lungs and exposed to the air. Measured at each circuit, the whole quantity of blood so exposed in a day amounts to 57 hogsheads, and by weight 540 lbs. every hour, or 12,960 lbs. in a day. The quantity of fresh air *imbibed* by this exposure of the blood amounts to 616 cubic inches, or about 2¼ gallons every minute, or upwards of two hogsheads per hour.

Life has often been compared to a burning flame, a sort of combustion which, like fire, can never be sustained without the consumption of fuel, and failing this, it flickers out, never again to be rekindled except new life be given. The simile is in some respects marvellously perfect. Both flame and life depend upon air. Most persons have witnessed the experiment of placing a lighted candle or a taper under a bell-glass, and know the result, that at first it burns brightly, gradually becomes feeble, and finally goes out altogether. If instead of flame, a bird or a mouse be placed under the glass, the effect on its life is precisely the same. In both cases the air is devitalized; it is not all used up, but that which is left will neither support a flame nor sustain life. A large proportion of the oxygen has been consumed, and the proportion of carbonic acid and moisture increased. In the one case oxygen has been used to support combustion, and in the other to sustain life; and air which has been respired, or in which anything has been burned, is always deficient in oxygen and contains an excess of carbonic acid and moisture. So far, then, as these conditions apply, every living animal represents combustion. In the free atmosphere, no creature ever suffered for the want of oxygen, or from an excess of carbonic acid; but in crowded and unventilated rooms great harm often results from both.

Brain culture is environed by the school-room. Upon the condition and management of the school-room depends the quality of the brain, and the brain is the *soil* of subsequent endowments. Education is the fruit, *it* contemplates a continuance of mental discipline and exertion far beyond the limits of the school-room, or college life. By education is acquired the mental and moral power to sustain the feelings, affections, propensities and passions, so that none of these may ever gain the mastery of the intelligence; a power which can never be acquired without proper brain culture. A fruitful harvest can never come of an impoverished soil. Most of the anxieties and miseries of life result from the want of a sound and strong brain; and as we trace back these to their source, they all seem to depend on the want of power to regulate impulse and feeling. A well-cultivated brain is unquestionably the true road to exalted virtues, and the union of a sound intellect and moral power the only stable foundation of true wisdom, by which health becomes, next to eternal salvation, the most important object of life. A pure atmosphere is the first need of the school-room, without it none of the vital functions can be sustained in health.—We have seen the wonderful activity with which the functions of life are performed; that within twenty seconds a poisonous gas drawn in with the breath permeates every tissue of the body. That every single respiratory act multiplies the carbonic acid a hundred-fold. No teacher, surely, will fail to appreciate the importance of these phenomena, nor should he fail to teach them to his pupils. A new series of questions in arithmetic should be devised for their inculcation, such as: If half a cubic inch of oxygen be consumed at every respiration, how many respirations will it take to consume 25 cubic feet? If air that has been once passed through the lungs contain five and a-half per cent. of carbonic acid, how many volumes of atmosphere will it require to reduce it to four parts per ten thousand? If a single pupil breathes 70 cubic feet of air in four hours, how many cubic feet will be required for 600 pupils seven hours? If a closet of 300 cubic feet capacity requires 2,000 cubic feet of air every hour to purify the air sufficiently for one individual, how many cubic feet of air will be required every hour to purify the atmosphere of a school-room 40x35x12, containing 75 pupils? Many other questions of similar practical utility will readily suggest themselves to the thoughtful teacher.

I cannot better close these remarks than by inviting attention to the recent action of the R. I. State Medical Society, as being eminently worthy of serious consideration. This action may not meet with general approval in all its particulars, but it is commendable, as being a practical and definite application of general principles, and a suggestion to all thoughtful persons who are in any way responsible for the modes and methods of education.

"*Whereas*, Although the present school system has been brought to a high degree of completeness in intellectual culture, and to an exalted position, of which its friends and the community may well be proud, yet, entertaining for its welfare a profound interest, and viewing it as we do from a physical standpoint, and believing that in the haste for intellectual culture the physical is too much neglected, the nervous system is developed to the omission of other portions of the body, thus giving rise to a long train of ills, and producing an unsymmetrical and distorted organization in the young, entirely unfitted for the stern duties of life; therefore,—

"*Resolved:* First—That physical culture is of primary importance in our public schools, and that gymnastic exercise should be made a part of our school system.

"Second—That the 'Kindergarten system' should be engrafted upon our public school system.

"Third—That the school buildings should not exceed two stories in height.

"Fourth—That three hundred cubic feet of space and twenty-five square feet of floor space should be the minimum for each child in a school-room in connection with good ventilation.

"Fifth—That proper warmth and pure air are of the first importance, and should always be considered before ornamentation.

"Sixth—That scholars should not maintain the same position more than half an hour at a time.

"Seventh—That two short sessions, daily, are better than one long one.

"Eighth—That no child should be admitted into our public schools, as now conducted, under seven years of age.

"Ninth—That under twelve years of age, three hours a day, and for twelve years and over, four hours a day, is sufficiently long confinement to mental culture.

"Tenth—That study out of school should not usually be permitted.

"Eleventh—That all incentives to emulation should be used cautiously, especially with girls.

"Twelfth—That the 'half-time system' should be introduced into our public schools."

PROTECTING INFLUENCE OF THE EARTH'S ATMOSPHERE.—Weilman, after reducing the hourly observations made at Berne, Switzerland, for seven years, and deducing therefrom the laws of diurnal change of temperature, has investigated the effect of cloudiness on the daily variation, especially at night. He finds that the radiating power of the earth's surface is everywhere and at all times the same. The temperature in the morning is, he finds, in cloudy weather, five or six degrees higher than in clear weather. And again, that the simple atmosphere of the earth surrounds it like a protecting layer of clouds, and that without this the earth would experience daily an enormous variation in temperature. Even the clear sky, or rather the moisture present, as an invisible vapor, protects the earth with an efficiency equal to about one-third of that exerted by a layer of clouds, against too strong a daily change of temperature.

PHYSICAL CULTURE.

THE BEST MEANS OF SECURING IT.

By H. L. Bartlett, M. D.

Having demonstrated the necessity of exercise, both for the well-being of the individual, and the good of society, it remains to consider the best means of securing it.

We can hardly expect to revive the ancient games, nor would it be well for us if we could, as modern life has too many demands upon our time to permit it. They tended to develop athletism rather than enduring health—to make soldiers rather than citizens—and yet there can be no doubt that an enforced military education like that which is practised by some of the governments of Europe is beneficial to a large class of their subjects. It inures them to privations and hardships, teaches subordination to wholesome restraints, inculcates industry and regularity, and a respect for law.

In the late war of the rebellion, many a young man went into service pale and muscleless and returned (if he returned at all) a bronzed, athletic veteran.

The recent popularity of ball playing, boat-racing, cricketing, and other athletic sports, has undoubtedly done much to develop the young men of the country; but they are not applicable to the great bulk of those needing exercise. Gymnasia have lately been introduced into most of our schools and colleges, but as at present managed, are far from being all that is required, even for students. The great defect in all the "manly sports," so called, is that they are too violent for delicate persons, and quite inapplicable for females. Besides they cultivate certain muscles, or groups of muscles, to the neglect of others. Thus foot-ball, cricket, rowing, and walking, or running, call into play the muscles of the lower limbs, while the arms and muscles of the chest are little used.

It has been said that the excessive exercise required to become a proficient in rowing or boxing, is injurious to health—that the system becomes exhausted and feels the strain upon the bodily powers in after years. That modern pugilists and gymnasts are short-lived is beyond contradiction, and we have the authority of both Galen and Hippocrates for saying that the same was the case with the ancient athletæ. Galen says, "The athletes became dull, sluggish and torpid, and only averaged five years of (athletic) life." He also says, "They were subject to mental diseases—constant excitement exalted or depressed them, according as they were victorious or defeated—thus producing diseases of the brain and nervous system." He further writes, that he had often witnessed in the contestants "loss of sense and motion—suffocation and rupture of blood-vessels." In fine, the testimony of history is, that the athletæ, as a class, possessed neither true health, nor permanent physical power. This is equally true of modern pugilists and gymnasts. It is well known by trainers that a man cannot be long kept in an exalted physical condition with impunity. He becomes, as they say, "trained too fine," and loses bodily power. His muscular system is developed at the expense of everything else, and he becomes a mere machine. He leads an exciting and precarious life, alternately pitied and scorned. To-day living an abstemious and chaste life—to-morrow given to gluttony and vice. No wonder such persons are short-lived, either killed by accident, or untimely cut off by acute disease, for it is well attested that inflammatory diseases are far more likely to prove fatal to those who are over plethoric than to those of an opposite habit.

These remarks, however, hardly apply to athletic sports as connected with student life. Here the contests of physical strength are wisely alternated with intellectual life. With the student, boat-racing and ball-playing are but recreations, and not the business of life—a mere amusement and relaxation from study and not a profession.

Some years since public attention was called to the subject of athletic sports, in connection with college and university life, and the statement was made by popular journals that the exercise requisite to make a student proficient as a champion in rowing or ball-playing, was dangerous to life, and detrimental to health. To settle this question, Dr. John Edward Morgan, of Oxford, England, took the trouble to learn the personal history of all the crews engaged in the Oxford and Cambridge boat-races from 1829 to 1869, a period of forty years, and comprising thirty-two crews, including two hundred and ninety-four oarsmen. Of these thirty-nine had died, in the mean time, of the following diseases: of fever, 11; consumption, 9; accidental causes, 6; heart affections, 3; diseases of the brain, 2; inflammatory attacks, 2; general paralysis, 1; calculus, 1; erysipelas, 1; Bright's disease of the kidneys, 1; cancer, 1; lupus, 1.

Surely these are not causes of death induced by over-exertion.

According to the report of the Register General of Great Britain, the mortality in civil life from diseases of the heart and lungs, is 46 per cent., and among soldiers and sailors still larger, while among the Oxford and Cambridge oarsmen the mortality was only 30 per cent. from the same causes.

According to Dr. Farr's Life Tables, the average duration of life after the age of 20, is 40 years. In other words, a person who has reached the age of 20 will probably live till the age of 60. Dr. Morgan found the average of the Oxford crew of 1829 to be 46 years, and the Cambridge crew, of the same year, to be 48.6, or an excess of from 6 to 8 years beyond the average of human life, and concludes that the University oarsmen, though their labor be excessive at times, are more robust, better scholars, and live longer than the other students.

Rev. Henry Arthur Morgan, brother of the above, says: "I have, myself, rowed in over 100 eight-oared races, on the Cambridge, and have mingled much with rowing men, but have never seen injurious effects from the rowing." The popular idea, therefore, that it is injurious to the students of our colleges and universities to join in athletic sports, even of a severe character, is not borne out by facts. On the contrary, experience proves that they who are the most successful ball-players and oarsmen are, as a rule, the best students. It is reasonable to suppose that this should be so, since study is a great tax upon the physical strength and endurance of a man, and he who has the most stamina, other things being equal, will win.

There are other causes, also, which tend in the same direction. A student who is engaged and interested in manly exercise has less inclination and less time to spend in vicious and indolent habits than he who cares for none of these things. Elevate any man or woman physically, and you elevate them intellectually and morally. This is the reason why the middling and working classes are the most contented and virtuous. So far, therefore, from discouraging manly exercise in students, whether academic or collegiate, the opposite course should be strenuously followed by all who have their best good at heart. But in the selection of the right kind and amount of exercise for each particular student, great care and judgment are requisite.

Here is where the present system is defective. To put all boys through the same drill is not only unscientific but often injurious.

Connected with every gymnasium there should be a medical man, specially educated for this work, whose duty it should be to examine into the history and physical condition of every student, and prescribe for each the kind and amount of exercise required. This is especially true in schools where girls are taught. The latter are more sensitive and excitable than boys, and sooner become exhausted; hence they require a different drill. And yet in their case, as well as in that of boys, the cardinal rule of physical development should never be lost sight of, viz.: that to develop a muscle it must be made to contract to its fullest extent. The law of muscular growth demands that to make a muscle stronger to-morrow, it must be taxed to its utmost to-day. Keeping this law in view, the so-called "light gymnastics," or "calisthenics," are almost worthless. Their object seems to be to produce celerity and precision of movement rather than to develop strength. As well might you expect the throw of the weaver's shuttle or the ceaseless ply of the seamstress's needle to produce muscular growth!

It is a very pretty sight to see a large class of youths, dressed in uniform, engaged in the calisthenic drill, each with his or her baton moving to the time of exhilarating music, but to me the thought ever uppermost is, "How tired the poor little things must be!" With the peculiar genius of our people, conductors of academies and colleges, finding a popular demand for gymnasia, at once erect a structure or appropriate a room, suitably furnished with all the appliances for the same, and inaugurate gymnastic exercises without knowing the first principles of the science of physical culture, or the rules by which they should be governed in order to prove beneficial to those who are engaged in them. In fact, I am inclined to the opinion that these institutions, as at present managed, do as much harm as they do good. They are frequently conducted in poorly-ventilated rooms, continued to the point of exhaustion, at least on the part of the feebler members of the class, and at a period of the day when the bodily powers have been already overtaxed by prolonged mental exertions. If these athletic sports and gymnastic drills come short of doing all that we could desire, what shall we say or do for those who have not even these advantages? The toiling millions need exercise, for labor is not exercise. Labor may and does develop certain muscles used in particular occupations, but it does not strengthen all of them; it does not develop the brain, the intellectual or imaginative faculties, or the feelings. Many kinds of labor are carried on in darkness, and amid foul and noxious airs, and are decidedly detrimental to digestion and assimilation. In its highest sense, exercise develops all the organs of the body; it produces growth in the muscles, both voluntary and involuntary, accelerates the circulation, and hastens from the body all useless and effete matters, enlarges the lung capacity and furnishes oxygen to the waste tissues, stimulates the brain and nervous energies; in fine, sends the pulses bounding with a new joy and life through the entire frame. Labor does not, and can not do this. Man, as a result of his disobedience, has been forced to work for his subsistence, and consequently work not only becomes a duty, but is honorable. But a condition of servitude, whether self-imposed or enforced, is not the highest condition of man.

Even farmers, who have the advantages of fresh air, nutritious food, and the control of their own movements, are only fourth on the list of longevity, according to life rates. Clergymen are the longest lived men, and this is accounted for by their mode of life, embracing pleasant mental occupation, with a moderate amount of physical exercise and agreeable social relations.

The effect of education and leisure combined, is shown in a still more marked degree, when we compare the aristocracy of a country with its peasantry. In England, the average length of life among the nobility is largely in excess of that of the lower classes. In answer, therefore, to the question, What shall we do for the working millions? we reply, teach them the laws of health, show them that to raise man to his highest estate we must develop all his faculties, physical, mental, and moral—that labor is a necessity, but a necessary evil of an earthly condition—that rational pleasure is needed as much as enforced labor——that to develop the muscles, they must be used vigorously and intensely for a short period every day. That to enlarge the lungs, full and prolonged respiration must be made in the open air, so that the deep cells of the lungs may be washed out, and the air changed, as it is not, and never can be, by ordinary breathing. That the brain, including all the mental faculties, must be used, for on this the well-being of the body largely depends. Do this, and digestion, assimilation and excretion, will take care of themselves, and the machinery of life will run smoothly on. To accomplish these objects, let every sound person become a gymnast, and every home a gymnasium. Begin the day with a cold sponge bath, not only for purposes of cleanliness, but more particularly to shock the cutaneous nerves, and accustom them to sudden transitions of temperature, and to drive the blood in upon the lungs for oxygenation—then rub vigorously with crash towels, and use dumb bells or Indian clubs till the crimson current ebbs back again with healthful glow through all the capillaries, and my word for it, a keener appetite will await with impatience the morning meal. Let that be a generous one, composed of both animal and vegetable food, not forgetting that by far the great bulk of mankind are underfed. When in the open air, walk with body erect, and with an elastic step, a step impelled by the power of the will, thus bringing

into active play the muscles of the lower limbs, meanwhile gesticulating with the arms, like a lunatic, if you like. Let your sleeping apartments be large, light, and airy, and guard against all noxious emanations from sewers and cesspools, as you would from the midnight assassin, and the curtains of sleep will fall sweetly and gently over your eyelids, and life will possess a charm and a joy before unknown.

THE CARE OF CANARIES.

A pair of canaries I give to your care.
Don't blind them with sunshine, or starve them with air,
Or leave them out late in the cold and the damp,
And then be surprised if they suffer from cramp;
Or open the window in all kind of weathers
Quite near to their cage till they puff out their feathers.
The birds that are free fly to bush and to grot,
If the wind be too cold or the sun is too hot;
But these pretty captives depend on your aid,
In winter for warmth, and in summer for shade.
When they chirrup, and ceaselessly hop to and fro,
Some want or discomfort they're trying to show;
When they scrape their bills sharply on perch or at wire
They're asking for something they greatly desire;
When they set every feather on end in a twinkling,
With musical rustle, like water a-sprinkling,
In rain or in sunshine, with sharp call-like notes,
They are begging for water to freshen their coats.
Cage, perches and vessels, keep all very clean,
For fear of small insects—you know what I mean!—
They breed in their feathers, and leave them no rest.
In buying them seed, choose the cleanest and best.
I feed my canaries (excuse me the hint)
On hemp and canary, rape, millet and lint.
I try them with all, till I find out their taste—
The food they don't care for they scatter and waste.
About their bright cages I hang a gay bower
Of shepherd's purse, chickweed, and groundsel in flower.
At a root of ripe grass they will pick with much zest,
For seeds and small pebbles, their food to digest.
But all should be ripe, and well seeded, and brown,
Few leaves on the groundsel, but plenty of down.
In summer I hang them out high in the shade
About our hall-door by a portico made;
In spring, autumn, winter, a window they share,
Where the blind is drawn down to the afternoon glare.
This window, if open beneath them, we close,
Lest the cramp should seize hold of their poor little toes.
A bath about noontide on every mild day
Will keep your small favorites healthy and gay.
In hot summer sunshine, some calico green,
As a roof to their cage, makes a very good screen.
On winter nights, cover from lamplight and cold;
And they'll sing in all weathers, and live to be old.

—*The Animal World*.

DEFECTIVE DRAINAGE AS A CAUSE OF DISEASE IN THE STATE OF NEW YORK.

Abstract of the Report of the Committee on Hygiene of the Medical Society of the State of New York. Annual Meeting, February 3d, 1875.

The Committee on Hygiene again reported progress—in continuation of the subject of *Defective Drainage;* submitted reports from eleven different counties, and two special reports—one on the *Cayuga Marshes*, by S. J. Parker, M. D., and the other on the *Development of Intermittent Fever, at Sing Sing, by Obstructed Drains,* by G. J. Fisher, M. D.

Albany County has for a basis of drainage a natural system of old creek beds, by which, there can be no doubt, the city has been spared much suffering, disease and death, from ailments of a zymotic character, owing to the favorable hygienic conditions secured by this natural drainage.

Indeed the death rate of Albany compares very favorably with that of any of the large cities of the Union. According to the report of the City Registrar, Mr. Thomas J. Lanahan, for the year ending April 30th, 1873, the number of deaths was 1786. Now assuming that the population of the city at that time was 85,000, which perhaps very nearly represents the fact, we find that the ratio of deaths was one to forty-eight, or 20.83 to each 1,000. While this ratio of mortality compares very favorably with some of our larger cities, it must be admitted it is by no means so favorable as ought to be secured to Albany, with its superior natural advantages and a well regulated system of drainage.

In looking over the above-mentioned report as to the assigned causes of death, we are struck with the large number of deaths attributed to diseases of a zymotic type. Among these may be enumerated—cerebro-spinal meningitis, 76; cholera infantum, 161; convulsions, 62; diarrhœa, 19; typhoid fever, 50; marasmus, 45; meningitis, 26; phthisis pulmonalis, 277; diphtheria, 12. Total, 728, or more than 40 per cent. of the whole number of deaths.

It is fair to presume that of the above number of deaths from causes in which we know defective drainage plays so important a part, at least one-half the mortality may be justly ascribed to this cause. And further, of the remaining thousand deaths, may we not aptly infer that many of the cases enumerated as congestion of the lungs or brain, debility, dropsy, paralysis, pneumonia, scarlatina, pertussis, or rubeola, may have been hastened to a fatal termination from the poisonous air generated from an imperfect drainage. If the vigorous and the strong are so often made to succumb before the deadly shafts of this unseen foe, who can depict all the baneful effects of sewage on the aged, the feeble and the sick?

It is apparent then that defective drainage kills at the rate of one person each day, in the city of Albany, throughout the year.

It will be remembered how a few months ago, when the dead body of a man was found in a ravine in the western part of the city, the whole community was horrified. A foul murder had been committed. Avenging justice was at once upon the track of the culprit, and did not sleep day or night in its search for the author of so great a crime. The world was not large enough to conceal him. His crime found him out, and swift and sure was the penalty the violated law imposed.

An enemy lurks beneath our feet; his very breath is full of poison; he sends no herald of his coming; he pollutes the water we drink and the air we breathe; he enters our chambers, and, while we sleep, saps the very foundations of our lives; he is ever ready to escape from his prison house to kill and to destroy. His annual victims in this fair city are only numbered by the days of the year. His name is sewerage. This is no fancy sketch, but stern sober truth; and yet because the victim is killed so quietly and noiselessly in his own house, and his pallid features bear no impress of the violent hands laid upon him, the community look on with no sense of horror at the great and unnecessary destruction of human life that is going on.

Scattered about the streets of Albany are a large number of wells, the water of which, owing to its coldness and apparent purity, is much used by the inhabitants of the city. Indeed, during the hotter months of summer these wells are often pumped dry early in the day.

Some of these wells undoubtedly furnich good and wholesome water, especially those which are located in a soil of clay and receive their supply of water from the bottom of the well. The greater number, however, including all that are located in the thickly populated parts of the city and in a sandy soil are almost certain to become, in a greater or less degree, the receptacles of street sewage. The earth removed, when these wells are cleaned (as is sometimes the case), presents a dark sewerage appearance, and offensive smell, indicating but too plainly that they receive the drainage of a sewage-saturated soil, the natural and inevitable result of their close proximity to the cesspools and drains which carry off the sewerage of the neighborhood.

On either side of many of these wells, perhaps ten or twenty feet distant, may be found the street sewers through which flow the refuse of the night closets and all manner of abominable filth, while down the centre of the street passes the drain carrying the sewerage of a hundred or a thousand families. Many of these drains are not intended to be water-tight, and readily allow their fluid contents to percolate through the sandy soil beneath. Can it be doubted that the water obtained from wells thus situated is entirely unfit for domestic use, and a fruitful source of the type of diseases we have been considering. The same objections apply with equal, if not greater force, to the so-called springs or wells, which are to be found in many basements and cellars in the city. Defective drains, the escape of their contents into sandy soil, and its reception into the well, are but precursors of intermittent and typhoid fever, diarrhœa, dysentery, or some other form of zymotic disease, and but too often of death.

Individual cases of the pernicious effects of insufficient drainage may be cited in this connection. An open drain carries the sewerage from a slaughter-house in the western part of the city. A family of father, mother and four children, removed from a healthy neighborhood to the vicinity of this drain. A few weeks later malignant scarlet fever carries off three of the children, while the fourth barely escapes with life. A healthy Irish family resided in an alley in a thickly populated neighborhood (in the immediate vicinity of a number of privy vaults). A visit to the house never fails to suggest to the olfactory nerves, the question of sewerage. A large family was born unto the parents. Phthisis pulmonalis took the father, then one after another of the children, till the mother is left almost alone. A stagnant pond caused by a street opening was allowed to fester for years in the rays of the sun, its rank and poisonous water tainting the neighborhood. A healthy German family of father, mother, and three children lived on low ground immediately contiguous to this pond. Malignant scarlet fever entered the household and left the parents without children. A family of nine persons received their supply of water from a well in the cellar. All were stricken down with typhoid fever; one died, the others recovered, one of whom became the victim a few months afterwards of phthisis pulmonalis. These cases are but types of hundreds that occur every year in our city which add largely to our mortuary statistics.

Two tenement-houses in the central part of the city have cellars underneath without drains. A fatal case of typhoid pneumonia in one, and a fatal case of cerebro-spinal meninigitis, which at this writing assumes a fatal character, in the other, are suggestive of sewage.

There can be no doubt that a vast deal of sickness and death in Albany is caused by the absence of proper drainage to basements and cellars, and the breakage and filling up of old drains, thereby causing the refuse of the privies, cesspools and sinks to percolate through the soil underneath the floors, from which the deadly poison escapes through all parts of the dwelling, bearing its bitter fruit of suffering and disease.

What is needed in Albany County, to secure a greater immunity from malarial diseases, is a more thorough system of small drains or sewers provided with traps, where the surface drainage is received, and an abundant supply of pure water, that it may be used both as a solvent for sewage and to hasten its transit to a point remote from our dense population. Your Committee believe that with a thorough system of drainage, Albany ought to be second to no large city of the Union in the smallness of its death rates, and that by proper effort its sanitary condition can be placed foremost among American cities.

LEVI MOORE, M. D.,
S. H. FREEMAN, M. D.,
JOHN M. BIGELOW, M. D.,
Committee on Hygiene,
Medical Society, County of Albany.

CAYUGA COUNTY.—In behalf of the Committee on Hygiene of the Cayuga County Medical Society, I regret that I can add nothing to my imperfect report of last year in regard to the state of the county in this respect. The members of the committee located in the several sections of the county have failed to report the result of any investigations they may have made. My own residence being in Auburn, I submit the following report upon the condition of the drainage and sewerage of this city and of that of its buildings. The street sewers, so far as constructed, are the only provision made for soil drainage in the city. Very few of the sewers are adequate for this purpose, not being sunk deep enough, and invariably following the street lines; some localities remain in the condition of swampy ground, covered in without drainage. The outlet of the Owasco Lake runs semicircularly through the city, cutting it in two nearly equal parts. Within the city limits there are some five dams upon this stream, constructed to obtain the water power to carry on manufacturing operations. Only one, however, of these dams, viz., the State Prison dam, interferes with the proper drainage and sewerage of any part of the city: and that only because for some years past this dam has been raised till its pond surface is nearly on a level with a street parallel to it on the south, which street is very appropriately called Water street. This locality is in the very heart of the city, and was originally swamp ground, which has been filled in. This section is covered with buildings, and two-thirds or more of Water street has no sewer even. North and east of the stream, and also in the centre of the city was formerly a frog-pond, now covered in and undrained, at the lower part of Franklin street, and a part of North street. South and William streets, thickly built up with handsome private residences, are inadequately drained, from the sewers being too superficial and not connected with an unconstructed sewer in the natural drain channel of that part of the city. I believe that hardly a sewer has been constructed in Auburn with reference to the original topography of the place, and I know of no adequate drainage for low swampy grounds which have been covered in, when the street sewer has not accidentally intersected them. Very much of the house drainage and sewerage has been provided for by sinking barrels and boxes filled with stones on the premises, and opening the drains and sewers of the buildings into these contrivances. Before the city was supplied, some eight or nine years since, with the Owasco Lake water, as it is now in great abundance for all domestic uses, and for the extinguishment of fires, these were the favorite methods of providing for sewerage and drainage of houses, and they are still largely relied on. In consequence, in the older parts of the city, the ground is all honeycombed with successive crops of these sewage barrels and accompanying privy vaults, intervening spaces being striped with wooden drain-pipes, saturating the whole soil with sewage matters, as they also in turn have rotted out, till in some of these localities on excavating new cellars after rainy weather, the water which would leach into them from the surrounding soil would be of the color of coffee. In consequence, as I believe, of this state of things, together with some others to be hereafter mentioned, there has not been, for the twenty-five years that I have practiced medicine here, one solitary week in all these years in which I have not had to treat disease of malarial or sewage gas origin, and this notwithstanding that Auburn is located on high ground, and no swamp of any considerable dimensions within seven miles of it, and the general atmosphere being almost always in a breezy or windy action.

Our building drainage and sewerage is also very improperly constructed, as may be seen from a description of it. The discharge pipes being common for both the drainage and sewerage, open into the cellars of the buildings, their outlets being into the street sewers, or the already described barrels. In consequence of this arrangement, cellars not dry from *natural* soil drainage are always damp, since the drainage water must always enter the cellar before it can find an outlet through the pipe so arranged. Sewage gases also enter the cellar, by this same opening, through the pipe. Practically as most of the street sewers and all of the barrels of stones are sunk not deep enough in the ground, these discharge pipes have no traps, the descent not being sufficient to admit of traps, which would become clogged at once, and where they were constructed with traps these have soon been taken out again for this reason,—a tolerably rapid descent being necessary to keep the trap clear. Even with good working traps on the discharge pipes, this opening, then, into the cellars is a bad arrangement in respect to the introduction of sewage gases into the cellar, in addition to their leaving the cellars damp, because it is well known that water soon becomes saturated with gases, and then they pass through it as they would through a sieve, this fact requiring that all water traps should be constantly or frequently renewed with fresh water, and this is left altogether to the supply from the occasional use of water-closets, etc. As the foundation walls of all buildings are or ought to be laid some eighteen inches or two feet deeper in the ground than the surface of the cellar bottom, it is plain that the bottom of this wall will act as a drain of the soil, if an outlet is furnished it. Of course it follows that the drain-pipe should be laid *outside* of the foundation wall and as deep as the bottom of it, thus furnishing the required outlet, and keeping the cellar always dry. Into the discharge drain-pipe so laid the sewage-pipe of the building can enter outside also of the wall, and the expense be saved of laying down a separate discharge sewage-pipe. There would then be no possible access of sewage gases into the building except through the traps of the water-closet, bath tub, wash stands, and kitchen sinks; and if the main sewage pipe of the building is located in close vicinity to some most constantly heated chimney flue and carried up to the roof so as to secure a decided ascending current, the draught would always be from the water-closet and other traps into the sewage-pipe and out into the general atmosphere (high up among the winds, which are the general purifiers for gases, as water courses are for the solid and liquid matters), instead of into the house from the sewage-pipe through these traps. I believe there is hardly a single building in Auburn with its drainage and sewerage so arranged. I have already stated what I believe to be the consequences in disease of the neglect of these evidently necessary arrangements to avoid the retention and introduction of the causes of disease into our buildings. A single instance may be mentioned by way of illustrating this point. Some years since I was saying in a mixed company of my neighbors, that I believed in a large number of instances I could point out in houses where severe cases of fever had occurred, the local causes of them in the drainage or sewerage of those houses. A wealthy and intelligent gentlemen standing by who had, as he supposed, spared no pains or expense in these respects in building his house, and in whose family a servant girl had died of fever, and his wife had barely escaped death after a long and dangerous attack of it, quite indignantly protested against my statement and defied me to prove it in the case of his house. Taking a pencil and a piece of paper, I drew on the paper a sectional outline of his cellar and of the street sewer, and connecting them with a pipe, asked him if that was not the way his house was drained. He acknowledged that it was. I then said to him, "Do you not see that you are ventilating your house through this drain-pipe from the street sewer?" Happily he did see it, and the same day had an effectual stop put to that method of ventilation, and equally happily there has not been a case of fever in his house since.

THEODORE DIMON, M. D.
Chairman of Committee on Hygiene.

CHAUTAUQUA COUNTY is nominally a well-drained county. It is divided into two water-sheds, the northern or Lake Erie shed being from 5 to 10 miles wide, with a descent of 600 to 900 feet to the lake. The other drains southerly into Chautauqua Lake or other tributaries of the Allegany.

The land within a mile of Lake Erie is clayey, rising abruptly from the lake by a sharp rocky bluff 30 to 50 feet, then about 80 feet to the mile for 2 to 5 miles, then much more abruptly to summit.

The soil on main east and west road, parallel with the lake, and 1 to 1½ miles distant, is gravel loam. There is no marsh land on northern slope.

The soil of southern water-shed is clayey, sandy, or a loam with hardpan subsoil. Around Chautauqua Lake there is some marsh land and also along the most level water courses.

There has been no systematic drainage in the county. Our diseases indicate defective drainage. We have typhoid fever, diphtheria, cerebro-spinal meningitis, epidemic dysentery, etc. Some four years since, cerebro-spinal meningitis prevailed as a fatal epidemic along the low land from Cassadaga Lake, near the summit between the water sheds, following its outlet to the south part of the county. In the spring of 1872, the same disease prevailed with unusual malignity in the village in Ripley, the northwest town in the county. The village is located along the main road, where the soil is gravel. Immediately south of the village is the Lake Shore Railroad, and south of this the soil is loam with hardpan subsoil. On the south bank of the railroad the water-courses crop out on the line of the hardpan at 2 to 6 feet below the soil surface. For half a mile to the steeper rise, the springs are near the surface and the ground is wet. This epidemic was confined to the east and extreme west ends of the village. An interesting fact may account for the immunity through the central portion. A large farm on south side of and adjoining the railroad has been thoroughly drained with tile, and not a single case occurred till its limits were passed to the east or west.

Other facts indicate to this Committee that great improvement in the general health is to be made by efficient drainage in this county, for which nature has done so much to relieve it of surface and stagnant water.

THOS. D. STRONG, M. D.,
Chairman Committee on Hygiene,
Chautauqua County Soc.

(*To be continued.*)

ABATTOIRS AND DROVE-YARDS.

By John H. Rauch, M. D.

Philadelphia, *Nov.* 21, 1874.

John H. Rauch, M. D., *Late Sanitary Superintendent of Chicago:*

Dear Sir—In behalf of the Committee of Citizens on the Schuylkill Drove-Yard and Abattoir, I would respectfully ask you to favor us with your opinion as to the advantages and disadvantages of the proposed location, and the probable influence of such an establishment upon the sanitary condition of this city; and if you should consider the proposed site to be objectionable, we would be glad to know where you think it ought to be located. * * * *

John Sellers, Jr., *Chairman.*

To John Sellers, Jr., Esq., *Chairman of Committee, etc.:*

Sir—Before replying to your communication I would state, by way of explanation, that my replies to the queries propounded before the American Public Health Association, at its recent meeting in this city, were of a general character, and did not apply specially to the abattoir and stock-yards, as proposed to be conducted at West Philadelphia. Since then I have carefully examined that site and considered all the conditions bearing upon it, and in this letter I propose to discuss the questions connected with that enterprise.

In response to your inquiry as to the advantages of the proposed location, in my opinion they are purely commercial, and in this respect it is, in some points, superior to any other within or near the limits of Philadelphia; but from a strictly sanitary standpoint it is one of the most undesirable that could be selected.

In your letter you state that the Pennsylvania Railroad Company designs the stock-yards eventually to have a capacity for storing 7,500 head of cattle, 8,000 hogs, and 12,000 sheep. It is, therefore, safe to assume that 3,000 head of cattle, 3,000 hogs, and 6,000 sheep, will generally be collected here at one time. From these, in spite of all possible care, exhalations will arise that cannot be prevented. It is true that on many days the presence of this number of animals will not be noticed a short distance beyond the inclosure, but there will be days when, owing to the location, high temperature, and certain atmospheric conditions, the air will be tainted for at least a mile in the direction of the wind. I have repeatedly noticed the "cattle odor" half a mile from a distillery where only 1,000 head were stabled, and in a locality where the atmospheric conditions were more favorable than they possibly could be at the proposed yards here.

The slaughtering of animals, under the most favorable circumstances, cannot be conducted without more or less smell. From its very nature it is a filthy operation, and it is not presuming too much to say that, even if conducted with the care proposed, there will be times when the atmosphere will be polluted from the abattoir. The killing of 800 head of cattle, 1,500 hogs, and 2,000 sheep daily in this locality, which will be about the amount required for consumption in this city in 1875, and if not then, certainly in 1876, cannot always be carried on without offence to the surrounding district.

From this amount of slaughtering there will have to be removed daily from the cattle about 20 tons of offal, from the hogs 15 tons, and from the sheep 7 tons, with about 2,500 gallons of cattle blood, 1,300 of hog blood, and 700 of sheep blood, making in all about 55 tons of refuse for rendering and utilization. Owing to the character of this material, decomposition soon takes place, and, therefore, at times it cannot be removed without being offensive. This is especially the case when, from accident or some other unavoidable cause, its removal is not promptly effected. The fat for rendering can, as a general rule, be taken away without any trouble, but the removal of the heads, hoofs, and manure cannot always take place from this locality without smell. It is true, that by the free use of disinfectants this objection can be partially obviated, but their application is not always practicable.

From the meteorological observations of Prof. Fitzgerald, as recorded in the Franklin Institute, I find that for the years 1872 and 1873, during the months of June, July, August, and September, when the exhalations from the proposed abattoir and stock-yards will be most rife, owing to high temperature, the wind was for two-thirds of this period from a westerly direction; most frequently from the S. W., next from the N.W. Then occur the N.E., S.E., W., S., N., and E. winds in the order named. The mean daily temperature for the same years was for June, 75°, July, 81°, August, 78°, and September, 69°.

With this high temperature during the prevalence of the S. W. wind, it is safe to assume that the odors of this establishment at times, without any rendering or the utilization of refuse being done, will be observable as far as Coates and Broad streets. When from the West, as far as Broad, and from the N.W., as far as Pine and 18th streets. Occasionally it will be noticed beyond these limits. The influence of these exhalations upon life will be felt in about two-thirds of the district indicated, according to density of population, compactness of buildings, and other local conditions, and especially at the Children's Hospital. While it is true that it would be difficult to point out a single case where these emanations have directly caused death, I have repeatedly observed their effect at Chicago, in increasing the death-rate of a particular locality when the wind was blowing in a south-easterly or south-westerly direction, from one of these establishments for several consecutive days, with a high temperature, while the death-rate was not increased in localities remote, with the wind in the same direction, and the other conditions that affect life being the same. It may be said that other influences destructive to life were at work at this time, but even taking these into consideration, I could not avoid the conclusion that the emanations from these establishments were an important factor in increasing the death-rate, especially of the infantile diseases incident to summer, as well as in cases debilitated by other diseases. In other words, they increase the destructive influence of certain atmospheric contaminations existent under high temperatures, especially where population is dense. On the west side of the Schuylkill the exhalations will be observed when the wind is from the N.E., in the neighborhood of the almshouse; when it is from the E., about 40th street; and when from the S.E, about Aspen street. The effect upon life will be less marked than on the east side, since the population is less dense, while the easterly winds are less frequent and such winds generally are of a lower temperature. It will, however, increase the death-rate in the University and Blockley Hospitals, particularly in the latter, as in institutions of this character the patients are necessarily more susceptible to such influences.

There will also be occasions when, owing to the fact that the establishment is to be located upon lower ground than the residences in the neighborhood, the odors from it will be noticed only at higher and more remote points. The topography of the locality prevents that free and constant access of air which is, from a sanitary standpoint, one of the most important preventives of foul odors. Thus there will result accumulations of this character, and then owing to certain atmospheric conditions they will ascend until they strike a current of air to be wafted to and be observed at a distance. In New York, the residents on Murray Hill are frequently annoyed by noxious odors when nothing is observed near the source from whence they emanate. These conditions obtain most frequently at night, and it is in this way that during the summer months sleeping rooms are contaminated, owing to the fact that the windows are open. If the establishment were to be located on a hill or a plain, so that there would be free access for the winds from all directions, or, in other words, its ventilation better, this objection would in a very great measure be obviated.

The most important objection, from a sanitary standpoint, to the proposed abattoir and stock-yards will be the necessary drainage of refuse matter into the Schuylkill River. In fact, without good drainage and a large supply of water it is impossible to conduct establishments of this magnitude without their becoming great nuisances, and just in proportion as they are kept in a cleanly condition will the river be polluted. I find upon examination of the records in the office of the City Engineer that the current of the river is on the east side, and that, generally speaking, there is but little on the west side, save such as is incident to the rise and fall of the tide, which, owing to the winding character of the river, and perhaps Fairmount Dam, is by no means as rapid as in the Delaware. If the cattle are slaughtered in the mode at present adopted in the best establishments, there will be at least five pounds of blood, meat, and other refuse from each animal, carried into the river. This is a low estimate, and no doubt frequently too low. From the hogs nearly two pounds each, and from the sheep about two ounces. There will also be daily carried into the river from the cattle stabled at least one pound per head of excreta, about the same quantity per hog, and about two ounces per sheep. This last calculation is based upon the supposition that the yards will be impervious to fluids, and that the drainage will be as complete as possible. Although the greater portion of the blood will be collected for utilization, there is necessarily some waste. This will be washed into the river, where it will coagulate and sink, and unless the current is very rapid it will remain at the bottom of the river until the temperature of the water is such as to cause the putrefactive process to take place. I have frequently found coagulated blood at the bottom of the Chicago River months after it had been deposited, and when its presence had become manifest by the escape of noxious gases, the result of its decomposition.

From the foregoing it will be observed that about 15,000 pounds of organic and decomposable material will daily enter the river from this source. Although this estimate may seem large, I do not think that the establishment can be kept clean without this amount of waste material being carried into the river by frequent flushing, for it is so much easier to remove refuse in this way—particularly when the drainage is good, and the water in abundance for this purpose—than by the slow process of collecting by hand, and removing to another locality. Indeed, much of it cannot be removed by hand; with the best intentions and most constant supervision it will be found impracticable, from the amount of time and labor required. Of course, this estimate does not include the manure—that can be readily disposed of.

As already remarked, the current of the Schuylkill is not rapid on this side, and it will soon be found, from the character of the refuse—as a large portion of it is animal matter—that at low tide much of it will be left in the docks and on the marshy grounds (overflowed at high tide) and shallow places on this side of the river for some distance below the abattoir. At low tide the action of the sun in midsummer would cause it to be the source of noxious exhalations, which would be carried by the winds over a much larger portion of the city than the emanations from the abattoir and stock-yards, and thus exercise a more widely spread influence upon health and comfort. I learn that the railroad company propose to build a sewer into the middle of the river, emptying into deep water, and where there is a more rapid current, so as to carry off this drainage. This will no doubt be better than if the mouth of the sewer should be at the west side of the river; but when there is little water flowing over the dam, it will not make much difference, as the ebb and flow of the tide, with the wind, will carry this material to every portion of the river.

From Mr. Smedley, the Chief Engineer of the city, I learn that only a small portion of the region lying west of the Schuylkill is sewered, and that, comparatively speaking, but little sewage from it empties into the river at this time, but that with the increase of population the sewers will have to be extended; also that the drainage of the lower part of the city lying east of the Schuylkill is limited. In this direction sewers are being rapidly built, the tendency of population being to the territory drained by the Schuylkill, so that with the natural increase and the addition from the proposed slaughtering and stock-yards (which will in itself be equal, at the lowest estimate, to the sewage of a population of 20,000), it will soon be found that the river will become so much contaminated as to prove offensive, and exercise an injurious influence upon the health of the city. The effect of this river pollution will be more marked when there is little or no water flowing over the dam at Fairmount, as frequently occurs, particularly in the summer months, since but little fresh water being added, the same water remains flowing upward and downward, while the daily addition of contaminating material remains the same. It should be borne in mind that the refuse matter from stock-yards and abattoirs, in undergoing the process of decomposition, gives off much more effluvia than ordinary sewage, so that combining the river pollution with the atmospheric contamination, I think it safe to say that the proposed establishment will be fully equivalent in its effects upon the atmosphere in the neighborhood of the river to the sewage derived from a population of at least 50,000 souls. The purification, by oxidation of the ordinary sewage with the proposed additional refuse materials from the yard and abattoir flowing into the Schuylkill River with its present water supply, cannot be accomplished before it joins the Delaware. The purification of the Illinois and Michigan Canal, at Chicago, with like contaminating material, and with a constant supply of fresh water from Lake Michigan, requires a distance of from twenty to thirty miles, at least double the distance being required for refuse animal matter that is needed for ordinary city sewage.

This river pollution will increase as population increases, until it will be necessary to construct an intercepting sewer, on one or both sides of the river, with pumping works near its mouth, to pump the sewage into the Delaware, at great expense.* This will become in the course of time a sanitary necessity.

Since the reception of your letter, and as attention has been called thereto, I have inspected the abattoir and stock-yards at Harsimus Cove, and do not hesitate to say, that, taking everything into consideration, they constitute the most complete and best adapted establishment of the kind in the country, and, perhaps in the world. In some respects, in mechanical construction, and certainly in location, they are superior to the Brighton abattoir and stock-yards near Boston, to the construction of which so much attention has been paid by the Massachusetts State Board of Health. At Brighton, however, hogs are slaughtered, and the rendering of fat and utilization of the refuse are carried on, which is not the case at Harsimus Cove. At the latter place albumen is manufactured from the blood, the remaining products being converted into a fertilizer without the process being specially disagreeable, while on the Schuylkill this operation cannot at all times be conducted without being offensive to a neighboring population. There is also a marked difference in climate, one being oceanic and the other continental. There is also at Harsimus a constant and free circulation of air, as there is no obstruction from any direction, and it is built at least four feet above the water, so that the air has even an opportunity to pass under it; while on the Schuylkill the site is, as it were, in a basin, and lower than the surrounding territory. In the summer, when most annoyance is experienced from establishments of this character, a stiff sea breeze is frequent at Harsimus Cove, blowing up the North River, so that it really does not affect any one, while at West Philadelphia the prevailing winds will carry the emanations to the most densely populated and best built-up portions of the city. Harsimus Cove is so situated that in three directions it cannot possibly affect pop-

* In the latter part of last July, while coming into the city on the West Chester Railroad, my attention was attracted by a foul and oppressive odor, and from habit, I looked out of the car window to see from whence it had its origin, I found that we were approaching the Schuylkill River, and that the tide was low, and that the effluvia came from the low and marshy ground. Afterwards in crossing Chestnut street bridge, I observed a similar odor coming from the docks, and, as I approached the east side, noticed the most offensive gas smell; altogether reminding me of the atmospheric impurities that several years ago were so common in the immediate neighborhood of the Chicago River.

ulation. In the remaining quarter there is comparatively no population within half a mile, and only about fifteen thousand within a mile. and with the wind rarely blowing towards that point, while on the Schuylkill there is at least a resident population of one hundred and twenty-five thousand, including several large hospitals and other public institutions within reach of its influence. At Harsimus the water supply is unlimited, with a rise and fall of the tide of eight feet, flowing swiftly with the full volume of the North River; while on the Schuylkill the rise and fall of the tide is only six feet, and not rapid, with at times a small water supply in the river, or, in other words, the drainage from Harsimus is to all intents and purposes daily removed, while at the Schuylkill it cannot be. The mean daily temperature, during the months of June, July, August, and September, is at least 5° lower at Harsimus Cove than at West Philadelphia, a very important difference, as high temperature is the chief factor in causing offensive smells. The day of my visit at Harsimus was one of the coldest of this season, and yet as I stepped into a small boat upon leaving the abattoir, at a point some distance from where the slaughtering was carried on, I noticed an odor as if it came from an old sewer or from blood and refuse that had been deposited in the river. I have no doubt that this will increase year by year.

It will, therefore, be seen that the conditions that obtain in the two localities are wholly unlike, and that to draw a comparison, or to say that what can be accomplished at one place in the conducting of this business can be done at the other, is simply impossible. I do not hesitate to say that at Harsimus Cove slaughtering is carried on with but little offence, and no injury to the public health; but I am equally positive in saying that it is not possible to do so at the proposed point on the Schuylkill.

In reply to the query, "At what distance should the rendering and utilization of the refuse be carried on from the built-up portions of the city?" I would state that this depends entirely upon the atmospheric conditions, the direction of the prevailing winds, the mode and character of the appliances for conducting these processes, the drainage and water supply. The *rendering* of clean, fresh fat or tallow is not necessarily an offensive operation, except in a warm, murky atmosphere, but the *rendering* of offal, and its utilization, under all circumstances, require constant care and attention, but even then, with all the improved machinery, cannot always be carried on without offence. In *rendering*, much water is used, and this, after the process is completed, is drawn off, necessarily impregnated with a large amount of organic material. The tank water or soup, as it may more properly be called, from rendering fresh fat and tallow, is not specially offensive, but that from rendering offal must necessarily be so from the fact that in this process the fatty matter is removed from the intestines, and the various glands and organs that are not otherwise used. It is estimated that from the offal of a bullock there are about 12 gallons of this liquid, which, if 800 are slaughtered daily, will amount to 9,600 gallons, 3 gallons to each hog that is slaughtered, making a total daily of 4,500 gallons, and one gallon per head of sheep, making 2,000 gallons more, or a total daily of 16,500 gallons of this tank fluid that must be daily removed. It is from this source mainly that the south branch of the Chicago River south of the Illinois and Michigan Canal is polluted. It is really a highly concentrated essence of the material that is rendered, containing variable quantities of ammonia, phosphorus, and nitrogen, products that are valuable as fertilizers. Glue has also been manufactured from this result of the rendering process. So far, however, but little progress has been made in the utilization of the tank fluid, and at this time it is necessarily one of the chief causes of the pollution of streams into which these establishments drain. The necessity of a large water supply for the removal of this waste will be apparent. These processes should, therefore, be conducted on the Delaware below the mouth of the Schuylkill, where water is abundant, and the remoteness from population would render it inoffensive.

This is the first time in the history of slaughtering, in this country, that it is proposed to locate a drove-yard and abattoir in what may be termed the heart of a city, or what certainly will soon be the centre of population. As a general rule, this business has been driven away from population, in consequence of the inseparable conditions that follow it, and while it is true that many improvements have been made in the mode of conducting these operations, especially within the last five years, both from a commercial and sanitary standpoint, still taking all these into consideration, judging from my experience, and the general principles of sanitary science, I am of the opinion that they should not be tolerated where population is dense, or likely to become so. In spite of everything that can be done, offence will sometimes arise. I have more than once been led to hope from many experiments, as well as from the great improvements in the machinery and appliances made to render the system a success, that the time might come when such establishments in the midst of population might be safe and proper, but in this I have so far been disappointed.

There is probably no practical sanitary question that at this time, especially in our large cities, is attracting so much attention as this, and even with all the improvements that have been made at Chicago, it is by no means yet conducted so as not to be offensive or prejudicial to health. In Baltimore this question is under discussion, and in New York steps are now being taken toward improvement. In Great Britain the hygienic considerations involved are now regarded as of so much importance that a recent act of Parliament has been passed defining how the work is to be carried on, not only in the great cities, but throughout the entire kingdom.

The best site for an abattoir for this city is on the Delaware, near the mouth of the Schuylkill, from sanitary considerations, and possibly, also, from a commercial point of view, as here slaughtering and packing for exportation might be carried on—a branch of business, I believe, not conducted in this city, and quite an important item in the export trade of Boston.

At the proposed location on the Schuylkill the sanitary difficulties will yearly become greater, owing to increasing density of population, diminished water supply, accumulation of refuse, and inevitable contamination of buildings and grounds. The expense, also, incident to conducting two establishments for slaughtering and rendering so far remote from each other as will have to be done, will go far toward equalizing any supposed commercial advantages of the proposed site on the Schuylkill. On the Delaware all the different processes can be carried on, if not under the same roof, at least in close proximity.

In speaking as I have, I do not wish to be understood as undervaluing an abattoir system in this city, but, on the contrary, I heartily commend it, and do not hesitate to say that if the location is a proper one, it is far preferable to the present mode of slaughtering. As a general rule, slaughtering should not be carried on as a purely commercial enterprise, but under the supervision and control of the municipality. This applies with special force to cities, where slaughtering is done for home consumption.

Dr. Rauch's views, as above expressed, have been endorsed by the leading physicians and Medical Societies of Philadelphia, and all sanitarian swho have examined the premises.—[*Ed.*

OZONE.—Ever since Ozone was discovered by Prof. Schönbein, in 1839, it has been a favorite study of physicians, chemists, and physiologists. Recent theories in regard to the bacterian origin of diphtheria would seem to give this study an additional impulse, or at least should tend to give Ozone a new application; for if this theory of the cause of diphtheria be true, and Ozone is as potent as it is said to be in the prevention and destruction of bacteria in the atmosphere, we see no reason why its local application would not be an important curative agent. According to the observations of Clemens, Schönbein, Bérigny, Hammond, Billard, and T. Boeckel, the quantity of Ozone in the atmosphere and the prevalence of malarious diseases bear an inverse proportion, and this is the case not only in point of time but also in respect of locality.

Dr. Ross, Medical Officer of Health for St. Giles, London, found that during the prevalence of relapsing fever in that part of the metropolis the amount of Ozone in the air decreased as the mortality from the disease increased, and *vice versa.* And at Salford, in 1869, it was remarked that "generally, as the amount of Ozone decreased, the seizures in measles, scarlatina, typhus, and continued fever increased." Similar observations were made in regard to the prevalence of the cattle plague.

"The evidence which we possess at present" (Dr. Cornelius Fox, *Ozone and Antozone*), "enables us to state with confidence that—

"1. A deficiency of Ozone in the air in all probability predisposes to disease, particularly of the epidemic form, by virtue of the depressing and debilitating effects of such air, in consequence of its feeble powers of oxidizing animal debris; and

"2. A permanent diminution in the normal amount of active Ozone probably favors the development of chronic diseases characterized by mal-nutrition, imperfect oxidation, and degeneration of tissues.

"As the recent investigations of Chauveau and Sanderson prove that the poison of an infectious disease, as scarlet fever, measles, etc., consists of excessively minute particles of living matter, which may be diffused through or wafted by the air, and that bacteria are carriers of infection, there is some reason for thinking that a *materies morbi* may be rendered inert by atmospheric Ozone."

Editor's Table.

THE PUBLIC HEALTH.

TO CONTRIBUTORS.—In the necessity for condensing this department, our intention is not to sacrifice any of its usefulness, but, on the contrary to make it as complete and accurate as possible. To this end we will esteem is a special favor to be accurately informed in regard to population and such other data in regard to the respective spheres of observers as will contribute to its value. Correspondents will also confer an obligation upon us, and mutually benefit one another, by more promptly forwarding their summaries. Reports to be in time for any issue, should be at hand *before the 10th* of the month next preceding.

New York, February 10, 1875.—The total number of deaths in the four weeks ending January 30, 1875, was 2,536. The course of mortality by the different classes of causes and from the predominant diseases in these four weeks may be stated as follows:

CAUSES OF DEATH, JAN. 2ND TO JAN. 30TH, 1875.	Week ending Jan. 9.	Week ending Jan. 16.	Week ending Jan. 23.	Week ending Jan. 30.
Total Mortality from all causes	612	696	624	604
Zymotic Diseases	164	236	158	164
Constitutional Diseases	117	131	126	118
Local Diseases	272	261	278	265
Developmental Diseases	35	42	38	33
Deaths by Violence	24	23	24	24
Small-pox	20	52	30	38
Scarlatina	21	17	16	9
Diphtheria	46	73	48	43
Typhoid Fever	4	10	7	5
Phthisis Pulmonalis	77	94	91	88
Bronchitis	28	30	36	37
Pneumonia	84	103	96	103
Deaths in Institutions	112	131	118	107
" of Persons 70 years old and over	45	34	45	42
" Children under 5 years of age	239	291	222	245
Mean Temperature	28.5°	19.9°	19.4°	26.8°
Range of "	38.0°	37.0°	41.0°	21.0°

The death-rate during the first month of the year was equivalent to 31.07 in the 1,000 per annum, the population being estimated at 1,060,800. This is a higher rate of mortality than has been experienced in any winter month since January 1865, when the death-rate became excessive from small-pox, diphtheria, scarlatina and typhoid fever and the unusual fatality of inflammatory diseases of the lungs. The excessive prevalence and fatality of the latter class of diseases during the past month (January) is more marked than in any preceding year in the present decade. The rapidly fatal invasion of pneumonia and bronchitis is certified by the daily death records in which a few days—say from three to seven, but often only a day or two in the infant cases,—are certified as the time from attack till death. This excessive fatality, and the probably unusual prevalence of the inflammatory diseases of the organs of respiration, being coincident with the excessive fluctuations and low average of temperature, the inference might not be unwarranted that this cold and changeable temperature has been the exclusive cause of this unusual mortality by lung diseases. But upon a close analysis of the circumstances and places of death by these pulmonary diseases, the fact appears that the overcrowded, badly drained and unventilated habitations of fully 80 per cent. of the victims of these maladies must be charged with contributing certain factors to this fatality. In short, there is no doubt that the poor and imprudent who are most exposed to these foes of healthful respiration, require the interposition of sanitary laws which shall limit the degree of domiciliary crowding as well as determine the ventilation of tenement dwellings, school-rooms and public halls. In this frigid season the close atmosphere of all classes of dwellings, and especially the highest and most heated structures, are most dangerously invaded by sewer gases, and from the suddenness and fatality of pneumonia in many persons exposed in such dwellings and hotels, there is reason to believe Sir WM. JENNER's opinion correct, that a very fatal type of pneumonia and congestive disease of the lungs is induced by sewer gas poisoning. Yet the chief factor in the causation of the recent excessive fatality of these maladies unquestionably consists in *excessive and continued cold*: and such long continued ice-bound weather is associated with an unflushed and unwholesome state of the street sewers.

During this protracted period of inclement temperature there has been a slight decrease in the weekly mortality from diphtheria and a marked increase in that from small-pox. There still continues to be less than the usual mortality from measles, whooping cough, scarlatina, and typhoid fever, and only the usual number of deaths from tubercular phthisis. Old age has suffered unusual fatality from numerous diseases, while the mortality in children under five years of age has not been excessive in a corresponding ratio.

ELISHA HARRIS, M.D., *Registrar.*

MORTALITY PER 1000 INHABITANTS ANNUALLY, FROM ALL CAUSES, AND CERTAIN SPECIAL CAUSES.

Population and Registration at most recent Estimates and Dates.	Deaths under 5 years.	Total number of deaths from all causes.	Per 1000.	By Violence.	Small-pox.	Diphtheria.	Scarlatina.	Measles.	Croup.	Whooping Cough.	Typhoid Fever.	Typhus Fever.	Puerperal Diseases.	Diarrhoeal Diseases.	Consumption.	Lung Diseases, excluding Consumption.	Other Causes.
New York, 1,050,890; 4 weeks ending Jan. 30	592	2736	31.06	95*	140	210	60	....	....	....	26	....	....	....	320	[illegible]	
Philadelphia, 775,000; " " "	561	1216	20.40	21		41	102	2	27	....	26	1	11	....	154	162	
Brooklyn, 450,000; " " "	154	505	20.33	11	15	81	59	2	19	7	4	1	2	7	130	216	
St. Louis, 450,000; " " "	209	501	14.47	16	109	7	15	....	2	....	12	....	7	2	51	72	
Chicago, 400,000; " " 28	211	255	16.58	16	....	7	11	1	8	....	11	....	11	3	54	88	
Boston, 375,000; " " "	....	605	21.05														
Baltimore, 250,000; " " 21	270	650	22.62	13	....	11	59	....	25	6	16	1	17	....	93	105	
Cincinnati, 260,000; 2 weeks, " 25	101	253	25.30	[illegible]	2	7	9	....	3	10	7	....	....	4	40	57	
New Orleans, 210,000; year, 1874		6758	32.87	154	587	102		....	....	....	....	....	....		820	258	
" 210,000; month ending Jan. 31	168	552	31.68	15	32	1	1	....	7	1	2	....	7	46	81	94	
Washington, 150,000; 4 weeks ending Jan 30	156	555	24.??	12	....	3	1	5	6	16	1	....	5	5	51	62	
Pittsburg, 110,000, month ending " "	132	285	21.16		2	2	23	2	....	6	13	....	2	....	61	165	
Richmond 65,000; 4 weeks ending " "	38	109	21.80	1	....	3		....	1	....	3	....	....	2	21	15	
New Haven, 60,000; month ending Jan. 31	40	105	21.00	3	1	....	....	....	1	....	3	....	2	3	18	11	
Charleston, 50,000; " " "	50	98	23.48	2		5	....			....	1	....	2	....	9	15	
Toledo, 50,000; month ending " 31	22	55	13.20	....	....	....	....	....	1	1	....	....	1	1	1	6	
Paterson, 40,000; year 1874	31	32	26.65	....	....	15	1	....	1		....	....		....	12	10	
Wheeling, 27,000; month ending Jan. 31	18	36	28.41	2	....	4	6	....		....	1	....	1	....	7	....	
" " year 1874	195	306	11.16	9	....	7	21	1	5	12	18	....	6	12	42	18	
Dayton, 34,000; month ending Jan. 31	12	36	†16.25	2	....	....	....	....	1	....	1	....	....	....	10	12	
Salem (1870) 21,117; month ending Jan. 31	....	16		1	....	....	2	....	....	....	....	....	....	....	7	6	
" year 1874	161	496	20.50	7	....	1	5	....	6	6	21	....	6	16	74	57	
Poughkeepsie, 21,000; year 1874	157	304	16.66	8	....	11	15	3	7		9	1	4	21	58	37	
Elmira, 21,000; month ending Jan. 31	7	25	14.00	2	....	....	4	....	....	....	....	....	....	....	3	4	
Norfolk, 21,000; year 1874	243	574	26.07	16	8	11	3	....	3	20	11	....	8	52	67	59	

New Orleans — Congestive Fever, 274; Other Fevers, 14.

* Gunshot Wounds, 66; Drowning, 93.

† By clerical error last month, the ratio per 1000 in Dayton was stated to be 9.21 instead of 14.08.

For the following table we are indebted to Dr. Jas. Watt, the accomplished Registrar of Vital Statistics, Brooklyn.

MORTALITY STATISTICS FOR 1874.

CITIES.	Population.	Total Number of Deaths.	Per 1,000.	Deaths from Consumption	Per cent of Consumption to Total Mortality.	Consumption per 1,000 population.
New York	1,040,000	28,727	27.62	4,033	14.04	3.88
Philadelphia	775,000	15,238	19.66	2,304	15.12	3.10
Brooklyn	450,000	11,011	24.46	1,267	11.45	2.81
St Louis	450,000	6,506	14.45	581	8.93	1.29
Chicago	395,000	8,025	20.29	630	7.85	1.62
Boston	375,000	7,812	30.83	1,309	16.75	3.46
Baltimore	350,000	7,401	21.14	1,036	14.	2.96
Cincinnati	260,000	5,321	20.46	....	....	....
New Orleans	207,000	6,798	32.76	....	....	....
Washington	150,000	2,959	19.72	471	15.90	3.14
Cleveland	145,000	2,195	15.13	178	8.10	1.23
Pittsburg	137,000	3,381	24.68	331	9.78	2.41
Jersey City	120,000	1,436	33.93	....	....	....
Milwaukee	100,000	1,909	19.09	136	7.12	1.36
Providence	99,608	1,983	19.90	269	13.58	2.70
Rochester	80,000	1,405	17.56	188	13.38	3.10
Albany	95,000	1,786	18.80	....	....	....
Richmond	65,000	1,591	24.47	231	14.52	3.55
New Haven	59,000	1,078	17.85	197	18.35	2.96
Troy	50,000	1,450	29.90	294	20.27	5.88
Charleston	50,000	1,948	38.96	98	5.05	1.96
Memphis	50,000	1,148	22.96	137	11.93	2.74
Hartford	45,000	588	13.06	55	9.35	1.22
Fall River	43,000	1,177	27.21	148	12.55	3.41
Paterson	40,000	892	22.30	125	14.01	3.12
Dayton	34,000	479	14.09	68	14.19	2.00
Galveston	34,000	626	18.41	16	.25	....
Quincy, Ill	30,000	555	18.60	52	9.37	1.73
Peoria	30,000	338	11.16	32	9.46	1.06
Lansing	7,445	69	9.26	10	14.49	1.47

SEWING MACHINES.

It is rumored that the effort of last winter, before the Legislature of New York, to force all sewing machine companies to adopt a fallacious contrivance—claimed to be an improvement for the benefit of health—on the ordinary treadle of sewing machines is to be again renewed. We hope the members of the Legislature are fully alive to the deception. That too much work on the sewing machine is injurious to health, is doubtless as true as that too much of any other kind of woman's work is injurious; but that it is more so, we very much doubt.

Sewing machines, however, are not all alike, any more than spinning-wheels or plows. Some run easy, and some hard; some require much strain on the muscles of the back, others of the feet; some require much stooping, others not. We have observed many, and seriously called in question the use of some; but one kind, at least, we have no complaint against.

WILLCOX & GIBBS' machine has been the subject of our personal observation for several years, and we have no hesitation in stating that it is not only a noiseless worker but that it can be used with perfect safety by delicate women with as little fatigue as any other household work within the scope of our observation.

ANALYTICAL AND FOOD DEPARTMENT.

TRICHINOSIS.—"Doctor, what is good for the cholera? My wife got it, and the neighbors also,"—said to me on New Year's day a German plasterer, living on F street.

I jumped from the cutter and ran to the house. There was a young woman, the mother of four little children, with all the symptoms of the cholera morbus. She had the diarrhœa for several days, and was now vomiting for several hours; pulse a hundred a minute, and threadlike.

While I was examining her, a sister of the patient came in, and complained also about diarrhœa, great prostration, and swelled arms and legs, and her husband appeared, who walked like a man who was just pulled from the water with wet clothes on. He was stiff all over, he said, and awful weak, and wanted to vomit up the whole inside. The well where both families obtained drinking water was a good distance from the privy, and I was told they cleaned the well only a few weeks ago.

So I inquired about their food—and espied a pigsty in the back part of the lot, which is about 165 feet long. Did you eat any pork? I asked. Yes, but we raised it ourselves, was the answer. In the woodshed there were two pigs salted down in a barrel. I cut a few lean pieces off—took also some sausage along; galloped home—examined the meat under the microscope, and found it full of trichinæ spiralis. Some of the meat I thought would make a nice New Year's present to the Editor of the Sanitarian, and I am glad you received it.

After the discovery of the pork worms it did not take my horse very long to go back to the patients, a distance of seven blocks. Castor oil, senna, and other physics were freely administered notwithstanding their diarrhœa, and a few hours afterwards a remarkable improvement was observed. Although some German physicians recommended the use of Picrotoxin and such preparations, I did not want to lose time with experiments. Picrotoxin, and Extract of Cocculus! I thought; there is plenty in the beer our people are drinking every day. So I appropriated some bottles of the best California port wine and claret, raised in the gardens near Los Angeles which I visited myself three years ago, and my patients got better, and are now able to work. For the swelling of the arms and legs, and fever—warm water with a little alcohol seems to do good.

The owner of the pigs did not get sick; perhaps because he takes his whiskey regularly, twice or three times a day, although he is by no means a drunkard, but a hard-working man, in good circumstances.

The pigs were bought from a Western drover. Amongst the lot were four dead ones, and the others were feeding on them. If any one wants a sample of the meat, I will send it. Very respectfully,

E. W. GERMER, *Health Officer.*

ERIE, Pa., Feb. 15, 1875.

About two weeks before the receipt of the above letter, we received from Dr. Germer specimens of the pork referred to, and our friend, Dr. Carroll being present at the time, we divided it for examination. A few days subsequently Dr. Carroll wrote:

To the Editor of the Sanitarian.

DEAR SIR—The specimen of pork which you handed to me for examination a few days ago contains numerous trichinæ, at the rate, roughly estimated, of about 2,000 to the cubic inch, some of them free, the majority encysted, and many of the cysts containing two embryones. Granular degeneration of some of the muscular fibres was well marked.

ALFRED L. CARROLL, M.D.

NEW BRIGHTON, STATEN ISLAND, *January* 25, 1875.

Our own examination corresponded with Dr. Carroll's.

BIBLIOGRAPHY.

Maintenance of Health. A Medical work for Lay Readers. By J. Milner Fothergill, M.D., Edin., member of the Royal College of Physicians of London, physician to West London Hospital, etc., etc. 8vo. pp. 399, London: Smith, Elder & Co., 1874.

A book admirably well suited to its purpose of household instruction on hygiene from infancy to old age. Not only giving the general care of health in regard to schooling, food, clothing and habitation; but clear common sense directions, divested of technicalities, in regard to the causes of disease in general, how to recognize them when they exist, and how to remove them with safety. The chapter on "What to do in Certain Emergencies," while waiting for the doctor, and the proper care of slight ailments is especially notable for its concise directions in various injuries and shocks by railroads or otherwise, hemorrhage, fainting, convulsions, choking, drowning, etc., etc., a kind of knowledge for which all persons are liable to have use, for the alleviation of suffering and the saving of life. We cordially commend Dr. Fothergill's work as one of the most useful books on hygiene for lay readers hitherto published.

Young Folks' History of the United States. By Thomas Wentworth Higginson, 12mo, illustrated, p. 370. Boston: Lee & Shepard. New York: Lee, Shepard & Dillingham. 1875.

By no means a Peter Parley history, but a more substantial work of sound knowledge. Evidently not intended to be a book of pretty pictures and pretty stories, but a book of instruction. And in this the author has well succeeded; giving, certainly, as much of the most useful history of the United States, as the capacity of "young folks'" minds may by any reasonable supposition be thought to be equal to, but leaving much yet to be learned. Had a little more pains been taken to avoid the repetition of certain popular inaccuracies just previous to, and at the conclusion of the civil war, it would have been better. But, taking it altogether, it is a good epitome of the history of the United States for both old and young. The blemishes are at the least based upon popular impressions, and possibly on that account excusable.

BOOKS RECEIVED.—Steiner's Compendium of Children's Diseases; Eating for Strength; Nature and Culture; Physicians' Pocket, and Office Case Records; Near Sight and Atropia; American Clinical Lectures, Vol. I, No. 1; Report of Commissioners of Lunacy, Mass.; Transactions of Texas State Medical Association; Rhode Island Registration; Papers from the National Bureau of Education; Report of Health Commission of New Jersey; The Coming Medical Man.

INDEX.

UNIVERSITY OF MICHIGAN
3 9015 07345 9508

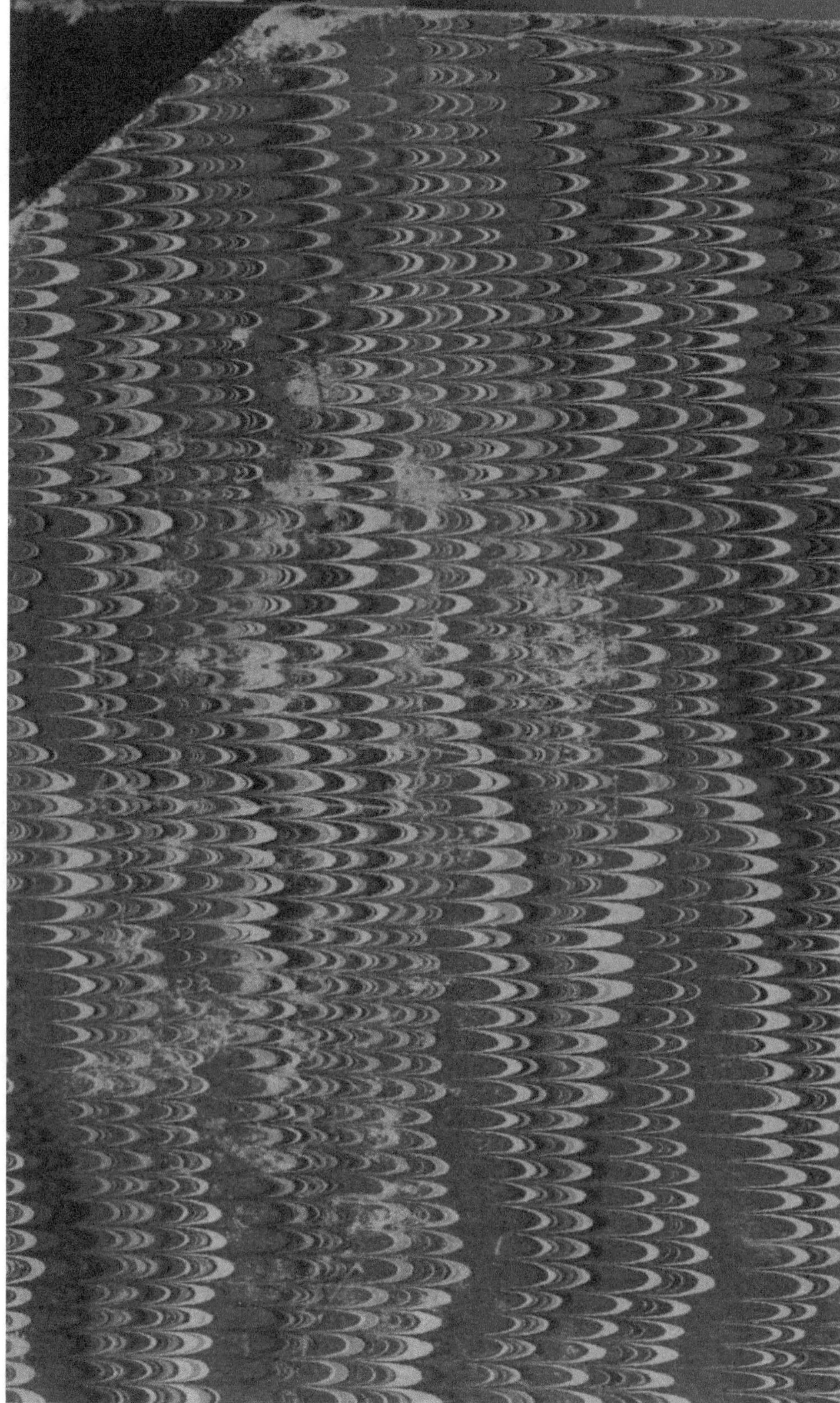

Check Out More Titles From HardPress Classics Series In this collection we are offering thousands of classic and hard to find books. This series spans a vast array of subjects – so you are bound to find something of interest to enjoy reading and learning about.

Subjects:
Architecture
Art
Biography & Autobiography
Body, Mind &Spirit
Children & Young Adult
Dramas
Education
Fiction
History
Language Arts & Disciplines
Law
Literary Collections
Music
Poetry
Psychology
Science
…and many more.

Visit us at www.hardpress.net

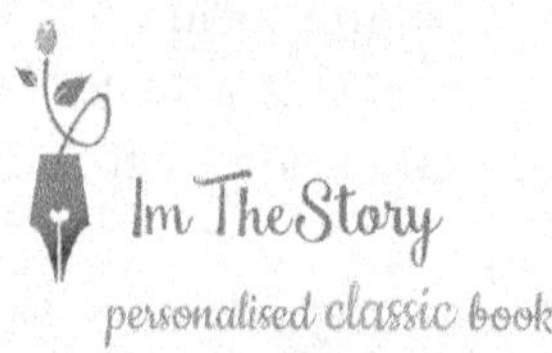

"Beautiful gift.. lovely finish,
My Niece loves it, so precious!"

Helen R Brumfieldon

FOR KIDS, PARTNERS AND FRIENDS

Timeless books such as:

Alice in Wonderland • The Jungle Book • The Wonderful Wizard of Oz
Peter and Wendy • Robin Hood • The Prince and The Pauper
The Railway Children • Treasure Island • A Christmas Carol

Romeo and Juliet • Dracula

Visit
ImTheStory.com
and order yours today!

CPSIA information can be obtained
at www.ICGtesting.com
Printed in the USA
BVHW040404120819
555626BV00005B/854/P